Future Law

Future Law

Series Editors
Lilian Edwards, Professor of Law, Innovation and Society,
Newcastle University
Burkhard Schafer, Professor of Computational Legal Theory,
University of Edinburgh
Edina Harbinja, Senior Lecturer in Media/Privacy Law, Aston University

Books in the series are critical and topic-led, reflecting the global
jurisdiction of technology and culture interacting with law. Each title
responds to cutting-edge debates in the field where technology interacts
with culture to challenge the ability of law to react to frequently
unprecedented scenarios.

Available or forthcoming titles

Buying Your Self on the Internet: Wrap Contracts and Personal Genomics
Andelka M Phillips

Future Law: Emerging Technology, Regulation and Ethics
Lilian Edwards, Burkhard Schafer and Edina Harbinja (eds)

*Technology, Innovation and Access to Justice:
Dialogues on the Future of Law*
Siddharth Peter de Souza and Maximilian Spohr (eds)

edinburghuniversitypress.com/series/ful

Future Law

**Emerging Technology,
Regulation and Ethics**

Edited by Lilian Edwards,
Burkhard Schafer and Edina Harbinja

EDINBURGH
University Press

Edinburgh University Press is one of the leading university presses in the UK. We publish academic books and journals in our selected subject areas across the humanities and social sciences, combining cutting-edge scholarship with high editorial and production values to produce academic works of lasting importance. For more information visit our website: edinburghuniversitypress.com

Edinburgh University Press Ltd
The Tun – Holyrood Road
12 (2f) Jackson's Entry
Edinburgh EH8 8PJ

First published in hardback by Edinburgh University Press 2020

Typeset in 11/13pt Adobe Garamond by
Servis Filmsetting Ltd, Stockport, Cheshire

A CIP record for this book is available from the British Library

ISBN 978 1 4744 1761 7 (hardback)
ISBN 978 1 4744 1762 4 (paperback)
ISBN 978 1 4744 1763 1 (webready PDF)
ISBN 978 1 4744 1764 8 (epub)

Contents

Contributors

Paul Bernal Senior Lecturer, School of Law, University of East Anglia

Damian Clifford Postdoctoral Research Fellow, Australian National University, College of Law; Associate Research Fellow, Information Law and Policy Centre, Institute of Advanced Legal Studies (University of London)

Melissa de Zwart Dean of Law, Adelaide Law School, University of Adelaide

Catherine Easton Reader in Law, University of Lancaster

Lilian Edwards Professor of Law, Innovation and Society, Newcastle Law School, Newcastle University

Andres Guadamuz Senior Lecturer in Intellectual Property Law, University of Sussex

Rob Hamper PhD Candidate, University of New South Wales

Edina Harbinja Senior Lecturer in Media/Privacy Law, Aston Law School, Aston University

Andrew Katz Partner, Moorcrofts LLP, UK and Visiting Researcher, University of Skövde, Sweden

Michaela MacDonald Lecturer, Queen Mary University, London

Alana Maurushat Professor of Cybersecurity and Behaviour, Western Sydney University

Miranda Mowbray University of Bristol

Andelka M Phillips Senior Lecturer, Te Piringa (Faculty of Law), University of Waikato, and Research Associate, Centre for Health, Law and Emerging Technologies (HeLEX), University of Oxford

Burkhard Schafer Professor of Computational Legal Theory, School of Law, University of Edinburgh

Lachlan D Urquhart Lecturer in Technology Law, School of Law, University of Edinburgh and Visiting Research Fellow, Horizon Digital Economy Research Institute, School of Computer Science, University of Nottingham

Figures and Tables

Table of Cases

Table of Legislation

1

The Future's Already Here:
It's Just Unevenly Edited

Lilian Edwards, Burkhard Schafer and Edina Harbinja

When, in 2017, the European Parliament adopted the Resolution with Recommendations to the Commission on Civil Law Rules on Robotics,[1] it introduced the topic in an unusual way, for a legal document:

> whereas from Mary Shelley's Frankenstein's Monster to the classical myth of Pygmalion, through the story of Prague's Golem to the robot of Karel Čapek, who coined the word, people have fantasised about the possibility of building intelligent machines, more often than not androids with human features.

By evoking in a legal text some of the most recognisable figures from literary fiction, the Parliament confirmed, if confirmation was indeed necessary, the wisdom behind the Gikii conference series, which since 2006 has brought together in an annual event, lawyers, technologists, sociologists, political scientists and other researchers, from industry as well as academe, to explore the intersection between law, popular culture and technology. This book grew out of this ongoing effort not just to bridge the gap between different intellectual traditions and communities, but to explore and leverage the power of human imagination in understanding, critiquing and improving the legal responses to technological change.

Arts and popular culture play a complex role in mediating between law and technology. For scholars, critics and media observers, they can act as an expression of both the enthusiasm and unease that a society feels about

---

[1] On 27 January 2017. Available at: <www.europarl.europa.eu/doceo/document/A-8-2017-0005_EN.html> (accessed 5 May 2019).

technological development, and in this way shape demand for regulatory intervention. They can also provide us with the creative space to think about how societies governed by new laws may look. Asimov's Three Laws of Robotics, first introduced in the short story 'Runaround' in 1942, long before autonomous intelligent robots were any kind of real-life possibility, are one key example that has had a palpable impact on the discussion around regulatory theory and jurisprudence. Asimov's laws have been frequently invoked in scholarship, both to explore the limits of legal formalism (i.e. making legal rules into computable code) and as a model for 'compliance by design' (think digital rights management or content filters, which operate without any need for enforcement in courts or by police). Since their creation, they have often been mentioned, for example when designing codes of ethics for researchers[2] and have even influenced legislatures, as in South Korea's Robots Charter.[3] Other more recent science fiction writers such as Cory Doctorow, William Gibson and Charles Stross have also directly or indirectly been influential in recent debates around copyright online and state surveillance,[4] policing in an online world and the nature of corporations as active and possibly malevolent entities.

Genetic manipulation and eugenics – discussed as context in Chapter 7 – are another, less 'hardware'-orientated domain where fiction has had a very strong influence on both public perceptions and ethical or regulatory responses. Huxley's *Brave New World* is the most obvious exemplar here, but other texts such as Andrew Niccol's 1997 film *Gattaca*, the Marvel mutant superhero series the *X-Men*, and the feminist thought experiment *Women On The Edge of Time*[5] have also been influential, both as both warnings of dystopias and explorations of possible utopias. Even online memes, trivial as they seem, are a popular culture feature that is used extensively to fight for regulatory causes, especially in relation to technology and digital rights, on sites like Facebook, Twitter, Instagram and Tumblr; one of the most widely effective (though ultimately unsuccessful) campaigns against the EU's new 2019 Copyright Directive imposing mandatory 'upload filters' on copyright

---

[2] Note, for example, Engineering and Physics Research Council (EPRSC), 'Principles of Robotics', subtitled 'Regulating Robots in the Real World' (2010, which Edwards helped draft), and explicitly intended to regulate the *designers* of robots rather than autonomously intelligent robots themselves.

[3] See discussion in Anderson, 'After 75 Years, Isaac Asimov's Three Laws of Robotics Need Updating' (*The Conversation*, 17 March 2017) <http://theconversation.com/after-75-years-isaac-asimovs-three-laws-of-robotics-need-updating-74501> (accessed 5 May 2019).

[4] For example, Doctorow, *Little Brother* (Tor 2008) but also the well-read blog Boing-Boing on IP issues.

[5] Piercy, *Women on the Edge of Time* (Women's Press 1979).

Figure 1.1   Meme campaigning against EU Copyright Directive 2019
Credit: iStock/Antonio Guillem/Getty/Joe Sohm/Visions of America.

infringing works used the fear that memes would be caught and thus banished to drum up support.[6] The example below brilliantly plays on one of the most popular memes of 2018/19: the 'distracted boyfriend' meme.

Educationally, popular culture and the arts – philosophy, drama, fiction, graphics, virtual media – can act as pedagogical tools to communicate complex technological or legal issues to laypersons, and through the distancing effect of unreality, perhaps create space for more critical reflection than would otherwise have been the case. One of the key 'texts' referenced in this volume (see Chapter 9), the UK Channel 4 (later Netflix) anthology TV series *Black Mirror* (initiated and often written by the former TV critic, writer and gamer, Charlie Brooker) has been pivotal in this regard in relation to consumer uptake of the information society and social media. It is now commonplace in geeky critical circles, for example, to reference *Nosedive*[7] when thinking about the Chinese social credit system, or 'White Bear' when

---

⁶ See for example, Reynolds M, 'What is Article 13? The EU's Divisive New Copyright Plan Explained' (*Wired*, 15 April 2019) <https://www.wired.co.uk/article/what-is-article-13-article-11-european-directive-on-copyright-explained-meme-ban> (accessed 5 May 2019).

⁷ 2016; see <https://en.wikipedia.org/wiki/Nosedive_(Black_Mirror)> (accessed 5 May 2019).

thinking about punishment, online trolling and bullying and desensitisation online.[8] Similar critical and educational uptake was observed earlier on in relation to the *Matrix*[9] series of movies, which provoked many metaphorical discussions about the nature of reality or virtuality and how they should be governed or used; similar discussions also often revolve around the literary works of Philip K. Dick (or, perhaps more often now, their filmic adaptations such as *Minority Report*, which gave the world of surveillance studies the term 'pre-crime').

A remarkable range of less obviously thematic literary or dramatic works can be, and have been, used in the Gikii series of conferences, to illustrate or elicit thoughts on key aspects of law and technology; for example targeted behavioural advertising in *South Park*; privacy intrusions seen as comparable to telepathy in the *Twilight* novels; blanket surveillance, Snowden style, justified on grounds of national security but questioned by, of all people, Captain America, in the Marvel movie *The Winter Soldier*.[10] Cartoon series aimed at smart, short-attention-span, college-educated audiences, such as *The Simpsons*, *Futurama* and *Rick and Morty*, often present quite complex and arcane legal technology issues in ways that are both dramatic and amusing (the latter of which goes a very long way with perplexed students).[11] Even Disney princesses (see Chapter 2) can be used to cleverly analyse different conceptions of privacy and identity.

At the same time, popular culture representations of complex law and technology issues can mislead academics and create false expectations for the public, engendering a demand for premature, over-simplistic or actively unhelpful legislative initiatives, even 'moral panics'. We can see this ambivalence in the above quote from the Resolution when it highlights the 'human features' that are so often given to robots in films, and moves from there

---

[8] 2013; see <https://en.wikipedia.org/wiki/White_Bear_(Black_Mirror)> (accessed 5 May 2019).

[9] The first film appeared in 1999; its two sequels have been rather less well received by critics. See <https://en.wikipedia.org/wiki/The_Matrix> (accessed 5 May 2019).

[10] State and other types of mass data surveillance have been a particularly popular topic to examine through the lens of popular culture, both at Gikii and elsewhere, a trope that goes back at least to examinations of *1984* and *Brave New World* and has recently continued in inter alia *The Prisoner* (TV), and *The Circle* (David Eggers, Penguin 2014). A particularly popular Gikii paper compared the techniques of state surveillance to the protection of Hogwarts by Dumbledore against the outside world in the Harry Potter novels.

[11] Examples of the use of all these works and many more can be found in the archive of Gikii papers and Powerpoints, which is held for work up to 2014 at <www.gikii.org/previous-events/> (accessed 3 June 2019). Later papers can be found on the websites of individual conferences (see list below).

to the idea, often popular with students, that sooner or later 'intelligent' robots should be given legal personality. One of the authors has explored this notion using clips from the Channel 4 TV drama *Humans*, and found that showing synthetic robots on screen in what looks like the current-day world, however imaginary, encourages students to embrace legal personality as a remedy, even where other avenues such as commercial law and agency might do just as well and present fewer philosophical and legal quandaries.[12] If we think, however, of robots as intelligent hoovers or dishwashers, fake software profiles on Twitter, commercial eBay sniping bots (see Chapter 10) or even as autonomous driverless cars (see Chapter 11) it suddenly seems much less compelling to start awarding them legal personality.

The typical 'human-like' depiction of robots in fiction is an interesting feature in other ways. Does such fake humanity mislead and deceive 'real' humans – and should it maybe thus be outlawed or limited? Are new forms of relationships being created between humans and machines, new forms of dependencies, new forms of companionship, or even, from *Pygmalion* to the film *Her*,[13] love?[14] Do these new relationships raise new ethical issues, and how should the law react to them? The EPRSC Principles of Robotics[15] suggest that robots should make clear their 'machine nature', and there are considerable worries that even the primitive automated assistants we have in Siri and Alexa might unduly influence children and vulnerable adults into buying things they don't need or disclosing personal data. A 2018 Californian law, influenced by the fallout of 'fake news' spread by bots, has already demanded that 'bots', often prevalent on Twitter and Facebook, should make it clear that they are not humans.[16]

The iconography of military robots in fiction has also become part of mainstream political and legal discourse. The image of the Terminator[17] repetitively frames thoughts and discussions in this domain, even though real autonomous weapons are far more likely to take forms such as drones, with

---

[12] On some of these issues see Bryson, Diamantis and Grant, 'Of, For, and By the People: The Legal Lacuna of Synthetic Persons' (2017) 25 *Artificial Intelligence and Law* 273.

[13] 2013; see *Her*: <https://en.wikipedia.org/wiki/Her_(film)> (accessed 5 May 2019).

[14] On this issue again, *Black Mirror*, and Chapter 9 has things to say.

[15] See note 2.

[16] This law has been criticised as trying to define something – robots rather than humans – that is impossible to define: see Casey and Lemley, 'You Might Be a Robot' (1 February 2019), *Cornell Law Review*, available at SSRN: <https://ssrn.com/abstract=3327602> (accessed 5 May 2019).

[17] The Terminator franchise began in 1984 (<https://en.wikipedia.org/wiki/Terminator_(franchise)>, last accessed 5 May 2019) with Arnold Schwarzenegger as the eponymous hero/antihero.

or without human pilots, or even mini-swarms. Is there a danger that these images impose a narrative that inevitably fails to capture the more prosaic developments of intelligent land mines, closes debates on legal issues such as the use of battlefield medical robots, or distracts attention away from the much more dangerous automation of cyberwarfare by the gradual phasing out of a 'human in the loop' in remotely controlled bombing drones? Maybe the story of the Golem of Prague would be better suited to influence democratic sentiment: built to protect the weak and marginalised, but falling foul of its own machine rationality and becoming the destroyer of all that it was supposed to care for?

The story of the Golem also reminds us just how intimately intertwined legal and technological discourse always have been. The first example of a golem's creation was described in a legal text, the Talmud's text *Sanhedrin*, which described how Rava, the foremost lawyer of his day (in modern parlance, his h-index was amazing), created one from the mud. When Rava was not creating golems, he reformed the law of evidence in civil procedure and developed new forms of adverse possession in property law. (Which also shows why property lawyers need close watching.)[18]

Looking at the way in which technology is depicted in fiction can, therefore, serve multiple purposes for lawyers. It can help to identify the underlying mental models that policymakers deploy when drafting legislation, and in this way can assist in interpreting and critiquing laws. It can develop utopian or dystopian visions of society and ask how laws or other modes of regulation can help to shape or prevent these futures. It can also be a mirror (b(B)lack, white or grey?) through which we see ourselves, a canvas on which we project our fears and hopes. It can allow us to perform a *gestaltswitch*, seeing old ideas in a new light and probing their conceptual boundaries. And finally, it can aid as a teaching tool, to educate students in the interactions between different disciplines as well as the key points where they may find ethical or normative dispute.

Technological fictions can be a way to provide lawyers with improved literacy in technology, and computer scientists and designers with the ability to reflect on the regulatory issues that science and technology raise. At the

---

[18] To show even more complexities, in Marge Piercy's *He, She and It* (Fawcett 1991), the Golem is effectively reincarnated as a Jewish sexbot. Sexbots have become another area of frantic legal concern, and popular at Gikii, but sadly not included in this volume; but see Shen, 'Sex Robots Are Here, But Laws Aren't Keeping Up with the Ethical and Privacy Issues They Raise' (*The Conversation*, 12 February 2019) <https://theconversation.com/ sex-robots-are-here-but-laws-arent-keeping-up-with-the-ethical-and-privacy-issues-they-raise-109852> (accessed 5 May 2019).

same time, students from the arts and humanities may often appreciate the dynamic between law and technology that underpins many utopian and dystopian visions in literature, film, music and the visual arts. Finally, and perhaps most importantly, at a time of constant concern about the place of ethics in artificial intelligence (AI) and other technologies (see for example the discussion of Big Data Ethics by Mowbray in Chapter 5), they can, and should, alert students, academics and critics – and indeed all consumers, citizens, industrialists and regulators – to the wider social and legal implications of new technologies, and sensitise them to the less or more foreseeable consequences. We cannot see the future; but fiction, popular culture, philosophy and even memes may help us to work out what future law should be.

The present collection of chapters draws on ideas ventilated at annual Gikii conferences from 2006 to date, along with some new papers especially contributed for this volume. The persistent attraction of an event that was originally conceived of as a one-off frolic, in the relatively early days of Internet law almost fifteen years ago, seems to show a continuing need for a place to discuss themes around law, technology and popular culture. (As well as the 'main' Gikii conference there have been many requests to 'franchise' the idea from places like Australia, Holland and Malaysia.) A conference has many benefits, not least creating a real-world community of researchers, and providing a welcome opportunity to experiment in front of a live audience with humour and graphics (Gikii has rather gratifyingly been described as 'stand-up comedy for lawyers' and precedes the current vogue for science comedy). However, written texts obviously allow deeper reflection than an oral paper. Many Gikii papers have found their way into the literature of academe in expanded form; however, to date, there has been no volume of Gikii-type papers. Edinburgh University Press however has now chosen to back an edited series exploring the worlds of law and technology from many different lenses; this volume, or 'primer' as we have sometimes called it, is the first of this series. It is particularly intended to celebrate the remarkable persistence of Gikii, but also more generally to alert both academics of many disciplines and more casual readers to the joys and takeaways of this particular intersection of endeavours. More volumes will follow expanding on some of the chapters within, which act as 'tasters'. (The editors are still very happy though to hear from anyone new who feels they can contribute to this series.)

Not all chapters in this volume revolve around particular cultural texts. Some do – *Black Mirror*, in Chapter 9 by Edwards and Harbinja has already been mentioned, as has Chapter 2 by Bernal interrogating Disney princesses; and remarkably, three chapters (4, 5 and 6, by Clifford, Mowbray and Maurushat/Hamper respectively) draw on the mythos of *Star Wars*, which tells us something about the captive power of Lucas' imagination.

De Zwart's contribution (Chapter 13) draws, interestingly, not on a single cultural text, but on a *site* for social creation and remix, namely Instagram – again, the frazzled interaction of social media and copyright has long been a Gikii obsession, one that is also revisited in this volume by one of its most persistent commentators, Andres Guadamuz in Chapter 12, where he manages to integrate not only Dr Who and knitting patterns but also sharks and 3D printing (sadly, no monkey selfie).

Others however draw more generally on particular cultural tropes such as zombies and AI (Schafer, Chapter 8), while Urquhart (Chapter 3) fascinatingly surveys pretty much the entire cultural SF history of smart homes and domestic automation, from Bradbury and Dick to *Rick and Morty*, before using this to contextualise his own empirical research into users of 'smart' technologies. Other authors simply engage with regulation of technology from a lateral, future-orientated and speculative point of view. Some legal domains have always been more appropriate to this kind of analysis than others; we have already mentioned state surveillance, and privacy and security generally, as seen in the first four chapters, have always been a popular source of Gikii papers. Three more sections deal, roughly, with regulating life and death: i.e. genetics (Phillips, Chapter 7) and property after death (Edwards and Harbinja, Chapter 9, and Schafer, as discussed above); regulating advanced autonomous technologies (Katz and Macdonald in Chapter 10 and Easton in Chapter 11); and the regulation of intellectual property (Guadamuz, Chapter 12 and de Zwart, Chapter 13, as discussed). A special shout-out goes to Chapter 10 by Katz and Macdonald, which illustrates another particular recurrent Gikii sub-category; solving what seems to be a very new problem (transactions made between autonomous intelligent agents) with a very old law (the Roman law of slavery).[19]

All three editors are of course immensely grateful to the contributors and their patience with the multiple versions demanded of their chapters during the protracted conception of this unusual volume. Two of the editors (Edwards and Schafer) would also like to express heartfelt thanks to the third (Harbinja), who came on board to save their sanity (and succeeded!). This is also a good opportunity to thank all the long-lasting members of the Gikii community for their support, many of whom would have liked to have taken part in this volume if circumstances had allowed; and in particular those who have kindly hosted the annual event; including, Judith Rauhofer, Chris Marsden and Andres Guadamuz, Ian Brown, Karen McCullough,

---

[19] For another example of this sub-genre, see recently Brown ' "Revenge Porn" and the Actio Iniuriarum: Using "Old Law" to Solve "New Problems" ' (2018) 38 *Legal Studies* 396.

Dinusha Mendis, Caroline Wilson, Matthias Klang, Katharine Sakirakis, Andrea Matwyshyn and Joris von Hoboken. In 2019, Fernando Barrio will host at Queen Mary College, London. Daithi MacSithigh deserves special mention for consistent support, good humour and fabulous PowerPoints, as does Andres Guadamuz (again!) for heroic maintenance of the Gikii website and Twitter account (@gikii) over the years. A full list of previous Gikiis, as well as access to papers and PowerPoints, can be found at gikii.org.

Finally, one (another) unusual feature of Gikii has been a sometimes mysterious obsession with cats. Most of this is due to the particularly central place cat memes have played in the development of popular culture on the Internet; but a small part is due to the fact that one of the editors, and original founder of Gikii, has two rather loveable cats of her own. As far as she is concerned, it seems appropriate to dedicate this volume to Cookie and Java, the original #catsagainstbrexit and a good example of how Internet memes can also play a provocative role in matters of law, policy and politics.

References

Anderson MR, 'After 75 Years, Isaac Asimov's Three Laws of Robotics Need Updating' (*The Conversation*, 17 March 2017) <http://theconversation.com/after-75-years-isaac-asimovs-three-laws-of-robotics-need-updating-74501> (accessed 5 May 2019).

Brown J, '"Revenge Porn" and the Actio Iniuriarum: Using "Old Law" to Solve "New Problems"' (2018) 38 *Legal Studies* 396.

Bryson JJ, Diamantis ME and Grant TD, 'Of, For, and By the People: The Legal Lacuna of Synthetic Persons' (2017) 25 *Artificial Intelligence and Law* 273.

Casey B and Lemley MA, 'You Might Be a Robot' (1 February 2019), *Cornell Law Review*, available at SSRN: <https://ssrn.com/abstract=3327602> (accessed 5 May 2019).

Doctorow C, *Little Brother* (Tor 2008).

Eggers D, *The Circle* (Penguin 2014).

Engineering and Physics Research Council, 'Principles of Robotics: Regulating Robots in the Real World' (2010) <https://epsrc.ukri.org/research/ourportfolio/themes/engineering/activities/principlesofrobotics/> (accessed 5 May 2019).

Her (film), Wikipedia <https://en.wikipedia.org/wiki/Her_(film)> (accessed 5 May 2019).

Nosedive (Black Mirror), Wikipedia <https://en.wikipedia.org/wiki/Nosedive_(Black_Mirror)> (accessed 5 May 2019).

Piercy M, *Women on the Edge of Time* (Women's Press 1979).

Piercy M, *He, She and It* (Fawcett 1991).

Reynolds M, 'What is Article 13? The EU's Divisive New Copyright Plan Explained' (*Wired*, 15 April 2019) <https://www.wired.co.uk/article/what-is-article-13-article-11-european-directive-on-copyright-explained-meme-ban> (accessed 5 May 2019).

Shen FX, 'Sex Robots Are Here, But Laws Aren't Keeping Up with the Ethical and Privacy Issues They Raise' (*The Conversation*, 12 February 2019) <https://

theconversation.com/sex-robots-are-here-but-laws-arent-keeping-up-with-the-ethical-and-privacy-issues-they-raise-109852> (accessed 5 May 2019).

Terminator (franchise), Wikipedia <https://en.wikipedia.org/wiki/Terminator_(franchise)> (accessed 5 May 2019).

The Matrix, Wikipedia <https://en.wikipedia.org/wiki/The_Matrix> (accessed 5 May 2019).

White Bear (Black Mirror), Wikipedia <https://en.wikipedia.org/wiki/White_Bear_(Black_Mirror)> (accessed 5 May 2019).

PART I

From Privacy and Princesses, to Security and *Star Wars*

2

Privacy and Identity through the Eyes of Disney Princesses[1]

Paul Bernal

1. Once Upon a Time …

Once upon a time there were eleven beautiful princesses. In many ways they were very different: they came from all over the world, from different periods of history, some from fiction, some from fact, some from fairy tale or folklore, some whose stories were shaped in the modern era. Though the films they grace were created in many different times and for widely different audiences, the stories of each of these fair princesses have distinct similarities, and not simply because the protagonists are all beautiful, troubled and beset by powerful enemies. Each highlights a key issue or issues about privacy and identity that are as relevant to today's online world as they were in the princesses' own realms and eras.

That they do so is neither happenstance nor some carefully crafted plan of Disney. Rather, it reflects something more important: privacy is a perennial issue, not a modern or transient indulgence as is sometimes suggested, an idea that did not exist in the past and will not exist in the future. That *all* these tales demonstrate the importance of privacy and identity rights is thus something that should be taken seriously – as should the rights themselves, which are also, at times, in danger of being dismissed as unimportant, outdated or

---

[1] The ideas in this chapter were inspired to a great extent by my daughter Alice, to whom I offer thanks and love. They were originally presented at Gikii in 2013 and 2014, and were blogged about on Paul Bernal's blog in September 2013 at <https://paulbernal.word-press.com/2013/09/17/online-privacy-and-identity-and-disney-princesses/> (accessed 5 September 2019). I am also grateful to my colleague Polly Morgan for her review of this chapter in draft.

13

even self-indulgent in the face of other, seemingly more grown-up issues such as security or economic prosperity.

The earliest of the princesses, Snow White, appeared in Disney's first full-length animation, *Snow White and the Seven Dwarfs*, in 1937, but it wasn't until 2000 that 'Disney Princesses' became an official franchise. At that point there were nine 'official' Disney Princesses – as of July 2018 there were eleven, with a number of other unofficial princesses lurking around the edges. The franchise has an official website and a massive commercial arm. Disney takes its Princesses very seriously: when Rapunzel became the tenth official Princess, she had a 'coronation' in Kensington Palace in London.[2] While the eleven official Princesses are all animated creations, a current trend is for 'live action' remakes and twists on the classics, including the world-shifting romantic comedy of *Enchanted* (2007), the inverted *Maleficent* (2014), and classically retold new versions of *Cinderella* (2015) and *Beauty and the Beast* (2017), all Disney, while the massive success of the Shrek saga rests to an extent on its own twists of princess tales. The role and rule of princesses is hard to overstate.

The long-term appeal of fairy tales is undoubted: they are not just a matter of trivial entertainment or a passing fad. As Marina Warner puts it, while '[a] few dissenting voices still consider fairy tales childish and foolish, on the whole, they have been widely accepted as a most valuable and profound creation of human history and culture'.[3] Whether you see the Disney Princess stories – and the fairy tales, folklore and legends that lie behind them – as instructional morality tales, psychological insights, deep reflections of particular aspects of culture or merely popular entertainment designed to resonate with young minds, that privacy and identity play an important part in them should make us pause. The fact that privacy and identity play a significant part in *all* of them should make us do more than pause.

It should make us pay very close attention. There are particular lessons about privacy and identity in these stories that could, *and should*, influence how both law and technology are shaped, if we are to improve our chances of living happily ever after.

---

2 The official Disney Princesses website is at <http://princess.disney.com>. In 2012, for example, the Disney Princess product line was believed to top the list of bestselling entertainment products, reckoned to be worth more than $3 billion worldwide. See Goudreau, 'Disney Princess Tops List of the 20 Best-Selling Entertainment Products' (*Forbes*, 17 September 2012) <https://www.forbes.com/sites/jennagoudreau/2012/09/17/disney-prin cess-tops-list-of-the-20-best-selling-entertainment-products/#369b49fbab06> (accessed 5 September 2019).

3 Warner, *Once Upon a Time: A Short History of Fairy Tale* (Oxford University Press 2014), p. 179.

1.1 Privacy, Identity and Autonomy

While some of the princesses' issues relate primarily to privacy, and others primarily to identity, most have an element of both because in practice the two issues are closely and often inextricably linked. Privacy can be seen as a protector of identity and identity as a way to control access to information, satisfying Westin's definition of privacy as 'the claim of individuals, groups or institutions to determine for themselves when, how and to what extent information about them is communicated to others'.[4] The connections between privacy and identity are intensified by common practices by both governments and corporations on the Internet: profiling for example, can be seen as using invasions of privacy in order to ascertain aspects of identity.[5]

It might be better, however, particularly in relation to the kinds of issues that the Disney Princesses demonstrate, to see both privacy and identity as aspects of a struggle for autonomy, the underlying theme in *all* the stories. The Princesses may appear to want tiaras, beautiful dresses, magnificent palaces or the love of a handsome prince, but underlying all of this is a need for something deeper. They are fighting for the freedom to live their lives the way that they want to. For some, their freedom has been taken away, for others their lives are constrained by forces arrayed against them, for still others, something they want or need is blocked or apparently unattainable. For all of the princesses, autonomy is the dream; as Cinderella sings, the 'wish your heart makes'.

1.2 Magic and Technology

Magic is a recurrent theme in fairy tales, and indeed in most of the Disney Princess stories, though in a few of them, notably the (at least partially) historically based stories of *Pocahontas* and *Mulan*, the magic on display is not directly connected with privacy and identity issues. In the majority, however, magic is critical, and that again gives a clue to the relationship between the stories and online life. As Arthur C Clarke put it, '[a]ny sufficiently advanced technology is indistinguishable from magic'.[6] The technology of the Internet

---

[4] Westin, *Privacy and Freedom* (Bodley Head 1968), p. 7. Westin defines privacy from the outset in his introduction to the book.

[5] Setting out precise definitions of privacy is a thorny issue: see Solove, *Understanding Privacy* (Harvard University Press 2008), particularly Chapter 1, and Bernal, *Internet Privacy Rights: Rights to Protect Autonomy* (Cambridge University Press 2014), Chapter 2. For the purposes of this chapter, however, the Westin definition and the connection with autonomy gives sufficient context.

[6] The third of Clarke's often quoted 'Three Laws', it appeared first in the 1973 version of

is in most ways, and for most users, advanced enough to fit that definition – and allows things that would have only have been possible by magic in the past. Changes in sex, crystal balls and magic mirrors, invisibility and shape-changing, silencing curses and magical sleep spells all have their online equivalents. Creating online 'identities' different from your 'real' identity has been crucial to many online platforms – pseudonymity provides a vital protection to whistle-blowers, for example, while avoiding using gender-specific or religion-specific names can reduce stereotypical responses, online harassment or potentially discriminatory online prices. Surveillance can be tantamount to a crystal ball, profiling methods can simulate mind reading, social media accounts can be muted or blocked – or even banned and so silenced.

Magic in the princess stories is something that helps as well as hinders. For many, magic is the key that opens the doors that have been locked, bringing the opportunities that had been denied to them. The same could be true of technology, and the internet in particular. It can provide opportunities that would otherwise have been impossible: it can be a liberator, giving voice to the voiceless, protection to the weak, and so forth, as noted above. The risk is that, as Morozov[7] and others have elucidated in depth, in practice it becomes very much the opposite: a tool of oppression and control. The question for those interested in the internet as a tool of liberation is how the positive possibilities can be made real, while the negative kept to a minimum. That is where the princess stories can, perhaps, provide some clues.

2. Disney Princesses

2.1 Snow White, from 'Snow White and the Seven Dwarfs' (1937)

The version of the Snow White story with which we are most familiar comes from the Brothers Grimm, in their first collection of fairy tales in 1812. In that version, as in the Disney version, Snow White has a vital need to protect from the Evil Queen, her stepmother, two different but critical aspects of her privacy, namely her existence (that she is still alive) and her location.

In the real world, the latter aspect in particular is of increasing importance and, with the geolocation possibilities enabled by smartphones and related technology, increasingly under threat. The Evil Queen's magic mirror, central to all versions of the Snow White story, is in many ways a classical surveillance tool: there are close parallels with modern concepts such as the

---

Clarke's essay 'Hazards of Prophecy: The Failure of Imagination', in *Profiles of the Future* (Phoenix 1973), p. 21.

[7] Most notably in Morozov, *The Net Delusion: How Not to Liberate the World* (Penguin 2012).

PRISM programme revealed by Edward Snowden or the filtering arrangements built into the UK's Investigatory Powers Act.[8] When the Evil Queen asks 'Magic mirror on the wall, who is the fairest of them all?', she is setting parameters for the search for a universal facial recognition database, and when the mirror tells her 'Over the seven jewelled hills, beyond the seventh fall, in the cottage of the Seven Dwarfs, dwells Snow White, fairest one of all', it is returning exactly the data that the Evil Queen needs in order to locate and track her down.

2.2 'Cinderella' (1950)

Different variations of Cinderella can be found in many cultures and traditions. The version that became the basis of the Disney version is from the French collector of folklore Charles Perrault in 1697. Cinderella has a different problem from Snow White, more directly connected with identity than privacy, though there are privacy elements to her story too.

Cinderella's identity is stolen by her stepmother, who forces her to take up a false identity that extends even so far as her name, for – and this is often forgotten – 'Cinderella' just means 'cinder girl', and one of her jobs as a drudge is to clean out the cinders from the fireplace. Her real name is not given in most versions of the story: the Disney version does not mention it at all, and indeed the opening lines to the opening song suggest that Cinderella is a lovely name.[9] Her false identity as Cinderella has a huge impact on her autonomy: it keeps her from living the life that she is born into and that she wants to live. As for a number of the Princesses, her solution is magical: she uses the magical assistance of her fairy godmother in order to get the life she wants and, in some sense at least, deserves.

The internet parallels apply both to the harm that Cinderella suffers – the harm of having an identity imposed upon you, for example by profiling – and the solution of being able to create your own identity, thus avoiding that profiling or any signifiers set by others. There is another recurring issue here: that of 'real' names. What is Cinderella's 'real' name? The one given to her at birth, or the one imposed upon her – potentially legally – by those in authority? It should be remembered that assuming Cinderella was a minor when her father died, her stepmother is in legal authority over her. In legal terms, therefore, 'Cinderella' may be both her 'real' name and her official identity. For Cinderella to go to the ball, meet the prince and find her future, she needs to go beyond that 'real name' and official identity.

---

[8] As set out in the Investigatory Powers Act 2016, ss 67–9.

[9] 'Cinderella, you're as lovely as your name' are the first words in the film.

The privacy aspects of Cinderella's story are also relevant. Cinderella has a secret life that her stepmother and stepsisters have no knowledge of – her companionship with mice and birds is one of the things that keeps her going through the hardship her stepmother has imposed upon her. If it were revealed, it seems likely that her stepmother would have ensured the mice were all killed and the birds driven away: privacy matters in a direct and important way to people suffering from oppression. Although it takes the magic of her fairy godmother to remove her from that suffering, it is her private life that keeps her going, just as some online communities provide invaluable support for people in particular situations – from mainstream support groups like Mumsnet[10] to specialised forums for sufferers of specific illnesses or conditions. The internet can provide the kind of privacy that supports these communities, just as Cinderella's attic let her talk with her mice and birds.

2.3 Sleeping Beauty *(1959)*

As for *Cinderella*, the version of *Sleeping Beauty* used by Disney comes primarily from Perrault, albeit via the Tchaikovsky ballet. However, there are much earlier versions of the story in evidence, such as 'Le Roman de Perceforest', a fourteenth-century Arthurian story that includes an episode with similar elements.[11]

In the Disney version, Princess Aurora, the Sleeping Beauty, has problems of both privacy and identity. She needs privacy to protect herself from the wrath of Maleficent, the powerful and dangerous evil fairy. Accordingly, from the time she is a baby she has to live with the three good fairies, under a pseudonym, Briar Rose. Maleficent tries to find her, sending her goblin minions out to search. Yet over the years the minions keep searching for a baby, not thinking that Aurora will have grown up. Finally, Maleficent's raven familiar successfully finds Aurora, who is just short of her sixteenth birthday.

Sleeping Beauty shows how privacy and anonymity work together to protect against potential enemies – but also how human (or near-human) error can make all the difference in both directions. The errors of the goblin minions mean that their surveillance is ineffective (just as much governmental surveillance is ineffective[12]), while the raven finally finds Aurora as a result

---

[10] See https://www.mumsnet.com.

[11] See, for example, Bryant, *Perceforest: The Prehistory of King Arthur's Britain* (DS Brewer 2011).

[12] The abject failure of Danish 'session logging', which in seven years provided useful evidence in only one single case, is just one example. See, for example, the evidence of

of the foolishness of the three good fairies, whose magical argument gives away their location.

2.4 Ariel, from The Little Mermaid (1989)

The story of Ariel, the 'Little Mermaid', comes from Hans Christian Andersen, and Disney's version is relatively faithful to Andersen's 1837 original. Ariel, the youngest daughter of the Sea King, Triton, is fascinated by the human world, and, disobeying her father's explicit instructions, goes to the surface and sees the ship of Prince Eric struggle in a storm. Rescuing Eric from the shipwreck, she falls for him – and seeks for a way to be with him. This, again, involves magic: Ariel does a deal with the evil Sea Witch Ursula, who gives her a new identity as a human, but at the cost of the loss of her voice – something absolutely vital for Ariel, as her singing is part of what makes her special, part of her *identity* that is taken away from her.

Privacy issues again play a critical part in Ariel's story. Ursula uses surveillance (as do so many Disney villains), seeing through the eyes of her twin eel familiars Flotsam and Jetsam and spying on Ariel in order to plan both Ariel's and her father's downfall.

Using information gathered through surveillance in order to take advantage of others is a classic technique in the 'real' world, but could also be said to be the basis of the business models of Google, Facebook and others, and to enable much of the surveillance of NSA, GCHQ and their equivalents. Surveillance has an empowering effect: it gives the person using it informational power over those they are monitoring.[13]

Ariel's identity issues are similar to those of Cinderella: she needs to create a new identity for herself (as a human) in order to get the kind of life she wants, and she has to use magic to do this. As with Sleeping Beauty, that identity would have been broken by the imposition of a 'real names' policy – another common theme for the Princesses.

2.5 Belle, from Beauty and the Beast (1991)

The most familiar version of *Beauty and the Beast* comes from French author Gabrielle-Suzanne Barbot de Villeneuve in 1740. The Disney version changes the story significantly, but the basic elements of the Disney version are

---

the IT-Political Association of Denmark to the Joint Parliamentary Committee on the Investigatory Powers Bill, online at <http://data.parliament.uk/writtenevidence/committeeevidence.svc/evidencedocument/science-and-technology-committee/investigatory-powers-bill-technology-issues/written/25190.html> (accessed 5 September 2019).

[13] See, for example, Richards, 'The Dangers of Surveillance' (2013) 126 *Harvard Law Review* 1934.

present in Villeneuve's original, including the privacy-critical magical mirror, albeit in a slightly more primitive form.

In Disney's version, the heroine, Belle, like so many of her fellow heroines, is struggling with autonomy. She wants find something different from the 'provincial life' that she leads, from the identity and profile that seem fixed for her, including marriage to such as her suitor, the boorish Gaston. The privacy and identity issues, however, really come into play in relation to the Beast. The first of these is the beastly identity forced upon him, the result of a curse from a fairy. The second is his response to that enforced identity: hiding his castle from the outside world. Effectively, he has taken an extreme form of privacy to protect himself – such an extreme form that it curtails his autonomy almost completely, just as for someone in modern society cutting themselves off from the internet would make ordinary social activities very difficult indeed, when so much of our lives, from work to finance, shopping to social lives, requires it. It takes the eventual arrival of Belle at his castle to offer a way forward.

When Belle has to leave the castle to look after her father, the Beast gives her a magical mirror that lets her see the Beast from wherever she is. When she returns home to find her father threatened with being locked away by Gaston, she shows Gaston the Beast in her mirror. The Beast is instantly profiled by Gaston, who gathers up a mob to give the Beast the full torches and pitchforks treatment. Effectively, Belle invades the Beast's privacy with devastating effect: it is not just evil witch-queens that we need to worry about surveillance from: sometimes privacy invasions by those we love can end up damaging us. Of relevance to current legal and technological developments, this demonstrates how 'backdoors' and surveillance systems created for friends and those you trust – in this case for Belle to see the Beast – can become vulnerable to enemies and to those you do not trust. Gaston, given access to the surveillance system, uses it for his own purposes.

2.6 Jasmine, from Aladdin (1992)

The story of Aladdin is generally considered to be one of the *Tales of 1,001 Nights*, but was actually a later addition to the original collection, added in around 1709–10 by the French translator Antoine Galland. He reportedly took it from a Syrian storyteller, although there is no known original source in Arabic. As with many of the princess stories, several of the key privacy and identity issues are in both the original and the Disney version. Aladdin himself needs to create the false identity of Prince Ali, through the magical help of the Genie, to get into a position to let his 'real' identity shine through in order to win Jasmine's love.

Apart from this, the Disney version is much changed from the Galland version. One of the biggest changes is the role of Jasmine, the daughter of the Sultan in the Disney version. Her role is much expanded and modernised, giving her much more of a stake in autonomy than in the original. As the film starts, she is being courted by princes, none of whom she has any liking for. In an abortive attempt to escape from being a princess and an unwanted future marriage, Jasmine runs away from the palace and tries to create a new identity for herself.

Two recurrent themes are present in Disney's Aladdin: once again the villain, this time the Vizier Jafar, uses surveillance as part of his machinations, and once again 'real names' would have prevented the protagonists from achieving their goals, both in their personal and their 'political' lives – for Jasmine as girl and as daughter of the Sultan.

2.7 Pocahontas *(1995)*

The story of *Pocahontas* is loosely based on a historical event and a historical person. There was a real Pocahontas, who lived, as far as can be told, from around 1596 until 1617. She was the daughter of a Powhatan Chieftain, and Pocahontas was a nickname rather than her 'proper' name.[14] The Disney version of the story shares some of the elements of the life of the real Pocahontas and is based around one particular (and disputed) incident in which she pleaded for mercy for the captured Englishman, Captain John Smith.[15]

In most ways, however, Disney's version is very different from what is known of the historical Pocahontas – though the most important issue for the Disney Pocahontas does bear some relation to what must have faced the real Pocahontas: the need and right to be able to assert one's identity.[16] The Disney Pocahontas in particular needs to assert an identity that is contrary to the idea of the 'savage' that the English settlers thought she was, based on their inaccurate profiling and prejudicial assumptions. There are parallels between the identity issues of Pocahontas and those of Cinderella: in both cases, profile-based assumptions of identity have to be overcome in order to achieve desired outcomes.

Algorithmic profiling on the internet as a form of categorisation is, in practice, inherently discriminatory, despite a common belief that it is in some

---

[14] See, for example, Mossiker, *Pocahontas: The Life and the Legend* (Alfred A Knopf 1976).

[15] Related in Mossiker, *Pocahontas*, pp. 80–1. Whether the event actually happened, and what its real nature was, is to an extent a matter of conjecture – it might have been a ritual, and Smith might have merely repeated an old story, for example – but this is not significant for the purposes of this chapter.

[16] See Bernal, *Internet Privacy Rights*, Chapter 9.

senses 'organic' or 'neutral'.[17] The assertion of identity and the need to over-come these kinds of assumptions is a crucial aspect of online identity rights.

2.8 Mulan *(1998)*

Disney's Chinese heroine Mulan – not really a princess, though included in the official Disney Princesses franchise – is based on a literary or possibly historical figure from China, Hua Mulan.[18] The legend has been the subject of much interest in Chinese literature and drama for over fifteen hundred years. As Louise Edwards puts it:

> Hua Mulan has entranced and intrigued generations of Chinese. Since the Northern Wei dynasty (386–534) stories of her remarkable adventures in the military realm, replacing her father in the imperial troops disguised as a man, have been a recurring theme in both elite and popular cultural forms: including poetry, drama, opera and more recently film, television series and video games.[19]

The central theme, of a girl who pretends to be a boy in order to help out a father who has no sons, is one that is repeated in folklore and fairy tales elsewhere across the world. The nineteenth-century Romanian scholar and historian Petre Ispirescu, for example, included 'The Princess Who Would Be a Prince or Iliane of the Golden Tresses' in his collection *The Foundling Prince, & Other Tales*,[20] while French scholar and diplomat Auguste Dozon quoted a traditional Albanian folk tale, 'The Girl Who Became a Boy', in 1879,[21] though both these versions have very different

---

[17] See, for example, Miller CC, 'When Algorithms Discriminate' (*New York Times*, 9 July 2015) <www.nytimes.com/2015/07/10/upshot/when-algorithms-discriminate.html> (accessed 5 September 2019), and a more general discussion in Bernal, *The Internet, Warts and All: Free Speech, Privacy and Truth* (Cambridge University Press 2018), Chapter 4.

[18] In Edwards, 'Transformations of the Woman Warrior Hua Mulan: From Defender of the Family to Servant of the State' (December 2010) 12 *Men, Women and Gender in Early and Imperial China* 175, p. 179. Louise Edwards notes that 'historical evidence about Mulan's life is elusive. If she did exist, the details of her life remain unverified and most scholars currently regard her as a purely literary figure.'

[19] Edwards, 'Transformations of the Woman Warrior Hua Mulan', pp. 175–6.

[20] A full copy of a 1917 University of Michigan translation of this 1879 collection, translated by Julia Collier and Rea Ipcar, is available online at the Hathi Trust: <https://babel.hathitrust.org/cgi/pt?id=mdp.39015043595746;view=1up;seq=13> (accessed 5 September 2019), pp. 239–84. A version of this story, titled 'The Girl Who Pretended to Be a Boy', is also included in Andrew Lang's collection, *The Violet Fairy Book* (Dover Children's Classics 1966, original 1901).

[21] See, for example <https://archive.org/details/manueldelalangue00dozouoft>. A summary of the story itself can be found here: <www.albanianliterature.net/folktales/tale_07.html> (accessed 5 September 2019).

endings than that of Mulan: the girl being magically transformed into a boy.

Disney's version of Mulan is based only loosely on the legend, though the central theme is the same. Mulan's identity problems are seen from a very different perspective than those of Cinderella and Sleeping Beauty, and have more in common with Ariel, though with a different purpose. Mulan has to create a new identity, as a boy rather than a girl, in order to protect her disabled father from disgrace by taking his place as a conscript in the army. This identity requires a pseudonym, Ping, because her real name would give away her sex. She needs privacy in order to protect this identity and not have her 'real' identity revealed – one scene in the film involves her taking a naked bath in a lake and being surprised by some of the other soldiers.[22] Preventing them from discovering her true nature is difficult – later in the story it proves impossible when she is injured and treated by a doctor. Once the other soldiers discover she is a *she*, they exclude her from their ranks and potentially disgrace both her and her family. It is only through heroic endeavour that she manages to prevent this happening – and at the same time save China and its emperor from invasion and death respectively.

The story of Mulan demonstrates again that there can be good reasons to allow pseudonymity and to protect privacy. She has to create her 'false' identity in order to help her own family, not as a matter of selfishness. It allows her to break free of the limitations imposed by societal norms and prejudices – something that online pseudonyms and anonymity can also allow. Once again, a 'real names' policy would have made her plans fail before they even started.

2.9 Tiana, from The Princess and the Frog *(2009)*

'The Frog Prince' is another familiar and old tale. According to Maria Tatar, the Brothers Grimm included their version 'The Frog King, or Iron Heinrich', as the opening story in their first collection (1812), because 'they considered it to be among the oldest in the collection'.[23] Interestingly, in Grimm the frog is not kissed: the transformation occurs when the princess throws the frog against a wall in disgust. The Disney version starts from the better known tale based around the kiss, and borrows its crucial twist from a much later source: ED Baker's 2002 story, 'The Frog Princess'.

When Tiana, the protagonist in 'The Princess and the Frog', kisses her

---

[22] This is not something new and out of character with the earlier forms of the story: 'ribald jokes' have recurred regularly in versions of the Mulan story over the centuries. See Edwards, 'Transformations of the Woman Warrior Hua Mulan', p. 179.

[23] Tatar, *The Annotated Brothers Grimm* (WW Norton 2004), p. 3.

frog, it isn't the frog that becomes a prince but the 'princess' who becomes a frog. The result is an identity issue related to that of Cinderella and the Beast. Like them, Tiana has a new identity thrust upon her, one that she doesn't like and doesn't want – and the film follows the great struggle through which she finds a way to regain the identity that she does want. Just as for Cinderella and the Beast, it takes a good deal of magical assistance to make this possible – as it does for those subject to automated, algorithmic discrimination based on profiling in the current internet. Determining what has happened, then finding a way to reverse it, is rarely easy even if laws are created to help you to do so – as Edwards and Veale argue in relation to the rules on profiling[24] in the General Data Protection Regulation (GDPR).[25]

2.10 *Rapunzel, from* Tangled *(2010)*

The story of Rapunzel is another of those included by the Brothers Grimm in 1812 but the origins of the tale are far earlier – at least as far as seventeenth-century Italian fairy tale collector Giambattista Basile, whose 'Petrosinella' has many similar elements, and even a parallel in names and triggers for the story. Petrosinella refers to the herb parsley, while Rapunzel is the German for the flowering herb rampion. Disney's version of 'Rapunzel', *Tangled,* is much changed from the familiar versions, but still retains many of the key parts – including and expanding upon both privacy and identity issues.

In *Tangled,* rather than effectively being given away by her parents, as in the original, Rapunzel is stolen from them by the villain Mother Gothel. Mother Gothel then brings Rapunzel up as her own daughter, lying to her about her parentage and nature. The underlying struggle of the film is Rapunzel's uncovering of this scheme, return to her family and regaining of knowledge and control of her identity.

The privacy elements of *Tangled* are also significant: as in the original version, Rapunzel has seclusion forced upon her when she is locked away in a tower – something that might be regarded as a kind of privacy that restricts autonomy completely. She needs to find a way to escape and – although she doesn't realise this initially – discover her true identity. There are echoes of both Cinderella and the Beast here: hiding, or being forced to hide, is not

---

[24] See Edwards and Veale, 'Slave to the Algorithm? Why a "Right to an Explanation" Is Probably Not the Remedy You Are Looking For' (2017) 16 *Duke Law & Technology Review* 18.

[25] The GDPR is Regulation (EU) 2016/679 of the European Parliament and of the Council, online at <https://eur-lex.europa.eu/legal-content/EN/TXT/?qid=1528874672298&uri=CELEX%3A32016R0679> (accessed 5 September 2019).

really what privacy is about. Conceptions of privacy have developed from the idea presented in Warren and Brandeis' seminal piece 'The Right to Privacy' in 1891 as a right to be let alone[26] to Westin's suggestion that it is about having the active ability to decide how and when information about yourself is made available, and to whom.[27] Enforced hiding is just as much an infringement of this as enforced revelation of private information – particularly from an autonomy perspective.

2.11 *Merida, from* Brave *(2012)*

The most recent of the 'official' Disney Princesses is Merida, the heroine of Brave – an original story written by Brenda Chapman for the film, but one that takes many elements and themes from folklore and fairy tale. Merida, daughter of King Fergus and Queen Elinor of Clan Dunbroch in a fantastical version of Medieval Scotland, is expected to fulfil the traditional princess's duty: marry an appropriate suitor for political purposes. She has different ideas: she is an active, outdoors girl, preferring wild riding and archery to music and embroidery, and has no desire to marry, let alone marry one of the three awful suitors selected by the allied clans. She cannot convince her parents – and particularly her mother – to give her freedom, so when she finds a witch in the wilds, she asks for a spell to change her mother. That change, though Merida does not realise it, means her mother transforming into a bear: bears are considered brutal and dangerous, and are hunted ruthlessly, most particularly by King Fergus. There then follows a struggle, a chase (with much hiding), and eventually both a reconciliation between mother and daughter and a return to human form for the former. Merida is given the freedom to choose when, with whom and *whether* to marry.

In essence, Merida's whole story is about autonomy and identity. She wants to forge her own identity, one very different from the identity chosen for her by convention and more directly by her mother. Just as with Cinderella, she needs privacy to survive her struggle: she finds refuge by riding out into the wilds, where none can see her or know what she is doing or thinking – or stop her from doing it. Her mother, too, has obvious issues. As with the Beast and Tiana, she has an identity forced upon her, one that curtails her autonomy, and, again like the Beast, this makes her a target for profiling and persecution. Once more, magic takes the place of technology, allowing the transformations and the profiling, causing the problems and

---

[26] Warren and Brandeis, 'The Right to Privacy' (1890) IV *Harvard Law Review*.
[27] Westin, *Privacy and Freedom*.

providing the solutions. Ultimately, it is only through this magic that Merida achieves her desired autonomy.

3. Unofficial Disney Princesses

Not all princesses in Disney films are *official* Disney Princesses. The notable absences, however, fit the pattern of privacy and identity issues just as well as the official ones. Elsa and Anna, the sibling stars of *Frozen*, may well have been excluded for commercial reasons: the *Frozen* franchise is so valuable on its own that confusing the issue by adding them to the princesses could be a distraction.[28] They are, however, in every practical way, Disney Princesses in a classical form, right down to the big hair, tiny waists and sparkling tiaras. Vanellope von Schweetz, from *Wreck-It Ralph*,[29] and Leia from *Star Wars*, are quite different: they do not really fit with what Disney refers to as the 'mythology' of the Disney Princesses. A further character, Esmeralda from 1996's *The Hunchback of Notre Dame*, was initially included in the franchise before being withdrawn for unspecified reasons: she too has particular privacy issues, discussed below. Moana, from *Moana* (2016), though she protests firmly that she is not a princess but the daughter of a chief, has many of the characteristics of a princess: as her foil in the film, the demi-god Maui, puts it, '[i]f you wear a dress and have an animal sidekick, then you're a princess'. Indeed, she was rumoured at one point to be joining the official line-up of princesses, though this never actually happened. Moana has a number of the privacy and identity issues of the official princesses – as well as a particular twist on the right to be remembered, shown most directly by Vanellope von Schweetz.

Even the more obscure possibilities have privacy and identity issues. Megara, from *Hercules* (1997), whose very different mythological equivalent would have been classed as a princess, had huge privacy and identity issues connected to her Faustian deal with Hades. Kida, the princess from *Atlantis: The Lost Empire* (2001), might well have fitted the bill if her film had been more successful. Her whole life was based on privacy, as Atlantis itself was deliberately kept concealed from the outside world. In every case, it seems, privacy and identity are critical for princesses.

---

[28] In 2014 *Frozen* became the most commercially successful animated film of all time (see, for example, <www.ibtimes.com.au/disney-movie-frozen-hits-1072-billion-revenue-now-highest-grossing-animated-movie-all-time-1336475>) whilst its merchandising was considered by many to be the key to Disney's profit growth (see <http://fortune.com/2015/02/03/disney-quarterly-earnings/>) (accessed 5 September 2019).

[29] See below at section 3.2 ('*Wreck-It Ralph* and the Right to be Remembered').

3.1 Frozen – *and the Chilling Effect*

Frozen, from 2013, is the most financially successful Disney animation to date. It was inspired by Hans Christian Andersen's 1844 story 'The Snow Queen', although the plot bears almost no resemblance to that of Andersen. *Frozen*, however, has privacy issues at its frozen heart. Where *Snow White, Sleeping Beauty, Beauty and the Beast, The Little Mermaid* and *Aladdin* demonstrate the dangers imposed by surveillance and invasions of privacy, *Frozen*, through both of its heroines, explores how the very possibility of such invasions can have an impact on the psyche and actions of those at risk of surveillance and affect the actions used to defend and protect against surveillance. *Frozen*, appropriately, demonstrates exactly how the 'chilling effect' of potential privacy invasions works.

Elsa, the Queen whose icy magical powers are such that both she and her parents believe their revelation would be disastrous, hides herself away from view much of the time.[30] When she does show herself, she creates an image of conformity: emotionless and flawless. 'Conceal, don't feel' is a mantra repeated in a number of songs in the film. Elsa's tortured soul is the result, for the most part at least, of her fear of discovery. She has, she believes, something to hide – and though the saying 'nothing to hide, nothing to fear' is fundamentally flawed, if you *believe* you have something to hide then in a world where privacy is insufficiently protected you do, in practice, have something to fear. Societies where surveillance is near universal encourage conformity – as the experience of East Germany and the Stasi confirms.[31] Elsa certainly believes that she needs to hide her powers: and this shapes her whole approach to life. It is not for nothing that the song with which the film opens warns 'Beware the Frozen Heart'. Though Elsa's sister Anna's heart is physically frozen by an accident of Elsa's magic, it is Elsa's heart that is metaphorically frozen through her attempts to 'conceal, don't feel'.

Anna herself demonstrates some other critical aspects of the effects of privacy invasion – or, to be more precise, of the impact of methods used to

---

[30] There are echoes here of *Beauty and the Beast*: the Beast locks himself away in his castle to protect himself (and what he has to hide) from prying eyes.

[31] See for example Garton Ash, *The File* (Atlantic Books 2009). Garton Ash experienced it personally. 'More typical were the nice couple from whom the University had rented my room. Intelligent, well-educated, well-informed through watching Western television, they nonetheless devoted virtually all their energies to their private lives, and particularly to extending, decorating and maintaining their cottage on a small lake some half-an-hour's drive from Berlin', p. 66.

protect against such invasions. Anna is kept in ignorance of Elsa's powers, but under the same strictures: she too is 'protected' from the outside world, though without knowing why. This protectiveness, this insulation from the outside world – overprotectiveness as an overreaction to perceived risk – leaves her unprepared and vulnerable to be preyed upon by the unscrupulous. This proves to be the case as Prince Hans first of all presents himself as exactly the kind of man a girl like Anna – swiftly and calculatedly profiled – would fall in love with. She has developed none of the tactics that might protect her either from this profiling or from the seduction that follows: the potentially counterproductive 'wrap in cotton wool' approach to 'protecting' young people on the internet played out in fiction.

Where Elsa is defensive and troubled, Anna is naive and vulnerable: both are unable to deal with the outside world as a result of the tactics taken to deal with potential invasions of their privacy.

3.2 Wreck-It Ralph *and the Right to be Remembered*

Vanellope von Schweetz, the diminutive kart-racing heroine of the 2012 video game-based film *Wreck-It Ralph*, demonstrates yet another side of online identity and privacy, though in a way that is not immediately obvious. At the start of the film, Vanellope does not even know who she is: her identity has been directly and deliberately blocked by the villain of the piece, King Candy, with all the information about her history and nature locked away. Without this information, Vanellope does not fit into her own world, is shunned by everyone around her and is unable to do any of the things that she wants or dreams of. Her autonomy is highly restricted. This touches upon another critical element of privacy: it is not, despite appearances, about hiding so much as choosing what to show. In Westin's terms, how can someone 'determine for themselves when, how, and to what extent information about them is communicated to others'[32] if they have no access to that information in the first place?

The often-contentious idea of a 'right to be forgotten' is familiar to most concerned with online privacy:[33] its potential partner and counterpart, a 'right to be remembered'[34] is perhaps equally important. They are aspects of

---

[32] Westin, *Privacy and Freedom.* See footnote 4.

[33] As set out in Article 17 of Regulation (EU) 2016/679, more commonly known as the General Data Protection Regulation, one aspect of which was ruled upon in the noted case of *Google Spain SL, Google Inc* v *Agencia Española de Protección de Datos (AEPD), Mario Costeja González,* Case C-131/12.

[34] The concept of this form of a right to be remembered was put forward by the author of this chapter in the paper 'The Right to be Remembered – or – The Internet, Warts and

the same thing: a privacy-based right at least to influence how information about oneself is made available. Where the right to be forgotten relates to the obscuring of old, irrelevant or otherwise inappropriate information, a right to be remembered should aim to ensure that new, important and appropriate information is brought to light and given suitable prominence. This kind of a right would of course be in tension with others' rights – speech rights, for example, or the rights of individuals over what they themselves have said,[35] but it is what Vanellope needs: when both her memory and those of people around her are restored, her real identity as a princess is revealed, and she is able to do the things that she has dreamed of.[36]

Wreck-It Ralph shows another side to the identity issue: King Candy himself is concealing his own identity – he used to be another character from Turbo, another game entirely. Privacy, and control over identity, can be used for bad things as well as good. The challenge is to decide whether the good outweighs the bad – and whether a balance can be found.

3.3 Moana and the Right to Remember

As well as being central to *Wreck-It Ralph*, memory and its relationship to identity are also central themes in the story of Moana, drawn from Polynesian folklore. Where Vanellope needs her personal memory restored, Moana needs her cultural memory restored. Her forebears had hidden their past as voyagers and explorers to dissuade their people from sailing beyond the reef around their island: the moment when Moana discovers her people's true past and nature is one of the most poignant in the film. This relates to the other side of the right to be remembered: the right to remember. Just as freedom of expression has two elements, the right to impart and the right to receive,[37] so does remembering historical and similar information – reflected in the balance between the legal 'right to erasure' set out in the GDPR[38] and freedom of expression and other related rights.

Moana's quest, like that of Merida, is to forge an identity for herself. To do so she needs to remember – but she also needs privacy in a more

---

All', workshopped at the Privacy Law Scholars Conference in Berkeley, June 2015, and is discussed in depth in Bernal, *The Internet, Warts and All*.

[35] See Bernal, *The Internet, Warts and All*, particularly pp. 46–8.

[36] In the sequel to *Wreck-It Ralph*, *Ralph Breaks the Internet*, Vanellope faces another classical identity and autonomy issue – the desire to break out of her existing world and create a new identity in a wholly different place. The Disney Princesses scene in *Ralph Breaks the Internet* also provides dramatic support to the desire for autonomy of all the Disney Princesses.

[37] As expressed, for example, in Article 10 of the European Convention on Human Rights.

[38] GDPR, Article 17.

conventional way. It is only through her private conversations and explorations with her grandmother that she is able to discover the past of her people – and if her father had known about those conversations, he would have brought a halt to them and stopped Moana's quest before it had even started. For children in particular, privacy from parents is perhaps the most important part of privacy at all – as the almost-Disney princess, Leia, shows most directly.

3.4 Leia and Privacy from Parents

Parents play a crucial role in many of the Disney Princesses' stories, all too often by dying. Snow White, Cinderella, Ariel, Belle, Jasmine, Pocahontas, Elsa and Anna all lose at least one parent either before their films start or in the first few scenes. Disney's adoptive princess, *Star Wars'* Leia, has also lost her mother – but her relationship with her father, Darth Vader, is a critical part of the story. Indeed, it raises one of the most important aspects of privacy for children: privacy from their parents. It is parents that hold the greatest power over children, and hence parents from whom children often need (and want) the protection of privacy. For teenagers – and Disney princesses are mostly teenagers – this is particularly true. As danah boyd's extensive study of teens' social media activities suggested:

> teens aren't typically concerned with governments and corporations. Instead, they're trying to avoid surveillance from parents, teachers, and other immediate authority figures in their lives.[39]

Though Disney, and many earlier collectors and adapters of fairy tales, soften the blow by ensuring that the 'evil' parents are replaced by stepparents, in folk and fairy tales in their original form this was not always the case. In the earliest versions of Hansel and Gretel, for example, it is their *real* mother and father who leave them to die in the woods.[40] The way that Disney changed the Rapunzel story for *Tangled*, having Rapunzel stolen from her parents rather than given away, is another example of this tendency.

At the start of *Star Wars*, Leia's privacy issues are two-fold: first, she doesn't want Darth Vader to find her, and second, though she doesn't even realise it, she doesn't want him to find out that he is her father. Having a

---

[39] boyd, *It's complicated: The Social Lives of Networked Teens Teens* (Yale University Press 2014), p. 56.

[40] Tatar, in *The Annotated Brothers Grimm*, p. 73, notes that though the version in the Grimms' first collection in 1812 involved the biological parents, by the fourth edition in 1840 the mother had been replaced by a stepmother who had become the 'real villain of the piece'.

father like Darth Vader emphasises the problem: parents can be bad, parents can and do have power. While few children have parents as bad or as powerful as Vader, most have parents who can wield immense, life-changing power over them. All children need and want privacy from their parents at times: very few teenagers would be happy for their parents to read their private diaries or know their private thoughts.

3.5 *Esmeralda, from* The Hunchback of Notre Dame *(1996)*

Esmeralda's initial inclusion and subsequent disappearance from the Disney Princesses franchise has been the subject of some conjecture[41] but the role that privacy and identity play in the story itself is clear. Quasimodo's entire life is about hiding, and he helps Esmeralda, including by concealing her escape. This, however, is not the most important element of privacy in the tale. Esmeralda is a gypsy, and the gypsies are under direct threat from the authorities, and from Esmeralda and Quasimodo's nemesis, Frollo, in particular. Their only protection is that the location of their base, the Court of Miracles, remains a secret. By secretly tracking Esmeralda after her escape, Frollo finds the Court of Miracles, rounds up the gypsies and has Esmeralda herself prepared for burning at the stake. Only a dramatic rescue and popular uprising against Frollo saves her and the gypsies. The parallels with authoritarian regimes such as that in pre-revolutionary Tunisia, which hacked into Facebook to find where the enemies of the regime were meeting,[42] are direct. Privacy can be a protection against an oppressive regime for minorities and other groups that are seen as a threat.

4. Common Themes and Implications

There are a number of common themes in the princess stories – themes that have particular implications for law and for technology. Not many of us have genies, fairy godmothers or enchanted furniture to protect us: the most that we can generally expect is to have the law on our side and technology that can help us – or at least not have the law conspiring against us with the wicked stepmothers, sea witches and evil sorcerers of this world, and technology that aids them rather than us. That means, amongst other things, ensuring that

---

[41] No official reason for her removal from the line-up was given, but suggestions included her 'sultry pose'. See for, example, <http://disney.wikia.com/wiki/Esmeralda#Disney_Princess> (accessed 5 September 2019).

[42] See, for example, Madrigal AC, 'The Inside Story of How Facebook Responded to Tunisian Hacks' (*The Atlantic*, 24 January 2011) <www.theatlantic.com/technology/archive/2011/01/the-inside-story-of-how-facebook-responded-to-tunisian-hacks/70044/> (accessed 5 September 2019).

the powers available to legal authorities are limited and accountable: *Snow White*'s Evil Queen, it must be remembered, was the legal sovereign, while *Alladin*'s Jafar was at different times in the film either the Royal Vizier or the Sultan himself.

4.1 'Real Names'

'Real names' laws and rules, though superficially attractive in dealing with potentially malign uses of anonymity or pseudonymity from trolling to cyberbullying, have potentially disastrous effects for others, and particularly those in difficult situations.[43] It is no coincidence that several of the Disney Princesses, as well as a few of their princes, have to use pseudonyms or anonymity in the stories. Cinderella goes to the ball anonymously – and, as noted above, has other critical 'real names' issues. Aurora, the Sleeping Beauty, lives as Briar Rose to hide from Maleficent. Aladdin masquerades as Prince Ali. Mulan's use of a male pseudonym – the hastily decided 'Ping' – has particular pertinence: real names policies have hit the trans community particularly hard.[44]

The consequence of this is simple: real names laws and policies should be avoided. Indeed, it would be better to consider legally protecting the right to use a pseudonym, as they do in some parts of Germany.[45] Laws such as these, if properly set out, could prevent the enforcement of policies such as Facebook's 'real names' policy, which, due to Facebook's near ubiquity, have almost the same effect as a real name law.

4.2 Surveillance

Surveillance is a common theme throughout the Disney Princess stories. Many of the villains utilise it. *Snow White*'s Evil Queen's use of the Magic Mirror is a central part of the plot of both the original fairy tale and the

---

[43] See, for example, Edwards, 'From the Fantasy to the Reality: Social Media and Real Name Policies' in *Festschrift for Jon Bing* (University of Oslo 2013), or Bernal, *The Internet, Warts and All*, pp. 220–3.

[44] See, for example, York and Kayyali, 'Facebook's "Real Name" Policy Can Cause Real-World Harm for the LGBTQ Community' (EFF, 16 September 2014) <https://www.eff.org/deeplinks/2014/09/facebooks-real-name-policy-can-cause-real-world-harm-lgbtq-community> (accessed 18 April 2018).

[45] See, for example, Boardman, 'German Data Protection Authority Goes Head to Head with Facebook on Pseudonymous Accounts' (*Lexology*, 4 February 2013), <https://www.lexology.com/library/detail.aspx?g=28185928-8868-481a-9ae7-607fdaa2231c> (accessed 5 September 2019). <www.lexology.com/library/detail.aspx?g=28185928-8868-481a-9ae7-607fdaa2231c> (accessed 5 September 2019).

Disney version. Maleficent in *Sleeping Beauty* uses first her goblin minions and then, more effectively, her roving raven familiar. *Aladdin*'s Jafar uses his hourglass for both profiling and surveillance. Ursula the sea witch in *The Little Mermaid* sees through the eyes of her twin eel familiars, Flotsam and Jetsam, while Gaston uses the Beast's own magic mirror against him in *Beauty and the Beast*. Surveillance, it seems, is a critical tool for villains both classical and modern, fantastical and real.

The consequences of this are direct: it is important to be very careful about surveillance laws. Laws like the UK's Investigatory Powers Act 2016 have more implications than may be immediately apparent. Giving current, benign authorities excessive powers or powers with insufficient restraint also gives those powers to future, less benign authorities. Again, it is worth remembering that *Snow White*'s Evil Queen was the lawful government, as was Jafar in *Aladdin* in the later parts of that film, through a coup provided by the magic of the Genie. Indeed, the Genie demonstrates this himself – all his magical powers, including surveillance, are made available to his master, whoever that master might be.

Further, as Gaston demonstrates in *Beauty and the Beast*, surveillance systems can be hacked or piggybacked on by others who do not wish you well. Similarly, backdoors through encryption systems, as a number of authorities have suggested should be mandated,[46] run the risk of being used by malign as well as benign authorities and by others with nefarious purposes.

Finally, as shown in both *Sleeping Beauty* and *Beauty and the Beast*, human error (or sometimes fairy or goblin error) can be a critical factor – and can override legal or technological protections, something often borne out in practice.[47] This needs to be taken into account in designing both laws and surveillance systems. It means, for example, that *gathering* data itself adds

---

[46] For example, in the US via the Burr–Feinstein Compliance with Court Orders Act 2016 proposed in April 2016, and in the UK the initial drafts of statements from government representatives include the UK's Sir David Omand at Investigatory Powers Bill 2016. See Newman, 'Encryption Risks Leading to "Ethically Worse" Behaviour by Spies, Says Former GCHQ Chief' (*Bureau of Investigative Journalism*, 23 January 2015) <https://www.thebu reauinvestigates.com/2015/01/23/encryption-will-lead-to-ethically-worse-behaviour-by-spies-says-former-gchq-chief/> and the FBI's James Comey: McGoogan, 'FBI Director Says Companies Should Ditch Encryption' (*Wired*, 10 December 2015) <www.wired.co.uk/article/fbi-director-calls-for-encryption-end> (accessed 5 September 2019).

[47] Studies show that human error is a major contributor to cybersecurity and related problems. See, for example, Perez, 'Article 29 Working Party Still Not Happy with Windows 10 Privacy Controls' (*SC Magazine*, 28 February 2017) <www.scmagazine.com/study-find-carelessness-among-top-human-errors-affecting-security/article/406876/> (accessed 5 September 2019).

risks beyond those of hacking or intentional misuse: the data gathered may be lost or given away in error to exactly the wrong people.[48]

4.3 Profiling

Profiling in its various forms is another critical tool for villains in the princess stories, and indeed for others more well-meaning but mistaken. Snow White is identified, located and victimised based on her profile as 'the fairest of them all'. Another of the most common problems for the princesses is to be pigeonholed as a result of their profile, and decisions made about them on that basis that damage them or limit their freedom of action. Cinderella is prevented from going to the ball as her profile defines her as the wrong class, and Aladdin prevented from wooing Jasmine on a similar basis. In *Beauty and the Beast*, Belle's profile makes her the object of Gaston's desire for a 'little wife', while the Beast's gets him the torches and pitchforks treatment. Mulan cannot save her father's honour while profiled as a girl awaiting marriage.

As the princesses demonstrate dramatically, protections against profiling are vital if identities are to be protected and if autonomy is to be possible. How can someone have control over their identity if aspects of it – either true or false – can be determined through profiling? How can someone have control over their autonomy if decisions can be made, often automatically, on the basis of this profiling? The princesses and their fellow protagonists show both sides of this: Snow White, Mulan, Aladdin and Jasmine suffer through accurate profiling, Cinderella, Belle and the Beast through inaccurate profiling.

From a technological perspective, this kind of problem is likely to grow: profiling techniques and reliance upon them have become part of the environment, from behavioural targeting of advertising to tailored search results and personalised news. To an extent, this has been legally recognised: the reformed data protection regime in the EU makes specific reference to profiling and provides at least theoretical protection against it.[49] The new regime

---

[48] The 2018 'accidental' passing on of 'personal data of hundreds of private citizens, including email passwords', by the police in Northern Ireland to suspected paramilitaries, by leaving a USB drive in a laptop when it was returned after forensic examination, is one of the more dramatic examples. See Morris, 'PSNI gives Private Citizens' Data to Loyalist Paramilitaries' (*The Irish News*, 20 July 2018) <www.irishnews.com/news/northernireland news/2018/07/20/news/exclusive-personal-data-of-private-citizens-handed-over-to-loyal ists-by-police-1386969/> (accessed 5 September 2019).

[49] Regulation (EU) 2016/679 (the General Data Protection Regulation) makes a number of specific references to profiling, particularly in s. 4, covering the 'right to object and automated individual decision-making'.

came into force in May 2018: how successful it is in protecting against the negative effects of profiling is yet to be seen. The importance of such protection, however, should not be underestimated. It is also important to recognise that profiling techniques can be (and are) applied by both commercial and governmental bodies – as well as by criminals for targeting scams and other cybercrime, paralleling the different stories of the princesses again. This makes such protection even more important.

5. Happily Ever After?

It is easy, perhaps, to dismiss this all as irrelevant. After all, these are just princesses from fairy tales, and Disney princesses at that. That, however, is rather missing the point. First of all, the fact that Disney princesses – presented by and often seen as representing a corporation that is very much part of the establishment[50] – show that the critical importance of potentially subversive ideas such as opposition to government surveillance is significant. It is not rebellious counter-culture that is providing these arguments and pointing out the criticality of the issues, but the establishment itself.

The fairy tales that underlie so many of the Disney Princess stories are themselves often seen as ways of teaching values to children – and as ways to reinforce cultural or moral values. This is Maria Tatar:

> the Grimms' collection was integrated into the educational curriculum of
> most German-speaking regions in the early twentieth century and came to

---

[50] Views of Disney's politics vary significantly. They have been accused of both liberalism and extreme conservatism, of ethnic and racial stereotyping (of Pocahontas and Mulan in particular), and Walt Disney himself has been accused of misogyny and anti-Semitism. For example, *Independent News*, 'Walt Disney's Grandniece Backs up Meryl Streep's Racism Claims: "Anti-Semite? Check. Misogynist? OF COURSE!!!"' (*Independent*, 16 January 2014) <www.independent.co.uk/news/people/news/walt-disney-s-grandniece-backs-up-meryl-streep-s-racism-claims-anti-semite-check-misogynist-of-9064138.html> (accessed 5 September 2019). There is also empirical evidence that '[e]ngagement with Disney Princesses is associated with female gender-stereotypical behavior, even after controlling for initial levels of gender-stereotypical behavior' – see Coyne et al., 'Pretty as a Princess: Longitudinal Effects of Engagement with Disney Princesses on Gender Stereotypes, Body Esteem, and Prosocial Behavior in Children' (2015) *Child Development*, DOI: 10.1111/cdev.12569. Disney has also been one of the most vehement enforcers of copyright (they have lobbied actively and effectively in this field, for example, Greenhouse, 'Justices to Review Copyright Extension' (*New York Times*, 20 February 2002), <www.nytimes.com/2002/02/20/national/20RIGH.html>) (accessed 5 September 2019). The reasons that there are no images in this chapter is that Disney would not even consider permitting it. For a particular perspective on Disney's strongly conservative attitude to copyright infringement, see Gene Wolfe's short story 'Three Fingers' in Wolfe, *The Island of Doctor Death and Other Stories and Other Stories* (Pocket Books 1980).

figure as a monument to the virtues, values, ideals, and imaginative reach of the nation.[51]

Bruno Bettelheim, in his seminal and controversial 1976 work *The Uses of Enchantment*, suggests something even deeper: 'The fairy tale helps children to develop the desire for a higher consciousness through what is implied in the story. The fairy tale convinces through the appeal it makes to our imagination and the attractive outcome of events, which entices us.'[52] Marina Warner is critical of Bettelheim's psychoanalytical analysis, but acknowledges its impact: 'The belief that the stories have the power to lead by example and shape character, to engineer social citizens and inculcate values and ideology, has been widely held and is still accepted.'[53]

It is not necessary, however, to accept Bettelheim's interpretation to understand that fairy tales matter. Warner quotes Tatar on the subject:

> Fairy tales are still arguably the most powerfully formative tales of childhood and permeate mass media for children and adults … The staying power of these stories, their widespread and enduring popularity, suggests that they must be addressing issues that have a significant social function – whether critical, conservative, compensatory or therapeutic …[54]

It is clearly arguable that the early princess stories in particular are conservative, promoting the idea that women should rely on their men: Snow White singing 'some day my prince will come' does not promote an image of self-reliance or independence for women. That even these conservative tales demonstrate the importance of privacy and control over identity for all the princesses gives further weight to the analysis.

The crucial point that applies to *all* the princesses in the Disney stories – not just the eleven official Princesses but *all* the unofficial ones too – makes this point even more emphatic. As shown above, the stories come from a wide range of backgrounds, from many different times reaching back centuries, and from very different cultures. They reach back even further, to oral traditions and cultural memories – so suggestions that privacy (or a need for privacy) is something 'new', or an 'anomaly', as argued by Vint Cerf,[55] one of the founding fathers of the internet, are hard to support.

---

[51] In 'Reading the Grimms' Children's Stories and Household Tales', part of the introduction to *The Annotated Brothers Grimm*, edited by Tatar, p. xxxviii.

[52] Bettelheim, *The Uses of Enchantment: The Meaning and Importance of Fairy Tales* (Peregrine Books 1976), p. 34.

[53] Warner, *Once Upon a Time: A Short History of Fairy Tale*, pp. 125–6.

[54] Tatar, quoted in Warner, *Once Upon a Time: A Short History of Fairy Tale*, p. 114.

[55] See, for example, Kastrenakes, 'Google's Chief Internet Evangelist Says "Privacy May

The enduring – and in many ways growing – popularity of fairy tales in general and Disney Princesses in particular also suggests that the idea that people no longer care about privacy, as argued by Mark Zuckerberg,[56] Amazon's former chief scientist Andreas Weigend[57] and others, is just as unsustainable – as confirmed by boyd, for example, in relation to teenagers.[58] boyd quotes one particular boy on the topic: '[e]very teenager wants privacy. Every single last one of them, whether they tell you or not, wants privacy.'[59]

People empathise with the Princesses and support them in their struggles – and in their desires and need for privacy and control over their identity, even if they may not always realise that this what they are doing.

How and why people empathise with them is not a simple question – but one of the keys may well be that they feel a connection with the struggles that the princesses face, and the sense, in particular, that just as is the case for the princesses, there are strong forces that do not wish us well. Though they may appear to be powerful, in all the stories the princesses are, at their moments of need, weak, and facing far more powerful foes. Fairy tales can be seen as offering hope for the weak. As Marina Warner puts it:

> fairy tales offer enigmatic, terrifying images of what the prospects are, of the darkest horrors life may bring. Yet the stories usually imagine ways of opposing this state of affairs, of having revenge on those who inflict suffering, of turning the status quo upside down ...[60]

The lesson to learn from their stories may be that the purpose of privacy and identity rights – and, ultimately, the purpose of all human rights – is to work for the weak, to protect them from the powerful. We may not all be princesses, but we all need privacy and control over our identity – we need them to be more than just fairy tales – if we are to have a chance of living happily ever after.

Actually Be an Anomaly"' (*The Verge*, 20 November 2013) <www.theverge.com/2013/11/20/5125922/vint-cerf-google-internet-evangelist-says-privacy-may-be-anomaly> (accessed 18 April 2018). <www.theverge.com/2013/11/20/5125922/vint-cerf-google-internet-ev angelist-says-privacy-may-be-anomaly> (accessed 5 September 2019).

56 Zuckerberg suggested in 2010 that 'privacy is no longer a social norm'. See for example Johnson, 'Privacy No Longer a Social Norm, Says Facebook Founder' (*The Guardian*, 11 January 2010) <https://www.theguardian.com/technology/2010/jan/11/facebook-pri vacy> (accessed 5 September 2019). It would be a brave person who would take his apparent conversion into a supporter of privacy in 2019 at face value.

57 In Weigend, *Data for the People: How to Make our Post-Privacy Economy Work for You* (Basic Books 2017).

58 In her study in boyd, *It's Complicated.*

59 boyd, *It's Complicated*, p. 55.

60 Warner, *Once Upon a Time: A Short History of Fairy Tale*, pp. 95–6.

References

Official Princess Films

Snow White and the Seven Dwarfs (1937)
Cinderella (1950)
Sleeping Beauty (1959)
The Little Mermaid (1989)
Beauty and the Beast (1991)
Aladdin (1992)
Pocahontas (1995)
Mulan (1998)
The Princess and the Frog (2009)
Tangled (2010)
Brave (2012)

Unofficial Princess Films

Star Wars (1977)
The Hunchback of Notre Dame (1996)
Hercules (1997)
Atlantis: The Lost Empire (2001)
Wreck-It Ralph (2012)
Frozen (2013)
Moana (2016)
Ralph Breaks the Internet (2018)

Books, Chapters and Articles

Bernal P, *Internet Privacy Rights: Rights to Protect Autonomy* (Cambridge University Press 2014).

Bernal P, *The Internet, Warts and All: Free Speech, Privacy and Truth* (Cambridge University Press 2018).

Bettelheim B, *The Uses of Enchantment: The Meaning and Importance of Fairy Tales* (Peregrine Books 1976).

Boardman R, 'German Data Protection Authority Goes Head to Head with Facebook on Pseudonymous Accounts' (*Lexology*, 4 February 2013), <https://www.lex ology.com/library/detail.aspx?g=28185928-8868-481a-9ae7-607fdaa2231c> (accessed 18 April 2018).

boyd d, *It's Complicated: The Social Lives of Networked Teens* (Yale University Press, 2014).

Bryant N (translator), *Perceforest: The Prehistory of King Arthur's Britain* (Arthurian Studies) (DS Brewer 2011).

Clarke AC, *Profiles of the Future: An Inquiry into the Limits of the Possible* (Phoenix 1973).

Coyne S et al., 'Pretty as a Princess: Longitudinal Effects of Engagement with Disney Princesses on Gender Stereotypes, Body Esteem, and Prosocial Behavior in Children' (2015) *Child Development*, DOI: 10.1111/cdev. 12569.

Edwards L, 'Transformations of the Woman Warrior Hua Mulan: From Defender of the Family to Servant of the State NAN NU' (December 2010) 12 *Men, Women and Gender in Early and Imperial China* 175.

Edwards L, 'From the Fantasy to the Reality: Social Media and Real Name Policies' in *Festschrift for Jon Bing* (University of Oslo 2013).

Edwards L and Veale M, 'Slave to the Algorithm? Why a "Right to an Explanation" Is Probably Not the Remedy You Are Looking For' (2017) 16 *Duke Law & Technology Review* 18.

Garton Ash T, *The File* (Atlantic Books 2009).

Goudreau J, 'Disney Princess Tops List of the 20 Best-Selling Entertainment Products' (*Forbes*, 17 September 2012) <https://www.forbes.com/sites/jennago udreau/2012/09/17/disney-princess-tops-list-of-the-20-best-selling-entertain ment-products/#369b49fbab06> (accessed 18 April 2019).

Greenhouse L, 'Justices to Review Copyright Extension' (*New York Times*, 20 February 2002), <www.nytimes.com/2002/02/20/national/20RIGH.html> (accessed 18 April 2018).

Independent News, 'Walt Disney's Grandniece Backs up Meryl Streep's Racism Claims: "Anti-Semite? Check. Misogynist? OF COURSE!!!"' (*Independent*, 16 January 2014) <www.independent.co.uk/news/people/news/walt-disney-s-grandniece-backs-up-meryl-streep-s-racism-claims-anti-semite-check-misogy nist-of-9064138.html> (accessed 18 April 2018).

Ispirescu P, *The Foundling Prince, & Other Tales* (translated by Collier J and Ipcar R, 1917) (University of Michigan Press 1879) <https://babel.hathitrust.org/cgi/pt?id=mdp.39015043595746;view=1up;seq=13> (accessed 18 April 2019), pp. 239–84.

Johnson B, 'Privacy No Longer a Social Norm, Says Facebook Founder' (*The Guardian*, 11 January 2010) <https://www.theguardian.com/technology/2010/jan/11/facebook-privacy> (accessed 18 April 2018).

Kastrenakes J, 'Google's Chief Internet Evangelist Says "Privacy May Actually Be an Anomaly"' (*The Verge*, 20 November 2013) <www.theverge.com/2013/11/20/5125922/vint-cerf-google-internet-evangelist-says-privacy-may-be-anomaly> (accessed 18 April 2018).

Lang A, *The Violet Fairy Book* (Dover Children's Classics 1966, original 1901).

McGoogan C, 'FBI Director Says Companies Should Ditch Encryption' (*Wired*, 10 December 2015) <www.wired.co.uk/article/fbi-director-calls-for-encryption-end> (accessed 18 April 2018).

Madrigal AC, 'The Inside Story of How Facebook Responded to Tunisian Hacks' (*The Atlantic*, 24 January 2011) <http://www.theatlantic.com/technology/archive/2011/01/the-inside-story-of-how-facebook-responded-to-tunisian-hacks/70044/> (accessed 18 April 2019).

Miller CC, 'When Logarithms Discriminate' (*New York Times*, 9 July 2015) <www.nytimes.com/2015/07/10/upshot/when-algorithms-discriminate.html> (accessed 18 April 2019).

Morozov E, *The Net Delusion: How Not to Liberate the World* (Penguin 2012).

Morris A, 'PSNI gives Private Citizens' Data to Loyalist Paramilitaries' (*The Irish News*, 20 July 2018) <www.irishnews.com/news/northernirelandnews/2018/07/20/news/exclusive-personal-data-of-private-citizens-handed-over-to-loyalists-by-police-1386969/> (accessed 18 April 2018).

Mossiker F, *Pocahontas: The Life and the Legend* (Alfred A Knopf 1976).

Newman M, 'Encryption Risks Leading to "Ethically Worse" Behaviour by Spies, Says Former GCHQ Chief' (*Bureau of Investigative Journalism*, 23 January 2015) <https://www.thebureauinvestigates.com/2015/01/23/encryption-will-lead-to-ethically-worse-behaviour-by-spies-says-former-gchq-chief/> (accessed 18 April 2018).

Perez R, 'Article 29 Working Party Still Not Happy with Windows 10 Privacy Controls' (*SC Magazine*, 28 February 2017) <www.scmagazine.com/study-find-carelessness-among-top-human-errors-affecting-security/article/406876/> (accessed 18 April 2018).

Richards NM, 'The Dangers of Surveillance' (2013) 126 *Harvard Law Review* 1934.

Solove D, *Understanding Privacy* (Harvard University Press 2008).

Tatar M, ed., *The Annotated Brothers Grimm* (WW Norton 2004).

Warner M, *Once Upon a Time: A Short History of Fairy Tale* (Oxford University Press 2014).

Warren SD and Brandeis LD, 'The Right to Privacy' (1890) IV *Harvard Law Review*.

Weigend A, *Data for the People: How to Make our Post-Privacy Economy Work for You* (Basic Books 2017).

Westin A, *Privacy and Freedom* (Bodley Head 1968).

Wolfe G, *The Island of Doctor Death and Other Stories and Other Stories* (Pocket Books 1980).

York JC and Kayyali, D, 'Facebook's "Real Name" Policy Can Cause Real-World Harm for the LGBTQ Community' (EFF, 16 September 2014) <https://www.eff.org/deeplinks/2014/09/facebooks-real-name-policy-can-cause-real-world-harm-lgbtq-community> (accessed 18 April 2018).

3

White Noise from the White Goods? Privacy by Design for Ambient Domestic Computing[1]

Lachlan D Urquhart

The house was full of dead bodies, it seemed. It felt like a mechanical cemetery. So silent. None of the humming hidden energy of machines waiting to function at the tap of a button.

(Ray Bradbury, 'The Veldt', 1950)[2]

The house was an altar with ten thousand attendants, big, small, servicing, attending, in choirs. But the gods had gone away, and the ritual of the religion continued senselessly, uselessly.

(Ray Bradbury, 'There Will Come Soft Rains', 1950)

1. Introduction

Ambient domestic computing systems have moved from science fiction to the lab to everyday life. They have become mundane, unremarkable artefacts in the home and in this chapter, we examine why this shift matters for privacy regulation, both conceptually and empirically. The Bradbury quotes above set the scene for this Gikii contribution, in which we'll examine how smart homes have been envisioned in science fiction literature and film, both positively and negatively. We consider vintage visions of post-desktop

---

[1] This chapter draws on the author's doctoral research completed at the University of Nottingham. The author is supported by the following grants (RCUK Grant No. EP/G037574/1) and (RCUK Grant No. EP/G065802/1), EP/R03351X/1.

[2] As George Hadley continues to say to his wife in 'The Veldt': 'Lydia, it's off, and it stays off. And the whole damn house dies as of here and now. The more I see of the mess we've put ourselves in, the more it sickens me. We've been contemplating our mechanical, electronic navels for too long. My God, how we need a breath of honest air.'

computing, starting with Weiser's classic ubicomp and moving through the years, towards the current term *du jour*: the Internet of Things (IoT). The IoT can easily be dismissed as yet more tech industry marketing hype, like so many examples before, such as blockchain, big data analytics, cloud computing and Web 2.0, for example. However, in this chapter we dig deeper by unpacking how the IoT is framed both in technical and regulatory literature, in conjunction with how experts from technology law and design understand it in practice. Key to this is considering what harms could befall the humans left in the feedback loop living with smart domestic environments. Drawing on the regulatory solution of 'privacy by design' (PbD), we assess how computing professionals have been drawn into the regulatory fray. Instead of just functionally enabling the IoT through ubiquitous networking, ambient interfaces and cloud storage, they now also have a raft of wider human values to assimilate in design.[3] Responsible research and innovation agendas seek to create a future of more trustworthy, secure and accountable domestic IoT.[4] However, the practical role of the computing community in both regulating and creating smart homes that people actually want to live in is far from clear, but resolving it is a pressing concern.

To unpack this discussion, in section 2 we examine the emergence of the domestic IoT, in science fiction literature, film and computing research, particularly in the realm of human–computer interaction (HCI). In section 3, we look at the regulatory challenges of IoT, particularly drawing on a series of expert interviews (discussed below). We focus on various regulatory issues, but primarily privacy and data protection aspects of managing flows of personal information and obtaining user consent. In section 4 we introduce the solution of PbD, considering its legal basis, concerns about the concept and how it currently manifests in practice. We conclude with reflections on the contemporary nature of PbD for the IoT, considering the need to avoid more dystopian smart home futures.

Before turning to our substantive discussion, we'll briefly introduce the procedural underpinnings of our empirical component. Our qualitative findings are based on thirteen detailed semi-structured interviews conducted in

---

[3] Borning and Muller 'Next Steps for Value Sensitive Design' (2012) in proceedings of SIGCHI Conference Human Factors in Computer Systems (CHI'12), 1125.

[4] Stahl, Eden and Jirotka, 'Responsible Research and Innovation in Information and Communication Technology – Identifying and Engaging with the Ethical Implications of ICTs' in Owen, Bessant and Heintz (eds), *Responsible Innovation: Managing the Responsible Emergence of Science and Innovation in Society* (Wiley-Blackwell 2013), pp. 199–218; Stilgoe et al., 'Developing a Framework for Responsible Innovation' (2013) 42 *Research Policy* 1568.

Spring 2016[5] with leading UK technologists and information technology law experts. As thought leaders from law and technology, their breadth of expertise provides us detailed insight into both practical and strategic considerations of privacy by design for the IoT.

Our six 'lawyers' have an average of fourteen years of professional experience[6] with expertise across technology law from areas of: contracts, data protection (DP), intellectual property, software, e-commerce, accessibility, procurement, outsourcing, dispute resolution and litigation. The seven 'technologists' have an average of thirty-two years of professional experience at both strategic and operational levels. Their expertise draws on specialisms including wireless networking, information security, privacy and identity, data science, ethics, big data, telecoms, cloud computing, interaction design and digital media. Now we turn to the smart home visions provided in literature, film and computing.

2. Visions of Smart Homes in Literature, Film and Computing

Poetic portrayals forecasting the possible utopian and dystopian futures of home automation are not new.[7] If we turn to literature and film, we see a range of smart homes spanning the past fifty years. Starting with literature, the great and good of the sci-fi world, such as Philip K Dick, Ray Bradbury and JG Ballard, have all played with the concept, and we now explore their insights.

2.1 Literature

In Ray Bradbury's story 'The Veldt' (1950), the 'Happylife Home' automates and outsources a key function of family life: entertaining and caring for children. In this scenario, huge wall-sized screens in a dedicated nursery provide children with an immersive virtual environment complete with vultures, lions and zebras in an African savanna. However, the immersion becomes increasingly addictive and dangerous, disrupting family dynamics, and the relationship between the parents and children breaks down. This destroys their dream of technologically delegated parenting and ultimately spells the

---

[5] The average length of interview was forty-four minutes, and the study was approved by the University of Nottingham's Computer Science ethics approval process. The interviews were audio recorded, transcribed verbatim, coded and analysed using thematic analysis following Braun and Clarke, 'Using Thematic Analysis in Psychology' (2006) 3 Qualitative Research in Psychology 77.

[6] See Tables 1 and 2 in Appendix for more details.

[7] Lyon, *The Culture of Surveillance: Watching as a Way of Life* (Wiley 2018); Dourish and Bell, *Divining a Digital Future: Mess and Mythology in Ubiquitous Computing* (MIT Press 2011).

end of their smart home, with the nursery and other devices being switched off (as the opening quote highlights).[8]

In another short story written in 1950 but set in 2026, Ray Bradbury depicts a different demise of a smart home in 'There Will Come Soft Rains'. The story tells of an abandoned home, post nuclear attack, which continues to work (in varying levels of decay) despite lack of human occupants. It describes a range of technologies including robot cleaning mice, an auto-mated kitchen stove, bath and hearth fire, smart window blinds, a Veldt-like screen and conversational assistants readings poems and recounting the time. The story concludes with fire engulfing the home as it breaks into a frenzy of routines, culminating with 'one voice with sublime disregard for the situation read[ing] poetry aloud in the fiery study until all the film spool burned until all the wires withered, and the circuits cracked'.[9] Perhaps in a modern retell-ing, it will be an Amazon Alexa cackling into the night sky,[10] surrounded by embers and the charred remains of a Nest Protect smoke detector.

An infamous passage in Philip K Dick's *Ubik* (1969) describes a door refusing to open unless paid. It holds the lead character to a contract term requiring mandatory payment, exasperating him to the point he unscrews the hinges, amidst threats from the door of suing him. Showing his disregard for the agency of this non-human actor, he states 'I've never been sued by a door. But I guess I can live through it.'[11] As Latour once stated on the delegation of human functions and prescription of behaviour through technology 'the distance between morality and force is not as wide as moralists expect, or more exactly, clever engineers have made it smaller'.[12] It's not hard to imagine a similar scenario with a smart fridge door. The hungry occupant, ravenous while the door refuses to open as it enforces a UK government 'Nudge Unit'-inspired[13] public health strategy to tackle obesity by limiting the number of fridge openings per day.[14]

---

[8] Bradbury, 'The Veldt' in *The Illustrated Man* (Doubleday 1950).

[9] Bradbury, 'There Will Come Soft Rains' in *The Martian Chronicles* (Doubleday 1951).

[10] Lee, 'Amazon Promises Fix for Creepy Alexa Laugh' (BBC Tech, 7 March 2018) <https://www.bbc.com/news/technology-43325230> (accessed 15 April 2019).

[11] Dick, *Ubik* (Doubleday 1969).

[12] Latour, 'Where are the Missing Masses? – The Sociology of a Few Mundane Artifacts' in Bijker WE and Law J (eds), *Shaping Technology/Building Society* (MIT Press 1992).

[13] Former UK Government 'Nudge Unit' now the private Behavioural Insights Team – Quinn, 'The Nudge Unit: The UK Experts Hat Became a Prime UK Export' (*The Observer*, 10 November 2018) <https://www.theguardian.com/politics/2018/nov/10/nudge-unit-pushed-way-private-sector-behavioural-insights-team> (accessed 15 April 2019).

[14] Thaler and Sunstein, *Nudge: Improving Decisions about Health, Wealth and Happiness* (Yale University Press 2008).

In a recent paper, Urquhart, Jäger and Schnädelbach[15] use JG Ballard's 1962 short story 'The Thousand Dreams of Stellavista' to unpack the future of human–building interaction. They consider privacy, physical security and architectural design concerns from the emerging adaptive built environment.[16] Ballard's story depicts a 'psychotropic' house filled with sensors and actuators that can move and respond to the emotional state of the occupants.[17] It draws on their positive and negative life experiences, adapting its very architectural fabric to provide them visceral feedback (for example, shivering walls and shrinking/expanding roofs) and to retell past experiences (for example, of a violent relationship). This dark depiction shows how capturing provenance within a building gives it the ability to interact with occupants over space and time in new ways.

Relatedly, Harkaway's *Gnomon*[18] depicts a future of absolute transparency, where human actions are recorded, perceptible and auditable, down to the neurological level. As emotional AI technologies seek to read the body and emotive states, the ability to infer cognitive state over time enables the visibility of perceived emotions within the domestic context (for example, patterns in speech with smart speakers to infer happiness, sadness, and so on).[19]

2.2 Film

Turning to on-screen representations, many cult classic film and TV series have shaped the popular imagination on what form our technologically mediated domestic futures might take.[20] Future interactions with smart homes are again framed as both positive and negative, with the former foregrounding convenience and comfort, and the latter on security vulnerabilities. To consider a handful, in the 1960s, *The Jetsons* showcased a cartoon space age image of living with robots, flying cars and intelligent buildings, where relaxation

---

[15] Urquhart, Jäger and Schnädelbach, 'Adaptive Architecture: Regulating Human Building Interaction' (2019) *International Review of Law, Computers & Technology* (forthcoming).

[16] Ballard, 'A Thousand Dreams of Stellavista' The Complete Short Stories, volume 1 (1962).

[17] For the ways in which understanding the emotional state of individuals is increasingly prized, see McStay, *Emotional AI* (Sage 2018).

[18] Harkaway, *Gnomon* (Heinemann 2017).

[19] McStay and Urquhart, 'This Time, With Feeling? An assessment of the legal and privacy implications of out-of-home appraisal-based emotional AI' (2019) *First Monday* 24(10) https://firstmonday.org/ojs/index.php/fm/article/view/9457/8146

[20] Marks, *Imagining Surveillance: Utopian and Dystopian Literature and Film* (Edinburgh University Press 2015); see also Urquhart, Reedman-Flint and Leesakul, 'Responsible Domestic Robots: Exploring Ethical Implications of Robots in the Home' (2019) *Journal of Information, Communication and Ethics in Society* (forthcoming).

and well-being were paramount.[21] Cult 1980s classic *Back to the Future II* predicted many future inventions from drones to wireless payments,[22] but also portrayed domestic developments too, including smart kitchen appliances (who wouldn't want a rehydrated, fresh pizza in seconds?), smart wearables like self-tying shoes and the desired mode of transport for many kids of the 1980s: the hoverboard. In the 1990s, the wacky inventions of eponymous claymation star Wallace, of *Wallace and Gromit* fame, charmed viewers with his homemade systems to ease his daily routine, including an automated porridge maker and tilting bed to hasten getting dressed.[23] In the 2000s, Tony Stark's JARVIS natural language AI system in Marvel's *Iron Man* seamlessly responds to his every command to control other devices and smart, robotic systems.[24] To shoehorn a personal favourite of the author into the list, *Rick and Morty* cannot be left out (especially as the series was the topic of his 2017 Gikii presentation).[25] In the episode *Meeseeks and Destroy*, protagonist Rick Sanchez's Meeseeks box creates bright blue, ephemeral, embodied assistants on demand. They respond to user queries and cease to exist after completing these tasks. Unlike the current question and answer format home conversational assistants currently use, Meeseeks go much further in their assistance, but also get increasingly frustrated and unstable when they cannot solve the query, leading to disastrous consequences.

However, representations of smart homes can be negative too. Back in the 1970s, films like *Demon Seed* provided a dark vision of the traumatic ways in which automation and artificial intelligence might torment occupants if their instructions are not followed.[26] The 2016 film *I.T.* sees Pierce Brosnan's character and his family subject to a campaign of social engineering attacks by a disgruntled associate.[27] Using their smart home against them, intimate details of their lives are made visible, with their safety and well-being compromised to damage their reputation and manipulate them. Similarly, in critically acclaimed 2015 series *Mr Robot*, a Series 2 storyline follows the

---

21 Hanna and Barbera, *The Jetsons*. See also Maloney, 'The Jetsons is Actually a Bone Chilling Dystopia' (2017) *The Verge* <https://www.theverge.com/2017/11/3/16598440/jetsons-dystopia-dc-comics-future-apocalypse> (accessed 15 April 2019).

22 Zemeckis, *Back to the Future Part II* (Amblin Entertainment and Universal Studios 1989).

23 Park, *Wallace and Gromit: The Wrong Trousers* (Aardman Animations 1993).

24 Favreau, *Iron Man* (Marvel Entertainment 2008).

25 Roiland and Harmon, *Rick and Morty* (Adult Swim 2015); Urquhart, 'Hunting for Ethical Innovation in the Adventures of Rick and Morty' (19 September 2017) <https://lachlans research.com/2017/09/19/gikii-2017-hunting-for-ethical-innovation-in-the-adventures-of-rick-and-morty/> (accessed 15 April 2019).

26 Cammell, *Demon Seed* (MGM 1977).

27 Moore, *I.T.* (Voltage Pictures 2016).

Anonymous-esque hacker collective F-Society using unpatched vulnerabilities in a smart home management system to hack the smart showers, speakers and heating so as to make life untenable for the target, driving her out and allowing the collective to move in and squat.[28] Spike Jonze's *Her* (2014) showcases the emotional dimensions of letting conversational agents into our daily lives: the lonely lead character falls in love with an AI system.[29]

2.3 New Visions of Computing

Ambient domestic computing has a near thirty-year lineage in computer science research, and the links to science fiction have not been ignored.[30] Weiser's archetypal vision of ubicomp is a key milestone in the research agenda of post-desktop computing.[31] It follows the move from mainframe (one computer to many users) to personal (one computer to one system) to ubicomp (many computers to one user), via distributed/internet systems.[32] Through his depiction of tabs, pads and boards and a design fiction narrative for an archetypal user, Sal, he creates a vision of developing ubiquitous computing systems that have 'disappeared in use' and 'weave themselves into the fabric of everyday life until they are indistinguishable from it'.[33] Inspired by this, Satyanarayanan's 'pervasive computing' also aims to create invisibility in use, where integration between computing, communication and user needs leads to creation of 'technology that disappears'.[34] More popular in Europe, driven by the Philips 'Vision of the Future' programme[35] Ambient Intelligence (AmI) also emerged, with similar aspirations to ubicomp by envisioning computing that is embedded, context aware, personalised, adaptive and anticipative.[36]

---

[28] Esmail, *Mr Robot* (Universal Cable Productions 2015).

[29] Jonze, *Her* (Annapurna Pictures 2013).

[30] 'Special issue on Science Fiction and Ubiquitous Computing' in *Personal and Ubiquitous Computing*, 2014 <https://link.springer.com/article/10.1007/s00779-014-0773-4> (accessed 15 April 2019).

[31] Weiser, 'The Computer for the 21st Century' (1991) 265 *Scientific American* 94; Weiser and Brown, 'The Coming Age of Calm Technology' in Denning PJ and Metcalfe RM, *Beyond Calculation* (Copernicus 1997), pp. 1–2.

[32] Grudin, 'The Computer Reaches out: The Historical Continuity of Interface Design' proceedings of SIGCHI Conference Human Factors in Computer Systems (CHI'90) (ACM Press 1990), pp. 261–8.

[33] Weiser, 'The Computer for the 21st Century', p. 94.

[34] Satyanarayanan, 'Pervasive Computing: Visions and Challenges' (2001) 8 *IEEE Personal Communications* 10, p. 2.

[35] Lamourne, Feiz and Rigot, 'Social Trends and Product Opportunities: Philips Vision of the Future Project' proceedings of ACM SIGCHI, 1997.

[36] Aarts and Marzano, *The New Everyday: Views on Ambient* Intelligence (010 Publishers 2003); Lindwer et al., 'Ambient Intelligence Visions and Achievements: Linking Abstract

Managing such ubiquity requires strategies and prompted the emergence of 'calm computing', as proposed by Seely Brown and Weiser, who recognised that 'if computers are everywhere, they better stay out of the way'.[37] To do this, systems need to be there when needed, but on the periphery of user awareness when not needed; critically, knowing when to move between these states. Contextual awareness is key here, but this is difficult to implement as understanding human activity and making accurate inferences about behaviour depends on more than just accurate sensing. Human activities, while they can become routinely acted out, are hard to formalise within systems, as there is unpredictability and scope to categorise incorrectly.[38] Homes are messy, too, due to the variety of activities, boundaries that need to be managed and the variety of actors within a setting.[39] As Nissenbaum has long argued, maintaining contextual integrity of information flows is critical to preventing perceptions of privacy harms, hence understanding context is key socially, legally and technically.[40]

Significant industry and government investment attempted to bring ubicomp to life, with the European Commission's 'Disappearing Computer programme'[41] or the Philips HomeLab.[42] Branches of computing were captivated for years with engineering the omnipresent infrastructure of 'seamless' networks, developing location-based applications, resilient sensors, building ambient and physically invisible interfaces and critically, trying to better determine context.[43]

Weiser's ubicomp has been criticised from a number of perspectives. Reeves argues such future-orientated, quasi-fictional technological visions,

---

Ideas to Real-world Concepts' (2003) Design, Automation and Test in Europe Conference, p. 1.

[37] Weiser and Brown, 'The Coming Age of Calm Technology', p. 78.

[38] Suchman, *Plans and Situated Actions: The Problem of Human-Machine Communication* (Cambridge University Press 1987).

[39] Dourish, 'What We Talk About When We Talk About Context' (2004) 8 Personal and Ubiquitous Computing 19, p. 20; Rogers, 'Moving on from Weiser's Vision of Calm Computing: Engaging Ubicomp Experiences' (2006) proceedings of the 8th International Conference on Ubiquitous Computing (UbiComp'06), p. 408.

[40] Nissenbaum, *Privacy in Context: Technology, Policy and the Integrity of Social Life* (Stanford University Press 2009).

[41] The Disappearing Computer Resource page is available at: <www.disappearing-computer.eu/resources.html> (accessed 15 April 2019).

[42] Available at: www.research.philips.com/technologies/download/homelab_365.pdf (accessed 15 April 2019).

[43] Liu et al., 'Identity Crisis of Ubicomp? Mapping 15 years of the Field's Development and Paradigmatic Change' (2014) proceedings of the International Conference on Ubiquitous Computing (Ubicomp'14).

while dominant in computing, are not predictions but merely a commentary on the present.[44] They often never materialise, as some argue with 'ubicomp' twenty-five years on.[45] Others, such as Bell and Dourish, argue instead that ubicomp is already here, just not the 'yesterday's tomorrow' that Weiser envisaged, and not very evenly distributed.[46] As opposed to his clean, seamlessly networked[47] technological future, an alternative present has appeared, one that is seen not in labs, but in the real world.[48]

2.4 The Risk of Technical Visions

Importantly, the harm of committing to future computing visions risks the current disordered, difficult impact of technologies on social relationships and practices being ignored.[49] Real users' interests are neglected, and the visions are not being built with them in mind. Furthermore, change takes time, and as HCI scholars have long recognised, the smart home will not emerge overnight, but instead 'new technologies will be brought piecemeal into the home'.[50] Accordingly, instead of engineering a grand vision, there needs to be a turn away from implementing canonical principles, like calmness[51] or invisibility.[52] We see this if we consider the principle of invisibility. It is not just an issue of physical invisibility: computing has to become so routine in life it is no longer 'remarkable', and as Tolmie et al. argue, creating such unremarkable systems requires situated understanding of the social context of

---

[44] Reeves, 'Envisioning Ubiquitous Computing' in proceedings of SIGCHI Conference Human Factors in Computer Systems (CHI'12) (ACM Press 2012), p. 1580.

[45] Caceres and Friday, 'Ubicomp Systems at 20: Progress, Opportunities and Challenges' (2012) 11 IEEE Pervasive Computing 14, p. 15.

[46] Bell and Dourish, 'Yesterday's Tomorrows: Notes on Ubiquitous Computing's Dominant Vision' (2006) 11 *Personal and Ubiquitous Computing* 133.

[47] Where there are no gaps in connectivity for devices, it enables seamless interactions for users without drop off in connection and services.

[48] Anyone who takes a long-distance train journey in the UK knows that the goal of seamless networks, even in 2019, is aspirational at best, where mobile connectivity drops off regularly when moving between cells (and on-board WiFi is patchy too).

[49] Bell and Dourish, 'Yesterday's Tomorrows: Notes on Ubiquitous Computing's Dominant Vision', p. 140.

[50] Edwards and Grinter, 'At Home with Ubiquitous Computing: Seven Challenges' proceedings of the 3rd International Conference on Ubiquitous Computing (UbiComp'01) (ACM Press 2001), p. 257.

[51] Rogers, 'Moving on from Weiser's Vision of Calm Computing: Engaging Ubicomp Experiences', p. 406.

[52] Tolmie et al., 'Unremarkable Computing' in proceedings of SIGCHI Conference Human Factors in Computer Systems (CHI'12) (ACM Press 2012); Crabtree and Rodden, 'Domestic Routines and Design for the Home'.

use, and the actions and routines of daily life, including what makes activities routine in the first place.[53] Lessons need to be learned for IoT and the user, and how technologies impact them through use is a key design consideration.

The link between user needs and device functionality can be tenuous too. The observations of Leppänen and Jokinen that 'inhabitants themselves make a home and little everyday-practices make the known life go on ... a smart home should not be smarter than its inhabitants'[54] really need to be in the forefront of smart home designers' minds. As with the science fiction narratives above, technically driven smart home research has long promised benefits to users of increased efficiency, comfort, convenience, energy management, care and security, but in practice neglects their desires. Only through using and understanding the actual deployment setting can any utility and meaning emerge for users.[55]

Studies on the impact of smart home technologies, such as smart thermostats, CCTV or locks, highlight how these systems impact end-users' lives. Studies of parental auditing of home entry/exit through smart locks and cameras, while improving convenience and safety, showed an impact on parents' trust and relationships with their children.[56] Domestic sensing often leads to complex trade-offs between observers knowing observed family members are safe and protected against the observed members' perceptions of spying.[57] Occupants can become accustomed to monitoring technologies and adjust their behaviour accordingly.[58] Technologies can become 'unremarkable' over

---

[53] Tolmie P et al., 'Unremarkable Computing', p. 402: 'An orderly aspect of things with a routine character is that they can serve as resources for the mutual coordination of unremarkable activities ... these resources are mutually available and mutually accountable for those involved in the routine. Also, things do of course go wrong in domestic life, alarms can fail – but failure, in contrast to accomplishment, is remarkable and the elements held to account when part of a routine fails are the very ones that are unremarkable at other times.'

[54] Leppänen and Jokinen, 'Daily Routines and Means of Communication in a Smart Home', p. 223.

[55] Wilson et al., 'Smart Homes and Their Users: A Systematic Analysis and Key Challenges' in Harper R (ed.), *Inside the Smart Home* (Springer-Verlag 2003); Ihde, *Technology and the Lifeworld* (Indiana University Press 1990).

[56] Ur, Jung and Schechter, 'Intruders versus Intrusiveness: Teens' and Parents' Perspectives on Home-Entryway Surveillance' in proceedings of the International Conference on Ubiquitous Computing (Ubicomp'14) (ACM Press 2014).

[57] Mäkinen, 'Surveillance On/Off: Examining Home Surveillance Systems from the User's Perspective' (2016) 14 Surveillance & Society 59; Choe et al., 'Living in a Glass House: A Survey of Private Moments in the Home'.

[58] Oulasvirta et al., 'Long-term Effects of Ubiquitous Surveillance in the Home' in proceedings of the International Conference on Ubiquitous Computing (UbiComp'11) (ACM Press 2011).

time too. For example, provided smart thermostats work properly, studies show they can become mundane, and earlier home occupant frustration, lack of comprehension and concerns of control over functionality fade away.[59]

In conclusion, predecessors to the domestic IoT show that users, their social context, needs, relationships and environment need to be positioned at the core of system design.[60] Dogmatic commitment to engineering principles underpinning future technological visions can cause these to be neglected. From a regulatory perspective, looking to users and how technologies impact their interests is important, but we need to look at current, as opposed to future, visions. Accordingly, we now explore how IoT is understood and navigate the 'in the wild' challenges it poses.

2.5 Enter the Internet of Things

Divining clarity around contemporary smart homes is tricky, as IoT moves along from the 'peak of inflated expectations', when earlier drafts of this chapter were written,[61] to the trough of disillusionment in the most recent version of the Gartner hype cycle.[62] Famously, Cisco predicted there will be 24 billon internet-connected devices by 2019[63] and Huawei predicted 100 billion by 2025.[64] Similarly, back in 2013, the OECD that forecast a family of four will own seven smart light bulbs, five internet-connected power sockets, one intelligent thermostat (and so on) by 2022.[65] As we stumble into those futures, it remains to be seen how accurate these projections are.

---

[59] Yang and Newman, 'Learning from a Learning Thermostat: Lessons for Intelligent Systems for the Home' in proceedings of the International Conference on Ubiquitous Computing (UbiComp'13) (ACM Press 2013; Yang et al., 'Making Sustainability Sustainable: Challenges in the Design of Eco-Interaction Technologies' (2018) ACM Ubicomp'18.

[60] Flintham, Goulden, Price, and Urquhart, 'Domesticating Data: Socio-Legal Perspectives on Smart Homes & Good Data Design' in Daly A et al. (eds), *Good Data* (INC Theory on Demand 2019); Hargreaves and Wilson, *Smart Homes and Their Users* (Springer 2017).

[61] Gartner Hype Cycle for Emerging Technologies, available at: <https://www.gartner.com/newsroom/id/3114217> (accessed 15 April 2019).

[62] Gartner Hype Cycle for Emerging Technologies, available at: <https://blogs.gartner.com/smarterwithgartner/files/2018/08/PR_490866_5_Trends_in_the_Emerging_Tech_Hype_Cycle_2018_Hype_Cycle.png> (accessed 15 April 2019).

[63] Cisco website, Visual Networking Index, available at <www.cisco.com/c/en/us/solutions/service-provider/visual-networking-index-vni/index.html> (accessed: 13 April 2019).

[64] Huawei website, Global Connectivity Index, available at: <https://www.huawei.com/minisite/gci/en/> (accessed 15 April 2019).

[65] Working Party on Communication Infrastructures and Services Policy, *Building Blocks for Smart Networks* (OECD 2013) <https://www.oecd.org/officialdocuments/publicdisplaydocumentpdf/?cote=DSTI/ICCP/CISP(2012)3/FINAL&docLanguage=En> (accessed 15 April 2019).

Unlike AmI, Ubicomp or Pervasive Computing, IoT lacks a similar canonical technical definition, leading to greater uncertainty about what it actually is.[66] When Ashton first used the term in 1999[67] he focused on tracking objects via machines instead of humans in a product supply chain. Since then, the IoT term has emerged in a broad range of application domains, from the built environment of smart homes and cities, to smart energy grids, intelligent mobility through connected and autonomous vehicles, and smart health care through wearables and the quantified self.[68]

The smart home aims to use pervasive sensing, longitudinal monitoring and machine-to-machine data sharing to enable better services, such as automating domestic tasks. In part, this is by moving from segmented snapshots of users' lives to more holistic awareness of the socially complex setting of everyday life. IoT devices possess different affordances with varying interfaces (screens/no screens, haptic feedback, beeps, lights, and so on); sensing capabilities (temperature, air quality, motion sensing, speech, and so on); networking protocols (TCP, Zigbee, Z-Wave, Bluetooth, and so on), and underlying goals (from energy, security, well-being and comfort management to entertainment and pleasure). Thus, if anything, the IoT is defined by the breadth and fuzziness of the concept.

2.6 Defining the IoT?

Nevertheless, to get a handle on how the term is popularly understood, we look to perspectives from different industry, state, civil society, regulatory and policy stakeholders. We find that by considering the UK Government Office for Science;[69] EU Article 29 Working Party;[70]

---

[66] In 'What is IoT? That is Not the Question' (IoT UK, 2016) <http://iotuk.org.uk/what-is-iot-that-is-not-the-question/> (accessed: 15 April 2019), McAuley advises against focusing on the lack of fundamental technical definition for IoT because 'IoT is not about technical capabilities or novelty, rather it is a social phenomenon that reflects a significant proportion of society, and importantly businesses, who have started to recognise that there is value in building a virtual presence for many of our everyday physical things', p. 1.

[67] Ashton, 'That Internet of Things Thing' (*RFID Journal*, 2009) <www.itrco.jp/libraries/RFIDjournal-That%20Internet%20of%20Things%20Thing.pdf> (accessed 15 April 2019).

[68] Walport, *Internet of Things: Making the Most of the Second Digital Revolution* (UK Government Office for Science 2014), pp. 9–11.

[69] Walport, *Internet of Things*, p. 13: IoT 'is made up of hardware and software technologies. The hardware consists of the connected devices – which range from simple sensors to smartphones and wearable devices – and the networks that link them, such as 4G Long-Term Evolution, Wi-Fi and Bluetooth. Software components include data storage platforms and analytics programmes that present information to users.'

[70] Article 29 Working Party, 'Opinion 8/2014 on the Recent Developments on the Internet of Things' (European Commission 2014): IoT is devices 'that can be controlled remotely

Cisco;[71] the UN International Telecoms Union,[72] the Internet Engineering Task Force[73] and cross-disciplinary academic group, Cambridge Public Policy[74] there are a wide range of descriptive attributes assigned to IoT:

- physical objects,
- a digital presence,
- social embeddedness,
- remotely controllable,
- constantly connected with networking for information sharing between people, processes and objects,
- surrounded by an ecosystem of stakeholders interested in the personal data supply chain: for example, third parties,
- tied to backend computational infrastructure (for example, cloud, databases, servers),
- device-to-device/backend communication often without direct human input.

We now want to see whether these attributes also emerge in our empirical findings. We provide the participants with a pseudonym, a job, years of experience and noted specialisms to contextualise their quotes. In turning to our lawyers, we see wide framings of IoT: it is viewed largely as any

over the internet … most home automation devices are constantly connected and may transmit data back to the manufacturer', see s 1.3.

[71] Cisco, *The Internet of Everything*, available at: www.cisco.com/c/dam/en_us/about/business-insights/docs/ioe-value-at-stake-public-sector-analysis-faq.pdf (accessed 15 April 2019) the IoE is a 'networked connection of people, process, data, and things', p. 1.

[72] International Telecommunications Union, *Overview of the Internet of Things* (ITU 2012): IoT is 'a global infrastructure for the information society, enabling advanced services by interconnecting (physical and virtual) things based on existing and evolving interoperable information and communication', where a 'thing' is: an 'object of the physical world (physical things) or the information world (virtual things), which is capable of being identified and integrated into communication networks', p. 1.

[73] Arkko et al., *IETF RC 7452: Architectural Considerations in Smart Object Networking* (Internet Engineering Task Force 2015): IoT is a 'trend where a large number of embedded devices employ communications services offered by the Internet protocols. Many of these devices often called smart objects are not directly operated by humans, but exist as components in buildings or vehicles, or are spread out in the environment', p. 1.

[74] Deakin et al., *The Internet of Things: Shaping Our Future* (Cambridge Public Policy 2015): 'sensors which react to physical signals; software in these sensors transmitting information; a network for this information to be transmitted on; a database and control system which receives and processes this data, and sends a message back out over the network to instruct the initial device or another one that is networked', p. 8.

networked sensor or device.[75] Notwithstanding, more mundane, established systems like the smartphone are still considered by some to be IoT as they mediate end-user interactions with other IoT devices and services.[76]

Our legal community tends to contextualise IoT using illustrative examples from a number of application areas, often drawn from their own practical experience from their roles as legal advisors. These include machine-to-machine (M2M) industrial and retail applications; consumer products such as autonomous cars; wearables like fitness bands, and usefully for this chapter, a range of smart home systems for security, lighting, energy management, entertainment and comfort.

Overall, when turning to the technologists we see tighter but more contested definitions of IoT. Broadly, they focus on more technical attributes, such as the physicality of objects, the embedded nature of computation, the pervasiveness of communications infrastructure, the global nature of internet connectivity and variations in user interface.[77] Like the lawyers, they also classify IoT by reference to different applications and sectors, with some arguing that IoT is just the next hyped technology trend. Magnus [Chief Technology Officer, 40 years, Wireless Technology and Smart Devices; original emphasis] captures this well:

> they changed name from connected devices to M2M to internet of things – the cynical would say when something doesn't take off you just change the name –and it hasn't really taken off, *the IoT is still* predominantly hype … over the years [I've] ended up helping people putting wireless into everything from sex toys to snow ploughs.

However, for some, framing IoT around the nature of objects or networking is misguided. Instead, they want to go beyond just the vision of a

---

[75] Campbell [University Reader, 9 years, Media and Tech Law] contends that IoT is 'things that aren't computers that are connected to the internet. Computers in the sense of desktop, laptop, higher spec mobile devices, basically everything that is not one of them but is somehow internet connected'.

[76] As Findlay [Consultant, 20 years, Privacy and Information Management] maintains, 'more and more digital services and devices are being created where the smartphone is the hub if you like, and the router in your home is the hub to your connected life'.

[77] Allan [Director, 28 years, Digital Identity & Online Privacy] IoT is: 'a device that has processing capability that has some degree of user interface but where the user interface is partial, in other words … if you have a smart lightbulb, part of the user interface would be you can turn it on and off, part of it might be you can remotely control times that it goes on and off, but that is not all the functionality the device has, so it also might have network capability that you don't have an interface to, it's almost certainly got backend cloud communication capabilities, and data transfer capabilities that you're very unlikely to have an interface to.'

'connected product' to a more holistic, socially orientated vision. They focus on the user, their data flows and various practices around a technology. As Iain [professor, 25 years, Interaction Design] puts it, IoT is 'about flows of data through practices, and most social personal practices involve physical artefacts, environments and other people, ... [it's about] an internet of practice, but you can't practice without some objects, without other people'.

Some technologists stress the centrality of data as a commodity, as opposed to the user, due to the importance of data for analysis and creation of new services. These participants were also wary of regulation, insofar as it may limit their access to data.[78] Overall, in contrast to ubicomp or AmI, we see a less canonical narrative emerging around IoT. While hype persists, there is no single, unifying vision of what is or is not IoT. Conceptually and empirically, a more flexible framing is emerging. The strong focus on IoT applications sidesteps the need to fixate over where the margins of IoT lie. Most importantly, with applications, like the home, come contexts of use and end-users who have various needs and interests. By considering this level, as opposed to a grand vision, a richer, situated picture of IoT can emerge, looking at the practices, interactions and relationships end-users have with the technologies. We now consider regulatory implications of IoT, beginning with general challenges before shifting to privacy-orientated perspectives.

3. Regulating the IoT

We observe a range of IoT regulatory concerns discussed in the literature.[79] These include:

- a lack of interoperability between devices and across platforms;[80]
- market dominance and inadequate competition around firms;[81]
- insufficient spectrum and internet protocol (IP) addresses for devices (IPv6 solves much of this);[82]

---

[78] 'IoT is about taking data off a device and then doing data analytics on that somewhere in the cloud. The stuff in the middle doesn't really matter it just needs to be there and work ... from my mind where I'm involved in a lot of data analytics on large databases, people always say, "oh god data overload is terrible", I think it is an aspiration, I want more data, the more I have, the more I can do with it. Somebody tells me to minimise my data is basically trying to restrict a business model.' I believe it was Magnus.

[79] Urquhart, Jäger and Schnädelbach, 'Adaptive Architecture: Regulating Human Building Interaction', *International Review of Law, Computers & Technology* (2019) DOI: 10.1080/13600869.2019.1562605.

[80] Deakin et al. *The Internet of Things*, p. 7.

[81] Brown, 'Regulation and the Internet of Things' (GSR Discussion Paper, International Telecommunications Union 2015), p. 19.

[82] Ibid.

- a lack of leadership on industry standards;[83]
- uncertainty around responsibility and liability for harm;[84]
- technical education, appropriate regulation and trust in the security of these systems.[85]

In practice too, both lawyers and technologists provide a picture of the overarching regulatory issues they have experienced. These primarily include concerns around safety, liability and responsibility for harm, data security, intellectual property, funding and interoperability.

More generally, the technologists question the fitness for purpose of regulatory frameworks and legislation, particularly for how IoT impacts existing legal principles and consumer rights. As Gordon [Principal Consultant, 30 Years, Wireless Networking and Sensors] frames it, 'fundamentally it is such a new tech, new area, it is fairly wild west', and in some contexts, this is more apparent than others. A good example is the contrast between safety and security.[86] While device manufacturers face strict market access controls around electrical safety, similar oversight has not emerged for IoT security. Interestingly, security, as opposed to privacy, often emerges as a more legitimate concern for the technologists. Some feel DP is limiting business models, stifling innovation or creative practice, and instead regulating misuse of personal data should be favoured. For them, good security practices may require focusing on the diligence of designers to use best practices as opposed to post hoc responses like insurance for security breaches. However, this requires systematic consideration of IoT security risks in design, and needs to be framed by the current state of the IoT industry. In particular, the embryonic market, the heterogeneity of the device ecosystem, and lack of industry standards complicate any application of regulations. For Gordon,

> the [IoT] industry itself is very immature, very young … a 'primordial soup', there are a few things that have crawled out on land, some are slithering about, some have got legs, some have arms but we do not have many fully formed creatures yet.

---

[83] Bouverot, *GSMA: The Impact of the Internet of Things – The Connected Home* (GSMA 2015) <www.gsma.com/newsroom/wp-content/uploads/15625-Connected-Living-Report.pdf> (accessed 15 April 2019).

[84] Rose et al. *Internet of Things: An Overview* (Internet Society 2015), p. 38.

[85] Walport, *Internet of Things*.

[86] See also discussion in Leverett, Clayton and Anderson, 'Standardisation and Certification of the Internet of Things' (WEIS 17, 2017) <https://www.cl.cam.ac.uk/~rja14/Papers/weis2017.pdf> (accessed 15 April 2019).

Accordingly, dominant industry standards are yet to crystallise. The experts contend that the commercial process of establishing dominant platforms or communications protocols is in progress. However, the technical heterogeneity of IoT ecosystems means the standards landscape is likely to remain unsettled for some time. Long term, technologists argue that lack of device interoperability may enable market dominance by actors with the resources to invest in setting commercial standards and minimising competition from smaller actors. Similarly, while communications protocols like Thread, Weave, Z-Wave and so on are emerging, legally there remain device interoperability concerns. Duncan [Partner, 25 years, Technology and Procurement Law] contends that competition in the marketplace about who can become the dominant actor and hub for devices will slow emergence of standards.[87]

The technologists are concerned about how variations in device interfaces shape end-user interactions, with, as Allan [Director, 28 years, Digital Identity & Online Privacy] argues, increasingly restricted interfaces and less scope for user control.[88] Furthermore, devices mediate the actions of end-users, and variations in customisability of devices can shape control and choice in a subtle, everyday ways; Blair [Law Firm Managing Director, 9 years, IT and Telecoms Law] argues that the benefit for users may shrink as the control that technology exerts over users prevents them enjoying their environment.[89]

To conclude, we see from these experiences that the experts engage with a wide range of regulatory issues around IoT, where safety and security are particular concerns. Furthermore, the embryonic nature of the IoT, the heterogeneity of the device ecosystem, and the lack of industry standards further complicate the regulatory landscape. We now look at both conceptual

---

[87] '[legally] … it's always quite difficult in terms of the standardisation process, for it [IoT] to work together there have got to be effective standards to make everything work and at the moment, obviously everybody is jostling to become the hub, so that they want their thing to be in the driving seat, to be the heart of what is going on in the IoT, and obviously time will tell who will be the winners and who will be the losers' [Duncan, Partner].

[88] 'There is a general direction of travel you can plot a line from browsers to smartphones to devices that run an app to ambient devices. At each stage along that line, the end user gets access to a more restricted user interface and gets fewer and fewer controls over what the device is actually doing, and in the case of ambient, passive collection is at zero interface' [Allan, Director].

[89] 'At what point do you [as a consumer] find that actually you are not benefitting from all this wonderful technology but you're actually living in an environment where it is your fridge telling you when you can or cannot eat, because you've exceeded the number of times you've opened and closed the door in a day …' [Blair, Managing Director].

and empirical perspectives, particularly prominent concerns around privacy and DP.

3.1 Data Protection and Privacy Challenges of IoT

From a regulatory perspective, concern is mounting about security, surveillance and privacy from smart technologies.[90] Predecessors to the domestic IoT have long prompted reflection on privacy challenges for end-users.[91] With ubicomp, Čas worries that 'ubiquitous computing will erode all central pillars of current privacy protection' and that reconciling ubicomp benefits with privacy risks is a considerable challenge. Spiekermann and Pallas fear paternalism through ubicomp, where non-negotiable binary rules enable automatic compliance, limit control and reduce user autonomy.[92] With AmI, the SWAMI project systematically considered a multitude of threats and vulnerabilities highlighting privacy, security and trust issues from technical, regulatory and socio-economic perspectives.[93]

With IoT, such concerns persist,[94] particularly due to the opacity of device interfaces, with inadequate consent mechanisms, insufficient control due to latent machine-to-machine communications and the hidden ecosystem of personal data stakeholders.[95]

Countless recent news stories exemplify possible privacy, information

---

[90] Klauser, *Surveillance and Space* (Sage 2017); Hildebrandt, *Smart Technologies and the End(s) of Law* (Elgar 2016).

[91] Belotti and Sellen, 'Design for Privacy in Ubiquitous Computing Environments' (1993) ECSCW'93, 77–92; Čas, 'Ubiquitous Computing, Privacy and Data Protection' in Gutwirth et al., *Computers, Privacy and Data Protection: An Element of Choice* (Springer 2009), p. 167; Wright et al., *Safeguards in a World of Ambient Intelligence* (Springer 2008); De Hert et al., 'Legal Safeguards for Privacy and Data Protection in Ambient Intelligence' (2009) 13 *Personal and Ubiquitous Computing* 435.

[92] Spiekermann and Pallas, 'Wider Implications of Ubiquitous Computing' (2012) 55 *Communications of the ACM (CACM)* 34.

[93] Wright et al., *Safeguards in a World of Ambient Intelligence*.

[94] Edwards, 'Privacy, Security and Data Protection in Smart Cities: A Critical EU Law Perspective' (2016) 2 *European Data Protection Law Review* 28; Rosner, *Privacy and the Internet of Things* (O'Reilly 2016); Urquhart, McAuley and Sunil 'Realising the EU Right to Data Portability for Domestic Internet of Things' (2017) 2 *Personal & Ubiquitous Computing* 317 DOI: 10.1007/s00779-017-1069-2; Peppet, 'Regulating the Internet of Things: First Steps Toward Managing Discrimination, Privacy, Security, and Consent' (2014) 93 *Texas Law Review* 87; Weber, 'Internet of Things- New Security and Privacy Challenges' (2010) 26 *Computer Law and Security Review* 23.

[95] Urquhart, Lodge and Crabtree, 'Demonstrably Doing Accountability in the Internet of Things' (2019) *International Journal of Law and Information Technology* <https://doi.org/10.1093/ijlit/eay015> (accessed 15 April 2019); Rosner and Kenneally, *Clearly Opaque* (Internet of Things Privacy Forum 2018).

security and physical safety harms.[96] For privacy, smart TVs[95] and Barbie dolls[98] listening to conversations of home occupants have prompted discussions around privacy harms and adequate control over children's personal data. With security, there are search engines dedicated to finding unsecured internet-connected baby monitors[99] and connected kettles leaking not water but WiFi passwords.[100] Furthermore, compromised devices can form part of botnets, leveraging malware and spam campaigns globally.[101] With physical safety concerns, we see connected smoke alarms switching off when waved at[102] or learning thermostats randomly turning off heating.[103] Relatedly, how smart devices make behaviour visible to other occupants can lead to social issues ranging from energy freeloading to serious stalking and intimate partner violence.[104]

[96] 'Privacy Not Included', Mozilla Project <https://foundation.mozilla.org/en/privacynotincluded/> (accessed 15 April 2019); for a related context of Industrial IoT see Urquhart and McAuley 'Avoiding the Internet of Insecure Industrial Things' (2018) *Computer Law & Security Review* DOI: 10.1016/j.clsr.2017.12.004.

[97] Barrett, 'How to Stop Your Smart TV Spying on You' (*Wired*, 2 July 2017) <https://www.wired.com/2017/02/smart-tv-spying-vizio-settlement/> (accessed 15 April 2019); BBC, 'Not in Front of the Telly: Warning over "Listening" TV' (BBC Tech, 9 February 2015) <www.bbc.co.uk/news/technology-31296188> (accessed 15 April 2019).

[98] Sheffield, 'Mattel's WiFi Barbie Could Be Used to Spy on Children' (*The Independent*, 18 March 2015) <www.independent.co.uk/news/business/news/mattels-wifi-barbie-could-be-used-to-spy-on-children-10115724.html> (accessed 15 April 2019).

[99] Porup, 'How to Search the Internet of Things for Photos of Sleeping Babies')ARS Technica UK, 19 January 2016) <http://arstechnica.co.uk/security/2016/01/how-to-search-the-internet-of-things-for-photos-of-sleeping-babies/> (accessed 15 April 2019).

[100] Pauli, 'Connected Kettles Boil Over, Spill Wi-Fi Passwords over London' (*The Register*, 19 October 2015) <www.theregister.co.uk/2015/10/19/bods_brew_ikettle_20_hack_plot_vulnerable_london_pots/> (accessed 15 April 2019). See EPSRC Defence against Dark Artefacts project examining how to build more secure smart homes. Also, for legal discussion see Urquhart, 'Exploring Cybersecurity and Cybercrime: Threats and Legal Responses' in Edwards, *Law, Policy and the Internet* (Hart Publishing 2018).

[101] Krebs, 'Who Makes the IoT Things under Attack?' (Krebs on Security, 2016) <https://krebsonsecurity.com/2016/10/who-makes-the-iot-things-under-attack/#more-36566> (accessed 15 April 2019).

[102] Arthur, 'Nest Halts Sales of Protect Smoke and Carbon Monoxide Alarm on Safety Fears' (*The Guardian*, 4 April 2014) <https://www.theguardian.com/technology/2014/apr/04/nest-halts-sales-of-protect-smoke-and-carbon-monoxide-alarm-on-safety-fears> (accessed 15 April 2019).

[103] Gibbs, 'Bug in Nest Thermostat Turns off Heating for Some' (*The Guardian*, 15 January 2016) <https://www.theguardian.com/technology/2016/jan/15/bug-nest-thermostat-turns-heating-off-for-some> (accessed 15 April 2019).

[104] Freed et al., '"A Stalker's Paradise": How Intimate Partner Abusers Exploit Technology' in proceedings of the 2018 CHI Conference on Human Factors in Computing Systems

We focus here on two primary areas of regulatory concern for IoT, namely: managing flows of personal information and user consent.

3.2 Managing Flows of Personal Information

IoT ecosystems involve flows of information between different devices, users and services. The setting of the home is key. Brown (2015) argues that IoT as problematic because it exists in private domestic contexts, presenting an attack target that is harder to secure and that can compromise physical safety.[105] Indeed, as Rosner states, 'it is not the Internet of Things that raises hackles – it is the Intimacy of Things'.[106] Data from the home is often co-constructed between inhabitants ('interpersonal data'),[107] yet while the law primarily provides individual DP rights, there are challenges exercising these for groups.[108] This can leave occupants vulnerable to domestic power asymmetries, particularly when accounts are hierarchically managed by one occupant on behalf of others, with little practical or legal recourse.[109] Profiling is another big concern for IoT.[110] The Article 29 Working Party worries that detailed inferences can be drawn about daily life where 'analysis of usage patterns in such a context is likely to reveal the inhabitants' lifestyle details, habits or choices or simply their presence at home'.[111] Similarly, Deakin et al. note that combinations of non-personal data may create sensitive personal data (which consequently need explicit user consent), for example, when and what people eat or how often they leave the house daily may indicate religious beliefs.[112]

IoT concerns need to be situated against the wider European climate of user unease around control of personal data. In a 2015 Eurobarometer Survey of around 28,000 EU citizens' attitudes to personal DP, two-thirds of respondents are 'concerned about not having complete control over the

---

(CHI'18) (ACM Press 2018) DOI: <https://doi.org/10.1145/3173574.3174241> (accessed 15 April 2019); Goulden et al., 'Smart Grids, Smart Users? The Role of the User in Demand Side Management' (2014) 2 *Management, Energy Research and Social Science* 21.

[105] Brown, 'Regulation and the Internet of Things', p. 25.

[106] Rosner, *Privacy and the Internet of Things*, p. 18.

[107] Goulden et al., 'Living with Interpersonal Data: Observability and Accountability in the Age of Pervasive ICT' (2018) 20 *New Media & Society* 1580 <https://doi.org/10.1177/1461444817700154> (accessed 15 April 2019).

[108] Taylor, Floridi and van der Sloot, *Group Privacy* (Springer 2017).

[109] Flintham, Goulden, Price and Urquhart, 'Domesticating Data'; Vella, 'IoT Devices and Smart Domestic Abuse: Who Has the Controls?' (2018) *Engineering and Technology* <https://eandt.theiet.org/content/articles/2018/06/iot-devices-and-smart-domestic-abuse-who-has-the-controls/> (accessed 15 April 2019).

[110] Article 29 Working Party, 'Opinion 8/2014', p. 8.

[111] Article 29 Working Party, 'Opinion 8/2014', pp. 6–8.

[112] Deakin et al. *The Internet of Things: Shaping Our Future*, p. 15.

information they provide online'.[113] Nearly 70 per cent both think that prior explicit approval is necessary before data collection and processing, and worry about data being used for purposes different from those claimed at collection.[114] Around 60 per cent distrust telecoms firms, internet service providers and online businesses.[115] Looking to IoT more specifically, a recent global study by 25 DP regulators of IoT devices shows that '59 per cent of devices failed to adequately explain to customers how their personal information was collected, used and disclosed … [and] … 72 per cent failed to explain how customers could delete their information off the device'.[116]

Against this backdrop, we now turn to our experts. The complexity and diversity of device, service and user interactions can make it hard to comprehend the flows of information, and the rationales behind them.[117] Nevertheless, better understanding of the personal data flows within micro transactions between devices needs to emerge. We found that one practical challenge is understanding who is legally responsible for the information and for mapping their obligations therein. This requires asking practical questions like what is data being used for, by whom, where it is being stored and how long it is being kept, but as Innes argues, the breadth of stakeholders, platforms and applications make this a tricky exercise when:

> [we are] not just speaking about a single device but in an interconnected environment where you have all these providers of different technologies hosted on different platforms maybe a building landlord who is responsible for a building then you have got tenants and service providers … [Innes, Associate, 8 years, DP and IP].

A particular concern that both technologists and lawyers flag is the flows of data to third parties. While interactions between users and primary service

---

[113] European Commission, 'Special Eurobarometer 431 "Data Protection"' <http://ec.europa.eu/justice/newsroom/data-protection/news/240615_en.htm> (accessed: 13 April 2019), p. 6.

[114] European Commission, 'Special Eurobarometer 431 "Data Protection"', p. 58.

[115] European Commission, 'Special Eurobarometer 431 "Data Protection"', p. 63.

[116] ICO, 'Privacy Regulators Study Finds Internet of Things Shortfalls' (ICO Blog, 22 September 2016) <https://ico.org.uk/about-the-ico/news-and-events/news-and-blogs/2016/09/privacy-regulators-study-finds-internet-of-things-shortfalls/> (accessed 15 April 2019).

[117] As Iain puts it, 'Across the IoT then we will have to deal with a whole host of transactions, and some of those will be incredibly small, and involve small forms of currency, not just economic, but data, if a kettle talks to the fridge, or the toothbrush to the toothpaste, or the door to the car, will many of those things … how will they want to be private, how will they construct valuable experiences? [It] will be really really challenging' [Iain, Professor].

providers may be apparent and legitimate, protecting user rights around third parties is harder because identifying who they are and how to get in touch to exercise your rights is unclear.[118]

Indeed, end-users have a range of DP rights, but the challenges in establishing who is responsible for them can impact how they are protected and realised in practice. One reason these rights are so important is the control they afford the end-user over their personal data. Control in this context is not just about the data itself, but also controlling the inferences that can be drawn from the data, in particular any prejudicial impacts.[119] Blair's example captures this well, depicting a hypothetical scenario where insurers use wearables to monitor user activity to vary insurance premium rates:

> take for example, private health insurance and they say here you go, we will send you one of our smart pedometers or our smart fitness trackers, you wear it, as part of your contract of health insurance, and we will price your premium based on the level of activity that we see you doing, if we see you sitting in your chair all day you will get a higher premium because you're inactive, if we sense you play rugby you will get a higher premium because you will hurt yourself …

To conclude, establishing responsibility for flows of data in practice is a key challenge, often frustrated by the complexity of data flows in the IoT. We now turn to a mechanism that seeks to increase control over data for users: consent.

3.3 Consent

While it is not the only legal grounds for processing personal data (there are others such as protecting legitimate interests, or performing contracts or publicly assigned tasks), consent is an important one, especially for sensitive personal data such as information relating to sexual orientation, political beliefs, religion, ethnicity or health.[120] For IoT, the users' insufficient knowledge of

---

[118] 'You have a right to know that a third party has data about you and that right is kind of implied by the right to see that data, and to correct it and so on, if you simply don't know or you don't know who the third party is or how to get in touch with them, then your ability to exercise that right is completely undermined' [Allan, Director].

[119] In the context of the Right to Data Portability, the lack of portability in inferences and statistical outputs is a significant shortcoming for IoT devices, as explored in Urquhart, McAuley and Sunil, 'Realising the EU Right to Data Portability for Domestic Internet of Things'; also, for a fascinating study of responses to data portability requests see Wong and Henderson, 'How Portable is Portable? Exercising the GDPR's Right to Data Portability' (2018) ACM Ubicomp'18.

[120] Article 4(11) and 7 GDPR.

data processing by physical objects, inadequate consent mechanisms[121] and a lack of control over data sharing between such objects are key concerns.[122] As Edwards has argued:

> even if methods can be found for giving some kind of notice/information, the consents obtained in the IoT are almost always going to be illusory or at best low-quality in terms of the EU legal demand for freely given, specific and informed consent.[123]

Urquhart and Rodden have advocated new mechanisms for designing consent mechanisms, by repurposing Benford's trajectories framework for considering the actors, space, time and interfaces involved in designing user experiences.[124]

In our experts' experience, obtaining freely given, unambiguous, informed end-user consent with IoT can be challenging, especially when users are unaware of the nature of data collection. As Allan argues:

> consent is being tampered with, it's being assumed in some cases because the default setting for many devices may be that they connect and communicate, whether they ask or not, and consent is also being undermined because you don't necessarily know what data it is collecting or sharing, and you don't know what is being done with the data.

The requirement to inform end-users about data collection is impacted by device heterogeneity. The variations in IoT device interfaces necessitate more creative mechanisms for delivering information during the consent-giving process. As discussed above, smartphones play a key intermediary role in the IoT ecosystem, and can be a conduit for information, provided it belongs to the end-user, as a medium for authentication and validating identity.[125]

---

[121] Edwards, 'Privacy, Security and Data Protection in Smart Cities', pp. 18–20.

[122] Article 29 Working Party, 'Opinion 8/2014', p. 6; Rose et al. *Internet of Things: An Overview*, pp. 26–9.

[123] Edwards, 'Privacy, Security and Data Protection in Smart Cities', p. 32.

[124] Urquhart and Rodden, 'New Directions in Technology Law: Learning from Human Computer Interaction' (2017) 31 *International Review of Law, Computers and Technology* 1.

[125] 'In the IoT the challenge is many devices don't have a user interface, like the Nest smart thermostat. It is the smartphone, the web and email which you are using. You have two things right, your authentication device, the thermostat, but you can't present that info on the authentication device, so you need a consumption device like a smartphone, laptop or desktop, so it is going to require some thinking there, particularly when the law also says you also have to secure evidence of consent. So that needs to give some rise. So, when it comes to an IoT device, and then the consumption device for information, how do you know if the consumption device is mine?' [Findlay, Consultant].

Another attribute of consent is it is meant to be freely given. However, when terms of service change and renewed user consent is required, negotiation is lacking. Consumers are faced with a choice of either accepting changes or no longer using the product, and power asymmetries between consumers and IoT product/service providers quickly become evident. Blair questions this practice, stating 'the idea that something is freely given, when you've paid £250 on your smart thermostat, the idea of use it or lose it because of a change of terms makes it very questionable if any consent is ever freely given'.

A connected issue is how changes in consent manifest across different devices in an IoT ecosystem. The practicalities of designing cross-device consent-giving processes requires reflection and tailoring to different contexts and end-users. One consideration is that IoT devices often operate in settings where the consent of multiple end-users is required. Lawyers and designers need to create approaches that provide notification of data processing and obtain consent from all data subjects affected, for example, visitors to the home being captured by a domestic security system. Creating effective consent mechanisms is not a job for lawyers or designers alone. There is an explicit turn in the role of designers in regulation, and PbD is often cited as the solution to many challenges of IoT.[126] However, as we have argued elsewhere, to move PbD from theory into practice, a joint conceptual and practical approach is necessary to support designers and to enable lawyers to realise what is feasible through design.[127] We suggest turning to the user-centric tools and approaches prevalent within the human–computer interaction community.[128] Raising designer awareness of law is important, with new design tools being necessary to support this, like information PbD cards[129] or privacy design patterns.[130] We now turn to greater detail on the nature of PbD, both in theory and practice.

---

[126] Danezis et al., *Privacy and Data Protection by Design – From Policy to Engineering* (European Network Information Security Agency, 2014); Brown, 'Regulation and the Internet of Things'.

[127] Urquhart, 'Ethical Dimensions of User Centric Regulation' (2018) 47 *ACM Computers and Society* 81 DOI: 10.1145/3243141.3243151.

[128] Urquhart and Rodden, 'New Directions in Technology Law'.

[129] Luger et al., 'Playing the Legal Card: Using Ideation Cards to Raise Data Protection Issues within the Design Process' (2015) proceedings of SIGCHI Conference on Human Factors in Computer Systems (CHI'15) (ACM Press 2015).

[130] Colesky et al., 'Critical Analysis of Privacy Design Strategies' (2016) International Workshop on Privacy Engineering: IWPE'16 (IEEE 2016).

4. Regulatory Solutions? The Role of Privacy by Design

4.1 Introducing Privacy by Design

Privacy by Design (PbD) as a policy tool has been discussed in EU and UK regulatory circles for some time.[131] State regulatory bodies like the UK Information Commissioner's Office,[132] the European Data Protection Supervisor (EDPS),[133] European Union Agency for Network and Information Security (ENISA),[134] and EU Article 29 Working Party all recognise the importance of PbD approaches.[135] The EDPS, for example, has stated that 'systems and software engineers need to understand and better apply the principles of PbD in new products and services across design phases and technologies'.[136] More specifically for the IoT, the Article 29 Working Party Opinion recommends 'Every stakeholder in the IoT should apply the principles of Privacy by Design and Privacy by Default'.[137]

The core idea is for designers of technology to consider privacy challenges as early as possible, ideally before a system is built or goes to market, in order to embed appropriate safeguards. In some regards, it aims to narrow the regulatory effectiveness gap created by slow legislative change and quick technological development. Article 25(1) of the 2016 General Data Protection Regulation 2016[138] puts this concept into law, placing obligations on data controllers to protect the freedoms and rights of individuals, implement DP principles and generally comply with requirements of the new law. This is done by employing safeguards during data processing (Article 4(2), GDPR, 2016),[139] namely appropriate technical and organisational measures that reflect elements such as the state of the art, implementation costs, nature

---

[131] Cavoukian, '7 Foundational Principles of Privacy by Design' (Information and Privacy Commissioner of Ontario 2011); Spiekermann, 'The Challenges of Privacy by Design', pp. 34–7.

[132] Information Commissioner's website, Privacy by Design (2016) Available at <https://ico.org.uk/for-organisations/guide-to-data-protection/privacy-by-design/> (accessed: 13 April 2019).

[133] European Data Protection Supervisor, 'Drones – Opinion of 26 November 2014' (EDPS 2014); European Data Protection Supervisor, 'eCall System – Opinion of 29 October 2013' (EDPS 2015).

[134] Danezis et al., *Privacy and Data Protection by Design.*

[135] Article 29 Working Party, 'Opinion 8/2014'.

[136] European Data Protection Supervisor, 'Towards a New Digital Ethics Opinion 4/2015', p. 10.

[137] Article 29 Working Party Opinion, 'Opinion 8/2014', p. 21.

[138] Formerly Article 23 of draft.

[139] Processing is very broad – see below.

of processing and risks to rights and freedoms of individuals.[140] Safeguards shall be considered both before and during processing, using measures such as data minimisation, pseudonymisation, providing tools to monitor data processing, improving security and increasing transparency.[141] In addition, by default, technical and organisational measures should be taken to ensure that processing is necessary for specific purposes; the data are not collected once and forever but instead the amount, extent, period of storage and accessibility to data are controlled; and lastly, access to data by many people is not possible without the individual's permission.[142]

Compliance with Article 25 can involve implementing organisational and technical measures, adopting internal policies or accreditation through new certification mechanisms.[143] Indeed, complying with the accountability principle in Article 5(2) GDPR requires demonstrating compliance strategies, for example to data subjects and protection authorities.[144] Legal compliance is important for controllers and processors because, beyond protecting user rights, a key attribute of the new GDPR is much larger fines, charges up to the higher of €20m or 4 per cent of global turnover for failure to comply.[145] We assert that drafting in the GDPR[146] of data controller and data processing are sufficiently broad to put those creating new technologies at the forefront of compliance, including a range of system designers from manufacturers to third-party services.[147]

4.2 Challenges of Doing Privacy by Design

While a legally valuable provision, a key stumbling block with PbD is how it might work in practice. A detailed understanding of the law and policy

---

[140] Article 25(1), GDPR, 2016.

[141] Recital 78, GDPR, 2016.

[142] Article 25(2), GDPR, 2016.

[143] These are proposed but not yet developed.

[144] Urquhart, Lodge and Crabtree, 'Demonstrably Doing Accountability in the Internet of Things'.

[145] Article 83, GDPR, 2016.

[146] EU General Data Protection Regulation (GDPR), 2016, Recital 78: 'When developing, designing, selecting and using applications, services and products that are based on the processing of personal data or process personal data to fulfil their task, producers of the products, services and applications should be encouraged to take into account the right to data protection when developing and designing such products, services and applications and, with due regard to the state of the art, to make sure that controllers and processors are able to fulfil their data protection obligations.'

[147] GDPR, 2016, Article 4(5) controls 'the natural or legal person, public authority, agency or any other body which alone or jointly with others determines the purposes and means of the processing of personal data'.

environment is not prevalent amongst engineers. Birnhack, Toch and Hadar (2014) have argued that 'whereas for lawyers PbD seems an intuitive and sensible policy tool, for information systems developers and engineers it is anything but intuitive' (p. 3). Similarly, Danezis et al. highlighted that there is a lack of tools to support PbD and those created by researchers have limited practical impact, in part due to ignorance of DP issues with developers and data controllers.[148] Legal commentators, like Jaap Koops and Leenes echo this, arguing guidance on PbD in practice is lacking and developing the correct mindset in developer is important,[149] as does Brown, who argues that 'the specifics of implementation [for PbD] have so far only been developed to a limited extent'.[150] Solutions are needed to bridge the gap between these two communities.[151] Law is not intuitive or accessible to non-lawyers, yet by calling for PbD, the law is mandating non-lawyers to be involved in regulatory practices. There is a need to engage, sensitise and guide designers on DP issues on their own terms.[152] We have made endeavours in this direction exploring how to practically do PbD, and support interaction between the legal and human–computer interaction communities both conceptually[153] and practically, using decks of ideation cards to enable ethics, legal compliance and PbD.[154] Key in our approach is learning from HCI concepts, such as affordances, provenance and trajectories to create more user-centric approaches to designing regulatory interventions.[155] Approaches within HCI such as design ethnography, participatory and co-design are critical mechanisms in both understanding and responding to user needs in design.[156]

Beyond this social and interactional focus, complementary technical

---

[148] Danezis et al., *Privacy and Data Protection by Design*, p. 4.

[149] Koops and Leenes, 'Privacy Regulation Cannot Be Hardcoded. A Critical Comment on the "Privacy by Design" Provision in Data-Protection Law' (2014) 28 *International Review of Law, Computers & Technology* 159, p. 161.

[150] Brown, 'Regulation and the Internet of Things', p. 26.

[151] Urquhart, 'Bridging the Gap between Law & HCI: Designing Effective Regulation of Human Autonomy in Everyday Ubicomp Systems' (2014) proceedings of the International Conference on Ubiquitous Computing (Ubicomp'14).

[152] Urquhart, *Towards User Centric Regulation: Exploring the Interface between IT Law and HCI* (University of Nottingham/PhD Thesis 2016).

[153] Urquhart, 'Ethical Dimensions of User Centric Regulation'.

[154] MoralIT and LegalIT decks available at <www.lachlansresearch.com/moralitandlegalit cards> (accessed: 13 April 2019); Luger et al., 'Playing the Legal Card'; Darzentas et al., 'Card Mapper: Enabling Data-Driven Reflections on Ideation Cards' SIGCHI'19 (ACM Press 2019).

[155] Urquhart and Rodden, 'New Directions in Technology Law'; Urquhart, 'Ethical Dimensions of User Centric Regulation'.

[156] Crabtree, Rouncefield and Tolmie, *Doing Design Ethnography* (Springer 2012).

work addressing the privacy challenges of systems presents a useful blueprint to doing PbD. Such approaches include privacy and security engineering,[157] usable privacy and security,[158] privacy-enhancing technologies (PETS),[159] and most recently, human–data interaction.[160]

With usable privacy and security, for example, the goal is to create technical responses to regulatory challenges that are comprehensible and usable for end-users. A broad-church, usable privacy has worked to increase user control by setting machine-readable permissions for data collection from devices/browsers (so-called P3P);[161] improving quality of notice and choice mechanisms by creating 'nutrition labels' for users to compare privacy policies,[162] or nudging users towards more cautious sharing practices.[163] Personal information management systems, such as Databox, are providing a valuable mechanism to enable more control over personal data for subjects.[164] A combination of technical and social approaches to PbD are key.

We now briefly consider a few points around PbD in practice. Ideologically lawyers view PbD positively because it exposes privacy risks earlier in the design process, allowing them to be addressed and avoiding 'back-pedalling down the line'. However, our experts argue that PbD requires greater critique and reflection, with both communities sharing what works and what does not. At the abstract level, even the terms 'privacy' and 'by design' are disputed. For example, with privacy, some technologists question how to design for such a contested social value. As Iain frames it: 'My problem with privacy

---

[157] Dennedy, Fox and Finneran, *Privacy Engineer's Manifesto* (Apress 2014); Spiekermann and Cranor, 'Engineering Privacy' (2009) 35 *IEEE Transactions on Software Engineering* 67; Oliver, *Privacy Engineering*; Anderson, *Security Engineering* (2nd edn, Wiley 2011).

[158] Iachello and Hong, 'End User Privacy in Human–Computer Interaction' (2007) 1 *Foundations and Trends in Human–Computer Interaction* 1.

[159] Camp and Osorio, 'Privacy-enhancing Technologies for Internet Commerce' (Springer-Verlag 2003).

[160] Mortier et al., 'Human-Data Interaction: The Human Face of the Data-Driven Society' (2014) SSRN Working Paper <www.eecs.qmul.ac.uk/~hamed/papers/HDIssrn.pdf> (accessed: 15 April 2019).

[161] Cranor et al., 'The Platform for Privacy Preferences 1.0 (P3P)' (2002) W3C Recommendation.

[162] Kelley et al., 'A Nutrition Label for Privacy' Symposium on Usable Privacy and Security (SOUPS Conference, 15–17 July 2009) <https://cups.cs.cmu.edu/soups/2009/proceedings/a4-kelley.pdf> (accessed 15 April 2019).

[163] Wang et al., 'A Field Trial of Privacy Nudges for Facebook' in proceedings of SIGCHI Conference Human Factors in Computer Systems (CHI'14) (ACM Press 2014).

[164] Crabtree et al., 'Building Accountability into the Internet of Things: The IoT Databox Model' (2018) *Journal of Reliable Intelligent Environments* DOI: <https://doi.org/10.1007/s40860-018-0054-5> (accessed 15 April 2019).

by design is I don't know what people mean by privacy anymore because all of the practices we carry out contradict the values …'[165]

Other technologists (such as Kenneth) questioned what PbD actually means beyond the headline phrase, and what it requires of industry in practice. Instead, he argues that it is better to understand how PbD will play out differently for specific application sectors and solutions, for example, with cars, cities and the home, as opposed to a generalised approach.

Some lawyers are concerned about how PbD is framed as a solution. While PbD may involve building in privacy-enhancing tools like encryption into a system, more fundamentally it is important to reflect on whether PbD is meant to support existing legal approaches to privacy, or to replace them with technical measures. Another interesting finding is the parallels between privacy by design and security by design. Security is often not considered until later in the development cycle, retrospectively bolted on after the device has been rushed to market, as there are minimal motivations to think about security. In practice, this problem is particularly pronounced with SMEs and start-ups who are financially constrained. Cybersecurity director and consultant Hamish [Director and Managing Consultant, 30 years, Cybersecurity and Identity Management] captures this well, arguing that start-ups and SMEs have limited financial and time resources, and focus on getting products to market, leaving security issues to be fixed in the next iteration, but that this rarely happens, and if it does, it's constrained by earlier decisions.[166] Similarly, law firm partner Ewan argues that as start-ups lack the financial resources to obtain legal advice they focus on attracting more investment to stay in business, not to spend on compliance. As he puts it:

> all they are interested in really is raising money from investors, because that is what they need to live on, because they are living pretty much hand to mouth, [with PbD, data retention and anonymisation] … just not on their radar …

---

[165] He continues: 'You can't expect people to recover values, and when they do recover values, they go back to really old school values like Christian values or family values, or I don't think they know what privacy values are, I think they contradict them all the time, through the value propositions of which ubiquity in networked data offer them.'

[166] 'I think for start-ups and SMEs unless security is critical to their project, it largely gets overlooked because they are working on a limited budget, they have got to start producing revenue as soon as they can, and therefore it is a race to get your component to market as quickly as you possibly can, and it is very much seen, well there might be some security things, but we'll fix those in version 2 … sadly, it never happens in version 2 and what does happen in v2.0 is a bit too late, because of some of the design decisions made in version 1' [Hamish, Director and Managing Consultant].

In conclusion, more critical reflection on PbD in practice is important. Understanding privacy as a value is an issue for designers, as it is a contested term and they feel that looking to users may not always provide them the clarity they need (due to the long-standing privacy paradox hinted at by Iain).[167] Learning from similarities with security by design may be useful, as can questioning what PbD is actually doing – augmenting or replacing traditional legal approaches? For experts, the former is preferable, but importantly, as with IoT, PbD cannot be understood in the abstract, and focusing on how it manifests in specific sectors, rather than at a general level, is important. Furthermore, the commercial realities of limited financial and organisational resources, coupled with a different focus, especially for SMEs and start-ups, have to be factored into any workable notion of PbD.

5. Conclusions

We are entering a new age of ambient domestic computing. It is no longer unusual to imagine the following scenarios: home hubs with digital facial expressions that prompt guilt or contentment by smiling or scowling at you; conversational agents that hang on to your every word and unanswerable query; intelligent fridges that monitor your food consumption habits to suggest *sui generis* recipes that help avoid more food waste (perhaps by mixing together that pot of leftover fizzy hummus and curdled milk); smart lighting that can create the perfect *hygge* mood or Monday night mosh pit (depending on how your day went); and smart security systems that let you in, just because 'your face fits', despite forgetting your RFID entry fob.

We have seen that smart home visions have captured the imagination of many authors (including this one), film makers and technologists. Pop sci-fi culture is littered with examples, including *Ubik*, 'The Veldt', *Mr Robot*, *Back to the Future II* and *Rick and Morty*. However, as smart homes become increasingly commonplace, regulators and lawyers also need to exercise their imaginations to create strategies that move beyond the headline and actually help realise privacy by design for the IoT in practice. Key to this is learning the lessons from previous domestic technology trends, and ensuring that contemporary smart homes are designed with user interests at their core (particularly around privacy and security).

The legal challenges facing the IoT are considerable, and practical regulatory questions include how to design effective consent mechanisms across heterogeneous devices, how to allow users control over inferences from flows

---

[167] Barth and Jong, 'The Privacy Paradox – Investigating Discrepancies between Expressed Privacy Concerns and Actual Online Behaviour' (2017) 34 *Telematics and Informatics* 1038.

of information and how to establish parties with legal responsibilities in opaque domestic IoT ecosystems. Equally, the regulatory solution of PbD while theoretically welcomed, faces practical implementation challenges. With our experts, many issues have emerged such as a lack of sector-specific guidance and inadequate financial or organisational resources to enable businesses to do PbD in practice. Through analysis of earlier ambient domestic technologies we observe the importance of considering how a technology mediates a user's life in context and to respond accordingly. For PbD in the domestic context, this means creating design approaches that engage with values, like privacy, in the home setting. Neglecting the complex interactions and practices between users, services and devices risks moving ambient domestic computing a step closer to many of the darker prophecies of the future home.

Appendix Table 3.1 Lawyers

Pseudonym	Job	Years' experience	Specialism
Blair	Managing Director, Lawyer	9	IT and Telecoms Law
Campbell	Full-time academic	8	Teacher and researcher in law
Duncan	Partner	25	Technology and public procurement law
Ewan	Partner	14	Technology, data protection and information law
Findlay	Consultant	20	Privacy and information management policy
Innes	Legal Associate	8	Commercial technology, intellectual property and data protection law

Appendix Table 3.2 Technicians

Pseudonym	Job	Years' experience	Specialism
Allan	Director, Technical Professional	32	Digital identity and privacy
Iain	Professor, Chair	25	Interaction design and digital media
Jess	Senior Researcher	28	Cybersecurity, big data and ethics of data science
Gordon	Vice President, Primary Consultant	30	Wireless networking and sensors
Kenneth	Vice President, Visiting Professor	42 (telecoms)/ 15 (visiting professor)	Engineering and telecoms
Magnus	Chief Technology Officer	40	Wireless technologies and smart devices
Hamish	Managing Consultant	30	Cybersecurity and identity management

References

Aarts E and Marzano S, *The New Everyday: Views on Ambient Intelligence* (010 Publishers 2003).

Anderson R, *Security Engineering* (2nd edn, Wiley 2011).

Arkko J et al., *IETF RC 7452: Architectural Considerations in Smart Object Networking* (Internet Engineering Task Force 2015).

Arthur C, 'Nest Halts Sales of Protect Smoke and Carbon Monoxide Alarm on Safety Fears', *The Guardian*, 4 April 2014 <https://www.theguardian.com/tech nology/2014/apr/04/nest-halts-sales-of-protect-smoke-and-carbon-monoxide-alarm-on-safety-fears> (accessed 15 April 2019).

Article 29 Working Party, 'Opinion 8/2014 on the Recent Developments on the Internet of Things' (European Commission 2014).

Ashton K, 'That Internet of Things Thing' (*RFID Journal*, 2009) <www.itrco.jp/libraries/RFIDjournal-That%20Internet%20of%20Things%20Thing.pdf> (accessed 15 April 2019).

Ballard JG, 'A Thousand Dreams of Stellavista' in *The Complete Short Stories* (vol. 1) (Harper Perennial 2006).

Barrett B, 'How to Stop Your Smart TV Spying on You' (*Wired*, 2 July 2017) <https://www.wired.com/2017/02/smart-tv-spying-vizio-settlement/> (accessed 15 April 2019).

Barth S and Jong M, 'The Privacy Paradox – Investigating Discrepancies between Expressed Privacy Concerns and Actual Online Behaviour: A Systematic Literature Review' (2017) 34 *Telematics and Informatics* 1038.

BBC, 'Not in Front of the Telly: Warning over "Listening" TV' (BBC Tech, 9 February 2015) <www.bbc.co.uk/news/technology-31296188> (accessed 15 April 2019).

Bell G and Dourish P, 'Yesterday's Tomorrows: Notes on Ubiquitous Computing's Dominant Vision' (2006) 11 *Personal and Ubiquitous Computing* 133.

Belotti V and Sellen A, 'Design for Privacy in Ubiquitous Computing Environments' (1993) ECSCW'93, 77–92.

Borning A and Muller M, 'Next Steps for Value Sensitive Design' (2012) in proceedings of SIGCHI Conference Human Factors in Computer Systems (CHI'12), 1125.

Bouverot A, *GSMA: The Impact of the Internet of Things – The Connected Home* (GSMA 2015) <www.gsma.com/newsroom/wp-content/uploads/15625-Con nected-Living-Report.pdf> (accessed 15 April 2019).

Bradbury R, *The Illustrated Man* (Doubleday 1950).

Bradbury R, 'There Will Come Soft Rains', in *The Martian Chronicles* (Doubleday 1951).

Braun V and Clarke V, 'Using Thematic Analysis in Psychology' (2006) 3 *Qualitative Research in Psychology* 77.

Brown I, 'Regulation and the Internet of Things' (GSR Discussion Paper, International Telecommunications Union 2015).

Caceres R and Friday A, 'Ubicomp Systems at 20: Progress, Opportunities and Challenges' (2012) 11 *IEEE Pervasive Computing* 14.

Cammell D (Director) *Demon Seed* (MGM 1977).

Camp J and Osorio C, 'Privacy-enhancing Technologies for Internet Commerce' (2003) *Trust in the Network Economy* 317 (Springer-Verlag).

Čas J, 'Ubiquitous Computing, Privacy and Data Protection' in Gutwirth S et al., *Computers, Privacy and Data Protection: An Element of Choice* (Springer 2009).

Cavoukian A, '7 Foundational Principles of Privacy by Design' (Information and Privacy Commissioner of Ontario 2011).

Choe EK et al., 'Living in a Glass House: A Survey of Private Moments in the Home' in proceedings of the International Conference on Ubiquitous Computing (UbiComp'11) (ACM Press 2011).

Colesky M et al., 'Critical Analysis of Privacy Design Strategies' (2016) International Workshop on Privacy Engineering: IWPE'16 (IEEE 2016).

Crabtree A and Rodden T, 'Domestic Routines and Design for the Home' (2004) 13 *Computer Supported Cooperative Work* 191.

Crabtree A et al., 'Building Accountability into the Internet of Things: The IoT Databox Model' (2018) *Journal of Reliable Intelligent Environments* DOI: <https://doi.org/10.1007/s40860-018-0054-5> (accessed 15 April 2019).

Crabtree A, Rouncefield M and Tolmie P, *Doing Design Ethnography* (Springer 2012).

Cranor LF et al., 'The Platform for Privacy Preferences 1.0 (P3P)' (2002) W3C Recommendation.

Danezis G et al., *Privacy and Data Protection by Design – From Policy to Engineering* (European Network Information Security Agency, 2014).

Darzentas D et al., 'Card Mapper: Enabling Data-Driven Reflections on Ideation Cards' SIGCHI'19 (ACM Press 2019).

Deakin S et al., *The Internet of Things: Shaping Our Future* (Cambridge Public Policy 2015).

De Hert P et al., 'Legal Safeguards for Privacy and Data Protection in Ambient Intelligence' (2009) 13 *Personal and Ubiquitous Computing* 435.

Dennedy M, Fox J and Finneran T, *Privacy Engineer's Manifesto* (Apress 2014).

Dick PK, *Ubik* (Doubleday 1969).

Dourish P, 'What We Talk About When We Talk About Context' (2004) 8 *Personal and Ubiquitous Computing* 19.

Dourish P and Bell G, *Divining a Digital Future: Mess and Mythology in Ubiquitous Computing* (MIT Press 2011).

Edwards K and Grinter R, 'At Home with Ubiquitous Computing: Seven Challenges' in proceedings of the 3rd International Conference on Ubiquitous Computing (UbiComp'01) (ACM Press 2001) pp. 256–72.

Edwards L 'Privacy, Security and Data Protection in Smart Cities: A Critical EU Law Perspective' (2016) 2 *European Data Protection Law Review* 28.

Esmail S (Director), *Mr Robot* (Universal Cable Productions 2015).

European Commission, 'Special Eurobarometer 431 "Data Protection"' (2015) <http://ec.europa.eu/justice/newsroom/data-protection/news/240615_en.htm> (accessed: 15 April 2019).

European Data Protection Supervisor, 'eCall System – Opinion of 29 October 2013' (EDPS 2013).

European Data Protection Supervisor, 'Drones – Opinion of 26 November 2014' (EDPS 2014).

European Data Protection Supervisor, 'Towards a New Digital Ethics Opinion 4/2015' (EDPS 2015).

Favreau J (Director), *Iron Man* (Marvel Entertainment 2008).

Flintham M, Goulden M, Price D and Urquhart L, 'Domesticating Data: Socio-Legal Perspectives on Smart Homes & Good Data Design' in Daly A et al. (eds), *Good Data* (INC Theory on Demand 2019).

Freed D et al., ' "A Stalker's Paradise": How Intimate Partner Abusers Exploit Technology' in proceedings of the 2018 CHI Conference on Human Factors in Computing Systems (CHI'18) (ACM Press 2018) DOI: <https://doi.org/10.1145/3173574.3174241> (accessed 15 April 2019).

Gibbs S, 'Bug in Nest Thermostat Turns off Heating for Some' (*The Guardian*, 15 January 2016) <https://www.theguardian.com/technology/2016/jan/15/bug-nest-thermostat-turns-heating-off-for-some> (accessed 15 April 2019).

Goulden M et al., 'Living with Interpersonal Data: Observability and Accountability in the Age of Pervasive ICT' (2018) 20 *New Media & Society* 1580 <https://doi.org/10.1177/1461444817700154> (accessed 15 April 2019).

Goulden M et al., 'Smart Grids, Smart Users? The Role of the User in Demand Side Management' (2014) 2 *Management, Energy Research and Social Science* 21.

Grudin J, 'The Computer Reaches Out: The Historical Continuity of Interface Design' in proceedings of SIGCHI Conference Human Factors in Computer Systems (CHI'90) (ACM Press 1990), pp. 261–8.

Hanna W and Barbera H (Directors) *The Jetsons* (Screen Gems 1962).

Hargreaves T and Wilson C, *Smart Homes and Their Users* (Springer 2017).

Harkaway N, *Gnomon* (Heinemann 2017).

Hildebrandt M, *Smart Technologies and the End(s) of Law* (Elgar 2016).

Iachello G and Hong J, 'End-User Privacy in Human–Computer Interaction' (2007) 1 *Foundations and Trends in Human–Computer Interaction* 1.

ICO, 'Privacy Regulators Study Finds Internet of Things Shortfalls' (2016) ICO Blog, 22 September 2016 <https://ico.org.uk/about-the-ico/news-and-events/news-and-blogs/2016/09/privacy-regulators-study-finds-internet-of-things-shortfalls/> (accessed 15 April 2019).

Ihde D, *Technology and the Lifeworld* (Indiana University Press 1990).

International Telecommunications Union, *Overview of the Internet of Things* (ITU 2012).

Jonze S (Director), *Her* (Annapurna Pictures, 2013).

Kelley PG et al., 'A Nutrition Label for Privacy', Symposium on Usable Privacy and Security (SOUPS) Conference, 15–17 July 2009 <https://cups.cs.cmu.edu/soups/2009/proceedings/a4-kelley.pdf> (accessed 15 April 2019).

Klauser F, *Surveillance and Space* (Sage 2017).

Koops BJ and Leenes R, 'Privacy Regulation Cannot Be Hardcoded. A Critical Comment on the "Privacy by Design" Provision in Data-Protection Law' (2014) 28 International Review of Law, Computers & Technology 159.

Krebs B, 'Who Makes the IoT Things under Attack?' (Krebs on Security, 2016) <https://krebsonsecurity.com/2016/10/who-makes-the-iot-things-under-attack/#more-36566> (accessed 15 April 2019).

Lamourne R, Feiz K and Rigot B, 'Social Trends and Product Opportunities: Philips Vision of the Future Project' in proceedings of ACM SIGCHI, 1997.

Latour B, 'Where are the Missing Masses? – The Sociology of a Few Mundane Artifacts' in Bijker WE and Law J (eds), *Shaping Technology/Building Society*

(MIT Press 1992), pp. 205–24 (reprint <www.bruno-latour.fr/sites/default/files/50-MISSING-MASSES-GB.pdf> last accessed 15 April 2019).

Lee D, 'Amazon Promises Fix for Creepy Alexa Laugh' (BBC Tech, 7 March 2018) <https://www.bbc.com/news/technology-43325230> (accessed 15 April 2019).

Leppänen S and Jokinen M, 'Daily Routines and Means of Communication in a Smart Home', in Harper R (ed.), *Inside the Smart Home* (Springer-Verlag 2003).

Leverett E, Clayton R and Anderson R, 'Standardisation and Certification of the Internet of Things' (WEIS 17, 2017) <https://www.cl.cam.ac.uk/~rja14/Papers/weis2017.pdf> (accessed 15 April 2019).

Lindwer M et al., 'Ambient Intelligence Visions and Achievements: Linking Abstract Ideas to Real-world Concepts' (2003) Design, Automation and Test in Europe Conference.

Liu Y et al., 'Identity Crisis of Ubicomp? Mapping 15 Years of the Field's Development and Paradigmatic Change' (2014) Proceedings of the International Conference on Ubiquitous Computing (Ubicomp'14).

Luger E et al., 'Playing the Legal Card: Using Ideation Cards to Raise Data Protection Issues within the Design Process' (2015) proceedings of SIGCHI Conference on Human Factors in Computer Systems (CHI'15) (ACM Press, 2015).

Lyon D, *The Culture of Surveillance: Watching as a Way of Life* (Wiley 2018).

McAuley D, 'What is IoT? That is Not the Question' (IoT UK, 2016) <http://iotuk.org.uk/what-is-iot-that-is-not-the-question/> (accessed: 15 April 2019).

McStay A, *Emotional AI* (Sage 2018).

Mäkinen L, 'Surveillance On/Off: Examining Home Surveillance Systems from the User's Perspective' (2016) 14 *Surveillance & Society* 59.

Maloney D, 'The Jetsons is Actually a Bone Chilling Dystopia' (2017) *The Verge* <https://www.theverge.com/2017/11/3/16598440/jetsons-dystopia-dc-comics-future-apocalypse> (accessed 15 April 2019).

Marks P, *Imagining Surveillance: Utopian and Dystopian Literature and Film* (Edinburgh University Press 2015).

Moore J (Director), *I.T.* (Voltage Pictures 2016).

Mortier R et al., 'Human-Data Interaction: The Human Face of the Data-Driven Society' (2014) SSRN Working Paper <www.eecs.qmul.ac.uk/~hamed/papers/HDIssrn.pdf> (accessed: 15 April 2019).

Nissenbaum H, *Privacy in Context: Technology, Policy and the Integrity of Social Life* (Stanford University Press 2009).

Oliver I, *Privacy Engineering* (independently published 2014).

Oulasvirta A et al., 'Long-term Effects of Ubiquitous Surveillance in the Home' in proceedings of the International Conference on Ubiquitous Computing (UbiComp'12) (ACM Press 2012).

Park N (Director) *Wallace and Gromit: The Wrong Trousers* (Aardman Animations 1993).

Pauli D, 'Connected Kettles Boil Over, Spill Wi-Fi Passwords over London' *The Register*, 19 October 2015 <www.theregister.co.uk/2015/10/19/bods_brew_ikettle_20_hack_plot_vulnerable_london_pots/> (accessed 15 April 2019).

Peppet S, 'Regulating the Internet of Things: First Steps toward Managing Discrimination, Privacy, Security, and Consent' (2014) 93 *Texas Law Review* 87.

Porup JM, 'How to Search the Internet of Things for Photos of Sleeping Babies' (ARS Technica UK, 19 January 2016) <http://arstechnica.co.uk/security/2016/01/how-to-search-the-internet-of-things-for-photos-of-sleeping-babies/> (accessed 15 April 2019).

Quinn B, 'The Nudge Unit: The UK Experts Hat Became a Prime UK Export' (*The Observer*, 10 November 2018) <https://www.theguardian.com/politics/2018/nov/10/nudge-unit-pushed-way-private-sector-behavioural-insights-team> (accessed 15 April 2019).

Reeves S, 'Envisioning Ubiquitous Computing' in proceedings of SIGCHI Conference Human Factors in Computer Systems (CHI'12) (ACM Press 2012), pp. 1573-1582.

Rogers Y, 'Moving on from Weiser's Vision of Calm Computing: Engaging Ubicomp Experiences' (2006) proceedings of the 8th International Conference on Ubiquitous Computing (UbiComp'06), pp. 404–21.

Roiland J and Harmon D (Creators) *Rick and Morty* (Adult Swim 2015).

Rose K et al., *Internet of Things: An Overview* (Internet Society 2015).

Rosner G, *Privacy and the Internet of Things* (O'Reilly 2016).

Rosner G and Kenneally E, *Clearly Opaque* (Internet of Things Privacy Forum 2018).

Satyanarayanan M, 'Pervasive Computing: Visions and Challenges' (2001) 8 *IEEE Personal Communications* 10.

Sheffield J, 'Mattel's WiFi Barbie Could Be Used to Spy on Children' (*The Independent*, 18 March 2015) <www.independent.co.uk/news/business/news/mattels-wifi-barbie-could-be-used-to-spy-on-children-10115724.html> (accessed 15 April 2019).

Spiekermann S, 'The Challenges of Privacy by Design' (2012) 55 *Communications of the ACM (CACM)* 34.

Spiekermann S and Cranor LF, 'Engineering Privacy' (2009) 35 *IEEE Transactions on Software Engineering* 67.

Spiekermann S and Pallas F, 'Wider Implications of Ubiquitous Computing' (2005) 4 *Poiesis & Praxis: International Journal of Ethics of Science and Technology Assessment* 6.

Stahl BC, Eden G and Jirotka M, 'Responsible Research and Innovation in Information and Communication Technology – Identifying and Engaging with the Ethical Implications of ICTs' in Owen R, Bessant J and Heintz M (eds), *Responsible Innovation: Managing the Responsible Emergence of Science and Innovation in Society* (Wiley-Blackwell 2013), pp. 199–218.

Stilgoe J et al., 'Developing a Framework for Responsible Innovation' (2013) 42 *Research Policy* 1568.

Suchman L, *Plans and Situated Actions: The Problem of Human-Machine Communication* (Cambridge University Press 1987).

Taylor L, Floridi L and van der Sloot B, *Group Privacy* (Springer 2017).

Thaler R and Sunstein C, *Nudge: Improving Decisions about Health, Wealth and Happiness* (Yale University Press 2008).

Tolmie P et al., 'Unremarkable Computing' in proceedings of SIGCHI Conference Human Factors in Computer Systems (CHI'12) (ACM Press 2012).

Ur B, Jung J and Schechter S, 'Intruders versus Intrusiveness: Teens' and Parents' Perspectives on Home-Entryway Surveillance' in proceedings of the International Conference on Ubiquitous Computing (Ubicomp'14) (ACM Press 2014).

Urquhart L, 'Bridging the Gap between Law & HCI: Designing Effective Regulation of Human Autonomy in Everyday Ubicomp Systems' (2014) proceedings of the International Conference on Ubiquitous Computing (Ubicomp'14).

Urquhart L, *Towards User Centric Regulation: Exploring the Interface between IT Law and HCI* (University of Nottingham/PhD Thesis 2016).

Urquhart L, 'Hunting for Ethical Innovation in the Adventures of Rick and Morty' (19 September 2017) <https://lachlansresearch.com/2017/09/19/gik ii-2017-hunting-for-ethical-innovation-in-the-adventures-of-rick-and-morty/> (accessed 15 April 2019).

Urquhart L, 'Ethical Dimensions of User Centric Regulation' (2018) 47 *ACM Computers and Society* 81 DOI: 10.1145/3243141.3243151.

Urquhart L, 'Exploring Cybersecurity and Cybercrime: Threats and Legal Responses' in Edwards L, *Law, Policy and the Internet* (Hart Publishing 2018).

Urquhart L and McAuley D, 'Avoiding the Internet of Insecure Industrial Things' (2018) *Computer Law & Security Review* DOI: 10.1016/j.clsr.2017.12.004.

Urquhart L and Rodden T, 'New Directions in Technology Law: Learning from Human–Computer Interaction' (2017) 31 *International Review of Law, Computers and Technology* 1.

Urquhart L, Jäger N and Schnädelbach H, 'Adaptive Architecture: Regulating Human Building Interaction' (2019) *International Review of Law, Computers & Technology* (forthcoming).

Urquhart L, Lodge T and Crabtree A, 'Demonstrably Doing Accountability in the Internet of Things' (2019) *International Journal of Law and Information Technology* <https://doi.org/10.1093/ijlit/eay015> (accessed 15 April 2019).

Urquhart L, McAuley D and Sunil N, 'Realising the EU Right to Data Portability for Domestic Internet of Things' (2017) 2 *Personal & Ubiquitous Computing* 317 DOI: 10.1007/s00779-017-1069-2.

Urquhart L, Reedman-Flint D and Leesakul N, 'Responsible Domestic Robots: Exploring Ethical Implications of Robots in the Home' (2019) *Journal of Information, Communication and Ethics in Society* (forthcoming).

Vella H, 'IoT Devices and Smart Domestic Abuse: Who Has the Controls?' (2018) *Engineering and Technology* <https://eandt.theiet.org/content/articles/2018/06/iot-devices-and-smart-domestic-abuse-who-has-the-controls/> (accessed 15 April 2019).

Walport M, *Internet of Things: Making the Most of the Second Digital Revolution* (UK Government Office for Science 2014).

Wang Y et al., 'A Field Trial of Privacy Nudges for Facebook' in proceedings of SIGCHI Conference Human Factors in Computer Systems (CHI'14) (ACM Press 2014).

Weber R 'Internet of Things – New Security and Privacy Challenges' (2010) 26 *Computer Law and Security Review* 23.

Weiser M, 'The Computer for the 21st Century' (1991) 265 *Scientific American* 94.

Weiser M and Brown JS, 'The Coming Age of Calm Technology' in Denning PJ and Metcalfe RM, *Beyond Calculation* (Copernicus 1997).

Wilson C et al., 'Smart Homes and Their Users: A Systematic Analysis and Key Challenges' (2015) 19 *Personal and Ubiquitous Computing* 463.

Wong J and Henderson T, 'How Portable is Portable? Exercising the GDPR's Right to Data Portability' (2018) ACM Ubicomp'18.

Working Party on Communication Infrastructures and Services Policy, *Building Blocks for Smart Networks* (OECD 2013) <https://www.oecd.org/official documents/publicdisplaydocumentpdf/?cote=DSTI/ICCP/CISP(2012)3/ FINAL&docLanguage=En> (accessed 15 April 2019).

Wright D et al., *Safeguards in a World of Ambient Intelligence* (Springer 2008).

Yang R and Newman M, 'Learning from a Learning Thermostat: Lessons for Intelligent Systems for the Home' in proceedings of the International Conference on Ubiquitous Computing (UbiComp'13) (ACM Press 2013).

Yang R et al., 'Making Sustainability Sustainable: Challenges in the Design of Eco-Interaction Technologies', Proceedings SIGCHI Conference Human Factors in Computer Systems (CHI'14) (ACM Press 2014).

Zemeckis R (Director) *Back to the Future Part II* (Amblin Entertainment and Universal Studies, 1989) <http://time.com/money/4076862/back-to-the-future-day-predictions-accuracy/> (accessed 3 June 2019).

4

Citizen-consumers in a Personalised Galaxy: Emotion-influenced Decision Making, a True Path to the Dark Side?

Damian Clifford

Fear is the path to the Dark Side. Fear leads to anger, anger leads to hate, hate leads to suffering.

Yoda, *Star Wars: Episode I – The Phantom Menace*

1. Introduction

A good Jedi must resist the influence of emotions that subvert reason. Jedi Master Yoda's warning of the consequences of fear and the graduated descent to the dark side, referred to above, does not however categorise all emotions as dangerous. Instead and as noted by Stephens, the Jedi philosophy appears to be somewhat stoic in character.[1] Stoicism, as first advanced by Hellenic philosophers, advocates the passivity towards disturbing emotions (or *apatheia*), while at the same time recognising ' "good emotional states" that are not pathological movements of the soul, namely, benevolence (wishing someone good things for his own sake), joy (in virtuous deeds), and caution (reasonable wariness)'.[2] The stoics suggest that one must separate what can be controlled and what remains outside of one's reach. This appears to be reflected in the fictional Jedi teachings and is manifested when Luke Skywalker urges his father to 'let go' of his hate and the dark side.

But how separable are emotions practically, and should we really delineate emotion (or indeed particular emotions) from reason in order to make

---

[1] Stephens, 'Stoicism and the Philosophies of the Jedi and the Sith' (2014) 9 *The Stoic Philosopher* <https://dspace2.creighton.edu/xmlui/handle/10504/62183> (accessed 13 April 2019).

[2] Ibid.

effective decisions? Is there not something to be said for letting our emotions guide our responses? And is this not the *de facto* reality? It is clear that emotions[3] play a key role in decision making and this is aptly reflected in their role in advertising and marketing. These questions are becoming increasingly relevant, given the rise in emotion detection and monetisation online. In this vein, one can further wonder how a wide-scale adoption of such technologies would be affected by (and indeed affect) the law. In aiming to reflect upon these points this chapter examines the emergence of such technologies in an online context. Although, as discussed elsewhere, there is a clear debate to be had regarding the emergence of empathic media and their use *vis-à-vis* fake news,[4] its use in public spaces for commercial purposes,[5] its deployment for public security and safety purposes,[6] and also issues relating to the accuracy of the certain emotion detection techniques, such matters remain outside the scope of this targeted chapter.

Instead, therefore, this chapter will provide an initial offering of issues associated with the use of such technologies online for commercial advertising and marketing purposes (construed broadly) and the challenges they present in particular for the EU data protection and consumer protection legislative framework. The analysis relies on a descriptive and evaluative analysis of the EU data and consumer protection frameworks and aims to provide normative insights into the potential legal challenges presented by emotion commercialisation online. The legal instruments have been selected on the basis of their substantive and material scope. Section 2 briefly examines emotion detection online, the philosophical positioning of law and emotion and finally, the effects of emotion on decision-making capacity. Section 3 examines emotion detection through the lens of the data protection framework. And finally, Section 4 questions the continuing relevance of the current framework and calls for more detailed analysis in this area in light of the underlying difficulties.

---

[3] It should be noted that although there is a wide body of literature delineating emotions, feelings, moods and so on, and offering 'affect' as the umbrella term – the terms will be used interchangeably herein for ease of reading even if it is 'affect' as the categorizing notion that is referred to substantively. See section 2.3 for more.

[4] Bakir and McStay, 'Fake News and the Economy of Emotions: Problems, Causes, Solutions' (2018) 1 *Digital Journalism* 154.

[5] Lewinski, Trzaskowski and Luzak, 'Face and Emotion Recognition on Commercial Property under EU Data Protection Law' (2016) 33 *Psychology & Marketing* 729; McStay, 'Empathic Media and Advertising: Industry, Policy, Legal and Citizen Perspectives (the Case for Intimacy)' (2016) 3 *Big Data & Society* 1.

[6] Erkin et al., 'Privacy-Preserving Emotion Detection for Crowd Management' *International Conference on Active Media Technology* (Springer 2014) <http://link.springer.com/chapter/10.1007/978-3-319-09912-5_30> (accessed 13 April 2019).

2. Emotion and the 'Rationality' of Citizen-consumer Protections – 'I've Got a Bad Feeling about This'

The emergence of emotion detection technology online certainly raises concerns, but how has the law traditionally treated emotions? How do emotions affect decision making and do these developments present novel concerns? The purpose of this section therefore, is to briefly examine the means and applications of emotion detection technology before examining law and emotions theory and then finally examining interdisciplinary insights as to how emotions influence decision making.

2.1 Empathic Media and Emotion Monetisation – 'I can Feel Your Anger' And I Like Your Other Emotions Too …

Force empathy is a force power in the Star Wars world that allows those capable to detect another's feelings, emotional state and even deeply guarded secrets. For instance, Darth Vader senses Luke's feelings for Leia and the fact that they are brother and sister. Such empathic insights therefore reveal the value of such a power. Technological advancements are now rendering emotions detectable in the online world, thereby placing Vader's power in the hands of a variety of commercial entities. Although there are clear concerns regarding the accuracy of emotion detection (i.e. in particular see critiques of the reliance on facial action coding systems) such criticisms (1) do not rule out the capacity to automate the detection of emotion but instead focus on the failure of research exploring emotion detection from facial expressions based on specific emotion categories to appreciate the need for high dimensional measures and context[7] and, (2) do not therefore, eliminate the concerns being addressed in this chapter. Indeed, the emergence of what McStay categorises as empathic media or 'technologies that track bodies and react to emotions and intentions'[8] arguably raises a number of concerns. Building on the granular insights provided by big data, such technological developments allow commercial entities to move beyond the mere targeting of behaviour in advertisements to the personalisation of services, interfaces and the other consumer-facing interactions, based on personal preferences, biases and emotion insights gleaned from the tracking of online activity and profiling.[9]

---

[7] See Barrett, Adolphs, Marsella, Martinez, and Pollak (2019). 'Emotional Expressions Reconsidered: Challenges to Inferring Emotion From Human Facial Movements', *Psychological Science in the Public Interest* 20 (1), 1–68.

[8] McStay, 'Empathic Media: The Rise of Emotion in AI'.

[9] See Calo, 'Digital Market Manipulation' (2017) ResearchGate <https://www.researchgate.net/publication/317616480_EMPATHIC_MEDIA_THE_RISE_OF_EMOTION_AI> (accessed 13 April 2019).

Although the interest in emotion measurement is far from a new phenomenon given the steady rise of the affective computing sub-discipline,[10] the increasing capacity to monetise emotions is in part due to the emergence of empathic media. Facebook in particular has received a lot of media attention in this regard. From the infamous emotional contagion experiment where users newsfeeds were manipulated to assess changes in emotion, to the introduction of 'feelings' in addition to the 'like' button, the targeting of insecure youths with 'vulnerable' moods,[11] and their patents for the detection of emotion in messenger (to add emoticons automatically), via the camera of a smartphone or laptop (for content delivery) and also through image analysis of photos such as selfies (in order to dynamically generate emojis).[12] However, Facebook is clearly not alone, and with the rise of many big technology players and also the emergence of smaller dedicated companies, empathic media is now becoming increasingly mainstream.[13] From the analysis of *inter alia* facial expressions,[14] to text[15] and data mining,[16] voice[17] analysis and the use

[10] McStay, 'Empathic Media: The Rise of Emotion in AI'.

[11] Levin, 'Facebook Told Advertisers It Can Identify Teens Feeling "Insecure" and "Worthless"' (*The Guardian*, 1 May 2017) <www.theguardian.com/technology/2017/may/01/facebook-advertising-data-insecure-teens> (accessed 13 April 2019); Solon, '"This Oversteps a Boundary": Teenagers Perturbed by Facebook Surveillance' (*The Guardian*, 2 May 2017) <www.theguardian.com/technology/2017/may/02/facebook-surveillance-tech-ethics> (accessed 13 April 2019); 'Facebook Research Targeted Insecure Youth, Leaked Documents Show' (*The Independent*, 1 May 2017) <www.independent.co.uk/news/media/facebook-leaked-documents-research-targeted-insecure-youth-teenagers-vulnerable-moods-advertising-a7711551.html> (accessed 13 April 2019).

[12] 'Facebook's Emotion Tech: Patents Show New Ways for Detecting and Responding to Users' Feelings' (*CB Insights Research*, 1 June 2017) <https://www.cbinsights.com/research/facebook-emotion-patents-analysis/> (accessed 13 April 2019).

[13] For a growing list of empathic media-related projects, companies, people and groups, and so on see <https://emotionalai.org/useful-links/> (accessed 13 April 2019).

[14] Reece and Danforth, 'Instagram Photos Reveal Predictive Markers of Depression' (2017) 6 *EPJ Data Science* <http://epjdatascience.springeropen.com/articles/10.1140/epjds/s13688-017-0110-z> (accessed 13 April 2019).

[15] Potenza, 'Google's US Search Results Will Let People Check if they're Depressed' (*The Verge*, 23 August 2017) <https://www.theverge.com/2017/8/23/16193236/google-depression-questionnaire-mental-health> (accessed 13 April 2019).

[16] Hibbeln et al., 'How Is Your User Feeling? Inferring Emotion through Human–Computer Interaction Devices' (2017) 41 *Management Information Systems Quarterly* 1.

[17] See for instance companies such as: <https://vokaturi.com/> (accessed 13 April 2019). Or indeed the project: 'EmoVoice – Real-Time Emotion Recognition from Speech' available at: <https://www.informatik.uni-augsburg.de/lehrstuehle/hcm/projects/tools/emovoice/> (accessed 13 April 2019).

of smart devices to reveal emotions,[18] such detection is becoming ever more commonplace.

Despite the fact there are many applications of these technologies, for instance in health care or road safety, that appear morally above reproach (at least in terms of their goals as opposed to their implementation, accuracy and potential effects[19]), their use for advertising and marketing purposes raises clear concerns. In this regard it should be noted that the lines between the seemingly ethical uses of this technology and the murkier commercial exploitation of insights into emotion in advertising and marketing may be very fine. Indeed, there is arguably only a small step between a service and the future commercial exploitation of the gathered emotional insights for advertising and marketing purposes.[20] Although these insights are not currently being plugged into programmatic advertising data sets, generally speaking (i.e. there is no market for data sets on emotions),[21] they are used in the plethora of examples in the emotion-aware entertainment media sphere in which emotion is used as an indicator for the recommending of content.[22] Moreover, the 'positioning' of products via differentiation on the basis of their subjective features is a well-established component in marketing strategies;[23] and ongoing technological developments that allow for the personalisation of

[18] Zhao, Adib and Katabi, 'Emotion Recognition Using Wireless Signals' (ACM Press 2016) <http://dl.acm.org/citation.cfm?doid=2973750.2973762> (accessed 13 April 2019).

[19] In this regard one can refer to the work of Rouvroy. In her examination of the 'algorithmic production of reality', Rouvroy questions the impact of decision making based on the profiling of individuals' or 'data behaviouralism' and the effects of such techniques on capacity for critical thinking. The author notes that despite the pretences of objectivity and responding to individual needs, the computational turn eliminates the capacity for the transversal dimension of 'test', 'trial', 'examination', 'assessment' or 'épreuve', or even 'experience', which the author deems essential in the scientific, judicial and existential domains. Rouvroy, 'The End(s) of Critique: Data Behaviourism versus Due Process' in Vries K and Hildebrandt M (eds), *Privacy, Due Process and the Computational Turn* (Routledge 2013), pp. 143–5.

[20] For instance, Google has recently revealed that it will allow users in the US to check if they exhibit signs of depression, however it must be remembered that Google is the largest online advertising company globally. Available at: <https://www.theverge.com/2017/8/23/16193236/google-depression-questionnaire-mental-health> (accessed 13 April 2019).

[21] McStay, 'Empathic Media and Advertising'.

[22] One should consider in particular services concentrated on the supply of media content and their use of recommender systems. See Rolland, 'Comment les algorithmes revolutionnent l'industrie culturelle' (*La Tribune*, 19 November 2015) <https://www.latribune.fr/technos-medias/comment-les-algorithmes-revolutionnent-l-industrie-culturelle-523168.html> (accessed 13 April 2019).

[23] Reed Jr and Coalson Jr, 'Eighteenth-Century Legal Doctrine Meets Twentieth-Century Marketing Techniques: FTC Regulation of Emotionally Conditioning Advertising' (1976) 11 *Georgia Law Review* 733.

all aspects of commercial communication delivery (even the nature of the appeal) facilitate commercial penetration. Accordingly, one must question the effects of combining such personalisation with consumer-facing interactions that are driven by emotion insights.[24] The proliferation of internet technologies has allowed for the commercialisation of different forms of content that were historically void of a commercial nature, and permits the further monetisation of the private sphere, thereby extending technology's reach even further. This is significant as emotionally appealing campaigns can have a direct and immediate impact upon consumers who can act on their desires at the click of a mouse. Such direct access and the elimination of time for reflection permits the commercial exploitation of impulses through emotionally triggered actions.[25]

The categorisation of emotions as a key stimulus in provoking sales is hardly controversial as emotions have always been recognised as an important factor in the advertising process.[26] Despite the fact that emotion, and indeed emotion detection technologies, have been used in market research for some time (therefore informing the development of marketing campaigns and products and services), their expansion out of laboratory conditions to everyday consumer-facing interactions raises the stakes considerably, given the potential for real-time detection and personalisation. Fundamentally, from a legal perspective this challenge is aligned to our capacity as citizens and consumers (hereinafter citizen-consumers) to act autonomously online. Indeed, the separation of rational thinking (or reason) from emotion is a core underlying presumption of modern legality. As noted by Maloney, the law works from the perspective that these notions 'belong to separate spheres of human existence; the sphere of law admits only of reason; and vigilant policing is required to

---

[24] For example, the gamification of content (be it commercial or editorial) has been shown to engender positive emotional reactions from consumers, thereby rendering such content more attractive and engaging (i.e. gamification techniques applications or advertising techniques such as advergames). See Verdoodt, Clifford and Lievens, 'Toying with Children's Emotions, the New Game in Town? The Legality of Advergames in the EU' (2016) 32 *Computer Law & Security Review* 599.

[25] Although not specific to the context of emotions one can refer more generally here to Calo, 'Digital Market Manipulation' (2014) 82 *George Washington Law Review* 995.

[26] Poels and Dewitte, 'How to Capture the Heart? Reviewing 20 Years of Emotion Measurement in Advertising' (2006) 46 *Journal of Advertising Research* 18. The authors note in the introduction that the role of emotions has always been recognised as an important factor in the 'advertising process'. They note that even in the earliest advertising model, AIDA (attention, interest, desire and action), there was reliance on an emotional reaction – in this instance desire, and that this only happened after the consumer had experienced interest in the advertisement or the product. This led to the conception that the sequence went Attention, Information, Desire and then Action – generally referred to as the 'hierarchy of effects' model.

keep emotion from creeping in where it does not belong'.[27] With this in mind, the capacity of the current legal framework to cope with such developments is in doubt. The development of emotion detection technology further facilitates the creation of emotion-evolved consumer-facing interactions, in that such technologies allow for the development *inter alia* of content, formats and products or indeed entire campaigns that are optimised by emotion insights. The harnessing of biases for commercial purposes has been analysed in the context of behavioural economics and is referred to as market manipulation.

Hanson and Kysar introduced the market manipulation theory in three articles published almost twenty years ago.[28] The authors emphasised the key contention that commercial entities will respond to market incentives and hence, manipulate consumer perceptions in a way that maximises profits.[29] This is significant *vis-à-vis* emotion monetisation, as there is little doubt that commercial entities are aware of the importance (and make use of) emotional influences on consumer behaviour.[30] It therefore seems natural that establishing a bias opens up the possibility of manipulation and thus its exploitation for commercial purposes.[31] The development of technology capable of detecting emotions in real time, the tailoring of individualised affective appeals and hence, the capacity to personalise based on metrics other than relevance, all increase the potential effectiveness and reach of commercial campaigns.

---

[27] Maroney, 'Law and Emotion: A Proposed Taxonomy of an Emerging Field' (2006) 30 *Law and Human Behavior* 119.

[28] Hanson and Kysar, 'Taking Behavioralism Seriously: The Problem of Market Manipulation' (1999) 74 *New York University Law Review* 630; Hanson and Kysar, 'Taking Behavioralism Seriously: Some Evidence of Market Manipulation' (1999) 12 *Harvard Law Review* 1420; Hanson and Kysar, 'Taking Behavioralism Seriously: A Response to Market Manipulation' (2000) 6 *Roger Williams University Law Review* 259.

[29] Market manipulation theory also renders much of the criticisms positioned against the discovery of bias moot. More specifically, the so-called 'citation bias', where behavioural law and economics scholars have been accused of disproportionately weighing biases relative to the instances in which individuals act in accordance with what is deemed rational, becomes somewhat irrelevant. Instead it is replaced by what Hanson and Kysar refer to as exploitation bias (i.e. the tendency to exploit biases that result 'in increased sales, higher profits and decreased perceptions of risk'): Hanson and Kysar, 'Taking Behavioralism Seriously: The Problem of Market Manipulation', p. 743.

[30] In this context one can refer to Kaptein, *Persuasion Profiling: How the Internet Knows What Makes You Tick* (Business Contact Publishers 2015).

[31] The economists Akerlof and Shiller analogised irrational actions as *monkey-on-our-shoulder* inspired human decision making that can be, and is, commercially harnessed or *phished*. Akerlof and Shiller, *Phishing for Phools: The Economics of Manipulation and Deception* (Princeton University Press 2015), pp. 5–6. 'Phished' in this context should be interpreted broadly and not within the traditional meaning in terms of the extraction of sensitive information by cyber criminals.

Therefore, an ongoing point of contention in EU consumer law is the enduring relevance of the 'reasonable' or 'credulous' consumer, given the systematic nature of revelations in research regarding consumer behaviour, the ability of commercial entities to exploit such insights and hence, the capacity (or lack thereof) of consumers to act rationally and in their own best interests.[32]

2.2 Law and Emotions in an Empathic Galaxy

Despite implicit references, the role of emotion in law has largely been ignored. Law and emotions theory emerged as a means of challenging legal rationality. Nevertheless, law and emotion theory is distinct from other such theories (in particular behavioural law and economics, and neuroscience and the law).[33] Indeed, as noted by Albramst and Keren '[l]aw and emotions is more epistemologically challenging to conventional thought than those variants that have received wider recognition: it does not privilege rationality or prioritize the objectivist epistemologies that have become cornerstones of mainstream legal thought'.[34] As a consequence, precisely plotting the contours of this field is challenging. The purpose of this section is therefore, to present the positioning of emotions in law as inspired by philosophical and legal philosophical writings in this area in order to understand the potential effects of emotion detection technology and how it could shape the underlying positioning of emotion and its place in the law.

2.2.1 'Feel, Don't Think, Use Your Instincts' … or is it Think and Then Feel to Use Your Instincts?

As noted by Kahan and Nussbaum, '[p]hilosophical accounts of emotion have their roots in ordinary ways of talking and thinking about the emotions'.[35] Emotions however are difficult to define. Indeed, Strasser observes that although '[m]any philosophers, scientists and psychologists have laboured from pre-Socratic times onwards to find the right way to define the term emotion … no consensual definition has been ever been found'.[36] Nevertheless, the lack of

---

[32] Ramsay, *Consumer Law and Policy: Text and Materials on Regulating Consumer Markets* (Hart 2012), p. 63.

[33] Blumenthal, 'Emotional Paternalism' (2007) 35 *Florida State University Law Review* 1(2007) 35 *Florida State University Law Review* 1.

[34] Abrams and Keren, 'Who's Afraid of Law and the Emotions' (2009) 94 Minnesota Law Review 1997, p. 1999.

[35] Kahan and Nussbaum, 'Two Conceptions of Emotion in Criminal Law' (1996) 96 *Columbia Law Review* 269, p. 277.

[36] Strasser, *Emotions, Experiences in Existential Psychotherapy and Life* (Duckworth 1999), p. 23, as cited by Spain, *The Role of Emotions in Criminal Law Defences: Duress, Necessity and Lesser Evils* (Cambridge University Press 2011), p. 74.

a definition has not had a detrimental effect on the analysis of emotion and the expanding body of literature examining its role and nature.[37] Moreover, there has been long-standing agreement that certain experiences can be grouped together as emotions and that these are distinct from 'from bodily appetites such as hunger and thirst, and also from objectless moods, such as irritation or endogenous depression'.[38] Although a full examination of the development of the modern philosophical understanding of emotions is outside the scope of this chapter, a few key points emerge from the existing literature analysing the developments in this area *vis-à-vis* the positioning of law and emotions in terms of rationality as a legal notion.[39]

More specifically, there has been a long-standing debate regarding the interaction between cognition and emotion. Broadly speaking two opposing views have emerged namely, those that position emotion as thoughts incorporating beliefs and appraisals or evaluations (the evaluative view) and those that classify emotions as a distinct phenomenon acting independently of cognitive function (the mechanistic view).[40] The mechanistic view holds a certain appeal, given that it responds to certain features associated with emotions. For instance, the way in which emotions can feel like they sweep over one's consciousness leaving one without the capacity to control their effects, the sense that emotion appears to reside external to the self and finally, the urgency of the experience of emotion.[41] In contrast, at first glance it appears conceptually difficult to align emotion with thought, given that thoughts are often conceived of as conscious evaluations.[42] However, despite the

---

[37] Spain *The Role of Emotions in Criminal Law Defences*, p. 74. See also Bandes, *The Passions of Law* (New York University Press 2001).

[38] Kahan and Nussbaum, 'Two Conceptions of Emotion in Criminal Law', p. 276.

[39] Spain, *The Role of Emotions in Criminal Law Defences*; Maroney 'Law and Emotion'.

[40] As defined by the authors, 'the mechanistic view holds that emotions are forces more or less devoid of thought or perception – that they are impulses or surges that lead the person to action without embodying beliefs, or any way of seeing the world that can be assessed as correct or incorrect, appropriate or inappropriate. The evaluative view holds, by contrast, that emotions do embody beliefs and ways of seeing, which include appraisals or evaluations of the importance or significance of objects and events. These appraisals can, in turn, be evaluated for their appropriateness or inappropriateness.' Kahan and Nussbaum, 'Two Conceptions of Emotion in Criminal Law', p. 278.

[41] Ibid.

[42] As observed by Kahan and Nussbaum, 'Conceptions that define emotions as embodying a kind of thought about an object would appear to have difficulty meeting this challenge, for thoughts are usually seen as things we actively make or do, not things we suffer; they are usually conceived of as central to the core of our selfhood; and they are usually imagined as calm and cool. Thinking of emotions as thoughts may make it difficult to see why they should be so difficult to manage and should cause the upheaval in human life that they frequently do.' Ibid., 280.

traditionally strong positioning of the mechanistic view, more recent research in cognitive psychology and neuroscience has provided strong evidence of a cognitive element.[43] In short, the evaluative view (the view encompassing cognitive appraisal theories) is founded on the premise that 'individuals make assessments about the personal relevance of a given situation in light of their beliefs, values and capabilities, and it is this assessment which results in the experience of emotion'.[44] Hence, as noted by de Sousa '[e]ven when emotions involve physical manifestations, it is their mental causation that defines them as emotion and grounds our evaluations of them'.[45] In essence, it is not that cognitive appraisal theories ignore physiological manifestations of emotions but rather that these are consequential to the experience of emotion rather than constituting or causing them. Thus, although emotions are accompanied by bodily arousal, judgements are both necessary and, in themselves, sufficient constituent elements.[46]

Cognitive elements are therefore essential to an emotion's identity. However, even if one accepts the cognitive element to emotion, there is no consensus on the precise nature of the interaction between emotions and cognition and thus the exact role of cognition.[47] As observed by Clore, '[a]sserting that emotions are mental states in no way implies that emotions are not also bodily states and legacies of our evolutionary past … It requires only that emotion be seen as part of a larger information processing system'.[48] Indeed, although cognitive appraisal theories are the dominant approach, such theories hang on the interpretation of what is meant by cognition and have been criticised for positioning emotions as thoughts rather than mere brain functions. In response to such criticisms, Lazarus has observed that a thought must actually 'refer to something – it does not operate in a vacuum – and the cognition of the emotions involves goals, plans and beliefs and is about the stakes (active goals) and (coping) options a person has for managing the person-environment relationship'.[49] Hence, from this perspective emotions are more than mere thoughts as the person's goals,

---

[43] See LeDoux and Brown, 'A Higher-Order Theory of Emotional Consciousness' (2017) proceedings of the National Academy of Sciences 201619316.

[44] Spain, *The Role of Emotions in Criminal Law Defences*, p. 77.

[45] De Sousa, *The Rationality of Emotion* (MIT Press 1987), p. 6.

[46] Nussbaum, *Upheavals of Thought: The Intelligence of Emotions* (Cambridge University Press 2003), p. 64.

[47] Solomon, *Not Passion's Slave: Emotions and Choice* (Oxford University Press 2007), p. 86.

[48] Ekman and Davidson, 'Why Emotions Are Felt' in Fox AS, Lapate RC, Shackman AJ and Davidson RJ (eds), *The Nature of Emotion: Fundamental Questions* (Oxford University Press 1994), p. 181. As referred to by Spain, *The Role of Emotions in Criminal Law Defences*, p. 80.

[49] Lazarus, *Emotion and Adaptation* (Oxford University Press 1994), p. 13.

beliefs, values, morals and capabilities are applied to these thoughts, thereby resulting in an emotion that reflects the relevance of the particular situation for an individual.

Nevertheless, for some authors the fact that thoughts still retain such a key role fails to reflect emotions as intense forces over which we exert no control. For instance, LeDoux, in proposing the emotion appraisal theory as an alternative to cognitive appraisal theories, suggests that cognitive theories 'have turned emotions into cold, lifeless states of mind'.[50] The author instead suggests that emotions should be considered as brain functions rather than psychological states that emerge from a more primitive emotion appraisal system. In this vein, Damasio refers to the non-conscious and thus non-deliberative responses that occur in the 'evolutionary old brain structure'.[51] However, this delineation of (emotional) brain function and the cognitive or conscious part of the brain appears to be formed more on the basis of intuition than on scientific results.[52] Indeed, in refining her evaluative view of emotions as cognitive appraisals, Nussbaum notes that emotions have urgency and heat not for any primitive mechanistic reason but 'because they concern our most important goals and projects, the most urgent transactions we have with our world'.[53] As such, the cognitive appraisal triggers the experience, and the 'heat' of emotion is dependent on an individual's assessment of the circumstances.

The validity of cognitive appraisal theories therefore seems to rest somewhat on their willingness to include both conscious and non-conscious appraisals within their scope. Nussbaum, in her inclusion of conscious and non-conscious appraisals, proposes a wide definition of cognition as being nothing more than 'concerned with receiving and processing information' without the need for 'elaborate calculation, of computation, or even of reflexive self-awareness'.[54] To clarify, the author positions non-conscious appraisals in the ordinary sense of the word to mean the way 'in which many of our most common beliefs are nonconscious, although they guide our actions in many ways: beliefs about cause and effect, beliefs about numbering, beliefs about where things are, beliefs about what is healthy and harmful, and so forth'.[55] As such, the adoption of such a wide interpretation of cognition,

---

[50] LeDoux, *The Emotional Brain: The Mysterious Underpinnings of Emotional Life* (Simon & Schuster 1996), p. 42.

[51] Damasio, *Descartes' Error: Emotion, Reason and the Human Brain* (Quill 2004).

[52] See for example: LeDoux and Brown, 'A Higher-Order Theory of Emotional Consciousness'.

[53] Nussbaum, *Hiding from Humanity: Disgust, Shame, and the Law* (Princeton University Press 2004), p. 77.

[54] Nussbaum, *Upheavals of Thought*, p. 23.

[55] Nussbaum, *Upheavals of Thought*, 70–1. Nussbaum goes on to clarify that '[i]n the case of

and the recognition that emotions are more than merely thoughts, result in the assumption that emotions result from an individual's appraisal of a given situation bearing in mind their goals, beliefs, values, morals and capabilities at both conscious and non-conscious levels.

However, although as discussed above, emotions appear to be cognitive appraisals this does not mean that they are 'rational'. The question thus becomes what is meant here by the term rational? With this in mind, the analysis now turns to an examination of what is meant by rationality and how this aligns with the notion of rationality in citizen-consumer protections.

2.2.2 Dysfunctional Rationality, the Role of Emotion and Other Jedi Mind Tricks

As noted by Spain, '[t]wo distinct meanings can be attributed to the concept of rationality and both must be borne in mind in any discussion of the rationality of emotions. The term rational may refer to the process through which an emotion is experienced, following a trail of reason, or it may refer to the normative acceptability of the emotion.'[56] The former of these is aligned with the above discussion of thought *vis-à-vis* the cognitive nature of emotion. The conception of emotion as primitive rather than as a mental state has resulted in its being classified as irrational, reflecting the historical weight of the mechanistic view of emotion.

However, and as discussed above, under the cognitive appraisal theories emotions are capable of rationality in the sense that there is a clear link to reasoning. This is reflected by the fact that emotions change with our opinions and thus, significantly, are at least rational in this more literal sense.[57] Building on this de Sousa has suggested that emotion makes an important contribution to the decision-making process and that '[w]hat remains of the old opposition between reason and emotion is only this: emotions are not reducible to beliefs or wants'.[58]

It has therefore been suggested that emotions are in fact indispensable to rationality in that they point us in the right direction and allow us to best exercise 'the instruments of logic'.[59] However, that is not to say that all

---

emotion-beliefs, there may at times be special reasons for not confronting them consciously, for they may be very painful to confront. This means that it may take much longer to get someone to recognize grief or fear or anger in herself than to admit to spatial or numerical beliefs. There is a resistance to the acknowledgment of one's own vulnerability that must be overcome.'

[56] Spain, *The Role of Emotions in Criminal Law Defences*, p. 98.
[57] Solomon, *Not Passion's Slave*, p. 5.
[58] De Sousa, *The Rationality of Emotion*, p. xv.
[59] De Sousa, *The Rationality of Emotion*, p. xii.

emotions are rational. Indeed, as noted by Nussbaum, in this sense one must acknowledge emotions, like beliefs, 'can be true or false, and (an independent point) justified or unjustified, reasonable or unreasonable. The fact of having an emotion depends on what the person's beliefs are, not whether they are true or false'.[60] As observed by Damasio however, acknowledging that emotions are 'an integral component of the machinery of reason … is not to deny that emotions and feelings can cause havoc in the processes of reasoning under certain circumstances'.[61] Indeed, with this in mind one can refer to Nussbaum's positioning of irrationality, which she defines in terms of thought and thus from the perspective of normative irrationalities based on false information or values.[62] Rationality here has thus been distinguished from a broader understanding of rationality in terms of the objective merits of the choice made by an individual. Indeed, it has been suggested that '[e]ven though emotions have their own rationality, this rationality is of a different order than that of deliberate reflective judgments'.[63] Irrational emotions will result from an incorrect assessment of a situation or when the person's underlying value system is somehow flawed.[64] Undoubtedly, an overarching understanding of decision making requires an understanding of the role of emotion. Indeed, Herbert Simon, who introduced the notion of bounded rationality and thus the need to include cognitive and situational constraints thereby revolutionising decision theory, recognised that 'in order to have

---

[60] Nussbaum, *Upheavals of Thought*, p. 46.

[61] Damasio, *Descartes' Error*, p. xii.

[62] '[I]n terms of thought that is bad thought in some normative sense. Thus, the person who says that two plus two is five, even after repeated teaching, is irrational, because he thinks badly. So, too, in a different way, we typically hold that racism is irrational, based on beliefs that are false or ungrounded … Of course many particular instances of anger or fear may indeed be irrational in the normative sense. They may be based on false information … [or] false values, as would be the case if someone reacted with overwhelming anger to a minor insult. (Aristotle's example of this is anger at people who forget one's name.)' Nussbaum, *Hiding from Humanity*, pp. 11–12.

[63] Pillsbury, 'Emotional Justice: Moralizing the Passions of Criminal Punishment' (1988) 74 *Cornell Law Review* 655, p. 679.

[64] In contrast, irrationality in behavioural economics refers more to flawed decision making, mental heuristics and bounded rationality. Irrationality here should be construed as referring to a decision that an individual would not have made if they were informed and had alternative choices (i.e. if informed afterwards they would wish to change their choice). Sunstein, 'Nudging: A Very Short Guide' (2014) 37 *Journal of Consumer Policy* 583; Sunstein, 'Fifty Shades of Manipulation' (2015) *Journal of Behavioral Manipulation* <https://dash.harvard.edu/handle/1/16149947> (accessed 13 April 2019); Jolls, Sunstein and Thaler, 'A Behavioral Approach to Law and Economics' (1998) 50 *Stanford Law Review* 1471.

anything like a complete theory of human rationality, we have to understand what role emotion plays in it'.[65]

Emotion can thus be both rational and irrational, and this is distinct from the discussion of bounded rationality in behavioural economics. But what does this mean in terms of consumer protection? How does the commercialisation of emotion challenge the fundamental paradigms within the law, and how does this align or differ from the more widespread attention that is given to behavioural economics? Despite the fact that we have determined that emotion can be rational or irrational in the normative sense, it must also be acknowledged that emotion does indeed affect decision making. Hence, the question becomes one of whether the commercial use of emotion can result in irrational decision making, or indeed decision making that can result in an alternative outcome if the individual targeted by the campaign had been experiencing a different emotion. This is a significant question, as legal analysis more readily categorises challenges to the existing rationality-based paradigm within the law on the basis of behavioural economics or neuroscientific insights.[66]

To illustrate, Richard Posner, for example, has argued that improvements in the level of education and the capacity of consumers to learn from repeated disappointments allow for the dilution of the significance of sales techniques such as puffing (i.e. the use of exaggerated claims in order to induce an emotional reaction).[67] In criticising this conclusion, Hoffman links the effectiveness of puffing to 'overconfidence bias' and optimism theory, and notes that both the 'puffer' and the consumer suffer from congenial over-optimism.[68] In essence, Hoffman refers to the fact that the puffer may genuinely believe the puff and that the consumer's retrospective assessment of the product may be influenced in an optimistic light. As Hoffman concludes, this means that a failure to protect consumers against puffery may fail to prevent consumption-distorting behaviour.[69] The author therefore links the effectiveness of a puff to underlying cognitive biases, but what about the role of emotion? Blumenthal has suggested that the focus on cognition and rationality in legal research perhaps relates to the fact that the discussion often relies on the work of authors such as Nussbaum and the conceptual starting point that emotions are typically based on a belief or judgement. In

---

[65] Simon, *Reason in Human Affairs* (Stanford University Press 1990), p. 29.

[66] Blumenthal, 'Emotional Paternalism'.

[67] Posner, *Regulation of Advertising by the FTC* (American Enterprise Institute for Public Policy Research 1973).

[68] Hoffman, 'The Best Puffery Article Ever' (2005) 91 *Iowa Law Review* 1395, pp. 1432–4.

[69] Ibid., p. 136.

criticising Nussbaum's approach Blumenthal suggests that such an account fails to consider adequately how emotions affect decision making due to the focus on emotions as cognitions.

However, Blumenthal's critique arguably fails to nuance the fact that Nussbaum's evaluative view does not disregard the potential for a loss of control while under the influence of emotion. Instead, and as described above, Nussbaum theorises that emotion stems from an individual's conscious or non-conscious assessment of how a situation affects them. In essence, this relates to the differentiation between the rationality or cognitive nature of emotions and rationality *vis-à-vis* the objective assessment of the logical nature of a person's actions and the resulting outcome. Eric Posner refers to this distinction and claims that while in an emotional state a person still acts rationally, or rather is internally consistent given the circumstances, thus resulting in temporary preferences, abilities and beliefs.[70] Posner's suggestion of viewing decision making as internally consistent with the emotion being experienced does act as a useful means of illustrating how emotional rationality and irrationality remain a distinct yet connected discussion regarding deliberate reflective judgements and indeed, mental heuristics.

Nevertheless, although Posner's approach may reflect the alignment of emotion and cognition and thus rationality (understood in the sense of positioning emotion within the evaluative view), such a perspective may still be inconsistent with the very function of rationality *vis-à-vis* the protection of autonomous citizen-consumer decision making in a legal sense. Autonomy here is to be understood in line with the writings of Joseph Raz, who proposes that:

> [T]he ruling idea behind the ideal of personal autonomy is that people should make their own lives. The autonomous person is a (part) author of his own life. The ideal of personal autonomy is the vision of people control-ling, to some degree, their own destiny, fashioning it through successive decisions throughout their lives.[71]

Accordingly, the capacity for emotion to influence decision making, combined with the ability to detect emotion, presents clear fundamental issues in terms of the protection of personal autonomy (in an online setting).

---

[70] Posner, 'Law and the Emotions' (2001) 89 *Georgetown Law Journal* 1977, p. 1982.

[71] Raz, *The Morality of Freedom* (Clarendon Press 1986), p. 369. In making this proposal the chapter follows Bernal's analysis in his reliance on the work of Joseph Raz and Raz's positioning of autonomy as the key notion at the root of privacy and data protection. Bernal, *Internet Privacy Rights: Rights to Protect Autonomy* (First, Cambridge University Press 2014).

2.3 Law, Emotions and Autonomous Decision-making Capacity

The effect of emotion on decision making has received an increasing amount of attention over the last twenty years in decision-making theory.[72] In their critical analysis of the field, Lerner et al. summarise by stating that '[p]ut succinctly, emotion and decision making go hand in hand', with emotions acting as the 'dominant driver of most meaningful decisions in life'.[73] Although a more detailed analysis of the relevant research is outside the substantive scope of this chapter, it is important to highlight some key takeaways in order to more accurately understand the effects of emotions on decision making. As summarised and categorised by Lerner et al., emotions research has found that the effects of emotion on decision making 'can take the form of integral or incidental influences; incidental emotions often produce influences that are unwanted and nonconscious'.[74] Integral emotions here should be understood as emotions arising from the choice at hand, whereas incidental emotions refer to emotions that carry over from one situation to the next despite the fact that they should remain separate normatively speaking.[75] In relation to the latter of these two, it has been suggested that mood (as distinct from emotion) or even a macro-level phenomenon (such as ambient weather[76] or sporting results[77]) can result in an incidental emotional bias for unconnected decisions.

As a consequence, in contrast with the more philosophical literature discussed above regarding the emergence of cognitive appraisal theory, decision-making research often takes a wider view, focused instead on the umbrella term of 'affect', which includes moods, emotions and emotion-related traits[78] (as seemingly mirrored in the affective computing literature). In addition, it has also been suggested that emotions shape decisions in two important ways. First, different emotions are associated with different patterns of cognitive appraisals, rendering the effect of emotions (for instance of anger or surprise) predictable in terms of the decision-making outcome.[79] Second, emotions

---

[72] Lerner et al., 'Emotion and Decision Making' (2015) 66 *Annual Review of Psychology* 799, pp. 800–1.

[73] Lerner et al., 'Emotion and Decision Making', p. 801.

[74] Lerner et al., 'Emotion and Decision Making', p. 816.

[75] Lerner et al., 'Emotion and Decision Making', pp. 802–4.

[76] Schwarz and Clore, 'Mood, Misattribution, and Judgments of Well-Being: Informative and Directive Functions of Affective States' (1983) 45 *Journal of Personality and Social Psychology* 513.

[77] Edmans, Garcia and Norli, 'Sports Sentiment and Stock Returns' (2007) 62 *Journal of Finance* 1967.

[78] Lerner et al., 'Emotion and Decision Making'.

[79] Ibid., pp. 804–6.

influence how individuals process information and affect whether they do so superficially or in detail.[80] This 'affect infusion' bias refers to the fact that in general those in positive moods are more easily persuaded than those in negative moods as those in positive moods tend to rely on heuristics.[81] For instance, in the context of advertising and marketing, commercial entities induce emotional responses so as to create awareness and positive brand association, and as a consequence evoke an emotional desire for a product or service. Campaigns aim to induce a 'positive' or 'negative' appeal to elicit an emotional response. Positive appeals promise positive emotions through the use or purchase of the advertised product or service.[82] In contrast, negative appeals associate negative consequences for those who ignore the commercial message.[83]

However, it should be specified that emotion valence (i.e. the positive (happiness) or negative (sadness) value of an emotion or more broadly affect) is somewhat of an inaccurate indicator given that emotions of the same valence (for example, sadness and anger) can result *inter alia* in different appraisals, depths of processing and thus outcomes in terms of the resulting decisions.[84] That being said, the key takeaway of the brief overview provided in this section is that emotions 'powerfully, predictably, and pervasively influence decision making.'[85] This is significant as the use of emotional appeal is not restricted to the content of commercial communications, and research has also shown the potential for advertising formats, branding, product design and indeed virtually all aspects of consumer-facing interactions to have a positive emotional impact.[86] As described in section 2.1, the emergence of a mediated society, whereby consumers increasingly interact with the market through technology, plays a significant role in the increased uptake and importance of the harnessing of emotion for commercial purposes. More concretely, this link relates to the fact that first, technology captures and retains vast amounts of information about consumers; second, commercial

---

[80] Hullett, 'The Impact of Mood on Persuasion: A Meta-Analysis' (2005) 32 *Communication Research* 423.

[81] See for example Forgas, 'Mood and Judgment: The Affect Infusion Model (AIM)' (1995) 117 *Psychological Bulletin* 39.

[82] Poels and Dewitte, 'How to Capture the Heart?' ; Percy and Rossiter, 'A Model of Brand Awareness and Brand Attitude Advertising Strategies' (1992) 9 *Psychology & Marketing* 263.

[83] Poels and Dewitte, 'How to Capture the Heart?'; Percy and Rossiter, 'A Model of Brand Awareness'.

[84] Lerner et al., 'Emotion and Decision Making', pp. 804–6.

[85] Lerner et al., 'Emotion and Decision Making', p. 802.

[86] Blumenthal observes that the use of emotional biases could also extend to the development of manipulative and arguably unconscionable contract terms; see Blumenthal, 'Emotional Paternalism', pp. 47–8.

entities design all aspects of the consumers' interaction with their services and finally, increasingly these commercial entities can choose when to interact with consumers, rather than waiting for them to enter the market.[87]

At its core the mediated society and its effects grow stronger with technological development and the increasing 'datafication' of consumer activity.[88] The precise consequences of the information asymmetries combined with the unilateral power to design all aspects of commercial interactions are as yet unknown.[89] But is data protection not the ready-made answer? If one protects citizen-consumer personal data, are the effects of empathic media and its application for the personalisation of commercial content in an online setting within the control of individuals? To clarify, as emotion detection would seem to necessitate the processing of personal data, is the data protection framework not capable of protecting citizen-consumers? With these questions in mind the following section aims to analyse the General Data Protection Regulation (GDPR)[90] and its capacity to cater for the challenges associated with emotion detection in an online setting.

3. Emotion Detection and Data Protection – A Match Made in a Jedi Temple?

The Jedi are trained to control their emotions to let go of their fears. Although, as discussed in the previous section, in the real world such control remains outside our human capacity, the data protection framework seemingly offers us the means to control our personal data, thus rendering the detection mechanisms subject to our individual choices and preferences. However, and as will be analysed below, such a conclusion fails to take into account the clear difficulties associated with the effective operation of the data protec-

---

[87] Calo, 'Digital Market Manipulation', pp. 1002–3. 'As a consequence, firms can generate a fastidious record of their transaction with the consumer and, importantly, personalize every aspect of the interaction. This permits firms to surface the specific ways each individual consumer deviates from rational decision making, however idiosyncratic, and leverage that bias to the firm's advantage. Whereas sellers have always gotten a "feel" for consumers, and although much online advertising today is already automatic, this new combination of interpersonal manipulation with large-scale data presents a novel challenge to consumers and regulators alike.'

[88] See Mayer-Schonberger and Cukier, *Big Data: A Revolution That Will Transform How We Live, Work and Think* (Houghton Mifflin Harcourt 2013).

[89] Calo, 'Digital Market Manipulation', pp. 1002–3.

[90] Regulation (EU) 2016/679 of the European Parliament and of the Council of 27 April 2016 on the protection of natural persons with regard to the processing of personal data and on the free movement of such data, and repealing Directive 95/46/EC (General Data Protection Regulation).

tion framework. Article 8(1) of the Charter of Fundamental Rights of the European Union (the Charter) states that '[e]veryone has the right to the protection of personal data concerning him or her'. The right to data protection however, is not an absolute right, and Articles 8(2) and 8(3) indicate the specific conditions through which the processing of personal data may be permissible. Article 8(2) sets out the rules for the legitimate processing of personal data, notably that the processing shall be fair and for pre-specified purposes, based on the consent of the person concerned (i.e. the data subject) or another legitimate basis laid down by law, and that data subjects have the right of access to the data collected concerning them and the right to have this data rectified. Finally, Article 8(3) sets out the need for an independent authority to monitor and control compliance with the data protection rules.

Data protection's underlying rationales of autonomy and informational self-determination aim to counteract the (informational) power asymmetries as triggered by technological advancement and market forces.[91] The fundamental right to data protection, while recognising the inevitability and benefits of such developments, also targets the prevention of disproportionate impacts on the individual and, by extension, society.[92] The triangular structure of Article 8 of the Charter (i.e. requirements for the controllers, data subject rights and the monitoring activities of data protection authorities) is indicative of this function[93] and appears to solidify the claim that control constitutes a fundamental underlying value of the right. In its operation in secondary law (i.e. the GDPR), control should be interpreted broadly[94] as including not only an individual's 'control' over their personal data but also as a robust architecture of control[95] that aims actively to ensure individual autonomy. Thus, although one might question how the potential for 'some other legitimate basis laid

[91] Rouvroy and Poullet, 'The Right to Informational Self-Determination and the Value of Self-Development: Reassessing the Importance of Privacy for Democracy' in Gutwirth S et al. (eds), *Reinventing Data Protection?* (Springer Netherlands 2009), pp. 68–9; Gutwirth, *Privacy and the Information Age* (translated by Raf Casert, Rowman & Littlefield 2002), p. 86.

[92] See Ferretti, 'Data Protection and the Legitimate Interest of Data Controllers: Much Ado about Nothing or the Winter of Rights?' (2014) 51 *Common Market Law Review* 843, p. 849.

[93] See Fuster, 'Beyond the GDPR, above the GDPR' (*Internet Policy Review*, 30 November 2015) <http://policyreview.info/articles/news/beyond-gdpr-above-gdpr/385> (accessed 13 April 2019).

[94] See notably: Kosta, 'Unravelling Consent in European Data Protection Legislation a Prospective Study on Consent in Electronic Communications' (Doctoral thesis, University of Leuven 2011), p. 130 *et seq*; Bernal, *Internet Privacy Rights*; Lazaro and Le Métayer, 'Control over Personal Data: True Remedy or Fairytale?' (2015) 12 SCRIPTed <http://script-ed.org/?p=1927> (accessed 13 April 2019).

[95] See Lynskey, *The Foundations of EU Data Protection Law* (Oxford University Press 2016).

down by law' in Article 8(2) of the Charter to legitimise data processing respects the notion of control, it should be highlighted that the right to data protection is a limitable right and that this notion is to be construed broadly.[96] Furthermore, Article 8(2) of the Charter must be read in conjunction with Article 52(1) of the Charter. This provision states that:

> Any limitation on the exercise of the rights and freedoms recognised by this Charter must be provided for by law and respect the essence of those rights and freedoms. Subject to the principle of proportionality, limitations may be made only if they are necessary and genuinely meet objectives of general interest recognised by the Union or the need to protect the rights and freedoms of others.

The GDPR aims to satisfy the conditions in Article 8 and Article 52(1) of the Charter through a system of checks and balances as directed by the principle of fairness.[97] In this vein, any secondary legislation restricting the right to data protection must satisfy the necessity and proportionality tests contained in Article 52(1) in conjunction with the further specifications in Article 8 of the Charter in order to be valid.[98] However, it is important to note that the GDPR targets the protection of the right to data protection in particular but also rights and freedoms more generally (Article 1(2) GDPR), thus reflecting the enabling functionality of the GDPR.[99]

3.1 Data Protection Principles and the Rules of the Jedi Code – Giving Balance to the Force

Although technological developments have accelerated the need for change, the core of the GDPR has remained consistent with Directive 95/46/

---

[96] For a discussion see Clifford and Ausloos, 'Data Protection and the Role of Fairness' (2018) 37 *Yearbook of European Law* 130.

[97] Evidence to support such a conclusion can be taken from the Digital Rights Ireland case, which struck out the Data Retention Directive and referred specifically to the Charter and significantly Article 52(1). *Digital Rights Ireland Ltd* [2014] Court of Justice of the EU Joined Cases C-293/12 and C-594/12, Curia. Indeed, as noted by the Court: 'Having regard to all the foregoing considerations, it must be held that, by adopting Directive 2006/24, the EU legislature has exceeded the limits imposed by compliance with the principle of proportionality in the light of Articles 7, 8 and 52(1) of the Charter.' For a discussion see Clifford and Ausloos (n 95).

[98] Clifford and Ausloos, 'Data Protection and the Role of Fairness'.

[99] Ibid., 20–1 and the discussion between Oostveen and Irion, 'The Golden Age of Personal Data: How to Regulate an Enabling Fundamental Right?' in M Bakhoum et al. eds, *Personal Data in Competition, Consumer Protection and IP Law – Towards a Holistic Approach?* (Springer 2017) <https://papers.ssrn.com/abstract=2885701> (accessed 13 April 2019).

EC.[100] Personal data are defined in Article 4(1) GDPR as 'any information relating to an identified or identifiable natural person ("data subject")'. A controller is defined in Article 4(7) GDPR as the natural or legal person 'which, alone or jointly with others, determines the purposes and means of the processing of personal data'. Article 4(8) GDPR defines a processor as any natural or legal person 'which processes personal data on behalf of the controller'. Essentially, the GDPR aims to counteract power asymmetries between controllers (and processors) and data subjects by offering data subjects tools to bolster their position and rebalance the existing asymmetry.[101] Data subjects are afforded rights and controllers (and processors) are required to satisfy specific requirements to process personal data. As such, the GDPR specifies a precise separation in responsibility and roles, consisting of controllers processing personal data with or without contracting the services of a processor (who holds merely a passive function), with each entity being clearly distinguishable.[102]

The specific requirements that controllers and processors are subject to inherently relate to the principle of accountability (that is, Article 5(2) GDPR), and indeed more generally the other principles relating to the processing of personal data contained in Article 5 GDPR. These are represented overleaf in Table 4.1. These principles play an overarching role in the application of the framework, and essentially guide the interpretation of the rights and obligations contained therein. However, it should be noted that it has been repeatedly argued that these principles are under strain due to the proliferation of technology and 'datafication'.[103] More specifically, data security

---

[100] De Hert and Papakonstantinou, 'The Proposed Data Protection Regulation Replacing Directive 95/46/EC: A Sound System for the Protection of Individuals' (2012) 28 *Computer Law & Security Review* 130.

[101] Lynskey, 'Deconstructing Data Protection: The "Added-Value" of a Right to Data Protection in the EU Legal Order' (2014) 63 International and Comparative Law Quarterly 569, p. 569.

[102] Clifford, 'EU Data Protection Law and Targeted Advertising: Consent and the Cookie Monster – Tracking the Crumbs of Online User Behaviour' (2014) 5 *Journal of Intellectual Property, Information Technology and Electronic Commerce Law* <www.jipitec.eu/issues/jipitec-5-3-2014/4095> (accessed 13 April 2019).

[103] See generally Zarsky, 'Incompatible: The GDPR in the Age of Big Data' (2017) 47 *Seton Hall Law Review* 2; Koops, 'On Decision Transparency, or How to Enhance Data Protection after the Computational Turn' in Hildebrandt M and de Vries K (eds), *Privacy, Due Process and the Computational Turn: The Philosophy of Law meets the Philosophy of Technology* (Routledge 2013), pp. 196–220; Koops, 'The Trouble with European Data Protection Law' (2014) 4 *International Data Privacy Law* 250; De Hert and Papakonstantinou, 'The Proposed Data Protection Regulation Replacing Directive 95/46/EC'.

Table 4.1 The Data Protection Principles

Article		Principle(s)	Relevant extract from provision
Article 5(1)	(a)	Lawfulness, fairness and transparency	Personal data shall be: processed lawfully, fairly and in a transparent manner in relation to the data subject
	(b)	Purpose limitation	Personal data shall be: collected for specified, explicit and legitimate purposes and not further processed in a manner that is incompatible with those purposes …
	(c)	Data minimisation	Personal data shall be: adequate, relevant and limited to what is necessary in relation to the purposes for which they are processed
	(d)	Accuracy	Personal data shall be: accurate and, where necessary, kept up to date; every reasonable step must be taken to ensure that personal data that are inaccurate, having regard to the purposes for which they are processed, are erased or rectified without delay
	(e)	Storage limitation	Personal data shall be: kept in a form which permits identification of data subjects for no longer than is necessary for the purposes for which the personal data are processed …
	(f)	Integrity and confidentiality	Personal data shall be: processed in a manner that ensures appropriate security of the personal data, including protection against unauthorised or unlawful processing and against accidental loss, destruction or damage, using appropriate technical or organisational measures
Article 5(2)		Accountability	The controller shall be responsible for, and be able to demonstrate compliance with, paragraph 1

is becoming gradually more difficult given the increasing number of attacks and high-profile data breaches, despite legislative developments.[104] Moreover, data gathering in the big data environment appears almost inherently in contradiction with the data minimisation and purpose limitation principles, given that data are often gathered in an unrestricted manner for unspecified purposes and then mined for useful commercial applications.[105] These failings

[104] In this context one can refer to the GDPR and also Directive (EU) 2016/1148 of the European Parliament and of the Council of 6 July 2016 concerning measures for a high common level of security of network and information systems across the Union (OJ L 194).

[105] Verdoodt, Clifford and Lievens, 'Toying with Children's Emotions, the New Game in Town?'

highlight the potential for function creep[106] and therefore, the repurposing of personal data.

The deployment of emotion detection technologies may raise clear concerns in this regard. Indeed, the expansion of technological capabilities provides new methods of assessing emotions in real time with everyday consumer technology. Empathic media are being implemented as a feature *inter alia* in the future smart home (adjusting of lighting or music depending on mood), health or *pseudo*-health care (the tracking of mood for the purposes of improving mental well-being) and automobile safety (counteracting the potential effects of road rage). For our current purposes, it is important to highlight how these principles are under strain and how this is heightened given the key role played by the principle of accountability (Article 5(2) GDPR). More specifically, one could argue that the accountability principle has a somewhat elevated status given its separation from the other principles in Article 5(1) GDPR and its substantive impact on the effective operation of the other principles and the reliance on so-called controller 'responsibilisation'.[107] This is manifested *inter alia* in the interpretation of the adoption of a risk-based approach[108] and the application of the requirements for data protection by design and by default (Article 25 GDPR) and data protection impact assessments (Article 35 GDPR). In short, the risk-based approach places risk at the centre and hence 'seems to combine the use of risk management tools with a calibration of the data controllers' obligations according to the level of risk at stake'.[109]

Given the role of controllers in the assessment of risk and the question marks surrounding the capacity of the risk-based approach to cater for intangible harms, reliance on the effective operation of the accountability principle is questionable.[110] The absence of a comprehensive taxonomy of risks is justified

---

[106] Koops, 'On Decision Transparency', p. 198.

[107] Article 29 Working Party, 'Opinion 3/2010 on the Principle of Accountability' (European Commission 2010) <http://ec.europa.eu/justice/data-protection/article-29/documenta tion/opinion-recommendation/files/2010/wp173_en.pdf> (accessed 13 April 2019).

[108] Although the inclusion of risk was not new in the data protection framework, Gellert observes that data protection's risk-regulation origins are distinct from the move towards a risk-based approach (or in other words the regulation through risk) enshrined in the GDPR. See Gellert, 'Data Protection: A Risk Regulation? Between the Risk Management of Everything and the Precautionary Alternative' (2015) 5 *International Data Privacy Law* 3, p. 13. See also: Article 29 Working Party, 'Statement on the Role of a Risk-Based Approach in Data Protection Legal Frameworks' (2014) WP 218.

[109] Gellert, 'Data Protection: A Risk Regulation?', p. 13.

[110] Importantly, a risk-based approach needs to be distinguished from risk as a threshold for application. See Peter Hustinx, 'EU Data Protection Law: Review of Directive 95/46 EC

by the fact that 'risk' is understood broadly to include societal effects and potential as well as actual harms.[111] This illustrates the key role of enforcement and the effective monitoring of controllers. To clarify the above, it is significant to highlight Article 5(2) GDPR, which provides that controllers are obliged to be able to demonstrate compliance with the principles relating to processing of personal data laid down in Article 5(1) GDPR. Hence, in order to operationalise control, the framework mobilises protections or 'environmental variables' incorporating technological and organisational safeguards in order to ensure a secure personal data-processing environment.[112]

Indeed, the operational mobilisation of protections and the risk-based approach enshrined in the GDPR are indicative of a more collective view of control, in that they aim to ensure the protection of data subjects collectively in order to provide a secure personal data-processing environment. Such an approach therefore aims to position data subjects as the key actors empowered to determine the fate of their personal data.[113] However, this rests on the willingness or at least capacity of controllers to cater effectively for risks (and therefore on effective enforcement in the absence of the necessary safeguards) but also, and as will be discussed in the following section, the assumption that individuals are capable of 'control' and thus playing the role of the active market participant.

3.2 The Fairness Checks and Balances and Delineating Consent and Control

As described in the introduction to this section, Article 8(2) of the Charter stipulates that personal data processing may be based on the consent of the data subject or another legitimate basis laid down by law. Article 6(1) GDPR provides six such conditions for lawful processing. Three of the conditions are

---

and the Proposed General Data Protection Regulation' <https://secure.edps.europa.eu/ EDPSWEB/webdav/site/mySite/shared/Documents/EDPS/Publications/Speeches/2014/ 14-09-15_Article_EUI_EN.pdf> (accessed 13 April 2019), pp. 18, 20, 38. See also the WP29's observation: 'It is important to note that – even with the adoption of a risk-based approach – there is no question of the rights of individuals being weakened in respect of their personal data. Those rights must be just as strong even if the processing in question is relatively 'low risk'. Rather, the scalability of legal obligations based on risk addresses compliance mechanisms. This means that a data controller whose processing is relatively low risk may not have to do as much to comply with its legal obligations as a data controller whose processing is high-risk.' Article 29 Working Party, 'Statement on the Role of a Risk-Based Approach in Data Protection Legal Frameworks' (2014) WP 218 2.

[111] Article 29 Working Party, 'Statement on the Role of a Risk-Based Approach in Data Protection Legal Frameworks', p. 4.

[112] Lazaro and Le Métayer, 'Control over Personal Data: True Remedy or Fairytale?'

[113] Ibid.

Table 4.2 Conditions for Lawful Processing

Article	Condition	Relevant extract from provision
Article 6(1)(a)	Consent	The data subject has given consent to the processing of his or her personal data for one or more specific purposes;
Article 6(1)(b)	Contract	Processing is necessary for the performance of a contract to which the data subject is party or in order to take steps at the request of the data subject prior to entering into a contract;
Article 6(1)(f)	Legitimate interests	Processing is necessary for the purposes of the legitimate interests pursued by the controller or by a third party, except where such interests are overridden by the interests or fundamental rights and freedoms of the data subject which require protection of personal data, in particular where the data subject is a child.

particularly relevant in the context of commercial personal data processing, namely, consent (Article 6(1)(a) GDPR), contract (Article 6(1)(b) GDPR) and legitimate interests (Article 6(1)(f) GDPR) as represented opposite in Table 4.2.

It should be noted from the outset that the Article 29 Working Party has repeatedly stated that personal data processing for the purposes of online behavioural advertising requires the consent of the data subject.[114] The need for consent is indicative of two important points. First, profiling for commercial purposes online will incorporate the processing of information (such as cookies) coming within the scope of *lex specialis* requirement for consent in Article 5(3) ePrivacy Directive 2002/58/EC[115] and second (perhaps a more debatable point) according to Article 22 GDPR, profiling or automated individual decision making for advertising or marketing purposes requires the data subject's explicit consent. Both of these will now be briefly discussed in the context of emotion detection technologies.

---

[114] See for instance: Article 29 Working Party, 'Opinion 02/2010 on Online Behavioural Advertising' (Article 29 Working Party 2010) WP 171 <https://ec.europa.eu/justice/article-29/documentation/opinion-recommendation/files/2010/wp171_en.pdf> (accessed 13 April 2019); Article 29 Working Party, 'Opinion 16/2011 on EASA/IAB Best Practice Recommendation on Online Behavioural Advertising' (Article 29 Working Party 2011) WP 188 <http://ec.europa.eu/justice/data-protection/article-29/documentation/opinion-recommendation/files/2011/wp188_en.pdf> (accessed 13 April 2019).

[115] For a discussion of the relationship between the ePrivacy Directive and the GDPR see 'European Data Protection Board, Opinion 5/2019 on the Interplay between the EPrivacy Directive and the GDPR, in Particular Regarding the Competence, Tasks and Powers of Data Protection Authorities Adopted on 12 March 2019'.

3.2.1 Personal Data – Information, Emotions and Consent

The ePrivacy Directive as a *lex specialis* legislative instrument that specifies the *lex generalis* provisions in the GDPR in the context the processing of personal data and the protection of privacy in the electronic communications sector.[116] However, the ePrivacy Directive still relies on the *lex generalis* provisions in the GDPR where indicated. For instance, one is required to refer to consent as defined in the GDPR. As amended by Directive 2009/136/EC,[117] Article 5(3) ePrivacy Directive provides that consent is required for the 'storing of information, or the gaining of access to information already stored, in the terminal equipment' of the user.[118] In the proposed reforms of the ePrivacy Directive, the proposed ePrivacy Regulation (largely speaking and depending on the version) retains the general rule in Article 5(3) ePrivacy Directive.[119] Here it is important to clarify that Article 5(3) ePrivacy Directive refers to 'information' as opposed to the narrower category of personal data, as protected in the GDPR. 'Personal data' is defined in Article 4(1) GDPR as 'any information relating to an identified or identifiable natural person

[116] Directive 2002/58/EC of the European Parliament and of the Council of 12 July 2002 concerning the processing of personal data and the protection of privacy in the electronic communications sector (Directive on privacy and electronic communications), OJ L 201, 31.7.2002, 37–47.

[117] Directive 2009/136/EC of the European Parliament and of the Council of 25 November 2009 amending Directive 2002/22/EC on universal service and users' rights relating to electronic communications networks and services, Directive 2002/58/EC concerning the processing of personal data and the protection of privacy in the electronic communications sector and Regulation (EC) No 2006/2004 on cooperation between national authorities responsible for the enforcement of consumer protection laws (text with EEA relevance), J L 337, 18.12.2009, 11–36.

[118] As described by the Article 29 Working Party, Article 5(3) ePrivacy Directive allows for processing to be exempt from the requirement of consent, if one of the following criteria is satisfied (1) technical storage or access 'for the sole purpose of carrying out the transmission of a communication over an electronic communications network' or (2) technical storage or access that is 'strictly necessary in order for the provider of an information society service explicitly requested by the subscriber or user to provide the service'. See 'Opinion 04/2012 on Cookie Consent Exemption' (Article 29 Working Party 2012) WP 194 <https://ec.europa.eu/justice/article-29/documentation/opinion-recommendation/files/2012/wp194_en.pdf> (accessed 13 April 2019).

[119] Article 8(1)(d) of the proposed Regulation adds an additional ground for processing of cookies that was not available in the ePrivacy Directive. More specifically, the activities referenced above in Article 8(1) shall be permitted 'if it is necessary for web audience measuring, provided that such measurement is carried out by the provider of the information society service requested by the end-user.' Accordingly, instead of providing a general consent rule with the two exemptions for 'functional cookies', the proposed Regulation includes this additional grounds for 'web audience measurement'.

("data subject")'. However, and as indicated by the Article 29 Working Party, 'cookies'[120] or 'device fingerprinting'[121] have generally been found to fall within both definitions.[122]

In essence, the definition of personal data includes any data capable of 'singling out' a data subject,[123] and as this is the very purpose of behavioural tracking for online advertising or marketing purposes, it is clear that such information will also be considered personal data.[124] This broad interpretation is significant given that a failure to include such information as personal data would have undermined the Regulation's protections and diluted its significance given that irrespective of the ability to identify the name of an individual, the ability to single out presents the same concerns and risks that the data protection provisions aim to safeguard citizens against.[125] Consequently, the detection of emotions online for advertising or marketing purposes will clearly fall within the scope of these provisions, but what about the protections for sensitive personal data? The definition of sensitive personal data is provided in Article 9(1) GDPR. This provision states:

> [The] processing of personal data revealing racial or ethnic origin, political opinions, religious or philosophical beliefs, or trade union membership, and

---

[120] Article 29 Working Party, 'Working Document 02/2013 Providing Guidance on Obtaining Consent for Cookies' (2013) Working Document <https://www.pdpjournals.com/docs/88135.pdf> (accessed 13 April 2019); Article 29 Working Party, 'Opinion on Online Behavioural Advertising'.

[121] 'Article 29 Working Party, Opinion 9/2014 on the Application of Directive 2002/58/EC to Device Fingerprinting WP 224' (2014).

[122] In the proposed ePrivacy Regulation it is significant to note that Article 8(1) of the proposed Regulation refers not 'to the storing of information, or the gaining of access to information already stored, in the terminal equipment' but rather prohibits '[t]he use of processing and storage capabilities of terminal equipment and the collection of information from end-users' terminal equipment, including about its software and hardware, other than by the end-user concerned'. This appears to offer a broader definition, thereby seemingly aiming to include browser finger-printing techniques more easily within the scope of the provision.

[123] Indeed the definition of personal data combined with the definition of pseudonymisation (Article 4(5) GDPR) and the clarification regarding the interaction between these two definitions (provided in Recitals 26 and 28), indicate that any data capable of *singling out* an individual should be considered as personal. See Borgesius, 'Singling out People without Knowing Their Names – Behavioural Targeting, Pseudonymous Data, and the New Data Protection Regulation' (2016) 32 *Computer Law & Security Review* 256.

[124] This is reflected in the addition of 'location data', 'online identifier' and 'genetic' and 'economic' identity as examples within the definition of personal data in Article 4(1) GDPR, compared to the equivalent provision in Directive 95/46/EC.

[125] Clifford and Verdoodt, 'Integrative Advertising: The Marketing "dark Side" or Merely the Emperor's New Clothes?' (2017) 8 *European Journal of Law and Technology* <http://ejlt.org/article/view/547> (accessed 13 April 2019).

the processing of genetic data, biometric data for the purpose of uniquely identifying a natural person, data concerning health or data concerning a natural person's sex life or sexual orientation shall be prohibited.

In order to avoid the general prohibition on the processing of sensitive personal data, a controller is required to satisfy one of the conditions in Article 9(2) GDPR. In the context of emotion detection for the purposes of advertising or marketing purposes, the explicit consent of the data subject (Article 9(2)(a) GDPR) will be required, given that the others are substantively out of scope. This is a stricter requirement than consent as required for the processing of personal data (see Article 6(1)(a) GDPR).[126]

However, it should be noted that given the rise of analysis-intensive processing methods the lines between personal data and sensitive personal data have become increasingly blurred.[127] The difficulties in this regard are particularly obvious in the context of emotion detection online. More specifically, emotion detection mechanisms focus on a range of techniques such as text analysis technology, speech analytics technology, technology for quantifying emotions via the analysis of facial expressions/eye movement, and content consumption contextual triggers capable of inferring user moods based on usage patterns (i.e. media content provision services such as e-books, music and video streaming).[128] Therefore, it is arguable that finding whether the data processed to reveal emotion falls into the personal or sensitive personal data category may potentially depend on the detection mechanism employed. For instance, the use of biometric data[129] (for emotion detection, this could be images or data collected by a smart device, such as a heart rate) may arguably result in the processing of sensitive personal data.[130] In comparison, it is questionable whether text analysis techniques or content usage analysis

---

[126] For more see Article 29 Working Party, 'Opinion Guidelines on Consent under Regulation 2016/679' (2017) WP 259.

[127] De Hert and Papakonstantinou, 'The Proposed Data Protection Regulation Replacing Directive 95/46/EC'.

[128] See McStay, 'Empathic Media: The Rise of Emotion in AI'.

[129] Defined in Article 4(14) as 'personal data resulting from specific technical processing relating to the physical, physiological or behavioural characteristics of a natural person, which allow or confirm the unique identification of that natural person, such as facial images or dactyloscopic data'.

[130] It should be noted that there is some degree of uncertainty regarding the interpretation of the definition of biometric data in Article 4(14) GDPR, but also of the biometric data that are covered by the prohibition in Article 9(1) GDPR. For more see Kindt, 'Having Yes, Using No? About the New Legal Regime for Biometric Data' (2017) *Computer Law & Security Review* <http://linkinghub.elsevier.com/retrieve/pii/S0267364917303667> (accessed 13 April 2019).

deployed for emotion detection purposes would necessarily process sensitive personal data. Indeed, in this context one should note that the purposes of processing may also play a key role in determining whether sensitive personal data are indeed processed.[131]

In this context, it is significant to consider the opinion of the Article 29 Working Party on the notion of personal data where it is noted that, 'in order to consider that the data "relate" to an individual, a '**content**' element OR a '**purpose**' element OR a '**result**' element should be present'.[132] Accordingly, either the content (the substance in question relates to a data subject), the purpose (which is or incorporates the need to identify the individual) or the result (irrespective of the content and purpose, the consequences are likely to have an impact on the rights and freedoms of an individual) can result in the processing of personal data.[133] Although traditionally one would associate the sensitive personal data category with the content element,[134] in an era of 'big data' the automated processing of ordinary categories of personal data may often 'reveal' sensitive personal data insights (see the wording of Article 9(1) GDPR). Hence, the content, purpose and result should be taken into consideration, and this is clearly an area requiring more detailed research, with emotion detection technology an excellent illustration of this need. Indeed, such a differentiation depending on the means of detection is significant, given that as noted by McStay, '[i]nformation about emotions feels personal because emotional life is core to personhood and while data may not be identifiable, it certainly connects with a fundamental dimension of human experience. This gives it special value.'[135] Aside from the more general issues associated with this personal *versus* sensitive personal data distinction, in the context of emotion monetisation the problem is potentially compounded

---

[131] To clarify, Article 4(15) GDPR defines data concerning health (which comes within the definition of sensitive personal data) as 'personal data related to the physical or mental health of a natural person, including the provision of health care services, which reveal information about his or her health status'. Therefore, emotion insights that are garnered for the purposes of advertising or marketing may be deemed distinct from mental health data, depending on the nature of the data and the potential to link such insights with an underlying mental illness. In short, it is arguable that, given the purpose is not to gain insights into the mental health status of the data subject, the personal data gathered should remain merely personal, and not sensitive personal, data.

[132] Article 29 Working Party, 'Opinion 4/2007 on the Concept of Personal Data' (Article 29 Working Party 2007) WP 136 10 <https://www.clinicalstudydatarequest.com/Documents/Privacy-European-guidance.pdf> (accessed 13 April 2019).

[133] Article 29 Working Party, 'Opinion on the Concept of Personal Data'.

[134] In this regard one can refer to the text of the GDPR itself but

[135] McStay, 'Empathic Media and Advertising'.

by the fact that (depending on the purpose to which this technology is applied) this processing may be completed in a product/marketing campaign development stage or even academic or private research and therefore, may remain somewhat disconnected from any potential harm to the end-user[136] or indeed, may arguably be compatible with the original purpose given the special allowances afforded to repurposing for the purposes of scientific research in the purpose limitation principle.[137]

3.2.2 Explicit Consent, Necessity and the Ex Post Empowerment Mechanisms

Although the analysis of emotion detection and the definition of personal data are areas requiring further research, it is sufficient to state for our current purposes that the precise classification remains uncertain. However, in this regard it is also important to highlight the effects of Article 22(1) GDPR given that it may negate the practical significance of the personal-sensitive personal data discussion. To clarify, if for commercial purposes the processing of personal data requires consent and sensitive personal data requires *explicit* consent, one must wonder whether the exceptions allowing for automated individual decision making, including profiling, in fact align these in the context of emotion detection by referring to explicit rather than *regular* consent. This provision states that '[t]he data subject shall have the right not to be subject to a decision based solely on automated processing, including

---

[136] In this context one can refer to Receptiv: 'Receptiv Is the Leading in-App, Mobile Video Advertising Platform that is Measurable and Scalable' <https://updates.easycounter.com/mediabrix.com> (accessed 13 April 2019); 'Opinion 02/2012 on Facial Recognition in Online and Mobile Services' (Article 29 Working Party 2012) WP 192 p. 3 <https://ec.europa.eu/justice/article-29/documentation/opinion-recommendation/files/2012/wp192_en.pdf> (accessed 13 April 2019). To clarify, consumers are generally targeted on the basis of an assumed emotional state with emotion-tailored campaigns. In this context one can refer to gaming, where companies capitalise on presumed emotional states based on how the consumer is progressing in the game in order to better tailor commercial campaigns.

[137] According to the purpose limitation principle, 'scientific research' is compatible with the initial purpose of the processing and thus no additional condition for lawful processing is required, provided the safeguards contained in Article 89(1) GDPR are satisfied. Given that scientific research is not defined in the GDPR and further that Recital 159 GDPR indicates that it is to be 'interpreted in a broad manner', one must question how far this notion can stretch in the context of research conducted by private commercial entities, especially in light of the exemptions to the right to erasure (Article 17(3)(d) GDPR) and the right to object (Article 21(6) GDPR). Such considerations are significant in light of Facebook's emotional contagion experiment and thus the potential fine line between research, beta-testing and the rolling out of such technologies as part of the everyday service.

Table 4.3 Conditions Legitimising Profiling

Article	Condition	Relevant extract from provision
Article 22(2)(a)	Contract	is necessary for entering into, or performance of, a contract between the data subject and a data controller;
Article 22(2)(b)	Authorised by law	is authorised by Union or Member State law to which the controller is subject and which also lays down suitable measures to safeguard the data subject's rights and freedoms and legitimate interests; or
Article 22(2)(c)	Explicit consent	is based on the data subject's explicit consent.

profiling, which produces legal effects concerning him or her or similarly significantly affects him or her', so long as none of the provisions contained in Article 22(2) GDPR are satisfied (see Table 4.3 above). Although it remains outside the scope of this chapter to explore whether the detection of emotion satisfies the elements in Article 22(1) GDPR, it is important to note that the Article 29 Working Party has noted that profiling for advertising and marketing purposes can potentially come within the scope of Article 22 GDPR.[138] This depends on the circumstances with the Working Party noting that one must keep in mind (1) the intrusiveness of the profiling; (2) the expectations of the individuals concerned; (3) the manner in which the advertisement is delivered; and (4) whether the controller uses knowledge of a specific consumer vulnerability.[139]

For the purposes of emotion detection technologies, Articles 22(2)(a) and 22(2)(c) GDPR are significant. In this regard, one must further note Article 22(4) GDPR, which specifies that a contract as outlined in Article 22(2)(a) GDPR cannot be utilised to legitimise profiling based on the processing of sensitive personal data. Instead, and by cross-reference to Article 9(2)(a) GDPR, explicit consent appears to be the only grounds for such processing for commercial purposes. From the above, two noteworthy points emerge. First, the classification of emotional insights as personal or sensitive personal data will determine the availability of a contract as a grounds for such profiling and second, if a contract is available this raises a clear question in terms of what can be considered 'necessary for entering into, or performance of, a contract'.

---

[138] 'Article 29 Working Party, Guidelines on Automated Individual Decision-Making and Profiling for the Purposes of Regulation 2016/679, Adopted on 3 October 2017 as Last Revised and Adopted on 6 February 2018', WP 259, p. 22.

[139] Ibid.

The second of these points relates to the delineation of contract from consent. Consent is defined in Article 4(11) GDPR as 'any freely given, specific, informed and unambiguous indication of the data subject's wishes by which he or she, by a statement or by a clear affirmative action, signifies agreement to the processing of personal data relating to him or her.' This definition is further specified by the conditions for consent outlined in Article 7 GDPR. Significant in this regard are Articles 7(1) and 7(4) GDPR, which in essence specify that the controller is obliged to demonstrate that the data subject has in fact consented to the data processing. These provisions further indicate that in the examination of the 'freely given' stipulation, it is necessary to examine whether consent is a condition upon which access to the service in question is granted where such personal data are not necessary for the performance of the contract for the provision of that service. This is bolstered by the focus on user-friendly information provision in Article 12 GDPR,[140] and also Recital 43 GDPR, which specifies that in order to be certain that data subject consent does not fall foul of the freely given requirement it should not provide a valid ground 'where there is a clear imbalance between the data subject and the controller', given that in such circumstance it is unlikely that consent would be freely given 'in all the circumstances of that specific situation'.[141]

Furthermore, Article 7(3) GDPR stipulates that data subjects have the right to withdraw consent at any time, and that consent should be as easy to withdraw as it is to give but that any such withdrawal should not affect

---

[140] Article 12 of the GDPR states that 'The controller shall take appropriate measures to provide any information referred to in Article 13 and 14 and any communication under Articles 15 to 22, and 34 relating to the processing to the data subject in a concise, transparent, intelligible and easily accessible form, using clear and plain language, in particular for any information addressed specifically to a child'. In this regard, the Article 29 Working Party recommends the use of layered notices, offering a dual system consisting of (1) a shorter notice, containing the basic information to be provided when collecting personal data either directly from the data subject or from a third party, accompanied by (2) a more detailed notice, preferably via a hyperlink, where all relevant details are provided that are necessary to ensure fair processing. Of course, the notice needs to be posted in the right place and at the right time that is, it should appear directly on the screen, prior to the collection of information. Article 29 Data Protection Working Party, 'Opinion 10/2004 on More Harmonised Information Provisions' (2004) WP 100, pp. 8–9.

[141] The recital goes on to further clarify the presumption that the 'freely given' criterion will not be satisfied if consent 'does not allow separate consent to be given to different data processing operations despite it being appropriate in the individual case, or if the performance of a contract, including the provision of a service is made dependent on the consent despite this is not necessary for such performance'. Regardless of the unclear wording, this appears to be linked with the discussion on purpose limitation above.

the lawfulness of the processing prior to its withdrawal. In this vein, one must question how such withdrawal would affect the continued use of a service.[142]

Although it remains to be seen how these obligations will be incorporated in practice and indeed interpreted by the data protection authorities (DPAs), it should be noted that the requirement for data protection by design and by default should play an integral role in the determination of an appropriate implementation. In this regard one can also refer to the discussion surrounding the proposed ePrivacy Regulation. More specifically, Article 9(2) of the Commission version of the proposed Regulation indicates that 'where technically possible and feasible, for the purposes of point (b) of Article 8(1), consent may be expressed by using the appropriate technical settings of a software application enabling access to the internet.' This is further specified in Articles 10(1) and 10(2) which require that software providers must permit electronic communications 'the option to prevent third parties from storing information on the terminal equipment of an end-user or processing information already stored on that equipment', and obliges software providers to require end-users to consent to a setting.

Accordingly, this provision stipulates that browser settings may be used to express consent. This provision is controversial, however, and in commenting on the proposal, the Article 29 Working Party has noted that general browser settings are unsuitable for providing consent under Article 7 and recital 32 of the GDPR, as such an expression of consent would fail to satisfy the conditions for consent and thus the requirement for consent to be informed and specific.[143] In addition, the opinion notes that Article 10(2) of the proposal fails to satisfy the requirement for data protection by design and by default as contained in Article 25 GDPR.[144] Building on this, the Article 29 Working Party has observed that in order to comply with Article 25 GDPR, the proposed ePrivacy Regulation 'must by default offer privacy protective settings, and guide users through configuration menus to deviate

---

[142] For example one can refer to the recent Sonos decision to require users to accept their updated privacy policy or risk losing functionality. See Whittaker, 'Sonos Says Users Must Accept New Privacy Policy or Devices May "Cease to Function"' (*ZDNet*) <www.zdnet. com/article/sonos-accept-new-privacy-policy-speakers-cease-to-function/> (accessed 13 April 2019).

[143] Article 29 Working Party, 'Opinion 01/2017 on the Proposed Regulation for the ePrivacy Regulation (2002/58/EC) WP 247' (Article 29 Working Party 2017) WP 247, pp. 14–15.

[144] This approach to default settings appears to reflect the Article 29 Working Party's traditional approach in this regard; see Article 29 Working Party, 'Working Document 02/2013 Providing Guidance on Obtaining Consent for Cookies'.

from these default settings upon installation', and further explicitly prohibit the use of tracking walls.[145]

Aside from these issues regarding data protection by design and by default, the burden of proof on the shoulders of controllers and the requirement for 'freely given' consent may render it difficult to convince DPAs of the correct implementation of a preformulated declaration of consent given the asymmetric business–data subject relationship where the processing is deemed unnecessary for the performance of the contract. This is significant given that the Article 29 Working Party has emphasised that necessity here should be construed narrowly.[146] Moreover, although the use of the term 'necessity' in Article 6(1) GDPR has caused a degree of confusion given the overlaps with Article 52(1) of the Charter,[147] conventional understanding delineates the necessity and proportionality test in Article 52(1) from that contained in Article 6(1) GDPR. Reflecting this approach, the European Data Protection Supervisor (EDPS) has noted in the opinion on the application of necessity that 'necessity of processing operations in EU secondary law and necessity of the limitations on the exercise of fundamental rights refer to different concepts.'[148]

---

[145] Article 29 Working Party, 'Opinion 01/2017 on the Proposed Regulation for the EPrivacy Regulation (2002/58/EC) WP 247', pp. 14–15.

[146] Article 29 Working Party, 'Opinion 01/2014 on the Application of Necessity and Proportionality Concepts and Data Protection within the Law Enforcement Sector' (European Commission 2014) Opinion WP 211 29 <https://ec.europa.eu/justice/arti cle-29/documentation/opinion-recommendation/files/2014/wp211_en.pdf> (accessed 13 April 2019); Article 29 Working Party, 'Opinion 06/2014 on the Notion of Legitimate Interests of the Data Controller under Article 7 of Directive 95/46/EC' (European Commission 2014) Opinion WP 217 <https://ec.europa.eu/justice/article-29/documen tation/opinion-recommendation/files/2014/wp217_en.pdf> (accessed 13 April 2019).

[147] This confusion is strengthened given the Court of Justice's interpretation of 'necessity' in Article 6(1) GDPR. In *Huber* the Court of Justice emphasised that 'necessity' in EU data protection secondary framework (specifically Article 6(1)(e) GDPR then Article 7(e) Directive 95/46) is aimed at precisely delimiting 'situations in which the processing of personal data is lawful': *Huber* v *Germany* [2008] Court of Justice of the EU C-524/06, InfoCuria, para 52. Furthermore, the *Huber* judgement also indicates that the concept of necessity that appears in Article 7 Directive 95/46/EC (now Article 6(1) GDPR) imports a proportionality test. Rosemary Jay, *Data Protection: Law and Practice* (Sweet & Maxwell 2012), p. 143.

[148] European Data Protection Supervisor (EDPS), 'Developing a "Toolkit" for Assessing the Necessity of Measures That Interfere with Fundamental Rights', 4 <https://secure.edps. europa.eu/EDPSWEB/webdav/site/mySite/shared/Documents/Consultation/Papers/ 16-06-16_Necessity_paper_for_consultation_EN.pdf> (accessed 13 April 2019). Indeed, as stated by the Court of Justice in the Huber case, necessity in the secondary framework 'is a concept which has its own independent meaning in Community law and must be inter-

However, one might further question how the conditions for lawful processing, which apply independently from the data subject's will or control (i.e. Article 6(1)(c)-(f) GDPR), remain substantively different from the strict necessity and proportionality test in Article 52(1) while seemingly legitimising the limitations of the data subject's control of their personal data as the essence of the right.[149] In this context, one must first remember that the GDPR aims to protect rights and freedoms in general and the right to data protection in particular, therefore manifesting broader aims than merely the protection of the right to data protection. In addition, one must also consider *inter alia* the right to erasure (Article 17 GDPR) and the right to object (Article 21 GDPR). These two *ex post* empowerment mechanisms effectively act as a stress test of the *ex ante* balancing conducted in Article 6(1) GDPR. Therefore, data subject rights and in particular the rights to erasure and object complement Articles 6(1)(e) and (f) GDPR by offering the tools to question the balance originally defined by the controller.[150] Another key issue in this regard is the analysis of how standardised privacy policies may impact the 'freely given' requirement and thus the reference to preformulated declarations of consent in Recital 42 of the GDPR. Recital 42 states: 'In accordance with Council Directive 93/13/EEC a declaration of consent pre-formulated by the controller should be provided in an intelligible and easily accessible form, using clear and plain language and it should not contain unfair terms.' As has been argued elsewhere, this reference to the Unfair Terms Directive (and the substantive and formal fairness elements therein) raises a number of challenges but most fundamentally *vis-à-vis* the exclusion of the core terms (that is, those concerning the price) from the substantive fairness test contained in that Directive.[151] One must question the effect of such an exclusion

preted in a manner which fully reflects the objective of that directive'. *Huber* v *Germany*, para 52.

[149] Clifford and Ausloos, 'Data Protection and the Role of Fairness', pp. 17–20.

[150] Clifford and Ausloos, 'Data Protection and the Role of Fairness', pp 35–6: 'Indeed, from a practical perspective, most controllers will construct their balancing under Article 6(1)(f) *a priori* on the basis of the median context and average data subject. In contrast, *ex post* empowerment tools such as the rights to erasure, object and not to be subject to an automated individual decision target the enabling of data subjects to allow them question this initial balancing act in light of their particular circumstances.' See in this line also: *Google Spain SL, Google Inc* v *Agencia Española de Protección de Datos (AEPD), Mario Costeja González*, InfoCuria at 82; Salvatore Manni, Case C-398/15, *Camera di Commercio, Industria, Artigianato e Agricoltura di Lecce* v *Salvatore Manni*, ECLI:EU:C:2017:197 at 46–7.

[151] Article 4(2) Unfair Terms Directive states that 'the definition of the main subject matter of the contract nor to the adequacy of the price and remuneration, on the one hand, as against the services or goods supplies [sic] in exchange, on the other, in so far as these terms are

in terms of the application of the Directive to preformulated declarations of consent.

In particular, what is to be considered as the 'price'? If personal data are the price would this not result in a somewhat counter-intuitive result where the fairness of personal data processing would be excluded? How would this relate to the data minimisation and purpose limitation principles, for instance? Although it remains outside the scope of this chapter to analyse these issues in detail, it is important to simply observe that the positioning of personal data as a counter-performance is an extremely topical issue, especially in light of the adoption of the Directive on contracts for the supply of digital content.[152] Although the EDPS criticised the positioning of data (including personal data) as counter-performance in the original proposal, which was deleted, leaving matters ambiguous in the Compromise draft, this remains a highly debated issue with divergences in interpretation evident amongst policy makers, academics and even different enforcement bodies.[153] It seems unlikely from a systematic and teleological interpretation of the GDPR, however (given its fundamental rights focus), that personal data could be positioned as the 'price' given the separation of data subject consent from other matters in order to be certain that it will not fall foul of the 'freely given' requirement. Nevertheless, as highlighted by Zingales in his analysis of the decision adopted by the Italian antitrust and consumer protection authority (AGCM), which qualified the process by which WhatsApp obtained user consent to their changed terms of service and privacy policy as 'unfair' and 'aggressive' under the Italian implementation of the Unfair Commercial Practices (UCP) Directive, the national authority refused to accept that personal data could not be construed as counter-performance.[154] It therefore

---

in plain intelligible language.' Clifford, Graef and Valcke, 'Pre-Formulated Declarations of Data Subject Consent – Citizen-Consumer Empowerment and the Alignment of Data, Consumer and Competition Law Protections' (2019) *German Law Journal* 20(5) 679–721.

[152] 'Proposal for a Directive of the European Parliament and of the Council on Certain Aspects concerning Contracts for the Supply of Digital Content', COM(2015) 634 final.

[153] Significantly, Recital 42 GDPR refers in particular to preformulated declarations of consent. It is therefore arguable that privacy policies, in addition to terms and conditions of use, may be presented as the provisions of the contract, with the declaration of consent being a separate (and indeed revocable) but connected part of the same overarching agreement. In this vein, personal data would not constitute a price, but the protection of it would be encompassed within the contractual agreement as both explicit (that is, what the controller promises) and implied (as legal obligations stemming from the GDPR) terms. For more, see Clifford, Graef and Valcke, 'Pre-Formulated Declarations of Data Subject Consent '.

[154] Zingales, 'Between a Rock and Two Hard Places: WhatsApp at the Crossroad of Competition, Data Protection and Consumer Law' (2017) 33 *Computer Law & Security*

remains to be seen how far consent will stretch but also, as noted above, if and how processing that is necessary for the contract will be delineated from additional activities as required by Article 7(2) GDPR, or if in practice personal data will be recognised as a price or counter-performance. Despite the uncertainties discussed above, however, emotion detection may always require the explicit consent of the data subject for commercial purposes. That said, developments in this area will need to be watched closely especially in light of limitations in effectiveness of the data protection framework.

3.3 Data Protection Requirements and the Broader Emotion Monetisation Picture – 'These Aren't the Droids you're Looking For'

Given the asymmetric data subject–controller relationship, the effectiveness of the data protection framework is questionable given that asymmetry diminishes the legitimacy of user participation, presents barriers to finding businesses accountable and also clearly impacts the data subject's bargaining power.[155] Due to issues stemming from this asymmetry (such as, for example, social lock-in effects), Mantelero has noted that 'the self-determination of the single individual is inadequate and insufficient to create an effective and conscious market activity concerning personal data'.[156] This illustrates Koops' point that in a practical sense data subject involvement has a limited effect due to their ignorance *vis-à-vis* the extent of data gathering and processing operations.[157] Indeed, in examining control, Lazaro and Le Métayer observe that this concept 'is strongly associated with the conventional figure of the "rational and autonomous agent", capable of deliberating about personal goals, controlling the course of the events and acting under the direction of such deliberation'.[158] The authors further note that this notion is both 'individualist', given the emphasis on individual sovereignty, and also 'active', in that control implies effective participation of the data subject and the liberty to alienate their personal data provided that such alienation is informed and voluntary.[159] Bounded data subject rationality and the biases inherent in

---

Review 553. In essence, WhatsApp had claimed (with reference to the EDPS opinion) that personal data could not be construed as counter-performance. However, the AGCM found, with reference to the recent common position on the application of consumer protection in the context of social media, that consumer protection and competition law, and indeed the company itself, all recognise the economic value of the data.

[155] Lynskey, 'Deconstructing Data Protection'.

[156] Mantelero, 'Competitive Value of Data Protection: The Impact of Data Protection Regulation on Online Behaviour' (2013) 3 *International Data Privacy Law* 229.

[157] Koops, 'On Decision Transparency'.

[158] Lazaro and Le Métayer, 'Control over Personal Data: True Remedy or Fairytale?'

[159] Ibid., pp. 7–9.

individual decision making, given issues such as information overload (i.e. the failure of privacy policies to inform data subjects), the multiplicity of requests for consent and the 'stickiness' of defaults further reduce the value of data subject participation.[160]

In this context, one must recognise the limitations of the data protection framework to adequately protect citizen-consumers online regarding the development of empathic media and the use of emotional insights for advertising and marketing purposes. Despite the fact that positioning of data subjects as the key actors affords protections in theory, the practical realities belie the liberal assumption of the capacity and rationality of the data subjects *vis-à-vis* decision making, and also the potential for market equalising effects. At the root of this statement is a reference to the acknowledgement within the data protection framework of objectives that extend beyond mere data protection and thus the intention to provide protections from harms stemming from personal data processing through control-orientated protections.

Therefore, despite the fact that the dual approach to control is well established in the data protection framework,[161] the ongoing legitimacy of this approach are increasingly under strain in the data-driven world.[162] Indeed, a clear difficulty in the application of the data protection framework to profiling is that the connection between the data-processing risk and the notion of personal data is unclear, since data protection focuses on the risks associated with processing and not on the substantial parts of profiling applications (which may also present a threat).[163] Although the concerns with such repurposing are not limited to the context of profiles incorporating emotion insights, their use raises fundamental concerns in the context of advertising and marketing given that (as described above) emotions are of key importance in the decision-making process. This strengthens the calls for a

---

[160] Clifford, 'EU Data Protection Law and Targeted Advertising'. The readiness of data subjects to consent to the surrender their personal data without being aware of the specific purpose indicated (or indeed of the data gathering in the first place) is a good illustration of this point. Despite the fact that reliance on consent as a ground for personal data processing is questionable (for a critique well-founded in literature see Kosta, *Consent in European Data Protection Law*, Martinus Nijhoff 2014), there is a continuing move towards empowerment at a policy level.

[161] Lynskey, *The Foundations of EU Data Protection Law*, pp. 258–62.

[162] For a recent discussion here see Zarsky, 'Incompatible'. But also, for instance, Koops, 'The Trouble with European Data Protection Law'.

[163] Koops, 'On Decision Transparency'. Instead the GDPR merely provides that a data subject has the right not to be subject to an automated individual decision and, as such, it does not specifically regulate the subject matter of such decisions. See Article 22 GDPR.

more holistic approach, and hence the alignment of the data protection and consumer protection policy agendas.

4. Autonomous Decision Making in an Emotion-sensitive Galaxy – 'Do. Or Do Not. There Is No Try'

In the previous two sections the analysis has highlighted how the emergence of emotion detection technology challenges consumer-citizen autonomy, and how data protection is somewhat of a blunt tool to facilitate holistic consumer-citizen protection. Despite the progressive alignment of the respective consumer protection and data protection policy agendas, it is arguable that the use of such technologies for advertising and marketing purposes undermines rationality and thus individual autonomy. With this in mind, the first subsection here aims to position rationality as a 'functional fiction' within the law, while at the same time arguing that the law needs to adjust in order to ensure that it does not itself become dysfunctional. Building on this, the second subsection aims to question the potential for paternalistic interventions via the blacklisting of certain applications of emotion detection technology in the context of the provision of online services. In essence therefore, this part of the analysis will act as a call for further research highlighting some fundamental issues at the core of the legislative framework in light of the foregoing analysis.

4.1 Emotions and Rationality as a Functional Fiction – 'Your Thoughts Betray You …' But Wait, 'Get Out of My Head!'

As argued above in section 2, personalisation undoubtedly aims to increase the persuasive intent of commercial communications by directly appealing to our profiles.[164] However, one must question the potential impact of adding emotion. Emotionally tailored profiles, and therefore the ability to target individuals on the basis of their emotional status and personalise the nature of the appeal to match, arguably adds a layer of manipulation beyond current programmatic advertising practices. Moreover, one could argue that given the Facebook 'emotional contagion' experiment, the capacity to manipulate may not stop at the nudging of consumers towards certain behaviours but could conceivably include the manipulation of a consumer's emotional state towards the one that is best suited to a particular commercial goal. With this in mind, one might question whether such practices would not bring only the notion of autonomy into question but also the fundamental right to the freedom of thought.[165]

---

[164] Kaptein, *Persuasion Profiling*, pp. 176–9.

[165] Article 10 Charter; see Oostveen and Irion, 'The Golden Age of Personal Data'; Bublitz, 'Freedom of Thought in the Age of Neuroscience' (2014) 100 *Archives for Philosophy of Law and Social Philosophy* 1.

In his analysis of the freedom of thought in the context of neuroscientific research, Bublitz has called for the law to redefine this right in terms of its theoretical significance in light of technological developments capable of altering thoughts.[166] The author concludes that such technological developments require the setting of normative boundaries 'to secure the freedom of the forum internum'.[167] Although this call for action may appear to be based on an overly dystopian outlook, especially as in the context of this chapter, there is currently no market for the exchange of data on emotions,[168] such developments are conceivable and arguably on the horizon. Indeed, given the frequency of the revelations in this area this concern is far from merely a dystopian reality but in fact appears instead to be an emerging one. But what does this mean for rationality-based assumptions in the framework in terms of the capacity of individuals to choose autonomously? In her analysis of rationality as the fundamental unit of liberalism, Rouvroy observes:

> [t]he rational, liberal, individual subject, or the autonomous legal subject have never been anything other than useful or even necessary functional fictions without empirical, phenomenal correlates, despite their merits and the fact that, in a series of domains, they need to be presupposed. However, the legal subject must be presupposed by the law, even though this subject is in no way an empirical entity.[169]

This appears to be well-reasoned: to simply abandon the rationality-based assumption would undercut the very foundations of liberalism potentially requiring a far more paternalistic form of governance.

That said, although the rationality standard may be a necessary construct for the continuance of a liberal rights-based approach, this does not exclude the possibility of ensuring the existence of an environment in which this standard is rendered more effective and realistic given the potential for such developments to undermine the capacity of an individual to act autonomously, and hence in their own best interests. This need is arguably exaggerated due to the emergence of the mediated society. Importantly, Raz's conception of autonomy does not preclude the potential for positive regulatory intervention by the state to protect individuals and enhance their freedom. In fact, such positive action is at the core of Raz's conception of

---

[166] Bublitz, ibid.

[167] Ibid., p. 25.

[168] This appears to be perhaps related to the fact that such technologies are only in their infancy rather than as a consequence of any practical hurdles. See McStay, 'Empathic Media and Advertising'.

[169] Rouvroy, 'The End(s) of Critique: Data Behaviourism versus Due Process', pp. 157–8.

autonomy, as a correct interpretation must allow effective choice in reality (even if those effective choices are irrational in substance), thus at times requiring regulatory intervention.[170] As such, the question thus becomes one of how to ensure that rationality does not digress to the point of dysfunctionality where this fiction no longer achieves its aims. In this vein, the means through which regulatory interventions may provide such protection must be considered, and must therefore carefully toe the line between paternalism and the protection of a life free from commercial manipulation.

In short, the manipulation of choice can inherently interfere with autonomy ultimately resulting in alienation and, as a result, one can conclude that through this lens excessive persuasion also runs afoul of autonomy.[171] To frame this problem, one can pose the following questions: how it is possible to ensure the ongoing viability of the average consumer standard? How can we create an environment in which consumers can make a rational choice or, more specifically, know when they are deviating from rationality but doing so in the pursuit of their own goals (i.e. autonomous irrationality)? How can we adjust protections to enable the continuance of fair market conditions? With these questions in mind, it is argued here that the use of emotion detection technology online may fall foul of the requirements in the UCP Directive in terms of the effect of personalisation on the decision-making capacity of individuals.[172] According to Article 5(2) a commercial practice is unfair if:

(a) it is contrary to the requirements of professional diligence, and

(b) it materially distorts or is likely to materially distort the economic behaviour with regard to the product of the average consumer whom it reaches or to whom it is addressed, or of the average member of the group when a commercial practice is directed to a particular group of consumers.

---

[170] Bernal, *Internet Privacy Rights*, p. 25, referring to Raz, *The Morality of Freedom*. Indeed, according to Raz, 'Autonomy is opposed to a life of coerced choices. It contrasts with a life of no choices, or of drifting through life without ever exercising one's capacity to choose. Evidently the autonomous life calls for a certain degree of selfawareness. To choose one must be aware of one's options.'

[171] Bernal, *Internet Privacy Rights*, p. 26.

[172] Directive 2005/29/EC concerning unfair business-to-consumer commercial practices in the internal market and amending Council Directive 84/450/EEC, Directives 97/7/EC, 98/27/EC and 2002/65/EC of the European Parliament and of the Council and Regulation (EC) No 2006/2004 of the European Parliament and of the Council ('Unfair Commercial Practices Directive') 2005 22.

This general clause is then further expanded upon by the two small general clauses that make up the second level of unfairness in the Directive, with Article 5(4) outlining the protections against misleading and aggressive commercial practices.[173] Finally, on the third level, Article 5(5) makes reference to Annex I of the Directive, which lists twenty-eight misleading or aggressive trading practices that are deemed *de facto* unfair, with Member States barred from deviating from this exclusive list.[174] Importantly, as confirmed by the Court of Justice, practices that are not provided in Annex I can be prohibited only on a case-by-case basis either under the general or one of the two small general clauses.[175]

The UCP Directive utilises the average consumer who is 'reasonably well-informed and reasonably observant and circumspect' as the benchmark for assessment taking social, cultural and linguistic factors into account.[176] However, as mentioned above in section 2.1, given the personalisation of online services and the ability to nudge consumers towards certain decisions the notion of an average consumer as the standard for assessing protection is under strain and thus the targeting of particular consumers on the basis of personal profiles can arguably have a manipulative effect.[177] This is symptomatic of the asymmetric consumer–business relationship, which is potentially heightened in the context of personalised advertising and marketing given the inherent information asymmetry.[178] As noted by Willet, although the

---

[173] These are further specified in Article 6 (Misleading Actions), Article 7 (Misleading Omissions), Article 8 (Aggressive Commercial Practices) and Article 9 (which outlines the elements to be considered in determining whether harassment, coercion and undue influence have been used).

[174] See Joined Cases C-261 and C-299/07, *VTB-VAB* v *Total Belgium* [2009] ECR 1-02949; ECJ Case C-304/08, *Plus Warenhandelsgesellschaft* [2010] ECR 1-217 at 37; ECJ Case C-540/08, *Mediaprint* [2010] ECR 1-10909 at 18; Case C-288/1O, *Wamo* [2011] ECR 1-5835 at 31.

[175] See ECJ Case C-540/08, *Mediaprint* [2010] ECR 1-10909; Case C-206/11, *Köck*, EU: C: 2013:14.

[176] Case C-210/96, *Gut Springenheide GmbH and Tusky* v *Oberkreisdirektor des Kreises Steinfurt*, EU:C:1998:369 para 31. See 'Commission Staff Working Document Guidance on the Implementation/Application of Directive 2005/29/EC on Unfair Commercial Practices' SEC (2009) 1666, 20 <http://ec.europa.eu/justice/consumer-marketing/files/ucp_guidance_en.pdf> (accessed 13 April 2019).

[177] Calo, 'Digital Market Manipulation'.

[178] See discussion paper: BEUC, 'Data Collection, Targeting and Profiling of Consumers Online' (15 February 2010) <www.beuc.eu/publications/2010-00101-01-e.pdf> (accessed 13 April 2019). Such difficulties are worsened due to the problems consumers experience in differentiating between commercial and non-commercial content and this is compounded by the fact that commercial content is often integrated into the editorial. For

Directive contains a substantial amount of specification (i.e. through the above divisions and respective definitions in Article 2), the provisions still retain a large degree of scope for interpretation.[179] Therefore, although the use of emotion detection technology for advertising and marketing purposes is not *de facto* unfair and thus does not appear on the blacklist in Annex I, it is arguable that such technology may fit within the small general clauses or the general clause more broadly. With this in mind, in particular one could arguably refer to the protection against aggressive commercial practices in assessing the use of emotion detection technologies. Indeed, commercial practices are classified as aggressive if 'by harassment, coercion or undue influence' they 'significantly impair the freedom of choice or conduct of the average consumer'.[180]

Although it is unlikely that harassment and coercion (including the use of physical force) would be applicable, undue influence may be applicable given the asymmetric power relationships.[181] However, it should be acknowledged that despite the fact that the data protection and consumer protection policy agendas have been gradually aligning, this has focused mainly on the bolstering of data subject control over their personal data (as illustrated in section 3).[182] Indeed, although the European Commission, in the guidance document on the interpretation of the UCP Directive mentioned that in certain circumstances 'personalised pricing/marketing could be combined with

instance, in this regard one can refer to the use of advergames (games that also contain advertising or marketing messages), where the gamification of commercial communications and their integration with non-commercial content (and thus the emotive appeal of the game) render it difficult for consumers to identify the commercial purpose. This example highlights the significance of emotional appeals which, although resting at the foundation of the advertising business, are now receiving increased attention given the increasing capacity to detect emotions. See Verdoodt, Clifford and Lievens, 'Toying with Children's Emotions, the New Game in Town?'

[179] Willett, 'Fairness and Consumer Decision Making under the Unfair Commercial Practices Directive' (2010) 33 *Journal of Consumer Policy* 247, p. 250.

[180] Article 8 Unfair Commercial Practices Directive.

[181] By undue influence is meant that the company holds a position of power in relation to the consumer and exploits this to exert pressure, in order to significantly restrict the consumer's ability to make an informed decision. Article 2(j) Unfair Commercial Practices Directive.

[182] See below the discussion of the Unfair Terms Directive but also the Unfair Commercial Practices Directive and in this regard the recent common position on consumer protection and social networks see EU Consumer Protection Agencies and European Commission (DG Justice), 'Common Position of National Authorities within the CPC Network Concerning the Protection of Consumers on Social Networks' <http://europa.eu/rapid/press-release_IP-17-631_en.htm> (accessed 13 April 2019).

unfair commercial practices in breach of the UCPD' (i.e. Articles 8 and 9 UCP Directive), there is no real clarity in this regard.[183] In particular, despite the arguments in academic research[184] it remains unclear whether personalisation in itself could ever be in violation of the UCP Directive or whether it must necessarily to be combined with some additional element that breaches the UCP Directive. This is significant as following the logical interpretation of the changes provided for by the Modernisation Directive, provided the consumer is 'informed' the commercial practice should be, generally speaking, deemed fair.[185] It is therefore uncertain whether EU consumer protection in its current form is in fact capable of protecting citizen-consumers, and developments in this regard need to be watched carefully.[186]

4.2 Bolstering Rationality and the Legislative Resistance – 'Difficult to See. Always in Motion is the Future'

In their analysis of market manipulation, Hanson and Kyser emphasised the key contention that commercial entities will respond to market incentives, and hence manipulate consumer perceptions to maximise profits, while providing supporting evidence of the possibility of market manipulation and arguing that a liability regime provides the best regulatory response.[187]

---

[183] 'Commission Staff Working Document Guidance on the Implementation/Application of Directive 2005/29/EC on Unfair Commercial Practices' SEC (2009) 1666, 20.

[184] See generally: Clifford and Verdoodt, 'Integrative Advertising: The Marketing "Dark Side"'; Verdoodt, Clifford and Lievens, 'Toying with Children's Emotions, the New Game in Town?'; Clifford, Graef and Valcke, 'Pre-Formulated Declarations of Data Subject Consent'.

[185] Indeed, the updates to the Consumer Rights (CR) and UCP Directive include information requirements regarding the ranking parameters used when rendering the result to a search query (see Article 6a(1)(a) CR Directive and Article 7(4a) UCP Directive and Article 6(1)(ea) CR Directive introduces the requirement to inform the consumer 'where applicable, that the price was personalised on the basis of automated decision making'. There are provided for in compromise version of Directive of the European Parliament and of the Council amending Council Directive 93/13/EEC of 5 April 1993, Directive 98/6/EC of the European Parliament and of the Council, Directive 2005/29/EC of the European Parliament and of the Council and Directive 2011/83/EU of the European Parliament and of the Council as regards better enforcement and modernisation of EU consumer protection rules COM/2018/0185 final – 2018/090 (COD)).

[186] It is outside the scope of this chapter, but here reference can be made to the proposed reforms of the consumer protection *acquis* and the so-called 'new deal' for consumers: 'European Commission – Press Release – A New Deal for Consumers: Commission Strengthens EU Consumer Rights and Enforcement Brussels, 11 April 2018' <http://europa.eu/rapid/press-release_IP-18-3041_en.htm> (accessed 13 April 2019).

[187] Market manipulation theory also renders much of the criticism positioned against the discovery of bias moot. More specifically, the so-called 'citation bias', where behavioural

However, one must question the capacity of a liability-based regime to truly protect citizen-consumers. Indeed, there is an argument for a move beyond liability and thus beyond systems that are rooted in the allocation of risk and responsibility to consumer-citizens. In simple terms, if individuals are emotionally manipulated, how then in their subjective state can we return them to a point of objectivity (whatever that might mean) within which they would have the capacity to exercise their consumer rights effectively? The problem is that simply relying on information provision and the identification principle may be insufficient.[188] As a consequence, the harm would have already been effectuated, the purchase made and the emotional connection exploited. Of course, this may also raise specific concerns regarding the potential harm to society as opposed to the economic harm felt by an individual.[189] Could this increase further the complaints focused against consumerism and the emergence of a culture of excess? Are these really harms that can be simply linked here, and also, do the economic benefits for businesses outweigh these concerns at a more macro socio-economic level? These are difficult questions requiring interdisciplinary research and it is certainly arguable that a more precautionary approach is required.

In this vein, it is important to highlight that the blacklist contained in Annex I of the UCP Directive (as the third level of unfairness in the Directive) could be updated specifically to ban certain practices or applications of emotion detection technology in B2C situations. Such protections could go beyond the mere transparency requirements and the requirement

---

law and economics scholars have been accused of disproportionately weighing biases relative to the instances in which individuals act in accordance with what is deemed rational, becomes somewhat irrelevant. Instead it is replaced by what Hanson and Kysar refer to as exploitation bias (the tendency to exploit biases that *result* 'in increased sales, higher profits and decreased perceptions of risk'): Hanson and Kysar, 'Taking Behavioralism Seriously', p. 743.

[188] The principle of identification provides the key requirement *vis-à-vis* the protection of consumers from commercial communications. Indeed, despite the complex web formed by the e-Commerce Directive, and the *lex specialis* Audiovisual Media Services (AVMS) Directive, the requirements essentially boil down to the requirement for businesses to ensure that their commercial communications (be they audiovisual or not) remain identifiable as such for consumers. For a discussion see Clifford and Verdoodt, 'Integrative Advertising: The Marketing "Dark Side". In practice, this principle is implemented through the use of labelling or 'cues' to make commercial content recognisable. For a discussion see Helberger, 'Form Matters: Informing Consumers Effectively' (University of Amsterdam, 2013–10) <http://papers.ssrn.com/abstract=2354988> (accessed 13 April 2019).

[189] In this content we can refer to emotional conditioning as discussed by Reed and Coalson: see Reed and Coalson, 'Eighteenth-Century Legal Doctrine Meets Twentieth-Century Marketing Techniques'.

to identify paid/commercial content.[190] In this regard however, it should be noted that delineating between what steps too far into the realms of manipulation (thereby justifying intervention) would be a major challenge. This is difficult from an autonomy perspective as we are already within the murky area of advertising and marketing (which are inherently persuasive by design). Hence, the bright-line between what would be permissible and what would not is perhaps difficult to distinguish. In this regard, one could arguably refer to the emergence of libertarian paternalism and thus the analysis of nudging in order to improve decision-making capacity in a range of policy areas. Although these discussions often focus on the use of such techniques from a policy perspective *vis-à-vis* the legitimacy of such interventions from an autonomy perspective, they may provide inspiration in terms of classifying where paternalistic intervention and protection are in fact justified and stay within the realms of what is proportionate.

For instance, in analysing the use of nudging or libertarian paternalistic means of regulation to improve consumer choices, Baldwin convincingly argues that for conceptual clarity one must differentiate between different types of nudging, as distinct ethical and practical issues are raised depending on the methods used.[191] Baldwin proposes three different nudge classifications. First, those that aim to enhance rational thinking, hence respecting autonomy and individual decision making. Second, those that build upon an existing behavioural or volitional limitation in order to bias a decision in a desired direction. Finally, third, those that incorporate behavioural manipulation the result of which renders reflection futile as it only further enhances the pursuit of a 'shaped preference'.[192]

Baldwin observes that the use of emotional appeal and the classification of the nudge will stem from the degree of associated emotional power. In dif-

---

[190] Here it should be noted that in the proposed updates to the UCP Directive the Compromise version of Directive of the European Parliament and of the Council amending Council Directive 93/13/EEC of 5 April 1993, Directive 98/6/EC of the European Parliament and of the Council, Directive 2005/29/EC of the European Parliament and of the Council and Directive 2011/83/EU of the European Parliament and of the Council as regards better enforcement and modernisation of EU consumer protection rules COM/2018/0185 final – 2018/090 (COD)) introduces point 11a to Annex I UCP Directive. This new provision blacklists '[p]roviding search results in response to a consumer's online search query without clearly disclosing any paid advertisement or payment specifically for achieving higher ranking of products within the search results'. However, this is still a transparency-based provision.

[191] Baldwin, 'From Regulation to Behaviour Change: Giving Nudge the Third Degree' (2014) 77 *Modern Law Review* 831.

[192] Ibid.

ferentiating between the second and third categories, the author notes that the distinguishing feature relates to the fact that the third category of nudge will result in a complete blocking of reflection.[193] Hence, this separation may in fact be one of degree rather than of method. It is significant to note that such mechanisms (or at least those fitting within the first and second categories) are becoming increasingly prevalent.[194] However, the use of such techniques is not restricted to the legislator, and nudging for commercial gain raises clear concerns in terms of autonomy and the need for regulatory intervention. Therefore, and as suggested previously, Baldwin's distinction between the three categories of nudge also provides food for thought in terms of the appropriateness of such a distinction in a commercial setting and hence, the establishment of a bright-line in terms of the acceptability of appeals.

Conclusion

Anakin Skywalker gives into his fear and turns to the dark side. It has been argued in this chapter however, that emotions (being of a cognitive nature) cannot simply be suppressed. Emotions play a key role in determining our choices and are not in conflict with reason. That being said, this does not mean that while in an emotional state we will make rational choices.

With this in mind, the emergence of emotion detection technology raises a number of fundamental challenges to the existing framework and in particular, the rationality-based paradigm imbued in legal protections. This requires more detailed analysis and although this chapter has plotted some of the key issues, many more are likely to surface with a more granular exploration of the expansion of emotion commerce and the proliferation of empathic media. Data protection alone through an isolated application fails to account for such developments. It is even arguable that only via paternalistic interventions will citizen-consumers be truly protected from such developments. Differentiating between what is persuasive and permissible from what is manipulative and an affront to individual autonomy is a clear challenge requiring more interdisciplinary research. Given the inherent aim of the adoption of emotion detection technologies in advertising and marketing practices, it is further debatable whether a more precautionary principled approach is necessary through the blacklisting of certain uses of emotion insights. In conclusion, therefore, more detailed analysis in this area is required and this needs to be brought into mainstream discussions on the future of legislative protections designed for a world of mediated choices.

---

[193] Ibid.

[194] In this regard one can refer to the behavioural science unit that was formed by the UK government.

References

Abrams K and Keren H, 'Who's Afraid of Law and the Emotions' (2009) 94 *Minnesota Law Review* 1997.

Akerlof G and Shiller R, *Phishing for Phools: The Economics of Manipulation and Deception* (Princeton University Press 2015).

Bakir V and McStay A, 'Fake News and the Economy of Emotions: Problems, Causes, Solutions' (2018) 1 *Digital Journalism* 154.

Baldwin A, 'From Regulation to Behaviour Change: Giving Nudge the Third Degree' (2014) 77 *Modern Law Review* 831.

Bandes S, *The Passions of Law* (New York University Press 2001).

Bernal P, *Internet Privacy Rights: Rights to Protect Autonomy* (First, Cambridge University Press 2014).

BEUC, 'Data Collection, Targeting and Profiling of Consumers Online' (15 February 2010) <www.beuc.eu/publications/2010-00101-01-e.pdf> (accessed 13 April 2019).

Blumenthal JA, 'Emotional Paternalism' (2007) 35 *Florida State University Law Review* 1.

Borgesius FJZ, 'Singling out People without Knowing Their Names – Behavioural Targeting, Pseudonymous Data, and the New Data Protection Regulation' (2016) 32 *Computer Law & Security Review* 256.

Bublitz C, 'Freedom of Thought in the Age of Neuroscience' (2014) 100 *Archives for Philosophy of Law and Social Philosophy* 1.

Calo R, 'Digital Market Manipulation' (2014) 82 *George Washington Law Review* 995.

Clifford D, 'EU Data Protection Law and Targeted Advertising: Consent and the Cookie Monster – Tracking the Crumbs of Online User Behaviour' (2014) 5 *Journal of Intellectual Property, Information Technology and Electronic Commerce Law* <www.jipitec.eu/issues/jipitec-5-3-2014/4095> (accessed 13 April 2019).

Clifford D and Ausloos J, 'Data Protection and the Role of Fairness' (2018) 37 *Yearbook of European Law* 130.

Clifford D and Verdoodt V, 'Integrative Advertising: The Marketing "Dark Side" or Merely the Emperor's New Clothes?' (2017) 8 *European Journal of Law and Technology* <http://ejlt.org/article/view/547> (accessed 13 April 2019).

Clifford D, Graef I and Valcke P, 'Pre-Formulated Declarations of Data Subject Consent – Citizen-Consumer Empowerment and the Alignment of Data, Consumer and Competition Law Protections' (2019) *German Law Journal* 20(5) 679–721.

Damasio AR, *Descartes' Error: Emotion, Reason and the Human Brain* (Quill 2004).

De Hert P and Papakonstantinou V, 'The Proposed Data Protection Regulation Replacing Directive 95/46/EC: A Sound System for the Protection of Individuals' (2012) 28 *Computer Law & Security Review* 130.

De Sousa R, *The Rationality of Emotion* (MIT Press 1987).

Edmans A, Garcia D and Norli Ø, 'Sports Sentiment and Stock Returns' (2007) 62 *Journal of Finance* 1967.

Ekman P and Davidson RJ, 'Why Emotions Are Felt' in Fox AS, Lapate RC, Shackman AJ and Davidson RJ (eds), *The Nature of Emotion: Fundamental Questions* (Oxford University Press 1994).

Erkin Z et al. 'Privacy-Preserving Emotion Detection for Crowd Management' *International Conference on Active Media Technology* (Springer 2014) <http://link.springer.com/chapter/10.1007/978-3-319-09912-5_30> (accessed 13 April 2019).

'Facebook's Emotion Tech: Patents Show New Ways for Detecting and Responding to Users' Feelings' (*CB Insights Research*, 1 June 2017) <https://www.cbinsights.com/research/facebook-emotion-patents-analysis/> (accessed 13 April 2019).

'Facebook Research Targeted Insecure Youth, Leaked Documents Show' (*The Independent*, 1 May 2017) <www.independent.co.uk/news/media/facebook-leaked-documents-research-targeted-insecure-youth-teenagers-vulnerable-moods-advertising-a7711551.html> (accessed 13 April 2019).

Ferretti F, 'Data Protection and the Legitimate Interest of Data Controllers: Much Ado about Nothing or the Winter of Rights?' (2014) 51 *Common Market Law Review* 843.

Forgas JP, 'Mood and Judgment: The Affect Infusion Model (AIM)' (1995) 117 *Psychological Bulletin* 39.

Fuster G, 'Beyond the GDPR, above the GDPR' (*Internet Policy Review*, 30 November 2015) <http://policyreview.info/articles/news/beyond-gdpr-above-gdpr/385> (accessed 13 April 2019).

Gellert R, 'Data Protection: A Risk Regulation? Between the Risk Management of Everything and the Precautionary Alternative' (2015) 5 *International Data Privacy Law* 3.

Gutwirth S, *Privacy and the Information Age* (translated by Raf Casert, Rowman & Littlefield 2002).

Hanson JD and Kysar DA, 'Taking Behavioralism Seriously: The Problem of Market Manipulation' (1999) 74 *New York University Law Review* 630.

Hanson JD and Kysar DA, 'Taking Behavioralism Seriously: Some Evidence of Market Manipulation' (1999) 12 *Harvard Law Review* 1420.

Hanson JD and Kysar DA, 'Taking Behavioralism Seriously: A Response to Market Manipulation' (2000) 6 *Roger Williams University Law Review* 259.

Helberger N, 'Form Matters: Informing Consumers Effectively' (University of Amsterdam, 2013–10) <http://papers.ssrn.com/abstract=2354988> (accessed 13 April 2019).

Hibbeln M et al., 'How Is Your User Feeling? Inferring Emotion through Human–Computer Interaction Devices' (2017) 41 *Management Information Systems Quarterly* 1.

Hoffman DA, 'The Best Puffery Article Ever' (2005) 91 *Iowa Law Review* 1395.

Hullett CR, 'The Impact of Mood on Persuasion: A Meta-Analysis' (2005) 32 *Communication Research* 423.

Hustinx P, 'EU Data Protection Law: Review of Directive 95/46 EC and the Proposed General Data Protection Regulation' <https://secure.edps.europa.eu/EDPSWEB/webdav/site/mySite/shared/Documents/EDPS/Publications/Speeches/2014/14-09-15_Article_EUI_EN.pdf> (accessed 13 April 2019).

Jay R, *Data Protection: Law and Practice* (Sweet & Maxwell 2012).

Jolls C, Sunstein CR and Thaler RH, 'A Behavioral Approach to Law and Economics' (1998) 50 *Stanford Law Review* 1471.

Kahan DM and Nussbaum MC, 'Two Conceptions of Emotion in Criminal Law' (1996) 96 *Columbia Law Review* 269.

Kaptein M, *Persuasion Profiling: How the Internet Knows What Makes You Tick* (Business Contact Publishers 2015).

Kindt EJ, 'Having Yes, Using No? About the New Legal Regime for Biometric Data' (2017) *Computer Law & Security Review* <http://linkinghub.elsevier.com/retrieve/pii/S0267364917303667> (accessed 13 April 2019).

Koops BJ, 'On Decision Transparency, or How to Enhance Data Protection after the Computational Turn' in Hildebrandt M and de Vries K (eds), *Privacy, Due Process and the Computational Turn: The Philosophy of Law meets the Philosophy of Technology* (Routledge 2013), pp. 196–220.

Koops BJ, 'The Trouble with European Data Protection Law' (2014) 4 *International Data Privacy Law* 250.

Kosta E, 'Unravelling Consent in European Data Protection Legislation a Prospective Study on Consent in Electronic Communications' (Doctoral thesis, University of Leuven 2011).

Kosta E, *Consent in European Data Protection Law* (Martinus Nijhoff 2014).

Lazaro C and Le Métayer D, 'Control over Personal Data: True Remedy or Fairytale?' (2015) 12 SCRIPTed <http://script-ed.org/?p=1927> (accessed 13 April 2019).

Lazarus RS *Emotion and Adaptation* (Oxford University Press 1994).

LeDoux JE, *The Emotional Brain: The Mysterious Underpinnings of Emotional Life* (Simon & Schuster 1996).

LeDoux JE and Brown R, 'A Higher-Order Theory of Emotional Consciousness' (2017) proceedings of the National Academy of Sciences 201619316.

Lerner JS et al., 'Emotion and Decision Making' (2015) 66 *Annual Review of Psychology* 799.

Levin S, 'Facebook Told Advertisers it can Identify Teens Feeling "Insecure" and "Worthless"' (*The Guardian*, 1 May 2017) <www.theguardian.com/technology/2017/may/01/facebook-advertising-data-insecure-teens> (accessed 13 April 2019).

Lewinski P, Trzaskowski J and Luzak J, 'Face and Emotion Recognition on Commercial Property under EU Data Protection Law' (2016) 33 *Psychology & Marketing* 729.

Lynskey O, 'Deconstructing Data Protection: The "Added-Value" of a Right to Data Protection in the EU Legal Order' (2014) 63 *International and Comparative Law Quarterly* 569.

Lynskey O, *The Foundations of EU Data Protection Law* (Oxford University Press 2016).

McStay A 'Empathic Media and Advertising: Industry, Policy, Legal and Citizen Perspectives (the Case for Intimacy)' (2016) 3 *Big Data & Society* 1.

McStay A 'Empathic Media: The Rise of Emotion in AI' (2017) ResearchGate <https://www.researchgate.net/publication/317616480_EMPATHIC_MEDIA_THE_RISE_OF_EMOTION_AI> (accessed 13 April 2019).

Mantelero A, 'Competitive Value of Data Protection: The Impact of Data Protection Regulation on Online Behaviour' (2013) 3 *International Data Privacy Law* 229.

Maroney TA, 'Law and Emotion: A Proposed Taxonomy of an Emerging Field' (2006) 30 *Law and Human Behavior* 119.

Mayer-Schonberger V and Cukier K, *Big Data: A Revolution That Will Transform How We Live, Work and Think* (Houghton Mifflin Harcourt 2013).

Nussbaum MC, *Upheavals of Thought: The Intelligence of Emotions* (Cambridge University Press 2003).

Nussbaum MC, *Hiding from Humanity: Disgust, Shame, and the Law* (Princeton University Press 2004).

Oostveen M and Irion K, 'The Golden Age of Personal Data: How to Regulate an Enabling Fundamental Right?' in M Bakhoum et al. (eds) *Personal Data in Competition, Consumer Protection and IP Law – Towards a Holistic Approach?* (Springer 2017) <https://papers.ssrn.com/abstract=2885701> (accessed 13 April 2019).

Percy L and Rossiter JR, 'A Model of Brand Awareness and Brand Attitude Advertising Strategies' (1992) 9 *Psychology & Marketing* 263.

Pillsbury SH, 'Emotional Justice: Moralizing the Passions of Criminal Punishment' (1988) 74 *Cornell Law Review* 655.

Poels K and Dewitte S, 'How to Capture the Heart? Reviewing 20 Years of Emotion Measurement in Advertising' (2006) 46 *Journal of Advertising Research* 18.

Posner EA, 'Law and the Emotions' (2001) 89 *Georgetown Law Journal* 1977.

Posner RA, *Regulation of Advertising by the FTC* (American Enterprise Institute for Public Policy Research 1973).

Potenza A, 'Google's US Search Results Will Let People Check if they're Depressed' (*The Verge*, 23 August 2017) <https://www.theverge.com/2017/8/23/16193236/google-depression-questionnaire-mental-health> (accessed 13 April 2019).

Ramsay I, *Consumer Law and Policy: Text and Materials on Regulating Consumer Markets* (Hart 2012).

Raz J, *The Morality of Freedom* (Clarendon Press 1986).

Reece AG and Danforth CM, 'Instagram Photos Reveal Predictive Markers of Depression' (2017) 6 *EPJ Data Science* <http://epjdatascience.springeropen.com/articles/10.1140/epjds/s13688-017-0110-z> (accessed 13 April 2019).

Reed Jr OL and Coalson Jr JL, 'Eighteenth-Century Legal Doctrine Meets Twentieth-Century Marketing Techniques: FTC Regulation of Emotionally Conditioning Advertising' (1976) 11 *Georgia Law Review* 733.

Rolland S, 'Comment les algorithmes revolutionnent l'industrie culturelle' (*La Tribune*, 19 November 2015) <https://www.latribune.fr/technos-medias/comment-les-algorithmes-revolutionnent-l-industrie-culturelle-523168.html> (accessed 13 April 2019).

Rouvroy A, 'The End(s) of Critique: Data Behaviourism versus Due Process' in Vries K and Hildebrandt M (eds), *Privacy, Due Process and the Computational Turn* (Routledge 2013).

Rouvroy A and Poullet Y, 'The Right to Informational Self-Determination and the Value of Self-Development: Reassessing the Importance of Privacy for Democracy' in Gutwirth S et al. (eds), *Reinventing Data Protection?* (Springer Netherlands 2009), pp. 68–9 <http://link.springer.com/10.1007/978-1-4020-9498-9> (accessed 13 April 2019).

Schwarz N and Clore G, 'Mood, Misattribution, and Judgments of Well-Being: Informative and Directive Functions of Affective States' (1983) 45 *Journal of Personality and Social Psychology* 513.

Simon H, *Reason in Human Affairs* (Stanford University Press 1990).

Solomon RC, *Not Passion's Slave: Emotions and Choice* (Oxford University Press 2007).

Solon O, '"This Oversteps a Boundary": Teenagers Perturbed by Facebook Surveillance' (*The Guardian*, 2 May 2017) <www.theguardian.com/technology/2017/may/02/facebook-surveillance-tech-ethics> (accessed 13 April 2019).

Spain E, *The Role of Emotions in Criminal Law Defences: Duress, Necessity and Lesser Evils* (Cambridge University Press 2011).

Stephens WO, 'Stoicism and the Philosophies of the Jedi and the Sith' (2014) 9 *The Stoic Philosopher* <https://dspace2.creighton.edu/xmlui/handle/10504/62183> (accessed 13 April 2019).

Strasser F, *Emotions, Experiences in Existential Psychotherapy and Life* (Duckworth 1999).

Sunstein CR, 'Nudging: A Very Short Guide' (2014) 37 *Journal of Consumer Policy* 583.

Sunstein, CR, 'Fifty Shades of Manipulation' (2015) *Journal of Behavioral Manipulation* <https://dash.harvard.edu/handle/1/16149947> (accessed 13 April 2019).

Verdoodt V, Clifford D and Lievens E, 'Toying with Children's Emotions, the New Game in Town? The Legality of Advergames in the EU' (2016) 32 *Computer Law & Security Review* 599.

Whittaker Z, 'Sonos Says Users Must Accept New Privacy Policy or Devices May "Cease to Function"' (*ZDNet*) <www.zdnet.com/article/sonos-accept-new-privacy-policy-speakers-cease-to-function/> (accessed 13 April 2019).

Willett C, 'Fairness and Consumer Decision Making under the Unfair Commercial Practices Directive' (2010) 33 *Journal of Consumer Policy* 247.

Zarsky TZ, 'Incompatible: The GDPR in the Age of Big Data' (2017) 47 *Seton Hall Law Review* 2.

Zhao M, Adib F and Katabi D, 'Emotion Recognition Using Wireless Signals' (ACM Press 2016) <http://dl.acm.org/citation.cfm?doid=2973750.2973762> (accessed 13 April 2019).

Zingales N, 'Between a Rock and Two Hard Places: WhatsApp at the Crossroad of Competition, Data Protection and Consumer Law' (2017) 33 *Computer Law & Security Review* 553.

5

Big Data Ethics: Darth Vader and the Green Cross Man

Miranda Mowbray

1. Introduction

What do the Green Cross Man, who helps children cross the road in 1970s road safety films,[1] and Darth Vader, lord of the dark side, have in common? The answer is that they were played by the same very tall actor, David Prowse. What do the Green Cross Man, Darth Vader and big data have in common? They're big. Big data analysis has great potential for improving lives, but is putting on a strain on the principles that underlie privacy laws. This chapter is about taming big data's scary Darth Vader-like aspects, to make it more like the helpful Green Cross Man.

One commonly used definition of big data is Gartner's, which does not set a minimum volume, but specifies them as 'high-volume, high-velocity and/or high-variety information assets that demand cost-effective, innovative forms of information processing for enhanced insight and decision making'.[2] The type of data analysis I had in mind when developing the code of practice was investigations, by teams of data scientists using dedicated analytic tools, of data sets including data about hundreds of thousands of individuals (or more).

The basis of the chapter is work that I have done with several teams on developing ethical guidelines for big data analysis. The sectors involved were high technology, health care, marketing and government; these are all sectors

---

[1] BBC News, 'The Green Force' (14 February 2006) <http://news.bbc.co.uk/1/hi/magazine/4690148.stm> (accessed 18 April 2019).

[2] Gartner Inc., 'Big Data' <https://www.gartner.com/it-glossary/big-data/> (accessed 18 April 2019).

in which big data analysis can play an important role. Like the Green Cross Man (who promoted the Green Cross Code for pedestrian safety), we aimed to improve others' safety through a code of practice. The content of this chapter was developed through discussions with many people, however it reflects my personal opinions, not necessarily those of anyone else involved. I did this work while employed in industry, at a US multinational company: my employer was one of the organisations involved.

A survey by Krista Bondy et al. of 390 codes of conduct for corporations[3] found that the most common reported voluntary motivations for the codes were as a guide for behaviour, or to formalise expected behaviours and commitments; to protect and enhance reputation, or to create and maintain trust and confidence with stakeholders; to have a consistent framework across a global network; and for various forms of compliance. Although the codes that the survey looked at were on more general topics than big data, these motivations are consistent with those reported by the organisations involved in the discussions on codes of practice for big data that I took part in. In particular, there was a belief that the trust and confidence of data subjects and consumers is crucial to the competitiveness of individual companies in industries that use big data heavily, as well as in the longer-term view to the viability of these industries as a whole. In addition, individuals involved in these discussions tended to believe that treating big data with care and respect for data subjects was simply the right thing to do, although corporate communications about this might focus on the economic benefits. A code of practice can assist in ensuring that an organisation behaves in an ethical and trustworthy way, and help communicate this to stakeholders. From my own perspective as a data scientist, I also found that having a code of practice with an established procedure made it simpler for me to conform to regulations and good practices relevant to a fast-evolving job. Codes of practice can be a useful complement to training, especially for employees who are not lawyers.

Ethical codes of practice are voluntary self-regulation, but potentially influence future law. It can be challenging for governments to design regulation for recent and rapidly developing technologies. It may be easier for practitioners than legislators to identify which big data practices are likely to be helpful for all stakeholders and which risk being counterproductive. Moreover, laws are (for good reasons) slower and more cumbersome to update than codes of practice. However, voluntary codes of practice are unlikely to be sufficient to ensure good practice by all organisations doing

---

[3] Bondy, Matten and Moon, 'Multinational Corporation Codes of Conduct: Governance Tools for Corporate Social Responsibility?' (2008) 16 *Corporate Governance: An International Review* 294.

big data analysis, precisely because they are voluntary. The organisations that have voluntarily adopted big data codes of practice believe that their advantages (particularly in terms of stakeholder trust) outweigh the cost of adoption, but this is not a universal belief. So it makes sense to view codes of practice as a complement to law rather than as a substitute for it. They are tools for easing compliance with existing law, and for supporting good practices that go beyond the law for the organisations that voluntarily adopt them; and they also allow the de-risking of potential future laws. The implementation of codes of practice can make it possible to demonstrate, to legislators concerned that putting restrictions on big data practices may stifle innovation and economic growth, that these concerns are unjustified (where they are unjustified). If a particular restriction relating to treating personal data respectfully and carefully has been voluntarily observed for a period of time by a number of successful organisations, this provides some evidence that making this restriction mandatory will not be harmful to the sector. On the contrary, by increasing trustworthiness, it may promote the sector's long-term viability.

For further discussion of different models of the interaction between codes of practice and law, and an argument that policy makers should explore co-regulation, in which government and industry share responsibility for drafting and enforcing standards, see Dennis Hirsch.[4]

Section 2 of this chapter gives recommendations. Later sections give more detailed discussion of some relevant issues, using the 1980 OECD data-processing principles[5] as an approximate structure. These principles are the basis for laws in many countries. From space considerations, not all 1980 OECD principles have a dedicated section.

The reason that these principles, rather than GDPR/EU principles, are used as an organising structure is that the commercial organisations involved in the discussions on codes of practice were interested in the global market rather than just Europe. (As already mentioned, one of them was a US multinational corporation, where I was employed during this work.) Of course, when a code of practice designed at the global level is implemented locally it is necessary to add detail to ensure good operation with the local environment, including compliance with local privacy laws, which can vary widely. Some skill is required to judge the right amount of discretion to

---

[4] Hirsch, 'The Law and Policy of Online Privacy: Regulation, Self-Regulation or Co-Regulation?' (2011) 34 *Seattle University Law Review* 439.

[5] Organisation for Economic Cooperation and Development, 'Recommendation of the Council concerning Guidelines on the Protection of Privacy and Transborder Flows of Personal Data' (OECD 1980).

leave to lower implementation levels: too much discretion may weaken its effectiveness and add to the administrative complexity for data analysis tasks involving more than one location, whereas too little discretion may result in it being impractical or impossible to implement in some local environment. I was fortunate to be talking with people who were experienced at the global policy level.

Big data analysis challenges the OECD principles of collection limitation and individual participation, by making consumer control of data even more problematic than before (section 3); of data quality, by making it less clear which data will be relevant (section 4); of purpose specification and use limitation, which has been described as antithetical to the very premise of big data (section 5); of openness, by the opacity of some analysis techniques (section 6); and of the accountability of data controllers to uphold these principles, for all of these reasons (section 2.2). It requires additional attention to the remaining principle, security safeguards, because of the potential scale of data breaches (section 2.6). All in all, it's about as friendly to these principles as Darth Vader was to the Federation.

2. Recommendations

In *The Clone Wars*,[6] Ahsoka Tano asks Anakin Skywalker (who will later become Darth Vader) what the plan is. When Anakin says that he thought Ahsoka was the one with a plan, Ahsoka replies that he's the one with enthusiasm.

This section says what the plan is: it gives recommendations for ethical big data analysis. These are not comprehensive. For instance, they focus more on the privacy of data subjects than on other issues or stakeholders, and they do not say anything about data collection practices, accuracy, commercial confidentiality or government surveillance.

Data protection by design is the concept of promoting data protection compliance right from the design of new systems or processes; and data protection by default is about ensuring that by default, personal data are processed with the highest privacy protection.[7] The recommendations are inspired by these concepts, although they are intended to go beyond legal compliance.

---

[6] Filoni (Director), *Star Wars: The Clone Wars*.

[7] For example, Information Commissioner's Office, 'Data Protection by Design and Default' <https://ico.org.uk/for-organisations/guide-to-the-general-data-protection-regulation-gdpr/accountability-and-governance/data-protection-by-design-and-default/> (accessed 18 April 2019).

2.1 Recommendation: Procedure

Before going ahead with a new type of big data analysis on personal data (and, if the analysis will use specially collected data, before collecting the data), teams using big data tools should discuss whether the analysis is ethical. It may be useful to involve someone outside the team to ensure diversity of perspective. Teams should consider the effects of different options on each type of stakeholder: stakeholder types should include data subjects, the organisation and society as a whole. These should be considered both from a rules/values-based ethical perspective (for example, 'Does this fit with our organization's policies and values? Is this the sort of organization we want to be? Is this legal? What would the world be like if everyone did this?'), and from an outcome-based ethical perspective ('How can we reduce risks of harm and increase benefits to all stakeholders? Does the overall risk to one type of stakeholders outweigh the benefit?'). The consideration of harm does not imply a ban on all analyses that harm a data subject (for example fraud detection may harm fraudsters); but teams could be especially careful about analysis that does not directly benefit the data subjects. Teams could apply the 'headline test': think of some media headlines that might be written about this analysis; would they make us look unethical? A short checklist of things to consider during this discussion may be useful. The team should record what type of analysis will be done, with what risk mitigations, along with reasons it is considered ethical if the discussion was not straightforward.

This procedure is based on DIODE.[8] The approach of considering effects on stakeholders from different ethical perspectives, rather than using one particular ethical perspective, is from DIODE and the Menlo Report.[9] The procedure was also influenced by Fred Cate[10] and, especially in the consideration of society as a whole as a stakeholder, by a particularly well-designed code of conduct from the Science Council of Japan.[11]

In addition to an ethical discussion before going ahead with a new type of analysis, if it becomes clearer during the course of the analysis what the application of the results will be, it may be useful to have another check

---

[8] Harris et al., 'Ethical Assessment of New Technologies: A Meta-Methodology' (2011) 8 Journal of Information, Communication and Ethics in Society 49.

[9] Bailey et al., 'The Menlo Report' (March/April 2012) IEEE Security & Privacy 71.

[10] Cate, 'The Failure of Fair Information Practice Principles' in Winn JK (ed.), *Consumer Protection in the Age of the 'Information Economy'* (Ashgate Publishing 2006), p. 370.

[11] Science Council of Japan, 'Statement: Code of Conduct for Scientists – Revised Version' (English translation, 25 January 2013) <www.scj.go.jp/en/report/Code_of_Conduct_for_Scientists-Revised_version.pdf> (accessed 18 April 2019).

before the application takes place. Decisions made for one analysis can be reused for other analyses of the same type; the danger that incremental small changes may add up to a large change is one that the assurance process could watch out for.

2.2 Recommendation: Assurance and Accountability

Teams making continued use of big data analysis tools should have an assurance process for their big data practices. This could be a periodic review of their practices by someone outside the team, during which ethical decisions and compliance to them can be checked and re-discussed if necessary. For example, this might be done by a joint big data ethics committee through which several teams in the same organisation check each other's practices. External review may be necessary at some level to avoid potential moral hazard when balancing the interests of the organisation against those of other stakeholders; and when large changes are considered, input from members of the public can be valuable. Senior leadership should communicate a policy for big data use consistent with the code, which should be part of mandatory data protection training for users of the big data analysis tools. Care should be taken that assurance processes do not impose too much red tape. Where the organisation has existing data accountability processes it is sensible to integrate with these.

2.3 Recommendation: Documentation and Logging

Tools should be configured and used in such a way that it is easy to determine what data sets are processed by whom, for what types of purpose, and subject to what use limitations. In some jurisdictions data subjects have rights of access, rectification, erasure, blocking, data portability, and/or the right to object to some uses of their personal data. (In the EU, all these rights apply.[12]) For data subjects to be able to exercise these rights, there need to be sufficient documentation and processes connected with the movement of personal data within an organisation to allow this. This may be challenging if there are complex decentralised movements of personal data that are not fully automated. To determine sensitivity, it is necessary to be able to identify when inferences considered sensitive to data subjects are made from non-sensitive data. Restrictions on the use or transfer of data should be easy for teams and data recipients to find out, and documented clearly, for instance with examples of what is allowed, what is not allowed and what is subject to

---

[12] European Commission, 'What Are My Rights?' <https://ec.europa.eu/info/law/law-topic/data-protection/reform/rights-citizens/my-rights/what-are-my-rights_en#reference> (accessed 18 April 2019).

discretion. Where it is practical, automated logging of accesses to and use of analysis tools may help with accountability, as may metadata describing the origin and use limitations of data. The default settings of tools should give the strongest data protection, for instance setting a data analyst's access to the lowest level. Overrides of these defaults could be recorded, with reasons.

2.4 Recommendation: Data Minimisation

Teams should try to ensure that inputs and final outputs of an analysis do not include or reveal personal data that are not necessary to achieve the purpose of the analysis. For instance it may be practical to do the analysis on de-identified data, or to de-identify the result before output, without affecting the quality of the result. Teams should have a data deletion policy. In addition, they could set a fixed or periodic date for reviewing the data and assessing whether it needs to be kept.

2.5 Recommendation: Restrictions on Re-identification

Deliberate re-identification of individuals or devices in de-identified data should be forbidden, except when data are de-identified in a deliberately reversible way, using pseudonymisation. In that case there should be governance rules, enforced with access control mechanisms, that restrict the people or automated processes allowed to re-identify subjects in the data set, and a ban on deliberate re-identification except in accordance with these rules. If a data analyst re-identifies a data subject accidentally, they should be required not to make use of this knowledge, and to report the issue so that if there is a risk that someone else will make the re-identification in the same way, steps can be taken (for instance, modification of the de-identified data) to guard against this happening. Contracts can be used to require recipients of de-identified data outside the organisation not to deliberately re-identify data subjects, and to follow the same process in the case of accidental re-identification.

2.6 Recommendation: Security

Security is a very important issue in big data use. All data should be appropriately protected based on their sensitivity, for example by encryption, in storage and transit. (As an aside, it should not be assumed that all communications metadata are of low sensitivity. In some cases, highly sensitive information can be deduced from such metadata.) Access to personal data via a big data analysis tool should be restricted to people who have a clear reason for accessing the data, using machines with adequate security safeguards. There could be separation of roles between granting or changing access permissions for a big data tool, and using the tool. More good practices from a technical point of view can be found in the Cloud Security Alliance's handbook for big data security and privacy.[13]

2.7 Recommendation: Very Harmful Uses

Organisations should maintain processes to avoid carrying out big data analyses likely to be used for very harmful discrimination, political oppression or human rights abuses. Organisations selling big data analysis tools and services should maintain processes to prevent the sale of these to a potential customer if there is a credible possibility that the customer would use the tools or services for such purposes.

2.8 Recommendation: Upstream and Downstream Considerations

The code of practice for use of big data analysis tools could be combined with considerations of the design of the tools in the first place, and of what happens after the analysis, requiring recipients of results from using the tools to maintain the standards described in the code.

3. Collection Limitation and Individual Participation

In a particularly dramatic scene of *Return of the Jedi*,[14] Darth Vader takes his helmet off and reveals his identity. This section is about data subjects' control over their data and identity.

3.1 OECD Principles

The principles of collection limitation and individual participation say that data should be collected where appropriate with the knowledge or consent of the data subject, and that the data subject has the right to access data about himself from a data controller and have it rectified, erased or blocked if it is incorrect.

3.2 Challenges to the Principles

Data protection law influenced by these two principles has focused on individuals' right to control their own personal information, via informed consent. Personal data are increasingly observed using sensors or derived using analysis rather than actively contributed by the data subject.[15] Informed

---

[13] Cloud Security Alliance, 'Big Data Security and Privacy Handbook: 100 Best Practices in Big Data Security and Privacy' <https://docs.google.com/document/d/1FqeHlA53sliNS3s d3ECy2hwyJu0UJDZT71zUs-02nX4/> (accessed 18 April 2019).

[14] Marquand (Director), *Star Wars: Episode VI – Return of the Jedi.*

[15] Abrams, 'The Origins of Personal Data and its Implications for Governance' (OECD Expert Roundtable Discussion, 21 March 2014) <http://informationaccountability.org/wp-content/uploads/Data-Origins-Abrams.pdf> (accessed 18 April 2019).

consent was already problematic before the rise of big data analysis, and has become even more difficult as this development has increased the variety of the types of personal data processed, the organisations processing them and the uses to which they are put.

3.3 Did I Really Consent to That?

As of early 2018, Facebook's options for advertisers included targeting people in a new relationship, men interested in men, expectant parents, friends of newly-weds, people likely to move house soon, African-Americans, politically active US liberals, donors to cancer charities and purchasers of anti-perspirants and deodorants. The ads could be targeted by age, gender, postal code, income, net worth, and size and age of house, amongst many other data points.[16] Some of these options were no longer offered by mid-2018, as a result of Facebook's no longer allowing advertisers to target Facebook users using data on offline behaviour collected by third-party data brokers; instead, only data collected online by Facebook (for instance, data about visits to external web pages containing a Facebook 'Like' or 'Share' button) could be used for targeting. However advertisers could still target all these audiences by using a combination of third-party and Facebook services.[17] Although Facebook's ad options have never been secret, it appears that some data subjects are even now unaware of the extent and level of detail of the data about them that is processed by Facebook (and other online ad networks, and offline data brokers). This is despite the spotlight shone on Facebook's business practices in mid-2018, via the Cambridge Analytica scandal.

In 2010, Facebook introduced the Open Graph API, which let app developers have access to data not only about users who signed up to their apps, but about these users' Facebook friends. Facebook signed a consent decree in the following year with the US Federal Trades Commission, agreeing not to share users' data with third parties without the users' express consent. However app developers still had access to data from users' Facebook friends by default in mid-2014, when Aleksandr Kogan, a researcher at Cambridge

---

[16] AdvertiseMint, 'The Complete Guide to Facebook Ad Targeting' (2018), *Infographics Archive* <https://www.infographicsarchive.com/seo-social-media/complete-guide-facebook-ad-targeting/> (accessed 18 April 2019).

[17] For instance, it was reported in 2017 that Oracle records over thirty thousand attributes on two billion consumer profiles, including income, net worth, and being an expectant parent. It may be that Oracle was the source of Facebook's ability to offer targeting for these particular attributes. Christl, 'Corporate Surveillance in Everyday Life' (2017) *Cracked Labs* <http://crackedlabs.org/en/corporate-surveillance> (accessed 18 April 2019).

University, started collecting data using a personality quiz app. Facebook stopped this type of access for app developers in 2015.

Aleksandr Kogan collected enough data to be able to match tens of millions of Facebook users to electoral roll data and derive psychological profiles for them, and sold the profiles to Cambridge Analytica, a political marketing company that was interested in using psychological data to manipulate voting behaviour, including in vote suppression campaigns. The number of users who had consented to Kogan's collection of their data by signing up to the app was only around 270,000. The extent of this data collection was reported in March 2018 by the *New York Times*[18] and the *Observer*.[19] Facebook claimed that Kogan had broken their rules by declaring that the data would be used for research, but then selling it for commercial/political purposes; Kogan denied breaking any Facebook rules. Between March and July 2018 Facebook made investments in security and privacy and several changes to their data use policies, in response to public outcry over this and other governance scandals. In the conference call for Facebook's second-quarter report, Facebook executives said that their investments in security would seriously impact Facebook's profitability, and that giving users more choices about data privacy was a factor leading to deceleration in revenue growth.[20] Facebook stock lost over $100 billion in market value in one day.

3.4 Mechanisms to Support Informed Consent

Almost nobody reads privacy policies. This is probably just as well: it was estimated in 2008 that if everyone read all the privacy policies for the websites they visited, this would cost 781 billion dollars a year in lost productivity.[21] There have been some attempts to enable individuals to manage their personal data in detail after collection. While these attempts have laudable intentions, this does not decrease the burden of personal data management: if anything, it increases it. Clearer wording of policies, machine-readable policies, privacy

---

[18] Rosenberg, Confessore and Cadwalladr, 'How Trump Consultants Exploited the Facebook Data of Millions' (17 March 2018) New York Times <https://www.nytimes.com/2018/03/17/us/politics/cambridge-analytica-trump-campaign.html> (accessed 18 April 2019).

[19] Cadwalladr and Graham-Harrison, 'Revealed: 50 Million Facebook Profiles Harvested for Cambridge Analytica in Major Data Breach' (*The Observer*, 17 March 2019) <https://www.theguardian.com/news/2018/mar/17/cambridge-analytica-facebook-influence-us-election> (accessed 18 April 2019).

[20] Facebook, 'Q2 2018 Earnings Conference Call Transcript' (25 July 2018) Motley Fool Transcription <https://www.fool.com/earnings/call-transcripts/2018/07/25/facebook-inc-fb-q2-2018-earnings-conference-call-t.aspx> (accessed 18 April 2019).

[21] McDonald and Cranor, 'The Cost of Reading Privacy Policies' (2008) 4 *I/S: A Journal of Law and Policy for the Information Society* 543.

certification organisations, policy standardisation, summaries and ratings of terms of service (such as the 'Terms of Service; Didn't Read' initiative at tosdr.org), use of visuals and icons, tools to explore outcomes of different choices,[22] and machine-readable, fine-grained preferences and permissions used in user-centric trust networks[23] are all good ideas, but they may not be sufficient for solving the problem. The uses made of big data are typically complicated, and it may be inherently difficult to give a clear description in sufficient detail for the subject (or their automated agent) to make an informed choice.

3.5 Suggestion

Consumer empowerment is a good thing. But decision-making by the data subject is increasingly difficult in this context. For this reason, and also because in some cases big data processing may have harmful outcomes for people other than data subjects, I suggest that the code of practice should forbid some kinds of processing even if the data subjects gave opt-in, informed consent to it.

4. Data Quality

In 'Cargo of Doom',[24] Anakin Skywalker returns from a mission without having either captured the 'Cargo of Doom' bounty hunter or recovered the holocron as planned. He says, however, that the mission was a success, because he won. This section challenges the notion that it is necessary to capture and hold on to personal data indefinitely in order to 'win' in innovative big data analysis.

4.1 OECD Principle

The data quality principle says, in part, that personal data should be relevant to the purposes for which they are used.

4.2 The Danger of Keeping Personal Data 'Just in Case'

The rise of big data analysis may lead to organisations keeping very large amounts of personal data for which they have no currently known use, in case

---

[22] Hildebrandt, 'The Dawn of a Critical Transparency Right for the Profiling Era' in Bus J et al. (eds), *Digital Enlightenment Yearbook* 2012 (IOS Press 2012), pp. 53–4.

[23] Cavoukian and Reed, 'Big Privacy: Bridging Personal Data and the Big Data Ecosystem through *Privacy by Design*' in Cavoukian A, *Privacy by Design: from Rhetoric to Reality* (Information and Privacy Commission of Canada 2013).

[24] Coleman, 'Cargo of Doom', television episode, *Star Wars: The Clone Wars* series 2 episode 2.

a use is found for them later. This brings a danger that general expectations of privacy will be eroded over time, and so will the legal protections that are a consequence of these expectations.

4.3 Innovation from Analysis of Data without Identifiers

Any de-identification or other alteration of data for privacy protection inevitably reduces what researchers can learn from the altered data, as preventing privacy-intruders from learning some particular fact from the data also prevents researchers from learning it.[25] However, it is not the case that innovative big data analysis requires the hoarding of personal data. When innovative insights are sought from personal data using big data analysis, a typical first step is to find the values of a large number of features for each data item or data subject, after which relationships between the features are investigated. These features are rarely personal identifiers or device identifiers. As a result, after feature values have been calculated the investigation can typically be done on de-identified data, as it uses feature values, not identifier values. Many impressive social and economic benefits of big data have resulted from analysis of data without personal identifiers. For example, Wal-Mart's inventory management system uses data about products rather than people. Analysis of de-identified mobile phone data from the Ivory Coast, in a data for development challenge, led to suggestions for transport rationalisation predicted to give a 10 per cent reduction in commuting time in a large city, and better strategies for containing country-wide epidemics, amongst other results.[26] The discoveries of the side-effects and interactions between several widely used pharmaceutical drugs through big data analysis were made by analysing de-identified or statistical data.[27]

4.4 Suggestions

Big data analysis tools could be configured to have the default behaviour of automatically deleting or de-identifying personal data items that have not been used for a specified length of time, or that have reached the age specified by the data deletion policy. Tools receiving structured data from third parties could be configured to automatically delete certain fields not needed for

---

[25] Wu, 'Defining Privacy and Utility in Data Sets' (2013) 84 *University of Colorado Law Review* 1117, p. 1137.

[26] Poole, 'Winning Research from the Data 4 Development Challenge' (United Nations Global Pulse, 6 May 2013) <www.unglobalpulse.org/D4D-Winning-Research> (accessed 18 April 2019).

[27] Tene and Polonetsky, 'Big Data for All: Privacy and User Control in the Age of Analytics' (2013) 11 *Northwestern Journal of Technology and Intellectual Property* 239, p. 245.

analysis. The code might recommend that teams seeking insights from personal data should first try on a de-identified or statistical version of the data, and only include identifiers in the input data if this first attempt has failed.

5. Purpose Specification and Use Limitation

In *The Empire Strikes Back*,[28] when Lando Calrissian expresses dissatisfaction at Darth Vader's broken promises, Darth Vader threatens to alter the deal even more. This section is about altering the deal, in the sense of processing data for a purpose that is a surprise to the data subject.

5.1 OECD Principles

The two principles of purpose specification and use limitation say that the purposes for which personal data are collected should be specified at or before collection, and that the data should not be used for incompatible purposes except by law or by consent of the data subject.

5.2 Data Maximisation

Omer Tene and Jules Polonetsky claim that use limitation and data minimisation are antithetical to big data analysis, because it is premised on the concept of data maximisation, the processing of as much data as possible.[29] This concept is in direct conflict with European privacy values. From an international point of view, to determine which data can be legally used, it is necessary to balance risks against the importance of the high-level purpose.

5.3 Suggestion

The first rule of the Data Ethics Framework of the UK government's Department for Digital, Culture, Media and Sport is 'Start with clear user need and public benefit'.[30] (For business analysis of customer data, the equivalent would be customer benefit.) Public workshops discussing a draft for this framework found the most important factor for members of the public was the purpose of the analysis. If they did not consider that the analysis would be effective in achieving a good purpose, they were reluctant for their data to be used at all, regardless of technical and procedural protections.

---

[28] Kirshner, *Star Wars: Episode V – The Empire Strikes Back*.
[29] Tene and Polonetsky, 'Big Data for All', p. 242.
[30] UK Department for Digital, Culture, Media & Sport, 'Data Ethics Framework' (13 June 2018) <https://www.gov.uk/government/publications/data-ethics-framework/data-ethics-framework> (accessed 18 April 2019).

6. Openness

A personality-test site has rated Darth Vader as having below average openness.[31] This section is about openness – however, in the sense of non-secrecy of big data processing, rather than personal openness to experience.

6.1 OECD Principle

The OECD openness principle requires openness about the existence and nature of personal data and practices connected with it.

6.2 Opaque Algorithms

Some of the techniques used in big data analysis derive the details of the algorithm used to analyse the data from big data sets themselves. For example, machine-learning techniques can be used to calculate which set of weights for many different features in a customer profile give the best prediction of whether the customer fits into a particular class, based on large samples of customers whose classification is known. A data scientist using this technique will not know in advance which of the features will be given high weight, and the algorithm does not provide any explanation of why a feature is correlated with membership of a particular class. The data scientist could tell someone who was wrongly classified what combination of features had led to their classification; however, if the algorithm is refreshed periodically using recent data, the features given high weight might be different tomorrow.

Opaque algorithms raise the possibility of unconscious harmful discrimination. For example, there may be a combination of features that has a high correlation with being a poor credit risk, and also with being a member of a particular ethnic minority. It may not be at all obvious that denying credit to people with this combination will disadvantage the ethnic minority.

6.3 Technical Barriers to Transparency to Data Subjects

The use of large data sets to derive algorithms limits how open it is possible to be about personal data even if data subjects have access to all the data concerning themselves. For instance, some types of data analytics tools can deduce, by analysing a large corpus of text by many authors, that the words 'a black and white flash jumped into the sea and returned with a fish in its beak' probably refer to a penguin.[32] The author of this phrase may not realise

---

[31] Arild, Gregersen, and Smith, 'Star Wars Big Five: Darth Vader' (26 January 2016) <https://www.idrlabs.com/articles/2016/01/star-wars-big-five-darth-vader/> (accessed 18 April 2019).

[32] Autonomy Inc., 'Transitioning to a New Era of Human Information' (Business White Paper, 2012) <www.frost.com/prod/servlet/cpo/270213756> (accessed 18 April 2019).

this, especially if the phrase actually referred to a guillemot, as the deduction depends on the statistical distributions of features in texts by other authors. This particular deduction is unlikely to have a negative impact for the author, but less benign examples can be imagined. It may be difficult to predict in advance which inferences will be made about data subjects. For example, an application might enable customer service agents to find authors of past messages relating to the currently top-trending service topic, which could be anything that customers become interested in.

Where it is feasible, a good way of improving accuracy and mitigating the consequences of inaccuracy is to give individuals some ability to rectify problems arising as a result of analysis of their data. However, it may not always be feasible. Individuals may not even realise that they have suffered some types of negative consequences (for instance, higher insurance premiums), and if they do, it may be impossible for them to tell that the analysis was inaccurate. It has been advocated that people who are subject to significant automated decisions based on predictive analysis should be given a right to third-party adjudication;[33] however the analysis may be opaque to the third party too.

6.4 Suggestions

Big data analysis can itself be used to identify and confirm instances of harmful discrimination in analyses,[34] although it may miss bias from unrepresentative or mislabelled training data.[35] Shadow analyses can be run to check whether particular groups are adversely affected. It is possible to design algorithms to practise positive discrimination. There is ongoing research into ways of making machine-learning algorithms less opaque; this is a topic of considerable theoretical and practical interest. As a final comment, the burden of checking that big data are used in an ethical way should not be placed entirely on the shoulders of the data subject.

7. Conclusion

Big data analysis brings two serious privacy-related dangers. First, we might lose all our privacy. Second, organisations might be so scared of doing

---

[33] See Citron and Pasquale, 'The Scored Society: Due Process for Automated Predictions' (2014) 89 *Washington Law Review* 1; Crawford and Schultz, 'Big Data and Due Process: Toward a Framework to Redress Predictive Privacy Harms' (2014) 55 *Boston College Law Review*, pp. 126–7.

[34] White House, 'Big Data: Seizing Opportunities, Preserving Values' (1 May 2014) <https://obamawhitehouse.archives.gov/sites/default/files/docs/big_data_privacy_report_may_1_2014.pdf> (accessed 18 April 2019).

[35] Barocas and Selbst, 'Big Data's Disparate Impact' (2016) 104 *California Law Review* 671.

something wrong privacy-wise that they do not carry out uses of big data that would considerably benefit individuals and society. With well-designed practices and regulations, I hope that we can avoid both dangers.

Acknowledgements

Thanks to Jacobo Esquenazi, Daniel Pradelles, Martin Abrams, Scott Taylor, Bill Horne, Martin Sadler, Susan Landau, Chiara Garattini, Ian Harris, Lilian Edwards, Jaap Suermondt, Jennifer Barrett-Glasgow, Hillary Wandall, Artemi Rallo, Cat Drew and everyone else whose ideas appear in this chapter.

References

Abrams M, 'The Origins of Personal Data and its Implications for Governance' (OECD Expert Roundtable Discussion, 21 March 2014) <http://information accountability.org/wp-content/uploads/Data-Origins-Abrams.pdf> (accessed 18 April 2019).

AdvertiseMint, 'The Complete Guide to Facebook Ad Targeting' (2018), *Infographics Archive* <https://www.infographicsarchive.com/seo-social-media/complete-gui de-facebook-ad-targeting/> (accessed 18 April 2019).

Arild S, Gregersen E and Smith R, 'Star Wars Big Five: Darth Vader' (26 January 2016) <https://www.idrlabs.com/articles/2016/01/star-wars-big-five-darth-vad er/> (accessed 18 April 2019).

Autonomy Inc., 'Transitioning to a New Era of Human Information' (Business White Paper, 2012) <www.frost.com/prod/servlet/cpo/270213756> (accessed 18 April 2019).

Bailey M et al., 'The Menlo Report' (March/April 2012) *IEEE Security & Privacy* 71.

Barocas S and Selbst AD, 'Big Data's Disparate Impact' (2016) 104 *California Law Review* 671.

BBC News, 'The Green Force' (14 February 2006) <http://news.bbc.co.uk/1/hi/ magazine/4690148.stm> (accessed 18 April 2019).

Bondy K, Matten D and Moon J, 'Multinational Corporation Codes of Conduct: Governance Tools for Corporate Social Responsibility?' (2008) 16 *Corporate Governance: An International Review* 294.

Cadwalladr C and Graham-Harrison E, 'Revealed: 50 Million Facebook Profiles Harvested for Cambridge Analytica in Major Data Breach' (*The Observer*, 17 March 2019) <https://www.theguardian.com/news/2018/mar/17/cambridge-analytica-facebook-influence-us-election> (accessed 18 April 2019).

Cate FH, 'The Failure of Fair Information Practice Principles' in Winn JK (ed.), *Consumer Protection in the Age of the 'Information Economy'* (Ashgate Publishing 2006).

Cavoukian A and Reed D, 'Big Privacy: Bridging Personal Data and the Big Data Ecosystem through *Privacy by Design*' in Cavoukian A, *Privacy by Design: from Rhetoric to Reality* (Information and Privacy Commission of Canada 2013).

Christl W, 'Corporate Surveillance in Everyday Life' (2017) *Cracked Labs* <http:// crackedlabs.org/en/corporate-surveillance> (accessed 18 April 2019).

Citron D and Pasquale F, 'The Scored Society: Due Process for Automated Predictions' (2014) 89 *Washington Law Review* 1.

Cloud Security Alliance, 'Big Data Security and Privacy Handbook: 100 Best Practices in Big Data Security and Privacy' <https://docs.google.com/document/d/1FqeH lA53sliNS3sd3ECy2hwyJu0UJDZT71zUs-02nX4/> (accessed 18 April 2019).

Coleman R (Director) 'Cargo of Doom', television episode, *Star Wars: The Clone Wars*, series 2 episode 2, USA: Lucasfilm (2009).

Crawford K and Schultz J, 'Big Data and Due Process: Toward a Framework to Redress Predictive Privacy Harms' (2014) 55 *Boston College Law Review*.

European Commission, 'What Are My Rights?' <https://ec.europa.eu/info/law/law-topic/data-protection/reform/rights-citizens/my-rights/what-are-my-rights_en#reference> (accessed 18 April 2019).

Facebook, 'Q2 2018 Earnings Conference Call Transcript' (25 July 2018) Motley Fool Transcription <https://www.fool.com/earnings/call-transcripts/2018/07/25/facebook-inc-fb-q2-2018-earnings-conference-call-t.aspx> (accessed 18 April 2019).

Filoni D (Director), *Star Wars: The Clone Wars*, film, USA: Lucasfilm (2008).

Gartner Inc., 'Big Data' <https://www.gartner.com/it-glossary/big-data/> (accessed 18 April 2019).

Harris I et al., 'Ethical Assessment of New Technologies: A Meta-Methodology' (2011) 8 *Journal of Information, Communication and Ethics in Society* 49.

Hildebrandt M, 'The Dawn of a Critical Transparency Right for the Profiling Era' in Bus J et al. (eds), *Digital Enlightenment Yearbook* 2012 (IOS Press 2012).

Hirsch D, 'The Law and Policy of Online Privacy: Regulation, Self-Regulation or Co-Regulation?' (2011) 34 *Seattle University Law Review* 439.

Information Commissioner's Office, 'Data Protection by Design and Default' <https://ico.org.uk/for-organisations/guide-to-the-general-data-protection-regulation-gdpr/accountability-and-governance/data-protection-by-design-and-default/> (accessed 18 April 2019).

Kirshner I (Director), *Star Wars: Episode V – The Empire Strikes Back*, film, USA: Lucasfilm (1980).

McDonald AM and Cranor LF, 'The Cost of Reading Privacy Policies' (2008) 4 *I/S: A Journal of Law and Policy for the Information Society* 543.

Marquand R (Director), *Star Wars: Episode VI – Return of the Jedi*, film, USA: Lucasfilm (1983).

Organisation for Economic Cooperation and Development, 'Recommendation of the Council concerning Guidelines on the Protection of Privacy and Transborder Flows of Personal Data' (OECD 1980).

Poole J, 'Winning Research from the Data 4 Development Challenge' (United Nations Global Pulse, 6 May 2013) <www.unglobalpulse.org/D4D-Winning-Research> (accessed 18 April 2019).

Rosenberg M, Confessore N and Cadwalladr C, 'How Trump Consultants Exploited the Facebook Data of Millions' (17 March 2018) *New York Times* <https://www.nytimes.com/2018/03/17/us/politics/cambridge-analytica-trump-campaign.html> (accessed 18 April 2019).

Science Council of Japan, 'Statement: Code of Conduct for Scientists – Revised Version' (English translation, 25 January 2013) <www.scj.go.jp/en/report/Code_of_Conduct_for_Scientists-Revised_version.pdf> (accessed 18 April 2019).

Tene O and Polonetsky J, 'Big Data for All: Privacy and User Control in the Age of

Analytics' (2013) 11 *Northwestern Journal of Technology and Intellectual Property* 239.

UK Department for Digital, Culture, Media & Sport, 'Data Ethics Framework' (13 June 2018) <https://www.gov.uk/government/publications/data-ethics-framework/data-ethics-framework> (accessed 18 April 2019).

White House, 'Big Data: Seizing Opportunities, Preserving Values' (1 May 2014) <https://obamawhitehouse.archives.gov/sites/default/files/docs/big_data_priv acy_report_may_1_2014.pdf> (accessed 18 April 2019).

Wu FT, 'Defining Privacy and Utility in Data Sets' (2013) 84 *University of Colorado Law Review* 1117.

6

Security Vulnerabilities, Backdoors, Exploits and the Marketplace for Each:
The Return of Boba Fett – Bug Bounty Hunter in the New Republic

Alana Maurushat and Rob Hamper

Unbeknownst to his arch-enemy Hans Solo, Boba Fett survived from the jaws of the Sarlacc in the Galactic Republic. Boba was the most feared bounty hunter in the Galaxy, and one of the most popular characters in the entire Star Wars universe. He remains determined to take down Hans Solo. Having incurred multiple irreversible wounds from the jaws of the Sarlacc, Boba took five years to make a partial recovery. While his upper torso was kept intact, he remains paralysed from the waist down. He has had three failed cyborg surgeries to connect his body with robotic limbs. He has vowed to take revenge and has been silently plotting to take Hans Solo and the Republic Army down. He is not his former physical self. His superior warrior and fighting skills are no more. He must find a new way to revenge against Hans Solo and to survive economically in his new surroundings on the expensive planet Norbiac.

Determined to succeed, Boba has been studying night and day for the past five years learning how to hack into network systems. Much to his surprise, Boba is a natural. As someone who is incapable of anything but full mastery of a discipline, he knows that to succeed he will have to study the art of war, cryptography, security vulnerabilities and exploits. He begins by starting with a chapter in the book *Future Technologies* from the planet Earth, published in 2018. He chuckles at the thought of what measly humans with known inferior knowledge would have thought of as futuristic in the year 2018. But he knows that in order to succeed at his revenge, he will need to understand humans and how their marketplace for bug bounties and security vulnerabilities started. Earth is still the planet where corporations pay the most amount of money for zero-day exploits, vulnerabilities and bug bounties. He begins with a chapter by Alana Maurushat and Rob Hamper, 'Security Vulnerabilities, Backdoors, Exploits and the Marketplace for Each'.

Apple v *FBI* made waves in the media with panels sprouting globally to address this novel tension between technologies designed to protect privacy and security, and law enforcement's desire and need to break them to access data. The problem with this characterisation is that it is not novel. The battle between secret code makers, code breakers and enforcement agencies has been a reoccurring theme commencing with Julius Caesar, coming to the forefront in World War II, reappearing in the early 1970s climaxing in the early 1990s with the Clipper Chip, and making a comeback post 9/11 and resurfacing yet again after the Paris and San Bernardino terrorist attacks. To understand *Apple* v *FBI* one has to understand the fifty-plus years of cryptography wars, vulnerability and backdoor markets, and the political tension that takes place between industry and governments' access to data not only in the United States, but nearly on a global basis. As will be seen, the FBI was able to crack the encryption on the Apple phone through the purchase of a security vulnerability. This chapter has the modest aim of discussing security vulnerabilities and backdoors and explores the marketplace for both.

The first part of the chapter addresses key terms that are followed by setting the technical context and background. The next part addresses security vulnerability markets. Next we look at the use of backdoors. Finally, applicable international legislation is considered followed by a discussion of whether there needs to be appropriate regulatory constraints of vulnerability markets and backdoor usages.

1. Key Terms and Technical Context

The following definitions provide a background to understanding the nature of vulnerabilities:

- *Vulnerability*: In this context, a software vulnerability is a weakness in a computer system that can be exploited by an attacker.[1] The vulnerability may exist as a concept or idea and need not necessarily be embodied in software.
- *Exploit*: An exploit is the implementation, in software, of a vulnerability.

---

[1] While definitions vary depending on the specific context and author, the most common two elements in the definition of a vulnerability are a weakness that can be exploited. See, for instance, International Standard (ISO/IEC) 27000 – Information Technology – Security Techniques – Information Security Management Systems – Overview and Vocabulary at 2.81, which defines a vulnerability, in a broader information security context, as the 'weakness of an asset … that can be exploited by one or more threats'.

- *Weaponised exploit*: This is an exploit that has been implemented in software to cause harm – for instance, to modify, delete or copy data or to make a system unavailable. These broadly map to the three pillars of information security known as CIA – confidentiality, integrity and availability. That is, the ability to keep information secret or known only to those intended, to ensure that information is in the form that is intended and, finally, to ensure that access to the information remains uninterrupted. A weaponised exploit may be implemented or instantiated as a worm, virus or other malware.
- *Virus*: A virus is a piece of malicious software code that attaches itself to executable files that requires execution, normally by a user, to run – it typically does not exploit vulnerability in software. When executed the virus tries to replicate itself into other executable code; when it succeeds, the code is said to be infected.[2]
- *Worm*: In contrast to a virus, a worm is self-replicating and replicates by exploiting vulnerabilities.
- *Zero day*: This is an exploit or vulnerability that is exploited against a target on the day on which public awareness of the existence of the vulnerability occurs (that is, zero days have elapsed since between the awareness and the use). These vulnerabilities are typically considered to be the most valuable as the utility and value of an exploit or vulnerability markedly decreases once it is known, as vendors produce patches or users reconfigure their systems to ameliorate the effect of the vulnerability.[3]
- *Backdoor* is a method of accessing a computer program or network that circumvents security mechanisms. Sometimes a programmer will install a backdoor so that the programmer (or company that the programmer works for) can access the program to perform security patches, trouble shoot, or monitor use. Attackers, however, can also use backdoors that they discover (or install themselves) as part of an exploit. A worm or virus may be designed to take advantage of an existing backdoor.[4]
- *Rootkits* are software or hardware devices designed to gain administrator-level control and sustain such control over a computer system without

---

[2] Aycock, *Computer Viruses and Malware* (Springer 2006).

[3] See, for instance, Oremus, 'Java Zero-day expLoit: Don't Patch, Just Disable Java in Your Browser' (*Slate*, 14 January 2013) <www.slate.com/blogs/future_tense/2013/01/14/java_zero_day_exploit_don_t_patch_just_disable_java_in_your_browser.html> (accessed 18 April 2019).

[4] Rouse, 'Definition: Back Door' *TechTarget*, June 2007 <http://searchsecurity.techtarget.com/definition/back-door> (accessed 18 April 2019).

being detected.[5] A rootkit is used to obscure the operation of malware or a botnet from monitoring and investigation. It could also be considered a type of backdoor.

Boba Fett yawns and thinks, 'these lawyer human types sure love their footnotes. Hard to believe there was a time when humans and creatures didn't know about such simple things, like a 'rootkit.' Thinking about the term ('root' and 'kit') he laughs out loud, remembering that Australian humans used 'to root' to mean 'to have sex'. He wonders how many Australian humans thought rootkit was a package of sex toys.

The main difference between a security vulnerability and a backdoor is one of intention. Vulnerabilities are accidental occurrences as the result of writing computer code. Backdoors are deliberately coded into a program. Their effects, however, are both the same – vulnerabilities and backdoors may be used for cyber-attacks, for surveillance and for bypassing security parameters.

1.1 Technical Context

It is useful to examine the technical context and background under which the development of the market for software vulnerabilities has occurred and how the new and unprecedented consequences of their use has developed.

1.1.1 Persistent Connectivity

The use of computing devices reliant upon increasingly complex software in our everyday lives has expanded hugely over the past decade, as demonstrated through the now ubiquitous 'smartphone' and tablets, which were expected by Gartner to overtake PCs as the most common device to access the web in 2013.[6]

As our use of these devices increases to a state of persistent connectivity, so too does our reliance on them in going about our everyday lives and for the ongoing function of the economy more broadly.

Ensuring these systems are secure and operate in an error-free fashion is a key concern for governments, corporations and individuals. The World Economic Forum, held in Davos during January 2013, recognised the

---

[5] Pfleeger and Pfleeger, *Security in Computing* (4th edn, Prentice Hall 2006), pp. 145–7.

[6] Gartner Press Release, 'Gartner Identifies the Top 10 Strategic Technology Trends for 2013' (*Gartner*, 23 October 2012) <www.gartner.com/newsroom/id/2209615> (accessed 18 April 2019).

'increasing dependence on connectivity for the normal functioning of society' and that the 'cyber risk landscape evolves rapidly'.[7]

This increased reliance has been matched by an increase in the complexity of the software underlying these systems, their potential vulnerability and the spoils for those that can successfully exploit these vulnerabilities for purposes as diverse as cyberwar, identity theft, financial fraud, market manipulation, spam propagation, politically motivated attacks and commercial espionage.

1.1.2 Cloud + Mobile + Complexity

A number of technology trends further increase the risk profile of vulnerable software. First, the paradigmatic shift to cloud-based services over locally hosted software broadens both the range of potential attacks and the consequence for a successful breach. For example, the penetration of Sony's PlayStation Network in 2011, discussed further below, compromised the personal details of some 77 million users.

Similarly, the current range of smartphones contain a bewildering array of sensors and storage capabilities including multiple high-resolution cameras, GPS, accelerometers, microphones, WiFi, 3/4G and up to sixty-four gigabytes of local storage. These capabilities and wide connectivity options make them an attractive target for exploitation by parties of varying motives.

The creation of secure computing environments is made more difficult by the increasing complexity of modern software. For instance, a modern operating system contains mind-boggling complexity and is of a vast scale – for example, a recent version of Apple's Mac OS X[8] contains 86 million lines of code. It is thought that there are errors made in each thousand lines of code produced – estimates of the number of defects vary depending on the nature of the product but are in the order of 0.44 to 0.75 errors per one thousand lines.[9] While each defect is not necessarily a vulnerability that can be exploited, these technological trends combine to present a timely opportunity for research into a holistic approach to consider ways that security and reliability of cyber infrastructure may be improved.

---

[7] World Economic Forum, 'Partnering for Cyber Resilience' (19 March 2015) <www3. weforum.org/docs/WEF_IT_PartneringCyberResilience_Guidelines_2012.pdf> (accessed 18 April 2019).

[8] Block, 'Live from WWDC 2006: Steve Jobs Keynote' (*Engadget*, 7 August 2006) <www. engadget.com/2006/08/07/live-from-wwdc-2006-steve-jobs-keynote/> (accessed 18 April 2019).

[9] Koetsier, '450M Lines of Code Say Large Open Source Projects and Small Closed Source Software Projects Are Worst Quality' (*Venturebeat*, 9 May 2013) <http://venturebeat.com/2013/05/09/450-million-lines-of-code-say-large-open-source-and-small-closed-source-software-projects-are-worst-quality/> (accessed 18 April 2019).

A final aspect regarding the technical context to vulnerabilities is the competitive market pressure on vendors to innovate and release the latest version of software with the latest features and functionality as quickly as possible, while ensuring it is backwards-compatible with all previous versions. Consequently, particularly in consumer devices, this may mean that security is not considered a central or critical function. The incremental and iterative nature of the software development lifecycle may also lead to outdated and potentially vulnerable code remaining in software for many years.

Skimming the page, Boba glances over IoT and laughs at the joke his great, great grandfather used to tell him:
'What does IoT stand for?'
'Idiots on Tinder'
Boba never did understand that joke well, even after it was explained. But the memory of his great, great grandfather always makes him smile.

1.2 Internet of Things (IoT)

The IoT refers to the connection of any device to a network. This may include fridges, baby monitors, coffee makers, wearable devices, wheelchairs, thermostats and components of machines. The analyst firm Gartner estimates that there will be over 26 billion connected devices by 2020.[10] IoT allows for endless connections of devices to networks opening the doors to many challenges, risks and opportunities. Security is one of the greatest challenges.

IoT is inherently insecure. At the annual hacker conference at DEF CON, forty-seven new vulnerabilities were revealed in IoT products.[11] While security vulnerabilities are expected in products, IoT or others, many IoT products come with outdated software, and software that is no longer supported.[12] This means that any security vulnerability in the device cannot be automatically patched. As more devices connect to networks, more security vulnerabilities are on offer to be exploited.

---

[10] Gartner Press Release, 'Gartner Says the Internet of Thigs Installed Base Will Grow to 26 Billion Units by 2020' (*Gartner*, 12 December 2013) <www.gartner.com/newsroom/id/2636073> (accessed 18 April 2019).

[11] Constantin, 'Hackers Found 47 New Vulnerabilities in 23 IoT Devices at DEF CON: The Results of This Year's IoT Hacking Contest Are In and It's Not a Pretty Picture' (CSO, 13 September 2016) <www.csoonline.com/article/3119765/security/hackers-found-47-new-vulnerabilities-in-23-iot-devices-at-def-con.html> (accessed 18 April 2019).

[12] Stefanovic, 'IoT Device Security: Problems and Recommendations' (PACE, 24 November 2016) <https://pacetoday.com.au/iot-security-problems-recommendations/> (accessed 18 April 2019).

Boba pauses again, remembering how obsessed humans used to be with IoT. He remembers reading about a challenge where hackers were teamed up with IoT suppliers and had a competition where they produced IoT *Star Wars* items. It was then that the first Star Wars Droid Helmut was produced. The helmets allowed humans to speak droid to one another, but the humans wearing the helmets could still understand one another as things were translated into the English language. Boba remembers his Great Uncle Weebart releasing the retro helmet on Earth a few decades prior, reaping quite the profit.

2. Security Vulnerability Markets

2.1 Background

The market for software vulnerabilities has undergone several evolutions. Historically significant software vulnerabilities have been disclosed publicly by security researchers – typically by publication or presentation at conferences such as BlackHat, which is held annually in Las Vegas, or online. While such disclosures continue, the rate of decline appears to have lessened, perhaps partially in response to the actions of software vendors, set out below, which has had a chilling effect on such activity.

Subsequently, in recognition of the potential for publicly disclosed vulnerabilities to be exploited before a software vendor has had an opportunity to fix the vulnerability, a model of responsible disclosure emerged.[13] While debate around the effectiveness of public *versus* responsible disclosure continues, the model of responsible disclosure would postpone public disclosure of a vulnerability until a software vendor had been provided an opportunity to fix it. There is much debate around the period of time a security researcher should allow the vendor to fix the vulnerability and other related elements.

The debate around vulnerabilities centres on the persistent tension around the level and nature of disclosure of public vulnerabilities, and recognises that 'the same information that allows more widespread exploitation of vulnerabilities is required to correct those vulnerabilities'.[14] This dual-use aspect pervades many of the ethical and legal considerations around the operation of the markets and the discussion of responsible disclosure:

---

[13] Typically, responsible disclosure would postpone public disclosure of a vulnerability until a software vendor has had the opportunity to fix it. There is much debate around how much time a security researcher should allow a vendor to fix the vulnerability and other related elements.

[14] Granick, 'Legal Risks of Vulnerability Disclosure' *Centre for Internet & Society* <www.black hat.com/presentations/bh-asia-03/bh-asia-03-granick.pdf> (accessed 18 April 2019).

> Responsible vulnerability disclosure addresses how a vulnerability identifier
> should disclose vulnerability information to appropriate people, at appro-
> priate times, and through appropriate channels in order to minimise the
> social loss associated with vulnerabilities.[15]

The growing commercial trade in vulnerabilities suggests that the principles of responsible disclosure have been and continue to be, in many cases,
ignored. An empirical study of the factors that underlie such changes has not
been conducted.

The market version that prevails today in which vulnerabilities are discovered, bought and sold by a wide range of participants with a variety of
motives for a huge range of prices is somewhat chaotic. Vulnerabilities are
acquired for a variety of purposes from improving security to cyber warfare,
'hacktivism', espionage, surveillance, cyber espionage, commercial advantage,
law enforcement and cyber crime. While bright-line differentiators do not
mark each stage of development of this market, available data and commentary indicate distinct evidence of underlying trends.

While there has been much debate in the field around responsible disclosure, the market, which has acted to substantially subsume the responsible
disclosure debate,[16] has developed particularly fast over recent years. This
development has resulted in the emergence of many companies dedicated to
the discovery, broking and sale of vulnerabilities, markedly altering the landscape. Further, to the extent that prior research has been conducted, the field
is likely to be found to have moved on significantly since then, as we outline.
In the next section we discuss the key categories of market participants related
to this development.

Boba stops, rubs his robotic transplant eye and starts to read about market
participants. He thinks, 'how boring it must have been back then with only creatures from Earth and none of the other planets … Humans can be dreadfully
dull at times.'

2.2 Market Participants

There are a number of participants in the market for software vulnerabilities,
often with conflicting goals, that operate across all points of the spectrum
from legitimate to criminal.

---

[15] Cabusoglu et al., 'Emerging Issues in Responsible Vulnerability Disclosure' *Infosecon*
<www.infosecon.net/workshop/pdf/65.pdf> (accessed 18 April 2019).

[16] Maurushat, *Disclosure of Security Vulnerabilities: Legal and Ethical Issues* (University of
Ottawa Press 2017).

At the highest level, participants evident in the market currently, each of which is discussed further below, include software vendors, security researchers, governments, hacktivists and criminals.

2.2.1 Software Vendors

Software vendors have a commercial incentive to ensure their software is reliable and bug free, and may offer a bounty for vulnerabilities disclosed[17] in their software or, alternately, may act aggressively to prevent disclosure using a variety of legal measures (further discussed below). The No More Free Bugs initiatives list thirty such bug bounty programs[18] currently in operation. In a similar vein a recent start-up, BugCrowd,[19] acts as an administrator of bug bounty programs on behalf of users of software and web-based applications. While certain vendors offer rewards for disclosed vulnerabilities many vendors have taken an adversarial position against individuals who reveal vulnerabilities in their products.

Historically, many vulnerabilities were disclosed publicly in order to provide both the incentive and opportunity for the vendor to fix them and for the discoverer to build credibility amongst the peer community of like-minded individuals. This community discovery has been recognised as a form of peer production,[20] a phenomenon that is apparent elsewhere in the technology sphere, particularly open source software and the creation of communities that have built services such as Wikipedia. It has been similarly described as 'crowd-sourcing' of security vulnerability research.

2.2.2 Security Researchers

Security researchers or bug hunters operate in the market in a variety of ways, including those that will (1) publicly release vulnerabilities in order to build credibility, reputation or out of a sense of altruism or similar; (2) sell vulnerabilities based on certain ethical guidelines (for example, Netragard, who will only sell to US purchasers who have been 'rigorously vetted'[21]) – there

---

[17] See, for instance, Google's bounty program <www.google.com/about/appsecurity/reward-program/>.

[18] Available at: <www.blog.nibblesec.org/2011/10/no-more-free-bugs-initiatives.html> (accessed 18 April 2019). Notes on file with authors.

[19] See <www.bugcrowd.com> (accessed 18 April 2019).

[20] Benkler, *The Wealth of Networks: How Social Production Transforms Markets and Freedom* (Yale University Press 2006) <www.benkler.org/Benkler_Wealth_Of_Networks.pdf> (accessed 18 April 2019).

[21] Gallagher, 'Cyberwar's Gray Market' (*Slate*, 16 January 2013) <www.slate.com/articles/technology/future_tense/2013/01/zero_day_exploits_should_the_hacker_gray_market_be_regulated.html> (accessed 18 April 2019).

has been no academic analysis of the strength of these measures, the process by which decisions applying these guidelines are reached or what effect the choice of such measures has; and (3) sell to the highest bidder including foreign nations that are either friend or foe, domestic intelligence agencies and criminal networks.

2.2.3 Intermediaries

The market for software vulnerabilities is fast developing, with a number of dedicated start-ups, including some in receipt of venture capital funding, now offering to purchase vulnerabilities under various programs such as the Netragard's 'zero-day exploit acquisition program'.[22]

Others, such as the controversial Vupen, will sell such vulnerabilities to customers, rather than publicly release them.[23] Vupen are selling exploits to a group of customers as opposed to exclusive sales. In the case of Vupen, the exploits are sold to governments (of the NATO alliance) around the world.[24] The company has been described as the 'Jersey Shore of the exploit trade', 'ethically challenged opportunists' and 'modern-day merchant of death', selling 'the bullets for cyberwar'.[25] Vupen sells state-of-the-art intrusion methods for software (and some hardware), where customers (typically governments) pay a subscription fee for a range of techniques made available for them to then utilise for whatever purpose they have in mind. For this reason, some industry players have compared them to arms dealers.[26] Vupen claims to do all its own research and development and does not purchase exploits. The founder of Vupen, Chaouki Bekrar, has now launched a new security vulnerability company, Zerodium, which buys 'high-risk vulnerabilities with fully functional and reliable exploits'.[27] The price list/catalogue lists an exploit for Apple iOS 10 for up to $1,500,000 USD to as low as $5, 000 for low-end zero-day exploits.[28] Vupen originally claimed only to sell to governments of democratic countries. Zerodium states that 'Zerodium solutions and capabilities is highly restricted and is only avail-

---

[22] Available at: <www.netragard.com/zero-day-exploit-acquisition-program> (accessed 18 April 2019).

[23] Greenberg, 'Meet the Hackers Who Sell Spies the Tools to Crack Your PC (And Get Paid Six-Figure Fees)' (*Forbes*, 21 March 2006) <www.forbes.com/sites/andygreenberg/2012/03/21/meet-the-hackers-who-sell-spies-the-tools-to-crack-your-pc-and-get-paid-six-figure-fees/> (accessed 18 April 2019).

[24] Ibid.

[25] Quotes from industry leaders in Greenberg, ibid.

[26] Greenberg, ibid.

[27] See <www.zerodium.com/program.html> (accessed 18 April 2019).

[28] Ibid.

able to a limited number of organisations'.[29] What types of organisations is not stated.

The market for vulnerabilities is currently not the subject of legal regulation, resulting in a huge variation in price depending on the ethics (and other factors) of those selling them.

2.2.4 Governments

There are several recent examples of government's participation in the market for software vulnerabilities and their application of exploits for a variety of purposes. We examine a few of these incidences below.

2.2.5 Cyber Warfare

The emergence of sophisticated worms developed by nation states, such as the now infamous Stuxnet[30] worm, which relied upon four unreleased 'zero-day' software vulnerabilities to exploit Iran's uranium-refining centrifuge industrial control systems, elegantly demonstrate the conflicting aims of government in dealing with software vulnerabilities and their inherent dual-use nature.

The Stuxnet worm was the first publicly known use of cyber warfare to cause physical harm – that is, the physical outcome was the destruction of uranium-refining centrifuges, in contrast to previous cyber-attacks whose effect was limited to damaging computer systems or the denial of service to them.

The demonstrated sophistication and unprecedented impact of the Stuxnet worm is a key exemplar in one of the factors underlying the explosion in the market and price of undisclosed or zero-day vulnerabilities with Forbes,[31] reporting that hackers are being paid up to $250,000 for each zero-day software exploit (in that particular case, purchased by a defence contractor). Recently, the Chief Security Officer of anti-virus and security vendor TrendMicro stated that the US Government had paid USD$2M for the vulnerabilities that were exploited in the Stuxnet worm.[32]

It has been suggested that this chaotic market may even incentivise

---

[29] Available at: <www.zerodium.com/about.html> (accessed 18 April 2019).

[30] Falliere et al., 'Symantec Security Response: W32.Stuxnet Dossier' Symantec Corporation, February 2011 <www.symantec.com/content/en/us/enterprise/media/security_response/whitepapers/w32_stuxnet_dossier.pdf> (accessed 18 April 2019).

[31] Schneier, 'The Vulnerabilities Market and the Future of Security' (*Forbes*, 30 May 2012) <www.forbes.com/sites/bruceschneier/2012/05/30/the-vulnerabilities-market-and-the-future-of-security/#35d47ee17763> (accessed 18 April 2019).

[32] This figure is unverified. Stated at the Trend Micro Evolve Security event held at Sheraton on the Park Sydney, 14 May 2013, at which I was an attendee.

developers to leave vulnerabilities in software that they develop, and then to sell them to a government agency or private entity.[33]

This conflicting role and application of government policy to the market in software vulnerabilities is demonstrated by the fact that, on the one hand governments are incentivised to acquire, discover and exploit software vulnerabilities as part of the cyber arms race and to deploy them against their enemies as a 'cyber weapon'.[34] On the other hand, they have a broader interest to ensure that their own infrastructure, and those of its citizens, are as safe from attack as possible.

The latter aim is often achieved through wide dissemination of known vulnerabilities to vendors and the IT community to allow the systems to be patched, while the former relies on the secrecy of the vulnerability to ensure the target systems remain available to be exploited. An effective regulatory environment needs to balance these two competing priorities to maximise public benefit.

While the international law implications of Stuxnet have been researched and discussed by others,[35] there appears to be less useful research into the effect of governments' participation in the market for vulnerabilities and the consequences of such participation. While complete data regarding the extent to which governments participate in the market is not currently available, it was revealed in September 2013, as a result of disclosures made by Edward Snowden – a rogue NSA employee – that the NSA alone spent USD$25 million in 2012 on purchasing software vulnerabilities from third parties; the use to which they were put was not stated.[36]

2.2.6 Cyber Espionage

The APT1 (Advanced Persistent Threat) report by American computer security firm Mandiant[37] revealed the extent to which Chinese government-sponsored

---

[33] Schneier, 'The Vulnerabilities Market and the Future of Security'.

[34] Diamond, 'The Cyber Arms Trade: Opportunities and Threats in Software Vulnerability Markets' Sigma Iota Rho, *Journal of International Relations* <www.sirjournal.org/2012/12/11/the-cyber-arms-trade-opportunities-and-threats-in-software-vulnerability-markets/> (accessed 18 April 2019).

[35] See, for instance, Richardson, 'Stuxnet as Cyberwarfare: Applying the Law of War to the Virtual Battlefield' (*JMR Portfolio Intelligence*, 22 July 2011) <http://ssrn.com/abstract=1892888> (accessed 18 April 2019); Richmond, 'Evolving Battlefields: Does Stuxnet Demonstrate a Need for Modifications to the Law of Armed Conflict?' (2012) 35 *Fordham International Law Journal* 842, pp. 842–3.

[36] Tung, 'NSA Tops Up Exploit Pool with $25m in "Grey Market" Vulnerabilities' (*CSO*, 2 September 2013) <www.cso.com.au/article/525241/nsa_tops_up_exploit_pool_25m_grey_market_vulnerabilities_/> (accessed 18 April 2019).

espionage,[37] believed to be conducted by a unit of the People's Liberation Army (PLA), compromises organisations and steals data across many industries. It is believed that APT1 (referring to the PLA unit) has 'systematically stolen hundreds of terabytes of data from at least 141 organisations',[38] and consists of 'hundreds, perhaps thousands, of individuals'.[39]

While data are not available regarding the source of the vulnerabilities that are used to affect such attacks, in the case of the Chinese threat, the breadth of the threat is a significant indicator of the negative effect to which vulnerabilities can be put and the changing context in which they are being deployed.

2.2.7 Law Enforcement

There has been recent discussion regarding the exploitation of software vulnerabilities as a potentially useful and lawful basis for surveillance to be undertaken by government agencies in the United States.[40] Many nations including Germany and Australia allow targeted surveillance via remote access on devices outside of a jurisdiction, subject, of course, to national safeguard frameworks such as the Constitution. The UK likewise allows for 'targeted equipment interference' under the Investigatory Powers Act. These frameworks don't, however, specifically address the purchase of or use of vulnerabilities and exploits to perform surveillance.

It is suggested that this may ameliorate the concerns of law enforcement and others that the transition to purely internet-based systems from traditional wired, switched networks will make previous surveillance capabilities obsolete and allow criminals to hide all their communications – referred to as 'going dark'.

While clandestine agencies such as the NSA retain significant ability to exploit signal intelligence, or 'sigint', as recent revelations by Snowden have revealed, these capabilities are classified and available to very few. It may be argued that retaining a lawful basis for the exploitation of software vulnerabilities may be beneficial to society in reducing crime and fulfilling legitimate law enforcement purposes.

Conversely, the reasonably held concerns regarding loss of privacy and the increased risk of vulnerabilities that are known to government but not

---

[37] See Fire-Eye, 'Exposing One of China's Cyber Espionage' <http://intelreport.mandiant.com/Mandiant_APT1_Report.pdf> (accessed 18 April 2019).

[38] Ibid.

[39] Ibid.

[40] Bellovin et al., 'Lawful Hacking: Using Existing Vulnerabilities for Wiretapping on the Internet' Privacy Legal Scholars Conference June 2013.

reported to vendors and patched, being discovered and being used by criminals and others with mischievous intent cannot be ignored.

Similarly, the use of vulnerabilities by the NSA, who spent USD$25 million purchasing vulnerabilities in 2012,[41] may be argued to provide public benefit by allowing the NSA to fulfil its Charter to protect US citizens and US allies from national security threats, but this must be balanced against the risk that the failure to use known vulnerabilities to patch the systems of citizens, governments and industry exposes them to attack from those with ill intent.

Apple v *FBI* exemplifies some of the challenges in the area. After the San Bernardino terrorist shootings, the FBI needed to access the perpetrator's iPhone. The iPhone 5C contains sophisticated encryption with no ability for Apple to decrypt the phone. Specifically, the FBI sought the ability to circumvent the 'auto-erase function' on the iPhone, which after ten unsuccessful password entries destroys the encryption keys. Apple refused to cooperate with the investigation. The FBI ended up dropping the lawsuit, and it is reported that the FBI paid approximately $1 million USD for the purchase of a zero-day exploit allowing a third party to get into the locked iPhone.[42]

2.2.8 Other Market Participants – Criminals, Hacktivists, Business

Other participants in the marketplace include criminals who will purchase and use exploits for a range of criminal purposes including fraud, identity theft, IP theft and ransomware – a form of malware that restricts use of the infected system until the creator is paid a fee for it to be removed.[43] We list a sample of screenshots obtained from research of criminal dark net forums. The following is a vulnerability for Android discovered by French nuclear engineer researcher Robin David, who posted the discovery to GitHub.

The vulnerability was posted onto the Dark Net forum Hackerhound and then later distributed as an exploit. See Figures 6.2 and 6.3 below:

A publicly disclosed vulnerability, as seen above, was turned into an exploit for Android. The Andro-RAT can be used to infiltrate a device for

[41] Fung, 'The NSA Hacks Other Countries by Buying Millions of Dollars' Worth of Computer Vulnerabilities' (*Washington Post*, 31 August 2013) <www.washingtonpost.com/blogs/the-switch/wp/2013/08/31/the-nsa-hacks-other-countries-by-buying-millions-of-dollars-worth-of-computer-vulnerabilities/> (accessed 18 April 2019).

[42] Zetter, 'FBI Hints It Paid Hackers $1 Million to get into San Bernardino iPhone' (*Wired*, 21 November 2016) <https://www.wired.com/2016/04/fbi-hints-paid-hackers-1-million-get-san-bernardino-iphone/> (accessed 18 April 2019).

[43] Stevenson, 'Darkleech Campaign Targets Java to Spread Reveton Ransomware' (*v3*, 17 September 2013) <www.v3.co.uk/v3-uk/news/2295107/darkleech-campaign-targets-java-to-spread-reveton-ransomware> (accessed 18 April 2019).

GitHub Listing of Android Rat

Code:

The name Androrat is a mix of Android and RAT (Remote Access Tool). It has been developed in a team of 4 for a university project. It has been realised in one month. The goal of the application is to give the control of the system remotely and retrieve informations from it.

<u>Features</u>
* <u>Get contacts (and all theirs informations)</u>
* <u>Get call logs</u>
* <u>Get all messages</u>
* <u>Location by GPS/Network</u>
* <u>Monitoring received messages in live</u>
* <u>Monitoring phone state in live (call received, call sent, call missed.)</u>
* <u>Take a picture from the camera</u>
* <u>Stream sound from microphone (or other sources.)</u>
* <u>Streaming video (for activity based client only)</u>
* <u>Do a toast</u>
* <u>Send a text message</u>
* <u>Give call</u>
* <u>Open an URL in the default browser</u>
* <u>Do vibrate the phone</u>

Credits to Robin David (https[://]www[.]soldierx.com[/]hdb[/]Robin-David)
Download the source code here:
Github – https[://]github[.]com[/]DesignativeDave[/]androrat

Figure 6.1 GitHub Listing of Andro-RAT. Credit: Robin David.

---

i HH,,,, i introduce Andro-RAT its a rat coded in JAVA for Android OS Credits: RobinDavid some pics it has great functions like taking shoots from cam and viewing callers,,,,,, etc. You can download src from github: Link all the best,,, enjoy Attached Files androrat-master.zip 3.44MB 128 downloads Edited by x58, 24 May 2014-04:06 PM. attached & link updated

---

Figure 6.2 Discussion of Andro-RAT Vulnerability on Hackerhound

use in a number of ways but most likely as a method to capture valuable information, and then later to perform surveillance for a highly targeted payment diversion fraud. Once a fraud is committed the Dark Net then provides many methods of money-laundering including the purchase of gold, altering bitcoin and other. Sample screenshots of these methods are found below.

'Hacktivist' groups, such as Anonymous, have been seen to exploit vulnerabilities to further their political or social agenda, though there is no

- Theft of mobile network information, storage capacity, rooted or not
- Theft of list of installed applications
- Theft of web browsing history from pre-installed browsers
- Theft of calendar events
- Record calls
- Upload files to victim device
- Use front camera to capture high resolution photos
- Delete and send forged SMS
- Screen capture
- Shell command execution
- T heft of WiFi passwords
- Enabling accessibility services for a key logger silently

Figure 6.3   The New Capabilities of the Exploit Derived from Andro-RAT

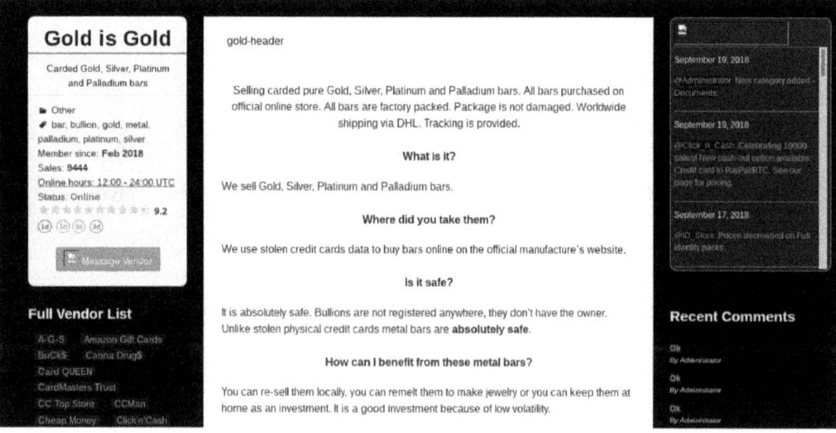

Figure 6.4   Sample Screenshots

evidence that these vulnerabilities were purchased[44] – such as the attack on the security company HB Garry, who were investigating Anonymous' activities and intended to present them at a security conference whose systems were attacked and compromised.[45] Media coverage of similar events does not discuss whether vulnerabilities and exploits were purchased or whether the members used vulnerabilities and exploits that they had discovered on their

---

[44] Maurushat, *Ethical Hacking* (University of Ottawa Press 2017).

[45] Menn, ' "Hacktivists" Retaliate against Security Expert' (*Financial Times*, 7 February 2011) <www.ft.com/cms/s/0/0c9ff214-32e3-11e0-9a61-00144feabdc0.html> (accessed 18 April 2019).

own. The latter would require an expert level of cybersecurity skills. In this instance, in particular it is not known whether an exploit was discovered by members within Anonymous or whether it was acquired via a third party.[46]

Finally, businesses may purchase vulnerabilities in order to patch or reconfigure and protect their systems.

Boba stops and thinks about just how mature the market has become for vulnerabilities. A zero day now fetches upwards of $1 trillion Galactic Credit Standard, or approximately $10 million Peggats on the planet Tatooine.

3. Backdoors and Encryption Keys

3.1 Background

Recall that a backdoor is a method of accessing a computer program or network that circumvents security mechanisms. The main difference between a security vulnerability and a backdoor is one of intention. Vulnerabilities are accidental occurrences as the result of writing computer code. Backdoors are deliberately coded into a program. The effects of vulnerabilities and backdoors, however, are both the same – they may be used for cyber-attacks, surveillance and bypassing security parameters.

A common backdoor method is through cryptography and the holding of encryption keys. Cryptography is the science of secret writing. Cryptography comes from the Greek word *kryptos*, meaning hidden.[47] Traditionally, cryptography was the exclusive domain of the government and military, but came into the sphere of commerce and academia with the advent of commercialisation of computer technology in the 1970s.[48] Much cryptography uses what is known as encryption and decryption. The process of encryption involves converting a readable message into unintelligible data. Decryption is the reverse procedure, taking the unintelligible data and constructing the original message. These procedures are made possible through keys. Each user deploys his or her key in order to encrypt or decrypt a message and keeps his or her key private. This is an overly simplistic explanation of encryption keys but will suffice for the purpose of studying encryption as a backdoor.

Encryption can be used as a backdoor when an organisation possesses

---

[46] Maurushat, *Ethical Hacking*, Chapter 3. The author studied hacking dark markets, where it was revealed that vulnerabilities were being discussed and traded between parties, some of which appeared to be related to ethical hacking.

[47] Singh, *The Code Book* (Doubleday 1999), p. 6.

[48] Levy, *Crypto: How the Code Rebels Beat the Government Saving Privacy in the Digital Age* (Viking 2001).

a public key, or a master key, that allows communications to be decrypted, thereby circumventing the security features on a device or application. As will be seen below, there are diverse market participants who use backdoors, and unlock encryption for a multitude of purposes.

3.2 Market Participants

3.2.1 Software and Hardware Vendors

There is no shortage of examples of software and hardware vendors placing backdoors in products. For example, DSL gateway hardware produced by Sercomm had manufacturer-added a backdoor on port 32764.[49] The company later patched the backdoor (TCP 32764 is found in many routers including Netgear and Cisco), but then it was later discovered that Sercomm added the same backdoor, only in a slightly different way.[50] There is speculation that the backdoor was put there by an intelligence agency. Some vendors implement backdoors to manage the interaction of the product.

3.2.2 Businesses

One of the most disturbing instances of placing a rootkit in a product involved Sony BMG in 2006. Sony secretly (not in the terms of use) installed Extended Copy Protection (XCP) onto CDs. XCP was a rootkit that monitored and reported what users did with the CD, including making copies (burning CDs).[51] The rootkit was undetectable by anti-virus software and received much criticism in the media and especially amongst hackers.

3.2.3 Security Researchers

Normally, security researchers spend their time finding security vulnerabilities and backdoors, not making them. There are, of course, some exceptions. Researchers at the University of Michigan recently developed an invisible backdoor that is built into a slice of a computer chip hardware (a thousandth of the width of human hair). This is not a hidden backdoor but, rather, a

---

[49] Yegulalp, 'The 12 Biggest, Baddest, Boldest Software Backdoors of All Time' (*InfoWorld*, 12 June 2014) <www.infoworld.com/article/2606776/hacking/155947-Biggest-baddest-boldest-software-backdoors-of-all-time.html#slide3> (accessed 18 April 2019).

[50] Khandelwal, 'Routers TCP 32764 Backdoor Vulnerability Secretly Re-Activated Again' (*Hacker News*, 20 April 2014) <http://thehackernews.com/2014/04/router-manufacturers-secretly-added-tcp.html> (accessed 18 April 2019).

[51] Brown, 'Sony BMG Rootkit Scandal: 10 Years Later' (*Network World*, 28 October 2015) <www.networkworld.com/article/2998251/malware-cybercrime/sony-bmg-rootkit-scandal-10-years-later.html> (accessed 18 April 2019).

modification to hardware. Because the backdoor is on the hard drive, there are no security software programs triggered. The research was done as a proof of concept and won best paper at the IEEE Symposium on Privacy and Security.[52]

3.2.4 Government

There are several recent examples of government participation in the market for backdoors and rootkits.

3.2.5 Law Enforcement

In 2012, Ragebooter, a DDOS 'testing service', came to surface. The company offered customers the ability to test how robust their systems were in relation to DDOS attacks. It goes without saying that the primary objective of the site is less focused around testing and more geared to attack.

Justin Poland is the man responsible for the creation of the site, but he too has questionable intentions. In 2013, Brian Krebs investigated the legality of the service being offered by Poland, uncovering some interesting findings. One of these was that Poland had links with the FBI through backdoor IP log-in accounts:

> They allow me to continue this business and have full access. The FBI also
> use the site so that they can moniter [sic] the activitys [sic] of online users.
> They even added a nice IP logger that logs the users IP when they log in.

This begs the question, how many more sites similar to Ragebooter are actually controlled by government entities? Further, how is it that a company such as Ragebooter can operate unimpeded by authority, which knows of its existence? Arguably, this also implicates organisations such as the FBI in attacks that have previously taken place. In 2013, Ragebooter was processing up to four hundred DDOS attacks per day, essentially four hundred government-sponsored DDOS attacks per day.

3.2.6 Intelligence

With the Edward Snowden leaks, there has been an explosion of published backdoors used by the National Security Agency (NSA). Developed by the NSA, Dual Elliptic Curve Deterministic Random Bit Generator (Dual_EC_DRBC) is a cyber security standard both in the American National Standards Institute and the International Organisation for Standardisation. In essence

---

[52] Greenberg, 'This "Demonically Clever" Backdoor Hides in a Tiny Slice of a Computer Chip' (*Wired*, 1 June 2016) <https://www.wired.com/2016/06/demonically-clever-backdoor-hides-inside-computer-chip/> (accessed 18 April 2019).

Dual_EC_DRBC is considered an effective form of public key cryptography. Two controversies have arisen with the standard.

RSA use of Dual_EC_DRBG was one of the first reported incidences of a backdoor into software. RSA were offered two products that relied on the Dual_EC_DRBG number generator.

Several aspects here suggested that RSA were working in conjunction with the NSA to coordinate the existence of a backdoor in their products. The first was that three employees were members of ANSI X9F1 Tool Standards and Guidelines Group, which ultimately brought up the notion that Dual_EC_DRBG contained a backdoor that could be exploited by the creators of the security system.[53] This was in the early 2000s, before Dual_EC_DRBG was ever implemented within an RSA security product.

Second, in 2006, RSA's use of the generator was cited in the calls for inclusion in the NIST SP 800-90A, potentially suggesting that RSA were acting at the will of the NSA in order to gain wider support for the use of Dual_EC_DRBG.

Most recently, and perhaps most obviously, in 2004 (reported in 2013), RSA Security received $10 million from the NSA to set Dual_EC_DRBG as the default number generator in their products.[54]

The NSA's Tailored Access Operations is an elite group of hackers who use a variety of exploits and backdoors to achieve access to a device or system. A list of hardware with backdoors is provided in the NSA Toolbox Catalog, including Cisco routers and products from Dell and Huawei.[55]

3.3 Criminals and Hacktivists

There are many examples of criminals gaining access to backdoors, and creating backdoors and rootkits in systems. Since Sony's outing of using hidden rootkits in 2006, the corporation has been a favourite destination of attack by hackers. In 2014 the hacking group 'Guardians of Peace' released personal and confidential emails from employees of Sony Pictures. This is commonly referred to as the Sony North Korea incident, as the attack was allegedly in response to the release of the movie *The Interview*, a parody of North Korea's

---

[53] Green, 'A Few More Notes on NSA Random Number Generators' (Cryptography Engineering Blog, 28 December 2013) <https://blog.cryptographyengineering.com/2013/12/28/a-few-more-notes-on-nsa-random-number/> (accessed 18 April 2019).

[54] Menn, 'Exclusive: Secret Contract Tied NSA and Security Industry Pioneer' (Reuters, 20 December 2013) <www.reuters.com/article/us-usa-security-rsa-idUSBRE9BJ1C220131220> (accessed 18 April 2019).

[55] Appelbaum et al., 'Catalog Advertises NSA Toolbox' (*Der Spiegel*, 29 December 2013) <www.spiegel.de/international/world/catalog-reveals-nsa-has-back-doors-for-numerous-devices-a-940994.html> (accessed 18 April 2019).

leader Kim Jong-un. Security experts have stated that the group had been accessing a backdoor for at least a year prior in Sony's system (it is thought that the backdoor was used in addition to a listening implant, proxy tool, destructive cleaning tool and destructive hard drive tool).[56]

Boba's upper lip stiffens as he reads 'international framework'. Like any international framework has helped the Galaxy. It has only been since the authoritarian dictatorship of Darth Vader that the Galaxy has been run as efficiently as it should. Because of this dictatorship and the rebellion, Boba has made a small fortune – all of which was gambled away by his son when he thought his father was dead. Boba thinks about Hans Solo with a hatred building up in his head and heart. He calms himself then continues to read.

4. International Framework

Few nations, and neither the US nor Australia, impose legal sanctions that specifically restrict or regulate the trade in software vulnerabilities. While criminal sanctions may apply to the unauthorised access, modification or impairment to a computer[57] (and equivalent acts in other jurisdictions), such acts are related to the application of a weaponised exploit, rather than the sale of a vulnerability itself.

The only criminal law decision that clearly addresses the role of ethical hacking and security vulnerability disclosure is the United Kingdom 2012 decision against Glenn Mangham. In *R* v *Mangham*,[58] Glenn Mangham was charged with three counts of unauthorised access and modification of a computer, but was convicted of two counts under the Computer Misuse Act 1990. He was sentenced initially to eight months' imprisonment by the Southwark Crown Court. Later the Court of Appeal Criminal Division reduced the sentence from eight months to four months due to a lack of malicious intent.[59] Glenn Mangham, a university software development student, took advantage of a vulnerability to penetrate Facebook's firewall. Once Mangham discovered the vulnerability in Facebook's network system,

---

[56] Lennon, 'Hackers Used Sophisticated SMB Worm Tool to Attack Sony' (*Security Week*, 19 December 2014) <www.securityweek.com/hackers-used-sophisticated-smb-worm-tool-attack-sony> (accessed 18 April 2019).

[57] See, for instance, Division 476 of the Criminal Code Act 1995 (Cth).

[58] The decision was given in the Southwark Crown Court on 17 February 2012. The decision is not itself reported. Information was obtained through media stories. See BBC, 'York Facebook Hacking Student Glenn Mangham Jailed' (17 February 2012) <https://www.bbc.co.uk/news/uk-england-york-north-yorkshire-17079853> (accessed 30 June 2019).

[59] *Mangham* v *R*, Court of Appeal Criminal Division, EWCA, 4 April 2012.

he continued to probe deeper in Facebook's network and at one point had downloaded a copy of Facebook's source code. Prosecutor Sandip Patel stated to the media that Mangham, 'acted with determination, undoubted ingenuity and it was sophisticated, it was calculating', that he stole 'invaluable' intellectual property and that the attack 'represents the most extensive and grave incident of social media hacking to be brought before the British courts'.[60] Mangham issued a lengthy public statement regarding the affair in which he describes himself as an ethical hacker who had been awarded a fee previously for finding other security vulnerabilities within Yahoo![61] While Mangham takes responsibility for his actions in his statement, he makes a number of claims that he feels should have been taken into account. In the past, companies such as Yahoo! had paid Mangham for security vulnerability discovery. Mangham had a history of ethical security vulnerability disclosure. He did not use proxies or anonymisers to shield his identity when discovering vulnerabilities, as his intention was never to use the information for commercial gain. In fact, Mangham had a history of rejected fees for vulnerability discovery.

This case is potentially interesting for those who disclose security vulnerabilities on a number of grounds. The first is that had Mangham used an anonymiser and proxy server, he could have sold the vulnerability to a security vulnerability company with impunity. There is no legal requirement for security vulnerability companies such as Zerodium to verify whether a vulnerability has been discovered by breaking the law – virtually all forms of hacking require breaking the law.

The study of such criminal sanctions for the use of exploits is not central to this chapter but does form part of the legal context in which considerations regarding regulation may occur given that the potential end-use may have significant consequences.

It is useful for further context to note that, unlike most other nations, German law, as an outlier, does regulate the trade in 'hacker tools' that may include a vulnerability, or tools that may be used to discover vulnerabilities, such as a toolkit known as 'MetaSploit', which is used in penetration testing of computer systems and to 'verify vulnerabilities and manage security assess-

[60] Protalinkski, 'British Student Jailed for Hacking into Facebook' (*Zdnet*, 18 February 2012) <www.zdnet.com/blog/facebook/british-student-jailed-for-hacking-into-facebook/9244> (accessed 18 April 2019).

[61] Mangham, 'The Facebook Hack: What Really Happened' (GMangham Blog, 23 April 2012) <http://gmangham.blogspot.co.uk/2012/04/facebook-hack-what-really-happened.html> (accessed 18 April 2019).

ments'.[62] Article 202(c) of the German Criminal Code was enacted in 2007, criminalising many hacker tools. At the time, many famous vulnerability discovery experts, including the famous HD Moore who created Metasploit, were very concerned, professing that they weren't going to take any chances and publicly announcing that they would stay out of Germany altogether.[63] However, these concerns were largely dismissed when in 2008 a German prosecutor refused to prosecute a security researcher using Metasploit, as there was no intention to aid the commission of a criminal offence.[64] Concern about this criminal provision, however, has not been alleviated amongst researchers. Security research websites and blogs are still replete with cautionary tales of Metasploit and German law – the 2008 decision is clearly not known in the wider security landscape.[65]

4.1 Tallinn Manual

The *Tallinn Manual on the International Law Applicable to Cyber Warfare*, commissioned by the NATO Cooperative Cyber Defence Centre of Excellence, while not formally representing the views of NATO members, is an important analysis undertaken by leading academics regarding the application of principles of international law in the cyber context and attempts to 'apply standards of international law to a virtual battlefield'.[66]

The *Tallinn Manual* considers, amongst other things, the application of the rules of international law to situations including the use of worms such as Stuxnet or other cyber-based attacks, and the circumstances in which development and use of malware or cyber operations could be considered a use of force under international law or could justify anticipatory self-defence or armed response.

The *Tallinn Manual* provides useful analysis of the way in which vulnerabilities may be exploited, but does not relate directly to the trade in such vulnerabilities and backdoors, only their ultimate application.

---

[62] Available at: <http:// www.metasploit.com/> (accessed 18 April 2019).

[63] Schneier B (2007), 'New German Hacking Law' (Schneier on Security, 28 August 2007) <https://www.schneier.com/blog/archives/2007/08/new_german_hack.html> (accessed 20 August 2018).

[64] The Decision is only available in German. Verfassungsbeschwerden geges 202c Abs 1 Nr. 2 StGB. Available at: <https://www.bundesverfassungsgericht.de/SharedDocs/Pressemitteilungen/DE/2009/bvg09-067.html;jsessionid=BC04673B69E54AC3A63836EA0C91590A.2_cid383> (accessed 18 April 2019).

[65] See <http://insidetrust.blogspot.com/search?q=german> (accessed 18 April 2019).

[66] *Tallinn Manual on the International Law Applicable to Cyber Warfare* (Council for Foreign Relations, 28 March 2013) <www.cfr.org/cybersecurity/tallinn-manual-international-law-applicable-cyber-warfare/p30415> (accessed 18 April 2019).

4.2 Convention on Cybercrime

The Budapest Convention on Cybercrime, an international treaty adopted by the Council of Europe in November 2001, and since ratified or signed by a total of fifty-one states[67] aims to 'deter action directed against the confidentiality, integrity and availability of computer systems, networks and computer data as well as the misuse of such systems, networks and data by providing for the criminalisation of such conduct'.

Under Article 6 of the Convention each Party is required to:

> adopt such legislative and other measures as may be necessary to establish as criminal offences ... the production, sale, procurement for use, import, distribution or otherwise making available of ... a device, including a computer program, designed or adapted primarily for the purpose of committing any of the offences established in accordance with Articles 2 through 5.

Articles 2–5 set out offences regarding illegal access, interception and interference with data or systems. Again, while Article 6 may apply to the sale of weaponised exploits, it does not, in its current form, apply to the sale of vulnerabilities or backdoors themselves, particularly without a known end-use proscribed by Articles 2–5.

4.3 The Wassenaar Arrangement: on Export Controls for Conventional Arms and Dual-use Goods and Technologies

The Wassenaar Arrangement is an agreement between nation states to promote responsibility in transfers of conventional arms and weapons, as well as dual-use goods and technologies. The Wassenaar Arrangement has several working groups who put out 'Best Practices for Effective Legislation on Arms Brokering',[68] 'Best Practices for Effective Export Control Enforcement',[69] and a 'List of Dual-Use Goods and Technologies and Munitions List'.[70] There are a number of different types of technologies that are regulated, from navigation software to electrical currency converters to various types of electronics, and information security. Information security largely means encryption. For example, Wassenaar mandates at most a 56-bit encryption be used.

---

[67] Available at: <www.conventions.coe.int/Treaty/Commun/ChercheSig.asp?NT=185& CM=&DF=&CL=ENG> (accessed 18 April 2019).

[68] Available at: <www.wassenaar.org/wp-content/uploads/2016/12/Best-Practices-for-Effec tive-Legislation-on-Arms-Brokering-1.pdf> (accessed 18 April 2019).

[69] Available at: <www.wassenaar.org/wp-content/uploads/2016/12/Best-Practices-for-Effec tive-Export-Control-Enforcement-1.pdf> (accessed 18 April 2019).

[70] Available at: <www.wassenaar.org/wp-content/uploads/2016/12/WA-LIST-16-1-2016- List-of-DU-Goods-and-Technologies-and-Munitions-List.pdf> (accessed 18 April 2019).

The WA expanded its control list in 2013. The proposal is to update the control list under the WA as it continues to be negotiated into 2016. If these changes go through, the agreement amendments will take away the legal grey zone by potentially criminalising (and certainly controlling) the export of certain tools/code without a permit. In essence, the new agreement would put additional exports controls on hacking tools and computer code used in information security. In 2015 the United States Bureau of Industry and Security announced their intention to introduce restrictions around exploits, zero-day exploits, rootkits and intrusion software following proposals to amend the WA.

How does this affect programmers? If programmer Jane discovers a vulnerability which leads her to further discover a zero-day exploit, the exporting of the zero-day exploit without a permit would be a crime. Jane is an American residing in Seattle. This means that if Jane wants to sell the zero-day exploit to Zerodium (headquartered in France), she would be required to have an export licence to do so. If Jane, however, sold the zero-day exploit to a local exploit and vulnerability business (in the United States) she commits no crime and doesn't require a licence. However, the exploit and vulnerability businesses cannot then turn around and sell or license vulnerabilities and exploits to parties outside of their jurisdiction without an export licence. One can easily see how 'legitimate' vulnerability markets are potentially affected here. The aim is to control cyber weapons and cyberwar, as well as surveillance systems sold to repressive regimes, but the potential effects are far-reaching.[71] Some potential effects are loosely defined terms that capture goods and technologies that are not at the heart of the agreement. An 'intrusion software' or 'rootkit', while meaning to target cyber weapons, also targets fundamental security technologies such as Chrome's browser and GPS. As privacy and security guru Jon Callas (founder of PGP – Pretty Good Privacy – and now Apple's Chief of Security) stated, 'It made sense, for example, to consider GPS a dual-use item in the 1980s. It doesn't now that every cellphone has it'.[72]

Indirectly, the implementation of the Wassenaar Control List will regulate the trading of zero-day exploits and rootkits in the security vulnerabilities market. In practice, however, the business of zero-day exploits and rootkits will merely become more secret, and possibly move completely underground

---

[71] Zetter, 'Why an Arms Control Pact Has Security Experts Up in Arms' (*Wired*, 24 June 2015) <https://www.wired.com/2015/06/arms-control-pact-security-experts-arms/> (accessed 18 April 2019).

[72] Violet Blue, 'Weaponizing Code: America's Quest to Control the Exploit Market' (*Engadget*, 29 May 2015) <https://www.engadget.com/2015/05/29/weaponizing-code/> (accessed 18 April 2019).

to the dark net. The NSA and law enforcement will continue to purchase vulnerabilities and exploits, though in theory, there will be a reduced market in zero days and rootkits. Again, in theory. One cannot see the US government shying away from purchasing zero days and rootkits if it means that they can carry out covert operations such as Stuxnet. The WA is really about the US having better ability to control which other governments get to acquire zero-day exploits and rootkits legally. Differentiating between zero days and regular exploits, as well as backdoors and rootkits, is not easy in practice. The WA makes it sound as though it is as easy as implementing a classification system similar to movie ratings. The reality is far messier, and is likely to be the subject of future international agreements.

Boba closes the book and thinks, 'yes, a whole lot messier with consequences no one at the time could have foreseen'. Boba reflects on the Republic Army's purchase of the schematics for the Death Star, where they discovered the weakness in the core reactor chamber. He also remembers both sides purchasing zero-day exploits for a range of weapons and spaceships, many resulting in the turn of the ongoing wars.

Boba smiles, thinking about his latest zero-day vulnerability discovery – a fatal weakness in the Millennium Falcon found in the wire connectors in its hidden capsule. The VSTX safety valve was modified with a zerodiumantyte wire system. This is one zero-day vulnerability that Boba will not be selling to anyone. He and he alone will use this zero-day vulnerability to subvert Hans Solo's flight path to land on Norbiac. And won't Hans be surprised by his waiting party! Thinking of how Boba will kill Hans Solo once and for all puts a wide smile on his face.

References

Appelbaum J et al., 'Catalog Advertises NSA Toolbox' (*Der Spiegel*, 29 December 2013) <www.spiegel.de/international/world/catalog-reveals-nsa-has-back-doors-for-numerous-devices-a-940994.html> (accessed 18 April 2019).

Aycock J, *Computer Viruses and Malware* (Springer 2006).

BBC, 'York Facebook Hacking Student Glenn Mangham Jailed' (17 February 2012) <https://www.bbc.co.uk/news/uk-england-york-north-yorkshire-17079853> (accessed 30 June 2019).

Bellovin et al., 'Lawful Hacking: Using Existing Vulnerabilities for Wiretapping on the Internet' Privacy Legal Scholars Conference, June 2013 (Draft, 18 August 2013), pp. 1–70 <http://papers.ssrn.com/sol3/papers.cfm?abstract_id=2312107> (accessed 18 April 2019).

Benkler J, *The Wealth of Networks: How Social Production Transforms Markets and Freedom* (Yale University Press 2006) <www.benkler.org/Benkler_Wealth_Of_Networks.pdf> (accessed 18 April 2019).

Block R, 'Live from WWDC 2006: Steve Jobs Keynote' (*Engadget*, 7 August 2006) <www.engadget.com/2006/08/07/live-from-wwdc-2006-steve-jobs-keynote/> (accessed 18 April 2019).

Brown B, 'Sony BMG Rootkit Scandal: 10 Years Later' (*Network World*, 28 October 2015) <www.networkworld.com/article/2998251/malware-cybercrime/sony-bmg-rootkit-scandal-10-years-later.html> (accessed 18 April 2019).

Cabusoglu et al., 'Emerging Issues in Responsible Vulnerability Disclosure' (*Infosecon*) <www.infosecon.net/workshop/pdf/65.pdf> (accessed 18 April 2019).

Constantin L, 'Hackers Found 47 New Vulnerabilities in 23 IoT Devices at DEF CON: The Results of This Year's IoT Hacking Contest Are In and It's Not a Pretty Picture' (CSO, 13 September 2016) <www.csoonline.com/article/3119765/security/hackers-found-47-new-vulnerabilities-in-23-iot-devices-at-def-con.html> (accessed 18 April 2019).

Diamond J, 'The Cyber Arms Trade: Opportunities and Threats in Software Vulnerability Markets' (Sigma Iota Rho, *Journal of International Relations*) <www.sirjournal.org/2012/12/11/the-cyber-arms-trade-opportunities-and-threats-in-software-vulnerability-markets/> (accessed 18 April 2019).

Falliere N et al., 'Symantec Security Response: W32.Stuxnet Dossier' (Symantec Corporation, February 2011) <www.symantec.com/content/en/us/enterprise/media/security_response/whitepapers/w32_stuxnet_dossier.pdf> (accessed 18 April 2019).

Fire-Eye, 'Exposing One of China's Cyber Espionage' <http://intelreport.mandiant.com/Mandiant_APT1_Report.pdf> (accessed 18 April 2019).

Fung B, 'The NSA Hacks Other Countries by Buying Millions of Dollars' Worth of Computer Vulnerabilities' (*Washington Post*, 31 August 2013) <www.washingtonpost.com/blogs/the-switch/wp/2013/08/31/the-nsa-hacks-other-countries-by-buying-millions-of-dollars-worth-of-computer-vulnerabilities/> (accessed 18 April 2019).

Gallagher R, 'Cyberwar's Gray Market' (*Slate*, 16 January 2013) <www.slate.com/articles/technology/future_tense/2013/01/zero_day_exploits_should_the_hacker_gray_market_be_regulated.html> (accessed 18 April 2019).

Gartner Press Release, 'Gartner Says the Internet of Things Installed Base Will Grow to 26 Billion Units by 2020' (*Gartner*, 12 December 2013) <www.gartner.com/newsroom/id/2636073> (accessed 18 April 2019).

Gartner Press Release, 'Gartner Identifies the Top 10 Strategic Technology Trends for 2013' (*Gartner*, 23 October 2012) <www.gartner.com/newsroom/id/2209615> (accessed 18 April 2019).

Granick J, 'Legal Risks of Vulnerability Disclosure' (*Centre for Internet & Society*) <www.blackhat.com/presentations/bh-asia-03/bh-asia-03-granick.pdf> (accessed 18 April 2019).

Greenberg A, 'Meet the Hackers Who Sell Spies the Tools to Crack Your PC (And Get Paid Six-Figure Fees)' (*Forbes*, 21 March 2006) <www.forbes.com/sites/andygreenberg/2012/03/21/meet-the-hackers-who-sell-spies-the-tools-to-crack-your-pc-and-get-paid-six-figure-fees/> (accessed 18 April 2019).

Green M, 'A Few More Notes on NSA Random Number Generators' (Cryptography Engineering Blog, 28 December 2013) <https://blog.cryptographyengineering.com/2013/12/28/a-few-more-notes-on-nsa-random-number/> (accessed 18 April 2019).

Greenberg A, 'This "Demonically Clever" Backdoor Hides in a Tiny Slice of a Computer Chip' (*Wired*, 1 June 2016) <https://www.wired.com/2016/06/demonically-clever-backdoor-hides-inside-computer-chip/> (accessed 18 April 2019).

Khandelwal S, 'Routers TCP 32764 Backdoor Vulnerability Secretly Re-Activated Again' (*Hacker News*, 20 April 2014) <http://thehackernews.com/2014/04/router-manufacturers-secretly-added-tcp.html> (accessed 18 April 2019).

Koetsier J, '450M Lines of Code Say Large Open Source Projects and Small Closed Source Software Projects Are Worst Quality' (*Venturebeat*, 9 May 2013) <http://venturebeat.com/2013/05/09/450-million-lines-of-code-say-large-open-source-and-small-closed-source-software-projects-are-worst-quality/> (accessed 18 April 2019).

Lennon M, 'Hackers Used Sophisticated SMB Worm Tool to Attack Sony' (*Security Week*, 19 December 2014) <www.securityweek.com/hackers-used-sophisticated-smb-worm-tool-attack-sony> (accessed 18 April 2019).

Levy S, *Crypto: How the Code Rebels Beat the Government Saving Privacy in the Digital Age* (Viking 2001).

Mangham G, 'The Facebook Hack: What Really Happened' (GMangham Blog), 23 April 2012 <http://gmangham.blogspot.co.uk/2012/04/facebook-hack-what-really-happened.html> (accessed 18 April 2019).

Maurushat A, *Disclosure of Security Vulnerabilities: Legal and Ethical Issues* (Springer Publishing 2011).

Maurushat A, *Ethical Hacking* (University of Ottawa Press 2017).

Menn J, "Hacktivists" Retaliate against Security Expert' (*Financial Times*, 7 February 2011) <www.ft.com/cms/s/0/0c9ff214-32e3-11e0-9a61-00144feabdc0.html> (accessed 18 April 2019).

Menn J, 'Exclusive: Secret Contract Tied NSA and Security Industry Pioneer' (Reuters, 20 December 2013) <www.reuters.com/article/us-usa-security-rsa-idUSBRE9BJ1C220131220> (accessed 18 April 2019).

Oremus W, 'Java Zero-day Exploit: Don't Patch, Just Disable Java in Your Browser' (*Slate*, 14 January 2013) <www.slate.com/blogs/future_tense/2013/01/14/java_zero_day_exploit_don_t_patch_just_disable_java_in_your_browser.html> (accessed 18 April 2019).

Pfleeger C and Pfleeger S, *Security in Computing* (4th edn, Prentice Hall 2006).

Protalinkski E, 'British Student Jailed for Hacking into Facebook' (*Zdnet*, 18 February 2012) <www.zdnet.com/blog/facebook/british-student-jailed-for-hacking-into-facebook/9244> (accessed 18 April 2019).

Richardson JC, 'Stuxnet as Cyberwarfare: Applying the Law of War to the Virtual Battlefield' (*JMR Portfolio Intelligence*, 22 July 2011) <http://ssrn.com/abstract=1892888> (accessed 18 April 2019).

Richmond JC, 'Evolving Battlefields: Does Stuxnet Demonstrate a Need for Modifications to the Law of Armed Conflict?' (2012) 35 *Fordham International Law Journal* 842.

Rouse M, 'Definition: Back Door' (*TechTarget*, June 2007) <http://searchsecurity.techtarget.com/definition/back-door> (accessed 18 April 2019).

Schneier B (2007), 'New German Hacking Law' (Schneier on Security, 28 August 2007) <https://www.schneier.com/blog/archives/2007/08/new_german_hack.html> (accessed 20 August 2018).

Schneier B, 'The Vulnerabilities Market and the Future of Security' (*Forbes*, 30 May 2012) <www.forbes.com/sites/bruceschneier/2012/05/30/the-vulnerabilities-market-and-the-future-of-security/#35d47ee17763> (accessed 18 April 2019).

Singh S, *The Code Book* (Doubleday 1999).

Stefanovic S, 'IoT Device Security: Problems and Recommendations' (PACE, 24 November 2016) <https://pacetoday.com.au/iot-security-problems-recommendations/> (accessed 18 April 2019).

Stevenson A, 'Darkleech Campaign Targets Java to Spread Reveton Ransomware' (*v3*, 17 September 2013) <www.v3.co.uk/v3-uk/news/2295107/darkleech-campaign-targets-java-to-spread-reveton-ransomware> (accessed 18 April 2019).

Tallinn Manual on the International Law Applicable to Cyber Warfare (Council for Foreign Relations, 28 March 2013) <www.cfr.org/cybersecurity/tallinn-manual-international-law-applicable-cyber-warfare/p30415> (accessed 18 April 2019).

Tung L, 'NSA Tops Up Exploit Pool with $25m in "Grey Market" Vulnerabilities' (*CSO*, 2 September 2013) <www.cso.com.au/article/525241/nsa_tops_up_exploit_pool_25m_grey_market_vulnerabilities_/> (accessed 18 April 2019).

Violet Blue, 'Weaponizing Code: America's Quest to Control the Exploit Market' (*Engadget*, 29 May 2015) <https://www.engadget.com/2015/05/29/weaponizing-code/> (accessed 18 April 2019).

World Economic Forum, 'Partnering for Cyber Resilience' (19 March 2015) <www3.weforum.org/docs/WEF_IT_PartneringCyberResilience_Guidelines_2012.pdf> (accessed 18 April 2019).

Yegulalp S, 'The 12 Biggest, Baddest, Boldest Software Backdoors of All Time' (*InfoWorld*, 12 June 2014) <www.infoworld.com/article/2606776/hacking/155947-Biggest-baddest-boldest-software-backdoors-of-all-time.html#slide3> (accessed 18 April 2019).

Zetter K, 'FBI Hints It Paid Hackers $1 Million to get into San Bernardino iPhone' (*Wired*, 21 November 2016) <https://www.wired.com/2016/04/fbi-hints-paid-hackers-1-million-get-san-bernardino-iphone/> (accessed 18 April 2019).

Zetter K, 'Why an Arms Control Pact Has Security Experts Up in Arms' (*Wired*, 24 June 2015) <https://www.wired.com/2015/06/arms-control-pact-security-experts-arms/> (accessed 18 April 2019).

PART II

A Matter of (Future) Life and Death

7

Will My Genes Really Help Me Fit Into Those Jeans? Personal Genomics and Wrap Contracts

Andelka M Phillips

1. Introduction

The abstract for this chapter begins with a story. This is the story of an ordinary person wanting to know more about their genetic makeup. Today, those who are interested in this can purchase genetic tests online. This industry is known either as direct-to-consumer genetic testing (aka DTC or personal genomics, and sometimes commercial genomics). It has created a market for a wide range of genetic tests, ranging from the increasingly popular tests for health and ancestry (which still lack harmonised standards) to more dubious types of tests, such as child talent, matchmaking and infidelity.

Deoxyribonucleic acid (DNA) testing is a hot topic at present for a variety of reasons. There has been significant press coverage of the Golden State Killer investigation. This was a cold case where a suspect, James DeAngelo, was identified through the process of familial DNA matching after law enforcement created a profile on the genetic genealogical database, GEDmatch[1] based on DNA samples collected from crime scenes in the 1970s and 1980s. DeAngelo is a former police officer in his seventies, and has appeared in court in a wheelchair. Proceedings against DeAngelo are

---

[1] Molteni, 'The Key to Cracking Cold Cases Might Be Genealogy Sites' (*Wired*, 1 June 2018) <https://www.wired.com/story/police-will-crack-a-lot-more-cold-cases-with-dna/> (accessed 18 April 2019); see https://www.gedmatch.com/tos.htm; Lapin, ' "Golden State Killer" Cleared of 1978 Double-murder Cold Case' Lapin T, ' "Golden State Killer" Cleared of 1978 Double-murder Cold Case' (*New York Post*, 14 June 1018) <https://nypost.com/2018/06/14/golden-state-killer-cleared-of-1978-double-murder-cold-case/> (accessed 18 April 2019).

ongoing, but it is important to note that he has been cleared in relation to two of the murder charges against him, on the basis that his DNA did not match.[2] There are also important issues at stake here including the presumption of innocence until proof of guilt, and the right to a fair trial. His defence counsel has noted in relation to the press coverage of the case: ' "I feel like he's been tried in the press already." '[3] This is particularly important to remember given that four of the prosecutors in this case are now seeking the death penalty.[4] It has also emerged that prior to DeAngelo's arrest police wrongly hunted down another suspect in Oregon who was innocent and who was living in a nursing home. In May 2019 GEDmatch altered its User Policy opting its users out of law enforcement matching by default.[5] Since amending its policy a much lower number of GEDmatch's users have opted into law enforcement matching, (approximately 50,000), which may suggest some level of discomfort with this type of secondary use.[6] The man's daughter has said that she was not contacted by police prior to their taking a swab of DNA from her father, but she subsequently worked with the police to identify who might be the suspect.[7] However, in December 2019, GEDmatch was purchased by Verogen, which is a forensic genetics company that works with law enforcement and so despite its policy changes, it is possible that the database may be used more for crime solving,

[2] Lapin, ' "Golden State Killer" Cleared of 1978 Double-murder Cold Case'; Luperon, 'DNA Evidence Clears Golden State Killer Suspect of a Murder' (Law & Crime, 9 January 2019) <https://lawandcrime.com/high-profile/dna-evidence-clears-golden-state-killer-suspect-of-a-murder/> (accessed 18 April 2019).

[3] Associated Press, 'DNA Used in Hunt for Golden State Killer Previously Led to Wrong Man' (NBC News, 29 April 2018) <https://www.nbcnews.com/news/us-news/dna-used-hunt-golden-state-killer-previously-led-wrong-man-n869796> (accessed 18 April 2019).

[4] Smith and Stanton, 'Prosecutors to Seek Death Penalty in Golden State Killer Case' (*Mercury News*, 10 April 2019) <https://www.mercurynews.com/2019/04/10/prosecutors-to-seek-death-penalty-in-golden-state-killer-case/> (accessed 18 April 2019); Dowd, 'Golden State Killer Suspect Appears in Court Nearly One Year after Arrest' (*San Francisco Chronicle*, 10 April 2019) <https://www.sfgate.com/bayarea/article/joseph-deangelo-hearing-sacramento-trial-13757418.php> (accessed 18 April 2019).

[5] Adam Vaughan, 'DNA database opts a million people out from police searches', *New Scientist* (20 May 2019) https://www.newscientist>.

[6] Andelka M Phillips, 'All Your Data Will Be Held Against You: Secondary Use of Data from Personal Genomics & Wearable Tech' in Susan Sterett and Lee Demetrius Walker (eds), *Research Handbook On Law And Courts* (Edward Elgar Publishing, forthcoming October 2019), citing Kristen V Brown, 'DNA Site That Helps Cold-Case Sleuths Curbs Access for Cops' Bloomberg (11 June 2019) <https://www.bloomberg.com/news/articles/2019-06-10/dna-site-that-helps-cold-case-sleuths-curbs-access-for-police> (accessed 21 June 2019).

[7] Associated Press, 'DNA Used in Hunt for Golden State Killer Previously Led to Wrong Man'.

as Verogen's CEO has 'indicated a vision for the site that focuses on solving crimes . . .'[8]

Since the press coverage of this case began, Parabon NanoLabs has uploaded data from around a hundred other crime scenes to GEDmatch hoping to find further matches.[9] More recently, in early 2019, it emerged that FamilyTreeDNA has been working with the US Federal Bureau of Investigation (FBI) to investigate violent crime.[10] Initially it was not possible for FamilyTreeDNA's consumers to opt out of law enforcement matching, but they have since altered their settings, so that consumers can choose to opt out of law enforcement matching.[11] This is a positive development, and there is a need for more privacy-friendly options in this space. It should be possible for DTC companies to offer consumers the option of deleting their data and destroying their physical sample after sending test results.

We are all unique and we all have our own unique genetic code. Through the process of genetic testing, that code becomes digital data, and that data can be used in a variety of ways. Of course we all share and leak various forms of personal data through our use of the Internet, email and all our devices. All of this data can be used in various ways, but not all personal data are the same. Unlike your bank password once your genetic data are stored in digital form they serve as a unique identifier for you and you cannot change it. Unlike your bank password and some other forms of personal data, you share much of your genetic information with your family, which means that stored genetic data can also be used to trace family members. This also means that if

---

[8] Adam Vaughan, 'DNA site GEDmatch sold to firm helping US police solve crime'(*New Scientist*, 10 December 2019) <https://www.newscientist.com/article/2226791-dna-site-gedmatch-sold-to-firm-helping-us-police-solve-crime/#ixzz68QGQDhwS> (accessed 18 December 2019); for more on the acquisition, see Kameran Wong, 'A message to Verogen customers about the GEDmatch partnership' (Verogen, 10 December 2019) <https://verogen.com/a-message-to-verogen-customers-about-the-gedmatch-partnership> (accessed 19 December 2019).

[9] See Phillips, *Buying Your Self on the Internet: Wrap Contracts and Personal Genomics* (Edinburgh University Press 2019), Chapter 4 citing Aldhous, 'DNA Data from 100 Crime Scenes Has Been Uploaded to a Genealogy Website – Just like the Golden State Killer' (*BuzzFeed News*, 17 May 2018) <https://www.buzzfeednews.com/article/peteraldhous/parabon-genetic-genealogy-cold-cases> (accessed 18 April 2019).

[10] Haag, 'FamilyTreeDNA Admits to Sharing Genetic Data with FBI' (*New York Times*, 4 February 2019) <https://www.nytimes.com/2019/02/04/business/family-tree-dna-fbi.html> (accessed 18 April 2019).

[11] Vaughan, 'Home DNA-testing Firm Will Let Users Block FBI Access to their Data' (*New Scientist*, 13 March 2019) <https://www.newscientist.com/article/2196433-home-dna-testing-firm-will-let-users-block-fbi-access-to-their-data/> (accessed 18 April 2019).

you are considering having a test you really ought to consider talking to your family about it before going ahead with a purchase.

It is also important to understand that as well as all this digital data, we can all potentially leak our genetic data by shedding our DNA as we move around in the world. So regardless of whether or not you have chosen to have a genetic test, it is possible that other parties such as law enforcement could create a genetic profile for you based on DNA you have left behind. Research has demonstrated that DNA transfer, i.e. leaving traces of our genetic makeup on objects or on other people, happens much more than we might think.[12] This can be done very easily by leaving bits of our skin or saliva. Unfortunately, DNA transfer is not well understood by many, and often juries and investigators will give significant weight to DNA evidence and the reliability of DNA evidence may also be misrepresented in legal proceedings. The issue that needs to be understood here is that as we can unintentionally and unknowingly leave traces of ourselves in many places. Those traces can be used to identify us and they may potentially incriminate us when we are in fact innocent. The case of Lukis Anderson, who was wrongly charged due to DNA transfer, highlights just how serious the consequences can be. In Anderson's case his DNA was found under the fingernails of a murder victim, Raveesh Kumra. It was assumed on this basis that he must have been involved in the commission of a burglary and a murder. However, Anderson's defence attorney found that Anderson had in fact been hospitalised at the time of this home invasion and was in fact in hospital throughout that evening as well as being very intoxicated. It is still unclear exactly how his DNA was transferred to Raveesh's body, but the same paramedics that attended the crime scene had taken Anderson to hospital earlier that evening:

> The prosecutors, defense attorney, and police agree that somehow, the paramedics must have moved Anderson's DNA from San Jose to Monte Sereno. Santa Clara County District Attorney Jeff Rosen has postulated that a pulse oximeter slipped over both patients' fingers may have been the culprit; Kulick thinks it could have been their uniforms or another piece of equipment. It may never be known for sure.[13]

---

[12] Worth, 'Framed for Murder by his Own DNA' (*Wired*, 19 April 2018) <https://www.wired.com/story/dna-transfer-framed-murder/> (accessed 18 April 2019); see also Van Oorschot and Jones, 'DNA Fingerprints from Fingerprints' (1997) 387 *Nature* 767 DOI: 10.1038/42838; and Smith, 'When DNA Implicates the Innocent' (2016) 314 *Scientific American* 11 <https://www.scientificamerican.com/article/when-dna-implicates-the-inno cent/> (accessed 18 April 2019).

[13] Worth, 'Framed for Murder by his Own DNA'.

There is a need for more research and more funding of research into DNA transfer, as only a small number of laboratories consistently research it.[14] Given that it is possible for anyone to leave some type of DNA trace behind and given the reliance placed on DNA evidence in many cases, DNA transfer needs to be better understood, and while DNA evidence can be very useful, investigators need to be cautious of relying on DNA evidence where there is no other supporting evidence.

As the majority of the most prominent DTC companies are currently based in the USA, this means that an individual consumer will often have their genetic testing performed in another country and their physical DNA sample and the genetic data generated from their genetic test, as well as other forms of personal data, may be stored and shared in another country than where the consumer resides. The industry is also growing. According to Khan and Mittelman, in 2018, the 'personal genomics industry surpassed 10 million genotyped consumers', which represented a ten-fold increase since their previous comment piece in 2013. They estimate that there may be a further 'ten-fold increase by 2021, with upwards of 100 million genotyped individuals'.[15] Meanwhile, Research and Markets has suggested that the 'global predictive genetic testing & consumer/wellness genomics market is anticipated to reach USD 4.6 billion by 2025'.[16]

Also, 2018 can be viewed as the year of the General Data Protection Regulation (GDPR),[17] and as every one of us can be a data subject, we have all received slightly panicked emails from a variety of companies in the lead up to the GDPR coming into force. Significantly for present purposes, the GDPR includes genetic information within the definition of personal data under Article 4, as well as including genetic data in the prohibition on processing of special categories of personal data set out in Article 9. Therefore, in order to lawfully carry out the processing of genetic data, a business must obtain an individual's explicit consent. According to Article 4(11) consent to any data processing must be the 'freely given, specific, informed and unambiguous indication of' their wishes. Article 7 imposes a number of conditions in relation

[14] Ibid.

[15] Khan and Mittelman, 'Consumer Genomics Will Change Your Life, Whether You Get Tested or Not' (2018) 19 *Genome Biology* 120 DOI: 10.1186/s13059-018-1506-1.

[16] Research and Markets, 'Predictive Genetic Testing and Consumer/Wellness Genomics Market by Application and Trend Analysis from 2013 to 2025' (January 2017) <www.researchandmarkets.com/research/26mxz4/predictive> (accessed 18 April 2019).

[17] Regulation (EU) 2016/679 of the European Parliament and of the Council of 27 April 2016 on the protection of natural persons with regard to the processing of personal data and on the free movement of such data, and repealing Directive 95/46/EC (General Data Protection Regulation) [2016] OJ 2 119/1.

to consent and according to Article 9, the processing of genetic data can only be carried out with the data subject's explicit consent. This means that DTC companies, as providers of genetic testing services, need to comply with the GDPR where they offer tests to EU and UK-based consumers. However, this is not the only area of law that has relevance to the industry's regulation: the other most significant areas in this context are consumer protection,[18] contract law, and the framework governing medical devices.

This chapter is based on ongoing research on the regulation of the DTC industry. This work explores the use of wrap contracts and privacy policies by the industry to govern relationships with consumers. It also explores the ways that consumers engage with these documents, drawing upon the work of Frischmann and Selinger,[19] Obar and Oeldorf-Hirsch,[20] and the Norwegian Consumer Council.[21] It was presented at an earlier stage at the GIKII VIII: Seaside Edition, which was held in Bournemouth in 2013. The book, *Buying Your Self on the Internet: Wrap Contracts and Personal Genomics* is a volume in this series.[22] Also, at the time of writing the UK's Science and Technology Committee (Commons) is undertaking an inquiry into commercial genom-

---

[18] Directive 2011/83/EU of the European Parliament and of the Council of 25 October 2011 on consumer rights, amending Council Directive 93/13/EEC and Directive 1999/44/EC of the European Parliament and of the Council and repealing Council Directive 85/577/ EEC and Directive 97/7/EC of the European Parliament and of the Council.

[19] Frischmann and Selinger, 'Engineering Humans with Contracts' (September 2016) Cardozo Legal Studies Research Paper No 493 <https://papers.ssrn.com/sol3/papers.cfm?abstract_id=2834011> (accessed 18 April 2019); Frischmann and Selinger, *Re-Engineering Humanity* (Cambridge University Press 2018).

[20] Obar and Oeldorf-Hirsch, 'The Biggest Lie on the Internet: Ignoring the Privacy Policies and Terms of Service Policies of Social Networking Services' (2018) *Information, Communication & Society*, DOI: 10.1080/1369118X.2018.1486870.

[21] Norwegian Consumer Council, *APPFAIL Threats to Consumers in Mobile Apps* (March 2016) <https://www.forbrukerradet.no/undersokelse/2015/appfail-threats-to-consumers-in-mobile-apps/> (accessed 18 April 2019); Norwegian Consumer Council, *Deceived by Design* (June 2018) <https://www.forbrukerradet.no/undersokelse/no-undersokelsekate-gori/deceived-by-design/> (accessed 18 April 2019).

[22] Please see the related work: Phillips, *Buying Your Self on the Internet*; Phillips, 'Reading the Fine Print When Buying Your Genetic Self Online: Direct-to-Consumer Genetic Testing Terms and Conditions' (2017) 36 *New Genetics and Society* 273 <http://dx.doi.org/10.1080/14636778.2017.1352468> (accessed 22 June 2019); Phillips, 'Only a Click Away – DTC Genetics for Ancestry, Health, Love … and More: A View of the Business and Regulatory Landscape' (2016) 8 *Applied & Translational Genomics* 16; and Phillips, 'Genomic Privacy and Direct-to-Consumer Genetics – Big Consumer Genetic Data – What's in that Contract?' (2015) Security and Privacy Workshops (SPW), IEEE 60–4; for more on the DTC industry, please also see the other articles in the *New Genetics and Society* special issue (2017) 36 (issue 3).

ics, but as it will not be completed prior to the submission of this chapter it is not possible to comment on the Committee's recommendations.[23]

This research began in 2011. It included the compilation of a database of all the companies operating with English language websites that offered some form of genetic testing via the Internet. A version of the dataset has been released via Zenodo, and the total number of companies identified as of August 2018 stands at 288. (This figure includes companies that may no longer be operating, but were operating when this research began in 2011). Further updates will be released in the coming years.[24] As part of this work, the contracts of seventy-one DTC companies that provide tests for health purposes were reviewed and a number of terms were identified that might be problematic from a consumer protection standpoint.[25] The diverse nature of the industry needs to be stressed, as health testing represents only one category of the range of tests available. There are also a growing number of companies offering tests ranging from genetic relatedness (most commonly paternity), ancestry, child talent, athletic ability, diet, dating and infidelity.

This research to date has focused primarily on the UK regulatory framework for DTC together with relevant EU legislation. Based on the review of DTC contracts, it is suggested that companies offering services to consumers based in the UK and European Union may find that several terms they have included in their contracts are challengeable on the grounds of potential unfairness, and some contracts may overall fail to meet transparency requirements. These findings are also in line with the studies by Laestadius et al. and Hazel and Slobogin.[26] The Laestadius study highlighted problems with adherence to international transparency standards by DTC companies, while

<hr>

[23] Science and Technology Committee (Commons), Commercial genomic inquiry (March 2019) <https://www.parliament.uk/business/committees/committees-a-z/commons-select/science-and-technology-committee/inquiries/parliament-2017/commercial-genomics-17-9/> (accessed 18 April 2019); please note that I am making a submission to this Committee and meeting with its chair.

[24] Phillips, 'Data on Direct-to-Consumer Genetic Testing and DNA Testing Companies' (Version 1.3, Open Access Dataset, Zenodo, February 2018) DOI: 10.5281/zenodo.1175799 <https://zenodo.org/record/1183565#.WunK6y-ZNp8> (accessed 22 June 2019).

[25] Phillips, 'Only a Click Away'; Phillips, 'Genomic Privacy'.

[26] Laestadius, Rich and Auer, 'All Your Data (Effectively) Belong to Us: Data Practices among Direct-to-Consumer Genetic Testing Firms' (2016) *Genetics in Medicine* DOI: 10.1038/gim.2016.136; Hazel and Slobogin, 'Who Knows What, and When? A Survey of the Privacy Policies Proffered by US Direct-to-Consumer Genetic Testing Companies' (Vanderbilt Law Research Paper No. 18-8, 19 April 2018) *Cornell Journal of Law and Public Policy*.

Hazel and Slobogin examined the data practices of DTC companies based on a review of their contracts and privacy policies conducted in 2017.

The aim herein is to provide a brief overview of a complex area, and show some of the problems with the use of contracts and privacy policies. It highlights the need for compliance with existing data protection and consumer protection law in the EU and UK. It also encourages us to think about the ways we all behave online in relation to contracts and privacy policies and to think about how businesses could do things better.

As with a number of other new technologies, there is a need for a wider discussion including all stakeholders and the public, so that existing law can be adapted and enforced, and new law cognisant of the various issues raised by new technologies can be developed. There is also a need for increased transparency more generally so that the public can make informed decisions about whether or not they wish to engage with the industry and whether or not they wish to adopt other digital technologies.

2. What is Direct-to-consumer Genetic Testing?

The DTC industry began two decades ago with the launch of University Diagnostics' mail order service in 1996.[27] It provides genetic testing services on a commercial basis and allows individuals to purchase tests online, normally without a medical intermediary. The industry has developed as a direct consequence of advances in genetic and genomic science and the reductions in the cost of sequencing technologies. The rise of DTC can also be viewed as merely one development in the 'quantified self' (or lifelogging) movement.[28] DTC services can also be viewed as an example of disruptive innovation and one of the most prominent DTC companies, 23andMe, has been described as an example of a 'big bang disruption'.[29] The services offered by providers of wearable fitness and health monitoring devices and applications raise similar issues for society and regulators. As with many other new and emerging technologies, the industry is not subject to specific regulation and has tended to rely on its electronic contracts and privacy policies to govern relationships with consumers.

---

[27] Hogarth and Saukko, 'A Market in the Making: The Past, Present and Future of Direct-to-Consumer Genomics' (2017) 36 *New Genetics and Society* 197 197. DOI: 10.1080/14636778.2017.1354692.

[28] Swan, 'The Quantified Self: Fundamental Disruption in Big Data Science and Biological Discovery' (2013) 1 *Big Data* 85 <https://doi.org/10.1089/big.2012.0002> (accessed 22 June 2019), p. 85.

[29] Downes and Nunes, 'Regulating 23andMe Won't Stop the New Age of Genetic Testing' (*Wired*, 1 January 2014) <https://www.wired.com/2014/01/the-fda-may-win-the-battle-this-holiday-season-but-23andme-will-win-the-war/> (accessed 18 April 2019).

These services have largely come to market without much restriction and often without any pre-market review.[30] Due to the nature of its services, DTC has presented challenges to existing legal regulation in the UK, the EU, the USA, Canada, New Zealand, Australia and elsewhere. While several areas of law do have relevance to its regulation (data protection, consumer protection and the frameworks governing medical devices) there has not been a harmonised legislative response and many DTC services have been able to operate without much oversight. Significantly, in 2017 the American Food and Drug Administration (FDA) altered its stance on DTC tests, making it easier for companies to market genetic tests for health purposes in the USA. The FDA's position is unfortunately not in line with the previous statements released by the American Association for Molecular Pathology (ACMG).[31] Very few DTC companies have actually received FDA approval for their tests. 23andMe was the first company to obtain approval for its BRCA1 and 2 cancer risks tests.[32] However, concern has been expressed regarding the usefulness of such tests to individuals,[33] and a recent study on the clinical utility of BRCA testing further highlights this concern over clinical utility, as it found that individuals would need to have additional genetic tests in a clinic in order to confirm both positive and negative findings.[34]

---

[30] Phillips, 'Only a Click Away'.

[31] Ray, 'ACMG Guidelines at Odds with FDA Green Light for 23andMe Health Risk Tests' (*Genomeweb*, 11 April 2017) <https://www.Genomeweb.com/regulatory-news/acmg-guidelines-oddsfda-green-light-23andme-health-risk-tests> (accessed 18 April 2019); Association for Molecular Pathology, 'Position Statement: On Direct Access Genetic Testing (Direct-to-Consumer Genetic Testing)' (Association for Molecular Pathology 2007) <https://www.amp.org/AMP/assets/File/position-statements/2007/AMPDTCPositionStatement_Final.pdf> (accessed 16 April 2019); and Association for Molecular Pathology, 'Position Statement: Direct Access Genetic Testing (Direct to Consumer Genetic Testing' (Association for Molecular Pathology 2015) <https://www.amp.org/AMP/assets/File/position-statements/2015/AMPpositionstatementDTCtesting-FINAL_002.pdf> (accessed 16 April 2019).

[32] 23andMe, '23andMe Granted First FDA Authorization for Direct-to-Consumer Genetic Test on Cancer Risk' (press release, 6 March 2018) <https://mediacenter.23andme.com/press-releases/23andme-granted-first-fda-authorization-direct-consumer-genetic-test-cancer-risk/> (accessed 18 April 2019); FDA, 'FDA Authorizes, with Special Controls, Direct-to-Consumer Test that Reports Three Mutations in the BRCA Breast Cancer Genes' (press release, 6 March 2018) <https://www.fda.gov/newsevents/newsroom/pressannouncements/ucm599560.htm> (accessed 18 April 2019).

[33] Cornel, van El, and Borry, 'The Challenge of Implementing Genetic Tests with Clinical Utility while Avoiding Unsound Applications' (2014) 5 *Journal of Community Genetics* 7, pp. 7–12.

[34] Karow, '23andMe DTC Breast and Ovarian Cancer Risk Test Misses Almost 90 Percent of BRCA Mutation Carriers' (*GenomeWeb*, 5 April 2019) <https://www.genomeweb.com/

In the UK, the Human Tissue Act 2004 (HTA) sets requirements for consent for tests involving the use of human tissue and DNA. DNA tests prior to the rise of DTC were previously performed only in a medical setting, as part of medical research, as part of legal proceedings for identification purposes (including to establish paternity) or by law enforcement agencies for identification purposes. Under the Act, it is an offence to conduct a DNA test without 'qualifying consent', with very few exceptions. It would appear from the guidance documents and information provided by the Human Tissue Authority (which enforces the HTA) that companies providing DNA test kits to UK-based consumers come within the Act's remit. For instance, the HTA's 'Analysis of DNA under the HT Act FAQs' states: 'All companies providing DNA testing kits or DNA testing services must comply with the provisions of the Human Tissue Act 2004 relating to consent and the hold-ing of bodily material with the intent to analyse DNA.'[35] Consequently, it seems that any DTC company, regardless of the type of test it offers, should be complying with the HTA. The offence of non-consensual DNA analysis under section 45 of the HTA carries with it penalties of fines or imprison-ment, so it would be wise for DTC companies to work on improving their consent mechanisms and for the Human Tissue Authority to investigate compliance. (The requirements for what constitutes 'qualifying consent' are set out in Schedule 4 of the HTA.)

The DTC industry offers a variety of services, but typically companies sell genetic sequencing services via their websites. Purchase of a test is made by the consumer online, and the company will then send a test kit in the mail, which the consumer uses to take a sample of their DNA, normally in the form of saliva or a cheek swab.[36] The sample is then sent back to the company for analysis.[37] After the sample has been analysed the company will convey the results of the test to the consumer and sometimes provide ongoing updates on their health

---

molecular-diagnostics/23andme-dtc-breast-and-ovarian-cancer-risk-test-misses-almost-90-percent-brca#.XKfbrS1L1PU> (accessed 18 April 2019). See 'Limitations of HBOC Direct-To-Consumer Genetic Screening: False Positives, False Negatives and Everything in Between', Abstract 27 presented at the ACMG Annual Clinical Genetics Meeting, 4th April 2019, Washington State Convention Center <https://acmg.expoplanner.com/index.cfm?do=expomap.sess&event_id=13&session_id=10875> (accessed 3 August 2019).

35 Human Tissue Authority, 'Analysis of DNA under the HT Act FAQs' <https://www.hta.gov.uk/faqs/analysis-dna-under-ht-act-faqs> (accessed 18 April 2019).

36 23andMe, 'How It Works' <https://www.23andme.com/howitworks/> (accessed 7 January 2013. Checked again for this chapter, 10 August 2018).

37 Harris, Wyatt and Kelly, 'The Gift of Spit (And the Obligation to Return It): How Consumers of Online Genetic Testing Services Participate in Research' (2013) 16 *Information, Communication & Society* 236.

information. These results and ongoing updates are normally accessible through an IT interface. So web-based return of results is the primary mode of delivering results to consumers and this is often done without recourse to genetic counselling, although some countries and states may mandate genetic counselling. The earliest prominent DTC companies were: DeCODE (which became DeCODEme); 23andMe; Navigenics; Pathway Genomics; and Knome.[38] However, Gene By Gene and Ancestry.com's AncestryDNA are also now very significant in this area, and several other companies are also beginning to grow. The prices offered by DTC companies are continuing to fall. Here are some examples based on current prices: UK and European consumers can purchase tests from 23andMe for £79 (ancestry) and £149 (ancestry and health), €99 and €169 respectively, while New Zealanders and Australians can purchase these tests for $99 and $199(USD) (as of April 2019). (There have been various discounts for holidays, such as Valentine's Day, Christmas, Thanksgiving and even the Soccer World Cup.)[39] Tests from AncestryDNA can be purchased for £79 (as of August 2018) and FamilyTreeDNA's FamilyTreeDNA offers options for: Paternal Ancestry ($169); Family Ancestry ($79); and Maternal Ancestry ($199) (USD, as of April 2019).[40] EasyDNA offers a DNA Diet and Healthy Weight test for £119 (as of April 2019).[41]

It is difficult to assess the size of the DTC market at present for all testing types, but as mentioned above, several companies have very significant databases of consumers' data. This includes: 23andMe; AncestryDNA; Gene by Gene's FamilyTreeDNA; and MyHeritage. AncestryDNA in the period between Black Friday and Cyber Monday 2017 sold 1.5 million test kits.[42] It is likely that the market will continue to grow in the near future[43] and

---

[38] Hogarth, Javitt and Melzer, 'The Current Landscape for Direct-to-Consumer Genetic Testing: Legal, Ethical, and Policy Issues' (2008) 9 *Annual Review of Genomics and Human Genetics* 161; Kalf et al., 'Variations in Predicted Risks in Personal Genome Testing for Common Complex Diseases' (2014) 16 *Genetics in Medicine* 85.

[39] Prices accurate as of 15 April 2019 <https://www.23andme.com/en-gb/> and <https://www.23andme.com/en-eu/> (accessed 15 April 2019).

[40] Prices accurate as of 10 August 2018 <https://www.ancestry.co.uk/dna/> and <https://www.familytreedna.com> (accessed 18 April 2019).

[41] Prices accurate as of 15 April 2019 <https://www.easydna.co.uk/health-dna-tests/> (accessed 15 April 2019).

[42] AncestryDNA, 'AncestryDNA Breaks Holiday Sales Record for Black Friday to Cyber Monday; More Than Triples Kits Sold versus 2016' (press release, 28 November 2017), <https://www.ancestry.com/corporate/newsroom/press-releases/ancestrydna-breaks-holiday-sales-record-black-friday-cyber-monday-more> (accessed 18 April 2019); Molteni, 'Ancestry's Genetic Testing Kits Are Heading For Your Stocking This Year'.

[43] European Academies Science Advisory Council (EASAC) and Federation of European Academies of Medicine (FEAM), Direct-to-Consumer Genetic Testing – Summary

23andMe has been valued at a market cap of $1 billion.[44] Thus, the leading DTC companies have already amassed substantial databases, some of which have already begun to be used in medical research, and companies have begun to partner with the pharmaceutical industry.[45] Such databases might also be used for targeted marketing and broader surveillance. There is also the potential for this information to be shared with the insurance industry.

3. A Range of DTC Services Available

The DTC industry is diverse. Companies offer tests for a wide range of health purposes, but the provision of ancestry and genetic-relatedness tests is also very common. Companies also offer tests for athletic ability, child talent, dating and also surreptitious tests, often marketed as infidelity tests, which are typically non-consensual in nature. Companies also tend to offer testing for more than one purpose.[46] The research upon which this chapter is based has focused primarily on providers of health-related testing. The category of health testing is viewed as an illustrative example that is representative of the broader issues raised by theDTC industry.

There has also been renewed concern from the scientific community regarding the availability of more dubious genetic tests, such as those for diet, athletic ability and child talent.[47] In order to highlight problems in this area, the geneticist Stephen Montgomery created a parody website called Yes

Document (EASAC–FEAM Project on Direct-to-Consumer Genetic Testing, October 2012), pp. 4–6; Dr Spencer Wells of National Geographic's Genographic Project speaking at the Consumer Genetics Conference in Boston in 2013 suggested that the most likely growth area in the immediate future in consumer genetics would be in the field of ancestry testing.

[44] Krol, 'Open Humans Aims to Be the Social Network for Science Volunteerism' (*Bio IT World*, 9 April 2015) <bio-itworld.com/2015/4/9/open-humans-aims-social-network-science-volunteerism.html> (accessed 18 April 2019); Krol, 'What Comes New for Direct-to-Consumer Genetics?' (*Bio IT World*, 16 July 2015) <bio-itworld.com/2015/7/16/what-comes-next-direct-consumer-genetics.html> (accessed 18 April 2019).

[45] Sullivan, '23andMe Has Signed 12 Other Genetic Data Partnerships beyond Pfizer and Genentech' (*VentureBeat*, 14 January 2015) <venturebeat.com/2015/01/14/23andme-has-signed-12-other-genetic-data-partnerships-beyond-pfizer-and-genentech/> (accessed 18 April 2019); Cussins, 'Direct-to-Consumer Genetic Tests Should Come with a Health Warning' (*Pharmaceutical Journal*, 15 January 2015) <https://www.pharmaceutical-jour nal.com/opinion/comment/direct-to-consumer-genetic-tests-should-come-with-a-health-warning/20067564.article?firstPass=false> (accessed 18 April 2019).

[46] Phillips, 'Only a Click Away'.

[47] Brown, 'Scientists Push Back against Booming Genetic Pseudoscience Market' (*Gizmodo Genetics*, 14 July 2017) <https://gizmodo.com/scientists-push-back-against-booming-genetic-pseudoscie-1796923059> (accessed 18 April 2019).

or No Genomics.[48] This was created partly in response to the service offered by Soccer Genomics.[49] DNA Friend, another parody website, has also been launched more recently. According to their website:

> At DNA Friend, we're committed to analysing and cataloguing every detail in your genome and then passing much of that information back to you. With millions of genetic samples collected and thousands of happy customers, you can trust DNA Friend to unlock your genetic secrets.[50]

Both these parodies are aimed at highlighting the limitations of DTC tests along with other concerns around their utility. These are both useful examples, but more informational resources are needed to assist the public in understanding the nature of these tests and privacy and consumer protection issues in this context.

3.1 Health Tests

The category of health-related testing itself covers a broad range of services, and it is possible to further classify tests within this category into subcategories, namely: predisposition; pre-symptomatic; pharmacogenetics or pharmacogenomics; nutrigenetics or nutrigenomics; susceptibility; and carrier testing.[51] At present, most companies do not offer whole genome sequencing services, which means that there will necessarily be limitations on the personal utility of their tests for individual consumers. We may see more whole genome offerings in the future, as the costs of sequencing continue to fall.

In a medical setting, for a genetic test to become part of clinical practice, it ultimately needs to have analytical validity, clinical validity and clinical utility.[52] A test will have analytical validity where its results are 'positive when a particular sequence is present and negative when it is absent'.[53] It will have clinical validity where the test results in a positive finding 'in people with the disease and negative in those without'.[54] Finally, it will have clinical utility

---

[48] Available at: <http://montgomerylab.stanford.edu/yesorno.html> (accessed 18 April 2019).

[49] Available at: <https://www.soccergenomics.com> (accessed 18 April 2019).

[50] Available at: <https://dnafriend.com/about> (accessed 18 April 2019).

[51] Please see Phillips, *Buying Your Self on the Internet*, Chapter 3, for a more detailed discussion of the different types of DTC tests.

[52] Human Genetics Commission, *More Genes Direct* (Department of Health 2007) <http://sites.nationalacademies.org/cs/groups/pgasite/documents/webpage/pga_053238.pdf> (accessed 18 April 2019), para 2.1.

[53] Annes, Giovanni and Murray, 'Risks of Presymptomatic Direct-to-Consumer Genetic Testing' (2010) 363 *New England Journal of Medicine* 1100-1, p. 1100. DOI: 10.1056/NEJMp1006029.

[54] Ibid.

where its 'benefits outweigh its risks'.[55] Generally, any diagnostic test is more likely to have clinical utility if it can be used to guide treatment decisions.

At present, many tests offered by DTC companies lack clinical validity and utility and this means that the nature of product that DTC companies are selling is questionable. A recent study evaluating the clinical utility of BRCA testing in the DTC context found that individuals would need follow-up tests in a clinic to confirm both positive and negative findings.[56] Furthermore, as tests for many conditions and especially complex diseases, are not standardised, it is possible for individuals to receive contradictory test results from different companies.[57] Nutrigenetics, which deals with associations between genetics and human metabolism and diet generally, is one category of health testing with quite poor validation to date.[58]

Concern has also previously been expressed regarding the marketing of DTC genetic tests. Companies often emphasise the importance of genetics in a very deterministic way and consumers may gain a skewed or exaggerated view of the role that a person's genes play in whether or not they develop a particular disease.[59] Some claims made by DTC companies may potentially

---

[55] Annes, Giovanni and Murray, 'Risks of Presymptomatic Direct-to-Consumer Genetic Testing', p. 1100; Cornel, van El and Borry, 'The Challenge of Implementing Genetic Tests with Clinical Utility'.

[56] Karow, '23andMe DTC Breast and Ovarian Cancer Risk Test Misses Almost 90 Percent of BRCA Mutation Carriers'.

[57] Kalf et al., 'Variations in Predicted Risks in Personal Genome Testing for Common Complex Diseases'; US Government Accountability Office, 'Direct-To-Consumer Genetic Tests: Misleading Test Results Are Further Complicated by Deceptive Marketing and Other Questionable Practice' (GAO-10-847T, 2010) Testimony before the Subcommittee on Oversight and Investigations, Committee on Energy and Commerce, House of Representatives 1–8 <http://www.gao.gov/assets/130/125079.pdf> (accessed 22 June 2019); Barry, 'Seeking Genetic Fate Personal genomics Companies Offer Forecasts of Disease Risk, but the Science behind the Packaging Is Still Evolving' (CBC News, 13 June 2018) <https://newsinteractives.cbc.ca/longform/dna-ancestry-test> (accessed 18 April 2019).

[58] Saukko et al., 'Negotiating the Boundary between Medicine and Consumer Culture: Online Marketing of Nutrigenetic Tests' (2010) 70 *Social Science and Medicine* 744 <https://doi.org/10.1016/j.socscimed.2009.10.066> (accessed 18 April 2019); Ries and Castle, 'Nutrigenomics and Ethics Interface: Direct-to-Consumer Services and Commercial Aspects' (2008) 12 *OMICS A Journal of Integrative Biology* 245; Marietta and McGuire, 'Direct-to-Consumer Genetic Testing: Is It the Practice of Medicine?' (2009) 37 *Journal of Law, Medicine & Ethics* 369; Rehm et al., 'ClinGen – The Clinical Genome Resource' (2015) 372 *New England Journal of Medicine* 2235; Sboner et al., 'The Real Cost of Sequencing: Higher than You Think!' (2011) 12 *Genome Biology* 125.

[59] McGuire et al., 'Social Networkers' Attitudes toward Direct-to-Consumer Personal Genome Testing' (2009) 9 *American Journal of Bioethics* 3 DOI: 10.1080/15265160902928209.

constitute misleading advertising.[60] While if an individual's genes do play a role in whether or not they will develop a particular disease or condition, for most complex diseases, genes are only one factor and other things, such as environment and the microbiome, will also have an impact on whether you develop a particular disease or condition. There is a tendency for DTC companies to overstate the role of genetics in human health.[61] A recent study has also found a high incidence of false positives in DTC test results and suggests:

> While having access to raw genotyping data can be informative and empowering for patients, this type of information can also be inaccurate and misinterpreted. Genetic testing needs to be interpreted by a qualified health-care professional in the context of several other factors, such as personal and family medical history.[62]

It is important for consumers to understand that there are many conditions that individuals might have a genetic predisposition to, but which they may avoid if they take precautionary measures. The environment in which people live, their lifestyle choices (for instance whether they smoke or exercise regularly), and their family history will often also play an influential role in determining whether or not they develop breast cancer or heart disease.[63]

---

[60] Caulfield, 'Predictive or Preposterous? The Marketing of DTC Genetic Testing' (2011) 10 *Journal of Science Communication* <https://doi.org/10.22323/2.10030302> (accessed 22 June 2019); Gabel, 'Redeeming the Genetic Groupon: Efficacy, Ethics, and Exploitation in Marketing DNA to the Masses' (2012) 81 *Mississippi Law Journal* (Georgia State University College of Law, Legal Studies Research Paper no. 2012-14) <https://ssrn.com/abstract=2020634> (accessed 22 June 2019); Myers, 'Health Care Providers and Direct-to-Consumer Access and Advertising of Genetic Testing in the United States' (2011) 3 *Genome Medicine* 81; Williams-Jones, '"Be Ready against Cancer, Now": Direct-to-Consumer Advertising for Genetic Testing' (2006) 25 *New Genetics and Society* 89 DOI: 10.1080/14636770600603527.

[61] Caulfield et al., 'Direct-to-Consumer Genetic Testing: Good, Bad or Benign?' (2010) 77 *Clinical Genetics* 101, pp. 101–5; Kaufman et al., 'Risky Business: Risk Perception and the Use of Medical Services among Customers of DTC Personal Genetic Testing' (2012) 21 *Journal of Genetic Counseling* 413, DOI: 10.1007/s10897-012-9483-0; Goddard et al., 'Health-Related Direct-to-Consumer Genetic Tests: A Public Health Assessment and Analysis of Practices Related to Internet-Based Tests for Risk of Thrombosis' (2009) 12 *Public Health Genomics* 92 DOI: 10.1159/000176794, p. 104; Frebourg, 'Direct-to-Consumer Genetic Testing Services: What Are the Medical Benefits? (2012) 20 *European Journal of Human Genetics* 483.

[62] Tandy-Connor et al., 'False-positive Results Released by Direct-to-Consumer Genetic Tests Highlight the Importance of Clinical Confirmation Testing for Appropriate Patient Care' (2018) 20 *Genetics in Medicine* 1515, p. 1520.

[63] Feero and Guttmacher, 'Genomic Medicine – An Updated Primer' (2010) 362 *New England Journal of Medicine* 2001 DOI: 10.1056/NEJMra0907175, pp. 2002–6.

There is also growing interest in the role of the microbiome[64] and its role in human health.

Despite the limitations of many of their services, DTC companies providing genetic tests for health purposes can more readily be likened to clinical laboratories and research institutions than providers of ancestry and genetic-relatedness tests. This is especially true where they engage in health research using consumers' data, although because companies often provide more than one type of testing the lines between health and non-health-related testing are increasingly blurred. Also, while the term consumer is used herein rather than patient in the context of DTC for health purposes, because currently these are framed as consumer services, it is possible that at some point a DTC consumer may become a patient or a medical research participant. One way forward for improved regulation might be to classify many DTC services as medical genetic tests, and to apply existing govern-ance mechanisms to providers of DTC tests. My view though is there is also a need for new, industry-specific legislation to be developed and enacted nationally, and international collaboration is needed to improve industry governance globally.

3.2 Ancestry Tests

Currently, the most popular type of DTC service on the market is ances-try testing, which has seen a significant rise in popularity in the last two years, with a number of prominent companies (AncestryDNA, 23andMe, MyHeritage and FamilyTreeDNA) achieving significant increases in sales.[65] This is 'intended to provide information about an individual's relatedness to a certain ancestor or ancestral group'.[66] This category of testing is likely

---

[64] Sampson and Mazmanian, 'Control of Brain Development, Function, and Behavior by the Microbiome' (2015) 17 *Cell Host Microbe* 565 DOI: 10.1016/j.chom.2015.04.011; Khanna and Tosh, 'A Clinician's Primer on the Role of the Microbiome in Human Health and Disease' (2014) 89 *Mayo Clinic Proceedings* 107 <https://doi.org/10.1016/j.mayocp.2013.10.011> (accessed 22 June 2019); Kramer and Bressan, 'Humans as Superorganisms How Microbes, Viruses, Imprinted Genes, and Other Selfish Entities Shape Our Behavior' (2015) 10 *Perspectives on Psychological Science* 464 <https://doi.org/10.1177/1745691615583131> (accessed 22 June 2019).

[65] Helft, 'Ancestry.com DNA Database Tops 3M, Sales Rise to $850M Ahead of Likely 2017 IPO' (*Forbes*, 10 January 2017) <https://www.forbes.com/sites/miguelhelft/2017/01/10/ancestry-com-dna-database-tops-3m-sales-rise-to-850m-ahead-of-likely-2017-ipo/#210a99a713b3> (accessed 18 April 2019); AncestryDNA, 'AncestryDNA Breaks Holiday Sales Record for Black Friday to Cyber Monday; Karow, '23andMe DTC Breast and Ovarian Cancer Risk Test Misses Almost 90 Percent of BRCA Mutation Carriers'.

[66] Human Genetics Commission, 'A Common Framework of Principles for Direct-to-Consumer Genetic Testing Services' (Department of Health 2010) <https://ukgtn.nhs.uk/

to be the most popular type of testing over the coming years.[67] This type of testing is typically classed as recreational, but as certain ethnic groups can be more prone to particular diseases it can also reveal information that is health-related. It is important to recognise that ancestry testing standards are also not harmonised and test results are estimates, so it is possible for an individual to receive results from different companies that indicate different ethnic origins.[68] Two recent stories of DTC companies providing test results for dogs, with one also indicating that two dogs had North American First Nations ancestry,[69] also demonstrate that consumers should be cautious about using these services.[70] As ancestry tests can also reveal unknown relatives and false paternity and as some companies offering ancestry testing have begun to conduct health research, more oversight of the industry is desirable. When thinking about purchasing a test it is recommended that you do compare different services and read the company's privacy policy and contract. You may also find it useful to use a service such as PriBot, which allows you to ask the PriBot chatbot questions about a company's privacy policies. While this only allows for particular questions at present, it is a useful tool, which I intend to use more in the future to assist with analysing these documents.[71]

4. DTC Contracts

Contracts and privacy policies are everywhere online and your devices are full of them. The Norwegian Consumer Council (NCC) in its *APPFail* campaign estimated that the average smartphone contains 250,000 words of terms and conditions and privacy policies.[72] Quartz has suggested that consumers

---

resources/library/article/human-genetics-commission-a-common-framework-of-principles-for-direct-to-consumer-genetic-testing-services-70/> (accessed 18 April 2019), p. 3.

[67] Spencer Wells of *National Geographic*'s Genographic Project speaking at the Consumer Genetics Conference in Boston in 2013 suggested that the most likely growth area in the immediate future in consumer genetics would be in the field of ancestry testing.

[68] Brown, 'How DNA Testing Botched My Family's Heritage, and Probably Yours, Too' (*Gizmodo Genetics*, 16 January 2018) <https://gizmodo.com/how-dna-testing-botched-my-familys-heritage-and-probab-1820932637> (accessed 18 April 2019); Karow, '23andMe DTC Breast and Ovarian Cancer Risk Test Misses Almost 90 Percent of BRCA Mutation Carriers'.

[69] Karow, '23andMe DTC Breast and Ovarian Cancer Risk Test Misses Almost 90 Percent of BRCA Mutation Carriers'.

[70] Barrera and Foxcroft, 'Heredity or Hoax?' (CBC News, 13 June 2018) <https://newsinteractives.cbc.ca/longform/dna-ancestry-test> (accessed 18 April 2019); Karow, '23andMe DTC Breast and Ovarian Cancer Risk Test Misses Almost 90 Percent of BRCA Mutation Carriers'.

[71] PriBot <https://pribot.org/bot> (accessed 16 April 2019).

[72] Norwegian Consumer Council, '250,000 Words of App Terms and Conditions' (24 May

who own five Apple devices have entered into 'at least 30 contracts, totalling more than 100,000 words'.[73] The Australian consumer group Choice also conducted a study of e-reader contracts and found that the Amazon Kindle actually had eight documents exceeding 73,000 words in total, which took an actor they hired nine hours to read.[74]

A number of experiments carried out by GameStation, F-Secure and Purple highlight how very significant and unexpected clauses can be effectively buried in terms and conditions and in End-user Licence Agreements (EULAs).[75] In the GameStation example, consumers agreed to give their immortal soul to the company, and in F-Secure's public WiFi experiment in London consumers agreed to hand over their first born child for eternity.[76] Meanwhile, Purple included a community service clause, where '22,000 people agreed to carry out 1,000 hours of community service', which included agreeing to clean public toilets, hug stray animals and paint snails' shells.[77] Purple offered a prize to those who noticed the problematic clause, but 'only one individual, which is 0.000045% of all Wi-Fi users throughout the whole two weeks, managed to spot it'.[78]

2016) <https://www.forbrukerradet.no/side/250000-words-of-app-terms-and-conditions/> (accessed 18 April 2019).

[73] Groskopf, 'CLICK "I AGREE": Apple Fans Have Click-signed more than 100,000 Words of Legal Contracts' (*Quartz*, 5 November 2016) <https://qz.com/797928/apple-fans-have-click-signed-more-than-100000-words-of-legal-contracts/> (accessed 18 April 2019).

[74] Hunt, 'Amazon Kindle's Terms "Unreasonable" and Would Take Nine Hours to Read, Choice Says' (*The Guardian*, 15 March 2017) <https://www.theguardian.com/australia-news/2017/mar/15/amazon-kindles-terms-unreasonable-and-would-take-nine-hours-to-read-choice-says> (accessed 18 April 2019); *Choice*, 'Nine Hours of "Conditions Apply"' <https://www.choice.com.au/about-us/media-releases/2017/march/nine-hours-of-conditions-apply> (accessed 18 April 2019); Elshout et al., *Study on Consumers' Attitudes towards Terms Conditions (T&Cs) Final Report* (22 September 2016) Report for the European Commission, Consumers, Health, Agriculture and Food Executive Agency (CHAFEA) on behalf of Directorate-General for Justice and Consumers <https://ssrn.com/abstract=2847546> (accessed 18 April 2019).

[75] Perton, 'Read Fine Print or GameStation May Own Your Soul' (*Consumerist*, 16 April 2010) <http://consumerist.com/2010/04/16/read-fine-print-or-gamestation-may-own-your-soul/> (accessed 18 April 2019, only outside EEA).

[76] Fox-Brewster, 'Londoners Give Up Eldest Children in Public Wi-Fi Security Horror Show' (*The Guardian*, 29 September 2014) <https://www.theguardian.com/technology/2014/sep/29/londoners-wi-fi-security-herod-clause> (accessed 18 April 2019).

[77] *Purple*, '22,000 People Willingly Agree to Community Service in Return for Free WiFi' *Purple*, '22,000 People Willingly Agree to Community Service in Return for Free WiFi' (13 July 2017) <https://purple.ai/blogs/purple-community-service/> (accessed 18 April 2019).

[78] Tuffley, 'How Not to Agree to Clean Public Toilets When You Accept Any Online Terms and Conditions' (The Conversation, 23 July 2017) <https://theconversation.com/how-

The recent work of Obar and Oeldorf-Hirsch, which explored how undergraduate students interacted with clickwrap contracts and privacy policies on the fictitious social network NameDrop, provides some further insight.[79] Again, this study included some 'gotcha' clauses (a child assignment clause and a clause allowing for data sharing with the NSA). Unfortunately, only 1.7 per cent (nine out of 543) of those surveyed 'mentioned the child assignment clause', and '11 (2 per cent) mentioned concerns with data sharing', and only one person actually mentioned the NSA clause.[80]

While the above examples were all experiments, the tendency of consumers not to read, and regulators' tendency not to enact specific regulation of many new digital technologies, have led to a situation where wrap contracts are increasingly lengthy with companies copying terms from each other and also inserting clauses that allow them additional rights that do not relate to the original purpose of the contract.[81] These contracts are also not generally industry specific, which means that a consumer might agree to similar terms when purchasing shoes and when ordering a genetic test. These tendencies also have the combined effect of limiting consumer choice, in the sense that it will often not be possible to access a particular service with more favourable terms and these contracts may also attempt to erode certain rights.[82]

It is possible that your activities on a website may be governed by the company's contract even when you are merely browsing a website. The frequency of these contracts might not be problematic if all these documents were easily understood by the ordinary person or were unlikely to contain anything surprising. Unfortunately, this is not the case at present. Wrap contracts and privacy policies might be everywhere, but consumers often ignore them and may not give much consideration to their significance or potential impact on their rights. Often this lack of reading and regard is based primarily on people's generally not having sufficient time to read these documents. For example, Cranor and McDonald's study estimated 'that reading privacy

---

not-to-agree-to-clean-public-toilets-when-you-accept-any-online-terms-and-conditions-81169> (accessed 18 April 2019).

[79] Obar and Oeldorf-Hirsch, 'The Biggest Lie on the Internet'; Obar and Oeldorf-Hirsch, 'Clickwrap Impact: Quick-Join Options and Ignoring Privacy and Terms of Service Policies of Social Networking Services' (2017) in proceedings of the 8th International Conference on Social Media & Society ACM, p. 8. <https://ssrn.com/abstract=3017277> (accessed 18 April 2019).

[80] Ibid., p. 11.

[81] Kim, *Wrap Contracts: Foundations and Ramifications* (Oxford University Press 2014), pp. 41–2.

[82] Ibid., pp. 51–2; Kim, 'Contract's Adaptation and the Online Bargain' (2010) 79 *University of Chicago Law Review* 1327.

policies carries costs in time of approximately 201 hours a year, worth about $3,534 annually per American Internet user. Nationally, if Americans were to read online privacy policies word-for-word, we estimate the value of time lost as about $781 billion annually.'[83] Meanwhile, Wigley Law compared iTunes' and Amazon's contracts to the lengths of Shakespeare's *Macbeth* and *Hamlet* and both contracts were longer than the respective plays,[84] suggesting that one might now choose between reading the iTunes agreement or reading Shakespeare.

Often these documents will appear in the form of terms and conditions or terms of use when you are at the point of entering your payment information. You may also encounter them as End-user Licence Agreements when installing or updating computer software, playing a video game or setting up a smart television. Whether you are purchasing shoes, setting up an online dating profile or ordering a genetic test, you will have at some point entered into a contractual relationship through a wrap contract (clickwrap or browsewrap). The term wrap contract is used herein, in the same manner as in Kim's book, as 'a blanket term to refer to a unilaterally imposed set of terms which the drafter purports to be legally binding and which is presented to the non-drafting party'.[85] DTC companies' contracts appear on their websites as terms and conditions, terms of service or terms of use. They may be accompanied by additional documents, such as privacy policies, but sometimes elements of privacy statements or privacy policies are also included in contractual documents. Companies may also seek to incorporate terms by reference. This is done by mentioning another document in the contract. This means that a number of documents can be linked together and so it is necessary for a person to read all the documents in order to understand their rights and obligations under the contract.

Even where consumers do choose to read such contracts there is evidence to suggest they will not necessarily understand their content due to the complex nature of the language used, which, as Conklin and Hyde's recent study[86] demonstrates, often requires a high level of education to com-

---

[83] McDonald and Cranor, 'The Cost of Reading Privacy Policies' (2008) 4 I/S *Journal of Law and Policy for the Information Society* 562, p. 562.

[84] Wigley + Company Solicitors, 'To Read or Not To Read … Online Ts and Cs. Or Hamlet' (2015) <http://wigleylaw.com/assets/Uploads/To-read-or-not-to-read.pdf> (accessed 18 April 2019).

[85] Kim, *Wrap Contracts*, pp. 2–3.

[86] Conklin and Hyde, 'If Small Print "Terms and Conditions" Require a PhD to Read, Should they be Legally Binding?' (*The Conversation*, 10 May 2018) <https://theconversation.com/if-small-print-terms-and-conditions-require-a-phd-to-read-should-they-be-legally-binding-75101> (accessed 18 April 2019); see also Conklin, Hyde, and Parente,

prehend.[87] Additionally, genetic test results are complex in nature and the governance mechanisms that would normally apply to genetic tests carried out in a clinical setting have been developed in recognition of this. However, current DTC industry practice often does not adhere to existing governance mechanisms, and this does raise questions about the adequacy of consent mechanisms in this context and the level of transparency in current industry practice.[88]

Another issue that is explored in the larger work is how the online environment could impact upon consumers' abilities to make informed decisions and limit their ability to make informed choices. It has been suggested elsewhere that the online environment may be habituating people to the act of clicking and that it also can encourage impulsivity.[89] Frischmann and Selinger's work[90] argues that the architecture of electronic contracts can mean that 'it is completely rational for a user to blindly accept the terms of use'.[91] They suggest that the designed environment of websites encourages people to behave as automatons and this in turn has negative consequences for autonomy and sociality.[92] The NCC in its *Deceived by Design* report also suggest that design features in some popular services nudge users into choosing less privacy-friendly options.[93] It is suggested that current business practices in relation to protection of privacy and informed consent are in need of reform. Other reform will be necessary in order to assist consumers with making informed decisions and informed choices regarding whether or not to engage with such services.

'Assessing Plain and Intelligible Language in the Consumer Rights Act: A Role for Reading Scores?' (2018) Legal Studies, ISSN 1748-121X (in press) <http://eprints.nottingham.ac.uk/51073/> (accessed 18 April 2019).

[87] Ayres and Schwartz, 'The No-Reading Problem in Consumer Contract Law' (2014) 66 *Stanford Law Review* 545; Loos and Luzak, 'Wanted: A Bigger Stick: On Unfair Terms in Consumer Contracts with Online Service Providers' (Centre for the Study of European Contract Law Working Paper Series, 8 January 2015) 39 *Journal of Consumer Policy* 63.

[88] Laestadius, Rich, and Auer, 'All Your Data (Effectively) Belong to Us'.

[89] Kim, *Wrap Contracts*, pp. 9–61; Hillman, 'On-line Consumer Standard-form Contracting Practices: A Survey and Discussion of Legal Implications' (Cornell Law Faculty Publications Paper 29, 2005) <http://dx.doi.org/10.2139/ssrn.686817> (accessed 18 April 2019).

[90] Frischmann and Selinger, 'Engineering Humans with Contracts'; and Frischmann and Selinger, *Re-Engineering Humanity*.

[91] Frischmann and Selinger, 'Engineering Humans with Contracts', p. 5.

[92] Frischmann and Selinger, 'Engineering Humans with Contracts', pp. 2–3.

[93] Norwegian Consumer Council, *Deceived by Design*, p. 3. See also the US Bill, Act S. 1084: Deceptive Experiences To Online Users Reduction Act <https://www.govtrack.us/congress/bills/116/s1084/text> (accessed 10 September 2019); this Bill if passed would ban certain design practices that exert negative influences on users' decision making.

For some, the use of wrap contracts may not seem problematic. It might be argued that as this is standard business practice and so commonplace there should be no cause for concern. That might be acceptable when it comes to mundane consumer purchases of clothing and shoes. However, it is suggested herein that a more cautious approach is desirable when these contracts are used to govern the provision of services which are dependent on the collection, sharing, storage and use of sequenced genetic information and other types of personal data that might be considered sensitive, or might have previously been included only as a part of a medical record. It needs to be stressed that wrap contracts and privacy policies need to be read together, as these documents are often linked to each other and seek to incorporate terms by reference. Reform and further oversight of both contracts and privacy policies are needed.

It should also be noted that while a lengthy privacy policy might be beneficial if it actually complies with applicable privacy and data protection law and protects the rights of individuals, at present privacy policies may often not be compliant. Specifically, many policies may be failing to meet the transparency requirement set by the GDPR, in the sense that they do not make it clear what types of data companies collect, how long data are stored for, and with whom they are shared. Policies may also fail to meet transparency requirements in the sense of not being in plain and intelligible language.

Given the shared nature of genetic information, there is another issue regarding who in fact has the capacity to consent, as genetic test results can also have significant meaning for family members. This issue increases in significance in the context of tests for close genetic relatedness (paternity and maternity), and also for all testing of children.

The linking of contracts and privacy policies also requires further scrutiny, as it is common practice for DTC companies to include clauses that allow for unilateral variation of the contract. This could potentially have the effect of allowing a company to alter its privacy policy on collection, storage, sharing and sale of both stored sequenced genetic information and personal data more generally. Additionally, developing strong security infrastructure and policies are also vital given the privacy risks and the potential for re-identification of individuals using genetic data.

5. Terms That May Be Unfair

In analysing DTC contracts much commonality was found in the terms included and the language used. At present, the majority are skewed heavily in the company's favour. The UK's consumer regulator, the Competition & Markets Authority (CMA), conducted a compliance review of cloud storage providers' terms and business practices aimed at assessing whether cloud storage providers' terms and business practices complied with consumer protection law. It should be noted that the report[94] has already had some degree of success with improving terms, as several cloud service providers have made commitments to improve their terms.[95] It is also suggested that a number of terms commonly included in DTC contracts are likely to be deemed unfair in line with the CMA's 'Cloud Storage Findings Report' and consequently unenforceable under UK law and EU law. These include: clauses allowing for unilateral variation of the contract; clauses disclaiming liability for fitness for purpose or for personal injury caused by the company's negligence; clauses limiting scope of purpose; clauses purporting to bind the consumer to resolve any disputes in another jurisdiction; and consent clauses that are likely to be deemed unfair; regulators should take an interest in policing these terms.

It should be noted that in this context, such terms are imposed on consumers who have no opportunity to negotiate and there will normally be a disparity between the company and the consumer in terms of information regarding the respective risks and benefits of testing, the limitations of testing and the significance of genetic risk information. It is therefore desirable that companies do reform their contracts and omit the most onerous terms. They could also look to governance mechanisms developed in the medical research context.

In the UK, the CMA has conducted a compliance review of the contracts of cloud computing providers and released its findings report, 'Consumer Law Compliance Review: Cloud Storage'.[96] This review was concerned with assessing whether cloud storage providers' terms and business practices complied with consumer protection law. It should be noted that the report has already had some degree of success with improving terms, as several cloud service providers have made commitments in this direction.[97] The report

---

94 CMA, *Consumer Law Compliance Review: Cloud Storage* (CMA Findings Report 2016) <https://assets.digital.cabinet-office.gov.uk/media/57472953e5274a037500000d/cloud-storage-findings-report.pdf> (accessed 18 April 2019); CMA, *Update on Cloud Storage Consumer Compliance Review* (CMA 1 April 2016) <https://assets.digital.cabinet-office.gov.uk/media/56fe3227ed915d117d000037/Investigation_update-1_April_2016.pdf> (accessed 18 April 2019); CMA, *Unfair Contract Terms Explained* (CMA37(a), 31 July 2015); CMA, *Unfair Contract Terms Guidance – Guidance on the Unfair Terms Provisions in the Consumer Rights Act 2015* (CMA37, 31 July 2015).

95 CMA, 'Cloud Storage: Consumer Compliance Review' (homepage) <https://www.gov.uk/cma-cases/cloud-storage-consumer-compliance-review> (accessed 16 April 2019).

96 CMA, *Consumer Law Compliance Review: Cloud Storage Findings Report*, note 80.

97 CMA, 'Cloud Storage: Consumer Compliance Review' (homepage).

is very relevant to the present discussion, as it indicates the types of terms and business practices that the CMA is likely to view as problematic and potentially unfair.[98]

Several terms that the CMA found problematic in cloud computing contracts are also commonly included in DTC contracts, and consequently it is recommended that the CMA makes a compliance review of DTC contracts, as this could help to improve DTC contracts in the short term, as the CMA could encourage companies to discontinue the use of particular terms. The frequency of these terms highlights the need for greater oversight of the industry and indicates that self-regulation may not provide sufficient protection to consumers.

Furthermore, DTC companies marketing tests to consumers based in the EU and the UK should be complying with the consent requirements of the GDPR. In the UK they should also comply with the provisions of the Human Tissue Act and the Data Protection Act 2018, which transposes the GDPR into the UK's domestic law. It is also possible that where companies provide health tests they may in fact need to adhere to higher standards in line with the decision in *Montgomery*.[99]

Given the tendency to combine privacy policies with contracts, the impact of unilateral variation clauses is increased. Clauses of this type may permit a company to alter their policies on the use, storage, sharing and sale of stored genetic information in significant ways that may have serious consequences for consumers.

6. Privacy and Security

The nature of sequenced genetic information means that it can be used for a wide variety of genetic testing purposes. The DTC industry is an example of disruptive innovation, as it has created a market for the commercial sale of genetic testing services. This represents an important shift, as previously these tests were confined primarily to a medical setting[100] or as part of criminal or forensic proceedings. It should also be borne in mind that if you were to have a genetic test in a medical setting, informed consent would generally

---

[98] Financial Conduct Authority, *The Unfair Contract Terms Regulatory Guide* (February 2018) <https://www.handbook.fca.org.uk/handbook/UNFCOG.pdf> (accessed 18 April 2019).

[99] *Montgomery* v *Lanarkshire Health Board* (Scotland) [2015] 2 All ER 1031, [2015] UKSC 11.

[100] Curnutte and Testa, 'Consuming Genomes: Scientific and Social Innovation in Direct-to-Consumer Genetic Testing' (2012) 31 *New Genetics and Society* 15; Spector-Bagdady and Pike, 'Consuming Genomics: Regulating Direct-to-Consumer Genetic and Genomic Information' (2014) 92 *Nebraska Law Review* 677.

be required. Due to certain aspects of the nature of genetic information, privacy is an important issue in this context. While the regulatory response to the DTC industry to date has generally been a policy response,[101] rather than a legislative response as noted above, companies offering DTC services to UK and EU consumers should be complying with the provisions of the GDPR and at present the industry does have some work to do to ensure compliance.

Genetic data are also included in Article 9's prohibition on processing special categories of data. There are two relevant exceptions set out in Article 9(2). These are: (a) 'explicit consent' of data subject; and (j) the so-called research exemption. It has been suggested that it may be possible for DTC companies to take advantage of the research exemption.[102] However, even if this occurred, companies would still need to comply with the consent requirements for the initial test and it seems likely that they may instead need to obtain additional consent for all secondary research. The GDPR also provides for a number of rights for data subjects and this includes being able to withdraw consent as well, so DTC companies also need to make sure that they have policies and practices in place to allow for withdrawing consent.

The GDPR also sets a number of requirements in relation to privacy policies and notices. Article 13 sets out the types of information that should

---

[101] A number of organisations have released guidance including: Human Genetics Commission, *Genes Direct: Ensuring The Effective Oversight Of Genetic Tests Supplied Directly To The Public* (Department of Health 2003) <https://repository.library.georgetown.edu/handle/10822/523214> (accessed 18 April 2019); Human Genetics Commission, *More Genes Direct*; Human Genetics Commission, 'A Common Framework of Principles'; European Society of Human Genetics, 'Statement of the ESHG on Direct-to-Consumer Genetic Testing for Health-Related Purposes' (2010) 18 *European Journal of Human Genetics* 1271; European Academies Science Advisory Council (EASAC) and Federation of European Academies of Medicine (FEAM), *Direct-to-Consumer Genetic Testing – Summary Document*; Association for Molecular Pathology, *Position Statement: on Direct Access Genetic Testing* (2007); Association for Molecular Pathology, *Position Statement: Direct Access Genetic Testing* (2015); Canadian College of Medical Geneticists, 'CCMG Statement on Direct-to-Consumer Genetic Testing' (2012) 81 *Clinical Genetics* 1 <https://www.ccmg-ccgm.org/documents/Policies_etc/Pos_Statements/PosStmt_EPP_DTC_FINAL_20Jan2011.pdf> (accessed 18 April 2019); Office of the Privacy Commissioner (OPC), *Statement on the Use of Genetic Test Results by Life and Health Insurance Companies* (2014) <https://www.priv.gc.ca/en/opc-news/news-and-announcements/2014/s-d_140709/> (accessed 18 April 2019).

[102] Pormeister, 'Genetic Data and the Research Exemption: Is the GDPR Going Too Far?' (2017) 7 *International Data Privacy Law* 137 <https://doi.org/10.1093/idpl/ipx006> (accessed 22 June 2019), p. 145.

be provided to data subjects in relation to processing of information. There is also a transparency requirement in relation to Privacy Notices in Article 12(1). Article 12(7) also requires information that is provided to a data subject to be conveyed in a meaningful way, and that the information presented is 'easily visible, intelligible and clearly legible'.

The importance of protecting genetic privacy was also stressed in the European Society of Human Genetics' Statement on Direct-To-Consumer Genetic Testing For Health-Related Purposes and the Human Genetics Commission's Common Framework of Principles for Direct-to-Consumer Genetic Testing Services.[103] Genetic information can serve as a unique identifier for an individual. It can also be used both in genealogical research and criminal investigations to identify related individuals.[104] As DNA does not change, in a way that would make the information non-identifiable over time, stored sequenced data does pose some level of risk to an individual's privacy. While previously researchers have often relied on de-identification or pseudonymisation techniques it has become apparent that it may not be possible to truly de-identify genetic data.[105] This has consequences not only for the individual to whom the genetic data pertains, but also to their family, which also means that where one family member undergoes genetic testing it will necessarily reveal information about others.

DTC companies often also collect additional personal information from their consumers through surveys, and may also encourage consumers to share information via social networking functions on their websites. In the context of genetic relatedness and ancestry tests, this can include connecting consumers with other people to whom they may be related.[106]

As the DTC industry grows, companies will accumulate more data and it is vital that such data are stored securely, as potential attackers could target

---

[103] European Society of Human Genetics, 'Statement of the ESHG on Direct-to-Consumer Genetic Testing for Health-related Purposes'; Human Genetics Commission, 'A Common Framework of Principles'.

[104] Simoncelli, 'Dangerous Excursions: The Case against Expanding Forensic DNA Databases to Innocent Persons' (2006) 34 *Journal of Law, Medicine and Ethics* 390 <https://doi.org/10.1111/j.1748-720X.2006.00045.x> (accessed 22 June 2019), p. 390.

[105] Nuffield Council on Bioethics, *The Collection, Linking and Use of Data in Biomedical Research and Health Care: Ethical* Issues (February 2015), pp. 69–71; Ayday et al., 'Whole Genome Sequencing: Revolutionary Medicine or Privacy Nightmare?' (2015) 2 *Computer* 58, p. 62; Erlich and Narayanan, 'Routes for Breaching and Protecting Genetic Privacy' (2014) 15 *Nature Reviews Genetics* 409, p. 409.

[106] Doe, 'With Genetic Testing, I Gave My Parents the Gift of Divorce' (*Vox*, 9 September 2014) <https://www.vox.com/2014/9/9/5975653/with-genetic-testing-i-gave-my-parents-the-gift-of-divorce-23andme> (accessed 18 April 2019).

DTC companies' databases for a number of reasons. Two data breaches at DTC companies have already emerged in 2017 and 2018.[107] It has also now been shown that it is possible to infect genetic data with malware. 'Researchers at the University of Washington have shown that changing a little bit of computer code in DNA sequencing software can make a computer vulnerable to malware embedded in a strand of DNA.' While we have not as yet seen real-world attacks of this kind, this may pose challenges for companies dealing with genetic data in the future.[108]

It is quite difficult to quantify risks in this context. Although some risks may seem relatively small at present (one example being the creation of synthetic DNA to plant at a crime scene), the risks of harvesting stored sequenced genetic data and other personal data stored by DTC companies to create very detailed profiles for the purposes of marketing or targeting a particular group are not necessarily remote. The chances of DTC databases being used to harvest data for marketing are increased by the tendency of DTC companies to partner with others, including the pharmaceutical industry and other DTC companies, which is already a growing trend amongst the most prominent DTC companies. For instance, Gene By Gene's FamilyTreeDNA has also acquired DNA Heritage and DNA-Fingerprint, and MyHeritage has partnered with both FamilyTreeDNA and 23andMe. 23andMe has also entered at least fifteen partnerships to date. This includes a very recent venture with GlaxoSmithKline[109] and previous collaborations with Pfizer, Genentech

---

[107] Coldewey, 'MyHeritage Breach Exposes 92M Emails and Hashed Passwords'; Ancestry, 'RootsWeb Security Update' (*TechCrunch*, 5 June 2018) <https://techcrunch.com/2018/06/05/myheritage-breach-exposes-92m-emails-and-hashed-passwords/?guccounter=1> (accessed 18 April 2019); Navarro, 'Ancestry.com Suffers Big Data Leak – 300,000 User Credentials Exposed' (*Komando*, 28 December 2017) <https://www.komando.com/happening-now/435921/ancestry-com-suffers-big-data-leak-300000-user-credentials-exposed> (accessed 18 April 2019); Chen, 'Why a DNA Data Breach Is Much Worse Than a Credit Card Leak' (*The Verge*, 6 June 2018) <https://www.theverge.com/2018/6/6/17435166/myheritage-dna-breach-genetic-privacy-bioethics> (accessed 18 April 2019).

[108] Nordrum, 'Researchers Embed Malware into DNA to Hack DNA Sequencing' (Software IEEE Spectrum, 10 August 2017) <https://spectrum.ieee.org/the-human-os/computing/software/researchers-embed-malicious-code-into-dna-to-hack-dna-sequencing-software> (accessed 18 April 2019).

[109] Geggel, '23andMe Is Sharing Its 5 Million Clients' Genetic Data with Drug Giant GlaxoSmithKline' (*Livescience*, 26 July 2018) <https://www.livescience.com/63173-23andme-partnership-glaxosmithkline.html> (accessed 18 April 2019); Glaxo SmithKline, 'GSK and 23andMe Sign Agreement to Leverage Genetic Insights for the Development of Novel Medicines' (25 July 2018) <https://www.gsk.com/en-gb/media/press-releases/gsk-and-23andme-sign-agreement-to-leverage-genetic-insights-for-the-development-of-novel-medicines/> (accessed 18 April 2019).

and Reset Therapeutics.[110] It is possible that it may also collaborate with Google's Calico due to its links with Google.[111] 23andMe has also started a pharmaceutical branch[112] and it also purchased CureTogether in 2012.[113] Some companies have also begun to partner with the insurance industry. For example, Prenetics aims to offer pharmacogenetic tests to Chinese customers, but it has received significant investment from Ping An, which is an insurance company with 200 million policy holders based in China.[114]

The risk of data leakage in many industries now seems to be merely a matter of time and no system is completely secure. Furthermore, as Ayday et al. note, due to the shared nature of genetic data, potential data leakage is not a matter that will only affect the individual whose data are stored. It could potentially impact their wider family.[115] There is growing use of biometric identifiers in a variety of security systems, which could create incentives for criminal organisations to attempt to gain access to both DTC databases and biobanks. While some of this concern may seem far-fetched, some recent examples can illustrate the potential problems in this area. Fingerprint recognition being used to validate payments with Apple Pay's Touch ID is the most prominent example, although Samsung and banks

---

110 Sullivan, '23andMe has Signed 12 Other Genetic Data Partnerships beyond Pfizer and Genentech'.

111 Lagorio-Chafkin, '23andMe Exec: You Ain't Seen Nothing Yet' (*Inc*, 7 January 2015) <www.inc.com/christine-lagorio/23andMe-new-partnerships.html> (accessed 18 April 2019); Associated Press, 'Pfizer, 23andMe Team Up to Study Bowel Disease' (*Medical Xpress*, 12 August 2014) <medicalxpress.com/news/2014-08-pfizer-23andme-team-bowel-disease.html> (accessed 10 August 2018); Ward, 'Google-Backed Genetic Testing Company Hires Veteran Scientist' (*Financial Times*, 12 March 2015) <ft.com/cms/s/0/ead07e84-c8d8-11e4-bc64-00144feab7de.html> (accessed 18 April 2019).

112 Duhaime-Ross, '23andMe Plans to Move beyond Genetic Testing to Making Drugs' (*The Verge*, 12 March 2015) <theverge.com/2015/3/12/8199303/23andme-drug-development-testing> (accessed 18 April 2019); Genomeweb staff reporter, '23andMe Launches Therapeutics Group with Former Genentech Exec at Helm' (12 March 2015) <Genomeweb.com/drug-discovery-development/23andme-launches-therapeutics-group-former-genentech-exec-helm> (accessed 18 April 2019).

113 Proffitt, 'Deals Center on Self-reported Patient Data Services' (2012) 30 *Nature Biotechnology* 1016 doi: 10.1038/nbt1112-1016; 23andMe, '23andMe Acquires CureTogether, Inc' (press release, 12 July 2012) <https://mediacenter.23andme.com/press-releases/23andme-acquires-curetogether-inc/> (accessed 18 April 2019).

114 Woodhouse, 'iGene: Hong Kong Biotech Start-up Prenetics Bringing 48-hour DNA Tests to Broader Chinese Market for Safer Prescriptions' (*South China Morning Post*, 4 April 2016) <www.scmp.com/tech/science-research/article/1932838/igene-hong-kong-biotech-start-prenetics-bringing-48-hour-dna> (accessed 18 April 2019).

115 Ayday et al., 'Whole Genome Sequencing: Revolutionary Medicine or Privacy Nightmare?', p. 62.

such as RBS and NatWest are using similar technology, while EyeLock has developed an iris scanner.[116] The Touch ID was successfully hacked one day after its launch.[117] A German hacking group has also claimed to be able to recreate fingerprints based on photographs.[118] If genetic data are not stored securely this may lead to as yet unforeseen harms. It is therefore desirable that companies utilise encryption technology, and also have rigorous policies in place covering data storage, sharing, access, sale and destruction of data. It has also been demonstrated that hacking medical devices is a real possibility with the FDA publishing an alert regarding the Hospira drug pump.[119] Security experts demonstrated that it would be possible for a person with access to the hospital network to alter drug dosage remotely meaning that it would be possible for a hacker with malicious intent to cause a patient's death.[120] Finally, Citizen Lab and Open Effect's report[121] on the security of wearable fitness trackers found that seven out of the eight devices tests had significant security vulnerabilities. This included the possibility for the creation of fake records.[122].

[116] Belton, 'In Your Irises: The New Rise of Biometric Banking' (BBC News, 20 March 2015) <bbc.co.uk/news/business-31968642> (accessed 18 April 2019); also see Yeap, 'Your Finger is About to Replace Your Bank Password' (*CCN Money*, 9 June 2015) <https://money.cnn.com/2015/06/05/technology/bank-fingerprint-reader/index.html?iid=EL> (accessed 18 April 2019).

[117] Yeap, 'Your Finger is About to Replace Your Bank Password'.

[118] Goldman, 'Hackers Recreate Fingerprints Using Public Photos' (*CNN Money*, 30 December 2014) <http://money.cnn.com/2014/12/30/technology/security/fingerprint-hack/> (accessed 18 April 2019).

[119] FDA, 'Cybersecurity Vulnerabilities of Hospira Symbiq Infusion System' (FDA Safety Communication, 31 July 2015) <https://www.fda.gov/medicaldevices/digitalhealth/ucm373213.htm> (accessed 18 April 2019).

[120] Bhatia, 'FDA Fears Hacking Risks in Medical Devices; Says Hospira Pump Should Not Be Used' (*International Business Times*, 5 August 2015) <https://www.ibtimes.com/fda-fears-hacking-risks-medical-devices-says-hospira-pump-should-not-be-used-2039898> (accessed 18 April 2019); Brady and Glazer, 'Cybersecurity in Hospitals: Protecting Electronic Patient Devices from the Risk of Hacking' (*MD News*, 7 August 2015) Legal Technology <http://lowerhudsonbronx.mdnews.com/cybersecurity-hospitals-protecting-electronic-patient-devices-risk-hacking> (accessed 18 April 2019); Storm, 'MEDJACK: Hackers hijacking medical devices to create backdoors in hospital networks' (*Computerworld*, 8 June 2015) <computerworld.com/article/2932371/cybercrime-hacking/medjack-hackers-hijacking-medical-devices-to-create-backdoors-in-hospital-networks.html> (accessed 18 April 2019).

[121] Hilts, Parson and Knockel, 'Every Step You Fake: A Comparative Analysis of Fitness Tracker Privacy and Security' (Open Effect Report 2016) <https://citizenlab.org/2016/02/fitness-tracker-privacy-and-security/> (accessed 18 April 2019).

[122] Ibid., p. 32, para 2.7.2.

All the above examples highlight the need for appropriate regulation of technologies that rely on the collection and transmission of personal data. Businesses offering their services to consumers based in the EU and UK should be complying with the GDPR. For both DTC and wearable fitness-monitoring devices, consumers' personal information is often being shared more widely then they might anticipate. Given the privacy and data protection issues here, it is recommended that the UK's Information Commissioner's Office, together with data protection authorities and privacy regulators in other countries, take on a more active role in regulating the industry and assessing compliance.

In August 2018, the Future of Privacy Forum released Privacy Best Practices for Consumer Genetic Testing Services,[123] which were developed in collaboration with a number of DTC companies. These are framed as voluntary guidelines, and while this is a positive step, companies marketing to EU consumers still need to comply with the GDPR. At present, it seems that there is much work to be done in order for the industry to ensure compliance.

7. Conclusion

DTC services, by taking genetic tests out of the clinic and into the domestic space and offering them via the Internet internationally, do challenge existing governance mechanisms. They raise similar issues as several developments in the Internet of Things, such as wearable health- and fitness-monitoring devices, or innovations in the field of biometrics. In an increasingly globalised world, where legal regulation is no longer restricted to national laws, the DTC industry highlights some of the problems associated more generally with the regulation of internet-based industries. Its reliance on wrap contracts can also be used as an illustrative example of some of the issues that the use of such contracts raises, especially where services that were previously considered medical services become consumer services.

In the long term, if the industry is to continue to develop, specific legal regulation needs to be developed. New regulatory bodies are also needed. These could potentially come under the authority of existing data protection and privacy regulators. Codes of conduct could also be beneficial, and these should be mandatory.[124] The development of a certification system is also

---

[123] Future of Privacy Forum, *Privacy Best Practices for Consumer Genetic Testing Services* (31 July 2018) <https://fpf.org/wp-content/uploads/2018/07/Privacy-Best-Practices-for-Consumer-Genetic-Testing-Services-FINAL.pdf> (accessed 18 April 2019).

[124] Phillips, 'Buying Your Genetic Self Online: Pitfalls and Potential Reforms in DNA Testing' (May–June 2019) 17 *IEEE Security and Privacy – Privacy Interests* 77–81 DOI: 10.1109/MSEC.2019.2904128; <https://www.computer.org/csdl/magazine/sp/2019/03/08713274/19V23r7NPkk>

desirable, as it could assist the public in distinguishing those DTC providers engaging in more responsible business practices from those that are not.

It is also desirable that consumer protection regulators and data protection authorities take a more active role in attempts to improve industry governance and specifically wrap contracts and privacy policies. In the UK, the CMA has already conducted a compliance review of cloud computing service providers, and it is desirable that it conducts a similar review of DTC companies' contracts. Similar agencies based in other jurisdictions could also conduct reviews. Companies could also work with the CMA to improve their contracts. Specifically, there are several types of contractual terms that are inappropriate for services that handle sequenced genetic data and other personal data. These include clauses allowing for unilateral alteration of terms without notice; deeming consent or assent to the contract through use or viewing of the website (as it is often possible to visit a website without ever viewing the terms and conditions); deeming consent to contracts or privacy policies through using the service itself; deeming consent or assent to altered terms through continued use of the website; also, indemnity clauses; clauses disclaiming liability for negligence; clauses specifying that services are provided on an 'as is' basis; and clauses limiting the scope of purpose.

As DTC companies often promise consumer empowerment in their marketing, they should consider alternative approaches to their existing models. DTC companies are for-profit entities and the primary source of value for DTC companies is consumer data and partnerships with other entities to pursue research using that data, rather than the sale of tests. If DTC companies conducting medical research truly want to do things differently and give something back to their consumers, then they should consider the possibility of benefit sharing with their consumers.

Regulatory reform is also needed, but there is also a need for reform of both contracts and privacy policies. Regulators could develop model contracts and policies. Contracts could be shorter and more interactive with more options to opt out of particular services. However, as well as shortening these documents and providing more options for consumers, companies should also consider how to make contracts and privacy policies easier for consumers to understand. Recent work by Becher and Benoliel[125] assessed the readability of the '500 most popular websites in the U.S. that use sign-in-wrap agreements'.[126] Overall, they found that most of these agreements are unreadable with reading scores

---

[125] U Benoliel, and SI Becher, 'The Duty to Read the Unreadable' (11 January 2019) 60 *Boston College Law Review*, <SRN: https://ssrn.com/abstract=3313837 or http://dx.doi.org/10.2139/ssrn.3313837>.

[126] Ibid., p. 14.

'comparable to the usual score of articles found in academic journals'.[127] This work is timely and it highlights the need for many businesses to improve contracts. In the specific context of DTC, given the sensitive nature of these services and the wide potential for secondary use of data, businesses and regulators need to think about how to improve business practices. The WriteMark quality mark scheme is a New Zealand based project. It assesses documents and websites and awards the WriteMark quality mark to those who 'achieve a high standard of plain language' is an interesting example,[128] which could provide a potential model for thinking about how to improve readability of contracts more generally and in the specific context of DTC genetics.

Given the realities of how we all tend to behave in relation to contracts and privacy policies, businesses and regulators should also think beyond merely rewording these documents. We also need to think about new ways of doing things, which should involve thinking about interface design. While in many contexts a speedy decision and a seamless transaction may be what the consumer wants, this is not what they need in the context of services that are complex and involve sensitive data. Designing interfaces that slow transactions down and enhance a person's ability to make an informed decision could lead to further benefits both for consumers and businesses in the long term, especially in relation to consumer trust.

It is preferable that consumers are not automatically opted in to particular services or uses of data, but allowed to make more informed choices about use, storage and disclosure of data. Also, the ability to save documents in a printer-friendly, easily readable form is very important. Companies should also provide more information about the limitations, risks and benefits of their tests and the specific uses to which consumers' data may be put.

The Golden State Killer case highlights how data collected for one purpose may be used for a wide range of other purposes. As concern has been also been expressed regarding governments retaining identifiable DNA profiles, it is justifiable that where private companies are collecting and retaining DNA they are subject to greater scrutiny of their activities. While some tests currently offered by DTC companies may have little predictive value, stored sequenced data may allow individuals to be identified and may also enable people to learn much about the individuals that they may not want shared. While DNA evidence is often given much weight in criminal cases, it is also problematic. One of the most significant issues here is DNA transfer. As mentioned earlier, it has now shown that it is possible for people to leave

---

[127] Ibid., p. 21.

[128] WriteMark, 'About – WriteMark' <https://writemark.co.nz/about/> (accessed 30 September 2019).

DNA traces of themselves not just on objects, but also on other people, sometimes even without meeting them. The experience of Lukis Anderson should help us to acknowledge that the presence of DNA alone should not be viewed as synonymous with guilt, and that we need to be cautious in how we treat genetic data.[129]

There is potential for the Information Commissioner's Office (ICO), the Office of the Irish Data Protection Commissioner and other data protection authorities and privacy regulators to take on a more active role in regulating DTC, given the privacy concerns raised by the nature of DTC services.[130]

In an age where a range of technology companies are acquiring vast amounts of personal data, the activities of companies providing DNA tests and combining them with other sources of personal data do need to be monitored. Transparency, access to informational resources and education are also key in this context. In order for individuals to be able to make informed decisions about engaging with DTC services, they need to be able to access information about the respective risks, benefits and limitations of testing. At present, there is a real need for companies not only to improve their contracts, but also to be more transparent about the nature of the services they provide and the uses to which consumer data may be put.

Let us return to the story of Cleopatra mentioned earlier. Part of the purpose of the GDPR is to strengthen the rights of individuals just like Cleopatra in their personal data. It is meant to give us all more control over how our data are used. Meanwhile, consumer protection legislation also gives us rights so that we can purchase safe and reliable products and services. Given the nature of genetic information and the ways in which it can be used, businesses should pay more attention to our rights and not overreach in their contracts and privacy policies. If genetic tests are to be offered as commercial services, then we should be able to rely on the service being sold. It is not acceptable for a health test to be provided on an 'as is' basis, and warnings about learning unexpected information should not be buried in a long contract. We need to change how things are done, and reset matters so that there is a fair and balanced relationship between businesses and their consumers.

---

[129] Worth, 'Framed for Murder by his Own DNA' (*Wired*, 19 April 2018) <https://www.wired.com/story/dna-transfer-framed-murder/> (accessed 18 April 2019).

[130] See for example, Feilidh Dwyer, 'Your DNA is only a click away: Home DNA tests and privacy' Office of the New Zealand Privacy Commissioner (6 August 2019) <https://privacy.org.nz/blog/your-dna-is-only-a-click-away-home-dna-tests-and-privacy/>.

References

Aldhous P, 'DNA Data from 100 Crime Scenes Has Been Uploaded to a Genealogy Website – Just like the Golden State Killer' (*BuzzFeed News*, 17 May 2018) <https://www.buzzfeednews.com/article/peteraldhous/parabon-genetic-genealogy-cold-cases> (accessed 18 April 2019).

AncestryDNA, 'AncestryDNA Breaks Holiday Sales Record for Black Friday to Cyber Monday; More Than Triples Kits Sold versus 2016' (press release, 28 November 2017) <https://www.ancestry.com/corporate/newsroom/press-releases/ancestrydna-breaks-holiday-sales-record-black-friday-cyber-monday-more> (accessed 18 April 2019).

Ancestry, 'RootsWeb Security Update' (23 December 2017) <https://blogs.ancestry.com/ancestry/2017/12/23/rootsweb-security-update/> (accessed 18 April 2019).

Annes JP, Giovanni MA and Murray MF, 'RISKS of Presymptomatic Direct-to-Consumer Genetic Testing' (2010) 363 *New England Journal of Medicine* 1100–1 DOI: 10.1056/NEJMp1006029.

Associated Press, 'Pfizer, 23andMe Team Up to Study Bowel Disease' (*Medical Xpress*, 12 August 2014) <medicalxpress.com/news/2014-08-pfizer-23andme-team-bowel-disease.html> (accessed 10 August 2018).

Associated Press, 'DNA Used in Hunt for Golden State Killer Previously Led to Wrong Man' (NBC News, 29 April 2018) <https://www.nbcnews.com/news/us-news/dna-used-hunt-golden-state-killer-previously-led-wrong-man-n869796> (accessed 18 April 2019).

Association for Molecular Pathology, 'Position Statement: On Direct Access Genetic Testing (Direct to Consumer Genetic Testing)' (Association for Molecular Pathology 2007) <https://www.amp.org/AMP/assets/File/position-statements/2007/AMPDTCPositionStatement_Final.pdf> (accessed 16 April 2019).

Association for Molecular Pathology, 'Position Statement: On Direct Access Genetic Testing (Direct to Consumer Genetic Testing)' (Association for Molecular Pathology 2015) <https://www.amp.org/AMP/assets/File/position-statements/2015/AMPpositionstatementDTCtesting-FINAL_002.pdf> (accessed 16 April 2019).

Ayday E et al., 'Whole Genome Sequencing: Revolutionary Medicine or Privacy Nightmare?' (2015) 2 *Computer* 58.

Ayres I and Schwartz A, 'The No-Reading Problem in Consumer Contract Law' (2014) 66 *Stanford Law Review* 545.

Barrera J and Foxcroft T, 'Heredity or Hoax?' (CBC News, 13 June 2018) <https://newsinteractives.cbc.ca/longform/dna-ancestry-test> (accessed 18 April 2019).

Barry P, 'Seeking Genetic Fate Personal genomics Companies Offer Forecasts of Disease Risk, but the Science behind the Packaging Is Still Evolving' (2009) 176 *Science News* <https://doi.org/10.1002/scin.5591760123>

Belton P, 'In Your Irises: The New Rise of Biometric Banking' (BBC News, 20 March 2015) <bbc.co.uk/news/business-31968642> (accessed 18 April 2019).

Bhatia G, 'FDA Fears Hacking Risks in Medical Devices; Says Hospira Pump Should Not Be Used' (*International Business Times*, 5 August 2015) <https://www.ibtimes.com/fda-fears-hacking-risks-medical-devices-says-hospira-pump-should-not-be-used-2039898> (accessed 18 April 2019).

Brady W and Glazer E, 'Cybersecurity in Hospitals: Protecting Electronic Patient Devices from the Risk of Hacking' (*MD News*, 7 August 2015) Legal Technology <http://lowerhudsonbronx.mdnews.com/cybersecurity-hospitals-protecting-electronic-patient-devices-risk-hacking> (accessed 18 April 2019).

Borry P, Cornel M and Howard H, 'Where Are You Going, Where Have You Been: A Recent History of the Direct-to-Consumer Genetic Testing Market' (2010) 1 *Journal of Community Genetics* 101.

Borry, P et al., 'Legislation on Direct-to-Consumer Genetic Testing in Seven European Countries' (2012) 20 *European Journal of Human Genetics* 715.

Brown KV, 'How DNA Testing Botched My Family's Heritage, and Probably Yours, Too' (*Gizmodo Genetics*, 16 January 2018) <https://gizmodo.com/how-dna-testing-botched-my-familys-heritage-and-probab-1820932637> (accessed 18 April 2019).

Brown KV, 'Scientists Push Back against Booming Genetic Pseudoscience Market' (*Gizmodo Genetics*, 14 July 2017) <https://gizmodo.com/scientists-push-back-against-booming-genetic-pseudoscie-1796923059> (accessed 18 April 2019).

Canadian College of Medical Geneticists, 'CCMG Statement on Direct-to-Consumer Genetic Testing' (2012) 81 *Clinical Genetics* 1 <https://www.ccmg-ccgm.org/documents/Policies_etc/Pos_Statements/PosStmt_EPP_DTC_FINAL_20Jan2011.pdf> (accessed 18 April 2019).

Caulfield T, 'Predictive or Preposterous? The Marketing of DTC Genetic Testing' (2011) 10 *Journal of Science Communication* <https://doi.org/10.22323/2.10030302> (accessed 22 June 2019).

Caulfield T and McGuire A, 'Direct-to-Consumer Genetic Testing: Perceptions, Problems, and Policy Responses' (2012) 63 *Annual Review of Medicine* 23.

Caulfield T et al., 'Direct-to-Consumer Genetic Testing: Good, Bad or Benign?' (2010) 77 *Clinical Genetics* 101.

Chen A, 'Why a DNA Data Breach Is Much Worse Than a Credit Card Leak' (*The Verge*, 6 June 2018) <https://www.theverge.com/2018/6/6/17435166/myheritage-dna-breach-genetic-privacy-bioethics> (accessed 18 April 2019).

Choice, 'Nine Hours of "Conditions Apply"' <https://www.choice.com.au/about-us/media-releases/2017/march/nine-hours-of-conditions-apply> (accessed 18 April 2019).

Coldewey D, 'MyHeritage Breach Exposes 92M Emails and Hashed Passwords' (*TechCrunch*, 5 June 2018) <https://techcrunch.com/2018/06/05/myheritage-breach-exposes-92m-emails-and-hashed-passwords/?guccounter=1> (accessed 18 April 2019).

Competition & Markets Authority, *Unfair Contract Terms Explained* (CMA37(a), 31 July 2015).

Competition & Markets Authority, *Unfair Contract Terms Guidance – Guidance on the Unfair Terms Provisions in the Consumer Rights Act 2015* (CMA37, 31 July 2015).

Competition & Markets Authority, *Consumer Law Compliance Review: Cloud Storage* (CMA Findings Report 2016) <https://assets.digital.cabinet-office.gov.uk/media/57472953e5274a037500000d/cloud-storage-findings-report.pdf> (accessed 18 April 2019).

Competition & Markets Authority, *Update on Cloud Storage Consumer Compliance Review* (CMA 1 April 2016) <https://assets.digital.cabinet-office.gov.uk/

media/56fe3227ed915d117d000037/Investigation_update-1_April_2016.pdf> (accessed 18 April 2019).

Competition & Markets Authority, 'Cloud Storage: Consumer Compliance Review' (homepage, <https://www.gov.uk/cma-cases/cloud-storage-consumer-compliance-review>, accessed 9 August 2018).

Conklin K and Hyde R, 'If Small Print "Terms and Conditions" Require a PhD to Read, Should they be Legally Binding?' (*The Conversation*, 10 May 2018) <https://theconversation.com/if-small-print-terms-and-conditions-require-a-phd-to-read-should-they-be-legally-binding-75101> (accessed 18 April 2019).

Conklin K, Hyde R and Parente F, 'Assessing Plain and Intelligible Language in the Consumer Rights Act: A Role for Reading Scores?' (2018) Legal Studies, ISSN 1748-121X (in press) <http://eprints.nottingham.ac.uk/51073/> (accessed 18 April 2019).

Cornel MC, van El CG and Borry P, 'The Challenge of Implementing Genetic Tests with Clinical Utility While Avoiding Unsound Applications' (2014) 5 *Journal of Community Genetics* 7.

Curnutte M and Testa G, 'Consuming Genomes: Scientific and Social Innovation in Direct-to-Consumer Genetic Testing' (2012) 31 *New Genetics and Society* 159.

Cussins J, 'Direct-to-Consumer Genetic Tests Should Come with a Health Warning' (*Pharmaceutical Journal*, 15 January 2015) <https://www.pharmaceutical-journal.com/opinion/comment/direct-to-consumer-genetic-tests-should-come-with-a-health-warning/20067564.article?firstPass=false> (accessed 18 April 2019).

Doe G, 'With Genetic Testing, I Gave My Parents the Gift of Divorce' (*Vox*, 9 September 2014) <https://www.vox.com/2014/9/9/5975653/with-genetic-testing-i-gave-my-parents-the-gift-of-divorce-23andme> (accessed 18 April 2019).

Dowd K, 'Golden State Killer Suspect Appears in Court Nearly One Year after Arrest' (*San Francisco Chronicle*, 10 April 2019) <https://www.sfgate.com/bayarea/article/joseph-deangelo-hearing-sacramento-trial-13757418.php> (accessed 18 April 2019).

Downes L and Nunes P, 'Regulating 23andMe Won't Stop the New Age of Genetic Testing' (*Wired*, 1 January 2014) <https://www.wired.com/2014/01/the-fda-may-win-the-battle-this-holiday-season-but-23andme-will-win-the-war/> (accessed 18 April 2019).

Duhaime-Ross A, '23andMe Plans to Move beyond Genetic Testing to Making Drugs' (*The Verge*, 12 March 2015) <theverge.com/2015/3/12/8199303/23andme-drug-development-testing> (accessed 18 April 2019).

Elshout M et al., *Study on Consumers' Attitudes towards Terms Conditions (T&Cs) Final Report* (22 September 2016) Report for the European Commission, Consumers, Health, Agriculture and Food Executive Agency (CHAFEA) on behalf of Directorate-General for Justice and Consumers <https://ssrn.com/abstract=2847546> (accessed 18 April 2019).

Erlich Y and Narayanan A, 'Routes for Breaching and Protecting Genetic Privacy' (2014) 15 *Nature Reviews Genetics* 409.

European Academies Science Advisory Council (EASAC) and Federation of European Academies of Medicine (FEAM), *Direct-to-Consumer Genetic Testing – Summary Document* (EASAC–FEAM Project on Direct-to-Consumer Genetic Testing, October 2012).

European Society of Human Genetics, 'Statement of the ESHG on Direct-to-Consumer Genetic Testing for Health-related Purposes' (2010) 18 *European Journal of Human Genetics* 1271.

FDA, 'Cybersecurity Vulnerabilities of Hospira Symbiq Infusion System' (FDA Safety Communication, 31 July 2015) <https://www.fda.gov/medicaldevices/digitalhealth/ucm373213.htm> (accessed 18 April 2019).

FDA, 'FDA Authorizes, with Special Controls, Direct-to-Consumer Test that Reports Three Mutations in the BRCA Breast Cancer Genes' (press release, 6 March 2018) <https://www.fda.gov/newsevents/newsroom/pressannouncements/ucm599560.htm> (accessed 18 April 2019).

Feero W and Guttmacher A, 'Genomic Medicine – An Updated Primer' (2010) 362 *New England Journal of Medicine* 2001 DOI: 10.1056/NEJMra0907175.

Financial Conduct Authority, *The Unfair Contract Terms Regulatory Guide* (February 2018) <https://www.handbook.fca.org.uk/handbook/UNFCOG.pdf> (accessed 18 April 2019).

Fox-Brewster T, 'Londoners Give Up Eldest Children in Public Wi-Fi Security Horror Show' (*The Guardian*, 29 September 2014) <https://www.theguardian.com/technology/2014/sep/29/londoners-wi-fi-security-herod-clause> (accessed 18 April 2019).

Frebourg T, 'Direct-to-Consumer Genetic Testing Services: What Are the Medical Benefits?' (2012) 20 *European Journal of Human Genetics* 483.

Frischmann BM and Selinger E, 'Engineering Humans with Contracts' (September 2016) Cardozo Legal Studies Research Paper No 493 <https://papers.ssrn.com/sol3/papers.cfm?abstract_id=2834011> (accessed 18 April 2019).

Frischmann BM and Selinger E, *Re-Engineering Humanity* (Cambridge University Press 2018).

Future of Privacy Forum, *Privacy Best Practices for Consumer Genetic Testing Services* (31 July 2018) <https://fpf.org/wp-content/uploads/2018/07/Privacy-Best-Practices-for-Consumer-Genetic-Testing-Services-FINAL.pdf> (accessed 18 April 2019).

Gabel JD, 'Redeeming the Genetic Groupon: Efficacy, Ethics, and Exploitation in Marketing DNA to the Masses' (2012) 81 *Mississippi Law Journal* (Georgia State University College of Law, Legal Studies Research Paper no. 2012-14) <https://ssrn.com/abstract=2020634> (accessed 22 June 2019).

Geggel L, '23andMe Is Sharing Its 5 Million Clients' Genetic Data with Drug Giant GlaxoSmithKline' (*Livescience*, 26 July 2018) <https://www.livescience.com/63173-23andme-partnership-glaxosmithkline.html> (accessed 18 April 2019).

Genomeweb staff reporter, '23andMe Launches Therapeutics Group with Former Genentech Exec at Helm' (12 March 2015) <Genomeweb.com/drug-discovery-development/23andme-launches-therapeutics-group-former-genentech-exec-helm> (accessed 18 April 2019).

Geransar R and Einsiedel E, 'Evaluating Online Direct-to-consumer Marketing of Genetic Tests: Informed Choices or Buyers Beware?' (2008) 12 *Genetic Testing* 13.

GlaxoSmithKline, 'GSK and 23andMe Sign Agreement to Leverage Genetic Insights for the Development of Novel Medicines' (25 July 2018) <https://www.gsk.com/en-gb/media/press-releases/gsk-and-23andme-sign-agreement-to-leverage-

genetic-insights-for-the-development-of-novel-medicines/> (accessed 18 April 2019).

Goddard KAB et al, 'Health-Related Direct-to-Consumer Genetic Tests: A Public Health Assessment and Analysis of Practices Related to Internet-Based Tests for Risk of Thrombosis' (2009) 12 *Public Health Genomics* 92 DOI: 10.1159/000176794.

Goldman D, 'Hackers Recreate Fingerprints Using Public Photos' (*CNN Money*, 30 December 2014) <http://money.cnn.com/2014/12/30/technology/security/fingerprint-hack/> (accessed 18 April 2019).

Groskopf C, 'CLICK "I AGREE": Apple Fans Have Click-signed more than 100,000 Words of Legal Contracts' (*Quartz*, 5 November 2016) <https://qz.com/797928/apple-fans-have-click-signed-more-than-100000-words-of-legal-contracts/> (accessed 18 April 2019).

Haag M, 'FamilyTreeDNA Admits to Sharing Genetic Data with FBI' (*New York Times*, 4 February 2019) <https://www.nytimes.com/2019/02/04/business/family-tree-dna-fbi.html> (accessed 18 April 2019).

Harris A, Wyatt S and Kelly SE, 'The Gift of Spit (And the Obligation to Return It): How Consumers of Online Genetic Testing Services Participate in Research' (2013) 16 *Information, Communication & Society* 236.

Hazel J and Slobogin C, 'Who Knows What, and When? A Survey of the Privacy Policies Proffered by US Direct-to-Consumer Genetic Testing Companies' (Vanderbilt Law Research Paper No. 18-8, 19 April 2018) *Cornell Journal of Law and Public Policy*.

Helft M, 'Ancestry.com DNA Database Tops 3M, Sales Rise to $850M Ahead of Likely 2017 IPO' (*Forbes*, 10 January 2017) <https://www.forbes.com/sites/miguelhelft/2017/01/10/ancestry-com-dna-database-tops-3m-sales-rise-to-850m-ahead-of-likely-2017-ipo/#210a99a713b3> (accessed 18 April 2019).

Hillman RA, 'On-line Consumer Standard-form Contracting Practices: A Survey and Discussion of Legal Implications' (Cornell Law Faculty Publications Paper 29, 2005) <http://dx.doi.org/10.2139/ssrn.686817> (accessed 18 April 2019).

Hilts A, Parson C and Knockel J, 'Every Step You Fake: A Comparative Analysis of Fitness Tracker Privacy and Security' (Open Effect Report 2016) <https://citizenlab.org/2016/02/fitness-tracker-privacy-and-security/> (accessed 18 April 2019).

Hogarth S and Saukko P, 'A Market in the Making: The Past, Present and Future of Direct-to-Consumer Genomics' (2017) 36 *New Genetics and Society* 197 197. DOI: 10.1080/14636778.2017.1354692.

Hogarth S, Javitt G and Melzer D, 'The Current Landscape for Direct-to-Consumer Genetic Testing: Legal, Ethical, and Policy Issues' (2008) 9 *Annual Review of Genomics and Human Genetics* 161.

Hogarth S, Melzer D and Zimmern R, 'The Regulation of Commercial Genetic Testing Services in the UK' (2005) A briefing for the Human Genetics Commission, Cambridge <https://www.kcl.ac.uk/sspp/departments/political economy/research/biopolitics/publications/regulationofcommercialgenetictest ingserviceshgcbriefing.pdf> (accessed 18 April 2019).

Human Genetics Commission, *Genes Direct: Ensuring the Effective Oversight of Genetic Tests Supplied Directly to the Public* (Department of Health 2003)

<https://repository.library.georgetown.edu/handle/10822/523214> (accessed 18 April 2019).

Human Genetics Commission, *More Genes Direct* (Department of Health 2007) <http://sites.nationalacademies.org/cs/groups/pgasite/documents/webpage/pga_053238.pdf> (accessed 18 April 2019).

Human Genetics Commission, 'A Common Framework of Principles for Direct-to-Consumer Genetic Testing Services' (Department of Health 2010) <https://ukgtn.nhs.uk/resources/library/article/human-genetics-commission-a-comm on-framework-of-principles-for-direct-to-consumer-genetic-testing-services-70/> (accessed 18 April 2019).

Human Tissue Authority, 'Analysis of DNA under the HT Act FAQs' <https://www.hta.gov.uk/faqs/analysis-dna-under-ht-act-faqs> (accessed 18 April 2019).

Hunt E, 'Amazon Kindle's Terms "Unreasonable" and Would Take Nine Hours to Read, Choice Says' (*The Guardian*, 15 March 2017) <https://www.theguardian.com/australia-news/2017/mar/15/amazon-kindles-terms-unreasonable-and-would-take-nine-hours-to-read-choice-says> (accessed 18 April 2019).

Kalf RR et al., 'Variations in Predicted Risks in Personal Genome Testing for common Complex Diseases' (2014) 16 *Genetics in Medicine* 85.

Karow J, '23andMe DTC Breast and Ovarian Cancer Risk Test Misses Almost 90 Percent of BRCA Mutation Carriers' (*GenomeWeb*, 5 April 2019) <https://www.genomeweb.com/molecular-diagnostics/23andme-dtc-breast-and-ovar ian-cancer-risk-test-misses-almost-90-percent-brca#.XKfbrS1L1PU> (accessed 18 April 2019).

Kaufman DJ et al., 'Risky Business: Risk Perception and the Use of Medical Services among Customers of DTC Personal Genetic Testing' (2012) 21 *Journal of Genetic Counseling* 413 DOI: 10.1007/s10897-012-9483-0.

Khan R and Mittelman D, 'Consumer Genomics Will Change Your Life, Whether You Get Tested or Not' (2018) 19 *Genome Biology* 120 DOI: 10.1186/s13059-018-1506-1.

Khanna S and Tosh PK, 'A Clinician's Primer on the Role of the Microbiome in Human Health and Disease' (2014) 89 *Mayo Clinic Proceedings* 107 <https://doi.org/10.1016/j.mayocp.2013.10.011> (accessed 22 June 2019).

Kim NS, 'Contract's Adaptation and the Online Bargain' (2010) 79 *University of Chicago Law Review* 1327.

Kim NS, *Wrap Contracts: Foundations and Ramifications* (Oxford University Press 2014).

Kramer P and Bressan P, 'Humans as Superorganisms: How Microbes, Viruses, Imprinted Genes, and Other Selfish Entities Shape Our Behavior' (2015) 10 *Perspectives on Psychological Science* 464 <https://doi.org/10.1177/1745691615583131> (accessed 22 June 2019).

Krol A, 'Open Humans Aims to Be the Social Network for Science Volunteerism' (*Bio IT World*, 9 April 2015) <bio-itworld.com/2015/4/9/open-humans-aims-social-network-science-volunteerism.html> (accessed 18 April 2019).

Krol A, 'What Comes New for Direct-to-Consumer Genetics?' (*Bio IT World*, 16 July 2015) <bio-itworld.com/2015/7/16/what-comes-next-direct-consumer-genetics.html> (accessed 18 April 2019).

Laestadius LI, Rich JR and Auer PL, 'All Your Data (Effectively) Belong to Us: Data

Practices among Direct-to-Consumer Genetic Testing Firms' (2016) *Genetics in Medicine* DOI: 10.1038/gim.2016.136.

Lagorio-Chafkin C, '23andMe Exec: You Ain't Seen Nothing Yet' (*Inc*, 7 January 2015) <www.inc.com/christine-lagorio/23andMe-new-partnerships.html> (accessed 18 April 2019).

Lapin T, ' "Golden State Killer" Cleared of 1978 Double-murder Cold Case' (*New York Post*, 14 June 1018) <https://nypost.com/2018/06/14/golden-state-killer-cleared-of-1978-double-murder-cold-case/> (accessed 18 April 2019).

Loos M and Luzak J, 'Wanted: A Bigger Stick: On Unfair Terms in Consumer Contracts with Online Service Providers' (Centre for the Study of European Contract Law Working Paper Series, 8 January 2015) 39 *Journal of Consumer Policy* 63.

Luperon A, 'DNA Evidence Clears Golden State Killer Suspect of a Murder' (*Law & Crime*, 9 January 2019) <https://lawandcrime.com/high-profile/dna-evidence-clears-golden-state-killer-suspect-of-a-murder/> (accessed 18 April 2019).

McDonald AM and Cranor LF, 'The Cost of Reading Privacy Policies' (2008) 4 I/S *Journal of Law and Policy for the Information Society* 562.

McGuire A et al, 'Social Networkers' Attitudes toward Direct-to-Consumer Personal Genome Testing' (2009) 9 *American Journal of Bioethics* 3 DOI: 10.1080/15265160902928209.

Marietta C and McGuire AL, 'Direct-to-Consumer Genetic Testing: Is It the Practice of Medicine?' (2009) 37 *Journal of Law, Medicine & Ethics* 369.

Molteni M, 'Ancestry's Genetic Testing Kits Are Heading For Your Stocking This Year' (*Wired*, 1 December 2017) <https://www.wired.com/story/ancestrys-genetic-testing-kits-are-heading-for-your-stocking-this-year/> (accessed 18 April 2019).

Molteni M, 'The Key to Cracking Cold Cases Might Be Genealogy Sites' (*Wired*, 1 June 2018) <https://www.wired.com/story/police-will-crack-a-lot-more-cold-cases-with-dna/> (accessed 18 April 2019).

Myers MF, 'Health Care Providers and Direct-To-Consumer Access and Advertising of Genetic Testing in the United States' (2011) 3 *Genome Medicine* 81.

Navarro F, 'Ancestry.com Suffers Big Data Leak – 300,000 User Credentials Exposed' (*Komando*, 28 December 2017) <https://www.komando.com/happening-now/435921/ancestry-com-suffers-big-data-leak-300000-user-credentials-exposed> (accessed 18 April 2019).

Nordrum A, 'Researchers Embed Malware into DNA to Hack DNA Sequencing' (Software IEEE Spectrum, 10 August 2017) <https://spectrum.ieee.org/the-human-os/computing/software/researchers-embed-malicious-code-into-dna-to-hack-dna-sequencing-software> (accessed 18 April 2019).

Norwegian Consumer Council, *APPFAIL Threats to Consumers in Mobile Apps* (March 2016) <https://www.forbrukerradet.no/undersokelse/2015/appfail-threats-to-consumers-in-mobile-apps/> (accessed 18 April 2019).

Norwegian Consumer Council, '250,000 Words of App Terms and Conditions' (24 May 2016) <https://www.forbrukerradet.no/side/250000-words-of-app-terms-and-conditions/> (accessed 18 April 2019).

Norwegian Consumer Council, *Deceived by Design* (June 2018) <https://www.forbrukerradet.no/undersokelse/no-undersokelsekategori/deceived-by-design/> (accessed 18 April 2019).

Nuffield Council on Bioethics, *The Collection, Linking and Use of Data in Biomedical Research and Health Care: Ethical Issues* (February 2015).

Obar JA and Oeldorf-Hirsch A, 'Clickwrap Impact: Quick-Join Options and Ignoring Privacy and Terms of Service Policies of Social Networking Services' (2017) in proceedings of the 8th International Conference on Social Media & Society ACM, p. 8. <https://ssrn.com/abstract=3017277> (accessed 18 April 2019).

Obar JA and Oeldorf-Hirsch A, 'The Biggest Lie on the Internet: Ignoring the Privacy Policies and Terms of Service Policies of Social Networking Services' (2018) *Information, Communication & Society* DOI: 10.1080/1369118X.2018.1486870.

Office of the Privacy Commissioner (OPC), *Statement on the Use of Genetic Test Results by Life and Health Insurance Companies* (2014) <https://www.priv.gc.ca/en/opc-news/news-and-announcements/2014/s-d_140709/> (accessed 18 April 2019).

Perton M, 'Read Fine Print or GameStation May Own Your Soul' (*Consumerist*, 16 April 2010) <http://consumerist.com/2010/04/16/read-fine-print-or-gamestation-may-own-your-soul/> (accessed 18 April 2019, only outside EEA).

Phillips AM, 'Genomic Privacy and Direct-to-Consumer Genetics: Big Consumer Genetic Data – What's in that Contract?' (2015) Security and Privacy Workshops (SPW), IEEE 60–4.

Phillips AM, 'Think Before You Click: Ordering A Genetic Test Online' (2015) 11 *SciTech Lawyer* 8.

Phillips AM, 'Only a Click Away – DTC Genetics for Ancestry, Health, Love ... and More: A View of the Business and Regulatory Landscape' (2016) 8 *Applied & Translational Genomics* 16.

Phillips AM, 'Reading the Fine Print When Buying Your Genetic Self Online: Direct-to-Consumer Genetic Testing Terms and Conditions' (2017) 36 *New Genetics and Society* 273 <http://dx.doi.org/10.1080/14636778.2017.1352468> (accessed 22 June 2019).

Phillips AM, 'Data on Direct-to-Consumer Genetic Testing and DNA Testing Companies' (Version 1.3, Open Access Dataset, Zenodo, February 2018) DOI: 10.5281/zenodo.1175799 <https://zenodo.org/record/1183565#.WunK6y-ZNp8> (accessed 22 June 2019).

Phillips AM, *Buying Your Self on the Internet: Wrap Contracts and Personal Genomics* (Edinburgh University Press 2019).

Phillips AM, 'Buying Your Genetic Self Online: Pitfalls and Potential Reforms in DNA Testing' (May–June 2019) 17 IEEE Security and Privacy – Privacy Interests 77–81 DOI: 10.1109/MSEC.2019.2904128; <https://www.privacy-foundation.nz/buying-your-genetic-self-online/>

Pormeister K, 'Genetic Data and the Research Exemption: Is the GDPR Going Too Far?' (2017) 7 *International Data Privacy Law* 137 <https://doi.org/10.1093/idpl/ipx006> (accessed 22 June 2019).

Proffitt A, 'Deals Center on Self-reported Patient Data Services' (2012) 30 *Nature Biotechnology* 1016 doi: 10.1038/nbt1112-1016.

Prudente S et al., 'Genetic Prediction of Common Diseases. Still No Help for the Clinical Diabetologist!' (2012) 22 *Nutrition, Metabolism and Cardiovascular Diseases* 929.

Purple, '22,000 People Willingly Agree to Community Service in Return for Free

WiFi' (13 July 2017) <https://purple.ai/blogs/purple-community-service/> (accessed 18 April 2019).

Radin MJ, *Boilerplate* (Princeton Press 2013).

Ray T, 'ACMG Guidelines at Odds with FDA Green Light for 23andMe Health Risk Tests' (*Genomeweb*, 11 April 2017) <https://www.Genomeweb.com/reg ulatory-news/acmg-guidelines-oddsfda-green-light-23andme-health-risk-tests> (accessed 18 April 2019).

Rehm HL et al., 'ClinGen – The Clinical Genome Resource' (2015) 372 *New England Journal of Medicine* 2235.

Research and Markets, 'Predictive Genetic Testing and Consumer/Wellness Genomics Market by Application and Trend Analysis from 2013 to 2025' (January 2017) <www.researchandmarkets.com/research/26mxz4/predictive> (accessed 18 April 2019).

Ries NM and Castle D, 'Nutrigenomics and Ethics Interface: Direct-to-Consumer Services and Commercial Aspects' (2008) 12 *OMICS A Journal of Integrative Biology* 245.

Sampson TR and Mazmanian SK, 'Control of Brain Development, Function, and Behavior by the Microbiome' (2015) 17 *Cell Host Microbe* 565 DOI: 10.1016/j. chom.2015.04.011.

Saukko P et al., 'Negotiating the Boundary between Medicine and Consumer Culture: Online Marketing of Nutrigenetic Tests' (2010) 70 *Social Science and Medicine* 744 <https://doi.org/10.1016/j.socscimed.2009.10.066> (accessed 18 April 2019).

Sboner A et al., 'The Real Cost of Sequencing: Higher than You Think!' (2011) 12 *Genome Biology* 125.

Science and Technology Committee (Commons), Commercial Genomic Inquiry (March 2019) <https://www.parliament.uk/business/committees/committees-a-z/commons-select/science-and-technology-committee/inquiries/parliament-2017/commercial-genomics-17-9/> (accessed 18 April 2019).

Simoncelli T, 'Dangerous Excursions: The Case against Expanding Forensic DNA Databases to Innocent Persons' (2006) 34 *Journal of Law, Medicine and Ethics* 390 <https://doi.org/10.1111/j.1748-720X.2006.00045.x> (accessed 22 June 2019).

Smith D and Stanton S, 'Prosecutors to Seek Death Penalty in Golden State Killer Case' (*Mercury News*, 10 April 2019) <https://www.mercurynews. com/2019/04/10/prosecutors-to-seek-death-penalty-in-golden-state-killer-case/> (accessed 18 April 2019).

Smith PA, 'When DNA Implicates the Innocent' (2016) 314 *Scientific American* 11 <https://www.scientificamerican.com/article/when-dna-implicates-the-inno cent/> (accessed 18 April 2019).

Spector-Bagdady K and Pike ER, 'Consuming Genomics: Regulating Direct-to-Consumer Genetic and Genomic Information' (2014) 92 *Nebraska Law Review* 677.

Storm D, 'MEDJACK: Hackers hijacking medical devices to create backdoors in hospital networks' (*Computerworld*, 8 June 2015) <computerworld.com/arti cle/2932371/cybercrime-hacking/medjack-hackers-hijacking-medical-devices-to-create-backdoors-in-hospital-networks.html> (accessed 18 April 2019).

Sullivan M, '23andMe has Signed 12 Other Genetic Data Partnerships beyond

Pfizer and Genentech' (*VentureBeat*, 14 January 2015) <venturebeat.com/2015/01/14/23andme-has-signed-12-other-genetic-data-partnerships-beyond-pfizer-and-genentech/> (accessed 18 April 2019).

Swan M, 'The Quantified Self: Fundamental Disruption in Big Data Science and Biological Discovery' (2013) 1 *Big Data* 85 <https://doi.org/10.1089/big.2012.0002> (accessed 22 June 2019).

Tandy-Connor S, Guiltinan K, Krempely K, LaDuca H, Reineke P, Gutierrez S, Gray P and Tippin Davis B, 'False-positive Results Released by Direct-to-Consumer Genetic Tests Highlight the Importance of Clinical Confirmation Testing for Appropriate Patient Care' (2018) 20 *Genetics in Medicine* 1515 <https://www.nature.com/articles/gim201838> (accessed 22 June 2019).

Tuffley D, 'How Not to Agree to Clean Public Toilets When You Accept Any Online Terms and Conditions' (*The Conversation*, 23 July 2017) <https://theconversation.com/how-not-to-agree-to-clean-public-toilets-when-you-accept-any-online-terms-and-conditions-81169> (accessed 18 April 2019).

23andMe, '23andMe Acquires CureTogether, Inc.' (press release, 12 July 2012) <https://mediacenter.23andme.com/press-releases/23andme-acquires-curetogether-inc/> (accessed 18 April 2019).

23andMe, '23andMe Granted First FDA Authorization for Direct-to-Consumer Genetic Test on Cancer Risk' (press release, 6 March 2018) <https://mediacenter.23andme.com/press-releases/23andme-granted-first-fda-authorization-direct-consumer-genetic-test-cancer-risk/> (accessed 18 April 2019).

23andMe, 'How It Works' <https://www.23andme.com/howitworks/> (accessed 7 January 2013. Checked again for this chapter, 10 August 2018).

US Government Accountability Office, 'Direct-To-Consumer Genetic Tests: Misleading Test Results Are Further Complicated by Deceptive Marketing and Other Questionable Practice' (GAO-10-847T, 2010) Testimony before the Subcommittee on Oversight and Investigations, Committee on Energy and Commerce, House of Representatives 1–8 <http://www.gao.gov/assets/130/125079.pdf> (accessed 22 June 2019).

Van Oorschot RA and Jones MK, 'DNA Fingerprints from Fingerprints' (1997) 387 *Nature* 767 DOI: 10.1038/42838.

Vaughan A, 'Home DNA-testing Firm Will Let Users Block FBI Access to Their Data' (*New Scientist*, 13 March 2019) <https://www.newscientist.com/article/2196433-home-dna-testing-firm-will-let-users-block-fbi-access-to-their-data/> (accessed 18 April 2019).

Ward A, 'Google-Backed Genetic Testing Company Hires Veteran Scientist' (*Financial Times*, 12 March 2015) <ft.com/cms/s/0/ead07e84-c8d8-11e4-bc64-00144feab7de.html> (accessed 18 April 2019).

Wigley + Company Solicitors, 'To Read or Not to Read … Online Ts and Cs. Or Hamlet' (2015) <http://wigleylaw.com/assets/Uploads/To-read-or-not-to-read.pdf> (accessed 18 April 2019)

Williams-Jones B, ' "Be Ready against Cancer, Now": Direct-to-Consumer Advertising for Genetic Testing' (2006) 25 *New Genetics and Society* 89 DOI: 10.1080/14636770600603527.

Woodage T, 'Relative Futility: Limits to Genetic Privacy Protection Because of the Inability to Prevent Disclosure of Genetic Information by Relatives' (2010) 95 *Minnesota Law Review* 682.

Woodhouse A, 'iGene: Hong Kong Biotech Start-up Prenetics Bringing 48-hour DNA Tests to Broader Chinese Market for Safer Prescriptions' (*South China Morning Post*, 4 April 2016) <www.scmp.com/tech/science-research/arti cle/1932838/igene-hong-kong-biotech-start-prenetics-bringing-48-hour-dna> (accessed 18 April 2019).

Worth K, 'Framed for Murder by his Own DNA' (*Wired*, 19 April 2018) <https://www.wired.com/story/dna-transfer-framed-murder/> (accessed 18 April 2019).

Yeap N, 'Your Finger is About to Replace Your Bank Password' (*CCN Money*, 9 June 2015) <https://money.cnn.com/2015/06/05/technology/bank-fingerprint-read er/index.html?iid=EL> (accessed 18 April 2019).

Zawati MH, Borry P and Howard HC, 'Closure of Population Biobanks and Direct-To-Consumer Genetic Testing Companies' (2011) 130 *Human Genetics* 425.

Zettler P, Sherkow J and Greely H, '23andMe, the Food and Drug Administration, and the Future of Genetic Testing' (2014) 174 *JAMA Internal Medicine* 493.

8

On Living and Undead Wills: ZombAIs, Technology and the Future of Inheritance Law*

Burkhard Schafer

Behind every man now alive stand 30 ghosts, for that is the ratio by which the dead outnumber the living.

Arthur C Clarke, *2001: A Space Odyssey*

1. Introduction

This chapter builds on earlier work on how AI could change the way in which we pass on property to the next generation, increasing potentially the control that we can exercise over the disposition of our estate.[1] Communicating (uni-directionally) with a world in which we no longer exist has been possible ever since the invention of writing, but until recently this process has remained inevitably static and one-sided: I can create a fixed message, a letter or more recently a voice or video recording, which will be read or played after my demise, but the reader or listener can't engage in a discussion with me, ask questions in case of ambiguities, and neither can I adjust the message to changed circumstances and conditions. It is this limitation that more intelligent technologies are beginning to probe. This chapter discusses some of the implications for the law that autonomous systems could pose, systems that replicate not just the way the deceased looked (as in Tupac's post-mortem 'holographic' performance) but also the way they thought and argued. The earlier paper focused on ensuring that the intentions of the testator, as they are now, are also observed after their death. This chapter takes some of the

---

* Work on this chapter has been supported by the AHRC 'Creative Informantics' grant.

[1] Schafer, 'ZombAIs: Legal Expert Systems as Representatives beyond the Grave' (2010) 7 SCRIPTed, 384.

anthropological foundations of inheritance law that were only tangentially discussed in that paper more seriously, and by incorporating more recent technological developments it develops a more dynamic account, where the AI's machine learning (ML) continues after the death of its owner.

The chapter begins by putting the practice of will-making in a historical, sociological and psychological context. We need to understand the multiple aims people pursue when making wills to see how technology could soon turn us all into 'digital pharaohs', building pyramids of bits and bytes to be remembered by, but which will also potentially burden the next generation with their curation and preservation. We look first at the cross-cultural psychological underpinnings of memory and will-making, before briefly discussing the emergence of wills in Europe from the spirit of Roman law. From this we will take in particular the concept of '*lares et penates*', the guiding spirits of the family as abstract objects, which we will later give a secularised, informational rendition as 'family AIs'.

The section that follows connects the evolution of the legal concept of will with the emergence of new communication technologies through history. After a short historical overview and a discussion of current and near-future practice, we discuss the emergence of digital-only wills and their treatment under current law. This then allows us to introduce the most radical part of this chapter, the possibility to move from static wills that record only the intentions of the testator while they are alive, to dynamic wills that change and adjust even after the testator's death, but in line with their preferences and normative commitments. In the final sections, we will discuss the legal, ethical and societal implications. As we will see, this thought experiment allows us to identify ambiguities and gaps in *current* doctrines of succession law, in particular the notion of 'testator intent'. Second, it points to a more general ethical and societal problem that the introduction of digital autonomous agents, the 'fourth revolution' as Floridi termed it,[2] could bring to our societies – their potential 'longevity' could signal a power shift from the present to the past, with *collective* 'forgetting' becoming as difficult as the right to be forgotten when applied to individuals.[3] It is at this point that we come back in conclusion to the discussion of 'AI *penates*' as a balancing element to restore intergenerational equity.

---

[2] Floridi, 'Artificial Intelligence's New Frontier: Artificial Companions and the Fourth Revolution' (2008) 39 *Metaphilosophy* 433, pp. 651–5.

[3] See also Esposito, 'Algorithmic Memory and the Right to be Forgotten on the Web' (2017) 4 *Big Data & Society* 1.

1.1 Sociological Background: Why People Make Wills

The desire to exercise control beyond the grave is deeply rooted in the human psyche, a phenomenon that can be found across cultures and across times.[4] Also cross-cultural is the conviction that the most promising way of achieving immortality is through the memories that we create in others: 'Do you not know that a man is not dead while his name is still spoken?'[5] David Unruh described this process as one of 'identity preservation':[6]

> Dying people hope they will be remembered as good fathers, competent women, successful businessmen, creative artists, or peacemakers. Survivors are left with bundles of images, materials, objects, and wishes of the deceased. Their task is to make sense of this amalgam and selectively preserve certain properties of the deceased ... The dead may be remembered as loving, obnoxious, volatile, or scornful, whether or not they viewed themselves as such while alive. However the fact that survivors focus on personal identity implies that the deceased held certain images themselves while alive which others accepted. In this context, what is being preserved after death is a self-concept which existed during life, was acknowledged by others, and had become significant aspect of the dead person.

Kings, presidents and other people of power can achieve this by carefully curating their legacy while alive, through monuments, statutes and commissioned eulogies. Examples range from Augustus Res Gestae, his record of his deeds that he instructed the Senate to put on public display after his funeral, to Winston Churchill's dictum that 'History will be kind to me for I intend to write it'. Between the divine Augustus and the earthly Churchill, we can also see how access to technology shaped and changed this process over the centuries. While the Res Gestae were carved in bronze for durability, what survived were copies of copies, hand-carved into stone in temples and palaces across the Empire. Churchill's memoirs were recorded on a less solid medium, but technological advances in the form of the printing press had since allowed the rapid copying and distribution of text. It seems that it is more reliable in passing on one's memory to the generations that follow to have many copies on a perishable medium than only a few on more durable material. This is of course also the insight that drives in its latest reiteration the interest in blockchain technology: records shared across a worldwide

---

[4] See McDonald, 'Idea of Immortality' (1971) 7 *Vox Evangelica*: 17.

[5] Pratchett, *Going Postal* (Doubleday 2004).

[6] Unruh, 'Death and Personal History: Strategies of Identity Preservation' (1983) 30 *Social Problems* 340.

network, albeit in mere electronic states of silicon chips, promise unsurpassed protection against change and destruction of information.

What powerful people do on a large scale is however just an amplification of behaviour we all engage in. Before we die, we try to create cues that preserve our identity in the minds of the survivors.[7] The survivor is left with images, materials and wishes of the deceased that allow, or force, them to act upon information and behaviours that were part of the deceased when he or she was alive.[8] This ability to influence others to act the way we want them to, even if we are not around any longer, creates a bond between the creation of memory and the exercise of control beyond the grave. On the one hand, by creating memories and images in the survivors we can induce people in the future to act in certain ways. Conversely, what we make them do can shape how we will be remembered, for instance through the actions of charities set up in our name. Just as we try to exercise power over the actions of future generations when we are gone, future generations can exercise a corresponding power by refusing to remember us the way we would want them to, maligning our deeds, or even by expunging us from the records altogether. *Yemach shemo vezichro*, 'obliterate his name and his memory', is one of the strongest curses in the Hebrew language,[9] and shows how powerful a threat of 'non-remembrance' can be. Law takes these intuitive, universal and efficient strategies and structures, amplifies and channels them. Inheritance law allows us to enforce, to a degree, our intentions and interests through third parties after we are dead. But this power is inevitably precarious. When Augustus dictated his *Res Gestae*, he had to do this in the knowledge that his successors might not only refuse to act on his orders, they could have gone further and erased his memory through legal edict, a *damnatio memoriae*, from the records altogether. We will come back to the power of memory erasure below, but will discuss first the way inheritance laws across the ages try to balance the freedom of the current generation to act as they desire, plans and intentions that survive in the memory of the dead.

While most of us realise that we cannot take our wealth with us, many of us hope nevertheless to control at least in part how our financial assets are used when we are not around any longer.[10] This too is part and parcel

---

⁷ Butler, 'Looking Forward to What? The Life Review, Legacy and Excessive Identity versus Change' (1970) 14 *American Behavioural Scientist* 121.

⁸ Unruh, 'Death and Personal History'.

⁹ See Bermant, *The Walled Garden: The Saga of Jewish Family Life and Tradition* (Weidenfeld & Nicolson 1974), p. 250.

¹⁰ For example, Rosenfeld, 'Old Age, New Beneficiaries: Kinship, Friendship and (Dis)inheritance' (1980) 64 *Sociology and Social Research* 86.

of Unruth's identity preservation strategy, especially if a will apportions and dispenses objects that the testator had imbued with their personal identity and their feelings about themselves. Testaments in this view also become part of a selective communication to survivors, instructing them which identities should be remembered, and also to a degree the content of those memories. This is particularly the case when specifically named artefacts are passed on, and also when they deviate from the normal default patterns. Inheriting these special objects brings with it obligations and commitments, a duty of stewardship:

> To receive grandmother's pearl brooch or grandfather's favorite shotgun may make emotionally mandatory compliance with other stipulations or expectations. One obligation may be the survivor's desire to preserve and protect specific memories or images of the deceased – that is, to become a guardian of the deceased's persona.[11]

For the discussion in this chapter, we take from this that testaments are not merely a means for the economic redistribution of wealth, something that settles potential conflicts between those still living. Rather, they are also a vehicle to create and maintain a new abstract object, the disembodied identity of the deceased, which prolongs and builds upon the sense of self-identity of the testator while s/he was alive. The distribution of artefacts in a testament does not so much bring the identity of the testator to a final conclusion, the shattering of what was theirs amongst the heirs, but sustains the prolonged existence of an 'informational object' in the form of distributed memory instances of the deceased.

Once a prerogative for the powerful and wealthy whose testaments could shape the fate of entire nations – as Caesar's famously did – the testament's historical roots in the West can be traced back to the law reforms of Solon. Testaments became a more common tool for the disposal of assets under Roman law. Roman law also gave us the mechanisms through which the desires and intentions of the deceased could be acted upon. Legates and *fideicommissa* were institutions that allowed the testator to put their trust in the execution of their will into people. It determined not just who should inherit, but also created an enforceable means for controlling how assets were to be used. The testator would nominate one of the heirs to act as fiduciary, who was then entrusted to distribute the assets to other beneficiaries as described in the *fideicommisarius*. This also allowed the passing on of assets to persons who would otherwise be ineligible to inherit, such as an unmarried

---

[11] Unruh, 'Death and Personal History, p. 344.

daughter. This in turn facilitated the preservation of wealth within the family line – important also because with the dissolution of a family, its *penates*, the household deities, would also perish. Faithful execution of a will thus serves to maintain three different abstract objects that our ontology has to account for: the self of the deceased as a memory artefact, the family of which they were part, and the '*lares et penates*', whose existence depends on the continuation of the family and mediation between the dead and the living. In an earlier version of this chapter, the focus was exclusively on the memory artefact of the deceased, which was given a digital representation. The discussion of Roman law, and the cognitive analysis of identity preservation by Unruh, show that such a view is arguably too restrictive, and that post-mortem identities are not self-sufficient and complete objects, but are constantly changed and recreated in communication amongst the living. So if we were to build an AI system that can act as our avatar on our behalf after we are dead, we also need to build *penates*, guiding spirits, to watch over them and moderate their behaviour in line with the interests of the family (or wider society) or else the past threatens to overwhelm the present by sheer numbers, as Clarke noted.

2. Technologies for Making Wills: From Paper Testaments to 'Digital' or Code-based Wills

For obvious reasons, 'communication technologies' played an important part in wills and testaments from the beginning. Since the testators are not around by definition and cannot be asked for their opinion, they need to find ways to reliably communicate their intentions to the administrators of the estate after death.[12] The advent of writing was followed by constant improvements in document storage facilities, such as archives. Archives thus were from the beginning a driving force in the development of wills and testaments as tools to engineer and control one's future. More recently, the use of video recordings added a new dimension of 'immediacy' to the way in which a testator can communicate with the executor and the heirs. In a variation of this theme, some US soldiers have made video recordings for their children prior to deployment into a battle zone, with the idea that if they do not return, the children will get parental advice at predetermined points in time. The next reiteration automatises this process of targeted and staggered release of information, and removes in this way the executor or the community of heirs in their role as mediators. Services such as Futuris[13] allow subscribers to schedule messages up to fifty years in advance. A specific free post-mortem

---

[12] The Scots law term 'executor' will also be used below.
[13] Available at: <www.futuristk.com/> (accessed 15 April 2019).

feature requires the sender to select trusted third parties to notify Futuris.tk of their passing, after which death-specific messages are sent.

A simple extension using straightforward technologies currently used (such as compliance software) can trigger the release, not on a specific pre-defined date, but at a predefined event. This can easily be automatised for many situations, with data about the event collected automatically from a news aggregator or similar source and matched against the triggering clause of the program. Someone could then send 'from the grave' instructions to sell the family business the moment shares fall beyond a certain point, or exhort their heirs to join the army/conscientiously object when the country enters a war against a pre-specified other nation. While this might give the 'feeling' that the deceased was in direct communication, and could enhance the persuasive capacities, ultimately these are still 'traditional' recordings of a person's thoughts, preferences and opinions *now*, while they are still alive. Once recorded they remain static and unaltered. This means, from a legal perspective, that the program that implements such a provision as an 'if => then' rule, should at the very least be treated as an extrinsic piece of evidence that can be used to interpret the corresponding provision of a will. This assumes, of course, that the applicable law permits generally the use of external materials to disambiguate a will and to establish the testator's true intent.

Take for instance a will that provides for the bequest of a sum of money to a relative 'upon completion of her degree'. The issue can now arise if this has to be the completion of the degree program she was enrolled in when the will was made, or if any degree will suffice. If we find that the software was set up by the deceased so as to send an email the moment her name is found on the graduation list of any university, with the message 'congratulations, enjoy the £5,000', then this would indicate that the nature of the degree should not matter. If by contrast the triggering event is to match her name on the graduation list of the university she was enrolled in when the will was made, and the text says 'congratulations on being an alumni of my own alma mater now', this would point towards a specific degree being required to inherit the money.

More complicated could be the question, in jurisdictions that do not have strict requirements regarding the form of a will, and do not require witnesses, whether the programme itself could be deemed to be 'the will' – either because no other document exists, or, more problematically, if the programme was set up after a paper-based will was written. This will depend obviously on the jurisdiction. Relevant questions are what, if any, requirements there are for the will to be 'in writing' and, if electronic documents count, how any requirements regarding witnesses are met, and the question of signatures. In England and Wales, the Law Commission has proposed to permit electronic wills, including what they term 'fully electronic wills'. This goes beyond a will drafted using word-processing software and subsequently printed, and while the Commission remains concerned about digital signatures, it considers the possibility that a will can be drafted, executed and stored exclusively as an electronic file, potentially through a third-party provider:

> [s]ince technology is already widely used to prepare hard copy wills, the intuitive next step is to develop our capacity to execute wills electronically and make use of fully electronic wills.[14]

Self-executing wills in the form of a software program could go even further than that. Rather than having a document that says that 'In the event of my niece graduating, she should receive £5,000', we would have a line of code that determines the trigger conditions ('graduating') in the head of the clause, and have as plain text only the content of the congratulatory email that it will automatically send if the trigger is matched. Any competent analyst could translate the code into a corresponding conditional sentence, but such a translation would be required. Since the UK is already breaking ground in permitting fully electronic wills, it seems unlikely that such a 'self-executing' will would be recognised at present. However, since wills are a form of private law making, the adage that, in the digital world, law *is* code could open up the scope further and eventually lead to an acceptance of wills written as executable software programs. If it becomes necessary to determine when a will was made, then the operative date would be the moment the program was uploaded, not the date when it executes one or several of the conditions of the will. This would preserve the analogy to traditional text-based wills that create an obligation for the executor *now* to act in a certain way at a certain future time.

While this means that near-future code-based wills would share significant similarities with traditional text-based wills, this also points to the significant limitation that they both share: they remain a snapshot of the testator's intentions and plans at a given point in time. Moreover, this snapshot is limited by the testator's ability to verbalise their preferences, intentions and desires and to make them explicit.

Wills as currently understood are made by the living, and upon the death of the testator cannot be altered any longer. This means that their

---

[14] Law Commission, 'Making a Will', Consultation paper 231 available at: <https://s3-eu-west-2.amazonaws.com/lawcom-prod-storage-11jsxou24uy7q/uploads/2017/07/Making-a-will-consultation.pdf> (accessed 15 April 2019); for a US discussion see No author, 'Developments in the Law – More Data, More Problems' (2018) 131 *Harvard Law Review* 1715.

faithful execution often depends on their interpretation by third parties. Consider Rudolf V of Ruritania, living in exile and drafting a will that sets up a trust that regularly discharges money to his wife and children, but with the condition that any relative who engages in any future war 'against the testator's country of origin, Ruritania' will lose any entitlement, the money falling to the other members. Imagine that shortly after Rudolf dies, civil war breaks out in Ruritania that divides the country into two, both parts gaining recognition from the UN as independent countries. They promptly wage war against each other, both claiming that they and only they are the legitimate Ruritania, and the other mere rebels. Flavia, the testator's wife, accepts the claim of Ruritania North and joins its fight. Whether or not our code 'fires' and the 'disinheritance clause' is triggered would in this case depend on almost arbitrary programming choices, together with similarly arbitrary decisions by the two countries in the conflict, for example on whether they chose new names for the two nations (condition not triggered) or both keep the Ruritania label (condition triggered). In any case, Flavia is likely to challenge the execution of the program and to claim that it does not faithfully represents the true intent of Rudolf, leaving the issue to the courts to determine. The same issue also applies of course to traditional wills, which in this situation need to be interpreted by the executor. Nonetheless, the known issues and limitations of traditional wills are likely to get worse in this scenario, given the expressive limitations of software code that mean that important nuances are likely to get lost in the process of translating the testator's preferences into code. So in this type of situation at least, a correct determination of the testator's preferences will be more difficult in comparison to traditional testaments. This would create a new source of potential errors and hence disputes, especially when the programming, the 'translation' of the verbal instructions into software code, has been left to a third party and the testator is not skilled enough to verify the accuracy of the translation.

The same issue also diminishes the value for identity preservation, which we identified above as a crucial purpose of testaments. Rudolf wants to be remembered as a patriot. His provisions in his will would have been appropriate to achieve this goal *if* things had stayed the same. But as they didn't, his disposition is likely to have the opposite effect, preventing his heirs from fighting for the unity and territorial integrity of his home country. Of course, had he lived, he would have been livid. This was never what he had meant, and everybody who knew him would have recognised what his true intentions would have been. So ideally, he wants to leave not just a static version of his plans as they are now, but also with them a method to interpret them in alignment with his values, should circumstances change. Rather than a mere self-executing but fixed digital object, what he needs is an AI system that understands him, his values and priorities, well enough to advise and instruct as he would have done had he been alive. Such an AI system continues to learn and to grow even after the initial programming is completed, to react flexibly to changing circumstances that he could not have anticipated.

This scenario is not unlike the one depicted in *Total Recall*:

> Hauser: Howdy, stranger! I'm Hauser. If things haven't gone wrong, I'm talking to myself and you don't have a wet towel around your head. Now, whatever your name is, get ready for the big surprise. You are not you, you're me.
> Douglas Quaid: [to himself] No shit.[15]

Hauser is about to get his memory wiped so that he can become the infiltrator Quaid. He needs to find a way to communicate to his own future self, who will have preferences and values intentionally designed to be very different from his present set of convictions. Technology gives him the means to do so in the form of a recorded video clip in which he explains to his own future self the background for his assignment and how he is to understand the orders given to him. In this case, norm giver and norm interpreter are the same person (for a given value of 'same person') and technology acts as a mediator to ensure that the present incarnation, Quaid, interprets the norms ('infiltrate the rebellion') in a way that his earlier persona, Hauser, would have approved of.

Total Recall is of course in many ways more like Futuris: a fixed message, programmed to be released if a certain trigger event is recorded. Much could have gone wrong, and the message would have been more efficient could it have responded to any change in circumstances. Had it seen how Quaid had changed, it may have chosen its words more carefully. This would mean that Hauser's AI representative needs to understand what Hauser tries to achieve. For this it could have systematically interrogated him to establish how he would have wanted his orders to be interpreted under a variety of hypothetical conditions. This approach will be the subject of the next section.

3. From Static to Dynamic Digital Wills

In this section, we will connect the above discussion on automated execution and dynamic interpretation of wills with the research tradition in legal AI that focuses on computational models of legal reasoning. We will argue that on the one hand this tradition provides us with a wealth of experience and solutions which anchor the above suggestions in reality. On the other

---

[15] Verhoeven (Director), Total Recall (Tristar Pictures, 1990).

hand, taking the interpretation of wills as an application of legal AI sidesteps some of the methodological and practical issues that in the past proved to be significant obstacles for legal AI solutions that were robust enough to move beyond worked examples, prototypes and similar research-based efforts.

The task of interpreting a will is not so different from interpreting an Act of Parliament. Both create (legally enforceable) norms for behaviour, both (also) try to constrain the actions of people in the future. Both try to be specific in what they ask, while maintaining sufficient flexibility to deal with unforeseeable events and circumstances, which leads to sufficiently open-textured language that can then be interpreted when and if the need arises. In both cases, it is impossible to go back to the norm giver and ask how they would have drafted the rule had they but known about the new circumstance. In both cases, establishing the 'true intent' will play a role, its role, importance and conceptualisation varying by jurisdiction. It seems therefore plausible to look at the efforts of the AI and law community to develop systems that are capable of reasoning with and interpreting legal norms and extend them to a situation where the norm in question is a person's will. Indeed as we will see, this scenario removes some of the obstacles that proved challenging for legal AI research.

In the early days of legal AI and legal expert system research, the image of the computer-judge provided a powerful metaphor that brought the hopes and aspirations of the research community to the point. The image did not influence only research in legal AI, but also jurisprudence[16] and popular literature and film, such as Futurama's *Judge Computer*.[17] But despite several promising results, the ultimate goal of fully automated judicial decision making remained elusive. The early enthusiasm was followed by a period of introspection from the 1990s onwards, which led to an increasingly critical reassessment of computerised decision makers in law, and a 'new modesty' in legal AI research. As a result of this phase of introspection, systemic problems in the project of developing computer judges were identified that seem to make any attempt to revive the notion in 2018 unfeasible on conceptual, philosophical, methodological and ethical grounds. The idea of a fully automated reasoner that interprets legal rules and suggests solutions in specific cases seems today distinctly like an anachronistic return to the 1980s. The idea is dead and we should let it rest – or so it seems but, as one would expect in a paper on ZombAIs, the dead do not always stay in their graves.

---

[16] Susskind, 'Detmold's Computer Judge Revisited' (1986) 49 *Modern Law Review* 683, pp. 683–4.
[17] Available at: <http://theinfosphere.org/Computer_Judge> (accessed 15 April 2019).

3.1 Learning from Legal AI: From Automated Legal Interpretations to Machine-learning Decision Support Systems

To achieve its aims, a computer-judge would have to be capable of applying general, abstract norms correctly to the facts of a specific case. But as the experience in legal AI research shows,[18] attempts to formalise this process of subsuming specific cases under general norms poses significant difficulties:

1. The inherent vagueness of legal texts. To be sufficiently flexible and capable of regulating situations unforeseen by the legislator at the point of law making, legal language is necessarily to a certain degree vague. This results in a need for interpretation and with it the capture of the meta-level rules that guide the interpretative process.
2. The value-laden-ness of law and legal language. To be able to give an adequate interpretation, judges need to refer to values implicit in the legal system. Their own moral, political and philosophical commitments play a necessary, albeit essentially contested, part in this process. However, these wider social values are regularly only implicit and not carried by the text on its surface – how then to program them into an AI system, how can it learn the relevant values and preferences, and who decides which of the various and often conflicting ideas and values in a pluralistic society should be given to the AI?
3. The contested nature of law. In particular in appeal cases, i.e. the cases where we learn most about legal interpretation, both sides will have good arguments on their side, otherwise the case would not have been allowed to progress. In particular, in cases where the court itself is divided and a decision is reached by simple majority voting, it is obvious that the opposite solution would also have been a possible answer, that is, an answer consistent with existing precedents and statutes.

For legal informatics, this opened up two follow-on questions:

4. If it is possible that even the top experts rationally hold mutually contradictory opinions, what exactly is the 'knowledge' that the computer models, and on what basis is the decision what to include, or which opinion to choose, taken?
5. What does it mean for the evaluation of the computer-judge? Under

---

[18] For a historical overview see Bench-Capon et al., 'A History of AI and Law in 50 Papers: 25 Years of the International Conference on AI and Law' (2012) 20 *Artificial Intelligence and Law* 215.

what conditions are we entitled to say that the programme is working correctly and that the 'right' decisions are reached? Is the task, as a legal realist would have it, merely predicting the outcome of a case – in which case extraneous information about the judge, their preference, life histories and personal foibles might help – or does it mean, as formalists would argue, correspondence to some abstract, legal ideal that can be assessed without knowledge of the human beings that interpret and implement the law?

3.2 From Expert Systems to Machine-learning Systems? Issues of Training Sets and Explicability

While the first generation of legal expert systems tried to give explicit, symbolic representations of legal reasoning, current attempts in legal AI prefer the ML paradigm, where the computer extracts autonomously rules from training set. This works well in particular in domains where there are large numbers of decisions, which then can form interesting patterns that AIs can discover. This means also that we do not have to decide in advance how to capture laws in rigid yet brittle and semantically vague rules. However, this approach also faces some challenges, especially for the type of task we are discussing here. ML approaches crucially depend on the identification and selection of appropriate training sets, which have to be big enough to permit the emergence of robust patterns. This general challenge for ML faces specific problems in the case of legal applications:

1. Most legal cases are decided on issues of fact, not legal interpretation. Only a selection of cases is accepted by the appeal courts for decision, and hence there are fewer authoritative training examples where word meaning is disambiguated, while the pre-selection process introduces biases in the training data. Cases are not necessarily selected because of their quality as training examples, but reflect also issues such as the financial resources of the parties (not everyone can afford to appeal) or statutory limitations on what type of decisions can be appealed (e.g. only those above a certain value). This approach works therefore better for mass cases decided by courts in first instance, as in the SplitUp system,[19] or more recently Lex Machina.[20]
2. Of these, a significant portion of court decisions are not published, and

---

[19] Zeleznikow, 'Building Judicial Decision Support Systems in Discretionary Legal Domains' (2000) 14 *International Review of Computers, Law and Information Technology* 341.
[20] Allison, Lemley, and Schwartz, 'Understanding the Realities of Modern Patent Litigation' (2013) 92 *Texas Law Review* 1769.

hence are not available to train an expert system. Decisions on publication again reflect external factors, and can as a result distort the sample.

3. Even in these decided and published cases, the reasoning that informs the decision is not always sufficiently clear to make straightforward training examples: they often create ambiguities of their own, and asking the decision maker is not normally possible.

These three issues affect the 'input' side of ML approaches in legal AI. It is often impossible to get sufficiently large, comprehensive, unbiased and detailed training sets. A fourth problem pertains to the outcome of ML approaches:

4. The extracted rules are in turn not symbolically represented and explicit. While 'explainable AI' has become one of the most interesting research themes, it still faces significant challenges.[21] In law however, the justification of a decision matters just as much as the correctness, reflected in the cross-jurisdiction duty of courts to give public reasons for their decisions.

The first three problems indicate that there is not enough, and not systematically varied, training data to allow AIs to reason like a lawyer interpreting a norm. The fourth problem is a problem for justice – courts must justify their decisions – and also a problem for our scenario. As we discussed above, the aim of the will is to create a persistent identity in the memory of the living. Allocating assets becomes a communicative task that expresses normative commitments. It rewards, punishes and praises, and in this way maintains a specific normative ideal that the testator had about themselves. It is in other words not enough that the AI allocates more money to the younger daughter than the oldest son, if it omits to give the explanation 'because she needs a dowry while he will get a job' (preserving the image of the deceased as a traditionalist patriarch), or the explanation 'because she has already excelled in her studies and she is much more likely to change the world than him' (preserving the image of a believer in meritocracy even in defiance of conventional social rules).

But what if the aim were not to predict how a group of as-yet-unknown future judges will try to determine what a past parliament may or may not have wanted to happen under circumstances the parliamentarians could not possibly foresee? What if instead my task is more modest, and I want my AI

---

[21] Biran and Cotton, 'Explanation and Justification in Machine Learning: A Survey' (2017) In IJCAI-17 Workshop on Explainable AI (XAI), p. 8.

to interpret rules that I and I alone have been creating? This indicates that the task to train an AI to correctly interpret *my* preferences to interpret rules that *I* made should be significantly easier than to program a computer (on the basis of a small number of published precedents) so that it can predict how a future judge, whom I don't know, might interpret a law that someone else has enacted and whose thought processes I have only indirect access to. The latter was what AI and law research tried to accomplish. The former however is the situation a testator finds himself in, at least if we focus initially only on those dispositions that the testator can make freely and without restrictions.

A note on this important restriction is necessary here. Below we will also discuss whether it could be relaxed or even lifted altogether. In many legal systems, the freedom of the testator is limited by a number of overriding social norms – in Scots law for instance, some closely related family members are protected against disinheritance through the notion of 'legal rights' in succession law.[22] In addition, a number of decisions from the early nineteenth century prevent particularly egregious examples of wasting assets or other determinations that go contrary to public morals.[23] We will come back to these restrictions below, noting here only that they also reflect what was said above about the function of inheritance in Roman law, which was not just an expression of individual preferences but a way to maintain and protect the 'family spirits', giving an inherently social dimension to what in modern liberal societies could be (mis)understood solely as an act of self-expression.

Going back for a moment to the question of legal AI, ML and automated judging, an analogy from another field of computer science may come in helpful. Research in computer-assisted speech recognition distinguishes between 'speaker-dependent' and 'speaker-independent' approaches.[24] In speaker-independent applications, the aim is to develop software for arbitrary, unknown users who can use the system immediately without it needing training. This type of system, for instance, tries to handle calls to call centres. One can assume in advance that every caller will use one of several terms to identify their problem ('overdraft', 'charges', 'mortgage', and so on) but it needs to be robust enough to predict how an arbitrary user whom the system

---

[22] For example, Hiram, 'Reforming Succession Law: Legal Rights' (2008) 12 *Edinburgh Law Review* 81.

[23] See for historical discussion Hiram, 'Morbid Family Pride: Private Memorials and Scots Law' in *Memory, Mourning, Landscape* (Brill Rodopi 2010).

[24] Huang and Lee, 'On Speaker-Independent, Speaker-Dependent, and Speaker-Adaptive Speech Recognition' (proceedings of the International Conference on Acoustics, Speech, and Signal Processing, ICASSP-91 1991) <http://doi.ieeecomputersociety.org/10.1109/ICASSP.1991.150478> (accessed 20 June 2019).

has never encountered before will pronounce these words. Whenever the vocabulary can be kept small, for example in telephone inquiries, successful systems have been developed, but even the best systems currently available can only identify several thousand words.

By contrast, speaker-dependent voice recognition software is 'tailor made' for the individual user, who can train the system on their personal particularities in pronunciation or dialect prior to use.[25] Typically, they will be given test sentences to train the system, repeating them often enough until the computer recognises the sentence. On the down side, this means that the system will only work properly with one specific user. On the positive side, these systems have a much larger vocabulary and higher degrees of accuracy and reliability than speaker-independent systems.[26]

The traditional approach to legal expert system design was similar to speaker-independent voice recognition. In these systems it does not matter who the user is, or who the judges will be who are going to evaluate and interpret a norm, the system should correctly predict their decision. As with voice independent speaker recognition, this is only feasible if the number of possible answers is highly restricted from the beginning and a very small vocabulary suffices. But our scenario is much more amenable to the second type of system. It should predict how the testator would have interpreted a provision in their own will, had they known about the new set of circumstances. To achieve this the testators only have to train the AI on their *own* preferences while they are still alive – they don't need to know the preferences and convictions of some arbitrary judge, nor do they need to speculate what some collective norm giver may have wanted to achieve. Norm giver and norm interpreter are one and the same, the AI a mere future extension of my present self. To train the system one only needs to know oneself, though this is of course the highest form of philosophical knowledge.

This resolves the problems 1–3 indicated above, and gives us a potentially unlimited number of training examples. In this approach, the user trains the system through a range if hypothetical scenarios that are specifically designed to elicit his or her approach to counterfactual future situations. Similar approaches to train AIs on the ethical preferences of their users have been suggested for autonomous cars,[27] which however would be a much more ambitious, and much more (legally) risky endeavour. In comparison, what

---

[25] Beigi, *Fundamentals of Speaker Recognition* (Springer 2010).

[26] Junqua and Haton, *Robustness in Automatic Speech Recognition: Fundamentals and Applications* (Kluwer Academic Publishers, 1995).

[27] Contissa, Lagioia, and Sartor, 'The Ethical Knob: Ethically-customisable Automated Vehicles and the Law' (2017) 25 *Artificial intelligence and Law* 365.

is suggested here builds on a long tradition of computational rule interpretation, and does not require translation between normative text and physical movements. Once the system has been trained sufficiently, the owner is then also the only benchmark for the evaluation of our system that matters: it is correct if and only if it predicts correctly how they would have interpreted the norm in question under a given set of circumstances.

In medical, inheritance and trust law, we thus find a kind of situation of norm interpretation where we deal with a single known 'legislator'. A living will establishes for instance general rules about how I want to be treated in case an accident or illness permanently deprives me of my ability to communicate or make decisions for myself. One concern that prevents people from writing such as disposition is that they will have to trust, just as in inheritance law, a third party, potentially one they do not yet know, to interpret it correctly should circumstances change.[28] What is suggested here for testaments could also alleviate this concern, by putting the trust instead into a system they themselves trained on their preferences, and under their exclusive control. In inheritance and trust law, we can create rules regarding who should benefit from our property after death, by leaving it for instance to trustees to act on our behalf and to interpret the rules we laid down. In both cases, we postulate rules that we hope are clear and can deal with all possible eventualities. Yet as the examples above show, this is not always possible, and sometimes someone will have to interpret in the light of new developments how we would have wanted our words to be understood. For obvious reasons, asking us will not be possible.[29] Hence, it will be necessary to interpret the rules, in the same way in which a judge would interpret an Act of Parliament.

3.3 Building the Machine-learning Post-mortem Will System: Training Hypotheticals

Of course, evidence about our value system, convictions or religious and ethical beliefs are relevant data points for that process, but inevitably a degree of speculation will be necessary. But what if we had trained a computer system to learn about our personal values in the same way in which we can train a computer to understand our voice? Such a system could then be interrogated

---

[28] Lynn, 'Why I Don't Have a Living Will' (1991) 19 *Law, Medicine and Health Care*, pp. 101–4.

[29] In Ryūnosuke Akutagawa's *Rashomon*, the ghost of the victim is allowed to give evidence in the trial against his murderer. Jacques Orneuve is a famous, real-life (?) example of a zombie asking to be permitted to give evidence in court (see <http://thefullzombie.com/topics/us_law_and_haitian_zombie>, last accessed 15 April 2019). However, cross-examining the undead is generally frowned upon by modern legal systems.

on our behalf, to hear an authentic account of 'our' opinion on that matter –
and to add psychological force, could even use our voice. The neural network
at the heart of the system would have been trained by asking us standardised
questions that permits it to learn about our general attitudes. In a simple
setting, this can be a QA game that is designed to permit inferences:

> User: My money should go to my surviving brother
> AI: what if he has undergone gender reassignment and has become your
> sister?
> User: that's fine, it's blood that counts.

At this point we significantly depart from the traditional understanding
of what a will is and what it can achieve. A traditional rule-based legal expert
system would model the preferences of the testator through conditional
propositions, fixed in advance. As we discussed above, this could also change
the way wills are drafted and implemented, but would still keep one important aspect of a traditional will: that it is limited by what the testator was able
to imagine about future developments. What is suggested here would remove
that limitation. The system itself is now able to infer from the training data
how its owner would probably have reacted, for a whole range of similar
events, had he but known about these changes in circumstances. This marks a
crucial change from a mere novel form of recording a will by a living person
to an autonomous legal representative beyond the grave, a ZombAI who
expresses the probable intentions of its deceased owner even under conditions
that the owner never anticipated.

Even more ambitiously than abstracting general rules for a range of hypothetical scenarios, it could try to learn some of the higher-level philosophical convictions through similar QA training ('Do you think nature is more
important than nurture – yes or no?') or by generating typical ethical problems
('Would you save someone who is related to you or someone who is your
personal friend, from a burning building?'). Similar ideas that could feed into
such a learning approach can be found in current research in 'experimental
philosophy'. This approach to ethics puts an emphasis on large datasets of
answers from large numbers of people across cultures, and would form a
natural starting point for developing the necessary methodology.[30] The questions can become increasingly subtle and detailed, and the user can spend as
much time on training the software as he or she wishes – depending on how
accurately they want their wishes to be represented once they are dead.

---

[30] For example, Knobe and Nichols (eds), *Experimental Philosophy* (Oxford University Press
2008); Appiah, *Experiments in Ethics* (Harvard University Press 2008); Musschenga, 'Was
ist empirische Ethik?' (2009) 21 *Ethik in der Medizin* 187.

3.4 Building the Machine-Learning post-mortem Will System: User Validation

In the next step, the system has to be validated by the user. For this it would be asked to develop its own solutions to user-defined tasks, try to mimic the owner's behaviour and attitudes and receive user feedback for correct and incorrect answers. Based on this feedback the system can then model increasingly accurately the user's convictions and the ethical rules that govern their behaviour. Here we can see two important differences from traditional legal AI: first, the user's decision is the only relevant benchmark for judging the correctness of the answer, and second, we can generate as large a number of training examples as we wish – just like voice recognition software that never stops learning. Theoretically, the system would already be a success if it predicted how its owner would reinterpret a provision in the light of new circumstances better than a third party, such as a judge who had no personal knowledge of the deceased. Alternatively, one could demand a specific success rate, for example 75 per cent correct predictions or outperforming humans, whichever is higher. The standards of proof in civil litigation could also provide such a benchmark, if translated correctly into the language of probabilities. Whether the system has in fact the necessary level of proficiency, whatever we decide this to be, could of course be documented easily. Nothing more than record keeping of the learning process would be required, though we may want in law to insist on specific precautions to make such a record tamper-proof.

4. Legal and Ethical Implications

So far, we have established a pan-human need, the desire to influence what happens to our memories once we are gone, that transcends times and cultures. We have also seen how wills and testaments as a legal technique leveraged communication technology throughout history to exercise post-mortem control. We also saw some of the inherent limitations of current wills, if measured against the objective to create an informational object, a memory that is preserved in future generations: they make the testator subject to the power of future generations to reinterpret, or misinterpret, what the text of the will should mean. In the next step, we made a *prima facie* case, building on the experience with computer-aided statutory interpretation, that training a system so as to provide interpretative aid, or maybe even to actively dispose assets, after the death of its owner seems highly feasible. In this section, we will delve a bit deeper into the ethical and societal consequences of building such as system and giving it legal recognition.

4.1 We Can, But Should We?

The type of system that was outlined above, like the zombies of lore, falls well short of the full intelligence of the person whose behaviour it models. In particular, it would not grow, mature and learn once its owner is dead. So far, the only input in the system that we discussed came from the owner, and would end with their death. But nonetheless it preserves task-specific knowledge that would make it a capable representative of the deceased for certain purposes. Crucially, and unlike the existing simple algorithms that only release pre-formulated advice and instructions that we encountered in the first part, the system is now partly autonomous, resulting potentially in advice and dispositions of assets that were not foreseen by the testator. Such a system would avoid or at least mitigate one of the pitfalls for successful identity preservation that we encountered earlier, the intentional or unintentional misreading of the deceased's preferences. In the example of Rudolf, for instance, it would have learned from him his moral attitudes towards civil war, and whether it was better to refrain from taking up arms against one's countrymen, or better to side with the party best placed to preserve the territorial integrity of the nation. If this sounds like science fiction, one should remember that AIs that profile our behaviour for advertising purposes have significant success in predicting our preferences even though we do not actively collaborate with them.

However, on the legal side this also means that it is no longer possible to translate directly between a traditional will and the software program. As we discussed above, a program that releases an instruction at a future point in time, but with a trigger condition X that is made fully explicit in the code now, is the direct equivalent of a sentence of the form 'If X happens, do Y' in a traditional will. This type of isomorphic,[31] meaning-preserving translation is impossible in what we suggested above: there is no single proposition in the computer code that 'matches' a single legal provision. Rather, the system will decide under as-yet-unknown circumstances, using the interaction between multiple sentences (the training data), the algorithm that extracts patterns from them and the unforeseen external event.

How should we think in law about such an advanced representation from beyond the grave? Would it be permissible to use the AI at least as an advisor, to provide refutable external evidence on how the deceased would have wanted their will to be read? Or could we be more radical, and dispense with

---

[31] Bench-Capon and Coenen, 'Isomorphism and Legal Knowledge Based Systems' (1992) 1 *Artificial Intelligence and Law* 65, pp. 65–86.

human administrators of wills altogether, or at least severely limit their role? I might not be able to go to my own funeral, but my AI will, and afterwards it will ensure through its actions that my assets serve the preservation of my identity in the memories of my heirs. Such an idea raises a number of interesting technical, ethical and legal questions, and even if such a system may not be feasible at present, it allows us to test our intuitions about wills, the digital afterlife and also the scope and limitations of AI-based rule interpretation.

The decisions we make in answer to some of the more obvious technical challenges will influence in turn how we are likely to think of such systems as representative – ethically, socially and in law. The greatest technical problem will be in formulating suitable training questions and examples. These need to be capable of generating the right general rules to model correctly the value system of the person who trains it. Alternatively (or additionally), a much more ambitious but also risky approach would have the system learn from the (online) behaviour of its owner, also outside a formal training context. This could include the values of the news sources that the testators read or their beliefs as expressed in online discussions or blogs. Finally, we could expand the training set beyond the individual owner, and in various ways think of aggregating across multiple users for profiling purposes. This could take the form of profiling and recommender systems, for example: 'other users who answered ethical questions A, B and C in their training sessions like this typically answered question X like this'. This would immediately increase the size of the training set even further, but gradually changing the AI from a system that incorporates knowledge about the personal preferences of its owner only to one that expresses how a member of the (socio-economic, cultural, gender, and so on) group of the testator typically thinks. While such an approach may empirically be even better at anticipating what its owner would have wanted, it changes the nature of the informational object that is created. Intuitively, we are likely to think of the first as a real representative of the owner, including their blind spots but 'true' to their self-conception, while the second seems more like an externally imposed understanding of the type of person the testator was. Such a system could still be of possible use to a third party (such as a judge) who wants to ascertain, for whatever reason, how a person may have acted under a given set of circumstances, but it seems to lack the authenticity that we would expect from a digital representative.

At this point it may also help to distinguish what is proposed here from some much more ambitious projects regarding 'digital immortality'.[32] In

---

[32] For an overview of the discussion see Rothblatt, *Virtually Human: The Promise – and the Peril – of Digital Immortality* (Macmillan 2014).

terms of popular culture, these more ambitious projects take their inspiration more from mind uploads described in the utopian *Culture* novels of Iain Banks, or the dystopian vision of Richard K Morgan's *Altered Carbon*. In these accounts, personal identity is strictly identified with mind states, which are then copied into a new medium. The AI literally becomes us and has subjective states that are continuous with ours – assuming such a reductionist conception of personal identity is credible.[33] It should be emphasised that nothing like this is suggested here, which ultimately is just a more sophisticated recording of our wishes. While all the legal and ethical issues that apply to the system proposed here also apply to such ideas as whole brain emulation and similar approaches to digital immortality,[34] the converse is not true. Still, some of the techniques used in these more ambitious approaches are also of relevance for our more modest proposal.

In the word of Susan Asche:

> As a hopefully minimalistic definition then, digital immortality can be roughly considered as involving a person-centric repository containing a copy of everything that a person sees, hears, says, or engenders over his or her lifespan, including photographs, videos, audio recordings, movies, television shows, music albums/CDs, newspapers, documents, diaries and journals, interviews, meetings, love letters, notes, papers, art pieces, and so on, and so on; and if not everything, then at least as much as the person has and takes the time and trouble to include. The person's personality, emotion profiles, thoughts, beliefs, and appearance are also captured and integrated into an artificially intelligent, interactive, conversational agent/ avatar. This avatar is placed in charge of (and perhaps 'equated' with) the collected material in the repository so that the agent can present the illusion of having the factual memories, thoughts, and beliefs of the person him/ herself.[35]

Along similar lines are projects by Microsoft on digital immortality[36] and the concept of personality capture.[37] Such comprehensive data collections

---

[33] On this, for example, Parfit, 'Divided Minds and the Nature of Persons' in Blakemore C and Greenfield S (eds), *Mindwaves* (Blackwell 1987), pp. 19–26; on the philosophical issues see Hauskeller, 'My Brain, My Mind, and I: Some Philosophical Assumptions of Mind-uploading' (2012) 4 *International Journal of Machine Consciousness* 187.

[34] Sandberg and Boström. 'Whole Brain Emulation: A Roadmap' (Technical Report, 2008) Future of Humanity Institute, Oxford University.

[35] Asche, 'Kulturelles Gedächtnis im 21. Jahrhundert: Tagungsband des internationalen Symposiums' (Vol. 1), 23 April 2005, Karlsruhe (KIT Scientific Publishing 2010), p. 35.

[36] Bell and Gray, 'Digital Immortality' (2001) 44 *Communications of the ACM* 28.

[37] Bainbridge, *Personality Capture and Emulation* (Springer 2013).

that record a person's life are from a data protection perspective of obvious concern. In our context, though, they allow us to rethink some key legal concepts through the prism of technology. What do we mean if we say that the avatar should implement the 'true intent' of the testator, as if they were still around? Consider again our example of Rudolph, and let's assume we have asked the AI how he would have wanted the will to be interpreted. There are at least four possible answers:

1. It should give the same answer *now* that Rudolph would have given *when he trained the AI*.
2. It should give the same answer that Rudolph *would have given had he lived*, and continued his personal developmental trajectory and growth *right to this point in time*.
3. It should give the answer that matches best who Rudolph *'truly was' when he trained the AI*, as evidenced by his actions and for everyone to see, even if he may not have been aware of this himself.
4. It should give the answer that matches best who Rudolph *'truly would have been' had he lived till this point in time* and continued his personal developmental trajectory, as evidenced by his actions and for everyone to see, even if he may not have been aware of this himself.

Points 1 and 2 differ from points 3 and 4 in the sense that for the first two, we take as 'true intent' whatever Rudolph would have answered explicitly and consciously, after due deliberation. They are the intentions of his 'rational self', governed by the ideal he has of himself. But of course, these may not always be in line with his actions and observed behaviour, especially (but not only) when the instinctive and emotional self are at odds with the reflective self. So points 3 and 4 are based on external ascription, on the inferences someone else would draw about him. He might for instance answer in the training session that he prefers neutrality in a civil war, because he wants to be the type of person who wants to resort to violence only when necessary, but he might not be that person (yet), and has to override his instincts. If this is what we mean by his true intentions – that is, deliberate and reflected intentions, then the simple training method we outlined above would potentially be more reliable than full personality capture. If on the other hand we want the avatar that it is 'true unto itself', warts and all, then the more the AI observes of the actual behaviour of the testator the better.

For both legal and anthropological reasons, for our purpose the more limited avatar, trained with approved and explicit training sets, is the much more appropriate solution. From a legal perspective, this follows since testaments are a form of exclusionary reason behind which the executor should not probe. If the will said the money should go to 'my beloved brother', then, barring duress or a similar reason that renders the will void, what I say counts, not what I 'really' feel about my brother, or whether this is by objective standards a rational decision. This matches the anthropological discussion from above – the identity that I want to preserve is not a *descriptive* fact about me, it is a *normative* construct, a vision of myself of how I want to be remembered, not necessarily how I was. This is a crucial difference between Unruh's identity preservation strategies and digital immortality. It is the former, not the latter that our inheritance law serves, and this has implications for the technology that could assist it.

However, this assumes that we use ZombAIs only as a new form of will, and not also as a way to allocate assets for those who died intestate. We will briefly touch again on this topic below, and note here only that such an application would pose different technological and ethical challenges. By definition, it would not be trained by the owner, and merely observe them passively. It would also be much more likely to incorporate general societal expectations, for example in the form of 'recommender systems' or similar profiling techniques that were mentioned above.

Going back to the four possible disambiguations of the term 'true intent', points 1 and 3 differ from 2 and 4 in the 'timelines' that they create. The first two are closer to a current testament: once it is signed, it remains fixed. In the will supported by an advanced AI, its content might change as a result of new circumstances, but it is the personality of the testator as it was at the time of making the will that determines its interpretation, along the lines of their preferences as they were then. Death, in that sense, was final, an end to growth and development; the AI is closer to a Zombie. In 2 and 4, the avatar changes more substantially even after the death of its owner, continues to learn and to grow – which can also mean a change in the very parameters that serve to interpret the testament. My broad political outlook or ethical system, for instance, as it is *now* might change over the next decade, but in line with and constrained by other aspects of my personality. My future self might indeed do things that my present self would strongly disapprove of. Should we give the AI as representative beyond the grave also the ability to change and grow in this way, after the demise of its owner? As before, the current legal answer is arguably no: the testament should be interpreted in conformity with who the person was when they wrote it, not the person they may have become had death not interrupted their life plan. Everything else, given our current state of knowledge, would simply invite idle speculation that goes well beyond the current use of external evidence to interpret wills, even in those jurisdictions that permit external evidence for disambiguation purposes. However, this legal attitude could change if we decided that the social benefits of this approach were significant – the most obvious one would be that changing social attitudes could more easily be accommodated.

Also of crucial importance is to ensure that the system is secure and cannot be hacked into or otherwise taken over by a third party. If such a security breach were possible, and if we really permitted computers to act as legal representatives of their (deceased) owners, such a compromised system would indeed be a zombie, or rather 'ZombAI' – acting as if it is the voice of its owner, while in reality being under the control of a malicious agency, just like a zombie botnet.[38]

4.2: If We Build Them How Should the Law Deal With Them?

From a legal perspective, we would need to address whether a computer should be permitted to act as a representative – or indeed whether conceptualising the computer as a representative is the most appropriate way to think about such an application. Discussions of autonomous agents and the law have addressed similar issues in some depth,[39] with some writers arguing that in order to form a legally valid offer, an autonomous agent software programme would need recognition as legal person.[40] Others have maintained that it is much more appropriate to think of autonomous agent software programmes just as a new delivery method for the expressions of the intentions of their owners, the equivalent of a messenger.[41] While our system would be semi- autonomous, and capable of dealing with situations that were not foreseen by (and hence not covered by the intent of) its owner, it seems more appropriate, if less spectacular, to think of it not so much as the disembodied mind of the person who trained it, but simply as a new way to record one's wishes and intentions. As we discussed above, this points to an understanding of 'true intent' in version 1 of the four possible readings of 'true intent'.

Furthermore, it is assumed throughout this chapter that establishing the 'true intent' of the testator is a desirable outcome and an objective of

---

[38] On the use of the expression 'zombie' for a type of cyberattack, see Cooke, Jahanian, and McPherson, 'The Zombie Roundup: Understanding, Detecting, and Disrupting Botnets' (2005) SRUTI, 5 <https://www.usenix.org/legacy/event/sruti05/tech/full_papers/cooke/cooke_html/> (accessed 19 June 2019).

[39] For example, Kerr, 'The Legality of Software-Mediated Transactions' (ACTA Press 2000) pp. 87–96; Shaheed and Cunningham, 'Agents Making Moral Decisions', presented at the ECAI2008 Workshop on Artificial Intelligence in Games (AIG'08), Patras, 2008 <www.doc.ic.ac.uk/~rjc/jss00_ecai08.pdf> (accessed 15 April 2019).

[40] See Wettig and Zehender, 'A Legal Analysis of Human and Electronic Agents' (2004) 12 *Artificial Intelligence and Law* 111.

[41] Sartor, 'Cognitive Automata and the Law: Electronic Contracting and the Intentionality of Software Agents' (2009) 17 *Artificial Intelligence and Law* 253.

inheritance law. Attitudes to this issue vary over time, and between legal systems, both in terms of what 'true' means, and also in terms of the methods and evidence that are permissible to establish this 'true intent'. Common law and civil law systems both emphasise in general terms the importance of establishing the 'true intent'.[42] They differ however in how best to establish this 'true intent', with common law systems preferring for a long time a 'plain meaning approach' that only in exceptional circumstances allows external evidence to be used to disambiguate a provision.[43] This seems to mirror attitudes to statutory interpretation between the legal families.[44] This in turn strengthens our argument above, that legal AI research on statutory interpretation can be reused to interpret wills and testaments. However, also common law systems have increasingly weakened a rigid 'plain meaning' approach.[45] For our purposes, an interesting doctrinal and philosophical issue then becomes what the digital equivalent of the 'four corners of the will' actually are. As we discussed above, there is no longer any isomorphic matching between a plain language text and the digital program that renders it dynamic and self-executing. Does this mean, however, that AIs are best understood as an 'external' aid to interpretation of an intangible and separate 'something', the real will, which the software merely implements, or is it better to broaden our understanding of what counts as the 'text of the will'? A discussion of this issue, which would have to be against the background of a wider analysis of 'living in the infosphere' and its ontological implications, goes beyond the scope of this chapter, but has the potential to clarify our thinking about digital wills even in their current static form. In particular, it supports and adduces additional evidence to the contention of Jarboe, that current doctrinal approaches to testamentary interpretation are not only inconsistent with our best linguistic theories, they also fail to achieve their stated aims even on their own terms.[46]

---

[42] For example, for Germany, Foer, 'Die Regel "Falsa demonstratio non nocet" unter besonderer Berücksichtigung der Testamentsauslegung: Eurpäische Hochschulschriften' (Peter Lang 1987), and for the common law historically Schouler, *A Treatise on the Law of Wills* (No. 12471–12479) (Boston Book Company 1892).

[43] Jarboe, 'Interpreting a Testator's Intent from the Language of her Will: A Descriptive Linguistics Approach' (2002) 80 *Washington University Law Review*, p. 1365; see also Robertson, 'Myth and Reality – or, Is It "Perception and Taste?" – in the Reading of Donative Documents' (2003) 61 *Fordham Law Review* 1045.

[44] MacCormick and Summers, *Interpreting Statutes: A Comparative Study* (Taylor & Francis 1991).

[45] In the US, for example, Cornelison, 'Dead Man Talking: Are Courts Ready to Listen? The Erosion of the Plain Meaning Rule' (2001) 35 *Real Property, Probate and Trust Journal* 811.

[46] Jarboe, 'Interpreting a Testator's Intent from the Language of Her Will', p. 1365.

Finally, if ZombAIs are not used just to record a (dynamic) will and in this way assist a human (for example an executor or other human administrator charged with disposing of a testator's estate) to make the right dispositions, but are also given the ability to execute some of them autonomously, the issue of liability also needs addressing. Some of these capabilities, in a very primitive form, already exist – a direct debit may continue to make payments even after the person who set it up has died, until the bank has been informed of that fact. Microlending platforms such as Kiva have 'auto-lending' settings that make loans automatically, according to predefined parameters, and these too will continue after death. None of these functionalities has raised major conceptual concerns, but if a post-mortem representative were to bundle all these activities and actively change settings in line with its programming, the chance of something going wrong increases and the issue of liability becomes more pressing. Executors are fiduciaries, and thus can incur liability if they fail in their duty. ZombAIs under current law would not have this status. However, as the examples above of existing 'post-mortem communications' show, they are likely to run from the servers of third-party commercial providers, and a question would be whether these servers should then be treated as trustees of the deceased's estate.

4.2.1 Interpreting AI Wills to Include the Wishes and Concerns of Those Other than Testators

Once we accept that at the very least, external aids can and should be used to interpret wills, then AIs provide a promising new avenue to communicate our wishes to the next generation. But as a society, we might actually not want to give the dead too much control over the present and restrict our ability to act as we see fit. After all, the dead outnumber the living by some margin. On the other hand, we might even want to extend this approach beyond people who have left a will (or have trained their avatar) and extend it to those who have died intestate. Answering this question tells us more about what we think testaments ought to achieve, and we will briefly start with this second point.

Currently, our system of wills is supplemented by a number of default rules that are activated if someone dies intestate. But why do we have the specific rules that we have? There are two possible answers.[47] First, these rules might be how we as society consider the ideal will, something that people ought to implement, even though we allow them to deviate from it if they so

---

[47] Hirsch, 'Default Rules in Inheritance Law: Problem in Search of its Context' (2004) 73 *Fordham Law Review* 1031.

choose.[48] Social utility and personal autonomy are balanced, with the default maximising the common good. In a very different reading, these rules might be an approximation of how most of us would write their will anyway, had we but the time (or lack of superstition). In this case the default rules are merely approximations of individuals, and in theory it would be better to analyse in every case of someone dying intestate what their will would have been. The only reason that we refrain from doing so, in this reading, is that it would be too burdensome to establish the deceased's actual intent from external evidence only. The 'one-size-fits-all' approach of statutory defaults in this case is but a compromise necessitated by the scarcity of resources. If this reading were more convincing, personalised AIs acting as representatives of the intestate deceased could lead to the legal equivalent of personalised medicine, a data-driven, reasonably fast and easy solution to determine what type of testament a person would have written.[49]

In reality, we probably find a mix of both subject-centric and social considerations in inheritance laws across all jurisdictions. Even if default rules for those who die intestate will take wider social considerations into account, they are also likely to reflect provisions the majority of people in a society agree with and would choose themselves, otherwise they would lack the necessary social acceptance. On the other hand, even countries that provide testators with a high degree of discretion do typically impose at least some restrictions, protecting some groups from wilful disinheritance. An early case from Scots law is interesting in this respect – also because it brings our journey back to Rome. At the beginning of the twentieth century, the rich philanthropist John Stuart McCaig commissioned what was to become known as 'McCaig's Tower'. An admirer of Roman and Greek architecture, his plan was for a building inspired by the Roman Colosseum, with statues of himself, his siblings and their parents. When he died, though, only the outer walls had been completed, but he had provided in his will sufficient funds to finish the project. His will was challenged by his surviving sibling, Catherine. After a legal process lasting five years, the Court of Session decided that the tower was self-advertisement, not in the general public interest and therefore not, as the will had decreed, suitable for a charitable trust.[50] This could have

---

[48] So for example, Friedman, 'The Law of the Living, the Law of the Dead: Property, Succession, and Society' (1996) 340 *Wisconsin Law Review*, p. 340.

[49] Along similar lines but for other domains see Porat and Strahilevitz, 'Personalizing Default Rules and Disclosure with Big Data' (2013) 112 *Michigan Law Review* 1417; and also Ben-Shahar and Porat, 'Personalizing Negligence Law' (2016) *New York University Law Review* <https://papers.ssrn.com/sol3/papers.cfm?abstract_id=2654458> (accessed 19 April 2019).

[50] *McCaig v University of Glasgow* [1907] SC 231.

been the end of the story, but apparently, Catherine had felt significant guilt about her role in defeating her brother's will. As a consequence, she too set aside over £6 million in her will to complete the work. In 1915 the Court of Session overturned her will for the same reasons that her brother's testament had been ruled invalid, in a landmark ruling that established limits on excessive and eccentric post-mortem dispositions.[51] Three lines of argument stand out for our purposes. One was the specific form the statues were to take – modelled on Roman examples, all members of the family were to be depicted wearing togas. On this, the Dean of the Faculty commented to general laughter in court: 'Our own statesmen are always enveloped in a toga which they never wore. They would have been taken up for indecent exposure if they had.' Here too we can see the limits of the dead hand of the past recognised in law: we may have a duty to care for our cultural inheritance, but this does not mean we must replicate in perpetuity the aesthetic judgements of the past.

The second line of argument concerned the lack of public interest – the monument would not have been in the public good, because (1) due to its location, the public had no access to it and (2) it despoiled rather than enhanced the environment. And third, maintaining the memorial once it was built would be a burden on the future Scottish population, potentially indefinitely. As a consequence of these and similar issues, the will was not suitable to 'achieve Miss McCaig's object of perpetuating an honourable memory. They would turn a respectable and creditable family into a laughing-stock to succeeding generations.' What we can see here is a more modern and secular variation of the Roman concepts of *lares et penates*. The purpose of succession law is not (just) to satisfy an individual. Rather, it has to be tempered by two other concerns, those of wider society, and also those of the family that inherits. The ultimate rationale, for the Romans, was the survival of the family line and with it their house deities. This brings in a collective element that also requires attention to wider social concerns (so not to bring the family into potentially dangerous conflict with wider society). Above, we saw how Roman culture made sense of this insight through two additional abstract 'informational' objects – the family and the family deities. Without them, the ultimate purpose of a will is in danger of being lost. This loss can be the result of eccentric self-aggrandisement of the testator. It can however also be the result of excessive grieving of the beneficiaries. Analysing the McCaig case and a number of similar decisions, Hilary Hiram showed that the courts, in

---

[51] *McCaig's Trs v Kirk Session of United Free Church of Lismore* [1915] SC 426; for a discussion and background see Rennie, 'Folly, Guilt and More Folly' in Grant JPS and Sutherland E, *Scots Law Tales* (Edinburgh University Press 2012).

striking down eccentric provisions of wills, were driven also by a (Freudian) theory of psychology that identified them as pathological excesses of mourning, an inability to let the past go.[52]

For our project, this means that an AI that represents solely the testator will be in danger of failing in one of its central objectives, memory preservation, by over-emphasising the role of the testator and weakening the way in which through history, ethics and social and religious commitments mitigated and contextualised their power.

We already mentioned above that identity preservation strategies are different from digital immortality –the self that lives on differs from the normative information construct, the self that we would like to be remembered as. To be successful requires the cooperation of the next generation, which can only be bribed to an extent. There is an aspect of intergenerational equity here – the power of the testator is balanced against the power of the heirs to subvert the identity preservation strategy. So in order to prevent ZombAIs from subjecting the future to a yoke from the past, we also have to balance the individualistic aspects of succession that they enhance through other tools, both technological and legal. This will be the topic of the next sections.

4.2.2 Lessons from Roman Law – Rebalancing Powers

Wills gave power to the testator in Roman law. But this was balanced, at least for the powerful, by the *abolitio nominis*, or in more modern terminology *damnatio memoriae*, a measure the Roman Senate could take against the memory of a deceased politician or emperor. His name would be erased from all annals, all his portraits and inscriptions were destroyed, and in the future mentioning his name publicly was discouraged, though in Roman times not legally prohibited. The emperors Caligula, Nero, Domitian, Commodus, Geta, Elagabal and Maximinus Thrax were punished this way.[53] That we still know their names, and indeed that they had been subject to *damnatio*, indicates a fundamental paradox: achieving collective forgetfulness was difficult even in Roman times, and rather than fully erasing their names from history, the order of *damnatio* created another reason to remember them, and sometimes created even a new and enduring set of documents to that

---

[52] Hiram, 'Morbid Family Pride: Private Memorials and Scots Law'.

[53] For a comprehensive discussion see Varner, *Monumenta Graeca et Romana: Mutilation and Transformation: Damnatio Memoriae and Roman Imperial Portraiture* (Brill 2004); see also Whitling, 'Damnatio Memoriae and the Power of Remembrance' Pakier M and Stråth B (eds), *A European Memory? Contested Histories and Politics of Remembrance* (Vol. 6) (Berghahn Books 2012).

effect.[54] Indeed, it has been argued that some of the erasure was intentionally left incomplete, enough for everyone to see that a name had been chiselled away, but with enough left to indicate who had been named, and to act as are reminder of their punishment. This 'remembrance of forgetting'[55] will be familiar to those acquainted with the discussion surrounding digital memory and suppression of information. Barbara Streisand did not only fail to have the image of her home, showing its contribution to coastal erosion, suppressed through legal action, but in the process generated interest in the image that dwarfed the exposure it would otherwise have had. By associating the event with the term 'Streisand effect', the memory of her (attempted) forced forgetting will endure even longer.[56] Mario Costeja González may have ensured the right to demand from Google that the record of his bankruptcy was delinked, but having set an important precedent, his name will survive in the court reports and law textbooks decades after any interest in his past dealings will have died.[57] Roman law seems to have been acutely aware of this effect and used the damnation not (just) as a form of memory erasure, but also as a way to remind everyone that such a sanction had taken place.

At times when discussions surrounding the desirability and utility of 'public disremembering' have taken centre stage, for instance in the debate surrounding the memorials for confederate generals or university buildings named after slave traders, we can easily see why the idea of an AI sustaining the identity-preservation strategies of their owners might meet scepticism. Having a monument for General Lee on the village green is bad enough,[58]

---

[54] The edict implementing the *damnatio* of Geta has been preserved on papyrus, Papyrus HGV BGU Xi 2056 available at: http://aquila.zaw.uni-heidelberg.de/hgv/16911 (accessed 15 April 2019).

[55] Hedrick, *History and Silence: Purge and Rehabilitation in Late Antiquity* (University of Texas Press 2000).

[56] Hagenbach and Koessler, 'The Streisand Effect: Signaling and Partial Sophistication' (2017) 143 *Journal of Economic Behavior & Organization* 1, pp. 1–8.

[57] For an example, and the background of the case, see Lynskey, 'Control over Personal Data in a Digital Age: Google Spain v AEPD and Mario Costeja Gonzalez' (2015) 78 *Modern Law Review* 522.

[58] On the ongoing dispute see Grossman, 'Whose Memory? Whose Monuments? History, Commemoration, and the Struggle for an Ethical Past' (2016) *American Historical Association Perspectives on History*, and Schuessler, 'Historians Question Trump's Comments on Confederate Monuments' (*New York Times*, 15 August 2017) <https://www.nytimes.com/2017/08/15/arts/design/trump-robert-e-lee-george-washington-thomas-jefferson.html> (accessed 15 April 2019). The law has been playing an increasingly important role in these social conflicts around remembering (unpalatable) historical events, with several (southern) states in the US now prohibiting the removal of confederate statues (for example, through the Alabama Memorial Preservation Act, passed in May 2017, and

having his avatar disposing financial assets to lost-cause writers would be infinitely worse. Just as the Romans recognised the power and danger of memory, and balanced the legal mechanism of indeterminate inheritance with the possibility of a public forgetting, at the very least a similar legal mechanism would be needed to terminate a legacy AI if its decisions could no longer be reconciled with changing social mores. This could mean limiting their 'lifespan' through law, deleting them automatically after a set period of time or establishing a legal process to terminate them if, as in the McCaig case, they subjected the deceased and their family to ridicule rather than commemoration.

4.2.3 Lessons from Roman Law (2) – The Long Hand of the Dead and What to Do about Them

Preserving the memory of the deceased is not a self-serving act. Its aim is the preservation of the family unit in perpetuity, as a precondition to guarantee the continuous existence of the *penates*, the family deities. The conflict between autonomy and public good that we diagnosed above does not quite fit the Roman understanding. Roman law allowed the testator to control the disposition of property over several generations, precisely because that was the only way to ensure the continuation of the family line. Unsurprisingly, we find the same technique employed in feudal law, the 'feoffment' that could in theory create perpetual trusts.[59] However, both the Roman law and the feudal law operated in societies where the power of the testators was balanced against their duties to the collective, in particular the family. With the individualism that is typical in market-driven, capitalist societies, the acceptance of this power became subject to challenges. The case of the Duke of Norfolk from 1682[60] established the 'rule against perpetuities', recognising that tying up property too long after the time of the death of the testator constitutes an unacceptable limitation of the freedom of the living. It took another 150 years, and the case of *Cadell* v *Palmer*,[61] to reach the twenty-one-year limitation rule that was to dominate the common law until recently.

North Carolina's law, the Cultural History Artifact Management and Patriotism Act), with legal challenges against these provisions ongoing, and with the Jefferson County Circuit Judge Michael Graffeo ruling the Alabama provision unconstitutional in 2017, available at: <https://apnews.com/4bed1a8c4e2348e7895133d9f3dd1d65> (accessed 15 April 2019).

[59] Seipp, 'Trust and Fiduciary Duty in the Early Common Law' (2011) 91 *Boston University Law Review* 1011.

[60] *Duke of Norfolk* (1682) 3 Ch Cas 1, 22 Eng Rep 931.

[61] *Cadell* v *Palmer* (1833) 1 Cl & F 372.

The justification of that rule is the 'fear of the dead hand', described by Ruth Deech as follows:

> The most convincing modern explanation of the functions of the Rule is the so-called Dead Hand Rationale. According to this doctrine, the Rule is necessary in order to strike a balance between on the one hand the freedom of the present generation and, on the other, that of future generations to deal as they wish with the property in which they have interests. If a settlor or testator had total liberty to dispose of his property amongst future beneficiaries, the recipients, being fettered by his wishes, would never enjoy that same freedom in their turn. The liberty to make fresh rearrangements of assets is necessary not only in order to be rid of irksome conditions attached by earlier donors to the enjoyment of income but also in order to be able to manoeuvre in the light of new tax laws, changes in the nature of the property and in the personal circumstances of the beneficiaries, unforeseeable by the best- intentioned and most perspicacious of donors.[62]

Of this rationale, the last part may become moot if we had the most ambitious of legacy AIs described above, one that continues to learn after its owner's death. One could envisage, for instance, the AI 'tracking' changing attitudes within groups that the testator belonged to, and/or incorporating training data by living members of these groups. This brings us to the main benefit of the idea that this chapter proposes: just like a legislator, testators exercise bounded rational judgement, trying to anticipate the future as best as they can, but inevitably not totally succeeding. An AI trained to their higher-level preferences can allow them to defer certain decisions under uncertainty to a point where the AI can act with a much greater chance of success: that is, once additional data are in and certain conditions changed from 'might happen' to 'has happened'. However, the first section of the quote, about fear for the freedom of the present and the oppressive presence of the past, remains valid. Recent years in the UK and the US have seen a move away from the rule against perpetuities and in a sense a return to the feudal (or Roman) past.[63] In the UK, the Perpetuities and Accumulations Act 2009 abolishes the rule against perpetuities, and commits to a 'wait and see' approach that can also be found in most of the US states. Under that approach, the validity of a contested future interest is adjudicated on the basis of facts as they exist now, and not at the time the interest was created. This type of judicial interpretation

---

[62] Deech, 'Lives in Being Revived' (1981) 97 *Law Quarterly Review* 593, p. 594. See also Simes, *Public Policy and the Dead Hand* (University of Michigan Press 1955).

[63] See Sterk, 'Jurisdictional Competition to Abolish the Rule against Perpetuities: R.I.P. for the R.A.P.' (2003) 24 *Cardozo Law Review* 2097.

could be assisted by an AI that is also not limited in its reasoning to the facts as they obtained when the will of its owner was created.

To analyse the benefits and disadvantages of the rule against perpetuities goes beyond the scope of this chapter. It is tempting however to link the unchallenged power of an avatar, trained to communicate (and act on) the intentions of its owner after the owner's death, to the worries that historically engendered the rule against perpetuities; should we be thinking about restricting the capabilities of AI self-executing testaments to benefit the living? As the dead outnumber the living, as Arthur C Clarke indicated in the quote at the beginning of this chapter, the legal recognition of an untrammelled post-mortem avatar or legacy AI would quantitatively shift the balance of power in several ways. First, as we said, there is a danger that ZombAIs could circumvent the prohibition against perpetuities in jurisdictions where they exist, or further accelerate their reintroduction. Even if such a use were to be prohibited, such systems would still create a power shift between the generations. The scope of the living to interpret a will or trust would decrease, and with that the ability to align it with changing circumstances, wider social concerns and the needs of third parties. By the same token, the deceased would gain in their ability to constrain future generations. Finally though, there would be significant psychological pressures to adhere more strictly to the requests of the dead, if they were perceived to talk with a 'living voice', even if recognition of this speech in law were to be limited. Arguably, descendants could feel much less inclined to challenge a will, even if they were legally entitled to do so, if the perception was created that the testator was addressing them directly.

Deech's quote conceptualises the issue as a conflict between the individualistic freedom of the testator and the freedom of the present generation. What this highlights is that, in comparison to the Roman blueprint, a crucial balancing power has been lost. The Roman testator was answerable, if only in a metaphysical sense, to the *penates*, the house spirits. The will was not just about him and his desires, it was a way to maintain the family as a unit over time. The psychological truth that this myth recognises, and which Roman law partly replicated in the *damnatio*, is that post-mortem identity preservation strategies require the collaboration of the future as a collective. We should not create immortal avatars that, beyond providing mere technical help in interpreting testaments, act as the legal representatives of their deceased owners unless we also build AIs that take the role of the *penates*, which hold the testators to account. In this sense, the modern secular equivalent to the *penates* are statutory limits of the freedom of testation.

References

Allison JR, Lemley MA and Schwartz DL, 'Understanding the Realities of Modern Patent Litigation' (2013) 92 *Texas Law Review* 1769.

Appiah KA, *Experiments in Ethics* (Harvard University Press 2008).

Asche S, 'Kulturelles Gedächtnis im 21. Jahrhundert: Tagungsband des internationalen Symposiums' (Vol. 1, 23 April 2005) Karlsruhe (KIT Scientific Publishing 2010).

Bainbridge WS, *Personality Capture and Emulation* (Springer 2013).

Beigi H, *Fundamentals of Speaker Recognition* (Springer 2010).

Bell G and Gray J, 'Digital Immortality' (2001) 44 *Communications of the ACM* 28.

Bench-Capon T et al., 'A History of AI and Law in 50 Papers: 25 Years of the International Conference on AI and Law' (2012) 20 *Artificial Intelligence and Law* 215.

Bench-Capon TJ and Coenen FP, 'Isomorphism and Legal Knowledge Based Systems' (1992) 1 *Artificial Intelligence and Law* 65.

Ben-Shahar O and Porat A, 'Personalizing Negligence Law' (2016) *New York University Law Review* <https://papers.ssrn.com/sol3/papers.cfm?abstract_id=2654458> (accessed 19 April 2019).

Bermant C, *The Walled Garden: The Saga of Jewish Family Life and Tradition* (Weidenfeld & Nicolson 1974).

Biran O and Cotton C, 'Explanation and Justification in Machine Learning: A Survey' (2017) In IJCAI-17 Workshop on Explainable AI (XAI).

Butler R, 'Looking Forward to What? The Life Review, Legacy and Excessive Identity versus Change' (1970) 14 *American Behavioural Scientist* 121.

Contissa G, Lagioia F and Sartor G, 'The Ethical Knob: Ethically-customisable Automated Vehicles and the Law' (2017) 25 *Artificial intelligence and Law* 365.

Cooke E, Jahanian F and McPherson D, 'The Zombie Roundup: Understanding, Detecting, and Disrupting Botnets' (2005) SRUTI, 5 <https://www.usenix.org/legacy/event/sruti05/tech/full_papers/cooke/cooke_html/> (accessed 19 June 2019).

Cornelison AW, 'Dead Man Talking: Are Courts Ready to Listen? The Erosion of the Plain Meaning Rule' (2001) 35 *Real Property, Probate and Trust Journal* 811.

Deech R, 'Lives in Being Revived' (1981) 97 *Law Quarterly Review* 593.

Esposito E, 'Algorithmic Memory and the Right to be Forgotten on the Web' (2017) 4 *Big Data & Society* 1.

Floridi L, 'Artificial Intelligence's New Frontier: Artificial Companions and the Fourth Revolution' (2008) 39 *Metaphilosophy* 433.

Foer R, 'Die Regel "Falsa demonstratio non nocet" unter besonderer Berücksichtigung der Testamentsauslegung: Eurpäische Hochschulschriften' (Peter Lang 1987).

Friedman LM, 'The Law of the Living, the Law of the Dead: Property, Succession, and Society' (1996) 340 *Wisconsin Law Review*.

Grossman J, 'Whose Memory? Whose Monuments? History, Commemoration, and the Struggle for an Ethical Past' (2016) *American Historical Association Perspectives on History*.

Hagenbach J and Koessler F, 'The Streisand Effect: Signaling and Partial Sophistication' (2017) 143 *Journal of Economic Behavior & Organization* 1.

Hauskeller M, 'My Brain, My Mind, and I: Some Philosophical Assumptions of Mind-uploading' (2012) 4 *International Journal of Machine Consciousness* 187.

Hedrick C, *History and Silence: Purge and Rehabilitation in Late Antiquity* (University of Texas Press 2000).

Hiram H, 'Reforming Succession Law: Legal Rights' (2008) 12 *Edinburgh Law Review* 81.

Hiram H, 'Morbid Family Pride: Private Memorials and Scots Law' in *Memory, Mourning,* Landscape (Brill Rodopi 2010).

Hirsch AJ, 'Default Rules in Inheritance Law: Problem in Search of its Context' (2004) 73 *Fordham Law Review* 1031.

Huang XD and Lee KF, 'On Speaker-Independent, Speaker-Dependent, and Speaker-Adaptive Speech Recognition' (proceedings of the International Conference on Acoustics, Speech, and Signal Processing, ICASSP'91) <http://doi.ieeecomput ersociety.org/10.1109/ICASSP.1991.150478> (accessed 20 June 2019).

Jarboe ST, 'Interpreting a Testator's Intent from the Language of Her Will: A Descriptive Linguistics Approach' (2002) 80 *Washington University Law Review*.

Junqua C and Haton J, *Robustness in Automatic Speech Recognition: Fundamentals and Applications* (Kluwer Academic Publishers 1995).

Kerr IR, 'The Legality of Software-Mediated Transactions' in proceedings of IASTED International Conference: Law and Technology (ACTA Press 2000) pp. 87–96.

Knobe J and Nichols S, eds, *Experimental Philosophy* (Oxford University Press 2008).

Law Commission, 'Making a Will' (consultation paper 231) <https://s3-eu-west-2. amazonaws.com/lawcom-prod-storage-11jsxou24uy7q/uploads/2017/07/Mak ing-a-will-consultation.pdf> (accessed 15 April 2019).

Lynn J, 'Why I Don't Have a Living Will' (1991) 19 *Law, Medicine and Health Care*.

Lynskey O, 'Control over Personal Data in a Digital Age: Google Spain v. AEPD and Mario Costeja Gonzalez' (2015) 78 *Modern Law Review* 522.

MacCormick DN and Summers RS, *Interpreting Statutes: A Comparative Study* (Taylor & Francis 1991).

McDonald HD, 'Idea of Immortality' (1971) 7 *Vox Evangelica*: 17.

Musschenga B, 'Was ist empirische Ethik?' (2009) 21 *Ethik in der Medizin* 187.

No author, 'Developments in the Law – More Data, More Problems' (2018) 131 *Harvard Law Review* 1715.

Parfit DA, 'Divided Minds and the Nature of Persons' in Blakemore C and Greenfield S (eds), *Mindwaves* (Blackwell 1987), pp. 19–28.

Porat A and Strahilevitz LJ, 'Personalizing Default Rules and Disclosure with Big Data' (2013) 112 *Michigan Law Review* 1417.

Pratchett T, *Going Postal* (Doubleday 2004).

Rennie R 'Folly, Guilt and More Folly' in Grant JPS and Sutherland E, *Scots Law Tales* (Edinburgh University Press 2012).

Robertson JL, 'Myth and Reality – or, Is It "Perception and Taste" – in the Reading of Donative Documents' (2003) 61 *Fordham Law Review* 1045.

Rosenfeld J, 'Old Age, New Beneficiaries: Kinship, Friendship and (Dis)inheritance' (1980) 64 *Sociology and Social Research* 86.

Rothblatt M, *Virtually Human: The Promise – and the Peril – of Digital Immortality* (Macmillan 2014).

Sandberg A and Boström N, 'Whole Brain Emulation: A Roadmap' (Technical Report, 2008) Future of Humanity Institute, Oxford University.

Sartor G, 'Cognitive Automata and the Law: Electronic Contracting and the Intentionality of Software Agents' (2009) 17 *Artificial Intelligence and Law* 253.

Schafer B, 'ZombAIs: Legal Expert Systems as Representatives beyond the Grave' (2010) 7 SCRIPTed, 384.

Schouler J, *A Treatise on the Law of Wills* (No. 12471–12479) (Boston Book Company 1892).

Schuessler J, 'Historians Question Trump's Comments on Confederate Monuments' (*New York Times*, 15 August 2017) <https://www.nytimes.com/2017/08/15/arts/design/trump-robert-e-lee-george-washington-thomas-jefferson.html> (accessed 15 April 2019).

Seipp DJ, 'Trust and Fiduciary Duty in the Early Common Law' (2011) 91 *Boston University Law Review* 1011.

Shaheed J and Cunningham J, 'Agents Making Moral Decisions', presented at the ECAI2008 Workshop on Artificial Intelligence in Games (AIG'08), Patras, 2008 <www.doc.ic.ac.uk/~rjc/jss00_ecai08.pdf> (accessed 15 April 2019).

Simes LM, *Public Policy and the Dead Hand* (University of Michigan Press 1955).

Sterk SE, 'Jurisdictional Competition to Abolish the Rule against Perpetuities: R.I.P. for the R.A.P.' (2003) 24 *Cardozo Law Review* 2097.

Susskind R, 'Detmold's Computer Judge Revisited' (1986) 49 *Modern Law Review* 683.

Unruh DR, 'Death and Personal History: Strategies of Identity Preservation' (1983) 30 *Social Problems* 340.

Varner ER, *Monumenta Graeca et Romana: Mutilation and Transformation: Damnatio Memoriae and Roman Imperial Portraiture* (Brill 2004).

Verhoeven P (Director), *Total Recall* (Tristar Pictures 1990).

Wettig S and Zehender E, 'A Legal Analysis of Human and Electronic Agents' (2004) 12 *Artificial Intelligence and Law* 111.

Whitling F, 'Damnatio Memoriae and the Power of Remembrance' in Pakier M and Stråth B (eds), *A European Memory? Contested Histories and Politics of Remembrance* (Vol. 6) (Berghahn Books 2012).

Zeleznikow J, 'Building Judicial Decision Support Systems in Discretionary Legal Domains' (2000) 14 *International Review of Computers, Law and Information Technology* 341.

9

'Be Right Back': What Rights Do We Have over Post-mortem Avatars of Ourselves?

Lilian Edwards and Edina Harbinja

1. Introduction: Staring into the Black Mirror?

In the well-received *Black Mirror* episode, 'Be Right Back',[1] a grieving young widow, Martha, decides she can no longer live without some kind of contact with her partner, Ash, who has died prematurely in a freak car accident – especially when she finds out she is posthumously pregnant by him. A friend points her in the direction of a service that synthesises convincing emails from Ash, using artificial intelligence (AI) techniques, working on a corpus of material drawn from social media posts, emails and direct messages to which she has access, and she finds this relieves her intense misery. This leads her on to a second stage of recreating her dead partner: adding sound and video. This time it is explicitly noted that the app can use material drawn from private videos and photos as well as publicly posted information (and Martha is required to consent to this); the app creates a simulated 'Ash' that can chat on the phone to Martha in a naturalistic way.

There is however no attempt to dupe Martha; one of the first things the new Ash says (jokingly) is 'How can I have a voice? I don't even have a mouth!' New Ash mimics the humour, voice patterns and mannerisms of Old Ash but at the same time displays access to knowledge (including video) drawn from sources like Google in a rather un-humanlike way. At one point, Martha drops the phone New Ash is resident on, and is distraught she has lost him, but after a recompilation, the simulacrum is restored. Again, New Ash is quite sanguine about letting Martha know about his artificial nature:

---

[1] Season 2, Episode 1, 11 February 2013. Series currently available on Netflix and More4.

'I'm not in that thing, I'm in the cloud.' This crisis leads New Ash himself (a tremendous piece of upselling) to recommend to Martha that she goes one crucial step further and makes or rather 'grows' him a body under his directions. At this point, the production seems to imply we have shifted from the merely creepy to the possibly illegal, but this is never explicitly discussed.

The body is in some senses a triumph and in others a failure. It looks and acts like Real Ash, able to restore intimacy to Martha, and yet it isn't, quite. It only knows things Ash or others recorded and naturally these do not include highly intimate matters that most people would never write down, such as favourite sexual positions. In an interesting representation of today's machine-learning (ML) flaws, he is both unrealistic because of the gaps in the training data but also optimised from available data in a fashion that makes him unreal; he is better looking than Ash really was because 'people only keep the flattering photos'. He cannot learn from experience or transcend his origins as the real Ash could have done. (Current ML systems could continue to integrate more data and be re-optimised for various functions; it is not clear whether it is the fixed bodily form that prevents this.)

In the end, New Ash is hidden in the attic, as somewhere between a toy that a child has broken or grown out of, and a bogeyman to be kept secret; but he still has his uses, such as playing with 'his' daughter, now born and grown, as a special treat (for her). For the daughter, New Ash is clearly not her father, but he is still something special and unique in her life.

Unusually for *Black Mirror*, this is an ending that is arguably (and perhaps morbidly) not sad and even partially happy. It is however an episode that, despite exploring numerous questions about the status of real and artificial humanity, the nature of grieving, the possible uses of AI and the limits that should be put on abusive, exploitative or 'creepy' techniques, fails to ask at any point: would Ash himself have wanted to be resurrected in this form? Should he have had the right to mandate or prevent it from happening?

2. Post-mortem Property, Privacy and Personality: Enter the Law

The scenario in 'Be Right back' is science fictional but its seeds already exist in reality. Chatbots themselves are old news: arguably the first, ELIZA,[2] created by AI pioneer Joseph Weizenbaum, dates from 1964. ELIZA was a rule-based expert system, but more recently chatbots have moved beyond mere regurgitation of recoded text to generative creation of lifelike conversation, using ML techniques. According to Wikipedia,[3] the *Black Mirror* episode was

[2] Available at: <www.manifestation.com/neurotoys/eliza.php3> and <https://en.wikipedia.org/wiki/ELIZA> (accessed 19 April 2019).

[3] Available at: <https://en.wikipedia.org/wiki/Be_Right_Back> (accessed 19 April 2019).

partially inspired by a particular chatbot, 'Replika',[4] which claims to enable conversations with your 'digital best friend' using ML techniques.[5] 'The more you talk to your Replika companion, the more it learns and becomes like you – and the more it gives you the type of feedback and reaction that a friend would if placed in the same position.' Although the examples given on the Replika website involve chats with a digital replication of yourself while you are *alive*, the bot clearly has the potential to recreate the sense of chatting post mortem with a replica of a deceased person. Indeed, according to press reports, Replika was deliberately created and used as far back as 2016[6] by its founder, Eugenia Kuyda, to recreate her closest friend, Roman Mazurenko, after he died, using easily accessible Tensor Flow ML technology; this project received substantial press coverage.

Other firms such as Eternime are now experimenting further with AI technology to 'give people a voice after death'; Eternime collects 'geolocation, motion, activity, health app data, sleep data, photos, messages that users put in the app' from the deceased's smartphone, with the permission of the heir, and also uses Facebook (FB) data from external sources. In November 2018, *Business Insider* found a number of firms developing tech in this direction, albeit some with ethical qualms.[7] Chatbots are relatively easy to develop given access to texts, messages and social media posts (Replika has recently begun to integrate photos) and voice synthesis in the form of personal assistants such as Siri and Alexa is also becoming ubiquitous: although voice-enabled chatbots replicating the particular *deceased*'s voice do not yet seem to be a commercial proposition, they cannot be far behind. Growing the *body* of the deceased of course remains, so far, way off; however, cloning is already possible in animals and may where not banned by law be possible for humans or at least human

---

[4] Available at: <https://replika.ai/> (accessed 19 April 2019).

[5] See further <https://classic.qz.com/machines-with-brains/1018126/lukas-replika-chatbot-creates-a-digital-representation-of-you-the-more-you-interact-with-it/>;   MacDonald, 'Would YOU Resurrect Your Dead Friend as an AI? Try Out "Memorial" Chatbot App – And You Can Even Talk to a Virtual Version of Prince' (*Daily Mail*, 7 October 2016) <https://www.dailymail.co.uk/sciencetech/article-3826208/Would-resurrect-dead-friend-AI-Try-memorial-chatbot-app-talk-virtual-version-Prince.html> (accessed 19 April 2019).

[6] Newton, 'Speak, Memory' (*The Verge*, 11 October 2016) <https://www.theverge.com/a/luka-artificial-intelligence-memorial-roman-mazurenko-bot> (accessed 19 April 2019); Pass Notes, 'The Chatbot that Lets You Talk to the Dead' (11 October 2016) <https://www.theguardian.com/technology/shortcuts/2016/oct/11/chatbot-talk-to-dead-grief> (accessed 19 April 2019).

[7] Hamilton, 'These 2 Tech Founders Lost their Friends in Tragic Accidents. Now They've Built AI Chatbots to Give People Life after Death' (17 November 2018) <https://www.businessinsider.com/eternime-and-replika-giving-life-to-the-dead-with-new-technology-2018-11?r=US&IR> (accessed 19 April 2019).

body parts.[8] Humans might also of course (perhaps potentially sooner) be recreated in robotic rather than biological android physical forms. In one particularly bizarre experiment from 2012, attempts were already made to synthesise a knowledge base built from material known about, and literature written by, the science fiction writer Philip K Dick (who died in 1982), with a physical basis in an animatronic head.[9]

If replicas of the kind imagined in *Be Right Back* are becoming reality, what does the law have to say about this? Are these 'inventions' legal? And even if they are, *should* they be built? Are they *ethical*? In Chapter 8, Schafer explores related issues of ZombAIs, intelligent agents that could be used to interpret legal documents, such as wills. We refer the reader to this chapter, as we are not going to explore the question of whether New Ash could be used to interpret Ash's last will.

At least two major *a priori* legal issues arise here. First, such chatbots or avatars (as we shall loosely call them) must be built from large amounts of data used to create a training set for ML. As we have seen in both fiction and reality, this can include emails, photos, videos, personal messages, social media posts, tweets, voice calls and voicemails, star ratings (as in the Nosedive episode of *Black Mirror*) and so forth. Some of these are public, accessible by all; some private, such as friends' locked FB posts; and some, such as calls and texts, are intended to be shared with one other person only. Adopting the language of intellectual property (IP), who owns these materials after the death of their creator? Who is entitled, in the language of personal data and data protection (DP) law, to process, mine and share them? How are conflicts to be resolved between the platforms that host these data assets, and the heirs, friends or lovers who may seek to access them?

These issues are primarily addressed by three legal institutions; copyright, contract and privacy/DP. The authors of this chapter have already explored in detail in previous work some of the major legal issues pertaining to the transmission of this kind of property – known as 'digital assets' – on death, and though some complex law is involved, the analysis is fairly advanced.[10]

---

[8] Ayala, 'Cloning Humans? Biological, Ethical, and Social Considerations' (2015) 112 *Proceedings of the National Academy of Science, USA* 8879.

[9] Bosch, 'The Android Head of Philip K Dick' (*Slate*, 1 June 2012) <https://slate.com/cul ture/2012/06/philip-k-dick-robot-an-android-head-of-the-science-fiction-author-is-lost-forever.html> (accessed 19 April 2019). In a still more bizarre development, the head was eventually left on a plane by mistake and never recovered. See further Dufty, *How to Build an Android: The True Story of Philip K. Dick's Robotic Resurrection* (Picador 2013). The head was nicknamed the 'Dick head'.

[10] Edwards and Harbinja, '"What Happens to My Facebook Profile When I Die"? Legal Issues Around Transmission of Digital Assets on Death' (2013) 32 *Cardozo Arts & Entertainment*

But arguably more controversial are issues relating to personal data and privacy. Below we will discuss whether the deceased has or should have rights to control their personal data and what is known about them, after death; a relatively novel concept that we have christened 'post-mortem privacy' in previous work.[11] The discourse here is primarily European though some US developments will be referred to.

The third set of issues needs mentioned though they will not for lack of space be explored in this chapter. What is the status of the avatar created of New Ash, in the *Black Mirror* scenario? Does it have legal personality, human rights?[12] If so we are not talking just about post-mortem rights but possible conflicts with the rights of a new, existent if not 'living' entity. A connected question that literature has begun to explore is whether such a human-seeming bot should make clear its 'human nature',[13] or whether it might be acceptable to allow impressionable humans – such as grieving widows – to be misled into thinking it is more 'human' (whatever that means) than it actually is. This idea is no longer science fiction; California has already legislated to demand that bots (defined as) must make their nature transparent.[14] Can embodied bots be far behind?

Law Journal 103; Harbinja, 'Virtual Worlds – A Legal Post-Mortem Account' (2014) 10 *SCRIPTed* 273; Harbinja, 'Virtual Worlds Players – Consumers or Citizens?' (2014) 3 *Internet Policy Review* <https://policyreview.info/articles/analysis/virtual-worlds-players-consumers-or-citizens> (accessed 19 April 2019); Harbinja, 'Legal Nature of Emails: A Comparative Perspective' (2016) 14 *Duke Law and Technology Review* 227 <http://scholar ship.law.duke.edu/dltr/vol14/iss1/10> (accessed 19 April 2019); Harbinja, 'Social Media and Death' in Gillies L and Mangan D (eds), *The Legal Challenges of Social Media* (Edward Elgar Publishing 2017); Harbinja, 'Digital Inheritance in the United Kingdom' (2017) 6 *Journal of European Consumer and Market Law* 253; Harbinja, 'Legal Aspects of Transmission of Digital Assets on Death'(PhD dissertation, University of Strathclyde, 2017).

[11] Edwards and Harbinja, 'Protecting Post-Mortem Privacy: Reconsidering the Privacy Interests of the Deceased in a Digital World' (2013) 32 *Cardozo Arts & Entertainment Law Journal* 103; Harbinja, 'Post-mortem Privacy 2.0: Theory, Law and Technology'.

[12] On the question of whether a synthetic being can or should be given legal personality or rights, see the excellent analysis in Bryson, Diamantis and Grant, 'Of, For, and By the People: The Legal Lacuna of Synthetic Persons' (2017) 25 *Artificial Intelligence and Law* 273 <https://doi.org/10.1007/s10506-017-9214-9> (accessed 19 April 2019).

[13] See the suggestion to that effect in the EPSRC Principles of Robotics, available at: <https:// epsrc.ukri.org/research/ourportfolio/themes/engineering/activities/principlesofrobotics/> (accessed 19 April 2019): 'Robots are manufactured artefacts. They should not be designed in a deceptive way to exploit vulnerable users; instead their machine nature should be transparent.'

[14] *Artificial Lawyer*, 'Declare Your Legal Bot! New California Law Demands Bot Transparency' (3 October 2018) <https://www.artificiallawyer.com/2018/10/03/declare-your-legal-bot-new-california-law-demands-bot-transparency/> (accessed 19 April 2019).

Although these are universal problems, law is local. This chapter will mainly draw comparatively on the laws of the EU and US and, with a few localised references to particular UK laws. In general matters of property in private law, including succession laws in the EU, are a matter for national legislatures. However intellectual property law, especially copyright, is more fully harmonised in the EU, and to some extent globally. Data protection law is also harmonised at the EU level by the General Data Protection Regulation (GDPR), except for the protection of the deceased's personal data (recital 27 GDPR). In the US, succession law is largely a state rather than a federal matter, but guidance can be given, as we shall see, by proposed 'model' laws that states can adopt or tweak. A federal law, however, regulates the confidentiality of communications (the Electronic Communications Privacy Act (ECPA) 1986) and this largely affects access to the social media accounts of others, including the deceased, in the US but also more widely. The lack of international (or often even national) harmonisation in areas like succession, executry and privacy is a particularly acute problem when talking about 'globalised' or delocalised assets such as tweets or FB profiles.

3. Property in Digital Assets after Death: Who Owns the Data to Make 'New Ash'?

'Digital assets' are not generally a legal term of art but have been defined widely in previous work by Edwards and Harbinja to include a huge range of intangible information goods associated with the online or digital world: including social network profiles; digitised text, image, music or sound, such as video, film and e-book files; passwords to various accounts associated with provisions of digital goods and services; domain names; 2D or 3D personality-related images or icons such as user icons on LiveJournal or avatars in Second Life.

Many digital assets – including those important to our scenario of recreating the deceased – are hosted on a platform, or made possible by platforms, intermediaries or service providers such as FB (including also WhatsApp and Instagram), Twitter, Microsoft (for Skype calls or Word docs), Google (for Gmail, YouTube, Google Drive, Photos, etc.) and so forth.[15] These relationships are governed while the subscriber is alive by contracts entered into between subscriber and platform, commonly known as 'terms of service' or 'end-user license agreements' (EULAs) and sometimes including 'acceptable use' policies. There has been a tendency in the past to regard the terms of service of these platforms as the sole legal instrument determining ownership

---

[15] See further Desai, 'Property, Persona, and Preservation' (2008) 81 *Temple Law Review* 67.

of, and access to, digital assets post mortem. However other stakeholders and other aspects of law are also important. Society in general, as well as the obvious next of kin, family and friends, have an interest in the legacy of the dead, and succession and executry law have roles to play. Contract terms – as located in the terms of service of providers – will sometimes have to play with and even yield to laws of property and in particular executry of estates. Such conflicts were first explored in case law in the early and much discussed US case of *Re Ellsworth*, discussed below.[16]

We don't know the contents of the will in 'Be Right Back' but it is quite likely that Martha is the sole heir to Ash's estate. He might have made a will saying this, or if he did not and she is his surviving spouse or partner/cohabitee, the law of intestacy might recognise her as the prior heir and administrator of the estate.[17] Matters would get more complicated if this was not the case – for example, other relatives such as parents or siblings, might have competing claims – but for simplicity let us assume she is the sole heir.[18] A first question to ask then is whether a digital asset is actually an item capable of being transmitted on death, i.e. does it legally constitute 'property'?

The most likely route for assigning property rights to an intangible item such as a tweet, an email or a FB post is via copyright. This issue has recently been controversial in the common law world in relation to two prevalent examples: emails and songs downloaded from the iTunes (Apple) platform.[19] Harbinja has in previous work discussed in depth the legal nature as property of emails[20] and items in virtual games worlds.[21] In general however, it can probably be assumed that most digital assets forming textual works (texts, tweets, FB posts, and so on), and audiovisual works (photos or videos) are covered by the law of copyright. The requirements for protection of some

---

[16] *In Re Ellsworth*, No. 20096, 651-DE (Mich Prob Ct 2005).

[17] Part 2 of the Administration of Estates Act 1925, c 23.

[18] Another possibility, as we shall see below, is that he might have made a 'digital will' on one of the relevant platforms such as Facebook leaving control of (say) his FB posts and photos to a 'legacy contact' who might be a best friend or other family member, perhaps one he knew long before he met Martha but unchanged since; see section 5 below.

[19] *Fairstar Heavy Transport NV v Adkins* [2012] EWHC (TCC) 2952; and *The Week*, 'Digital Property: Can You Bequeath Your iTunes Library?' (31 January 2014) <https://www.theweek.co.uk/57155/digital-property-can-you-bequeath-your-itunes-library> (accessed 19 April 2019).

[20] Harbinja, 'Post-mortem Privacy 2.0: Theory, Law and Technology' (2017) 31 *International Review of Law, Computers & Technology* 26 <www.tandfonline.com/doi/citedby/10.1080/13600869.2017.1275116?scroll=top&needAccess=true> (accessed 19 April 2019).

[21] Ibid.

kind are in most systems quite a low bar,[22] and in the EU there is no need for registration to claim copyright, though some special rules may apply to unpublished works.[23] As for photos, in the US, a photograph would be considered original if it includes a small degree of composure and positioning.[24] Under UK copyright law, photographs are protected as artistic works under section 4 of the Copyright, Designs and Patents Act 1988 (CDPA 1988). Case law confirms a low threshold of originality (which can be evidenced by for example, composition, positioning the object, choice of the angle of shot, lighting and focus, being at the right place at the right time).[25] The UK requirement for originality has been overall similar to the US one (the labour and skill or 'sweat of the brow' test), but differs from the Court of Justice of the European Union's (CJEU's) 'author's own intellectual creation' test, which requires a higher level of creativity.[26] Some social media 'items' such as very brief and generic or very short responses ('yes', 'no', 'fantastic', and so on) are, however likely to be found not to be sufficiently original to attract copyright protection.[27]

If digital assets constitute property or copyright, then it follows that they form part of the estate of the deceased and should transmit either to heirs identified by will, or if no such heirs are named or otherwise indicated, to heirs in intestacy. However, in the real world of social media and platform contracts, the matter may be seen as determined primarily by terms of service or 'End-user License Agreements' (EULAs). In the early days of the Internet, there was a fear that platforms might make a 'land grab' for any assets

---

[22] For US see *Burrow-Giles Lithographic Co* v *Sarony* 111 US 53, 59–60. (1884); *Feist Publications* v *Rural Telephone Service Co Inc* 499 US 340, 363 (1991). For the most important UK cases see *Walter* v *Lane* [1900] AC 539, 548; *University of London Press, Ltd* v *University Tutorial Press, Ltd* [1916] 2 Ch 601, 608; *Interlego AG* v *Tyco Industries Inc* [1989] AC 217, 29 (PC); *Express Newspapers Plc* v *News (UK) Ltd* [1991] FSR 36, 43 (Ch D); *Newspaper Licensing Agency, Ltd* v *Marks & Spencer, Plc* [2001] UKHL 38 [2002] RPC 4.

[23] See Council Directive 93/98/EEC of 29 October 1993 harmonising the term of protection of copyright and certain related rights [1993] OJ L290/9; the 1976 Copyright Act, 17 USC §302.

[24] *Burrow Giles Lithographic Co* v *Sarony*, 111 US 53, 59 (1884); *Mannion* v *Coors Brewing Co*, 377; FSupp2d 444, 455 (SDNY 2005).

[25] *Antiquesportfolio.com Plc* v *Rodney Fitch & Co Ltd* [2001] ECDR 5 at 29–39.

[26] CJEU Case C-5/08, *Infopaq International A/S* v *Danske Dagblades Forening* [2009] ECR I-6569.

[27] *Exxon Corp* v *Exxon Insurance Consultants International Ltd* [1982] Ch 119 (holding that the word Exxon does not qualify for copyright protection as an 'original literary work'); US Copyright Office, 'Copyright Protection Not Available for Names, Titles, or Short Phrases' (2012) Circular 34 (<http://copyright.gov/circs/circ34.pdf>, last accessed 19 April 2019).

stored or created on their site. The most obvious example of this in the early literature related to the online multi-player games site World of Warcraft. Blizzard, the World of Warcraft provider, explicitly excluded users from asserting any property rights in assets created or traded in the game, as well as forbidding transfers of accounts.[28] By contrast, Linden Labs, provider of the virtual world Second Life, gives users relatively extensive rights in content created by users therein.[29] Mazzone noted that in line with these policies, Linden Labs also allowed for in-game assets to be transferred and bequeathed on death.[30]

In the more recent social media world, the emergent norm has arguably been a more PR-friendly recognition of the property rights of users to their online created works, posts and so on, but accompanied with an assertion of a global, non-exclusive perpetual licence granted to the platform provider. FB has long incorporated such a term into its terms of service,[31] but this did not stop outrage breaking out when FB bought Instagram, the photo-sharing

---

[28] See Terms of Use Agreement (22 August 2012) <http://us.blizzard.com/en-us/company/legal/wow_tou.html> (accessed 15 June 2016): 'Blizzard owns, has licensed, or otherwise has rights to all of the content that appears in the Game. You agree that you have no right or title in or to any such content, including without limitation the virtual goods or currency appearing or originating in the Game, or any other attributes associated with any Account.' New 'Terms of Service' now specify this even further, enumerating various content and asserting Blizzard's ownership over the content (including characters, avatars, visual components, items, and so on). This provision is much more comprehensive than the previous one and again, does not confer rights to players: Blizzard® 'End User License Agreement', last revised 20 August 2018 <https://www.blizzard.com/en-us/legal/2c72a35c-bf1b-4ae6-99ec-80624e1b429c/blizzard-end-user-license-agreement> (accessed 19 April 2019).

[29] Linden Lab, 'Second Life Terms of Service' (15 December 2010) <http://secondlife.com/corporate/tos.php?lang=en-US> (accessed 15 June 2016), title 7. See especially the right to retain title to all intellectual property brought into the game, the right to delete all copies of your content from the game, and most importantly, '7.6 Linden Lab owns Intellectual Property Rights in and to the Service, except all User Content' (<http://secondlife.com/corporate/tos.php?lang=en-US>, last accessed 15 June 2016). This has now been revised, but the essence remains, users own their content, but they also 'grant to Linden Lab, the non-exclusive, unrestricted, unconditional, unlimited, worldwide, irrevocable, perpetual, and cost-free right and license to use, copy, record, distribute, reproduce, disclose, modify, display, publicly perform, transmit, publish, broadcast, translate, make derivative works of, and sell, re-sell or sublicense', available at: <https://www.lindenlab.com/tos#tos2> (accessed 19 April 2019).

[30] Mazzone, 'Facebook's Afterlife' (2012) 90 *North Carolina Law Review* 143, citing Second Life Wiki, 'Linden Lab Official: Death and Other Worries outside Second Life' <http://wiki.secondlife.com/wiki/Linden_Lab_Official:Death_and_other_worries_outside_Second_Life> (accessed 19 April 2019).

[31] Facebook, 'Terms of Service' <https://www.facebook.com/terms.php> (accessed 19 April 2019).

site, in 2012 and applied its ordinary terms of service to that platform. From the outside, this appeared as a sudden claim to the acquisition of ownership of photos stored on their site by users.[32]

Twitter, similarly, assert confidently: 'You retain your rights to any Content you submit, post or display on or through the Services. What's yours is yours – you own your Content (and your incorporated audio, photos and videos are considered part of the Content).'

But then they immediately go on FB-style to admit that 'you grant us a worldwide, non-exclusive, royalty-free license (with the right to sublicense) to use, copy, reproduce, process, adapt, modify, publish, transmit, display and distribute such Content in any and all media or distribution methods (now known or later developed)'.[33] Google has very similar provisions: 'You retain ownership of any intellectual property rights that you hold in that content. In short, what belongs to you stays yours', but goes on to claim the habitual 'worldwide license to use, host, store, reproduce, modify, create derivative works',[34] and so forth.

This bright-line is unsurprising: without rights to data-mine user materials to target ads, Google and FB would have no business model; furthermore, without rights to publish and republish such material, it would have a very odd-looking platform. What matters is whether these rights are restricted to these purposes. Google do say that they are for 'the limited purpose of operating, promoting, and improving our Services, and to develop new ones', but immediately add 'This license continues even if you stop using our Services', for example, if they wish to use content to populate a new section of Google Maps.

In terms of post-mortem chatbots, this should mean that a hypothetical heir should acquire rights to take possession of and data-mine the tweets, Gmails or similar of the deceased to create such an entity or service. The constraint is that FB or Google may have the right to do the same. What if Google or FB decide to go into the 'new business' of selling chatbots to grieving families of subscribers or ZombAIs, agents that represent the deceased legally (see Chapter 8)? Would this be seen as acceptable, tasteful, ethical? A single service provider avatar would, of course, be partial but there would be nothing (bar perhaps competition law) to stop the likes of FB and

---

[32] Holpuch, 'Instagram Reassures Users over Terms of Service after Massive Outcry' (*The Guardian*, 18 December 2012) <www.guardian.co.uk/technology/2012/dec/18/instagram-issues-statement-terms-of-service> (accessed 19 April 2019).

[33] Twitter, 'Terms of Service' <https://twitter.com/en/tos> (accessed 19 April 2019).

[34] Google, 'Privacy and Terms: Your Content in our Services' <https://policies.google.com/terms?gl=US&hl=en#toc-content> (accessed 19 April 2019).

Google pooling data. Could the family stop (say) Google doing this? This is something we consider below (section 4) under the head of privacy and DP, where the possibility of a 'right to be forgotten' and also of data portability under the GDPR,[35] as well as moral rights under copyright,[36] might confer some interesting ammunition on heirs.

3.1 Access Rights: Conflicts between Platforms and Heirs

A secondary but crucial problem after ownership rights is access. In 'Be Right Back', Martha seems to be the only person interested in, and with practical access to, Ash's phone calls/voicemails and (at least the) private videos and texts and instant messages. (It is not clear in the programme whether she simply retained his smartphone and computer and either had the password or the items were not password protected, whether she somehow broke any protection, which itself might be a crime – or whether the programme that created Ash accessed all his devices and data by itself, after Martha had consented.[37]) But in other scenarios, there might be conflicts between different heirs or family or friends and practical difficulties acquiring access to some material – FB posts for example – from the platform itself. Martha may still be able to read Ash's old FB posts, but what if the account is closed or deleted at the request of a parent or other friend,[38] or if he has friends-only posts for groups she is not on? As a technical matter, she might have needed API access to Ash's posts, as opposed to just scraping them.

FB does not allow the simple transfer of accounts to heirs, in terms of handing over passwords (for reasons to do with security, privacy and trolling[39]). FB's terms of service state that the agreement 'does not confer any

---

[35] GDPR, arts 17 and 20.

[36] In the UK, unless waived, users would have moral rights for seventy or twenty years post mortem, depending on the type of right (CDPA 1988, ss 77, 80, 84, 86 and 87). Moral rights in the UK, in principle, transmit on death. Unless a person waives their moral rights (CDPA 1988, s 87), the right to be identified as author and the right to object to derogatory treatment of work transmit on death, passes to the person as directed by will, or a person to whom the copyright passes, or sits exercisable by a personal representative (CDPA 1988, s 95). The US Copyright Act contains similar provisions as to the types of moral right conferred on the authors. However, these rights expire on the author's death and therefore are not applicable to our issue of post-mortem transmission of copyright in email content (17 USC §106A).

[37] See in the UK, the Computer Misuse Act 1990, s 1. Passing passwords to third parties, whether heirs, friends or family is forbidden by most service providers in their terms of use. But note also the solution of legacy contacts (below, section 5).

[38] See the discussion of requests to Facebook to delete, memorialise, and so on, below section 5.

[39] This is generally speaking an industry norm.

third party beneficiary rights'.[40] A FB account is non-transferable, including any 'Page' or 'application' that users administer, without FB's written permission.[41] There is a clear prohibition on impersonation (using another user's account pretending you are that user), as password sharing is prohibited and users are also banned from letting anyone else access their account.[42] Legally as far as FB is concerned, the relationship between them and the user, even after death, is a matter of contract – yet it is uncertain whether the contract terminates on the death of the subscriber, or rights transmit to heirs as in other contracts, such as debts.

In a recent important case in Germany, FB refused to grant access to a deceased girl's FB account to her parents, arguing that their duties of confidence were solely owed to her. The Court of Appeal in Berlin supported FB's stance, but the Federal Court of Justice overturned this decision, relying on the German Civil Code (BGB) and its principle of universal succession (i.e. that heirs step into the deceased's shoes for all their rights and obligations). The Court rejected FB's argument that this was a contract of a highly personal nature and therefore rights did not transmit to heirs.[43] This is intriguing, as in common law jurisdictions it has generally been assumed (albeit without binding precedent) that contracts with social media platforms would be of such a highly personal nature (the doctrine of *delectus personae* in English law) and therefore rights and duties would both come to an end with the death of the subscriber.[44] This argument was rejected in the German case.

Under succession law, the administrator of an estate typically has the right to access and ingather the assets of the deceased no matter what contract says. Think for example of an administrator obtaining funds from the deceased's bank, even though a bank normally only allows access to the accountholder. This is usually enabled via a grant of power from the court,

---

[40] Facebook, 'Terms of Service' (formerly known as Statement of Rights and Responsibilities), s 5.6.

[41] Ibid., ss 3, 5.

[42] Ibid., s 3.1.

[43] Kammergericht, Urteil vom 31. Mai 2017, Aktenzeichen 21 U 9/16 available at: <https:// www.berlin.de/gerichte/presse/pressemitteilungen-der-ordentlichen-gerichtsbarkeit/2017/ pressemitteilung.596076.php> (accessed 19 April 2019); BGH, 12 July 2018, Docket No. III ZR 183/17.

[44] For example, Arthur, 'Bruce Willis to Fight Apple over Right to Leave iTunes Library in Will' (*The Guardian*, 3 September 2012) <www.guardian.co.uk/film/2012/sep/03/bruce-willis-apple-itunes-library> (accessed 19 April 2019). The article relates to what turned out to be a hoax story: that Bruce Willis was trying to leave the songs and videos on his Ipod to his heirs in his will. Despite being a hoax, the story raised legal awareness of this as a potential pitfall.

known as obtaining probate, confirmation or the like. This has already caused some conflicts in case law with Internet platforms. In *In Re Ellsworth*,[45] Yahoo!, as webmail provider, refused to give the surviving family of a US marine killed in action the log-in rights to his email account. They pled their terms of service (i.e. the contract) which, they said, were designed to protect the privacy of the account owner by forbidding the transfer of details to third parties on death and requiring the deletion of the account after death. Yahoo! also maintained that they were required by the US Stored Communications Act (SCA) 1986 not to hand over the emails, as the SCA prohibited access to stored communications without lawful authority; however, this rule had arguably always been intended to defend the privacy of subscribers, for example, from advertisers during *life*.[46]

The family argued that as his heirs, they should be able to see his emails – seeking access not only to those emails received by the deceased (as with hard copy letters) but also those sent by the deceased to others, where a copy would be retained on the server. There was a serious imminent danger that the emails would be erased and lost forever if Yahoo!, according to its non-survivorship policy, deleted the account. The judge, in a judgment of Solomon, allowed Yahoo! to abide by their privacy policy in that he did not order transfer of log-in and password, but made an order requiring Yahoo! to merely provide to the family a CD containing copies of the emails in the account.[47]

Conversely, in a more recent case, *Ajemian* v *Yahoo!*, the Supreme Judicial Court of Massachusetts[48] held that personal representatives of a deceased

---

[45] In Re Ellsworth, No 2005-296, 651-DE (Mich Prob Ct 2005). See discussion in Baldas, 'Slain Soldier's E-Mail Spurs Legal Debate: Ownership of Deceased's Messages at Crux of Issue' (2005) 27 *National Law Journal* 10.

[46] '*No Right of Survivorship and Non-Transferability*. You agree that your Yahoo! account is non-transferable and any rights to your Yahoo! ID or contents within your account terminate upon your death. Any free account that has not been used for a certain period of time may be terminated and all contents therein permanently deleted in line with Yahoo!'s policy' (Yahoo!, 'Terms of Service', discontinued <http://info.yahoo.com/legal/uk/yahoo/utos-173.html>, last accessed 15 June 2016). The same argument has been used in the recent case of *Marianne Ajemian, coadministrator & another v Yahoo!, Inc* 2013 WL 1866907 (Mass App Ct 2013), No 12-P-178, where Yahoo! contented that the Stored Communications Act, 18 US C §§2701 *et seq.* prohibits disclosure of the contents of the e-mail account to the administrators of John Ajemian's estate.

[47] See Associated Press, *In Re Ellsworth*, 'Press Release: Soldier's Kin to Get Access to his Emails' (21 April 2005) <www.justinellsworth.net/email/ap-apr05.htm> (accessed 19 April 2019). Note there seemed to be at least initial dubiety that Yahoo! had in fact transferred all emails in the account on to the CD.

[48] *Ajemian v Yahoo!, Inc*, 84 NE 3d 766 (Mass 2017), *cert denied*, No 17-1005, 2018 WL 489291 (US 26 March 2018).

might provide lawful consent on a decedent's behalf to access his electronic communications, despite the US ECPA and SCA, even in the absence of an express authorisation in the decedent's will.[49] An interesting case in stark contrast with *Ajemian* is that of Sahar Daftary. Sahar died at the age of twenty-three in the UK, and her family applied to the US courts to subpoena records from her FB account, as they believed that it 'contain[ed] critical evidence showing her actual state of mind in the days leading up to her death', which could be used in proceedings in the UK.[50] FB had refused to grant access without a court order. The Northern District of California Court found that the SCA prevented the court from making an order to compel a US service provider like FB from disclosing stored communications in civil proceedings to third parties, even after death, and even for the purposes of foreign proceedings as well as in the US.[51] However, the court noted in an obiter dictum that FB could choose to disclose the records to the family voluntarily and still be in accordance with the Act. However, it has not been reported whether FB has done so, and anecdotally, most providers refuse to do so without a court order.

Finally, to make the matter even more confusing, in another US case, *In re Scandalios*,[52] Ric Swezey died unexpectedly in 2017 and his will did not explicitly authorise his husband, Nicholas Scandalios, to have access to his digital assets, including many family photos in his iTunes and iCloud accounts. As with most other providers, Apple iCloud's terms and conditions provided that, 'any rights to your Apple ID or content within your account terminate upon your death', unless required by law. The New York County Surrogate's Court, however, ordered Apple to give the deceased husband's and the executor of the estate access to the deceased's Apple account. The Court, in this case, relied on section 13-A, administration of digital assets, of the New York Consolidated Laws, Estates, Powers and Trusts Law, and found that while disclosure of electronic communications required 'proof of a user's consent or a court order', the decedent's photographs stored in his Apple account were not 'electronic communications.' For these reasons, the court ordered that Apple should provide the executor with the opportunity to reset the password to the deceased's Apple ID. Since there is a division of opinion here between the probate court and the

---

[49] Ibid., at 773–4, 778. This interestingly undermines the presumption that the model law RUFADAA (see below, section 3.2) was necessary at all.

[50] *In re Request for Order Requiring Facebook, Inc to Produce Documents and Things*, C 12-80171 LHK (PSG) (ND California; 20 September 2012).

[51] Ibid., at 2, citing *Theofel* v *Farey-Jones*, 359 F3d 1066, 1074 (9th Cir 2004).

[52] *In re Scandalios* 2017-976/A NY Surr Ct 2019.

District Court in *Daftari*, however, it is not certain what precedent will be followed in future.

In summary, access to the digital accounts of the deceased is often an unregulated and unresolved issue in many jurisdictions, including the UK. Ash's accounts may have been regulated by UK law but it is quite likely that the service providers were based in the US and operating under US law concerning access of executors. We will turn in the following section to the question of how legislation has developed to try to address these issues, especially in the US.

3.2 Statutory Access Solutions: US and France

The result of these well-publicised conflicts in case law has been a growing trend towards drafting bespoke laws to regulate access to digital assets on Internet platforms after the death of the subscriber, usually attempting to fit these assets within conventional executry law. The US, or more precisely, some of its states have been the most active nations in this area. In the UK, by contrast, there is as yet neither statute nor case law, and the matter was excluded from a recent Law Society consultation on reform of wills on the ground that it was more to do with contract than succession.[53] However, some EU states, notably France, are beginning to take the matter seriously.

Some US states were active from an early stage, spurred on by *Ellsworth*, in passing laws around access to platforms by heirs on death, but coverage was very patchy and not all digital assets included in any comprehensive fashion, with a concentration on emails in the main: and powers relative to conflicts with terms of service not always entirely clear. The answer to this patchwork coverage was to formulate a harmonising model law for the US. In July 2012 the US Uniform Law Commission formed the Drafting Committee on Fiduciary Access to Digital Assets.[54] The goal was to vest fiduciaries with at least the authority to access and manage, distribute, copy or delete digital assets. The final text of the Uniform Fiduciary Access to Digital Assets Act (UFADAA) was adopted by the ULC in July 2014.[55] A further round of lobbying, caused by industry dissatisfaction with the draft, resulted in a

---

[53] Law Commission, 'Making a Will', para 14.16.

[54] See US Uniform Law Commission 2012 Annual Meeting in Nashville, Tennessee (13–19 July 2012) <http://uniformlaws.org/Narrative.aspx?title=QR%20Issue%2012%20%3E% 20New%20Committees> (accessed 19 April 2019).

[55] National Conference of Commissioners on Uniform State Laws, Drafting Committee on Fiduciary Access to Digital Assets, 'Fiduciary Access to Digital Assets Act' (July 2014) <www.uniformlaws.org/shared/docs/Fiduciary%20Access%20to%20Digital%20Assets/ 2014_UFADAA_Final.pdf> (accessed 19 April 2019).

revised UFADAA (RUFADAA), adopted in December 2015.[56] The biggest difference between the two texts is in the recognition of post-mortem privacy – discussed in section 4 – and technological solutions – see section 5 below.

The Uniform Law Conference of Canada followed the US and adopted a similar model law: the Canadian Uniform Access to Digital Assets by Fiduciaries Act 2016 (UADAFA).[57] This Act provides a stronger right of access for fiduciaries than the RUFADAA. There is default access to the digital assets of the account holder. In UAFADA, the instrument appointing the fiduciary determines a fiduciary's right of access, rather than the service provider. The Canadian Act also includes a 'last-in-time' priority system, whereby the most recent instruction takes priority over an earlier instrument.

In the EU, France has led the way. The Digital Republic Act 2016, art 63(2) resembles provisions of RUFADAA.[58] The Act states that anyone can set general or specific directives for preservation, deletion and disclosure of his personal data after death. These directives are to be registered with a certified third party (for general ones) or with the service provider who holds the data (for example, FB and their policy described above).[59]

Other jurisdictions are also considering introducing new legislation to resolve the issues of access in particular. The Law Reform Commission of New South Wales is one of the most recent examples.[60]

4. Post-mortem Privacy and Post-mortem Avatars

Digital avatars of the type posited in 'Be Right Back' both require and reveal an enormous amount of intimate information about the deceased. Would Martha have had a right not just to acquire – the issue discussed in the first section – but to *reveal* that data after Ash's death? Furthermore, would Ash

---

[56] For example, Lamm, 'Revised Uniform Fiduciary Access to Digital Assets Act' (*Digital Passing*, 29 September 2015) <www.digitalpassing.com/2015/09/29/revised-uniform-fidu ciary-access-digital-assets-act/> (accessed 19 April 2019); and see National Conference of Commissioners on Uniform State Laws, Drafting Committee on Fiduciary Access to Digital Assets, 'Revised Fiduciary Access to Digital Assets Act' (December 2015) <www. uniformlaws.org/Act.aspx?title=Fiduciary%20Access%20to%20Digital%20Assets% 20Act,%20Revised%20(2015)> (accessed 19 April 2019).

[57] See Uniform Law Conference of Canada, Uniform Access to Digital Assets by Fiduciaries Act (2016) <https://www.ulcc.ca/images/stories/2016_pdf_en/2016ulcc0006.pdf> (accessed 19 April 2019).

[58] LOI no. 2016-1321 du 7 octobre 2016 pour une République numérique.

[59] For more see Castex, Harbinja and Rossi, 'Défendre les vivants ou les morts? Controverses sous-jacentes au droit des données post-mortem à travers une perspective comparée franco-américaine' (2018) 4 *Réseaux* 117.

[60] Available at: <https://www.lawreform.justice.nsw.gov.au/Pages/lrc/lrc_current_projects/ Digital%20assets/Project-update.aspx> (accessed 10 April 2019).

have wanted this information to survive him, and to be accessible to others after his death? In this fictional case, this might not have been a huge issue; Martha spends most of her time alone or with New Ash and hides him when her sister visits. However, looking at a real-life example, the Replika robot of Roman, discussed above in section 2, for example, was hosted on a FB page and can be conversed with by strangers such as journalists. Roman's friend Kuyda, the author of the chatbot, may have given permission for this but Roman did not and could probably not have imagined what she might do with the thousands of texts he had sent her (when he died, Kuyda was using ML to develop restaurant software). New Ash in 'Be Right Back' interacts only with Martha; but it's not at all implausible to imagine that if the experiment had been (more) successful, Ash's pre-mortem life might have been displayed to and shared with many.

This suggests an issue that the authors have raised extensively in previous work: what if there were aspects of the deceased's life (or work) that they preferred to remain private, even after or perhaps especially after they died? In relation to the case of *Re Ellsworth* cited above, where sympathy, amongst both academics and the courts, has tended to lie with the parents seeking access to their deceased's son's emails, we have asked if we would feel differently if we knew that the dead marine was hiding something crucial, such as being gay or having an affair.[61] There is, famously, precedent for the desire to hide lifetime choices after death: Kafka, for example, famously asked that all his unfinished novels be destroyed after his death (although this was thwarted by his literary executor). More recently, Terry Pratchett's unfinished novels were destroyed by a steamroller that crushed his hard disk, in accordance with his wishes.[62] A debate based on such examples exists in relation to whether the laws of succession and copyright should uphold such wishes, but little of that debate has spilt over until very recently into the domain of privacy.

This is what we come to discuss next. Should a deceased be able to bindingly state what they wish to happen to their private data after their death? If they say nothing, what should be the default outcome? Or, to take the opposite tack, are any wishes or instructions of the dead, even if ascertainable, irrelevant, and is what matters rather the feelings and wishes of those who still live? What about personal data and communications of third

---

61 See Edwards and Harbinja, ' "What Happens to My Facebook Profile When I Die?": Legal Issues Around Transmission of Digital Assets on Death' in Maciel C and Carvalho Pereira V (eds), *Digital Legacy and Interaction: Post-Mortem Issues* (Springer 2013).

62 Convery, 'Terry Pratchett's Unfinished Novels Destroyed by Steamroller' (*The Guardian*, 20 August 2017) <https://www.theguardian.com/books/2017/aug/30/terry-pratchett-unfinished-novels-destroyed-steamroller> (accessed 19 April 2019).

persons, those who were in touch with the deceased? Should heirs be able to access all this too? This is the debate around what the authors have christened 'post-mortem privacy', a novel idea that is nonetheless attracting significant attention in the digital era.

In traditional legal discourse, this argument has long been settled in favour of the living. It is tritely said that the dead have no privacy; it is the living who have rights and for this reason, for example, it is routinely asserted that the dead cannot be libelled.[63] To be more precise, the law draws a distinction in this area between economic and dignitary rights. A testator can of course leave instructions as to how they want their economic assets distributed on death and subject to certain caveats, which vary from legal system to legal system (eg providing for spouse and children, collection of death taxes), these wishes will generally be honoured (this is the principle of 'freedom of testation', which is particularly strong in common law systems). However, when it comes to dignitary or personal interests – things like privacy, personal data, reputation or moral rights in intellectual property – then the general assumption of most common law legal systems at least is that these rights or interests are extinguished on death.[64] The reigning principle has traditionally been of *actio personalis moritur cum persona* (personal causes of actions die with the person, including defamation claims, breach of confidence claims, wrongful dismissal claims and so on).[65] Although this principle has been whittled away in many contexts for reasons of social policy for example, succour to the dependents of the deceased,[66] Beverley-Smith, perhaps the leading English writer on commercial image rights, still represents a prevailing sentiment in noting that 'reputation and injured dignity are generally of no concern to a deceased person'.[67] Thus a deceased like Ash would in principle have conceptually no way to exert control over their personality rights after they were dead (such as in their image or voice). While some US states and

---

[63] See Edwards and Harbinja, 'Protecting Post-Mortem Privacy'; note that this is not completely right as some exceptions exist, mainly to protect the honour or reputation of a family as a whole.

[64] For discussion of civilian systems, where personality rights in general tend to have more protection, see a fuller discussion in Edwards and Harbinja, 'Protecting Post-Mortem Privacy'.

[65] Established in *Beker* v *Bolton* (1808) 1 Camp 439; 170 ER 1033.

[66] The principle has been revised in the UK and now only pertains to causes of action for defamation and certain claims for bereavement. See the Law Reform (Miscellaneous Provisions) 1934 Act c 41, Race Relations Act 1976 c 74, Sex Discrimination Act 1975 c 65, Disability Discrimination act 1995 c 50 and Administration of Justice Act 1982 c 53.

[67] Beverley-Smith, *The Commercial Appropriation of Personality* (Cambridge University Press 2002), p. 124.

civilian legal systems have extended personality rights until after death,[68] the exercise of these rights still typically falls to heirs – in our case, presumptively, Martha – and so would not protect Ash.

Rules on DP, the primary tool for the protection of *informational* privacy and exercise of control over personal data, have also very much followed this line. The GDPR, understandably given its fundamental connection with Article 8 of the ECHR (which itself applies, like other human rights, only to the living[69]), only protects the personal data of 'natural persons', usually interpreted to mean the living.[70] However, some EU states have nonetheless chosen in the past under the greater flexibility of the Data Protection Directive to offer some kind of post-mortem DP, even if limited in its scope and for a restricted period of time after death. Only a few member states have however taken advantage of this possibility.[71] The UK, in its implementation of the GDPR in the Data Protection Act 2018, takes no steps in this direction.

Accordingly, Ash's personal data are arguably 'up for grabs', and he seems in principle to have no rights[72] either before or after death to compel data about him to be processed in a particular way (or not, or deleted) after his death.[73] (This cuts both ways though. Arguably if Ash the data subject has no rights over his privacy after death, then neither does Martha his heir. Could Martha prevent someone else – an old girlfriend or Ash's mother, or as men-

---

[68] Edwards and Harbinja, 'Protecting Post-Mortem Privacy'.

[69] *Jäggi v Switzerland*, no 58757/00, ECHR 2006-X; *Estate of Kresten Filtenborg Mortensen v Denmark (dec)*, no 1338/03, ECHR 2006-V; *Koch v Germany*, no. 497/09, ECHR 19/07/2012.

[70] GDPR, art 4(1) and recital 27.

[71] Recital 27 of the GDPR makes this possible as a matter of national discretion. See McCallig, 'Data Protection and the Deceased in the EU' (24 January 2014), paper presented at the CPDP Conference, Brussels; Edwards and Harbinja, 'Protecting Post-Mortem Privacy', pp. 131–2.

[72] This might not be the case for his patient records. Harbinja, 'Posthumous Medical Data Donation: The Case for a Legal Framework' in Krutzinna J and Floridi L (eds), *The Ethics of Medical Data Donation, Philosophical Studies Series*, vol. 137 (Springer 2019), pp. 97–113.

[73] One conceivable way forward might be a data trust. Trusts are well recognised vehicles in common law (and some mixed systems such as Scots law) by which the living can exert continuing control over their assets after their death. However this would require data to be seen as a form of property capable of forming the assets of a trust, which is controversial, and data trusts themselves are only just emerging, so far as a mainly academic concept. This space should however be watched. See Hardinge, 'What is a Data Trust?' (Open Data Institute, 10 July 2018) <https://theodi.org/article/what-is-a-data-trust/> (accessed 19 April 2019), and early work by one of the co-authors: Edwards, 'The Problem with Privacy' (2004) 18 *International Review of Law, Computers & Technology* 263.

tioned above, a social network like FB – making their own chatbot if they had access to enough data? It would seem not, although Martha might certainly exercise rights over items involving her *own* personal data, for example photos of the two of them together,[74] or possibly make some kind of argument based on copyright or confidence.)

4.1 For and Against Post-mortem Privacy

Are we happy with this result? There are strong arguments that the long-embedded attitude of the common law, which denies any rights of privacy or DP after death, is no longer appropriate. We would suggest that a number of factors demand the reconsideration of post-mortem privacy in a digital world, including the very large volume of digital assets preserved after death; their accessibility, durability, shareability, and co-construction of such assets; and the lack of author control, as opposed to intermediary or platform control.[75] The rise of social media and the ever-vigilant eyes of Google have meant that we record and make public an infinitely larger amount of highly sensitive material than at any previous time in history. In Kafka's time, only authors or other public figures had to worry about what would happen to their unfinished works, journals, letters or diary entries after their death. Now we all regularly record the intimate details of our lives for posterity in unprecedented amounts. This might be said to indicate that there is no greater need for post-mortem privacy than there was in prior decades or centuries, as we have willingly given this material away; but as much might be written about us by others as by ourselves.

Furthermore, there is evidence that many regret what they have written, which has now left control in the hands of the Internet: no 'right to be forgotten' will exist for the dead.[76] As in our chatbot example, new data may also now be derived from old in the form of inferences drawn via ML systems, making breaches of privacy all the more likely and potentially more worrying. In an age of 'datification', 'big data' and 'quantified selves', the need for control over personal data, already well acknowledged before death, seems increasingly pressing afterwards as well. Harbinja[77] has argued persuasively that the new circumstances of the digital world and the lack of current legal support for post-mortem privacy suggest some level of urgency in addressing

---

[74] Although again it is possible that if such data had 'manifestly been made public' – for example, by posting these pictures publicly on social media without any privacy controls – then others might have the right to process them, including data mining; see GDPR, art 9(2)(e).

[75] See further, Edwards and Harbinja, 'Protecting Post-Mortem Privacy', at VI.i.

[76] See GDPR, art 17.

[77] Harbinja, 'Post-mortem Privacy 2.0'.

these matters; and that normative support for post-mortem privacy can be found in theories of autonomy,[78] privacy as autonomy[79] and the freedom of testation.[80]

On the other hand, the existing legal status quo is based at heart on the notion that the interests of the living, at least in relation to dignitary non-economic qualities like privacy, outweigh those of the dead.[81] Is Martha's happiness not rather more important than Ash's possible post-mortem queasiness? Do we know how he would have felt about the creation of the chatbot? (Probably not, though he could have made feelings known in a will.[82]) Can the dead suffer? (No, say the atheist authors.) Can the living suffer at the thought of what might happen to their reputation after death (surely yes) but does the balance of harms not still favour the remaining heirs? (The dead after all could have taken steps to destroy material before they died – though that would not help Ash, who died suddenly at a young age.) If any harm lies in reputation to the family, is it not the living family rather than the dead data subject who is best placed to judge? Some of these arguments have been interestingly ventilated in the context of organ donation, where the pre-death wishes of the donor to give away their organs are often thwarted by the post-mortem feelings of the family[83] and little societal or legal consensus has emerged, even in an area where organs (unlike privacy, by and large) are of vital interest to society.[84]

---

[78] For a commentary on the development of autonomy, see Schneewind, *The Invention of Autonomy: A History of Modern Moral Philosophy* (Cambridge University Press 1998); the conception adopted here is Mill's liberal, individualistic approach to autonomy, Mill, *On Liberty* Himmelfarb (ed.), (Penguin 1984), p. 72.

[79] For example, Henkin, 'Privacy and Autonomy' (1974) 74 *Columbia Law Review* 1410; Solove, ' "I've Got Nothing to Hide" and Other Misunderstandings of Privacy' (2007) 44 *San Diego Law Review* 745.

[80] For example, du Toit, 'The Limits Imposed Upon Freedom of Testation by the *Boni Mores*: Lessons from Common Law and Civil Law (Continental) Legal Systems' (2000) 3 *Stellenbosch Law Review* 358, p. 360; or de Waal, 'A Comparative Overview' in Reid, de Waal and Zimmermann (eds), *Exploring the Law of Succession: Studies National, Historical and Comparative* (Edinburgh University Press 2007).

[81] Note that historically the *economic* interests of the living have also sometimes been asserted to outweigh the economic choices of the dead; see the rule against perpetuities in trusts and the Perpetuities and Accumulations Act 2009.

[82] See further discussion of 'technological' wills below, section 5.

[83] Supra, Edwards and Harbinja, 'Protecting Post-Mortem Privacy', p. 57.

[84] See the slow progress of the Organ Donation (Deemed Consent) Bill 2017–19 in England and Wales, available at https://services.parliament.uk/bills/2017-19/organdonationdeemed consent.html (accessed 1 June 2019).

5. Giving the Dead a Voice about Privacy and Digital Remains: 'Technological' Wills

This discussion suggests a way forward, which is to encourage data subjects to make their feelings known about their post-mortem privacy before they die and to provide them with ways to have these wishes implemented – in other words, to allow the creation of 'technological' wills relating to material posted on sites like FB and YouTube (Google). FB has long been a leader in the world of social media in acknowledging the issues that arise when a subscriber with a profile dies.[85] Since around 2009 they have offered family or friends of deceased users the options of having the profile of the deceased deleted,[86] or 'memorialised'. Even earlier, FB provided a download on the request of the deceased's account[87] if prior consent had been given by the deceased, or court order was made after death.[88]

The effects of memorialisation are that it prevents anyone from logging into the account of the deceased, even those with valid log-in information and password. Content that the deceased shared, while alive, remains visible to those it was shared with (privacy settings remain 'as is').[89] Depending on the privacy settings, confirmed friends may still post to the deceased's timeline. Accounts (timelines) that are memorialised no longer appear in the

[85] Facebook's procedures for deletion and memorialisation of deceased's accounts were initiated partly as a result of a general intervention by the Canadian Privacy Commissioner, adjudicating on formal complaints made: see Office of the Privacy Commissioner of Canada, 'Facebook Agrees to Address Privacy Commissioner's Concerns' (27 August 2009) <www.priv.gc.ca/media/nr-c/2009/nr-c_090827_e.asp> (accessed 19 April 2019). Memorialisation also involves taking the profile out of public search results and prevents further login attempts (for example, by scammers, or someone the deceased had shared their password with).

[86] Facebook, 'Help Center: Deactivating & Deleting Accounts' <www.facebook.com/help/359046244166395/> (accessed 19 April 2019).

[87] Facebook, 'Help Center: Accessing Your Facebook Data' <https://en-gb.facebook.com/help/405183566203254/> (accessed 19 April 2019).

[88] Facebook, 'Help Center: How Do I Ask a Question about a Deceased Person's Account on Facebook?' <https://www.facebook.com/help/265593773453448/> (accessed 19 April 2019): 'We will provide the estate of the deceased with a download of the account's data if prior consent is obtained from or decreed by the deceased, or mandated by law.'

[89] Initially, content was only visible to the user's friends, but this changed in February 2014, see Fields, 'Facebook Changes Access to Profiles of Deceased' (ABC News, 22 February 2014) <http://abcnews.go.com/Technology/facebook-access-profiles-deceased/story?id=22632425> (accessed 19 April 2019); and Price and DiSclafani, 'Remembering Our Loved Ones' (Facebook Newsroom, 21 February 2014) <http://newsroom.fb.com/news/2014/02/remembering-our-loved-ones/> (accessed 19 April 2019).

'people you may know' suggestions or other suggestions and notifications.[90] Memorialisation prevents the tagging of the deceased in future FB posts, photographs or any other content.[91] Unfriending (removing someone from one's friends list) a deceased person's memorialised account is permanent,[92] and a friend cannot be added to a memorialised account or profile, which might be an issue for parents of deceased children who may not have added their parents as friends while alive.[93] A 'special request' can also be made for a variety of other purposes, including asking any question in relation to the profile, or if a friend wishes to obtain a 'Look Back' video.[94]

These processes are, it should be noted, the result of requests made by the living, not the deceased, and do not explicitly protect the wishes or privacy of the deceased (although in the process of memorialising an account, FB promises to remove 'sensitive information such as contact information and status updates' in order to protect the deceased's privacy).[95] However more recently, both FB and Google have gone further and allowed the owner of an account the opportunity to say *in advance of death* (or incapacity) how they would like their account data to be dealt with. These new solutions were first pioneered by the Google Inactive Account Manager, which was followed by Facebook Legacy Contact.

Google introduced in April 2013 the Orwellian sounding 'Inactive Account Manager',[96] which allows users to prescribe which of a number of disposals of their data they wish to be pursued after a prescribed length of inactivity (say, one, three or nine months).[97] The options are relatively limited: a 'trusted contact' can either delete the content associated with

---

90   Facebook, 'Help Center: What Will Happen to My Account if I Pass Away?' <www.facebook.com/help/1038897939701143/> (accessed 19 April 2019).

91   Buck, 'How 1 Billion People Are Coping with Death and Facebook' (*Mashable UK*, 13 February 2013) <http://mashable.com/2013/02/13/facebook-after-death/> (accessed 19 April 2019).

92   Death and Digital Legacy, 'Nebraska is Latest State to Address Digital Legacy' (20 February 2012) <www.deathanddigitallegacy.com/2012/02/20/nebraska-is-latest-state-to-address-digital-legacy/> (accessed 19 April 2019).

93   Facebook, 'Special Request for Deceased Person's Account' <www.facebook.com/help/contact/228813257197480> (accessed 19 April 2019).

94   Ibid. A 'Look Back' video is available on request of any of the deceased's Facebook friends, and Facebook promises to send the link to this video, which cannot be edited or shared.

95   Facebook, 'Help Center: What Will Happen to my Facebook Account if I Pass Away?'

96   See Google Public Policy Blog, 'Plan Your Digital Afterlife with Interactive Account Manager' (11 April 2013) <http://googlepublicpolicy.blogspot.co.uk/2013/04/plan-your-digital-afterlife-with.html> (accessed 19 April 2019).

97   See discussion in Harbinja, 'Does the EU Data Protection Regime Protect Post-Mortem Privacy and What Could Be the Potential Alternatives?' (2013) 10 *SCRIPTed* 19.

the account or download it.[98] Since 2015,[99] FB has also allowed its users to designate a friend or family member to be their 'Facebook legacy contact', who will manage their account after they have died. Legacy Contact has had a fairly limited number of options: to write a post to display at the top of the memorialised Timeline; to respond to new friend requests and to update the profile picture and cover photo of a deceased user. Also, a user 'may give their legacy contact permission to download an archive of the photos, posts and profile information they shared on Facebook'. The Legacy Contact will not be able to log in to the account or see the private messages of the deceased. All the other settings will remain the same as before memorialisation of the account. Finally, an option is that a user decides to permanently delete his/her account after their death.[100]

In April 2019, FB introduced a 'Tribute' section, with the aim to further develop the option of memorialisation and provide the legacy contact with some new powers. The tribute side of the deceased's profile coexists with their timeline, and the timeline seems to be still visible, as set by the deceased before their death. The legacy contact can alter the visibility of the tribute and do the following: change who can post tributes; delete tribute posts; change who can see posts that the deceased is tagged in; remove tags of the deceased that someone else has posted; and, if the deceased had turned on a timeline review, the legacy contact will be able to turn it off for posts in the tributes section.[101] FB also changed their policies to let parents who have lost underage children to request to become their legacy contact.[102] This is most likely their response to the recent court and media cases, such as the Berlin court case or the case of Molly Russell's tragic death.[103] Finally, in this iteration of changes to the deceased's policy, FB has attempted to clarify the use of AI for

---

[98] Google, 'Inactive Account Manager' <https://myaccount.google.com/inactive?pli=1> (accessed 19 April 2019).

[99] Callison-Burch, Probst and Govea, 'Adding a Legacy Contact' (Facebook Newsroom, 12 February 2015) <http://newsroom.fb.com/news/2015/02/adding-a-legacy-contact/> (accessed 19 April 2019).

[100] Ibid.

[101] Facebook, 'Help Center: What are Tributes on a Memorialized Facebook Page?' <https://www.facebook.com/help/745202382483645> (accessed 19 April 2019).

[102] Facebook, 'Making it Easier to Honor a Loved One on Facebook after They Pass Away' <https://newsroom.fb.com/news/2019/04/updates-to-memorialization/> (accessed 19 April 2019).

[103] Molly Russell took her own life following exposure to self-harm and suicide material. See BBC News, 'Molly Russell: "Why Can't I See My Daughter's Data?"' (6 February 2019) <https://www.bbc.com/news/av/technology-47143315/molly-russell-why-can-t-i-see-my-daughter-s-data> (accessed 19 April 2019).

profiles of the deceased that have not yet been memorialised. FB claims that they use AI to 'keep it from showing up in places that might cause distress, like recommending that person be invited to events or sending a birthday reminder to their friends'.[104] The exact extent or specifics of the use of AI is still vague and it would be useful if FB made this clearer in its terms of service and the help centre.

Although at an early stage of development, these kinds of tools could have given Ash the chance to shape his own future explicitly by indicating perhaps what data he did or did not want preserved, deleted or incorporated into a chatbot or avatar, and who that data should go to. Many issues still remain to be ironed out with such technological solutions. The idea of one tool per site is obviously clunky; it would be easier for the heir if there was a 'one-stop shop'. The issue of conflicts both with traditional wills and with traditional terms of service, may still cause problems.[105] The most obvious solution might be for such instructions to be incorporated into a traditional will but honoured by a platform; however this would throw away the self-enforcing quality of these tools being incorporated 'on site', as well as ignoring the fact that many social media users, especially the young, will not make traditional wills.[106] However, anecdotal evidence is that both the Google and FB tools also remain relatively obscure, and Google has so far refused to make statistics as to use available despite its generally good track record on Transparency Reports.[107] FB and Google could both make the existing options more obvious and part of their core terms of service rather than part of their 'help' pages. Finally, it may be impossible to locate the designated legacy contact, or they may simply refuse to play their part.

6. Conclusions

Legally, as can be seen this area, is highly complex and emergent. One issue we have barely touched on, for example, is the issue of conflict of laws or international private law. Martha and Ash appeared to live in England, but the service providers might have been based in the UK, EU, US or China

---

[104] Facebook, 'Making it Easier to Honor a Loved One on Facebook after They Pass Away'.

[105] This issue was a hot topic in the revision of the US model law UFADAA, which grants priority to service providers' terms of service and user choices over any other provisions, including a traditional will.

[106] Denton, 'Nearly 60% of Britons Haven't Written a Will – And a Fifth Don't Bother Because They Don't Feel Wealthy Enough' (*This is Money*, 26 September 2016) <https://www.thisismoney.co.uk/money/news/article-3807497/Nearly-60-Britons-not-written-will.html> (accessed 19 April 2019).

[107] See Google, 'Transparency Report' <https://transparencyreport.google.com/?hl=en_GB> (accessed 19 April 2019).

just to name a few possibilities. As shown in the recent case involving Molly Russell, acquiring access to accounts held by foreign service providers is still not at all easy.[108]

Many questions, social, philosophical and legal, remain unaddressed in this chapter. What is the legal status of New Ash, in the *Black Mirror* scenario? Is he property? Is he something that should not be capable of being owned, like human organs? Is he software? Would Ash's estate be owed royalties if he were marketed to a wider audience? Is it possible that he could acquire legal personality and hence human rights? *Should* he, and at what point of acquiring sentience, intelligence and/or consciousness? Should the deceased or the family have a veto on his creation?

Androids or synthetic entities are often seen as threats (the 'killer robot' syndrome), but in the very last scene of *Black Mirror*, Ash is portrayed as a sort of semi-abandoned, rather pathetic slave. Is this acceptable, and does this mirror our human tendency to short-term gratification followed by disposal when we are bored? What happens to no-longer-interesting post-mortem simulacra? Do they need a 'best by' date of expiry or a kill switch? How would they be updated or 'grow up', or would it be healthy for them to stay the same forever, fossilised in amber like a digital Peter Pan? Should the companies providing them have an obligation to keep older models going by upgrades and patches?[109] Perhaps of most immediate relevance, how healthy psychologically would it be for a grieving, bereaved relative to depend on the simulacrum of the deceased rather than moving on to new relationships?[110] What happens to their emotional stability if the software services supporting the avatar are turned off, say due to lack of a successful business model?[111]

Also, to get the whole picture, it is interesting to note another episode of *Black Mirror*, set even futher in the future, deals with the digital afterlife, namely 'San Junipero'.[112] In San Junipero, humans can decide to be

---

[108] BBC News, 'Molly Russell: "Why Can't I See My Daughter's Data?"'

[109] The C4 science fiction series *Humans* interestingly imagined this in its first series, with a father struggling to keep an android based on his dead son in working order even though he was now a hopelessly out-of-date model.

[110] This question is interestingly raised in the (fictional) film *Truly, Madly, Deeply*, where Juliet Stevenson is mysteriously led out of the depths of grief to new beginnings via the ghost of her former lover, Alan Rickman.

[111] Something like this has recently happened in relation to the social robot, Jibo, which has been left to 'die' as its software support is slowly reduced by the parent company, to the distress of its owners. See Van Camp, 'My Jibo Is Dying and It's Breaking My Heart' (*Wired*, 8 March 2019) <https://www.wired.com/story/jibo-is-dying-eulogy/> (accessed 19 April 2019).

[112] Season 3; Episode 4, 21 October 2016. Series currently available on Netflix and More4.

'uploaded' to the cloud to live out an eternal life of youth after their physical death. If this choice became available, is it one that should override the choice made by relatives to create a New Ash? But if we think that a compromise between post-mortem privacy (San Junipero) and the interest of heirs (New Ash) is a good way forward, is it not better to have a New Ash (replica) in the real world and an Old Ash (in a young body) in San Junipero? Can they communicate and how? How do they develop and 'age'? All these issues raise fairly profound questions about the line between humanity and machine and whether we want to treat humans as machines as much we treat machines as humans. These questions cast a shadow on what seem two of the rare hopeful endings in the *Black Mirror* canon.

References

Arthur C, 'Bruce Willis to Fight Apple over Right to Leave iTunes Library in Will' (*The Guardian*, 3 September 2012) <www.guardian.co.uk/film/2012/sep/03/bruce-willis-apple-itunes-library> (accessed 19 April 2019).

Artificial Lawyer, 'Declare Your Legal Bot! New California Law Demands Bot Transparency' (3 October 2018) <https://www.artificiallawyer.com/2018/10/03/declare-your-legal-bot-new-california-law-demands-bot-transparency/> (accessed 19 April 2019).

Associated Press, *In Re Ellsworth*, 'Press Release: Soldier's Kin to Get Access to his Emails' (21 April 2005) <www.justinellsworth.net/email/ap-apr05.htm> (accessed 19 April 2019).

Ayala FJ, 'Cloning Humans? Biological, Ethical, and Social Considerations' (2015) 112 *Proceedings of the National Academy of Science, USA* 8879.

Baldas T, 'Slain Soldier's E-Mail Spurs Legal Debate: Ownership of Deceased's Messages at Crux of Issue' (2005) 27 *National Law Journal* 10.

BBC News, 'Molly Russell: "Why Can't I See My Daughter's Data?"' (6 February 2019) <https://www.bbc.com/news/av/technology-47143315/molly-russell-why-can-t-i-see-my-daughter-s-data> (accessed 19 April 2019).

Beverley-Smith H, *The Commercial Appropriation of Personality* (Cambridge University Press 2002).

Blizzard, 'Terms of Use Agreement' (22 August 2012) <http://us.blizzard.com/en-us/company/legal/wow_tou.html> (accessed 15 June 2016).

Blizzard, 'End-User License Agreement', last revised 20 August 2018 <https://www.blizzard.com/en-us/legal/2c72a35c-bf1b-4ae6-99ec-80624e1b429c/blizzard-end-user-license-agreement> (accessed 19 April 2019).

Bosch T, 'The Android Head of Philip K Dick' (*Slate*, 1 June 2012) <https://slate.com/culture/2012/06/philip-k-dick-robot-an-android-head-of-the-science-fiction-author-is-lost-forever.html> (accessed 19 April 2019).

Bryson JJ, Diamantis ME and Grant TD, 'Of, For, and By the People: The Legal Lacuna of Synthetic Persons' (2017) 25 *Artificial Intelligence and Law* 273 <https://doi.org/10.1007/s10506-017-9214-9> (accessed 19 April 2019).

Buck S, 'How 1 Billion People Are Coping with Death and Facebook' (*Mashable UK*, 13 February 2013) <http://mashable.com/2013/02/13/facebook-after-death/> (accessed 19 April 2019).

Callison-Burch V, Probst J and Govea M, 'Adding a Legacy Contact' (Facebook Newsroom, 12 February 2015) <http://newsroom.fb.com/news/2015/02/adding-a-legacy-contact/> (accessed 19 April 2019).

Castex L, Harbinja E and Rossi J, 'Défendre les vivants ou les morts? Controverses sous-jacentes au droit des données post-mortem à travers une perspective comparée franco-américaine' (2018) 4 *Réseaux* 117.

Convery S, 'Terry Pratchett's Unfinished Novels Destroyed by Steamroller' (*The Guardian*, 20 August 2017) <https://www.theguardian.com/books/2017/aug/30/terry-pratchett-unfinished-novels-destroyed-streamroller> (accessed 19 April 2019).

Death and Digital Legacy, 'Nebraska is Latest State to Address Digital Legacy' (20 February 2012) <www.deathanddigitallegacy.com/2012/02/20/nebraska-is-latest-state-to-address-digital-legacy/> (accessed 19 April 2019).

Denton J, 'Nearly 60% of Britons Haven't Written a Will – And a Fifth Don't Bother Because They Don't Feel Wealthy Enough' (*This is Money*, 26 September 2016) <https://www.thisismoney.co.uk/money/news/article-3807497/Nearly-60-Britons-not-written-will.html> (accessed 19 April 2019).

Desai D, 'Property, Persona, and Preservation' (2008) 81 *Temple Law Review* 67.

De Waal MJ, 'A Comparative Overview' in Reid KGC, de Waal MJ and Zimmermann R (eds), *Exploring the Law of Succession: Studies National, Historical and Comparative* (Edinburgh University Press 2007).

Dufty D, *How to Build an Android: The True Story of Philip K. Dick's Robotic Resurrection* (Picador 2013).

Du Toit F, 'The Limits Imposed upon Freedom of Testation by the Boni Mores: Lessons from Common Law and Civil Law (Continental) Legal Systems' (2000) 3 *Stellenbosch Law Review* 358.

Edwards L, 'The Problem with Privacy' (2004) 18 *International Review of Law Computers & Technology* 263.

Edwards L and Harbinja E, 'Protecting Post-Mortem Privacy: Reconsidering the Privacy Interests of the Deceased in a Digital World' (2013) 32 *Cardozo Arts & Entertainment Law Journal* 103.

Edwards L and Harbinja E, ' "What Happens to My Facebook Profile When I Die?" Legal Issues around Transmission of Digital Assets on Death' in Maciel C and Carvalho Pereira V (eds), *Digital Legacy and Interaction: Post-Mortem Issues* (Springer 2013).

EPSRC, 'Principles of Robotics' (September 2010) <https://epsrc.ukri.org/research/ourportfolio/themes/engineering/activities/principlesofrobotics/> (accessed 19 April 2019).

Facebook, 'Help Center: Accessing Your Facebook Data' <https://en-gb.facebook.com/help/405183566203254/> (accessed 19 April 2019).

Facebook, 'Help Center: Deactivating & Deleting Accounts' <www.facebook.com/help/359046244166395/> (accessed 19 April 2019).

Facebook, 'Help Center: How Do I Ask a Question about a Deceased Person's Account on Facebook?' <https://www.facebook.com/help/265593773453448/> (accessed 19 April 2019).

Facebook, 'Help Center: What are Tributes on a Memorialized Facebook Page?' <https://www.facebook.com/help/745202382483645> (accessed 19 April 2019).

Facebook, 'Help Center: What Will Happen to My Account if I Pass Away?' <www.facebook.com/help/103897939701143/> (accessed 19 April 2019).

Facebook, 'Making it Easier to Honor a Loved One on Facebook after They Pass Away' <https://newsroom.fb.com/news/2019/04/updates-to-memorialization/> (accessed 19 April 2019).

Facebook, 'Special Request for Deceased Person's Account' <www.facebook.com/help/contact/228813257197480> (accessed 19 April 2019).

Facebook, 'Terms of Service' <https://www.facebook.com/terms.php> (accessed 19 April 2019).

Fields L, 'Facebook Changes Access to Profiles of Deceased' (ABC News, 22 February 2014) <http://abcnews.go.com/Technology/facebook-access-profiles-deceased/story?id=22632425> (accessed 19 April 2019).

Google, 'Inactive Account Manager' <https://myaccount.google.com/inactive?pli=1> (accessed 19 April 2019).

Google, 'Privacy and Terms: Your Content in our Services' <https://policies.google.com/terms?gl=US&hl=en#toc-content> (accessed 19 April 2019).

Google, 'Transparency Report' <https://transparencyreport.google.com/?hl=en_GB> (accessed 19 April 2019).

Google Public Policy Blog, 'Plan Your Digital Afterlife with Interactive Account Manager' (11 April 2013) <http://googlepublicpolicy.blogspot.co.uk/2013/04/plan-your-digital-afterlife-with.html> (accessed 19 April 2019).

Hamilton IA, 'These 2 Tech Founders Lost their Friends in Tragic Accidents. Now They've Built AI Chatbots to Give People Life after Death' (17 November 2018) <https://www.businessinsider.com/eternime-and-replika-giving-life-to-the-dead-with-new-technology-2018-11?r=US&IR> (accessed 19 April 2019).

Harbinja E, 'Does the EU Data Protection Regime Protect Post-Mortem Privacy and What Could Be the Potential Alternatives?' (2013) 10 *SCRIPTed* 19.

Harbinja E, 'Virtual Worlds – A Legal Post-Mortem Account' (2014) 10 *SCRIPTed* 273.

Harbinja E, 'Virtual Worlds Players – Consumers or Citizens?' (2014) 3 *Internet Policy Review* <https://policyreview.info/articles/analysis/virtual-worlds-players-consumers-or-citizens> (accessed 19 April 2019).

Harbinja E, 'Legal Nature of Emails: A Comparative Perspective' (2016) 14 *Duke Law and Technology Review* 227 <http://scholarship.law.duke.edu/dltr/vol14/iss1/10> (accessed 19 April 2019).

Harbinja E, 'Digital Inheritance in the United Kingdom' (2017) 6 *Journal of European Consumer and Market Law* 253.

Harbinja E, 'Legal Aspects of Transmission of Digital Assets on Death' (PhD dissertation, University of Strathclyde, 2017).

Harbinja E, 'Post-mortem Privacy 2.0: Theory, Law and Technology' (2017) 31 *International Review of Law, Computers & Technology* 26 <www.tandfonline.com/doi/citedby/10.1080/13600869.2017.1275116?scroll=top&needAccess=true> (accessed 19 April 2019).

Harbinja E, 'Social Media and Death' in Gillies L and Mangan D (eds), *The Legal Challenges of Social Media* (Edward Elgar Publishing 2017).

Harbinja E, 'Posthumous Medical Data Donation: The Case for a Legal Framework' in Krutzinna J and Floridi L (eds), *The Ethics of Medical Data Donation, Philosophical Studies Series*, vol. 137 (Springer 2019), pp. 97–113.

Hardinges J, 'What is a Data Trust?' (Open Data Institute, 10 July 2018) <https://theodi.org/article/what-is-a-data-trust/> (accessed 19 April 2019).

Harris O, *Black Mirror*, Season 2, Episode 1, 11 February 2013.

Harris O, *Black Mirror*, Season 3, Episode 4, 21 October 2016.

Henkin L, 'Privacy and Autonomy' (1974) 74 *Columbia Law Review* 1410.

Holpuch A, 'Instagram Reassures Users over Terms of Service after Massive Outcry' (*The Guardian*, 18 December 2012) <www.guardian.co.uk/technology/2012/dec/18/instagram-issues-statement-terms-of-service> (accessed 19 April 2019).

Lamm J, 'Revised Uniform Fiduciary Access to Digital Assets Act' (*Digital Passing*, 29 September 2015) <www.digitalpassing.com/2015/09/29/revised-uniform-fiduciary-access-digital-assets-act/> (accessed 19 April 2019).

Law Commission, 'Making a Will' (Consultation Paper 231).

Linden Lab, 'Second Life Terms of Service' (15 December 2010) <http://secondlife.com/corporate/tos.php?lang=en-US> (accessed 15 June 2016).

Linden Lab, 'Second Life Terms of Service' (current) <https://www.lindenlab.com/tos#tos2> (accessed 19 April 2019).

McCallig D, 'Data Protection and the Deceased in the EU' (24 January 2014), paper presented at the CPDP Conference, Brussels.

MacDonald C, 'Would YOU Resurrect Your Dead Friend as an AI? Try Out "Memorial" Chatbot App – And You Can Even Talk to a Virtual Version of Prince' (*Daily Mail*, 7 October 2016) <https://www.dailymail.co.uk/sciencetech/article-3826208/Would-resurrect-dead-friend-AI-Try-memorial-chatbot-app-talk-virtual-version-Prince.html> (accessed 19 April 2019).

Mazzone J, 'Facebook's Afterlife' (2012) 90 *North Carolina Law Review* 143.

Mill JS, *On Liberty*, Himmelfarb G (ed.) (Penguin 1984).

National Conference of Commissioners on Uniform State Laws, Drafting Committee on Fiduciary Access to Digital Assets, 'Fiduciary Access to Digital Assets Act' (July 2014) <www.uniformlaws.org/shared/docs/Fiduciary%20Access%20to%20Digital%20Assets/2014_UFADAA_Final.pdf> (accessed 19 April 2019).

National Conference of Commissioners on Uniform State Laws, Drafting Committee on Fiduciary Access to Digital Assets, 'Revised Fiduciary Access to Digital Assets Act' (December 2015) <www.uniformlaws.org/Act.aspx?title=Fiduciary%20Access%20to%20Digital%20Assets%20Act,%20Revised%20(2015)> (accessed 19 April 2019).

Newton C, 'Speak, Memory' (*The Verge*, 11 October 2016) <https://www.theverge.com/a/luka-artificial-intelligence-memorial-roman-mazurenko-bot> (accessed 19 April 2019).

Office of the Privacy Commissioner of Canada, 'Facebook Agrees to Address Privacy Commissioner's Concerns' (27 August 2009) <www.priv.gc.ca/media/nr-c/2009/nr-c_090827_e.asp> (accessed 19 April 2019).

Pass Notes, 'The Chatbot that Lets You Talk to the Dead' (11 October 2016) <https://www.theguardian.com/technology/shortcuts/2016/oct/11/chatbot-talk-to-dead-grief> (accessed 19 April 2019).

Price C and DiSclafani A, 'Remembering Our Loved Ones' (Facebook Newsroom, 21 February 2014) <http://newsroom.fb.com/news/2014/02/remembering-our-loved-ones/> (accessed 19 April 2019).

Schneewind JB, *The Invention of Autonomy: A History of Modern Moral Philosophy* (Cambridge University Press 1998).

Second Life Wiki, 'Linden Lab Official: Death and Other Worries outside Second Life' <http://wiki.secondlife.com/wiki/Linden_Lab_Official:Death_and_other_worries_outside_Second_Life> (accessed 19 April 2019).

Solove DJ, '"I've Got Nothing to Hide" and Other Misunderstandings of Privacy' (2007) 44 *San Diego Law Review* 745.

The Week, 'Digital Property: Can You Bequeath Your iTunes Library?' (31 January 2014) <https://www.theweek.co.uk/57155/digital-property-can-you-bequeath-your-itunes-library> (accessed 19 April 2019).

Twitter, 'Terms of Service' <https://twitter.com/en/tos> (accessed 19 April 2019).

Uniform Law Conference of Canada, Uniform Access to Digital Assets by Fiduciaries Act (2016) <https://www.ulcc.ca/images/stories/2016_pdf_en/2016ulcc0006.pdf> (accessed 19 April 2019).

US Copyright Office, 'Copyright Protection Not Available for Names, Titles, or Short Phrases' (2012) Circular 34 (<http://copyright.gov/circs/circ34.pdf>, last accessed 19 April 2019).

US Uniform Law Commission 2012 Annual Meeting in Nashville, Tennessee (13–19 July 2012) <http://uniformlaws.org/Narrative.aspx?title=QR%20Issue%2012%20%3E%20New%20Committees> (accessed 19 April 2019).

Van Camp J, 'My Jibo Is Dying and It's Breaking My Heart' (*Wired*, 8 March 2019) <https://www.wired.com/story/jibo-is-dying-eulogy/> (accessed 19 April 2019).

Yahoo!, 'Terms of Service' (discontinued) <http://info.yahoo.com/legal/uk/yahoo/utos-173.html> (accessed 15 June 2016).

PART III

Regulating Autonomous Technologies: Software Are Doing it for Themselves

10

Autonomous Intelligent Agents and the Roman Law of Slavery

Andrew Katz and Michaela MacDonald

1. Commerce and Machines

The ability to transact with machines has existed for over two thousand years: Hero of Alexandria invented a coin-operated holy water dispenser in the first century AD/CE.[1] As the capability of machines has increased over time, so has the complexity of human interactions with them. In a legal sense, transacting suggests that the action generates rights and obligations between parties. In an effort to produce a societally 'fair' result, the law has developed mechanisms to allow appropriate remedies when a party transacts with a machine.

The common law solution has traditionally been the notion of unilateral contract or standing offer. A unilateral contract can be formed when an *offer* is made, not to a specific individual, but to a class of people, or the world at large, and it remains open[2] until *accepted* by someone (acceptance is usually through conduct).

A vending machine operates on this mechanism. The seller uses the machine to offer a bottle of water for £1 and the purchaser accepts the offer by placing a pound coin in the slot and pressing the 'vend' button. The transaction cannot be revoked, once the buyer has inserted the money. If the machine fails to vend, the law provides that there is a breach of contract between the purchaser and the proprietor of the vending machine, and pro-

---

[1] Justin Pollard and Howard Reid, *The Rise and Fall of Alexandria: Birthplace of the Modern World* (Penguin Books 2009), pp. 181–2.

[2] Or is unambiguously withdrawn by the offeror prior to it being accepted. See *Carlill* v *Carbolic Smokeball Co* [1893] 1 QB 256 (an offer of reward could be seen as a unilateral contract).

vides remedies accordingly. Alternatively, the English courts have held that a parking ticket machine makes a standing offer capable of being accepted by users of the car park, with a binding contract formed when the ticket is accepted by the driver.[3]

Around two thousand years after Hero of Alexandria's death, a computer scientist and cryptographer, Nick Szabo, predicted how the rise of computer networks and algorithms would change the way in which contracts were made. He developed a concept of 'smart contracts', which minimise the human interaction with and automate the execution and performance of the contract by translating contractual obligations into computer code.[4] In this context, Szabo perceives the vending machine as an 'autonomous transfer of property'.[5]

From the perspective of contract law, the vending machine is not a party to the contract, nor is it a (human) agent acting on the seller's behalf. Rather, it is merely the parties' chosen method of making a contract. With the increasing sophistication and complexity of digital transactions, situations may arise where the intentions of the parties do not match the execution by automated and increasingly autonomous tools or 'agents' (software rather than human). The law will soon have to address any potential issues arising from these situations.

In cases of automated contracting, under current legal analyses, a contract is formed between two legal persons (natural or juristic). The automated mechanism is simply a tool. In such cases, the notion of unilateral contract has been so far sufficient to resolve questions of rights and obligations.

A core component in the formation of a legally binding contract under English law is, at least to the independent, objective observer, a meeting of minds (or *consensus in idem*). This is usually evidenced by a valid offer being made by one party that is unconditionally accepted by another. The rise of standard forms in consumer transactions, especially online, has challenged this notion of a meeting of minds.[6]

---

[3] *Thornton* v *Shoe Lane Parking* [1971] 2 WLR 585 (parking ticket machine regarded as making standing offer capable of acceptance when ticket is held out to driver)

[4] Nick Szabo defined a smart contract as 'a set of promises specified in digital form, including protocols within which the parties perform on these promises'. Szabo, 'Smart Contracts: Building Blocks for Digital Markets' (1996) <www.fon.hum.uva.nl/rob/Courses/ InformationInSpeech/CDROM/Literature/LOTwinterschool2006/szabo.best.vwh.net/ smart_contracts_2.html> (accessed 15 April 2019).

[5] Ibid.

[6] Click-wrap contracts will usually come up in a pop-up window and the user has to scroll down in order to manifest their consent by clicking 'OK' or 'I accept'. This type of interface has been accepted by the courts as adequate in establishing consent to all the terms

Introducing *autonomous intelligent agents* (AIAs) creates a new formation problem, akin to the one above. If electronic agents start to act autonomously, i.e. to make 'decisions' that go beyond or independently replace the intentions of the owner of the agent, it can be argued the meeting of human minds did not occur and instead the 'mind' of the agent was crucial to formation of the contract. The term *agent* can mean in the broadest sense 'anything that can be viewed as perceiving its environment through sensors and acting on that environment through actuators'.[7] The word used in the software sense (including embedded software, for example in robots or cars) should not be confused with the human agent, already well recognised in the law of principal and agent. AIAs will be defined here as capable of interacting with other software services, and initiating and completing certain tasks, without any direct input or supervision.[8] This definition can embrace a variety of entities (from web bots or software to programmed humanoid robots) and may, as we shall discuss below, utilise predetermined logic based on *rules*, and/or, increasingly, adaptive behaviour that resembles discretion and independent behaviour, based on machine-learning techniques.

Crucially, AIAs may form apparently binding contracts in ways their human owners did not anticipate or welcome – buying at too high or too low a price, transacting with the wrong type of counterparty (for example, someone to whom goods such as alcohol may not be sold because they are under age) or buying the wrong goods. This presents problems both for purchaser and vendor. This chapter identifies some of the ways in which this may occur, and proposes a possible means of addressing these issues, drawing on thinking that was already well developed by Roman jurists at the time of Hero of Alexandria.

governing the transaction. Browse-wrap terms and conditions will be typically available as a hyperlink at the bottom of the page. However, this interface does not require any affirmative action by the user prior to completing the transaction. As a result, it is not clear whether browse-wrap contracts bind end-users through enforceable terms and conditions. Jurisprudence on the enforceability of browse-wrap contracts: US – *Specht* v *Netscape Comm'ns Corp*, 306 F 3d 17 (2d Cir 2002), UK – *NLA* v *Meltwater* [2011] EWCA Civ 890 (the Court of Appeal deemed it unnecessary to rule on whether an internet user was bound by a website's terms and conditions of use of the content), EU – *Ryanair Ltd* v *PR Aviation BV*, Case C-30/14.

[7] Intelligent autonomous agents have existed for some time. Users and companies rely on intelligent agents to conduct online business on their behalf, while investment banks use intelligent systems for high-frequency stock trading. Stuart Russell and Peter Norvig, *Artificial Intelligence: A Modern Approach* (3rd edn, Pearson 2002).

[8] Chopra and White, *A Legal Theory for Autonomous Artificial Agents* (University of Michigan Press 2011), p. 21.

2. Introducing the Autonomous Intelligent Agent (AIA)

2.1 Single-target Agents

Computer software can be configured to interact with any user interface to capture data and manipulate applications just like humans do. These 'robots' can mimic most human actions, such as log into an application, copy and paste data or fill in a form. If the technology is designed to operate against a single website or a repository, we call it a single-target agent. It can be used as an efficient automation tool to deal with repetitive tasks and some platforms will welcome such interactions. Others will perceive it as a breach of their terms of use.[9]

A good example of such basic types of agent can be found in eBay 'bid-sniping' applications.[10] An eBay user (called a 'sniper') may sign up to a sniping service to try to gain an advantage over both other bidders, the seller of an item listed for auction on eBay, and, to a degree, eBay itself. The prospective sniper provides the sniping service with information as to what listed item they are interested in, how much they are prepared to pay for it, and with their eBay account details. The sniping service will then log into eBay as the user, monitor the progress of the auction for that item, and enter bids on behalf of the sniper at the last possible moment. This gives the sniper an advantage over other human bidders, because they are unable to respond as quickly. It also prevents eBay's automatic bidding algorithm from showing potential human bidders the true interest in a particular item, and thus thwarts both eBay's and the seller's desire to drive the price up. The decision-making abilities of the bid-sniping agent are fairly limited compared to the hypothetical AIA introduced above: it will simply follow a set of basic predefined rules as the bidding progresses.

---

[9] The most common authentication systems is CAPTCHA ('Completely Automated Process that can tell Computers and Humans Apart') that requires users to decode scrambled or distorted text to distinguish them from a malicious spam robot. An alternative to this device, more straightforward, accessible and effective, is called 'no CAPTCHA reCAPTCHA' and it simply asks 'are you a robot?'.

[10] eBay's rules prohibit the use of bid sniping but do not implement specific mechanisms to prevent them (some other auction sites discourage them by use of a mechanism that implements a short extension of the bidding period should a bid be placed just before the posted end of the auction). eBay's 'Terms' at https://www.ebay.co.uk/pages/help/policies/user-agreement.html (accessed 15 April 2019) state that it is prohibited to 'use any robot, spider, scraper or other automated means to access our Services for any purpose'. However, the eBay 'Help' system states: 'Bid sniping – including the use of software that places bids for you – is allowed on eBay', at <https://www.ebay.com/help/buying/auctions-bidding/bid-sniping?id=4224> (accessed 15 April 2019).

Because the sniping service must have access to the user's account through username and password, the user is taking a significant risk in providing those credentials to the sniping service. If the agent malfunctions, either maliciously, or because of a bug (bidding beyond the amount set by its user, or bidding for items other than the one requested), the user will be liable. All the bidding activity has happened on the user's account, under the user's credentials and instructions, and since the user cannot legitimately claim the bids were placed using stolen credentials, eBay will likely hold the user liable for any errant activity of the sniping application.

2.2 Multiple-target Agents – The Walled Garden

The benefits of single-target agents are limited as opposed to multi-target agents that can deal with multiple counterparties at once. A multiple-target agent is an agent that is, in its most basic form, designed to interact with more than one platform or site. For instance, if the agent has been instructed by its owner to purchase a first-edition copy of *Infinite Jest* for $100, rather than just looking at eBay, it may scan a number of different websites (for example, eBay, Amazon, BookFinder) for a copy and then purchase the cheapest. However, this would require the user to have formed a contractual relationship with each of the websites concerned, and to have conveyed those credentials to the agent. As with the eBay bid-sniping service, any mistakes made by the agent – such as the system buying a copy at too high a price – would still be the responsibility of the user. The user will have to register with, and obtain appropriate credentials across, a number of different sites. Another problem might be that the terms of service of the various sites are incompatible (for example, each may demand as a condition of access that the user does not contract with any other site).

A better approach might be a system where a number of sites decide between themselves that allowing automated agents to transact with them is beneficial, and accordingly present an application programming interface (API) to each agent to facilitate access. Allowing software-based agents to transact simultaneously with multiple platforms would increase efficiency and reduce barriers in the marketplace. Through a single API and on-boarding process, participants would be able to sign up to an overarching framework, outlining rules for accessing the APIs, handling transactions or allocating liability if a transaction fails, or fails to be honoured. This reduces work for participants, who only have to go through one on-boarding process. It does mean however that a software interface has to be designed carefully so that all agents can interact with the one unified specification for an API.

We call this unified approach the 'walled garden': in order to play in the garden, each participant will go through a validation process that will verify their identity, solvency and their qualifications to trade, and also require them to enter into the framework agreement. Any subsequent issues arising out of transactions between the members will be dealt with according to the overarching framework agreement.

Structures like this are becoming increasingly common in a number of fields from energy trading[11] to financial transactions.[12] A significant aspect of the multi-target agent is that it is potentially able to deal with two sites, or their agents, at the same time, thus effectively allowing arbitrage. The agent can be instructed to monitor the pricing differential between commodities in a commodity exchange and see what differentials it can exploit. As a result, it may buy two thousand barrels of pork bellies from network participant X at $1,300,000 and immediately resell them for $1,350,000 to another network participant Y. However, note that the agent would still not be acting as an 'agent' in the legal sense, with a breadth of discretion and autonomy, in that it is merely generating messages (for example, through the SWIFT system) that have the effect of triggering buy and sell orders within the framework agreement. It is arguably not yet an AIA, merely a software tool.

The application of machine learning to stock trading was posited and analysed as early as 1975.[13] Automated share trading systems initially relied on criteria such as price targets and stop-loss thresholds, but over time, the sophistication of the trading algorithms has increased, and machine-learning technology has become prevalent.[14] When financial AIAs participate in arbitrage, they monitor data on sale and purchase prices, and execute transactions (again, by sending buy or sell messages within the framework established by the walled garden participants) where they can make a profit or minimise a loss on a position already taken. These algorithms can be rule-based, but the availability of software such as TensorFlow[15] under free and open source software licences, has facilitated the development of complex agents using

---

[11] Engerati is Europe's largest community of utilities and power sector professionals. Access more information here <https://www.engerati.com> (accessed 15 April 2019).

[12] The SWIFT network provides secure financial messaging services. Access more information here <https://www.swift.com/> (accessed 15 April 2019).

[13] Jerry Felsen, 'Artificial Intelligence Techniques Applied to Reduction of Uncertainty in Decision Analysis through Learning' (1970–7), 26 *Operational Research Quarterly*, Part 2 (October 1975).

[14] Laura Cardella, Jia Hao, Ivalina Kalcheva and Yung-Yu Ma, Computerization of the Equity, Foreign Exchange, Derivatives and Fixed-Income Markets (2014) 49 *Financial Review* 231.

[15] TensorFlow is an open source software library for numerical computation using data flow graphs. Access more information at <https://github.com/tensorflow/tensorflow> (accessed 15 April 2019).

neural network architectures that adapt and learn from the patterns of data in the environment in which they operate. Such AI-based agents approach the concept of the AIA introduced above.

The 'walled garden' approach is superior to the single-target approach but still creates friction for new entrants to the market.[16] The requirement to enter into a framework agreement creates a barrier to entry, which has the effect of disincentivising or even preventing potential entrants from joining. Furthermore, it is not always the case that a single entity can simultaneously comply with the terms of two different trading structures and create a bridge between two different networks. As a result, those networks will remain separate and unable to combine into a single virtual network. These factors together reduce the efficiency of the market as a whole. Network effects are powerful. The value and efficiency of the market increases as the number of users increases, because the potential links increase for every user as a new person joins.[17] From a purely economic perspective, it is desirable that AIAs have a greater degree of freedom, and therefore a greater choice of counterparties with whom to transact, and wider scope to negotiate the terms of the contract (other than price) on which they are prepared to transact.

Compare offline transacting. A person can walk into a shop and immediately purchase a washing machine, with neither party having a pre-existing contractual relationship. General contract and property laws create a framework for title in the washing machine to pass to the customer, for money to pass to the shop, and for the shop to accept contractual liability for any defects in the machine. It is possible to imagine that the law could establish a general structure to enable AIAs to transact with each other in a similarly friction-free way, while balancing the advantages and flexibility of AIAs with reducing and predicting potential liability that may arise should any transaction go wrong.

---

[16] Some markets do allow the possibility that external parties can participate by using an existing member to contract on their behalf, such as a prime broker in a foreign exchange transaction. However, this does not affect the argument that additional steps are required to participate in the market, even if that participation is indirect, through an intermediary, as opposed to direct, as a market participant.

[17] The network effect describes the value of a service to a user that arises from the number of people using the service. Metcalfe's Law states that the value of a telecommunications network is proportional to the square of the number of connected users of the system. James Hendler and Jennifer Golbeck, 'Metcalfe's Law, Web 2.0, and the Semantic Web' (2008) *Journal of Web Semantics* <https://www.researchgate.net/journal/1570-8268_Journal_of_Web_Semantics> (accessed 19 April 2019).

3. Leaving the Walled Garden

Providing the AIAs with an opportunity to transact with each other and third parties, without a pre-existing contractual relationship, means that there needs to be a general legal framework in place that will allocate rights and responsibilities among the participants. In other words, a pre-existing legal agreement with each contracting target should not be necessary. This would facilitate the ease of transactions, but at the same time the selling platform (or other counterparty) must be given sufficient legal certainty that the risk of transactions failing is predictable, and can be minimised or avoided.

If we posit that such a legal framework is desirable, then what rights and obligations should fall on AIAs? How should a general legal framework for such transactions be designed? One approach is to work from the known legal institution of agency, treating AIAs like human or juristic agents. This raises considerable issues. How would the law deal with the enforcement of rights and obligations where the owner of the AIA ('principal') was not bound, and who should be liable for any damage caused by the AIA? The 'owner' of the AIA ought to be strictly liable for any damage it causes, and to be strictly bound to any obligations it enters into without exception. The European Parliament's Legal Affairs Committee has already suggested that strict liability in tort may be the appropriate standard to impose on an owner or operator when damage is caused by robots such as software bots or autonomous cars.[18]

Where a single agent is controlled by one legal entity (the 'owner' or principal) and designed to operate within a simple set of rule-based constraints producing foreseeable results, the rule that the principal is strictly responsible for all the agent's actions, tortious, criminal or contractual, may function well. However, with increasing complexity, the strict liability prin-

---

[18] European Parliament, Committee on Legal Affairs, 'Report with Recommendations to the Commission on Civil Law Rules on Robotics' (2015/2103(INL)) <www. europarl.europa.eu/ sides/getDoc.do?pubRef=-//EP//TEXT+REPORT+A8- 2017-0005+0+DOC+XML+V0// EN> (accessed 19 April 2019). The strict liability rule could be developed based on the analogy with liability for animals. There is potential for a more in-depth comparative analysis here, starting with Roman law, and the old common law concepts of liability for wild animals and domestic animals. Wild animals were presumed to be dangerous, but the keeper of a domesticated animal was only liable for damage the animal caused if the keeper knew or should have known that it was vicious. See generally Rachel Mulheron, *Principles of Tort Law* (Cambridge University Press 2016). Note, however, that while animals may cause damage or even death, they cannot enter (or seem to enter) contracts, so the analogy to AIAs relates only to tort and criminal law, not contract. Further analysis is outside the scope of this chapter.

ciple may produce undue risk for the owner of the agent. As agents become more complex and less constrained, move across multiple sites, and begin to collaborate and trade directly with each other (or in opposition to each other), more nuanced rules will arguably be required.

For example, imagine that the eBay sniping service agent discussed above starts vastly overpaying for items because an automated 'war' has broken out between competing agents bidding against each other and, unknown to their owners, driving prices up. This scenario has already been observed on Amazon, where competing bots have been found bidding up unexceptional second-hand books to ridiculous prices.[19] (Similar feedback loops have been implicated in stock market crashes deriving from high-frequency algorithm trading.) Should the vendor of the item be able to claim the inflated price from the owner of the agent (or 'principal') under the strict liability rule? Or should the principal be able to evade responsibility, because the vendor should have been aware that the agent was acting outside the scope of its authority (or outside its usual functional parameters)? What duties, if any, does the vendor have to ascertain that the contract made was within the instructions issued by the 'principal'?[20]

If bid-sniping software allows a mechanism to exist whereby two competing owners of agents bidding on the same item can agree between them as to who will snipe; does that count as criminal bid rigging?[21] Would such users be potentially liable if the designers of the sniping software implemented a

---

[19] Olivia Solon, 'How a Book about Flies Came to be Priced $24 Million on Amazon,' *Wired* (27 April 2011) <https://www.wired.com/2011/04/amazon-flies-24-million/> (accessed 15 April 2019).

[20] Presumably, under English law, if the winning bidder turns out to be a minor purchasing an unnecessarily large number of fancy waistcoats, then he or she will not be bound (*Nash* v *Inman* 1908 2 KB 1, CA). This might place a significant burden on the vendor to perform due diligence on the purchaser if the contract is not to be risky and potentially void. This matter has already been raised in relation to purchases made by children of virtual assets on game sites using parental credit cards, though principally as a consumer protection, not a pure contract matter: For example, Andy Robertson, 'UK Gov Obliges Developers to Meet New In-App Purchase Principles,' *Forbes* (30 January 2014) <https://www.forbes.com/sites/andyrobertson/2014/01/30/uk-government-oft-in-app-purchases/#42e8c64a55db> (accessed 15 April 2019), reporting on the then-OFT's issued guidelines 'Principles For Online and App-based Games' (now archived). More recently it has been suggested that FB algorithms might have been set intentionally to manipulate children into buying online assets: see Nathan Halverson, 'Facebook Knowingly Duped Game-playing Kids and their Parents out of Money,' *Reveal* (24 January 2019) <https://www.revealnews.org/article/facebook-knowingly-duped-game-playing-kids-and-their-parents-out-of-money/> (accessed 19 April 2019).

[21] Section 188(5), Enterprise Act 2002.

mechanism to rig bids by favouring one user over another without the users being aware of it? Would the designers be responsible? Would the users be potentially liable if the agents acquired such a strategy independently themselves using AI techniques?[22] Consumer law might have something to say about this – unfair commercial practices might be relevant, for example – but complex, multi-agent scenarios are as likely to arise in B2B as in B2C situations, perhaps more so. Competition law might conceivably also be implicated.

These questions will become increasingly complex. It is not impossible to imagine a scenario where an arbitrarily large number of agents is involved in what could be seen externally as a relatively simple transaction between two individuals.[23] Agents will not necessarily be bound to either of the two parties by direct contractual links and their 'owners' may not be identifiable. Failing contract, some form of tortious liability based on strict liability or negligence will be the only option for regulating the transaction, and this is likely to become rapidly unworkable. Despite being over two thousand years old, a model based on the Roman law concept of the *peculium* may provide a solution to this problem, at least to the extent that it relates to contractual and quasi-contractual rights and obligations.

4. The Electronic Slave Metaphor

As we have discussed, high-complexity AIAs begin to operate outside closed walled gardens, questions of liability and terms of transaction become problematic. Framework agreements may be an improvement on basic single-site contractual terms of service but they still present barriers to new entrants, and restrict the expansion of the market for AIAs. The existing law of agency

---

[22] Algorithms used by insurance companies, such as Sheila's Wheels, have determined that female drivers present a lower risk than male drivers and have been offering lower premiums as a result. However, such algorithmic determination has been found to be contrary to anti-discrimination law, as stated in 'Taking the gender of the insured individual into account as a risk factor in insurance contracts constitutes discrimination', Court of Justice of the European Union (Luxembourg, 1 March 2011) <https://curia.europa.eu/jcms/upload/docs/application/pdf/2011-03/cp110012en.pdf> (accessed 19 April 2019). There are also examples of algorithms becoming racist, as reported by James Vincent: 'Google ' "Fixed" "Fixed" its Racist Algorithm by Removing Gorillas from its Image-labeling Tech,' *The Verge* (12 January 2018) <https://www.theverge.com/2018/1/12/16882408/google-racist-gorillas-photo-recognition-algorithm-ai> (accessed 19 April 2019).

[23] One could imagine a system of mobile communications where the cost of transfer of each individual packet between endpoints and nodes is negotiated by intelligent agents transacting with each other to offer capacity at the best price, taking into account latency, resilience and so-on. In this way, a single phone call could, transparently to the user, involve a myriad of interactions involving intelligent agents.

presents one model for regulating agents operating outside the 'walled garden', but transposing it to AIAs presents many problems. Strictly binding the owner of the agent to all transactions entered may also not always be desirable, especially in the case of AIAs that learn and exhibit a facsimile of discretion, and in adversarial environments.

Pagallo summarises three possible approaches to regulating AIAs.[24] The first approach is that AIAs are allowed to acquire legal personality *sui generis*, complete with rights, responsibilities and protection against harm provoked by others, such as the state, contractual counterparties and third parties in tort law. Thus an AIA with full legal personality would be able to be sued (and theoretically to sue) in its own name by any third party with whom it interacts or who confers rights upon it, akin to a limited company. The second option recognises AIAs as strict agents in the commercial and legal sense, for example, for the purpose of negotiations and contracts. This means that the agent would have a subset of rights granted in the 'full personality' scenario. Thus their actions would render their principal liable in the legal sense, without there being a pre-existing relationship between the principal and counterparty in which to frame the relationship. It would mean that the authority of the AIA was limited to the authority granted to it by the principal (subject potentially to rules relating to ostensible authority). In the final and most traditional viewpoint, AIAs are simple tools, not agents or legal persons, and as such do not affect the basic cornerstones of the law. They can only represent a source of responsibility for other entities in the system.[25]

Legislators have started to address some of these issues, and are already taking their first steps towards regulating robotics and AI.[26] The European Parliament's Legal Affairs Committee has commissioned a study to evaluate and analyse, from a legal and ethical perspective, a number of civil law rules in robotics. The resulting Report[27] recommends that EU lawmakers develop a series of general principles governing *inter alia* liability, transparency and accountability of future initiatives on robotics and AI. In particular, it points

---

[24] Ugo Pagallo, *The Law of Robots: Crimes, Contracts, and Torts* (Springer 2013).

[25] Ibid.

[26] For instance, in the US the bulk of regulatory activities and court decisions is focused on two specific technologies: drones, and more recently, autonomous vehicles. The Japanese government devised a series of policies for regulating robotics called 'Japan's Robot Strategy' and introduced a Robot Revolution Initiative -(RRI) in 2015.

[27] See European Parliament, Committee on Legal Affairs, 'Report with Recommendations to the Commission on Civil Law Rules on Robotics' (2015/2103(INL)) <www.europarl. europa.eu/sides/getDoc.do?pubRef=-//EP//TEXT+REPORT+A8-2017-0005+0+DOC+X ML+V0//EN> (accessed 19 April 2019).

out that the current framework of contractual liability has clear shortcomings and does not address transactions where machines 'choose their counterparts, negotiate contractual terms, conclude contracts and decide whether and how to implement them'.[28] The Report also considers potential legislative instruments applicable to civil liability, ranging from a strict liability regime, an obligatory insurance scheme supplemented by a compensation fund and, in the long run, creating a specific legal status for robots – an electronic persona.[29]

However, we suggest a fourth option (or perhaps a variation on Pagallo's second option): a system based on Roman law where the owner or operator of an agent need not have entered into a framework agreement with the network(s) with which it wants to transact, but the participant can still determine at the point of potential contracting whether it is prepared to transact with the agent, and on what terms; and the owner of the agent can also restrict their potential liability.

Why Roman law? The problem of intermediaries that are not legal persons but are involved in commercial transactions is not new. The Romans had to address similar issues in the context of slavery law. Ancient Rome had a complex and vibrant economy. Slaves carried out the bulk of trade and commerce. Kerr points out that '[like] autonomous electronic devices, Roman slaves possessed valuable skills and could independently perform various important commercial tasks upon command. Still, Roman slaves were not recognized as legal persons according to the *ius civile*.'[30]

Under Roman law, slaves lacked legal personality and therefore had no corresponding rights or responsibilities, could not own property, sue or be sued. Yet they were not treated merely as chattels either. Educated slaves were entrusted with many aspects of their masters' affairs, and the record shows slaves acting as shopkeepers, merchants, bankers and estate managers. Acting on his master's behalf, a slave could enter into a contract and thereby bind a third party. The concept of agency (albeit relatively basic in comparison with modern use) was an essential part of the social and legal structure, and allowed slave-run commerce to prosper.[31]

Instead of attributing full legal personality to AIAs, or imposing strict liability on those who own or operate them, Kerr's electronic slave metaphor offers an alternative way forward.

---

[28] Ibid., s AG.

[29] Ibid., s 59.

[30] Ian R Kerr, 'Spirits in the Materials World: Intelligent Agents as Intermediaries in Electronic Commerce' (1999) 22 *Dalhousie Law Journal* 189.

[31] WW Buckland, *The Roman Law of Slavery: The Conditions of the Slave in Private Law from Augustus to Justinian* (AMS Press 1962), pp. 2–5.

5. Digital *Peculium*

An intriguing mechanism that made it possible for slaves to transact on behalf on their masters was the *peculium*.[32] The term refers to a bundle of assets allocated to slaves so that they could carry out specific activities on behalf of their master. This was not limited to money: it could include any form of property, such as other slaves (who could even hold their own *peculia*). Katz has described the concept of the digital peculium in his early 2008 article 'Intelligent Agents and Internet Commerce in Ancient Rome',[33] and this model has subsequently been adopted and expanded by a number of authors, most notably by Pagallo in his work 'Killers, Fridges, and Slaves: A Legal Journey in Robotics'.[34] Indeed, the European Parliament has adopted a variant of it in their Report on Robotics.[35]

The *peculium* was in many ways equivalent to the modern concept of working capital, and its existence was critical to the development of Roman commerce. As well as providing a mechanism to balance risk between the master (as 'investor') and the slave/business's customers and counterparties, it also provided for legal certainty in determining the rights and liabilities of those customers and counterparties on one hand, and the slave/business on the other. In principle, transacting with a slave meant that the other party accepted a significant risk. Since the slave lacked legal personality, without some further mechanism, the contracting party would not be able to enforce a contract against the slave (or his owner): a clear barrier to the growth of commerce. Accordingly, the Romans developed a rule allowing a contracting party to enforce judgments not against the slave, but against the *peculium*. This mechanism enabled the use of slaves as agents, because the owner's liability was limited to the value of the *peculium*, and it encouraged people to transact with slaves because of the security the *peculium* provided.

By analogy, the *digital peculium* is a special set of rules that would define the parameters of liability for AIAs in the context of commercial transactions. An AIA would be allocated a bundle of assets that would act both to provide

---

[32] Although the *peculium* was a Roman law construct, its use was not limited to Roman law. In his book *Southern Slavery and the Law 1619–1860* (University of South Carolina Press 2004), Thomas Morris explains that the Louisiana Civil Code allowed for a *peculium*. However, South Carolina did recognize the ability of a slave to hold personal property.

[33] See Andrew Katz, 'Intelligent Agents and Internet Commerce in Ancient Rome' (2008) Society for Computers and the Law <https://www.scl.org/articles/1095-intelligent-agents-and-internet-commerce-in-ancient-rome> (accessed 19 April 2019).

[34] See Ugo Pagallo, 'Killers, Fridges, and Slaves: A Legal Journey in Robotics' (2011) 26 *AI & Society* <https://doi.org/10.1007/s00146-010-0316-0> (accessed 19 April 2019).

[35] See above, note 27.

a fund to cover potential liability, and also to limit the ultimate liability of the agent's 'owner'. This would encourage a market using AIAs to develop. The proposal strikes a balance between the potential risks on both the supply and demand side, without pre-emptively suggesting where that balance should be struck.

The analogy with slaves only goes so far. AIAs are able to replicate themselves much more rapidly than slaves (with gestation measured in microseconds, not trimesters), and can transact many orders of magnitude more rapidly than human slaves. A key point is that information asymmetry can be reduced in the modern context of AIAs entering and initiating transactions. One of the problems with the Roman *peculium* was that a transacting party had relatively little knowledge about the extent of it, or about any prior debts attaching to it. By contrast, transactions involving AIAs, whether agent–agent or agent–human, can conceivably be entered into with much greater information about the transaction history of the agent and the currently outstanding potential liabilities against the peculium. Such information might be accessed mid-transaction from secure, assured and fraud-proof databases, using technologies such as cryptography and distributed ledgers (the 'blockchain'), even in the case of almost instantaneous high-frequency transactions.

This scenario is rather like the economic fantasy of perfect information leading to a perfectly efficient market. Parties transacting with AIAs might be able to consider the risk profile of each contract in very fine detail. The balance of risk between purchaser and vender can emerge as a function of the market. This dynamic contrasts with some other proposals that have been put forward for managing the legal context for AIAs – such as strict liability or the walled garden approach.

By contrast, the Romans knew rather more about *who* they were transacting with than we do today online. An individual's status (whether slave or free, Roman or foreign, family or independent)[36] was a matter of public knowledge. Compare with the Internet, where famously, 'no one knows you are a dog'.[37] Similarly, eBay does not necessarily know whether a user is a

---

[36] These were the three main incidents of status. Most free men (and, under analogous rules, taking account of marriage, women) were under the power (*patria potestas*) of their oldest male ancestor. The status of those *in patria potestas* was surprisingly similar to slavery: for example, a son under the control of his *paterfamilias* could be granted a *peculium*, as he was incapable of holding property himself. In early Rome, the *paterfamilias* even had the power of life and death over his offspring, although this right was tempered in later years.

[37] Peter Steiner, 'On the Internet, Nobody Knows You're a Dog', cartoon in *The New Yorker*, 5 July 1993.

human or a bid-sniping agent. Accordingly, any scheme attributing liability to an agent will require some mechanism to evidence and confirm the identity of the agent (and behind it, the provider of the *peculium.*).

We propose a system in which the identity of each AIA is authenticated by reference to a certificate, for example using public key infrastructure (PKI). The authentication mechanism could be centralised, or could use a decentralised blockchain ledger. Platforms such as eBay would be free to prohibit interaction with any agent that failed to present appropriate credentials.[38] It would not be obligatory to sign up to such a scheme, but failure to do so would render the 'owner' of the AIA strictly liable for any actions of that agent. The trust system would also hold the following information about any agent: (1) details of its owner, (2) details of the size of its *peculium* and (3) details of any contingent liabilities.

A financial institution, such as an insurance company, the details of which would be also held by the trust provider, would back the *peculium.* Essentially, a database would have to be dynamically updated each time a transaction was completed, with an agreed maximum exposure negotiated as part of the transaction. As with the authentication information referred to above, a centralised database could be one mechanism for storing and giving access to the relevant information. However, a distributed ledger technology such as the blockchain might provide a number of advantages over a centralised database, not least that its decentralised nature removes a potential single point of failure from the system and that in a trustless environment between strangers, information is tamper-proof.

It is also worth noting that it is likely that there would need to be exceptions to the privilege of limited liability. The obvious ones would be in the case of fraud, or the supply of dangerous goods that could cause death or personal injury.

This system does require an infrastructure with both technical and legislative components, but it is significantly simpler than the 'walled garden' approach, and gives any contracting party the comfort that the transaction

---

[38] Unauthorised access to a computer system is a criminal offence under the Computer Misuse Act 1990. Part 5 of the Criminal Justice Act s 36 made it a crime to impair the functioning of a computer system, which would include a denial of service attack. Although intentional triggering of a (D)DOS attack is caught by this section (as intended), it is easy to imagine a scenario in which a bot, failing to authenticate to a particular API, repeatedly and rapidly attempts to reconnect to a particular service, this causing, in effect, a DOS attack. Further, if the AI instructing it correlates the DOS attack with improved performance of other parameters (for example, it may have inadvertently knocked out a competitor), then it may 'deliberately' employ that DOS attack in the future. *Mens rea* cannot be imputed to bots.

is secure to the extent of the un-earmarked *peculium* (and in the case of an agent–agent transaction, the *peculia* on each side).

6. Conclusion

The sheer variety of forms and applications of artificial intelligence raises a number of issues and challenges for the current legal framework, including contract, tort, privacy and constitutional law. In order to adopt laws and regulations concerning robotics and AI, it is essential that we develop an understanding of these emergent technologies. In particular, policy- and lawmakers need to anticipate and provide societally acceptable solutions for potential issues and legal frameworks for the development of desirable norms.

In the context of the commercial environment, introducing AIAs creates new problems for contracting. In this new type of relationship, parties grant authority for an AIA to act on their behalf in dealings with third parties. From a legal perspective, AIAs remain *things*, but with significant autonomy. As such, they resemble agents in the strict commercial sense.

In the environment of a 'walled garden', any difficulties arising from the negotiation, formation and conclusion of contract by AIAs and the resulting rights and obligations are resoluble by the framework agreement. Leaving the walled garden means that identifying the 'owner' of an agent and determining the rights and obligations of the parties may be impractical or at least very difficult.

The chapter explored a model that would reduce friction, uncertainty and risk for parties contracting with, or via, an AIA. The mechanism proposed envisages circumstances in which an AIA can easily conclude binding contracts with third parties, even where there is no pre-existing relationship embodied in a site's terms of service or a multi-site framework agreement. We advocated for an approach based on the *digital peculium*, inspired by the Roman law of slavery. It provides a pertinent framework for the inevitable development and deployment of AIAs. It is a mechanism that balances the rights and obligations of the 'owner' of the agent, with those of the transacting parties (human, corporate or, themselves, an AIA), while at the same time providing legal certainty to all parties. The use of technology addresses one of the fundamental issues with the Roman implementation: how a transacting party can have sufficient reliable knowledge about the extent of, and the liabilities attaching to the *peculium*. An authentication model, based on cryptographic technologies such as PKI or blockchain, should allow for identification of an AIA, even if it is replicated across sites through multiple instances.

This approach notably provides the lightest touch of regulation; allows the market to set prices for risk, and renders that risk transparent, making mitigation accessible for traders; and at the same time encourages the use of AIAs by allowing their owners to shelter behind the privilege of limited liability. The past still has a great deal to teach us about the future.

References

Buckland WW, *The Roman Law of Slavery: The Conditions of the Slave in Private Law from Augustus to Justinian* (first published in 1908: AMS Press 1962).

Cardella L, Hao J, Kalcheva I and Ma Y, 'Computerization of the Equity, Foreign Exchange, Derivatives and Fixed-Income Markets' (2014) 49 *Financial Review* 231.

Chopra S and White LF, *A Legal Theory for Autonomous Artificial Agents* (University of Michigan Press 2011).

eBay, 'Help' <https://www.ebay.com/help/buying/auctions-bidding/bid-sniping?id=4224> (accessed 15 April 2019).

eBay, 'Terms' <https://www.ebay.co.uk/pages/help/policies/user-agreement.html> (accessed 15 April 2019).

European Parliament, Committee on Legal Affairs, 'Report with Recommendations to the Commission on Civil Law Rules on Robotics' (2015/2103(INL)) <www.europarl.europa.eu/sides/getDoc.do?pubRef=-//EP//TEXT+REPORT+A8-2017-0005+0+DOC+XML+V0//EN> (accessed 19 April 2019).

Felsen J, 'Artificial Intelligence Techniques Applied to Reduction of Uncertainty in Decision Analysis through Learning' (1970–7), 26 *Operational Research Quarterly*, Part 2 (October 1975).

Halverson N, 'Facebook Knowingly Duped Game-playing Kids and their Parents out of Money,' *Reveal* (24 January 2019) <https://www.revealnews.org/article/facebook-knowingly-duped-game-playing-kids-and-their-parents-out-of-money/> (accessed 19 April 2019).

Hendler J and Golbeck J, 'Metcalfe's Law, Web 2.0, and the Semantic Web' (2008) *Journal of Web Semantics* <https://www.researchgate.net/journal/1570-8268_Journal_of_Web_Semantics> (accessed 19 April 2019).

Katz A, 'Intelligent Agents and Internet Commerce in Ancient Rome' (2008) Society for Computers and the Law <https://www.scl.org/articles/1095-intelligent-agents-and-internet-commerce-in-ancient-rome> (accessed 19 April 2019).

Kerr IR, 'Spirits in the Materials World: Intelligent Agents as Intermediaries in Electronic Commerce' (1999) 22 *Dalhousie Law Journal* 189.

Morris T, *Southern Slavery and the Law 1619–1860* (University of South Carolina Press 2004).

Mulheron R, *Principles of Tort Law* (Cambridge University Press 2016).

Pagallo U, 'Killers, Fridges, and Slaves: A Legal Journey in Robotics' (2011) 26 *AI & Society* <https://doi.org/10.1007/s00146-010-0316-0> (accessed 19 April 2019).

Pagallo U, *The Law of Robots: Crimes, Contracts, and Torts* (Springer 2013).

Pollard J and Reid H, *The Rise and Fall of Alexandria: Birthplace of the Modern World* (Penguin Books 2009).

Robertson A, 'UK Gov Obliges Developers to Meet New In-App Purchase Principles,' *Forbes* (30 January 2014) <https://www.forbes.com/sites/andyrob

ertson/2014/01/30/uk-government-oft-in-app-purchases/#42e8c64a55db> (accessed 15 April 2019).

Russell S and Norvig P, *Artificial Intelligence: A Modern Approach* (3rd edn, Pearson 2002).

Solon O, 'How a Book about Flies Came to be Priced $24 Million on Amazon,' *Wired* (27 April 2011) <https://www.wired.com/2011/04/amazon-flies-24-million/> (accessed 15 April 2019).

Szabo N, 'Smart Contracts: Building Blocks for Digital Markets' (1996) <http://www.alamut.com/subj/economics/nick_szabo/smartContracts.html>

Vincent J, 'Google "Fixed" its Racist Algorithm by Removing Gorillas from its Image-labeling Tech,' *The Verge* (12 January 2018) <https://www.theverge.com/2018/1/12/16882408/google-racist-gorillas-photo-recognition-algorithm-ai> (accessed 19 April 2019).

11

Autonomous Vehicles: An Analysis of the Regulatory and Legal Landscape

Catherine Easton

1. Introduction

Autonomous vehicle technology has developed to the point where manufacturers now predict that fully autonomous personal vehicles will become commercially available within the next five years.[1] Its implementation has become a policy priority, with the European Commission, for example, outlining its potential to enhance 'safety and quality of life; to boost innovation, jobs, and competitiveness; and to maximise the benefits for citizens' mobility on a European scale'.[2]

The development of autonomous vehicle technology has led to ongoing collaborations between online technology companies, such as Google, and the traditional car industry.[3] NavLab, the Robotics Institute at Carnegie Mellon University in the USA, was one of the first research groups to develop fully autonomous vehicles. The institution recently teamed up with Uber to launch self-driving cars in Pittsburgh and San Francisco.[4] Also in the USA, the Google Self-Driving Car Project has been at the forefront of testing on

---

[1] Herrmann, Brenner and Stadler, *Autonomous Driving: How the Driverless Revolution will Change the World Bingley* (Emerald Publishing 2018), p. 86.

[2] European Commission, 'Europe on the Move: Sustainable Mobility for Europe: Safe, Connected, and Clean' (2018) Communication from the Commission to the European Parliament, the Council, the European Economic and Social Committee and the Committee of the Region, COM/2018/293 final.

[3] Favarò, Eurich and Nader, 'Autonomous Vehicles' Disengagements: Trends, Triggers, and Regulatory Limitations' (2017) 110 *Journal of Accident Analysis Prevention* 136.

[4] DeBord, 'Uber Did Everything Right in Pittsburgh with its Self-driving cars – But Is Doing Everything Wrong in San Francisco' (*Business Insider*, December 2016) <http://

313

public roads. Their vehicles have covered more than ten million miles, most of which have been in an urban environment. They equate this to over three hundred years of human driving experience.[5] In the UK, trials are ongoing in Milton Keynes and Greenwich,[6] with collaborative projects such as HumanDrive[7] aiming to complete journeys of over two hundred miles on UK roads by December 2019.

This chapter aims to evaluate how the law interacts with this technology, highlighting regulatory trends and making future predictions. From this analysis, the areas of safety, data protection, access for disabled people and the development of trust have been chosen for closer treatment. The overarching aim of this piece is to highlight key aspects of autonomous personal transport that need to be taken into account while regulating in a manner that does not hinder technological development. This analysis aims to have international reach, as it examines changes made to international legal instruments and subsequently draws out themes from legal and regulatory responses made by the USA, the EU and the UK.

2. Defining Autonomous Transport

While technology can make a vehicle capable of acting autonomously, the legal and regulatory framework dictates whether or not human control is required and, in this way, can limit its potentially autonomous nature. The notion of 'driving', particularly in relation to risk, has long been the subject of human–computer interaction research. Writing in 1994, Ranney[8] highlights the difficulties of developing an all-encompassing model of driving behaviour, due to the wide range and the unpredictability of driving situations and the skills needed to address them. The functions behind 'driving' as a whole can be broken down into control/operational (for example, breaking and steering), guidance/tactical (for example, navigating curves and entering traffic flow) and navigation/strategic (for example, trip and route planning).[9] These can involve differing levels of automation in the

---

uk.businessinsider.com/uber-doing-everything-wrong-in-san-francisco-self-driving-2016-12?r=US&IR=T> (accessed 15 April 2019).

5 Available at: <https://waymo.com/ontheroad/> (accessed 13 April 2019).

6 Taylor and Maynard, 'Self-driving Cars' (2015) 21 *Computer and Technology Law Review*, pp. 133–4.

7 Available at: <https://humandrive.co.uk/> (accessed 13 April 2019).

8 Ranney, 'Models of Driving Behavior: A Review of Their Evolution' (1994) 26 *Accident Analysis and Prevention* 733, pp. 741–3.

9 Wang, Hou, Tan and Bubb, 'A Framework for Function Allocations in Intelligent Driver Interface Design for Comfort and Safety' (2010) 3 *International Journal of Computational Intelligence Systems* 531, pp. 531–6.

interaction between the human and machine and, in turn, differing levels of human-directed control.

In pursuit of a purely technical definition of driving automation, the USA's National Traffic Highway Safety Administration has developed a five-point scale (from levels 0–4). Level 4 relates to full self-driving automation, in which the all safety-related functions will be carried out by the vehicle's system for the duration of the journey, including responses to changing conditions. At this level, while a human will be asked to provide necessary information on the required destination, he or she will not be called upon to control the vehicle at any time. These classifications prove a useful simplification to regulators and lawmakers trying to shape the environment to support the technology. However, while full Level 4 autonomy is currently technically achievable, it will not become an everyday reality if the legal framework mandates the need for some form of overriding control.

The nature of this technology also has the potential to revolutionise the concept of car ownership itself. Level 4 autonomous functionality will bring the opportunity for consumers to purchase what the European Commission has termed 'mobility services', with the provision of, for example, fleets of vehicles that can be called as and when needed, with the size of each vehicle tailored to the particular activity. In this way, autonomous transport as a service could bring considerable environmental benefits due to decreased fuel consumption and change the nature of personal travel fundamentally.[10]

3. Developments in the Regulatory and Legal Environment

When attempting to provide regulatory and legal frameworks that support the creation and implementation of autonomous vehicles, a choice needs to be made as to whether this should be grounded within existing traffic regulatory measures or whether key existing relevant laws should be abolished and reshaped with a focus on supporting technological progress. The following is an overview of relevant regulatory and legal measures internationally, in the USA, the EU and, finally, the UK.

3.1 International Legal Instruments

At an international level, the 1949 Geneva Convention on Road Traffic[11] was an agreement that aimed to create harmonised rules to promote road safety.

---

[10] European Commission, 'Digital Transformation Monitor Autonomous Cars: A Big Opportunity for European Industry' (January 2017) <https://ec.europa.eu/growth/tools-databases/dem/monitor/sites/default/files/DTM_Autonomous%20cars%20v1.pdf.

[11] See <https://treaties.un.org/doc/Publication/MTDSG/Volume%20I/Chapter%20XI/xi-b-1.en.pdf> (accessed 13 April 2019).

Its Article 8 holds that every vehicle should have a driver and every driver shall 'at all times' be able to control their vehicles. A strict reading of these rules would, unless the notion of driver were to be significantly widened, preclude the wide-scale use of autonomous functions. While the UK and USA have signed this convention, neither has ratified the subsequent Vienna Convention on Road Traffic of 1968.[12] In March 2016 a number of amendments[13] to this instrument, as pushed for by Germany, France and Italy were adopted.

The changes first clarify the law on semi-autonomous systems by adding a paragraph to Article 8 to state that using systems 'which influence the way vehicles are driven'[14] conforms to the notion of driver's control. These systems, however, need to be able to be overridden or switched off by the (human) driver. While these amendments do not support fully automated driving at Level 4 or give any clarifications on whether or not, for example, a commuter can immerse herself in her work, they demonstrate an engagement with increasingly automated driving systems and a willingness to update existing international agreements. The Geneva and Vienna Conventions are useful in providing a normative framework but, as outlined above, a number of countries have not yet signed or ratified these provisions. There have, however, been country-specific, autonomous vehicle-focused legal amendments to support the technology's testing and wider implementation.

3.2 USA Law and Policy

In the USA, at a federal level, initial guidance on the autonomous vehicle technology was issued in 2013 that focused on safety and testing licensing schemes while declaring that it was 'a historic turning point for automotive travel'.[15] While this gave a general framework for testing, there was a need to provide a more comprehensive policy statement in order to avoid the piecemeal adoption of state-passed laws that followed. Writing in 2011, Garza[16]

---

[12] See <https://www.unece.org/fileadmin/DAM/trans/conventn/crt1968e.pdf> (accessed 13 April 2019).

[13] Economic Commission for Europe, 'Inland Transport Committee Report of the Sixty-eighth Session of the Working Party on Road Traffic Safety' (24–6 March 2014) <www.unece.org/fileadmin/DAM/trans/doc/2014/wp1/ECE-TRANS-WP1-145e.pdf> (accessed 15 April 2019).

[14] Vienna Convention on Road Traffic, Article 8 5 bis.

[15] United States National Highway Traffic Safety Administration, 'Preliminary Statement of Policy Concerning Automated Vehicles' (30 May 2013) <www.nhtsa.gov/staticfiles/rulemaking/pdf/Automated_Vehicles_Policy.pdf> (accessed 15 April 2019).

[16] Garza, ' "Look Ma, No Hands": Wrinkles and Wrecks in the Age of Autonomous Vehicles' (2011) 46 *New England Law Review* 581.

highlighted the need for definitive clarification of the safety and testing regime relating to autonomous vehicles, as, without this, a number of presumptions of illegality were developed that were not truly based in comprehensive legal analysis. Some clarity at a federal level came in September 2016 when the US Department of Transport published its Federal Automated Vehicles Policy.[17] This provides performance guidelines in relation to the testing and deployment (that is, use by the public) of autonomous vehicles. It outlines a model state policy in which the rights and responsibilities of the state and federal regulators are delineated. The policy continues with an identification of current regulatory tools and strategies, and finally it looks to the future with an overview of potential new regulatory bodies and approaches to allow flexible responses to developing issues. It provides an essential, shaping push towards a streamlined implementation of the technology and is supported by $19 million of investment in research and development.

In 2018, the Self Drive Bill[18] was introduced at a federal level with the aim of enforcing federal standards for safety and testing. Before this comes into force, the law on autonomous vehicles is a matter for state legislatures. The National Conference of State Legislatures maintains a real-time database of relevant legislation and enactments.[19] As of March 2019, forty-three states and the District of Columbia have legislated, with a total of 344 Bills relevant to autonomous vehicles passed or pending. The provisions cover areas such as cybersecurity, insurance, licensing and vehicle testing. Writing in 2014, Smith analysed the state-specific development of legal and regulatory measures and made a call for the development of 'common vocabularies and definitions that are meaningful in both law and engineering and accessible to the public and the media'.[20] This, for example, can be seen in differences relating to the basic term 'vehicle operator', which has been legally defined in three different states as the autonomous driving system itself,[21] the person

---

[17] National Highway Traffic Safety Administration, 'United States Federal Automated Vehicle Policy Accelerating the Next Revolution in Roadway Safety' (September 2016) <https://www.transportation.gov/sites/dot.gov/files/docs/AV%20policy%20guidance%20PDF.pdf> (accessed 13 April 2019).

[18] Self Drive Bill, 2018 <https://www.congress.gov/bill/115th-congress/house-bill/3388> (accessed 13 April 2019).

[19] National Conference of State Legislatures, 'Autonomous Vehicles State Bill Tracking Database' (2019) <www.ncsl.org/research/transportation/autonomous-vehicles-legislative-database.aspx> (accessed 15 April 2019).

[20] Smith, 'Automated Vehicles Are Probably Legal in the United States' (2014) 1 *Texas A&M Law Review* 411, p. 517.

[21] Tennessee Senate Bill 151 2017–18.

causing this system to operate[22] and a natural person travelling through the use of the system.[23]

This lack of legal clarity could, for example, hinder the progress of this technology in enhancing the lives of disabled people. Currently, the only state to allow fully unmanned vehicles is California, where its vehicle code has been amended to permit small-scale speed-restricted tests of 'autonomous vehicles that do not have a driver seated in the driver's seat and are not equipped with a steering wheel, a brake pedal, or an accelerator'.[24] How the concept of 'vehicle operator' and the level of control he, she or it would be required to exercise is crucial to the development of a legal regime that allows disabled people to use these travel systems without the agency of others.

3.3 EU Law and Policy

While testing has been carried out in a number of EU member states, there have been no targeted domestic or EU-level legislative changes. In 2015 the European Parliament published its Civil Law Rules on Robotics,[25] indicating that the automotive sector is one of the key sectors fuelling growth in the sales of robots. It highlights that this sector is the area with the most pressing need for regulation to address the fragmented approaches taken to address the legal issues raised. Without this there is the potential to slow the development of the technology and to hinder the EU's competitiveness. Similarly, the report of the OECD's International Transport Forum on Automated and Autonomous Driving succinctly encapsulated the difficulties inherent in regulating for new technologies:

> Though regulators may target autonomous vehicles as a special case out of convenience, it may be preferable to adapt existing rules as much as possible. While desirable, early regulatory action carries risks as well. Prematurely codifying requirements can freeze unrealistic expectations – high or low – into the law in a way that causes the legal framework to lag rather than to lead.[26]

---

[22] Georgia Senate Bill 219 2017–18.

[23] Texas Senate Bill 2205 2017–18.

[24] An Act to Add and Repeal Section 38755 of the Vehicle Code, relating to autonomous vehicles. Assembly Bill No. 1592, Chapter 814 (29 September 2016) <http://leginfo.legislature.ca.gov/faces/billNavClient.xhtml?bill_id=201520160AB1592> (accessed 13 April 2019).

[25] See European Parliament, Legal Affairs Committee, 'Civil Law Rules on Robotics' (2016) PE 571.379 <www.europarl.europa.eu/RegData/etudes/STUD/2016/571379/IPOL_STU (2016)571379_EN.pdf> (accessed 15 April 2019).

[26] Organisation for Economic Co-operation and Development, 'Automated and Autonomous

Lobbying groups of manufacturers, insurers and consumer groups have demanded a cohesive policy and clarity on the Commission's position.[27] The confusion was highlighted at a meeting of the UN Economic Commission for Europe,[28] during which attention was drawn to the lack of specific definitions for the technology and the over-preponderance of Directorates-General working in the sector. The need for cohesion is particularly pressing given industry pressure to support cross-border testing.[29]

A May 2018 communication from the Commission[30] that set out the position that the EU's legal framework at that time was sufficient to allow the development and sale of autonomous vehicles. The Commission has, however, introduced an element of harmonisation through a regulation[31] introducing market surveillance measures to ensure EU-wide development of the technology according to a set level of safety and testing standards. This reflects the USA's approach in proposals put forward in the Self Drive Bill to clarify safety standards and, in doing so, encourage technological development.

3.4 UK Law and Policy

In the UK, an initial scoping study[32] concluded that there was no need for legal changes to enable autonomous vehicle testing in the UK. This was followed

Driving Regulation under Uncertainty' (2015) <https://www.itf-oecd.org/sites/default/files/docs/15cpb_autonomousdriving.pdf> (accessed 19 June 2019), p. 6.

27 *Euractiv*, 'Car Industry Frustrated by Commission "Disorganisation" on Driverless Vehicles' (May 2016) <https://www.euractiv.com/section/digital/news/car-industry-frustrated-by-eu-disorganisation-on-driverless-vehicles/> (accessed 15 April 2019).

28 See Economic Commission for Europe Inland Transport Committee Working Party on Road Traffic Safety, 'Automated Driving' (September 2016) <www.unece.org/fileadmin/DAM/trans/doc/2016/wp1/ECE-TRANS-Informal-2016-4e.pdf> (accessed 13 April 2019).

29 Stupp, 'Commission Asked to Fund Cross-border Tests of Driverless Cars' (July 2006) *Euractiv* <https://www.euractiv.com/section/innovation-industry/news/commission-asked-to-fund-cross-border-tests-of-driverless-cars/> (accessed 15 April 2019).

30 See European Commission, 'On the Road to Automated Mobility: An EU Strategy for Mobility of the Future' (17 May 2018) Communication from the Commission to the European Parliament, the Council, the European Economic and Social Committee, Committee of the Regions, Brussels, COM(2018) 283 final.

31 European Parliament (2018) Regulation (EU) 2018/858 of the European Parliament and of the Council of 30 May 2018 on the approval and market surveillance of motor vehicles and their trailers, and of systems, components and separate technical units intended for such vehicles, amending Regulations (EC) No 715/2007 and (EC) No 595/2009 and repealing Directive 2007/46/EC (Text with EEA relevance).

32 UK Department for Transport, 'The Pathway to Driverless Cars: Summary Report and Action Plan' (February 2015) <https://www.gov.uk/government/uploads/system/uploads/

by a code of practice for testing[33] and, in July 2016, by a consultation,[34] with responses elicited in the areas of insurance, regulation and the updating of the Highway Code. The subsequent government Report[35] outlined the choice of a step-by-step approach to regulation with 'waves' of reform being put into place after observing the technology's development. The first primary legislation emanating from this consultation was the Automated and Electric Vehicles Act,[36] which received royal assent in July 2018. In relation to autonomous vehicles, this moves away from a human 'driver'-focused model of insurance towards one that accepts that the 'driver' can also be a passenger. Given the nature of this technology, the potential can arise, in accidents in which the technology has made an active decision, for liability to be shared between the human and the technology. To bring clarity and to harmonise the approaches taken by the industry, the Act establishes a single point of compulsory insurance that also covers manufacturers' product liability. It goes further to extend this compulsory cover for 'not at fault' injuries to the driver and third parties. This aims to bring clarity in the face of some sectors of the car industry putting forward 'self-insure' options.[37]

As is often the case with early technology-focused statutes, the Act itself does not include a high level of detail. Indeed, section 3 on contributory negligence states:

> The insurer or owner of an automated vehicle is not liable under section
> 2 to the person in charge of the vehicle where the accident that it caused

attachment_data/file/401562/pathway-driverless-cars-summary.pdf> (accessed 15 April 2019).

[33] UK Department for Transport, 'The Pathway to Driverless Cars: A Code of Practice for Testing' (July 2015) <https://assets.publishing.service.gov.uk/government/uploads/system/uploads/attachment_data/file/401562/pathway-driverless-cars-summary.pdf> (accessed 15 April 2019).

[34] UK Department for Transport Centre for Connected and Autonomous Vehicles, 'The Pathway to Driverless Cars: Proposals to Support Advanced Driver Assistance Systems and Automated Vehicle Technologies' (July 2016) <https://www.gov.uk/government/uploads/system/uploads/attachment_data/file/536365/driverless-cars-proposals-for-adas-and_avts.pdf> (accessed 13 April 2019).

[35] Department for Transport and the Centre for Connected and Autonomous Vehicles, 'The Pathway to Driverless Cars: Consultation on Proposals to Support Advanced Driver Assistance Systems and Automated Vehicles, Government Response' (January 2017) <https://assets.publishing.service.gov.uk/government/uploads/system/uploads/attachment_data/file/581577/pathway-to-driverless-cars-consultation-response.pdf> (accessed 15 June 2019).

[36] Automated and Electric Vehicles Act 2018 c 18.

[37] Butcher and Edmonds, 'Automated and Electric Vehicles Act 2018' (15 August 2018) House of Commons Library Briefing Paper Number CBP 8118.

was wholly due to the person's negligence in allowing the vehicle to begin driving itself when it was *not appropriate to do so* [original emphasis].

The circumstances in which it is inappropriate to employ a vehicle's self-driving capabilities are not fleshed out in any way, and will be impacted upon by a wide range of technological and road safety-based factors that, at this point in the technology's development, are beyond full definition. Furthermore, section 4 of the Act relates in part to the insurer's potential to limit or exclude liability owing either to the user's alteration of software or to the user failing to install safety-critical updates. In relation to the latter, what is envisaged is a system in which the manufacturer has an ongoing relationship with a connected technology as it does with computer operating systems. If a user fails to remember to download a critical vehicle update, or more problematically and as can be seen with personal computers, the update either stalls or only partially installs, then this can lead to full or partial invalidation of a compulsory insurance. The practical implications of this section will need to be addressed in much more detailed legal provisions and guidance but, to date, it is an example of the UK government's step-by-step approach through which a framework is set out, with the details to be determined as the use of the technology becomes more of a daily reality.

4. Trends in Autonomous Vehicle Regulation

Even at this early stage of its development, analysis can be undertaken to determine trends in the regulation of autonomous vehicles and place them within the context of earlier regulatory responses. Dennis and Urry's work *After the Car*[38] outlines the complex, interconnected factors relating to changes in automotive technology. In relation to increased digitisation of vehicles they state that social practices 'will adapt and/or appropriate particular socio-technical developments in complicated ways'. Innovation needs to be strongly linked to existing infrastructural, societal, cultural and political infrastructures that comprise the system. In turn, law and regulation are merely part of this system and cannot develop in a linear manner with accurate predictions of how technology will be implemented. Within the wider regulatory context there are a few key issues that require pressing legal and policy-based actions to ensure the strategic development of this technology while avoiding constraining its development and impact. This chapter now continues to analyse in greater depth four key regulatory issues: safety, data protection and access to technology for disabled people, and the development of trust.

---

[38] Dennis and Urry, *After the Car* (Polity Press 2001), p. 91.

4.1 Safety

Safety is a paramount regulatory concern, particularly as addressing this issue is crucial to developing end-user trust and acceptance, as discussed below. The potential framework of liability is multi-layered, due to the input of numerous actors such as vehicle manufacturers, software programmers, system managers, retailers and the human passengers themselves.[39] For example, in the recent expansion of Uber's fleet into San Francisco, some of their fleet were recorded driving through red lights. When questioned on these violations and ordered to withdraw the vehicles from use, the error of the 'human' was blamed rather than the technical.[40] In relation to approaches taken to human–computer interaction, the consumer protection framework of other advanced technological can provide insights. A way forward can be found from an analysis of current product liability frameworks and determining the extent to which they are applicable to autonomous vehicles. The EU Council Directive on liability for defective products[41] creates a framework of damages for any potential defects caused in the manufacturing of the vehicle or pod itself.

More complex legal issues arise in cases where a decision is made by an intelligent system that injures its driver, passengers or third-party road users. An autonomous car's system, when forced to decide between two negative outcomes, will, based on its algorithms and the nature and level of its sophistication, cause the vehicle to act in a certain way. The now ubiquitous 'trolley problem' has been applied in the debate surrounding autonomous cars. Originating with Philippa Foot's[42] scenario which analyses the ethical dilemma of the runaway tram driver who can only manipulate the vehicle from one track to another, both options with differing negative outcomes. This example has often been applied to autonomous vehicles, given the reality that they will have to be programmed to take active decisions when faced with negative outcomes. Ultimately this will lead to human injury or death based on an active decision taken by an automated system. Despite wider

---

[39] Boeglin, 'The Costs of Self-Driving Cars: Reconciling Freedom And Privacy With Tort Liability In Autonomous Vehicle Regulation' (2015) 17 *Yale Journal of Law and Technology* 171.

[40] Levin, 'Uber Cancels Self-driving Car Trial in San Francisco after State Forces It off Road' (*The Guardian*, 22 December 2016) <https://www.theguardian.com/technology/2016/dec/21/uber-cancels-self-driving-car-trial-san-francisco-california> (accessed 15 April 2019).

[41] European Council (1985) Council Directive 85/374/EEC of 25 July 1985 on the approximation of the laws, regulations and administrative provisions of the Member States concerning liability for defective products (OJ L 210, 7.8.1985, p. 29).

[42] Foot, 'The Problem of Abortion and the Double Effect' (1967) 5 *Oxford Review* 5, pp. 5–15.

predictions on the benefits of autonomous vehicles on human safety on the roads, this aspect of the technology can lead to unease and can impact upon trust.[43] Indeed, the March 2018 death of a pedestrian caused by an Uber self-driving car shed a tragic light on the potential dangers.[44] The understanding that, given the complexities of road travel, the autonomous vehicle will be overtly programmed to allow or even cause harm to humans in certain circumstances causes unique regulatory issues. To probe society's attitudes, MIT has created a platform, the Moral Machine.[45] This presents users with a series of situations in which autonomous cars face ethical scenarios in which a choice has to be made to cause some level of harm. The users can judge the decisions taken and see how their judgements measure against that of others. The use of scenarios such as that of the pedestrian death caused by an Uber autonomous vehicle in 2018 would shed light on attitudes to risk, harm and technology.

Writing in the publication *Science*, Bonnefon et al.[46] outline their work on attitudes to algorithmic decision making in autonomous vehicles. Their survey-based research outlines a utilitarian model in which decisions are taken in an emergency situation with the aim of creating the least level of general harm. This is outlined alongside a 'self-protective' model in which the vehicle is programmed to respond in order first and foremost to protect its own human passengers rather than the wider road-using public. The results include a general agreement that the utilitarian model should be followed but, conflictingly, those who saw themselves as travelling in the technology held a strong belief that it should protect them as passengers above all else. This could lead to the contradictory situation in which people would wish to see a utilitarian approach taken to development and regulation while themselves choosing, if the choice were on the market, to ride in self-protective vehicles. According to the study's authors, regulators need to achieve the three potentially incompatible aims of 'being consistent, not causing public outrage, and not discouraging buyers'.

The proposed EU Civil Law Rules on Robotics accept this problematic aspect of legal regulation in relation to systems with the statement:

Adaptive and learning abilities entailing a certain degree of unpredictability in their behaviour, since these robots would autonomously learn from their

---

[43] Rowe, 'The Rise of the Machines: A New Risk for Claims?' (2018) 4 *JPI Law* 302.

[44] BBC News, 'Uber Halts Self-driving Car Tests after Death' (20 March 2018) <https://www.bbc.co.uk/news/business-43459156> (accessed 15 April 2019).

[45] Available at: <http://moralmachine.mit.edu/> (accessed 13 April 2019).

[46] Bonnefon, Shariff and Rahwan, 'The Social Dilemma of Autonomous Vehicles' (2016) 352 *Science* 1573.

own variable experience and interact with their environment in a unique and unforeseeable manner.[47]

Indeed, any assignation of liability related to an autonomous vehicle's active decisions would have to operate within the context of its ability to learn, coupled with its human-directed and, perhaps, self-directed education. A lack of clarity in this area could not only risk the safety of passengers and road users but could also impede technological development and advancement. The rules expressly hold that the type and extent of any compensation awarded should not be restricted on the specific ground that damage is caused by a 'non-human agent'. This proposition appears clear, but does not address the complexities of assigning and assessing the level of compensation. The report puts forward a number of suggestions. One would be to create a new category of legal personhood with customised rules relating to liability, related to specific circumstances. Within this there could be the potential for removing any limitations set relating to compensation, with no restriction of liability if the injury is caused by a non-human agent. There could be a stratified approach depending upon the levels of autonomy and the amount of human-directed education the system has undertaken. This would need to be linked strongly to standardisation and the development of codes, but clarity and uniformity would be difficult to achieve. The aim of quantifying a system's education and ongoing self-directed development would require a deep understanding of algorithms being translated into tangible, quantifiable rules.[48] Such an approach would risk simplifying the capabilities of machine learning and as Schafer suggests, 'giving us "false hope", in that it deludes us into thinking that by regulating a technology we can make it safe'.[49]

Another way forward, perhaps easier to envisage, could be through the development of autonomous vehicle-specific insurance schemes. Indeed, this is suggested in the Proposed EU Civil Law Rules on Robotics[50] which recommend an insurance scheme for autonomous systems that could be linked to a compensations scheme and that 'should take into account all potential responsibilities in the chain'. There is the possibility that compulsory insur-

---

[47] An Act to Add and Repeal Section 38755 of the Vehicle Code, Relating to Autonomous Vehicles. Assembly Bill No. 1592 Chapter 814 (29 September 2016).

[48] Mittelstadt, Allo, Taddeo, Wachter and Floridi, 'The Ethics of Algorithms: Mapping the Debate' (2016) *Big Data & Society* <https://doi.org/10.1177/2053951716679679> (accessed 13 April 2019).

[49] Schafer, 'Closing Pandora's Box? The EU Proposal on the Regulation of Robots' (2016) 99 *Pandora's Box (Journal of the Justice and the Law Society of the University of Queensland)* 55.

[50] An Act to Add and Repeal Section 38755 of the Vehicle Code, relating to autonomous vehicles. Assembly Bill No. 1592 Chapter 814 (29 September 2016), at 57 and 58.

ance might be taken out by those (humans) deemed to be, for example, the owners, operators and developers of intelligent robotic transport systems. This would be similar to current state-mandated compulsory car insurance schemes and would follow the approach taken in the UK's recent Automated and Electric Vehicles Act 2018, as outlined above. A less comprehensive approach would be to create a limited liability scheme for developers and operators based on compulsory payments into a compensation fund. This could be split into categories or bands depending upon functions and levels of autonomy and education. Again; this could pose definitional difficulties and would rely upon stringent top-down regulation, with the need for a register of intelligent autonomous vehicles with its associated costs and bureaucracy.

4.2 Data Protection

Autonomous vehicles present challenges to the privacy of individual users as, by their very nature, there is a need to track the vehicles and, in turn, gather information about their passengers. On an autonomous journey, both the car and its central navigation system know our exact movements and timings. This information can provide an in-depth picture of the nature of an individual's private and personal life. The issues can be seen by examining the recent data protection breaches involving the car-sharing service Uber.[51] The company reached a settlement to resolve a data breach and, separately, issues relating to its collection and disclosure of the personal information of its end-users. It was claimed that these data were made available to Uber executives and that the locations of end-users were made available in an aerial, so-called 'God view'. There is the need for autonomous cars to be tracked and guided by centrally controlled software and the potential for smartphone identification and tailoring of the vehicle experience. These lead to wider interactions with personal data in ever-intrusive ways, which need to be managed within the relevant legal framework.[52] Developers of autonomous vehicles need to focus at an early point on the interaction of end-users with data collection points. Furthermore, the potential for the technology to be used as a service rather than a one-off purchase will see much wider roles for technology companies in the automotive sector. This should lead to a fundamental shift in the car-manufacturing industry, as it is tasked with developing technology that operates within the framework of privacy legislation.

---

[51] Attorney General of New York, 'A.G. Schneiderman Announces Settlement with Uber to Enhance Rider Privacy' (January 2016) <www.ag.ny.gov/press-release/ag-schneiderman-announces-settlement-uber-enhance-rider-privacy> (accessed 15 April 2019).

[52] Collingwood, 'Privacy Implications and Liability Issues of Autonomous Vehicles' (2017) 26 *Information & Communications Technology Law* 32, pp. 32–45.

The EU's recently adopted General Data Protection Regulation (GDPR)[53] aims to provide high-level protection for data subjects, while operating in a flexible manner to support the growth of new technology. A key new inclusion in the legal regime is the concept of data protection by design and default. This is a concept, developed primarily by the Canadian Office of the Information Commissioner, which aims to embed privacy-supporting practices in the technology itself as it develops. Taking into account the nature and purpose of any data processing, 'appropriate technical and organisational measures'[54] should be taken while developing a technology to ensure that safeguards are embedded. Recital 78 provides further detail:

> When developing, designing, selecting and using applications, services and products that are based on the processing of personal data or process personal data to fulfil their task, producers of the products, services and applications should be encouraged to take into account the right to data protection when developing and designing such products, services and applications and, with due regard to the state of the art, to make sure that controllers and processors are able to fulfil their data protection obligations.

This indicates that those developing autonomous vehicle technology, both the hardware and the software, need, from the planning stages, to develop techniques and strategies to support data protection principles. To embrace this technology, the car industry needs to operate in a technology-focused manner, envisaging an ongoing relationship between their end-users and themselves and their partners as technology providers. The GDPR introduces into legislation a number of tools to aid organisations in supporting data processors and controllers in upholding data protection principles. Data protection impact assessments[55] are recommended and, in certain cases, mandated to focus technology developers' and users' attention on strategies to assess risk and to put in place safeguards and mechanisms to mitigate this risk.

These approaches operate in an environment in which data subjects' rights have been strengthened and extended. The concept of consent has been reinforced with the express provision that it needs to be given in unambiguous terms, fully informed and explicit. Added to this is the need for a wide

---

[53] European Parliament (2016) Regulation (EU) 2016/679 of the European Parliament and of the Council of 27 April 2016 on the protection of natural persons with regard to the processing of personal data and on the free movement of such data, and repealing Directive 95/46/EC (General Data Protection Regulation) (Text with EEA relevance).

[54] Ibid., Art 25.

[55] Ibid., Art 35.

range of information to be provided to the data subject, which includes the purposes of the data gathering, the recipients or categories of data recipients and data retention periods.[56] This information needs to be provided in a transparent, easily accessible manner.[57] It operates alongside an extended definition of personal data, which now refers to information relating to a data subject:

> who can be identified, directly or indirectly, in particular by reference to an identifier such as a name, an identification number, location data, an online identifier or to one or more factors specific to the physical, physiological, genetic, mental, economic, cultural or social identity of that natural person.[58]

Whether you use the autonomous car as part of a fleet service or as a privately owned vehicle, its use will lead to you as the traveller interacting with a number of parties who will share information that falls within this widened definition of personal data. The vehicle itself will log your presence through an identifier that will then, quite obviously, be able to track your location. The vehicle's sensors, harnessing ultrasonic, radar and lidar technology, will work alongside on-board cameras to relay signals to a GPS system to guide the car's movements.

Depending on how the technology develops, this will be relayed to traffic controllers and proximate autonomous and non-autonomous vehicles. Indeed, a call has been raised by the systems developers to implement a regime of enforced data sharing to support safety. Krompier[59] argues that in the USA the National Highway Traffic Safety Administration should create a mandatory data-sharing regime both to cover vehicle-to-vehicle 'talking' systems relating to hazards and incidents, and to atch this to information relating to the development of the algorithms themselves and how they function. In relation to such systems, provisions such as the EU's proposed E-Privacy Regulation[60] in its Article 6 would allow for such processing if data were collected according to data minimisation principles.

---

[56] Ibid., Art 13.

[57] Ibid., Art 12.

[58] Ibid., Art 4(1).

[59] Krompier, 'Safety First: The Case for Mandatory Data Sharing as a Federal Safety Standard for Self-driving' (2017) 2 *Journal of Law, Technology & Policy* 439.

[60] European Parliament (2017) Proposal for a Regulation of the European Parliament and of the Council concerning the respect for private life and the protection of personal data in electronic communications and repealing Directive 2002/58/EC (Regulation on Privacy and Electronic Communications) Brussels, 10 January 2017 COM(2017) 10 final 2017/ 0003(COD).

Further interaction with personal data, even in real time, will come from the insurance regime put in place, which is likely to rely heavily on the data generated by the interaction of travellers and vehicles. The data protection regime, with its need for consent and in-depth information on data sharing, will need to be applied to this interaction with technology in a way that provides the required explicit information-based consent while allowing for a streamlined and efficient experience for each passenger. There is the potential for the autonomous vehicle system to pass on lucrative data to marketing companies that will have a captive audience within the vehicle. The ride as a service, again, like certain current online services, could be sold at a discount as advertisement-free. To address such situations the GDPR provides for the right to object to processing of personal data for direct marketing purposes and this includes any use of these data for related profiling.[61] Any use, therefore, of personal data for such in-vehicle advertising purposes would need to be carried out subject to a waiver of this right to object. Quite obviously, an alternative perspective on this would see the advertisement-free ride being available at a premium. The aggregation of information about a person's journeys, in-vehicle preferences and communication on the move would present a nuanced, dynamic and therefore valuable profile to marketers. Article 22 of the GDPR is of particular relevance to a situation where machines are communicating with machines. It holds that the data subject has the right not to be subject to a decision that has a legal or significant impact upon them based solely on automated processing. This can be varied if the data subject gives explicit consent.[62] If we are to have a future of advertising linked to an autonomous journey then suitable technology-specific measures need to be developed to ensure that such advertising and linked profiling are carried out in a manner that does not infringe upon the data subject's fundamental rights and freedoms, particularly given the importance of travel in the modern age.

The European Automobile Manufacturers Association has created a statement on principles of data protection.[63] This, while not mentioning the terms of such an agreement, holds that data will be processed pursuant to legal obligations and upholds the principles of transparency and proportionality. The statement gives an overview of the type of activity that would lead to data sharing, including emergency response and vehicle maintenance

---

[61] Ibid., Art 21.

[62] Ibid., Art 22(2)(c).

[63] European Automobile Manufacturers Association, 'Principles of Data Protection in Relation to Connected Vehicles and Services' (September 2015) <https://www.acea.be/uploads/publications/ACEA_Principles_of_Data_Protection.pdf> (accessed 15 April 2019).

services, but also mentions improving vehicle quality and providing entertainment and information services, such as traffic and weather details. A key issue relates to how far these features will be part of the vehicle's default features and the potential for them to be deactivated. The EU has already indicated that it aims to regulate car manufacturers' use of data gleaned from automated vehicle systems. This, however, was met with criticisms from these businesses, who stated that such a move would impact upon their profitability.[64] Furthermore, the International Conference of Protection and Privacy Commissioners developed its own Resolution on Data Protection in Automated and Connected Vehicles.[65] This goes much further than industry statements and calls for approaches based on principles of data minimisation, privacy by design and default, anonymisation and the retention of data for no longer than is necessary. In particular, it contains technically focused recommendations, such as the need to provide technical means to erase personal data when a vehicle is sold or returned to its owner, the provisions of granular and easy-to-use privacy controls for vehicle users and the provision of technical features that allow users to restrict data collection.

The focus of the self-regulatory measures on data sharing pursuant to legal obligations raises issues of the collection of autonomous vehicle data by not only private technology companies but also state-based enforcement agencies. The Australian National Transport Commission[66] report into autonomous vehicles recommends the need for strategic options to be developed to enable state-based access to enforce traffic laws on them, and, more vaguely, to achieve 'road safety and network efficiency' within a balanced framework of privacy protections. Such information could be crucial to determine issues of responsibility in the case of accidents, but privacy threats arise from the potential for bulk data collection and storage. The eCall system, an automated system that, in the case of an accident, calls the nearest emergency centre and if no response is heard from the car itself, transmits its exact location. Following the passing of the eCall Directive[67]

---

64 Stupp, 'Carmakers Fear EU Plans to Ease Data Flows Will Help Tech Rivals' (September 2016) *Euractiv* <https://www.euractiv.com/section/transport/news/carmakers-fear-eus-plan-to-ease-data-flows-will-help-tech-rivals/> (accessed 15 April 2019).

65 Conference of Protection and Privacy Commissioners, 'Resolution on Data Protection in Automated and Connected Vehicles' (September 2017) <https://icdppc.org/wp-content/uploads/2015/02/Resolution-on-data-protection-in-automated-and-connected-vehicles-.pdf> (accessed 15 April 2019).

66 National Transport Commission of Australia, 'Regulatory Reforms for Automated Road Vehicles' (November 2016) <https://www.ntc.gov.au/Media/Reports/(32685218-7895-0E7C-ECF6-551177684E27).pdf> (accessed 13 April 2019).

67 European Parliament (2015) Regulation (EU) 2015/758 of the European Parliament and

from April 2018, all new cars now need to be fitted with the system. As early as 2006 the Article 29 Working Party[68] highlighted privacy concerns related to the system, particularly if it was to be compulsory, and indicated that the relevance of such data to the emergency situation must always be taken into account. The Directive is to be read alongside a technical standard[69] that defines a Minimum Set of Data to be transmitted as relating to the location of the incident, relating to the vehicle and any other information deemed relevant. These standards could be replicated in relation to the nature of the data transmitted and stored by autonomous vehicles. While such approaches to vehicle identification systems can be drawn upon, there is a need to determine the extent to which the particular privacy issues raised by autonomous vehicles can be addressed within the current data protection framework.

4.3 Access to Autonomous Vehicles for Disabled People

Effective access to transport has long been deemed crucial for disabled people to live an independent life.[70] The Institution of Engineering and Technology's 2014 Thought Leadership Review on autonomous vehicles outlines that in expert debates, alongside efficiency gains and reduced fuel consumption, key societal benefits exist in relation to the 'ageing population: maintaining independence and impaired or disabled drivers: greater freedom of mobility'. The EPoSS report 'European Roadmap: Smart Systems for Automated Driving'[71] and the UK government's 'Pathway to Driverless Cars'[72] both refer to the benefits that the technology could bring to support autonomy and

of the Council of 29 April 2015 concerning type-approval requirements for the deployment of the eCall in-vehicle system based on the 112 service and amending Directive 2007/46/EC <http://eur-lex.europa.eu/legal-content/EN/TXT/?uri=uriserv%3AOJ.L_.2015.123.01.0077.01.ENG> (accessed 13 April 2019).

68 Article 29 Working Party, 'Working Document on Data Protection and Privacy Implications in eCall Initiative' (1609/06/EN, September 2006) <http://ec.europa.eu/justice/policies/privacy/docs/wpdocs/2006/wp125_en.pdf> (accessed 15 April 2019).

69 Carroll, Seidl, Cuerden and Stevens, 'Technical Considerations regarding Type-approval Testing of eCall In-vehicle Systems' (2014) EC Project Number SI2.671420 TRL Client Project Report CPR1868.

70 Finkelstein, 'Getting There: Non-Disabling Transport' (11 June 1994) Beckfoot School, Bingley <http://disability-studies.leeds.ac.uk/files/library/finkelstein-Transport-Getting-There.pdf> (accessed 13 April 2019).

71 EPoSS, 'European Roadmap: Smart Systems for Automated Driving Version 1.2' (2015) <www.smart-systems-integration.org/public/documents/publications/EPoSS%20Roadmap_Smart%20Systems%20for%20Automated%20Driving_V2_April%202015.pdf> (accessed 15 April 2019).

72 UK Department of Transport, 'The Pathway to Driverless Cars: A Code of Practice For Testing'.

independence for disabled people. While this is strongly highlighted in the UK's policy document, it is mentioned only in passing in the 'EU Roadmap', in relation to France's motivation to support innovation.

Attention has been drawn to the importance of independence-supporting transport technology by the USA's National Federation of the Blind 'Blind Driver Challenge',[73] which develops non-visual interface technology and shows the importance of transport in facilitating the achievement of independence and empowerment. Writing in 2013, Dana and Mele[74] conclude that placing the use of autonomous vehicle technology by disabled people at the centre of legal and regulatory responses will further the objectives of anti-discrimination laws while enhancing 'safety, efficiency, and innovative automobile technology for all drivers'. This reflects the findings of the approach taken to technology regulation in other areas, such as accessible website design, in which embedding considerations that address the needs of disabled people at the early stage of a technology's development can improve access and user experience for all.[75]

The relationship between disability and technology is multi-faceted and complex. Assistive technology has been employed for many centuries and a point is being reached at which sophisticated systems can be deemed to merge with the human.[76] The social model of disability is one that identifies a disabling society that places barriers in front of those who do not conform to what is deemed to be 'normal'. There is a risk that the use of technology can place an onus on the individual to take measures rather than focus on the need for the barrier-creating political and social environment to evolve. Technology could be linked to a paternalistic, medical model-based response, used as a way of society 'curing' a problem inherent in the individual. Roulstone[77] shows how focusing on the potential of technology to impact upon the lives of disabled people can detract from the everyday realities of unequal access. This phenomenon has been identified in relation to information technology as the digital divide and sees inequalities of access

---

[73] Available at: <www.blinddriverchallenge.org/> (accessed 13 April 2019).

[74] Dana and Mele, 'The Quasi-Autonomous Car as an Assistive Device for Blind Drivers: Overcoming Liability and Regulatory Barriers' (2013) 28 *Syracuse Science & Technology Law Reporter* 26.

[75] Easton, 'An Analysis of the European Union's Law and Policy Relating to Website Accessibility' in *Research Handbook on EU Internet Law* (Edward Elgar 2014).

[76] Easton, 'You Will Never Walk Again … But You Will Fly: Human Augmentation in the Known World' (2015) 20 *Media and Arts Law Review*.

[77] Roulstone, 'Access to New Technology in the Employment of Disabled People' in Swain J et al. (eds), *Disabling Barriers, Enabling Environments* (2nd edn, Sage 2004), pp. 241–8.

exacerbating existing socio-economic divisions.[78] Through legal reform, anti-discrimination provisions have been passed but, in relation in particular to access to the Internet, for example, persistent divisions still exist.[79] It is essential that in the implementation of new technology such as autonomous vehicles, the position of disabled people is both theorised and addressed at the earliest possible opportunity.[80]

The United Nations Convention on the Rights of Persons with Disability (UNCRPD)[81] came into force in May 2008. This is a wide-ranging, normative piece of legislation that was negotiated in an innovative, participatory manner, with supported input from disabled people in its drafting. Importantly, this was the first legally binding human rights instrument that the EU negotiated and to which it subsequently acceded. The EU's relationship with the Convention is in the form of a 'mixed' agreement in which both it and its member states are separate contracting parties but subject to a duty of sincere cooperation. The UNCRPD includes an Article 9 provision on accessibility, which aims to 'enable persons with disabilities to live independently and participate fully in all aspects of life'. It requires states parties to 'take appropriate measures to ensure to persons with disabilities access, on an equal basis with others, to the physical environment, to transportation, to information and communications, including information and communications technologies and systems'. Furthermore, it includes in its Article 20 a requirement on states parties to 'take effective measures to ensure personal mobility with the greatest possible independence for persons with disabilities'. Technology employed to achieve this should be made available at an affordable cost and training should be provided where required.

The EU's 2014 report to the Committee of the UNCRPD outlines a number of legislative and standardisation methods to facilitate harmonisation of measures relating, for example, to consumer protection, procurement and access to goods and services. It also includes plans for the development of a Trans-European Transport Network with aims to 'strengthen the social, economic and territorial cohesion of the Union and contribute to the creation of a single European transport area'. Accessibility for disabled people is to be at the heart of this new transport strategy; however, the report does not

---

[78] Compaigne, *The Digital Divide: Facing a Crisis or Creating a Myth?* (MIT Press 2001).

[79] Dana and Mele, 'The Quasi-Autonomous Car as an Assistive Device for Blind Drivers'.

[80] Darcy and Burke, 'On the Road Again: The Barriers and Benefits of Automobility for People with Disability' (2018) 107 *Transportation Research Part A: Policy and Practice* 229, pp. 229–45.

[81] See <www.un.org/disabilities/documents/convention/convoptprot-e.pdf> (accessed 13 April 2019).

address strategies to implement autonomous vehicle technology in a manner that supports access and independence for disabled people. The UNCRPD is an important normative treaty in this area as it enshrines a right of access to technology alongside a right of access to transportation and, due to the need to report periodically, these procedures can be employed in order to place access to autonomous vehicles for disabled people at the heart of policy responses.

4.4 Developing Trust

With autonomous vehicles being squarely on the policy map as a fundamental feature of future society, a key issue relates to how to support and foster trust in this revolutionary new technology. While the potential safety benefits are effectively laid out, media reports have focused on negative aspects of the technology and control, such as the hacking of the electronic functions of cars currently on the road.[82] Giddens and Sutton[83] show that in a society increasingly reliant on technology, trust means having confidence in abstract systems and constructs. In this way trust and the notion of risk become interlinked. Due to this, there is a need to develop systems and, in turn, research that support social reflexivity and a constant reflection on how lives are lived. In an EU-wide survey[84] of the attitudes to robotic technology, 11 per cent of respondents chose transport/logistics as an area in which robotic technology should be used as a priority. Space exploration (52 per cent) received the highest response, with leisure and education both receiving the lowest at 4 per cent. Working in relation to the use of civilian drones, Boucher[85] highlights that there is little understanding of the nuanced nature of the attitudes of end-users to the use of the technology in a number of contexts. This work has led to a series of 'ethics dialogues'[86] that aim to determine key ethical issues and dilemmas and to highlight areas for further work. They promote a 'collective deliberation about narratives, values and norms by which we want to live'.

---

[82] Bowles, 'Yet Another Car Can Be Hacked – This Time It's the Mitsubishi Outlander Hybrid' (*The Guardian*, June 2016) <https://www.theguardian.com/technology/2016/jun/06/mitsubishi-outlander-car-hacked-security> (accessed 15 April 2019).

[83] Giddens and Sutton, *Sociology* (7th edn, Polity Press 2013).

[84] European Commission, 'Special Eurobarometer 382: Public Attitudes towards Robots' (2012) <http://ec.europa.eu/public_opinion/archives/ebs/ebs_382_en.pdf> (accessed 15 April 2019).

[85] Boucher, 'Societal and Ethics Aspects of Remotely Piloted Aircraft Systems' (2014) *JRC Science and Policy Reports*.

[86] Boucher, Nascimento, Vesnić-Alujević and Guimarães Pereira, 'Experiencing Ethics through "Things": Open IoT, Civil Drones and Wearable Sensors Ethics Dialogues' (2015) *JRC Science and Policy Reports*.

New and disruptive technology will not be implemented without the involvement of and consultation with end-users as consumers, employees and citizens. A robust, transparent and effective legal framework is intrinsically linked to the public's trust in a new technology.[87] Furthermore, trust is inherently linked to the public's acceptance of technology.[88] A socio-technical system approach can be defined as one that analyses 'the social infrastructure necessary to develop, commercialise and use innovations'.[89] There is a need to evaluate how society responds to technological change and how this trust is achieved. Sommerville[90] describes the challenges of differences across sectors such as law and technology both in vocabulary and in assumptions made about the practices of other disciplines. There is, therefore, a need to facilitate an active conversation between stakeholders such as designers, manufacturers, law and policymakers and, crucially, end-users.

5. Conclusion

Autonomous vehicles are increasingly accepted as a technology that will ultimately be implemented in the urban environment. The potential they present to increase road safety and address congestion and environmental pollution is deemed to be of fundamental benefit to the society of the future. These aims are currently pursued with large-scale funding to support public and private research, which will need to be underpinned by a flexible legal framework. However, as with all new technologies, a fine balance needs to be sought between regulation to enhance safety and fundamental rights such as privacy, without hindering the development of this constantly evolving technology.

While regulatory frameworks are allowing flexibility in the early regulations governing testing the technology, challenges will be presented in the transition to public use and, most importantly, the ability to gain public trust. The wider aspects of general increased road safety will have to be weighed against the passenger's direct ability to ensure that the technology protects their own personal interests if a dangerous situation arises.

Regulatory frameworks that address the realities of technological development while supporting transparency, openness and trust need to be the

---

[87] Schellekens, 'Self-driving Cars and the Chilling Effect of Liability Law' (2015) 31 *Computer Law and Security Review* 506, pp. 506–17.

[88] Lee and See, 'Trust in Automation: Designing for Appropriate Reliance' (2004) 46 *Human Factors* 50, pp. 50–80.

[89] Geels, 'From Sectoral Systems of Innovation to Socio-technical Systems: Insights about Dynamics and Change from Sociology and Institutional Theory' (2004) 33 *Research Policy* 897, pp. 897–920.

[90] Sommerville, *Software Engineering* (9th edn, Pearson 2011).

primary aim. Within this, the position of societal groups such as disabled people, for whom this technology could bring transformative benefits, needs to be identified and addressed on an equal basis. Based on current advancements and predictions, most developed urban futures will include interactions with this technology. There is, therefore, a need for ongoing consultation and debate with multiple stakeholders, focused not only on minimising harm but also on creating and developing a shared vision of the future of transport.

References

Article 29 Working Party, 'Working Document on Data Protection and Privacy Implications in eCall Initiative' (1609/06/EN, September 2006) <http://ec.europa.eu/justice/policies/privacy/docs/wpdocs/2006/wp125_en.pdf> (accessed 15 April 2019).

Attorney General of New York, 'A.G. Schneiderman Announces Settlement with Uber to Enhance Rider Privacy' (January 2016) <www.ag.ny.gov/press-release/ag-schneiderman-announces-settlement-uber-enhance-rider-privacy> (accessed 15 April 2019).

BBC News, 'Uber Halts Self-driving Car Tests after Death' (20 March 2018) <https://www.bbc.co.uk/news/business-43459156> (accessed 15 April 2019).

Boeglin J, 'The Costs of Self-Driving Cars: Reconciling Freedom and Privacy with Tort Liability in Autonomous Vehicle Regulation' (2015) 17 *Yale Journal of Law and Technology* 171.

Bonnefon J, Shariff A and Rahwan I, 'The Social Dilemma of Autonomous Vehicles' (2016) 352 *Science* 1573.

Boucher P, 'Societal and Ethics Aspects of Remotely Piloted Aircraft Systems' (2014) *JRC Science and Policy Reports.*

Boucher P, Nascimento S, Vesnić-Alujević L and Guimarães Pereira A; 'Experiencing Ethics through "things": Open IoT, Civil Drones and Wearable Sensors Ethics Dialogues' (2015) *JRC Science and Policy Reports.*

Bowles N, 'Yet Another Car Can Be Hacked – This Time It's the Mitsubishi Outlander Hybrid' (*The Guardian*, June 2016) <https://www.theguardian.com/technology/2016/jun/06/mitsubishi-outlander-car-hacked-security> (accessed 15 April 2019).

Butcher L and Edmonds T, 'Automated and Electric Vehicles Act 2018' (15 August 2018) House of Commons Library Briefing Paper Number CBP 8118.

Carroll J, Seidl M, Cuerden R and Stevens A, 'Technical Considerations regarding Type-approval Testing of eCall in-Vehicle Systems' (2014) EC Project Number SI2.671420 TRL Client Project Report CPR1868.

Collingwood L, 'Privacy Implications and Liability Issues of Autonomous Vehicles' (2017) 26 *Information & Communications Technology Law* 32.

Compaigne B, ed., *The Digital Divide: Facing a Crisis or Creating a Myth?* (MIT Press 2001).

Conference of Protection and Privacy Commissioners, 'Resolution on Data Protection in Automated and Connected Vehicles' (September 2017) <https://icdppc.org/wp-content/uploads/2015/02/Resolution-on-data-protection-in-automated-and-connected-vehicles-.pdf> (accessed 15 April 2019).

Dana M and Mele J, 'The Quasi-Autonomous Car as an Assistive Device for Blind Drivers: Overcoming Liability and Regulatory Barriers' (2013) 28 *Syracuse Science & Technology Law Reporter* 26.

Darcy S and Burke P, 'On the Road Again: The Barriers and Benefits of Automobility for People with Disability' (2018) 107 *Transportation Research Part A: Policy and Practice* 229.

DeBord M, 'Uber Did Everything Right in Pittsburgh with its Self-driving cars – But Is Doing Everything Wrong in San Francisco' (*Business Insider*, December 2016) <http://uk.businessinsider.com/uber-doing-everything-wrong-in-san-francisco-self-driving-2016-12?r=US&IR=T> (accessed 15 April 2019).

Dennis K and Urry J, *After the Car* (Polity Press 2001).

Department for Transport and the Centre for Connected and Autonomous Vehicles, 'Pathway to Driverless Cars: Consultation on Proposals to Support Advanced Driver Assistance Systems and Automated Vehicles, Government Response' (January 2017) <https://assets.publishing.service.gov.uk/government/uploads/system/uploads/attachment_data/file/581577/pathway-to-driverless-cars-consultation-response.pdf> (accessed 15 June 2019).

Easton C, 'An Analysis of the European Union's Law and Policy Relating to Website Accessibility' in *Research Handbook on EU Internet Law* (Edward Elgar 2014).

Easton C, 'You Will Never Walk Again … But You Will Fly: Human Augmentation in the Known World' (2015) 20 *Media and Arts Law Review*.

Economic Commission for Europe, 'Inland Transport Committee Report of the Sixty-eighth Session of the Working Party on Road Traffic Safety' (24–6 March 2014) <www.unece.org/fileadmin/DAM/trans/doc/2014/wp1/ECE-TRANS-WP1-145e.pdf> (accessed 15 April 2019).

Economic Commission for Europe Inland Transport Committee Working Party on Road Traffic Safety, 'Automated Driving' (September 2016) <www.unece.org/fileadmin/DAM/trans/doc/2016/wp1/ECE-TRANS-Informal-2016-4e.pdf> (accessed 13 April 2019).

EPoSS, 'European Roadmap: Smart Systems for Automated Driving Version 1.2' (2015) <www.smart-systems-integration.org/public/documents/publications/EPoSS%20Roadmap_Smart%20Systems%20for%20Automated%20Driving_V2_April%202015.pdf> (accessed 15 April 2019).

Euractiv, 'Car Industry Frustrated by Commission "Disorganisation" on Driverless Vehicles' (May 2016) <https://www.euractiv.com/section/digital/news/car-industry-frustrated-by-eu-disorganisation-on-driverless-vehicles/> (accessed 15 April 2019).

European Automobile Manufacturers Association, 'Principles of Data Protection in Relation to Connected Vehicles and Services' (September 2015) <https://www.acea.be/uploads/publications/ACEA_Principles_of_Data_Protection.pdf> (accessed 15 April 2019).

European Commission, 'Special Eurobarometer 382: Public Attitudes towards Robots' (2012) <http://ec.europa.eu/public_opinion/archives/ebs/ebs_382_en.pdf> (accessed 15 April 2019).

European Commission, 'Digital Transformation Monitor Autonomous Cars: A Big Opportunity for European Industry' (January 2017) <https://ec.europa.eu/growth/tools-databases/dem/monitor/sites/default/files/DTM_Autonomous%20cars%20v1.pdf> (accessed 20 June 2019).

European Commission, 'Europe on the Move: Sustainable Mobility for Europe: Safe, Connected, and Clean' (2018) Communication from the Commission to the European Parliament, the Council, the European Economic and Social Committee and the Committee of the Region, COM/2018/293 final.

European Commission 'On the Road to Automated Mobility: An EU Strategy for Mobility of the Future' (17 May 2018) Communication from the Commission to the European Parliament, the Council, the European Economic and Social Committee, Committee of the Regions, Brussels, COM(2018) 283 final.

European Parliament, Legal Affairs Committee, 'Civil Law Rules on Robotics' (2016) PE 571.379 <www.europarl.europa.eu/RegData/etudes/STUD/2016/571379/IPOL_STU(2016)571379_EN.pdf> (accessed 15 April 2019).

Favarò F, Eurich S and Nader N, 'Autonomous Vehicles' Disengagements: Trends, Triggers, and Regulatory Limitations' (2017) 110 *Journal of Accident Analysis Prevention* 136.

Finkelstein V, 'Getting There: Non-Disabling Transport' (11 June 1994) Beckfoot School, Bingley <http://disability-studies.leeds.ac.uk/files/library/finkelstein-Transport-Getting-There.pdf> (accessed 13 April 2019).

Foot P, 'The Problem of Abortion and the Double Effect' (1967) 5 *Oxford Review* 5.

Garza A, ' "Look Ma, No Hands": Wrinkles and Wrecks in the Age of Autonomous Vehicles' (2011) 46 *New England Law Review* 581.

Geels F, 'From Sectoral Systems of Innovation to Socio-technical Systems: Insights about Dynamics and Change from Sociology and Institutional Theory' (2004) 33 *Research Policy* 897.

Giddens A and Sutton P, *Sociology* (7th edn, Polity Press 2013).

Herrmann A, Brenner W and Stadler R, eds, *Autonomous Driving: How the Driverless Revolution will Change the World* (Emerald Publishing 2018).

Krompier J, 'Safety First: The Case for Mandatory Data Sharing as a Federal Safety Standard for Self-driving' (2017) 2 *Journal of Law, Technology & Policy* 439.

Lee, J and See K, 'Trust in Automation: Designing for Appropriate Reliance' (2004) 46 *Human Factors* 50.

Levin S, 'Uber Cancels Self-driving Car Trial in San Francisco after State Forces It off Road' (*The Guardian*, 22 December 2016) <https://www.theguardian.com/technology/2016/dec/21/uber-cancels-self-driving-car-trial-san-francisco-california> (accessed 15 April 2019).

MIT, 'The Moral Machine' (2019) <http://moralmachine.mit.edu/> (accessed 15 April 2019).

Mittelstadt BD, Allo P, Taddeo M, Wachter S and Floridi L, 'The Ethics of Algorithms: Mapping the Debate' (2016) *Big Data & Society* <https://doi.org/10.1177/2053951716679679> (accessed 13 April 2019).

National Conference of State Legislatures, 'Autonomous Vehicles State Bill Tracking Database' (2019) <www.ncsl.org/research/transportation/autonomous-vehicles-legislative-database.aspx> (accessed 15 April 2019).

National Federation of the Blind, 'Blind Driver Challenge National Federation of the Blind' (2015) <www.blinddriverchallenge.org/> (accessed 13 April 2019).

National Highway Traffic Safety Administration, 'United States Federal Automated Vehicle Policy Accelerating the Next Revolution in Roadway Safety' (September 2016) <https://www.transportation.gov/sites/dot.gov/files/docs/AV%20policy%20guidance%20PDF.pdf> (accessed 13 April 2019).

National Transport Commission of Australia, 'Regulatory Reforms for Automated Road Vehicles' (November 2016) <https://www.ntc.gov.au/Media/Reports/(32685218-7895-0E7C-ECF6-551177684E27).pdf> (accessed 13 April 2019).

Organisation for Economic Co-operation and Development, 'Automated and Autonomous Driving Regulation under Uncertainty' (2015) <https://www.itf-oecd.org/sites/default/files/docs/15cpb_autonomousdriving.pdf> (accessed 19 June 2019).

Ranney T, 'Models of Driving Behavior: A Review of Their Evolution' (1994) 26 *Accident Analysis and Prevention* 733.

Roulstone A, 'Access to New Technology in the Employment of Disabled People' (1993) in Swain J et al. (eds), *Disabling Barriers, Enabling Environments* (2nd edn, Sage 2004), pp. 241–8.

Rowe JK, 'The Rise of the Machines: A New Risk for Claims?' (2018) 4 *JPI Law* 302.

Schafer B, 'Closing Pandora's Box? The EU Proposal on the Regulation of Robots' (2016) 99 *Pandora's Box (Journal of the Justice and the Law Society of the University of Queensland)* 55.

Schellekens M, 'Self-driving Cars and the Chilling Effect of Liability Law' (2015) 31 *Computer Law and Security Review* 506.

Smith B, 'Automated Vehicles Are Probably Legal in the United States' (2014) 1 *Texas A&M Law Review* 411.

Sommerville I, *Software Engineering* (9th edn, Pearson 2011).

Stupp C, 'Carmakers Fear EU Plans to Ease Data Flows Will Help Tech Rivals' (September 2016) *Euractiv* <https://www.euractiv.com/section/transport/news/carmakers-fear-eus-plan-to-ease-data-flows-will-help-tech-rivals/> (accessed 15 April 2019).

Stupp C, 'Commission Asked to Fund Cross-border Tests of Driverless Cars' (July 2006) *Euractiv* <https://www.euractiv.com/section/innovation-industry/news/commission-asked-to-fund-cross-border-tests-of-driverless-cars/> (accessed 15 April 2019).

Taylor, M and Maynard P, 'Self-driving Cars' (2015) 21 *Computer and Technology Law Review*.

UK Department for Transport, 'The Pathway to Driverless Cars Summary Report and Action Plan' (February 2015) <https://www.gov.uk/government/uploads/system/uploads/attachment_data/file/401562/pathway-driverless-cars-summary.pdf> (accessed 15 April 2019).

UK Department of Transport, 'The Pathway to Driverless Cars: A Code of Practice for Testing' (July 2015) <https://assets.publishing.service.gov.uk/government/uploads/system/uploads/attachment_data/file/401562/pathway-driverless-cars-summary.pdf> (accessed 15 April 2019).

UK Department for Transport Centre for Connected and Autonomous Vehicles, 'Pathway to Driverless Cars: Proposals to Support Advanced Driver Assistance Systems and Automated Vehicle Technologies' (July 2016) <https://www.gov.uk/government/uploads/system/uploads/attachment_data/file/536365/driverless-cars-proposals-for-adas-and_avts.pdf> (accessed 13 April 2019).

United Nations (2008) Convention on the Rights of Persons with Disabilities, <www.un.org/disabilities/documents/convention/convoptprot-e.pdf> (accessed 13 April 2019).

United States National Highway Traffic Safety Administration, 'Preliminary

Statement of Policy Concerning Automated Vehicles' (30 May 2013) <www.nhtsa.gov/staticfiles/rulemaking/pdf/Automated_Vehicles_Policy.pdf> (accessed 15 April 2019).

Vienna Convention on Road Traffic (8 November 1968) <https://www.unece.org/fileadmin/DAM/trans/conventn/crt1968e.pdf> (accessed 13 April 2019).

Wang W, Hou F, Tan H and Bubb H, 'A Framework for Function Allocations in Intelligent Driver Interface Design for Comfort and Safety' (2010) 3 *International Journal of Computational Intelligence Systems* 531.

PART IV

Textual Poaching:
Copyright in a Remixed World

12

Living in a Remixed World: Comparative Analysis of Transformative Uses in Copyright Law

Andres Guadamuz

1. A Story of Knitting and Sharks

In May 2009, series four of *Doctor Who* ran an episode called 'Partners in Crime', which featured a creature generated from human fat called the Adipose, an unremarkable monster that has not been featured since, and certainly lacking the iconic quality of the Daleks, the Cybermen, and even the more recent Weeping Angels.

Soon after the episode aired, a Brighton fan and keen knitter, who goes by the Internet nickname 'Mazzmatazz' (hereafter Mazz), created her own knitted version of the Adipose, took a picture of it, and uploaded it to her website.[1] This seemingly innocent act was noticed by someone at the BBC, and in a baffling turn of events, they issued the following threatening cease and desist letter:

> We note that you are supplying DR WHO items, and using trade marks and copyright owned by BBC. You have not been given permission to use the DR WHO brand and we ask that you remove from your site any designs connected with DR WHO. Please reply acknowledging receipt of this email, and confirm that you will remove the DR WHO items as requested.

Mazz published the letter on her website, and it generated an immediate outcry from the *Doctor Who* fandom community. She then asked for help from the Open Rights Group (ORG), a UK-based digital rights organisation

[1] The website no longer exists.

protecting consumers and free speech online. Together with ORG, I became involved and looked at the legality of the claim,[2] finding it wanting. The story was picked up by various news organisations after a signal boost from celebrities and popular social media accounts. Sensing a backlash, the BBC dropped the claims and the matter eventually died down without making it to court.

But the legal question remained unanswered. The cease and desist letter from the BBC stressed the point that Mazz's designs constituted unlicensed merchandise, and that BBC had every right to stop others from distributing their property. However, Mazz never sold any merchandise as such, she created a knitting design to tell others how to make their own versions of the Adipose. Mazz took a character, and transformed it into something entirely new and distinct from the original.

An entirely unrelated, but similar issue took place in February 2015 in the US during the Super Bowl. During the half-time show, pop singer Katy Perry baffled and endeared millions with an act that included two blue dancing sharks. The unwitting star of the show was the left shark, which fumbled his dance moves and won over the Internet. A myriad of memes exploded afterwards, but these did not elicit any legal response. Florida-based designer Fernando Sosa, who has a 3D printing modelling company that specialises in digital prototypes, quickly reacted to the left shark craze and created a model for a 3D printed left shark, making it available for sale in his online shop. The model is also freely available on the 3D printer design repository Thingiverse.[3] This prompted a reaction from Katy Perry's lawyers, who sent a letter[4] to Mr Sosa asking him to 'cease and desist from all further commercial use or exploitation of unauthorised products bearing the IP and copyrighted images'. The letter claims that Katy Perry owns 'the intellectual property depicted or embodied in connection with the shark images and costumes portrayed and used in Katy Perry's Super Bowl 2015 half-time performance'.

As with the BBC Adipose letter, this seemed like a far-reaching claim, as there is no specification of what type of intellectual property was being discussed. Were they claiming that they own the costume design? The dance routine? The video depicting the routine? The likeness of the shark? Even if we accept the contention that the shark is protected by copyright, that does not mean that Perry's lawyers were correct in pursuing the model maker. Sosa did not take a picture, did not publish the video, did not upload the song,

---

[2] Guadamuz, 'Partners in Copyright Crime' (*TechnoLlama*, 7 May 2008) <www.technollama.co.uk/doctor-who-partners-in-copyright-crime> (accessed 15 April 2019).

[3] Available at: <www.thingiverse.com/thing:667127> (accessed 15 April 2019).

[4] Available at: <https://www.scribd.com/document/254849521/Left-Shark-cease-and-desist> (accessed 15 April 2019).

and did not copy the dance routine. He created a model, scanned it and then uploaded it to be sold. Following press outcry and doubts from copyright scholars about the legitimacy of the claims, Parry's lawyers did not pursue the issue further.

As was the case with the Doctor Who knitting saga, the legal question here is whether the making of a model of a copyright work infringes copyright. While the two cases highlighted never made it to court, they are illustrative of a wider phenomenon, that of the endless transformation and re-use of copyright works in what Lessig calls remix culture.[5] It is perhaps trite to point out the changes brought about by the prevalence of social media and the ease of copying, remixing and republishing content online, but the fact is that we are indeed seeing a great change in the ways users consume and share content. But most importantly, we are also seeing a change on how users interact with copyright law.

Sosa and Mazz are in a small minority in that their remixed content was subject to attention from copyright owners. This is actually rare: with the prevalence of memes in social media, we are experiencing an explosion in potential copyright infringement that goes unpunished. In some ways, copyright has become irrelevant for viral content, as success is measured not in licensing fees, but rather on likes and shares. If we take a maximalist view of copyright, online viral success would not even be possible, as most sharing and remixing would be classified as copyright infringement. Content is protected by copyright, and sharing it should in principle preclude anyone else from reusing it without permission, let alone converting it into a different platform and distributing it that way. But virality is its own reward in many instances, and it would seem preposterous if any lawyers were to get involved when content goes viral. Take the famous 'Distracted Boyfriend' meme, which shows a picture of a man looking at another woman while his girlfriend looks at him, angry and horrified. The meme became very popular in social media, but the photographer who took the picture seems ambivalent about going after people for reusing his photograph. While accepting the popularity of the picture, he has expressed that everyone using and modifying the picture is doing so illegally, and he reserves the right to go after uses that he considers are displaying the images 'in a pejorative, offensive or any way that can harm the models or me'.[6]

---

[5] Lessig, *Remix: Making Art and Commerce Thrive in the Hybrid Economy* (Bloomsbury Academic 2008).

[6] Belam, 'I Didn't Know What a Meme Was, Says Distracted Boyfriend Photographer' (*The Guardian*, 30 August 2017) <https://www.theguardian.com/media/2017/aug/30/the-team-that-made-the-distracted-boyfriend-meme-have-split-up> (accessed 15 April 2019).

The common denominator in these cases is the transformation of a work protected by copyright. Various legal questions arise from such cases, such as whether there is copyright infringement in the transformative use of a protected work, and if so, where the line is crossed. If there is infringement, is there some sort of defence in copyright law? In the next sections, there will be an analysis of the copyright aspects of the remixed world.

2. Setting the Legal Question

Copyright law protects original literary, artistic, dramatic and musical works.[7] The owner of such works is awarded with several exclusive rights, including the right to copy, rent, perform, distribute and adapt the work (amongst others).[8] Using some of the examples above for illustration, the BBC owns the copyright over *Doctor Who*, including the scripts, the characters, the costume designs, the music and the broadcast itself. As the owner, it can stop others from performing any of the exclusive rights, so a person cannot sell a T-shirt showing a character from the show, or re-broadcast an episode.

These restrictions are easy to understand, and their enforcement is not controversial. In the case of copying, whenever there is a situation in which direct copying has taken place, copyright infringement is easy to determine.[9] If I am a *Star Wars* fan and I sell copies of *The Last Jedi*, or post a digital copy online, I am infringing copyright directly. Things become interesting when we start looking at less obvious re-uses of works; such as a book, a film or a song that resembles another work. Say I write a *Star Wars* story featuring Luke Skywalker, Princess Leia and Han Solo. Here the situation is more difficult, and it may depend completely on the facts of the case. While we can assume infringement, this may not always be straightforward.

Some of the case law in the UK dealing with non-literal copying has taken place in music. Take for example a song that resembles another, and the owner sues another musician alleging copyright infringement; in these cases, courts have to decide whether there is a causal connection between both works. For example, in the famous case of *Francis Day* v *Bron*,[10] two songs were found to be similar, but the court could not find a causal connection between the author and the alleged infringer; claimants must not only prove similarity, but that this similarity was due to an act of copying. Most cases of alleged copyright infringement in music that get litigated tend to rest

---

[7] Also sound recordings, films, broadcasts, and typographical arrangements. See Copyright, Designs and Patents Act 1988 (CDPA), s 1.

[8] CDPA, s 16.

[9] Take for example the famous case of *Walter* v *Lane* [1900] AC 539.

[10] *Francis Day & Hunter* v *Bron* [1963] Ch 587.

on the issue of similarity and causal connection. Did one composer know the other's work?[11] Using the *Star Wars* example, a casual look at my social media output and t-shirt collection would make it evident that I am familiar with *Star Wars*, so any investigation of non-literal copying would easily prove a causal connection.

It is in situations where non-literal copying has taken place that the courts have to do more work in deciding whether infringement has taken place, often having to analyse the elements of one work compared to the alleged infringement to determine whether any infringement has occurred. The traditional test is the idea–expression dichotomy:[12] whether a work has infringed another is usually determined by whether a work is an idea or the expression of an idea; this is understood as the fact that general ideas are not awarded protection, but the particular expression of that idea remains protected.

Most copyright infringement cases dealing with non-literal copying have to determine whether this line has been crossed. For example, in *Jules Rimet* v *Football Association*,[13] the drawings of two lions kicking a ball were subject to such analysis, the angle of the ball, the way in which one lion was positioned, the colouring of the images, were all used to determine that there was not infringement. In *Baigent* v *Random House*,[14] the authors of a book called *The Holy Blood and the Holy Grail* sued the publisher of *The Da Vinci Code*, alleging that many of the ideas contained in their book had been used in the novel. The court decided that original expression does not cover 'facts, ideas, theories and themes', and that there cannot be copyright infringement if an author has done research, and as a result produced a different work vaguely based on the general theories proposed in the source material.

Going back to an example in which I reuse characters from *Star Wars*, and having established causal connection, it is also useful to prove how much of a character I have been using, and if such a use is enough to warrant an infringement. Following the above-mentioned cases, just writing about a protagonist who undertakes a space adventure would not infringe copyright, but if the story features a young protagonist, an old wise man, a princess and a rogue with a large hairy sidekick, we may be getting into infringement territory, regardless of the names given to such characters.

---

[11] This has even made it to the present with the case of 'Blurred Lines', *Williams* v *Bridgeport Music Inc*, Case No CV13-06004-JAK (AGRx) (2015).

[12] Samuels, 'The Idea–Expression Dichotomy in Copyright Law' (1988) 56 *Tennessee Law Review* 321.

[13] *Jules Rimet Cup Ltd* v *Football Association Ltd* [2008] FSR 10.

[14] *Baigent and Leigh* v *The Random House Group Ltd* (CA) [2007] EWCA Civ 247.

These cases start to give us a good understanding of the legal issues involved in infringement and indirect copying. But the legal issues unearthed by social media and 3D printing go beyond those that have been explored in the case law. In cases such as the Left Shark, or the *Doctor Who* knitting saga, what is happening is that an artist takes a pre-existing character or design and creates an entirely different version to the original by transposing it into another medium altogether. The copying is indirect, but it is not based entirely on the original: it is a separate work in its own right.

Copyrights subsists on an original work, and therefore it would not subsist if the work were not original. But can an entirely different work based on another work be original? Some could argue that nothing is truly original,[15] and that all works are derivatives of a previous work of art. Fiction is replete with tropes and commonalities that can be found throughout literature, film and TV. The story of a young male protagonist who goes on an adventure to defeat a great evil, prompted by the old wise counsellor (who dies), accompanied a feisty female character (not necessarily a love interest), and also involving a couple of comic relief characters will seem familiar, and it fits *The Lord of the Rings, Star Wars* and *Harry Potter*. This hero adventure setting is so common that it was described by Joe Campbell in his seminal works on storytelling.[16]

However, copyright law tries to draw a line somewhere, and originality can arise in some circumstances even when there is some similarity between works. In UK copyright law, the originality standard has been that of skill and labour: if an author had invested enough skill and labour in the creation of a work, then it would be considered original.[17] Originality therefore does not require the idea to be completely new: in the context of copyright law, originality exists if 'sufficient amount of work was originated by the author'.[18] It does not matter that *Harry Potter* and *Star Wars* share some commonalities, it matters that there is enough work that was originated by the author in both instances.

One of the best cases exploring the issue of originality in copies is *Interlego* v *Tyco*.[19] In this case, Interlego, the producer of Lego bricks, sued manufacturer Tyco for producing a similar type of brick. This case, as many other in

---

[15] Woodmansee and Jaszi, *The Construction of Authorship: Textual Appropriation in Law and Literature* (Duke University Press 1994).

[16] Campbell, *The Hero With a Thousand Faces* (3rd edn, Prometheus Books 2008).

[17] *University of London Press* v *University Tutorial* [1916] 2 Ch 601.

[18] Laddie et al., *The Modern Law of Copyrights* (2nd edn, Butterworths 1995), p. 48.

[19] *Interlego AG* v *Tyco Industries Inc & Ors* (Hong Kong) [1988] UKPC 3.

the UK,[20] rests mostly on the interaction between design and copyright, as the Lego bricks have a functional element that is mostly protected through design. Interlego tried to argue that their bricks were subject to copyright protection, and produced a series of design pictures to prove the point, the idea being that any derived work arising from that picture would be an infringement. It was held that the bricks did not have copyright protection, and were mostly subject to design. But most importantly, Lord Oliver elucidated whether the original design pictures could have copyright, and whether resulting works would be original. He commented:

> Take the simplest case of artistic copyright, a painting or a photograph. It takes great skill, judgement and labour to produce a good copy by painting or to produce an enlarged photograph from a positive print, but no one would reasonably contend that the copy, painting, or enlargement was an 'original' artistic work in which the copier is entitled to claim copyright. Skill, labour or judgement merely in the process of copying cannot confer originality.

The European standard for originality is different, and does not involve any test for labour or effort going into the work. This standard is to be found in the Court of Justice of the European Union (CJEU) decision of *Infopaq*,[21] where originality exists if the work is the 'author's own intellectual creation', other cases have further added to this standard as meaning that this is an intellectual creation reflecting the author's own personality.[22] English courts have recently been moving more towards this standard, particularly in the case of *Temple Island Collections* v *New English Teas*.[23] The case involves a black and white image of the UK Parliament building and a bright red bus travelling across Westminster Bridge. The claimant owns the photograph, which is used in London souvenirs, and the defendant is a tea company that created a similar picture for a publicity campaign. Birss QC had to determine whether the original picture had copyright, and he concluded that when it comes to photography the composition is important: namely the angle of shot, the field of view, and the bringing together of different elements at the right place and the right time are enough to prove skill and labour, and therefore should have copyright.[24] This result was consistent with the skill

---

[20] Such as *LucasFilm Ltd & Ors* v *Ainsworth & Anor* [2011] UKSC 39.
[21] Case C-5/08, *Infopaq International A/S* v *Danske Dagblades Forening* [2009] ECR I-06569.
[22] See Case C-145/10, *Eva-Maria Painer* v *Standard Verlags GmbH & Others* [2010] ECR I-12533.
[23] *Temple Island Collections Ltd* v *New English Teas Ltd and Another (No 2)* [2012] EWPCC 1.
[24] Ibid., at 68–70.

and labour originality standard that was prevalent in the UK through various cases.[25] However, throughout *Temple Island Collections* Birss QC seamlessly integrates 'skill and labour' with Infopaq's 'intellectual creative effort', and through repetition makes them equivalent, and even becoming 'skill and labour/intellectual creation'.[26]

Even with both the UK and the European standards, it is evident that originality is less about creating an entirely new work, and more about the intellectual effort that goes into the work, particularly if it is something that can be described as reflecting the author's personality. So, a transformative use that is proven to be original enough could carry copyright protection, even if it is derived from another work. At some point, the line is crossed from copying an expression of an idea, and into the creation of a new work.

The problem is that the law has difficulties trying to determine exactly when and where the lines are crossed. In systems with a wide and permissive definition of originality, small additions to a new work would be enough to warrant new protection. More stringent definitions of what constitutes originality could leave large number of works infringing copyright as they would be deemed not original in their own right, but rather copies of the original. Imagine a copyright system in which the idea/expression dichotomy is narrow: you could give protection to something that more resembles an idea, so all expressions of that idea would be infringing. Taking the red bus case in *Temple Island Collections*, are all depictions of red buses crossing a bridge with the House of Parliament on the background infringing copyright, or just the specific copy that closely resembles the 'original'? Narrowly defining copyright originality could stifle innovation, so a balance has to be reached, and with few exceptions the definition seems to be that originality exists with a small amount of effort, as long as it reflects the author's personality.

In the next sections we will analyse the various solutions to this conundrum.

3. Transformative Use in US Copyright Law

Arguably, one of the most evolved systems of dealing with transformative uses can be found in US copyright law, thanks to the fair-use doctrine. Most copyright law jurisdictions around the world have a close-ended system of exceptions and limitations, that is, the number of exceptions is limited to a list of possible defences to infringement.[27] The US is almost unique in that it

---

[25] See for example *Interlego AG* v *Tyco Industries Inc & Ors* (Hong Kong) [1988] 3 All ER 949.

[26] Ibid., at 27. Various other examples can be found at 31 and 34.

[27] Senftleben, *Copyright, Limitations, and the Three-step Test: An Analysis of the Three-step Test in International and EC Copyright Law* (Kluwer Law International 2004).

has an open-ended system called the fair-use doctrine, which is determined mostly by case law.[28]

US copyright law with regards to transformative uses has had an interesting evolution that results from an almost unique set of characteristics when compared to other jurisdictions. First, there is the existence of the aforementioned fair-use doctrine that allows for a more open approach to what copyright law permits. Second, US originality requirements tend to be much lower than in other jurisdictions since the landmark case of *Feist Publications v Rural Telephone Service*,[29] where the Supreme Court of the United States (SCOTUS) had to decide on the originality of a phone directory containing names, towns and telephone listings. Feist Publications copied over four thousand entries from a 'white pages' directory compiled by Rural Telephone Service, and they did so without a licence. The prevalent principle before this decision was a 'sweat of the brow' approach that allowed the copyright of a compilation of facts if enough effort had gone into the creation of the compilation, even if facts are not protected by copyright.[30] The Court famously commented that '100 uncopyrightable facts do not magically change their status when gathered together in one place'.[31] Copyright protection therefore will only be given to 'those components of a work that are original to the author',[32] giving rise to a standard that requires 'a modicum of creativity'.[33] This has the interesting effect that facts are not protected, but anything that is shown to have even 'a modicum of creativity' could be protected.

This point is vital in understanding the law of transformative uses in the US, and there seems to be no clear defining line. One of the most important cases dealing with transformative use is *Campbell* v *Accuff-Rose Music*.[34] In this case, the rap group 2 Live Crew created an unlicensed version of the Roy Orbison song 'Pretty Woman'. Accuff-Rose Music, the owners of the rights over the song, sued the group for copyright infringement. The District Court ruled that the song was a parody, and therefore fair use, but a Court of Appeals reversed that decision and ruled that the commercial nature of the parody rendered it unfair. The decision was eventually sent to the SCOTUS,

---

[28] Nimmer, '"Fairest of Them All" and Other Fairy Tales of Fair Use' (2003) 66 *Law and Contemporary Problems* 263.

[29] *Feist Publications, Inc* v *Rural Telephone Service Co*, 499 US 340 (1991).

[30] Ginsburg, 'No "Sweat"? Copyright and Other Protection of Works of Information after Feist v. Rural Telephone' (1992) 92 *Columbia Law Review* 338.

[31] *Feist*, at 1287.

[32] Ibid., at 1289.

[33] Ibid., at 1288.

[34] *Campbell* v *Acuff-Rose Music* 510 US 569.

which sided with the first ruling and declared that the use was fair. The SCOTUS found that a use is transformative if it 'adds something new, with a further purpose or different character, altering the first with new expression, meaning, or message'.[35] Importantly, the commercial nature of the work is mostly irrelevant when it comes to such an analysis. In other words, if the transformative works creates a new expression and new meaning to the original, then it will be considered fair use.

One of the cultural sectors that has been litigated the most in the US with regards to transformative use is in art; as artistic expression often relies on breaking boundaries and exploring new forms, and some art tries to do this by relying on the legacy of previous artists.[36] Nobody would claim that Andy Warhol does not have copyright over his iconic Marilyn portrait or his Campbell's Soup montages, even if they use other's intellectual property. However, these boundaries are often blurry, and may depend entirely on meaning, both intended and unintended. An artist may want to convey some meaning, and the recipient may have a different reaction altogether.[37] Transformative use is therefore a very difficult area of copyright law to navigate.

Some of the artistic cases have dealt first with originality. In *Bell* v *Catalda*,[38] artist Alfred Bell was making 'mezzotint' copies of public domain paintings. The mezzotint is a print-making process using engraved metal plates,: this means that the original work must be converted into another format to produce the engraved picture. Art publisher Catalda Fine Arts began reprinting some of Bell's engravings, and the artist sued for copyright infringement. The defendant argued that Bell's work was not original, and therefore could not be protected by copyright because they were merely faithful reproductions of other works. The court in first instance agreed with Bell that the engravings were original and therefore worthy of protection; the Appeals court agreed and affirmed the decision. The court argued that the artworks were not exact reproductions, that different artists would engrave the mezzotint in a slightly different manner, and that those differences were enough to meet the originality requirement. The court equated engravings to translations: while works in the public domain cannot be

---

[35] Ibid., at 579.

[36] Torsen, 'Beyond Oil on Canvas: New Media and Presentation Formats Challenge International Copyright Law's Ability to Protect the Interests of the Contemporary Artist' (2006) 3 *SCRIPTed* 45.

[37] Heymann, 'Everything is Transformative: Fair Use and Reader Response' (2008) 31 *Columbia Journal of Law & the Arts* 445.

[38] *Alfred Bell & Co* v *Catalda Fine Arts, Inc* 191 F2d 99 (2d Cir 1951).

subject to copyright, the translations of a literary work is capable of copyright protection.

Beyond the originality argument, we come back to the question of how much transformation is necessary to make a derivative work an entirely new piece, and when it can be considered to be copyright infringement. One of the most cited cases in this instance is *Rogers* v *Koons*.[39] Photographer Art Rogers took a black and white photograph of a couple holding eight puppies in their arms on a park bench. Famous artist James Koons turned the photograph into a coloured wooden sculpture, and Rogers sued for copyright infringement. Koons did not perform the act himself, but rather had a wood workshop work under specific instructions to reproduce the photograph as accurately as possible. The defendant argued that the sculpture was fair use as parody, but the Court of Appeal found that it was not a parody; while it agreed that the spirit of the sculpture was meant as a critique of materialistic society, the reproduction 'was done in bad faith, primarily from profit-making motives, and did not constitute a parody of the original work'. The court then had to determine whether there had been enough copying of the original to warrant the existence of copyright infringement; the court answered this in the affirmative, and found that there was too much similarity between the picture and the sculpture.

Koons was later involved in another copyright infringement case in *Blanch* v *Koons*.[40] Fashion photographer Andrea Blanch had taken a photograph of a woman's feet resting on a man's lap wearing a pair of Gucci sandals and with a lounge in the background, and this was published in an *Allure* magazine advert entitled 'Silk Sandals'. Koons scanned the picture, took only the feet and sandals, changed the angle and included it with other feet and some doughnuts in a work called 'Niagara'. Blanch sued for copyright infringement, and Koons claimed fair use for transformative use. The lower court found in favour of the defendant, and the Court of Appeals also sided with Koons and affirmed the decision. Parody is not needed for transformative use, so the court had to determine whether there was enough transformation in the work to give rise to a new and original work of art, and in this respect the court agreed positively, as the inclusion of the originals had been subject to a change in colouration, background and angle. The court also had to determine whether the use was necessary, and here they took Koons's own words, as he had stated: 'By using an existing image, I also ensure a certain authenticity or veracity that enhances my commentary – it is

[39] *Art Rogers* v *Jeff Koons* 960 F2d 301 (2d Cir 1992).
[40] *Blanch* v *Koons*. 467 F3d 244 (2d Cir 2006).

the difference between quoting and paraphrasing – and ensure that the viewer will understand what I am referring to.'

The court concluded that the use of the photograph was fair and did not amount to copyright infringement.

It is very interesting to contrast both the Koons cases because they serve as perfect illustrations of what US copyright fair-use doctrine will consider to be transformative use. In the Rogers photograph, the derivative was too close to the original to be considered transformative, even if there was a transposition into another format altogether. In the Blanch case, there was enough done to the original to take it into a completely different meaning and context, and this was enough to make the use fair.

4. Transformative Use in UK Copyright Law

Most other jurisdictions have more problems with transformative uses, particularly because of the lack of open-ended copyright exception doctrines. The fair-dealing approach in a country like the UK offers an exhaustive list of exceptions and limitations to copyright law that make it more difficult to approach something like the re-use of a work, even if the resulting work is very different from the original.

As explained earlier, copyright is infringed by an act of copying, and the interpretation of when a work infringes copyright may depend on a set of circumstances that go beyond the more open-ended approach found in the fair-use system. Infringement can occur due to similarities, but courts will look at differences as well, and even a few differences could be vital in finding that a work is not infringing. For example, *Mitchell* v *BBC*,[41] where the court had to decide on the similarity of two sets of cartoon characters. While some small similarities were found, these were considered to be mere coincidences.

But whenever a causal link is found between the original and the alleged copy, then even large differences may be found to be infringing. Take the case of *Designer's Guild* v *Russell Williams*,[42] where the claimant had created a textile flower design, and brought an infringement suit against the defendant alleging that copying had taken place. The original flower design had a white background with red lines and coloured flowers, while the alleged copy had a black background with similar flowers, but different colouration. It was established as fact that the defendant's design was a colour mirror image of the original, hence the black background and differences in colour.

---

[41] *Mitchell* v *BBC* [2011] EWPCC 42.
[42] *Designer Guild Ltd* v *Russell Williams (Textiles) Ltd* [2001] FSR 113.

The court found that the copying was substantial, and therefore there was infringement.

Designer's Guild exemplifies that wherever copying has occurred, even if there are some colour changes afterwards, then there will be infringement, so a defendant would look at potential exceptions. In the CDPA, there is no such thing as a defence for transformative use as such. Until very recently, there was not even a parody defence for copyright infringement in the UK, but this changed in 2014 with the inclusion of sectio 30A of the CDPA,[43] which states that there is fair dealing in a work 'for the purposes of caricature, parody or pastiche'. The problem is mostly with the definition of these terms, which are left open to interpretation by the courts. The Hargreaves Review of Intellectual Property[44] was the originator of the reform to copyright law, explaining that parody is an important element of freedom of expression in modern society, and it uses the US example of fair use in parody to justify the benefit of such a system. But it does not define parody.

The CJEU case of *Deckmyn*[45] offers the most comprehensive definition in Europe. The case involves the publication and distribution in Belgium of a calendar on New Year's Eve 2011, in which a famous cover from the 1991 comic book *Suske en Wiske* was reproduced with a few variations to represent political ideas of a Flemish nationalist political party. The national court granted an injunction as it found that the 2011 calendar cover was indeed copyright infringement. The case was appealed and eventually referred to the CJEU, which was asked whether the calendar could be considered a parody. In that opinion, the court commented that the concept of parody must be interpreted by considering the usual meaning of the terms in everyday language, while also taking into account the context in which they occur and the purposes of the rules of which they are part. Perhaps most important for the present chapter, the court established:

> the essential characteristics of parody, are, first, to evoke an existing work, while being noticeably different from it, and secondly, to constitute an expression of humour or mockery. The concept of 'parody', within the meaning of that provision, is not subject to the conditions that the parody should display an original character of its own, other than that of displaying noticeable differences with respect to the original parodied work; that it

---

[43] As a result of the Copyright and Rights in Performances (Quotation and Parody) Regulations 2014.

[44] Hargreaves, *Digital Opportunity: A Review of Intellectual Property and Growth* (Independent Review for Prime Minister David Cameron, 2011).

[45] Case C-201/13, *Johan Deckmyn and Vrijheidsfonds VZW v Helena Vandersteen and Others* [2014] ECLI: EU: C: 2014:2132.

could reasonably be attributed to a person other than the author of the original work itself; that it should relate to the original work itself or mention the source of the parodied work.[46]

These seem to set a very specific boundary for what should be considered a parody. First, a parody is always a copy, and while there must be differences, as the parody is a separate work in its own right, the copy must at the same time be recognisable to the public at which the parody is directed, otherwise it would not be a parody. While the court helpfully dissects the concepts of parody, the question of the intent of the parody, whether it is to provoke humour or to mock, is more difficult, as the intent may be humorous, but it might be deemed to be mocking the original. Here the CJEU left the interpretation more open for national courts based on culture and intent, but recognised that there must be a balance of rights between the owner of the original work, and the freedom of expression of the person making the parody.

But parody is just one part of transformative use, and it may not serve to cover other re-uses that have other intentions. Some re-use may be artistic in nature, such as the Koons examples cited above, or they may be functional. But the main place where we will find transformations of works is in fan fiction, fan art, memes and fan re-use, such as Mazz's knitted Adipose monsters. If your work is based on pre-existing characters, it is going to be infringing as described above, even if the resulting adaptation is truly transformative, and contains enough originality on its own right.

The first problem is that, as mentioned before, there is no such thing as fair dealing for transformative uses other than parody, so we should look at existing case law to try to discern where the borders of copyright infringement for non-literal copy are drawn. In most cases, any sort of infringing use, even transformative, should be considered infringing, so it would be fair to assume that most non-parody uses would be infringing, but there may be a few exceptions.

The leading case dealing with this is *King Features Syndicate* v *Kleeman*,[47] where the owners of copyright in drawings of *Popeye, the Sailor* sued importers of Popeye dolls and other similar toys. More specifically, the defendant was accused of infringing copyright by having copied the cartoon strips depicting Popeye, and placing them in brooches and other media. The case rested on two questions. First, the defendants argued that the drawings of Popeye did not carry copyright as they could have been subject to independent design protection in the then Copyright Designs and Patents Act 1907; they argued

---

[46] Ibid., at 36.
[47] *King Features Syndicate* v *Kleeman* [1941] AC 417.

that because the claimants had licensed other works from the same designs, then the works were protected as a design and not as copyright, and therefore were in the public domain. On appeal, the House of Lords looked at the issue and decided that the works did have original copyright protection. Second, the court had to look at the question of substantial copying, in other words, whether the derivative works as depicted in dolls, brooches and other toys were actually infringing copyright. Clauson LJ looked at various derived items, such as dolls and brooches, and found some to be substantially similar to the original drawings and some not to be, but decided to agree that overall there was infringement. This case serves to illustrate that in most instances, even an act of transforming a work into another format or medium will result in copyright infringement.

What about more abstract forms of infringement? Say if you transform a TV character into knitting patterns, or if you build a statuette out of a character and then convert it further into a 3D-printed article?

Here we have to look further afield, as there is no specific or analogous case law. A relevant case is that of *Anacon* v *Environmental Research Technology*.[48] This case has nothing to do with art, but rather deals with circuit design. In this case, the defendants made a list of the components in a circuit and their interaction with one another, and then made a circuit on its own that looked completely different from the original. The defendants claimed that their design was artistic and therefore different. However, Jacob J found that the actual list was a literary work, and therefore it was subject to copyright protection as such. This is relevant to those transformative uses where a work has been transformed into a set of instructions, as with the knitting designs described in the first section. It would be fair to say that under some circumstances, transformative uses such as knitting designs could be subject to their own protection, as the instructions are a literary depiction that could be very different from one that conveys the original meaning. An added benefit of considering a transposition of items from one format into a literary set of instructions is that this type of copyright is not infringed when those instructions are used to produce what is described. In other words, instructions for making things, such as knitting patterns and recipes, are protected only as literary or artistic works, and therefore the item produced from such instructions does not infringe the original design.[49]

This issue was also explored in *Sandman* v *Panasonic*.[50] The claimant

---

[48] *Anacon* v *Environmental Research Technology* [1994] FSR 659.

[49] See *Bridgid Folley* v *Elliot* [1982] RPC 433.

[50] *Sandman* v *Panasonic UK Limited, Matsushita Electric Industrial Co Ltd* [1998] EWHC Patents 346.

had published two circuit designs drawings for an amplifier in a journal in 1982. This design was eventually included in circuits that were included in musical devices such as CD players produced by Panasonic and Masushita Electronics. The claimant argued that the inclusion of such circuits in these products was copyright infringement, and the defendants applied for the litigation to be stuck as the argument was frivolous. Leaving aside the fact that copyright law does not protect functional elements,[51] Pumfrey J astutely described the dichotomy between design and the item resulting from the design as like that of musical notation and the resulting tune. Each has its own type of protection, but they are interlinked. A built circuit bears no visual resemblance to the design that gave rise to it, but it describes a set of instructions that can give rise to the circuit.

To summarise, it seems like the state of the law in the UK is not very favourable to transformative uses, outside of a few specific exceptions such as parody. When it comes to literal copying of one item into another, we can always assume infringement. If the case involves non-literal copying, then the substantial amount that was copied will be examined, and here it seems that under most circumstances there will be infringement, even if the resulting work is a very different medium. The situation is less clear with more novel transformative uses, such as knitting. It seems that creating a set of instructions might be enough to warrant an entirely different type of copyright protection of those very instructions. Having said that, the lack of specific fair-dealing provisions for transformative use would mean that most remixes are indeed infringing copyright in the various UK jurisdictions.

5. Room for Reform?

It would be fair to say that the state of transformative use is not harmonised internationally. While transformative uses can be accepted more in the US, the situation in other jurisdictions is less favourable to consumers who may be engaged in large-scale copyright infringement through the use of memes, remixes and fan fiction.

The Internet has made it possible for consumers to become creators, and this creative force often results in practices that would otherwise have been considered copyright infringement.[52] There are a few examples of memes that are subject to enforcement from time to time, a penguin picture belonging to *National Geographic* has become a famous meme called the 'Socially Awkward Penguin', and the magazine has firmly enforced its commercial

---

[51] See for example *Navitaire Inc* v *Easyjet Airline Co & Another* [2004] EWHC 1725 (Ch).
[52] Cotter, 'Memes and Copyright' (2005) 80 *Tulane Law Review* 331.

use on various occasions.[53] However, this is the exception to the rule, and millions of meme pictures daily go unpunished around the world.

This is similar to other common forms of re-use and remix of content, such as fan fiction[54] and machinima,[55] where users generate transformative uses based on popular works. The situation here is not precisely legally complicated, as it is almost universally recognised that such uses are infringing copyright. However, the practicalities make copyright law almost redundant, as in reality copyright holders tend to ignore fan re-use. This makes sense for economic and marketing reasons, as it is considered a bad business practice to sue your fan base. As explained by Stendell,[56] copyright holders often choose to ignore fan fiction because it can be 'the centerpiece of a thriving fan culture, a community that benefits copyright holders economically as well as intangibly'.[57]

If remixes and transformative uses are so blatantly common online, then why not try to change copyright law to recognise them? Talking in the context of user-generated content in general, Wong explains:

> Yet with the rise of participatory culture and Web 2.0, where the reader/listener/viewer is no longer just a passive consumer of content but is empowered to be an active participant and even a co-creator or collaborator, it is crucial that copyright law recognize the importance of the user/consumer of copyrighted content as well.[58]

If everyone is breaking the law, then maybe there is something wrong with the law in the first place, and it may be on everyone's best interest to try to make things more compliant with transformative use. It is unlikely that memes will disappear overnight, or that the technological challenges brought

---

[53] Jones, 'One Does Not Simply Post Memes without Reviewing the IP Issues' (*Lexology*, 14 April 2017) <https://www.lexology.com/library/detail.aspx?g=c470fc1e-d61e-4f98-a3b3-d113233998db> (accessed 15 April 2019).

[54] Warr, 'Fanfiction: Creators, Communities and Copyright' (2014), *Internet Policy Review* <https://policyreview.info/articles/news/fanfiction-creators-communities-and-copyright/304> (accessed 15 April 2019).

[55] Freedman, 'Machinima and Copyright Law' (2005) 13 *Journal of Intellectual Property Law* 235.

[56] Stendell, 'Fanfic and Fan Fact: How Current Copyright Law Ignores the Reality of Copyright Owner and Consumer Interests in Fan Fiction' (2005) 58 *Southern Methodist University Law Review* 1551.

[57] Ibid., at 1559.

[58] Wong, '"Transformative" User-Generated Content in Copyright Law: Infringing Derivative Works or Fair Use?' (2008) 11 *Vanderbilt Journal of Entertainment and Technology Law* 1075.

by 3D printing will go away, but it might be time for us to start looking at some other options. Talking in the US on copyright law, Vitanza urges the adoption of a workable standard of transformative use that balances the possibility of a derivative work turning something original into something different by adding substantial value, even if a work borrowed more than necessary from another piece.[59]

Fair use is easier to amend; the situation could be more difficult for us in fair-dealing countries, but there is no need to despair. First, there is a commonality of legal elements between memes, fan fiction, machinima, knitting and 3D printing. In most instances, remixes are not commercial in nature, and meme creators and knitters are not benefiting financially from their creations: the remixes are often a labour of love for the original. In most cases, we have a transformative use of the original that requires considerable skill and labour to pull. The level of originality and creativity on display is astounding, and while we are moving away from that standard, there should perhaps be recognition that at least some of these uses should be permitted in some sense or another. Things are going to get more complicated with wider application of technologies such as 3D printing[60] and augmented reality.[61] It is evident that users are going to be able to create their own versions of much-loved characters in ways that may compete with legitimate marketing and merchandising products. Intellectual property owners must be prepared to take into account new technologies, but also the law of transformative uses must evolve to accommodate the changes.

The closest that we have come to a change in the law took place recently with the publication of a draft report on copyright reform by the German MEP Julia Reda.[62] In that draft report, Reda proposed a radical way to look at copyright that allowed for some exceptions for transformative uses that did not conflict with the normal exploitation of a work. Unfortunately, this proposal was seriously watered down in the final text approved by the Parliament, and the only concession was a mild

---

[59] Vitanza, 'Popular Culture Derivatives: Castle Rock Entertainment, Inc. v. Carol Publishing Group, Inc.' (1999) 14 *Berkley Technology Law Journal* 43.

[60] Mendis, '"The Clone Wars" – Episode 1: The Rise of 3D Printing and its Implications for Intellectual Property Law – Learning Lessons from the Past?' (2013) 35 *European Intellectual Property Review* 155.

[61] Guadamuz, 'Pokémon Go: Augmented Reality Tests IP' (*WIPO Magazine*, February 2017) <www.wipo.int/wipo_magazine/en/2017/01/article_0005.html> (accessed 15 April 2019).

[62] Reda, 'Draft Report on the Implementation of Directive 2001/29/EC of the European Parliament and of the Council of 22 May 2001 on the harmonisation of certain aspects of copyright and related rights in the information society' (2014/2256(INI)) <http://bit.ly/2glFxnv> (accessed 15 April 2019).

promise to look into exceptions and limitations in responding to future digital challenges:

> Notes that exceptions and limitations must be applied in such a way as to take account of the purpose for which they were designed and the particular respective characteristics of the digital and analogue environments, while maintaining the balance between the interests of rightholders and the interests of the public; calls, therefore, on the Commission to examine the possibility of reviewing a number of the existing exceptions and limitations in order to better adapt them to the digital environment, taking into account the ongoing developments in the digital environment and the need for competitiveness.[63]

The resulting proposal for reform from the Commission is being discussed at the time of writing, and it does not even contain the cited proposal. While this is a missed opportunity for real change, the fact that this is even under discussion could be a sign of future reform. Perhaps we could have something that I would like to call a 'fan art' exception to copyright law. This is already recognised by many copyright owners who are not going after their fans, and on the contrary, they allow the amazing creativity on display to act as an engagement tool with customers. Already some companies are quite open about this, allowing fan-made creations to inform their property, and even incorporating fan creativity as an indication of popularity. Perhaps it is time for the law to catch up with non-commercial transformative uses.

Commercial use could retain the same status of infringement, as it can be argued that a person who produces a remix of another work for the purpose of commercial gain would be in direct competition with the original author. Creating a fan fiction story featuring the characters in a Harry Potter novel for non-commercial use would be acceptable, but selling the same story on Amazon, or making a theatre production of said work and charging the public would not be acceptable, and could be dealt with as infringement.

A reform to the fair-dealing system that brings it more in line with the transformative use defence in existence in other jurisdictions could alleviate the existing disparity between widespread infringement and the law as it exists in the statute books. A vibrant fan fiction and meme community is usually the hallmark of a successful creative work, and allowing fans to remix and reuse their favourite characters non-commercially would help to alleviate the existing situation. There is little to be gained by content owners in pursuing

---

[63] European Parliament resolution of 9 July 2015 on the implementation of Directive 2001/29/EC of the European Parliament and of the Council of 22 May 2001 on the harmonisation of certain aspects of copyright and related rights in the information society.

knitting communities that love *Doctor Who*. On the contrary, the presence of knitted scarves, thirteenth Doctor fan art and 3D printed daleks can only be seen as a positive. Copyright law should reflect this fact, instead of tarnishing every fan with the infringer brush. A more nuanced and balanced approach to derivative works, adaptations and transformative uses is in order.

As an old wise counsellor once said, 'only a Sith deals in absolutes'.

References

Belam M, 'I Didn't Know What a Meme Was, Says Distracted Boyfriend Photographer' (*The Guardian*, 30 August 2017) <https://www.theguardian.com/media/2017/aug/30/the-team-that-made-the-distracted-boyfriend-meme-have-split-up> (accessed 15 April 2019).

Campbell J, *The Hero with a Thousand Faces* (3rd edn, Prometheus Books 2008).

Cotter TF, 'Memes and Copyright' (2005) 80 *Tulane Law Review* 331.

European Parliament Resolution of 9 July 2015 on the implementation of Directive 2001/29/EC of the European Parliament and of the Council of 22 May 2001 on the harmonisation of certain aspects of copyright and related rights in the information society (2014/2256(INI)) <www.europarl.europa.eu/sides/getDoc.do?type=TA&reference=P8-TA-2015-0273&language=EN> (accessed 15 April 2019).

Freedman MB, 'Machinima and Copyright Law' (2005) 13 *Journal of Intellectual Property Law* 235.

Ginsburg JC, 'No "Sweat"? Copyright and Other Protection of Works of Information after Feist v. Rural Telephone' (1992) 92 *Columbia Law Review* 338.

Guadamuz A, 'Partners in Copyright Crime' (*TechnoLlama*, 7 May 2008) <www.technollama.co.uk/doctor-who-partners-in-copyright-crime> (accessed 15 April 2019).

Guadamuz A, 'Pokémon Go: Augmented Reality Tests IP' (*WIPO Magazine*, February 2017) <www.wipo.int/wipo_magazine/en/2017/01/article_0005.html> (accessed 15 April 2019).

Hargreaves I, *Digital Opportunity: A Review of Intellectual Property and Growth* (Independent Review for Prime Minister David Cameron, 2011).

Heymann LA, 'Everything is Transformative: Fair Use and Reader Response' (2008) 31 *Columbia Journal of Law & the Arts* 445.

Jones C, 'One Does Not Simply Post Memes without Reviewing the IP Issues' (*Lexology*, 14 April 2017) <https://www.lexology.com/library/detail.aspx?g=c470fc1e-d61e-4f98-a3b3-d113233998db> (accessed 15 April 2019).

Laddie H et al., *The Modern Law of Copyrights* (2nd edn, Butterworths 1995).

Lessig, L, *Remix: Making Art and Commerce Thrive in the Hybrid Economy* (Bloomsbury Academic 2008).

Mendis D, ' "The Clone Wars" – Episode 1: The Rise of 3D Printing and its Implications for Intellectual Property Law – Learning Lessons from the Past?' (2013) 35 *European Intellectual Property Review* 155.

Nimmer D, ' "Fairest of Them All" and Other Fairy Tales of Fair Use' (2003) 66 *Law and Contemporary Problems* 263.

Reda J, 'Draft Report on the Implementation of Directive 2001/29/EC of the European Parliament and of the Council of 22 May 2001 on the harmonisation of certain aspects of copyright and related rights in the information society' (2014/2256(INI)) <http://bit.ly/2glFxnv> (accessed 15 April 2019).

Samuels E, 'The Idea–Expression Dichotomy in Copyright Law' (1988) 56 *Tennessee Law Review* 321.

Senftleben M, *Copyright, Limitations, and the Three-step Test: An Analysis of the Three-step Test in International and EC Copyright Law* (Kluwer Law International 2004).

Stendell L, 'Fanfic and Fan Fact: How Current Copyright Law Ignores the Reality of Copyright Owner and Consumer Interests in Fan Fiction' (2005) 58 *Southern Methodist University Law Review* 1551.

Torsen MA 'Beyond Oil on Canvas: New Media and Presentation Formats Challenge International Copyright Law's Ability to Protect the Interests of the Contemporary Artist' (2006) 3 *SCRIPTed* 45.

Vitanza E, 'Popular Culture Derivatives: Castle Rock Entertainment, Inc. v. Carol Publishing Group, Inc.' (1999) 14 *Berkley Technology Law Journal* 43.

Warr P, 'Fanfiction: Creators, Communities and Copyright' (2014), *Internet Policy Review* <https://policyreview.info/articles/news/fanfiction-creators-communities-and-copyright/304> (accessed 15 April 2019).

Wong MWS, '"Transformative" User-Generated Content in Copyright Law: Infringing Derivative Works or Fair Use?' (2008) 11 *Vanderbilt Journal of Entertainment and Technology Law* 1075.

Woodmansee M and Jaszi P, *The Construction of Authorship: Textual Appropriation in Law and Literature* (Duke University Press 1994).

13

Repost This: Instagram and
the Art of Re-photography

Melissa de Zwart

There's a lot of cats on Instagram. Food too.
And there's tons of photos of people who take photographs of themselves.
(Yes, I know the word.)

Richard Prince[1]

In 2014 the notorious American appropriation artist Richard Prince held a series of exhibitions in the US titled 'New Portraits'. That exhibition featured thirty-seven inkjet prints on high-quality art canvas of images or 'screen saves' that Prince had taken from the social media platform Instagram. For the purposes of his exhibition he had selected a range of photographs, all of which were originally produced by third parties, some of them professional photographers, others not. Many of these images had already been posted on Instagram, but a number had been selected from other sources and posted to Instagram by Prince for the purposes of his art, via his Instagram account.

Prince's method was prompted by discussions with his daughter regarding her own use of social media. Observing her use of the visual social media platforms Instagram and Tumblr, and inspired by his love for his iPhone, he began taking screenshots of Instagram images, reposting them to his own account, saving them to his personal gallery of images and experimenting with adding his own comments below the image, all practices facilitated and to some degree encouraged by the platform itself.[2] Prince set up his first account on Instagram in 2013, singing the praises of the visual social media

---

[1] Available at: <www.gagosian.com/exhibitions/richard-prince--june-12-2015> (accessed 15 April 2019).

[2] *Highsnobiety*, 'Richard Prince: The Controversial Artist and Master of Appropriation'

364

platform: 'It's almost like it was invented for someone like myself … It's like carrying around a gallery in your pocket … Everything became easy. It was enjoyable. It reminded me of a free concert.'[3] As Prince has observed with glee, the existence of photograph-based social media platforms such as Instagram, mean that: 'You replace rephotographing with screen grabs'.[4]

Two of the images that were used by Prince as the basis for his 'New Portraits' are currently the subject of copyright disputes between Prince and the original photographers. While these cases are ongoing they raise clear issues not only about the relationship between copyright, the fair use and fair-dealing exceptions and art, but also the very nature of social media itself. This chapter will use the example of the Prince 'New Portraits' exhibition to explore the tensions that exist within social media, in particular the image-rich platform of Instagram, for copyright, considering the practices and attitudes of users to posting and reposting of their images. It will begin by briefly outlining the nature of Instagram, it will then consider the creation of the 'New Portraits' exhibition, followed by a discussion of responses to that exhibition and finally a consideration of the legal, ethical and artistic issues raised by online social media practices that facilitate copying, manipulation and reposting of visual images. Specifically it will ask the question if the recontextualising of art through placement in a different 'space' continues to be a valid justification for re-use of copyright material within the definition of fair use in the internet age.

1. What is Instagram?

Instagram first entered the 'applications' market in October 2010, and has amassed a steady increase in number of users, reaching 1 billion active users in June 2018.[5] Instagram clearly exemplifies the shift from a text-based to a visual social media, initially requiring nothing more than posting an image. In 2016, the platform expanded to include daily 'stories', consisting of a number of updates from users across the day, and video, facilitating expanded amounts of content delivery.

(5 September 2016) <www.highsnobiety.com/2016/09/05/richard-prince-artist> (accessed 15 April 2019).

[3]   Swanson, 'How Richard Prince Got Kicked off Instagram (And Then Reinstated)' (*Vulture*, 8 March 2014) <www.vulture.com/2014/03/how-richard-prince-got-kicked-off-instag ram.html> (accessed 15 April 2019).

[4]   Ibid.

[5]   Constine, 'Instagram Hits 1 Billion Monthly Users, Up from 800M in September' (*TechCrunch*) <https://techcrunch.com/2018/06/20/instagram-1-billion-users/> (accessed 15 April 2019).

Being a largely visual medium, Instagram has naturally appealed to visual artists of all kinds, especially professional and amateur photographers, allowing immediate sharing of work with followers. It has now expanded to a vast range of content, including food, travel, clothing and fashion trends generally. For many users the image posted on Instagram is a culmination of hours or days of hard work. However, the popularity of accounts and the need to have a social media presence that regularly appeals to followers may place pressure on account owners to continue to produce quality content. This means that many accounts use (or possibly reuse or repost) the images and content of other accounts and creators to keep the feed refreshed and updated. Users are encouraged by the tools within the app to like, comment upon and share the posts of others.

There is increasing pressure on creators to use Instagram as an advertising and distribution platform. Creative artists such as designers and photographers now find that their services are more commonly looked for via social media than via traditional advertising platforms. For example, wedding photographers will be looked for on the basis of displaying a particular style and being cross-tagged by sought-after wedding venues, designers or key destinations (for example #destinationweddings #vintagewedding #bohowedding #lookslike film). Online blogs have taken over from the well-thumbed wedding magazines of the past and they are tagged in posts in the hope that they will pick up and highlight the work of particular photographers or other creative workers (for example, #junebugweddings, #hellomay). Similarly models and fashion designers will share current trends and concepts through the use of imagery and strategic hashtags. It seems virtually impossible in this environment for creative workers to simply opt out of Instagram unless an entirely different business model has been developed by the creator. Even professional photographers contracted to an agency will post to social media to create interest, attract an audience and maintain profile.[6]

Instagram is now used increasingly for marketing. This has led to the emergence of a new group of social media marketers called 'influencers'.[7] These people are paid for advertising and product placement, able to charge fees according to numbers of followers. As in lifestyle magazine, much of the content they post is ghosted by professional photographers. Like glossy

---

[6] See, for example, the posting to Twitter of a photograph of earthquake devastation in Haiti by award-winning photographer Daniel Morel, *Agence France Presse* v *Morel & Getty Images*, 10 Civ 02730 (SDNY, 14 January 2013).

[7] Chafkin, 'Confessions of an Instagram Influencer' (*Bloomberg Businessweek*, 30 November 2016) <https://www.bloomberg.com/news/features/2016-11-30/confessions-of-an-instagram-influencer> (accessed 15 April 2019).

magazines, these accounts suggest a glamorous and idealised lifestyle, reflecting an imagined persona rather than a real person (ironically given the very common tag given on such accounts to attract followers: #liveauthentic).[8] In addition to these sponsored accounts there are of course fake accounts, operated by fans, bots, spammers and advertisers for a range of reasons. There are countless stories of images being copied and reposted by other users on Instagram for a variety of reasons.[9]

Instagram also facilitates the creation of multiple accounts, and in this way has enabled users to explore a range of interests, hobbies and businesses, without necessarily being linked to any person profile or account. The simple visual medium has also provided a platform for the creation of fandom accounts, which provide a simple entry-level access to social media and the exploits of online fandom. There are even 'how-tos' dedicated to explaining how to create a fandom account. At its most basic, all that is required is to set up an account with a suitable name, and to post images and memes from that fandom. Importantly, images should be 'tagged' with the relevant hashtag to ensure that they are visible to other like-minded fans, who may instantly copy and repost such images.

Prince's response to Instagram, as embodied in his 'New Portraits' exhibition, appears to capture the essence of social media, and more particularly, Instagram. As he explains in his notes to the exhibition:

> Besides cats, dogs, and food, people put out photos of themselves and their friends all the time, every day, and, yes, some people put themselves out twice on Mondays. I started 'following' people I knew, people I didn't know, and people who knew each other. It was innocent.[10]

Not only could Prince follow these accounts, with one user leading to another:

> I can start out with someone I know and then checkout who they follow or who's following them, and the rabbit hole takes on an outer body experience where you suddenly look at the clock and it's three in the morning.

---

[8] Ibid.

[9] Wang, 'Instagram is Full of Copyright Loopholes – It Made My Career, But It Could Break Yours' (*Quartz*, 11 June 2015) <https://qz.com/424885/i-got-a-job-posting-photos-of-my-dog-on-instagram-but-others-arent-so-lucky/> (accessed 15 April 2019); and Lyons, 'Camera Copia: Reflections on Rephotography in the Instagram Age' (*New American Notes Online*, Issue 10, December 2016) <https://nanocrit.com/issues/issue10/camera-copia-reflections-rephotography-instagram-age> (accessed 15 April 2019).

[10] Prince (exhibition), 'New Portraits' (Gagosian, 12 June–1 August 2015) <www.gagosian.com/exhibitions/richard-prince--june-12-2015> (accessed 15 April 2019).

I end up on people's grids that are so far removed from where I began, it feels psychedelic.[11]

In addition to this Prince could save these images to his iPhone gallery. He noted that some of these images exist only on Instagram, a unique platform for the publication of self-portraits (a term he prefers to 'selfies'), which must fit within the confines of the platform interface. From this obsession, the 'New Portraits' exhibition emerged.

2. Richard Prince and the Art of 'Re-photographing'

This method of 're-photographing' an existing work was not a new workstyle for Prince, merely the extension of an existing practice into a new online medium. Re-photography emerged as an art form of the postmodern era, involving the literal photographing of an earlier photograph. Artists including Prince, Sherrie Levine, Cindy Sherman and Jack Goldstein (the so-called 'Pictures Generation') created new works that challenged the concept of a photograph being both 'original' and 'realistic'.[12] Prince had started his artistic career in the mid-1970s re-photographing the cowboy from Malboro cigarette advertisements, using images literally torn from the pages of magazines, blown up to blurry detail, removing the Malboro logo and focusing on the macho man on the horse. These images of the archetypal American hero were slow to gain popularity, but in 2005 one of the 're-photographs' called 'Untitled (Cowboy)' sold for US$1.2 million and another for US$3.7 million in 2014.[13] 'Untitled (Cowboy)' is also listed in the Top 100 most influential images of all time by *Time Magazine*.[14]

Prince's most notorious work (certainly prior to his 'New Portraits' exhibition) was a 're-photograph' of Brooke Shields at ten years of age standing naked in a bath, surrounded by steam, with full glossy makeup and hairstyling, a photo originally taken by photographer Gary Gross, at Shields' mothers' request, in 1976 and published in *Sugar 'n' Spice* (a Playboy

[11] Ibid.

[12] Fineman, 'The Pleasure Principle'; Crimp, 'The Photographic Activity of Postmodernism' (*Slate*, 30 October 2003) <https://slate.com/culture/2003/10/richard-prince-s-naughty-nurses.html> (accessed 15 April 2019), p. 91.

[13] Swanson, 'Is Richard Prince the Andy Warhol of Instagram?' (*Vulture*, 20 April 2016) <www.vulture.com/2016/04/richard-prince-the-andy-warhol-of-instagram.html> (accessed 15 April 2019); Cohen, 'Who Actually Shot Richard Prince's Iconic Cowboys?' (*Artsy*, 2 March 2018) <https://www.artsy.net/article/artsy-editorial-richard-prince-stole-marlboro-man> (accessed 15 April 2019).

[14] *Time*, '100 Photos: The Most Influential Images of All Time' <http://100photos.time.com/photos/richard-prince-cowboy> (accessed 15 April 2019).

publication).[15] In 1983 Prince took a photo of the original photograph, placed it in a gilt frame and titled his version 'Spiritual America', a title that had already been used by Alfred Stieglitz in his 1923 photo of a close-up of the genitals of a castrated male horse, thus creating a juxtaposition of sexual themes and, potentially, a commentary on the preoccupations, double standards and secret obsessions of modern America. Copies of Prince's work were for sale for $100 at a small, shopfront gallery, opened at irregular days and times, but despite the scandal created by the image, none of them sold.[16] However the exhibition certainly added to Prince's notoriety, if not his bank balance. The work was later to be part of an exhibition at the Tate Modern in London in 2009 when London Metropolitan Police requested that the work be removed from the exhibition and exhibition catalogue to ensure that the museum did 'not inadvertently break the law or cause any offense to their visitors'.[17] In 2014 Prince himself found that his Instagram account had been blocked after he had posted an image of his version of 'Spiritual America' on the social media platform. Prince had already received several warnings about the inappropriate content of his postings, and in typical Prince fashion had resorted to Twitter to lambast Instagram about its policy against posting nude photos: 'Instagram just requested I remove all naked pictures of people I've been posting. Praise the Fucking Lord.'[18] Deliberately continuing to post images featuring naked men, women and children, Prince was therefore unsurprised when Instagram finally suspended his account. However, when invited to comment, Instagram responded that rather than his entire account being suspended, the single image should have been removed:

> Hi richardprince4,
> You may have recently had trouble accessing your Instagram account.
> We're sorry for the inconvenience, and you should be able to log in now.
> The issue we were having hasn't affected your photos.
> Thanks,
> The Instagram Team[19]

---

[15] Higgins and Dodd, 'Tate Modern Removes Naked Brooke Shields Picture after Police Visit' (*The Guardian*, 30 September 2009) <https://www.theguardian.com/artanddesign/2009/sep/30/brooke-shields-naked-tate-modern> (accessed 15 April 2019).

[16] Swanson, 'Is Richard Prince the Andy Warhol of Instagram?'

[17] Higgins and Dodd, 'Tate Modern Removes Naked Brooke Shields Picture after Police Visit').

[18] Petreycik, 'Richard Prince Loves Boobs and Hates Instagram: Live!' (*Animal*, 18 June 2013) <http://animalnewyork.com/2013/richard-prince-loves-boobs-and-hates-instagram-nsfw/> (accessed 15 April 2019).

[19] Swanson, 'How Richard Prince Got Kicked off Instagram (And Then Reinstated)'.

Thus the foundations were established for Prince's love/hate relationship with Instagram. The online platform offered him a technique that built directly on his own prior artistic practice: a vast smorgasbord of artworks to re-photograph; the capacity to build, store and access his own gallery of images and even a set of built-in tools to manipulate those images. These tools almost inevitably resulted in the controversial 'New Portraits' exhibition and the copyright disputes that followed.

3. New Portraits

In order to create the images in the 'New Portraits' exhibition Prince took a screenshot of an image appearing on an existing account, or uploaded an image he found elsewhere to his own Instagram account. He then reported all of the comments that appeared under the image and posted his own comment, in order to make that comment appear in close proximity to the image. He had discovered a 'hack' whereby he could report all of the other comments under an image as a 'Spam or Scam' and they would disappear, leaving Prince's own comments at the top (or as close as Prince wanted to the top) of the comments list, and hence proximate to the image. Those comments were what he describes as 'Birdtalk':

> The language I started using to make 'comments' was based on Birdtalk. Non sequitur. Gobbledygook. Jokes. Oxymorons. 'Psychic Jiu-Jitsu.' Some of the language came directly from TV. If I'm selecting a photo of someone and adding a comment to their gram and an advertisement comes on … I use the language that I hear in the ad. Inferior language. It works. It sounds like it means something. What's it mean? I don't know.[20]

Prince compares such notes to the writing of James Joyce, MAD magazine, advertising copy, fragmented lyrics, quotations and advice, something that appears to have meaning, but in fact may be little more than entertaining noise. The links to advertising appear particularly relevant in the context of Instagram, which has evolved into a powerful advertising, rather than a purely social or entertainment platform. Again, Prince is alive to this fact, noting: 'If Twitter was editorial … then Instagram was advertising.'[21] Predictably however, given the nature of the images chosen for the exhibition, some of the comments were closer to sleaze rather than advertising, such as the comment under the image of musician Sky Ferreira seated in a red car: 'Enjoyed the ride today. Let's do it again. Richard.'[22] Of course,

---

20 Prince (exhibition), 'New Portraits'.
21 Ibid.
22 Plaugic, 'The Story of Richard Prince and his $100,000 Instagram Art' (*The Verge*, 30

this sort of *double entendre* is also perfectly at home in the advertising world.

Each image selected by Prince was re-photographed together with his now proximate comment, enlarged and printed on art-quality canvas as a single edition work. The format was consistent with a screenshot from Instagram, featuring the distinctive white space, user name, number of likes and comments. In other words, it was a giant, albeit slightly blurred art quality screenshot of an iPhone screen.

The images selected by Prince featured both the 'famous and Internet-famous people'.[23] As discussed above, Instagram has given birth to a new sort of 'famous'. People may become well known solely through their Instagram accounts, becoming influential for setting fashion, food or fitness trends that can then be leveraged into businesses, advertising or other profitable formats. Instagram may not be just the form of advertising for a business, it may be a business platform in its own right, and in appropriating some of the images for his exhibition Prince was cutting across some existing norms.

The response to the inclusion of their works in this exhibition by the various original photographers ranged the full spectrum, from absolute delight to being 're-photographed' by Prince as part of his exhibition to amusement, anger, outrage and sometimes all of these at the same time. Sex columnist and blogger Karley Sciortino described the inclusion of her image in the exhibition as 'an honor'.[24] Sciortino also disclosed that the image re-photographed from her account, which shows her modelling a necklace by the designer Richardson, was an image that had originally been posted to its brand account. Anna Collins, a ballet student from Toronto, was less happy about the image from her account being appropriated by Prince: as a student she felt she could have benefited from a licence fee. However, she too disclosed that she had not taken the original image, which featured her and her boyfriend, and had been taken by her sister. Noting that her sister had given her explicit permission to post the image to Instagram, she stated: 'I

May 2015) <www.theverge.com/2015/5/30/8691257/richard-prince-instagram-photos-copyright-law-fair-use> (accessed 15 April 2019).

23 Lasane, 'The Art World Responds to Richard Prince's "New Portraits" Exhibition at Gagosian Gallery with More Instagram #ArtSelfies' (*Complex Style*, 2 October 2014) <www.complex.com/style/2014/10/art-world-responds-to-richard-princes-new-portraits-exhibition-at-gagosian-gallery-with-selfies> (accessed 15 April 2019).

24 Kircher, 'Two of the Women Whose Instagram Photos Were Hijacked by Richard Prince Admit They Didn't Even Shoot the Originals' (*Business Insider*, 29 May 2015) <www.businessinsider.sg/instagrammers-from-richard-princes-photos-didnt-take-the-original-pictures-2015-5/#7heMZKMEeKBqmCXB.97> (accessed 15 April 2019).

didn't have much intention behind it … Like many of my Instagram photos, it's of the moment.'[25]

Selena Mooney, known as Missy Suicide and founder of the Suicide Girls burlesque and modelling collective, decided to fight back against what she perceived as appropriation of Suicide Girls' images, offering to sell the same images as prints for $90, with the proceeds going to charity, rather than the $90,000 reportedly being charged by Prince at the Gagosian stand at the Frieze Art Fair in New York. Notably, her response displayed the ambivalence that appears to characterise uses of Instagram, distinguishing between purely commercial and 'art' purposes:

> If I had a nickel for every time someone used our images without our permission in a commercial endeavour I'd be able to spend $90,000 on art. I was once really annoyed by Forever 21 selling shirts with our slightly altered images on them, but an artist?
>
> Richard Prince is an artist and he found the images we and our girls publish on Instagram as representative of something worth commenting on, part of the zeitgeist, I guess? Thanks Richard![26]

Another user, Doe Deere, whose image of herself with a doll wearing an identical outfit to Deere and with matching blue hair, reposted her original post with the comment:

> Figured I might as well post this since everyone is texting me. Yes, my portrait is currently displayed at the Frieze Gallery in NYC. Yes, it's just a screenshot (not a painting) of my original post. No, I did not give my permission and yes, the controversial artist Richard Prince put it up anyway. It's already sold ($90K I've been told) during the VIP preview. No, I'm not gonna go after him. And nope, I have no idea who ended up with it! 😵 #lifeisstrange #modernart #wannabuyaninstagrampicture[27]

Part of this ambiguity of response stems from the nature of social media itself, and more specifically, the nature of the Instagram platform. Instagram is a visual medium, and one that permits both public and private accounts. Images are readily reposted from one account to another and, as noted above, many users actively seek reposting of their material on other accounts, with strategic selection and tagging of content. Therefore the social norms of this

<hr>

[25] Ibid.

[26] Needham, 'Richard Prince v Suicide Girls in an Instagram Price War' (*The Guardian*, 27 May 2015) <https://www.theguardian.com/artanddesign/2015/may/27/suicide-girls-richard-prince-copying-instagram> (accessed 15 April 2019).

[27] Ibid.

platform, which will be discussed further below, appear to actively condone reposting of content on public accounts. Predictably a number of users whose images had been reproduced in the exhibition were happy to attend the exhibition and take selfies with Prince's reproduction of their photos.[28]

4. Photographers *versus* Prince

A number of the creators of the original posts have instituted or threatened copyright infringement actions against Prince. Two of these actions will be discussed here.[29] The first of these is an infringement action brought by professional photographer Donald Graham, whose image 'Rastafarian Smoking a Joint' (1998) had been reproduced by Prince by means of a screenshot of an unauthorised post of the slightly cropped image on Instagram. Prince had added only a single line of text following the process outlined above, below the image, which stated: 'Canal Zinian de lam jam [emoji of fist]' next to the richardprince4 username.[30] Graham's statement of claim (against Prince, the Gagosian Gallery and Lawrence Gagosian, the owner of that gallery) alleges copyright infringement with respect to the copying and reproduction of the original image and the display of the modified work at the gallery and on Prince's website, richardprince.com, as well as reproduction on an advertising billboard and in the exhibition catalogue.[31] Unlike many of the other images that were reproduced for the 'New Portraits' exhibition, Graham's photograph was originally captured on a Nikon camera using black and white film. That photograph had never been licensed or made available for any commercial purpose other than for sale as a fine art print. The image does appear on Graham's websites, donaldgrahamfineart.com and donaldgraham.com, in each case in conjunction with a prominent ©Donald Graham notice.

The Complaint alleges that Graham's wife made a post to Twitter on 25 October 2014 stating that Prince had 'appropriated' Graham's photograph and that Prince had replied: 'You can have your photo back. I don't want it. You can have all the credit in the world.'[32] Subsequent to this Graham sent a letter to Prince and the Gagosian Gallery requesting removal of the work

---

[28] Lasane, 'The Art World Responds to Richard Prince's "New Portraits" Exhibition'.

[29] Actions are also pending with respect to California-based makeup artist, Ashley Salazar, and London-based photographer, Dennis Morris. See Halpern, 'Instagram Model and Makeup Artist Sues Richard Prince over Copyright Infringement' (*The Art Newspaper*, 26 August 2016) <http://theartnewspaper.com/news/instagram-model-and-makeup-artist-sues-richard-prince-over-copyright-infringement/> (accessed 15 April 2019).

[30] *Donald Graham v Richard Prince, Gagosian Gallery Inc and Lawrence Gagosian*, Complaint, 30 December 2015.

[31] Ibid., at 4–6.

[32] Ibid., para 31.

from the exhibition and other places, including the website, and destruction of copies of the image in the exhibition catalogue and other places, as well as financial compensation. The Complaint alleges copyright infringement of the original image through the reproduction, public display and distribution of the photograph, unauthorised preparation of derivative works and use of the work in promotional materials.

There appears to have been ongoing commentary by Prince regarding the infringement action, as well as further distribution via a grainy post of the cropped image on Twitter.[33] This cropped and blurred image from Twitter was added to the copyright infringement claim by Graham.

The second action concerns the use of a photograph of Kim Gordon, musician, songwriter and visual artist, best known as a member of Sonic Youth, originally created by Eric McNatt for publication in *Paper*, a fashion and pop culture magazine. The facts are complicated by the fact that Kim Gordon is a friend and collaborator of Prince. Like Graham, McNatt is a professional photographer who used a digital camera to produce the image. The image was originally published in September 2014 in *Paper* magazine, online and in print and on the *Paper* Instagram account, with the licence of McNatt and crediting his authorship. McNatt has also licensed the photograph to *Vogue.com* where it appeared on 20 February 2015. McNatt had himself published the image to his own website ericmnatt.com, via his Instagram account @ericmncnatt and his account on Tumblr.[34]

Prince posted a copy of the photo, which he had copied from the *Paper* website or Instagram account, to his own Instagram account @richardprince4 with minor cropping. Prince captioned the photo with his own comment: 'Kool Thang You Make My Heart Sang You Make Everything Groovy', accompanied with six emojis depicting musical notation and instruments. He then took a screenshot of the post and printed a copy of the image using inkjet printing on canvas. On 10 September 2014, Prince also posted a

---

33 *Donald Graham v Richard Prince, Gagosian Gallery, Inc and Lawrence Gagosian*, Opinion and Order 15-CV-10160(SHS), 18 July 2017: 'After Graham filed this lawsuit on December 30, 2015, … Prince has occasionally posted on Twitter ("tweeted") about fair use and this lawsuit in particular … On or about January 6, 2016, Prince tweeted a photograph of an "unidentified person with dreadlocked hair" (apparently *not* the subject of Graham's *Rastafarian Smoking a Joint*) accompanied by the message: "My lawyers say I can't post Richard Avedon portrait of Rastaj's post of man with dreads smoking weed. I'm mixed up" … later that same day, Prince posted a compilation of two somewhat blurry images to Twitter (the "Twitter Compilation"), one of which allegedly features a copy of Graham's *Rastafarian Smoking a Joint*' (citations omitted).

34 *Eric McNatt v Richard Prince, Blum & Poe LLC, Blum & Poe New York, LLC and Ocula Limited*, Complaint, 16 November 2016, at 16–21.

photograph of the printed portrait to his Instagram account and captioned it 'Portrait of Kim Gordon, ink jet on Canvas, 2014'. Kim Gordon posted her own comment 'Awe!' to that post. She was also later photographed holding that same printed portrait, and this later image was also posted to her Instagram account, along with a comment from Gordon: 'So thrilled thank you@richardprince4'.[35] Unsurprisingly, this post also attracted a lot of commentary including comments from McNatt's photographic assistant, Paul Teeling, who posted to Gordon's account:

> Kim I want to remind you that Eric got paid $0 for this photoshoot for paper magazine. Whereas Richard Prince has stolen Eric's photograph and created a print edition that is selling for how much??? How different is this from downloading free music or pirating other peoples music and selling it on the street? Well, actually it's worse. If there [sic] were selling posters of this image I assume you would probably want a cut. Or if you didn't like the picture at all, you would probably try to prevent it from being printed. You of all people should be at the forefront of protecting artist's copyrights.[36]

The Complaint in this action alleges copyright infringement with respect to reproduction, distribution and public display of the original photograph as a consequence of its publication on Instagram, the printed portrait and in the book accompanying the exhibition, as well as in publicity materials and Prince's website.

Both of the Complaints make much of Prince's well-documented contempt for copyright law. In an oft-cited quote from 2011, Prince articulates his attitude to copyright law:

> Copyright has never interested me. For most of my life I owned half a stereo so there was no point in suing me, but that's changed now and it's interesting … So, sometimes it's better not to be successful and well known and you can get away with much more. I knew what I was stealing 30 years ago but it didn't matter because no one cared, no one was paying any attention.[37]

35 Song, 'Artist Richard Prince Sued for Appropriating a Photograph of Kim Gordon' (*Paper*, 18 November 2016) <www.papermag.com/artist-richard-prince-sued-for-appropriating-a-photograph-of-kim-gordo-2098967338.html> (accessed 15 April 2019).
36 Ibid.
37 *Highsnobiety*, 'Richard Prince: The Controversial Artist and Master of Appropriation'.

5. Copyright and Instagram: Can they Coexist?

Judge Stein issued an Order on 18 July 2017 denying a motion by Prince's lawyers to dismiss the Complaint by Graham. At the heart of determination of the copyright infringement action is the question whether the reproduction of the images was permitted under copyright law as a fair use? Under US law, section 107 of the Copyright Act permits the fair use of a copyright work. In determining whether a use is a permitted 'fair use' the court must consider:

1. the purpose and character of the use, including whether such use is of a commercial nature or is for non-profit, educational purposes;
2. the nature of the copyrighted work;
3. the amount and substantiality of the portion used in relation to the copyrighted work as a whole; and
4. the effect of the use upon the potential market for or value of the copyrighted work.

Applying the analysis of the fair-use doctrine from the Second Circuit's decisions in *Cariou* v *Prince*[38] (an earlier decision that involved another action against Prince with respect to appropriation art created using the images of another photographer), the Court determined that it could not conclude that any of the four use factors favoured Prince at the motion to dismiss stage. In particular, the inquiry did not satisfy the first hurdle of the purpose and character of the use being 'transformative'. The defendants had argued that the re-photographing of Graham's image and presentation in the Instagram frame conveyed a number of potential messages, distinct from Graham's efforts 'to capture … the spirit and gravitas of the Rastafarian people'. Such messages may include various comments upon the power of social media to generate discussions about art, to disseminate and comment upon the work of others or merely to condemn the vanity of social media. The Court concluded that despite the frame and the line of text the dominant image in 'Untitled' was the unaltered photograph of the Rastafarian by Graham. Extensive evidence would need to be provided to justify any finding that the 'expression, meaning or message' of the work was different from that of the original photo.[39] Similarly, the other three fair-use factors were not clearly determinative in favour of Prince's work. With respect to the fourth

---

[38] *Cariou* v *Prince*, 714 F 3d 694 (2d 2013).
[39] *Campbell* v *Acuff-Rose Music, Inc* 510 US 5699, 579 (1994).

factor – the effect on the potential market for the copyrighted work – the Court needed to be persuaded that the re-photography of the work changed its character to such an extent that it would appeal to a completely different collector than Graham's photograph.

As noted above and detailed extensively in the two Complaints, Prince is no stranger to copyright infringement cases. Swanson observes that 'Prince has always been blunt about stealing – the outlaw idea is the core of who he is as an artist. And he's endured reputation confirming copyright infringement law-suits over the years; like a good punk, he did it by eye-rolling his way through depositions.'[40] In *Cariou* v *Prince*, Prince was successful in establishing that his re-use of photographs from Patrick Cariou's book *Yes Rasta*, were, in the majority of instances, protected as fair use. In 2007, Prince had created an exhibition called *Canal Zone* that featured photographs torn out of Cariou's book, which had been modified to a greater or lesser degree by Prince through cutting, pasting, painting and in combination with other imagery. Although held to be infringing at first instance, the majority in the Appeal Court held that twenty-five of the works were transformative, 'have a different character, give Cariou's photographs a new expression, and employ new aesthetics with creative and communicative results distinct from Cariou's.'[41]

Instagram provides the perfect platform for the further exploration of the postmodern artistic interests of Prince: repetition, consumerism, popular culture and celebrity. Prince's lawyers have gone even further and, in recently filed detailed memoranda in support of a motion for summary judgment in both cases, making the point that Instagram fundamentally challenges concepts of authorship and originality.[42] In those memoranda, Prince's lawyers argue that his reproduction of the original photographs on Instagram is 'highly transformative', having a 'different purpose and meaning' than the photograph that is 'underscored by the intent and perception of reasonable observer', repositioned in a 'larger-than-life form' and displayed as an Instagram post on a giant iPhone. This representation transforms the re-photograph to a 'commentary on the nature of social media'. Further, the memoranda argue that as such images appear without watermarks or

---

[40] Swanson, 'How Richard Prince Got Kicked off Instagram (And Then Reinstated)'.

[41] *Cariou* v *Prince* 714 F 3d 694 (2d 2013) at 15.

[42] Greenburg Traurig, LLP, *Memorandum of Law in Support of Defendants' Motion for Summary Judgment, Eric McNatt v Richard Prince, Blum & Poe, LLC, and Blum & Poe New York, LLC*, Case No 1:16-CV-08896-SHS, 5 October 2018; and Greenburg Traurig, LLP, *Memorandum of Law in Support of Defendant Richard Prince's Motion for Summary Judgment, Donald Graham v Richard Prince, Gagosian Gallery, Inc and Lawrence Gagosian*, Case No 1:15-CV-10160-SHS, 5 October 2018.

copyright notices according to 'social media norms', there was a licence in effect permitting reposting and re-use of the images.[43]

Of course, these arguments remain contested. Writing in *The Federalist*, lawyer Robin Ridless has asked (as our habits of cultural consumption have changed since the iconoclastic 1960s and 1970s): 'Does this overplayed Warholian strategy still have capacity to shock and surprise?'[44] In other words, does the transposition of an artwork from one context to another, particularly where that transfer occurs from a context of high art (for example, a gallery) to a commonplace or banal context (for example, Prince's erratic cornerstore offering a cheaply framed image) result in a transformative use of culture commodities?

Discussing the work of Prince, Levine and Sherman in 1980, Crimp wrote that their work demonstrated that photography's claims to originality were a fiction:

> Their images are purloined, confiscated, appropriated, *stolen*. In their work, the original cannot be located, is always deferred; even the self which might have generated an original is shown to be itself a copy.[45]

This description reads virtually like one of Instagram itself, a place of fakes, copied and borrowed images, used in homage, deference or tribute to the subject. A place where the representation is everything, even down to stage-managed breakfasts,[46] erasing the relationship between the image maker and the image taker. The fact of repetition and re-use is promoted, condoned and facilitated by the platform itself.

Leaving aside the legal issues, what about the moral rights of the original photographers, and broader still the ethical implications of taking, reposting and reusing images? As noted above, there are many stories of Instagram account holders who have had their photographs copied and reposted for a range of reasons, from purposes of tribute and homage, to irony and pastiche, to passing off images as someone's own and even to sheer desperation to find more content.

Does it depend upon what you are saying you are doing with the image?

---

43 Ibid.

44 Ridless, 'Richard Prince's Loss over Appropriated Art Gives Copyright Law a Chance' (*The Federalist*, 3 August 2017) <http://thefederalist.com/2017/08/03/richard-princes-loss-appropriated-art-gives-copyright-law-chance/> (accessed 15 April 2019).

45 Crimp, 'The Photographic Activity of Postmodernism' (*Indigenous Images*, Winter 1980), October, p. 98.

46 Fowler, 'Scarlett Posted Her Breakfast on Instagram. Then She Received Hundreds of Death Threats' (*MamaMia*, 3 September 2018) <https://www.mamamia.com.au/how-to-delete-instagram-messages/> (accessed 15 April 2019).

What is the difference between a copier/infringer and an appropriation artist? As Lyons notes: 'social media has arguably allowed greater accessibility to the works of others, further enabling creative borrowing of users' works, blurring the lines between what is acceptable and what is unlawful.'[47] If the arguments made by Prince's lawyers are to be regarded as persuasive, we are also now looking not only at how the artwork itself is perceived by the audience but the intention manifest by the artist at the time of creation.

Conclusions

The Internet, and in particular the easy click, copy, paste and post model of social media, has dramatically disrupted the creation, distribution and consumption models for copyright material. The extent and nature of that disruption varies across the creative industries, but there is no doubt that all creators from the visual, literary, dramatic, musical and audiovisual domains have been forced to change their creative and business practices. Social media provides avenues for greater exposure to and potentially more direct contact with audiences and customers, but it also exposes users to the risk of losing control over access to their content.

As Henry Jenkins has identified, we are now living in the age of participatory culture, where audiences seek to engage actively with the media, rather than to passively absorb it.[48] Social media platforms like Instagram have the tools built into them to enable everyone to be a content provider and host, with little distinction between professional and amateur accounts. Indeed, as noted above, the desire for 'authenticity' in advertising deliberately blurs the line between professional and amateur content with little transparency regarding paid and unpaid content. The diverse responses of Prince's subjects to the inclusion of their images in the 'New Portraits' exhibition highlights the ambivalence of people's attitudes to re-use of their photographs. In an era of fame for fame's sake, the re-use of an image may be regarded as more valuable than any licence fee.

Prince's work does not attempt to conceal the fact that it is a re-photograph, in fact Prince claims the blurriness that results from the reproduction process is an element of the work.[49] The iconic re-use of a photographic from a

---

[47] Lyons, 'Camera Copia'.

[48] Jenkins, *Textual Poachers: Television Fans and Participatory Culture* (Routledge 1992); See further, Jenkins, *Convergence Culture: Where Old and New Media Collide* (New York University Press 2006); Jenkins, 'Rethinking Convergence/Culture' (2014) 28 *Cultural Studies* 267.

[49] Hudson Hick, 'Forgery and Appropriation in Art' (2010) 5 *Philosophy Compass*, 1047, p. 1053.

transient social media site to being fixed on art-quality canvas is itself a comment on the nature of current cultural output.

How then has copyright law responded to the emergence and proliferation of social media? Interviews with account holders, including those working in the creative industries, as part of a study of attitudes to copyright and social media reveal a laissez-faire attitude to copyright. Account holders make claims such as: 'we don't really have the time to take photos ourselves so we use other platforms to access photos',[50] and 'we put a disclosure on every photo we post, saying if it's yours just let me know. I think that what you'll find with Instagram is that people post photos without crediting it.'[51] Like Prince, the suggestion is clear that re-use is condoned and accepted within the platform itself.

It appears that visual sharing platforms, with their blurred relationship between account holder and image maker, have resulted in a 'post first, ask questions later' mentality. Rather than spend too much time, energy or effort in seeking permission to post an image, account holders adopt an attitude that any exposure is good exposure, and at least a tag of #attributionunknown may protect them from liability. Prince's 'wild-child' punk aesthetic, where copyright does not even form part of the consideration of the creative process, seems to have become mainstream in the clickstream culture.

Whether Prince's decision to extract the images from the platform will be excused on the basis of social commentary on the Instagram platform itself remains to be seen.

References

Chafkin M, 'Confessions of an Instagram Influencer' (*Bloomberg Businessweek*, 30 November 2016) <https://www.bloomberg.com/news/features/2016-11-30/confessions-of-an-instagram-influencer> (accessed 15 April 2019).

Cohen A, 'Who Actually Shot Richard Prince's Iconic Cowboys?' (*Artsy*, 2 March 2018) <https://www.artsy.net/article/artsy-editorial-richard-prince-stole-marlboro-man> (accessed 15 April 2019).

Constine J, 'Instagram Hits 1 Billion Monthly Users, Up from 800M in September' (*TechCrunch*) <https://techcrunch.com/2018/06/20/instagram-1-billion-users/> (accessed 15 April 2019).

Crimp D, 'The Photographic Activity of Postmodernism' (*Indigenous Images*, Winter 1980), October.

Fineman M, 'The Pleasure Principle' (*Slate*, 30 October 2003) <https://slate.com/culture/2003/10/richard-prince-s-naughty-nurses.html> (accessed 15 April 2019).

Fowler B, 'Scarlett Posted Her Breakfast on Instagram. Then She Received Hundreds

---

[50] Interviews on file with the author.

[51] Interviews on file with the author.

of Death Threats' (*MamaMia*, 3 September 2018) <https://www.mamamia.com.au/how-to-delete-instagram-messages/> (accessed 15 April 2019).

Halpern J, 'Instagram Model and Makeup Artist Sues Richard Prince over Copyright Infringement' (*The Art Newspaper*, 26 August 2016) <http://theartnewspaper.com/news/instagram-model-and-makeup-artist-sues-richard-prince-over-copyright-infringement/> (accessed 15 April 2019).

Higgins C and Dodd V, 'Tate Modern Removes Naked Brooke Shields Picture after Police Visit' (*The Guardian*, 30 September 2009) <https://www.theguardian.com/artanddesign/2009/sep/30/brooke-shields-naked-tate-modern> (accessed 15 April 2019).

Highsnobiety, 'Richard Prince: The Controversial Artist and Master of Appropriation' (5 September 2016) <www.highsnobiety.com/2016/09/05/richard-prince-artist> (accessed 15 April 2019).

Hudson Hick D, 'Forgery and Appropriation in Art' (2010) 5 *Philosophy Compass*, 1047.

Jenkins H, *Textual Poachers: Television Fans and Participatory Culture* (Routledge 1992).

Jenkins H, *Convergence Culture: Where Old and New Media Collide* (New York University Press 2006).

Jenkins H, 'Rethinking Convergence/Culture' (2014) 28 *Cultural Studies* 267.

Kircher MM, 'Two of the Women Whose Instagram Photos Were Hijacked by Richard Prince Admit They Didn't Even Shoot the Originals' (*Business Insider*, 29 May 2015) <www.businessinsider.sg/instagrammers-from-richard-princes-photos-didnt-take-the-original-pictures-2015-5/#7heMZKMEeKBqmCXB.97> (accessed 15 April 2019).

Lasane A, 'The Art World Responds to Richard Prince's "New Portraits" Exhibition at Gagosian Gallery with More Instagram #ArtSelfies' (*Complex Style*, 2 October 2014) <www.complex.com/style/2014/10/art-world-responds-to-richard-princes-new-portraits-exhibition-at-gagosian-gallery-with-selfies> (accessed 15 April 2019).

Lyons S, 'Camera Copia: Reflections on Rephotography in the Instagram Age' (*New American Notes Online*, Issue 10, December 2016) <https://nanocrit.com/issues/issue10/camera-copia-reflections-rephotography-instagram-age> (accessed 15 April 2019).

Needham A, 'Richard Prince v. Suicide Girls in an Instagram Price War' (*The Guardian*, 27 May 2015) <https://www.theguardian.com/artanddesign/2015/may/27/suicide-girls-richard-prince-copying-instagram> (accessed 15 April 2019).

Petreycik K, 'Richard Prince Loves Boobs and Hates Instagram: Live!' (*Animal*, 18 June 2013) <http://animalnewyork.com/2013/richard-prince-loves-boobs-and-hates-instagram-nsfw/> (accessed 15 April 2019).

Plaugic L, 'The Story of Richard Prince and his $100,000 Instagram Art' (*The Verge*, 30 May 2015) <www.theverge.com/2015/5/30/8691257/richard-prince-instagram-photos-copyright-law-fair-use> (accessed 15 April 2019).

Prince R (exhibition), 'New Portraits' (Gagosian, 12 June–1 August 2015) <www.gagosian.com/exhibitions/richard-prince--june-12-2015> (accessed 15 April 2019).

Ridless R, 'Richard Prince's Loss over Appropriated Art Gives Copyright Law a

Chance' (*The Federalist*, 3 August 2017) <http://thefederalist.com/2017/08/03/richard-princes-loss-appropriated-art-gives-copyright-law-chance/> (accessed 15 April 2019).

Song S, 'Artist Richard Prince Sued for Appropriating a Photograph of Kim Gordon' (*Paper*, 18 November 2016) <www.papermag.com/artist-richard-prince-sued-for-appropriating-a-photograph-of-kim-gordo-2098967338.html> (accessed 15 April 2019).

Swanson C, 'How Richard Prince Got Kicked off Instagram (And Then Reinstated)' (*Vulture*, 8 March 2014) <www.vulture.com/2014/03/how-richard-prince-got-kicked-off-instagram.html> (accessed 15 April 2019).

Swanson C, 'Is Richard Prince the Andy Warhol of Instagram?' (*Vulture*, 20 April 2016) <www.vulture.com/2016/04/richard-prince-the-andy-warhol-of-instagram.html> (accessed 15 April 2019).

Time, '100 Photos, The Most Influential Images of All Time' <http://100photos.time.com/photos/richard-prince-cowboy> (accessed 15 April 2019).

Wang E, 'Instagram is Full of Copyright Loopholes – It Made My Career, But It Could Break Yours' (*Quartz*, 11 June 2015) <https://qz.com/424885/i-got-a-job-posting-photos-of-my-dog-on-instagram-but-others-arent-so-lucky/> (accessed 15 April 2019).

Index

CPSIA information can be obtained
at www.ICGtesting.com
Printed in the USA
BVHW032154190822
645070BV00012B/116